Major Problems in American
Indian History

MAJOR PROBLEMS IN AMERICAN HISTORY SERIES

GENERAL EDITOR
THOMAS G. PATERSON

Major Problems in American Indian History

Documents and Essays

THIRD EDITION

EDITED BY

ALBERT L. HURTADO
University of Oklahoma

PETER IVERSON
Arizona State University

WILLIAM J. BAUER, JR.
University of Nevada, Las Vegas

STEPHEN KENT AMERMAN
Southern Connecticut State University

Australia • Brazil • Japan • Korea • Mexico • Singapore • Spain • United Kingdom • United States

CENGAGE
Learning·

Major Problems in American Indian History: Documents and Essays, Third Edition
Edited by Albert L. Hurtado, Peter Iverson, William J. Bauer, Jr., and Stephen Kent Amerman

Product Director: Suzanne Jeans

Senior Product Manager:
  Ann West

Content Developer: Terri Wise

Product Assistant: Liz Fraser

Media Developer: Kate MacLean

Marketing Manager:
  Kyle Zimmerman

IP Analyst: Jessica Elias

Manufacturing Planner:
  Sandra Milewski

Art and Design Direction,
  Production Management, and
  Composition: PreMediaGlobal

Cover Image: Maidu Creation
  Story, 1 999; Harry Fonseca
  (Nisenan Maidu, Hawaiian,
  Portuguese) 1 946-2006

For product information and
technology assistance, contact us at **Cengage Learning
Customer & Sales Support, 1-800-354-9706**

For permission to use material from this text or product,
submit all requests online at **www.cengage.com/permissions**
Further permissions questions can be emailed to
permissionrequest@cengage.com

Library of Congress Control Number: 201 4933044

ISBN-13: 978-1-133-94419-5

ISBN-10: 1-133-94419-1

Cengage Learning
200 First Stamford Place, 4th Floor
Stamford, CT 06902
USA

Cengage Learning is a leading provider of customized learning solutions with office locations around the globe, including Singapore, the United Kingdom, Australia, Mexico, Brazil, and Japan. Locate your local office at **www.cengage.com/global**

Cengage Learning products are represented in Canada by Nelson Education, Ltd.

To learn more about Cengage Learning, visit **www.cengage.com**

Purchase any of our products at your local college store or at our preferred online store **www.cengagebrain.com**

For Our Friends and Mentors
Wilbur R. Jacobs
and
Allan G. Bogue

Contents

PREFACE   xv

Chapter 1   Approaching American Indian History   1

ESSAYS   2

Devon Mihesuah (Choctaw) • Countering Colonization   2

R. David Edmunds (Cherokee) • Practicing Inclusion   13

FURTHER READING   22

Chapter 2   Early American History   24

DOCUMENTS   24

1. The Skagit Describe Their Origins, n.d.   25

2. The Arikira Tell of Their Creation, n.d.   27

3. The Iroquois Depict the World on the Turtle's Back, n.d.   28

4. The Cherokees Narrate Their Beginnings, n.d.   31

5. The Hopis Describe Blue Corn Ear Maiden's Revenge, n.d.   33

6. The Pueblos Sing of the Sky Loom, n.d.   36

7. Dohasan (Kiowa) Records History as a "Winter Count," 1832–1892   36

8. Dudley and Ruth Patterson (Western Apache) See Their History in Places, ca. 1979–1984   37

9. Selected Native American Centers in North America, ca. 1250   41

ESSAYS   42

Neal Salisbury • The Indians' Old World: A Continental
View   42

Dennis Wall and Virgil Masayesva (Hopi) • The Old World and the
Modern World: A Hopi View   49

FURTHER READING   59

Chapter 3   **Strangers on the Shores, 1492–1600   61**

DOCUMENTS   61

1. Columbus Describes the Caribs, 1492   62

2. Spain Requires the Indians to Submit to Spanish Authority,
1513   63

3. Cabeza de Vaca Recounts His Experiences with the Indians of
Mexico, 1536   65

4. Rangel and Oviedo Tell of De Soto's Invasion of Florida,
1539   68

5. Cartier Records His Meeting with the Micmacs, 1534   70

6. An Englishman Discusses Trading with Indians on the Atlantic
Coast, 1584   71

ESSAYS   74

Bruce Trigger • The Shores: Native Responses to Early European
Contact   75

Cody Newton • The Interior: Comanche Mobility Before
European Contact   85

FURTHER READING   94

Chapter 4   **Southern and Northern Encounters,
1600–1700   96**

DOCUMENTS   96

1. Pedro Naranjo (Keresan Pueblo) Provides His Explanation for
the Pueblo Revolt, 1681   97

2. Juan (Tiwa Pueblo) Offers His Account of the Pueblo Revolt,
1681   100

3. Casañas Assesses the Native Peoples of Texas, 1691   101

4. Van den Bogaert Journeys into Mohawk and Oneida Country,
1634–1635   105

5. A French Missionary Describes the Iroquois, 1659–1660   106

6. A Micmac Responds to the French, 1677   109

7. Selected Native American Centers in North America,
ca. 1645   111

ESSAYS   112

Stefanie Beninato • Southern Encounters: Indian Leaders in the Pueblo Revolt of 1680   112

Jan Noel • Northern Encounters: Haudenosaunee Women and the Fur Trade   122

FURTHER READING   132

Chapter 5   Eastern Encounters, 1600–1700   134

DOCUMENTS   134

1. Captain John Smith Describes Powhatan Women and Men, 1624   136

2. Powhatan (Chief of Powhatan Confederacy) Speaks to Captain John Smith, 1609   137

3. An Englishman Reports on Violence in Virginia, 1622   138

4. William Bradford Tells of Samoset, Squanto, and Massasoit, 1620   140

5. William Wood Records His Impressions of the Indigenous Peoples of New England, 1634   141

6. Captain John Underhill Describes the Pequot War, 1638   143

ESSAYS   144

Helen C. Rountree • The "Virginia" Encounter: Powhatan Women and the English   145

Katherine A. Grandjean • The "New England" Encounter: The Pequot War   154

FURTHER READING   165

Chapter 6   War and Survival, 1700–1763   167

DOCUMENTS   167

1. Delaware Indians Discuss the French and Indian War, 1758   169

2. Neolin (Delaware) and Pontiac (Ottawa) Urge Tribes to Fight the British, 1763   169

3. William Trent Describes Pontiac's Uprising, 1763   172

4. Naomai Omaush (Wampanoag) Records Her Will, 1749   173

5. The Mashpee Wampanoags Petition the Massachusetts General Court, 1752   174

6. Joseph Fish Preaches to the Narragansett Indians, 1768   175

7. Samson Occom (Mohegan) Gives a Short Narrative of His Life, 1768   177

ESSAYS   **179**

Ian Steele • War: The Shawnees and the Seven Years' War   179

Jean M. O'Brien (Ojibwe) • Survival: Indian Women in Eighteenth Century New England   191

FURTHER READING   **202**

Chapter 7   Continental Transformations, 1763–1815   204

DOCUMENTS   **204**

1. The United States Speaks to the Iroquois, 1776   205

2. Colonel Gist of Virginia Addresses the Cherokee Chiefs, 1777   206

3. Dragging Canoe (Cherokee) Replies to Colonel Gist, 1777   207

4. Mary Jemison Remembers the American Revolution, 1775–1779   208

5. The Iroquois and the U.S. Make the Treaty of Fort Stanwix, 1784   210

6. Pablo Tac (Luiseño) Recalls His Life in a California Mission, 1835   211

7. Lorenzo Asisara (Costanoan) Tells of an Indian Response to a Priest's Authority, 1812   213

ESSAYS   **218**

Colin G. Calloway • Eastern Transformations: The Aftermath of the American Revolution in Indian Country, 1783–1800   218

Albert L. Hurtado • Western Transformations: Indians, Sexuality, and the California Missions, 1760–1840   229

FURTHER READING   **241**

Chapter 8   A Tightening Circle, 1750–1840   243

DOCUMENTS   **243**

1. A Spanish Soldier Describes the Comanche Destruction of the San Saba Mission in Texas, 1758   244

2. A Spanish Official Assesses the Comanche, 1758   245

3. Chief Sharitarish (Pawnee) Voices Concern for His People, 1822   245

4. The United States Issues the Northwest Ordinance, 1787   246

5. Tecumseh (Shawnee) Speaks Out Against Land Cessions, 1810   247

6. Indian Commissioner Thomas L. McKenney Explains Removal, 1828   248

7. Elias Boudinot (Cherokee) Opposes Removal, 1828   248

8. George Harkins (Choctaw) Laments His People's Forced Exile, 1832   249

ESSAYS   251

Pekka Hämäläinen • A Western Nation's Rise and Decline: Comanche Economy on the Southern Plains   251

Donna L. Akers (Choctaw) • An Eastern Nation's Removal: Choctaws Leave the Homeland   269

FURTHER READING   280

Chapter 9   Native People, Families, and Nations Confront American Western Expansion, 1840–1865   283

DOCUMENTS   284

1. Sarah Winnemucca (Paiute) Recalls Her Father's Encounter with Overland Emigrants, c. 1845   285

2. William Joseph (Nisenan) Describes the Gold Rush, c. 1849   286

3. Lucy Young (Lassik) Discusses the Dangers Native Women Faced in California, c. 1861   288

4. Black Hawk (Oglala) Asserts Lakota Land Claims on the Plains, 1851   295

5. Wabasha (Dakota) Explains How Nefarious Trading Practices Caused the 1862 Minnesota War, 1868   295

6. President Abraham Lincoln Orders the Execution of 39 Dakotas Involved in the Minnesota War, 1862   297

ESSAYS   299

Waziyatawin (Dakota) • Grandmother to Granddaughter: Remembering the Minnesota War of 1862   299

David A. Chang • Indigenous Families in the Borderlands: Concows and Native Hawaiians in Gold Rush California   305

FURTHER READING   317

Chapter 10   Resistance, Restrictions, and Renewals On and Off Reservations, 1865–1890   319

DOCUMENTS   320

1. Barboncito (Diné) Demands that the Diné Leave Bosque Redondo, 1868   320

2. Paiutes Explain How Settlers Threaten to Usurp Land on Pyramid Lake Reservation, 1875   321

3. George Manypenny, Commissioner of Indian Affairs, Discusses United States Conflict with the Lakota, 1876   323

4. Mountain Wolf Woman (Ho-Chunk) Describes Women's Work and Labor in Wisconsin, c. 1890   324

5. Ace Daklugie, Charlie Smith, and Jasper Kanseah (Chiricahua Apaches) Remember Geronimo, n.d.   328

6. Lakotas Describe the Wounded Knee Massacre, 1891   330

ESSAYS   332

William J. Bauer, Jr. (Wailacki and Concow) • Off the Reservation: Migrant Labor and Native Communities in California, 1865–1887   332

Tracy Neal Leavelle • On the Reservation: Agriculture and Adaptation in Oregon, 1856–1887   345

FURTHER READING   359

Chapter 11   Education, Land, and Sovereignty in the Assimilation Era, 1890–1920   361

DOCUMENTS   362

1. Henry Dawes Supports the Allotment of the Cherokee Nation, 1885   363

2. Cherokee Delegates Defend Their Land and Institutions, 1895   364

3. The General Allotment Act (Dawes Act), 1887   367

4. Queen Lili'uokalani (Hawaiian) Protests the United States' Annexation of Hawai'i, 1905   369

5. Dorothy Peche (Shoshone) Recalls Attending a Government Boarding School, c. 1917   371

6. Minnie Wilburn (Nomlacki) Wants Her Son, Clarence, to Come Home from the Sherman Indian Institute, 1918   374

ESSAYS   375

Brenda Child (Ojibwe) • Ojibwe Children and Boarding Schools   376

Malinda Maynor Lowery (Lumbee) • Creating Community and a Native Identity in Jim Crow Georgia, 1890–1920   387

FURTHER READING   399

Chapter 12   New Deals and Old Deals, 1920–1940   401

DOCUMENTS   402

1. Lewis Meriam Summarizes the Problems Facing American Indians, 1928   402

2. Wisconsin Residents Detail the Poor Health Conditions of Native People, 1929   406

3. The Indian Reorganization Act (Wheeler-Howard Act), 1934   408

4. Rupert Costo (Cahuilla) Condemns the Indian New Deal, 1986   411

5. Ben Reifel (Brule Lakota) Praises the Legacy of John Collier, 1986   414

ESSAYS   417

Marsha Weisiger • Diné Women and Livestock Reduction in the New Deal Era   417

John R. Finger • The Eastern Cherokees and the New Deal   429

FURTHER READING   443

Chapter 13   **Wars Abroad and at Home, 1941–1960   445**

DOCUMENTS   446

1. Codetalker Keith Little (Diné) Emphasizes the Importance of the Navajo Language in World War II, 2004   446

2. Ella Deloria (Yankton Dakota) on Indian Experiences During World War II, 1944   449

3. House Concurrent Resolution 108 Terminates the Trust Relationship, 1953   453

4. Ruth Muskrat Bronson (Cherokee) Criticizes the Proposed Termination of Federal Trusteeship, 1955   454

5. John Wooden Legs (Northern Cheyenne) Outlines the Fight to Save the Land, 1960   457

6. Mary Jacobs (Lumbee) Relates How Her Family Made a Home in Chicago, n.d.   459

ESSAYS   464

Peter Iverson • Building Toward Self-Determination: Plains and Southwestern Indians in the Mid-Twentieth Century   464

Myla Vicenti Carpio (Jicarilla Apache) • Fighting Colonization in the Urban Southwest: Laguna Pueblos in Albuquerque   471

FURTHER READING   484

Chapter 14   **Taking Control of Education, Land, and Lives, 1960–1981   486**

DOCUMENTS   486

1. Clyde Warrior (Ponca) Delineates Five Types of Indians, 1965   487

2. A Proclamation from the Indians of All Tribes, Alcatraz Island, 1969   489

3. Emil Notti (Athabaskan) Describes Economic Changes in Alaska and Calls for Self Determination, 1968   491

4. President Richard Nixon Advocates Self-Determination for Native Nations, 1970   492

5. Ada Deer (Menominee) Explains How Her People Overturned Termination, 1974   495

6. Michael Hughes (O'odham/Hopi) Describes Schools in Phoenix, 2001   498

ESSAYS   499

Stephen Kent Amerman • Making an Indian Place in Urban Schools   500

Daniel Cobb • Talking the Language of the Larger World: Politics in Cold War America   514

FURTHER READING   524

Chapter 15   Identity, History, and Economic Development in the Twenty-First Century   526

DOCUMENTS   527

1. Eddie Tullis (Poarch Band of Creek Indians) Outlines the Benefits of Bingo and Gaming, 1985   527

2. Senator Harry Reid Requests State Control of Indian Gaming, 1987   528

3. James Riding In Presents a Pawnee Perspective on Repatriation, 1996   530

4. Kai'opua Fyfe Opposes Federal Recognition of Kanaka Maoli (Native Hawaiians), 2000   532

5. Elouise Cobell (Blackfeet) Describes the History of Land Litigation, 2008   534

6. Steve Russell (Cherokee) Argues for a Hemispheric Indigenous Identity, 2010   535

7. Charlene Teters (Spokane) Asks "Whose History Do We Celebrate?" 1998   537

ESSAYS   539

Eileen Luna-Firebaugh (Cherokee and Choctaw) • The Border Crossed Us: Identity and Sovereignty on the Borders of Indian Country   539

Nicolas G. Rosenthal • Dawn of a New Day?: Indian Gaming in Southern California   554

FURTHER READING   565

Preface

In the early 1970s in Phoenix, Arizona, Michael Hughes's high school American history textbook contained little on American Indian history. Hughes, whose experiences related to his Hopi and O'odham heritage are further conveyed in Chapter 14, recalled, "I think there were two sentences on Indians in the whole book [...] One was at the very beginning, when the Pilgrims came over and they met the Indians, and then another one was in the 1800s when the settlers were trying to settle and the Indians were being hostile to them, always fighting with the settlers." Though only a teenager, Hughes knew that this somehow was not the full story. In fact, the text's minimal and skewed depiction of Native Americans upset him enough that he inscribed a pointed criticism right onto the pages of the book: "Bullsh★★."

We hope you will not write the same comment about this book. Indeed, American history textbooks have come a long way since the early 1970s. Since then, scholars have produced a growing number of textbooks like this one, concentrating specifically on American Indian history, designed for the increasing number of undergraduate college classes devoted to the topic. When Albert Hurtado and Peter Iverson published the original edition in 1994, it was among the first to improve and expand the textbook offerings on Native American history. Only seven years later, in 2001, a second edition was published, indicating the rapid growth of the field. In the past decade, American Indian history has continued its robust development—increasing both its breadth and depth—and so now, a third edition is warranted.

This edition retains many of its predecessors' core ideas and goals. When considering new essays and documents, we chose material that we believed was important, thought-provoking, engaging, accessible to undergraduates, and authored by a mix of senior as well as newer scholars. As before, we also strived to include as many Native authors—in both the essays and the documents—as possible. This edition continues to emphasize American Indian history beyond the year 1900, with nearly a third of the book devoted to the 20th and 21st centuries. And, the book as a whole continues to advance the general theme of Indian agency over victimization. That is, while it does and must acknowledge the oppressive structures that outsiders have imposed on Native peoples, it also recognizes the constant efforts and abilities of Indians to resist, respond, adjust, adapt, and survive. That they have somehow been able to do so, that they continue to exist as Native peoples in the 21st century, remains one of the truly impressive, inspiring stories in all of human history.

While staying true to the principles and purposes of the first two editions, in this edition we have made a number of changes and improvements. For the third edition, two additional co-editors, William Bauer and Stephen Amerman, join the co-editors of the first two editions, Albert L. Hurtado and Peter Iverson. We have changed nearly half of the documents and essays to bring in fresh material and perspectives. With the acknowledgment that no organizational scheme is perfect, this time we have opted to hew more to a chronological, as opposed to a more thematic, approach. We hope this framework helps further our goal of telling an Indian-centered, rather than European-directed, story. For instance, we have integrated the American Revolution and the Civil War into Chapters 7 and 9, rather than organizing chapters around those events. Chapter 3, which covers the period from 1492 to 1600, contains an essay entitled "The Interior: Comanche Mobility Before European Contact," by Cody Newton, that looks at Indian history on the southern Plains, where direct European contact had not yet occurred. Within this chronological framework, we also strive to maintain a continental view. As in previous editions, we try to eschew an Anglo-centric, east-to-west view of American history, where Indians only enter the story once they encounter the English and, later, the United States. In some instances, we do disrupt the standard timeline. There is sometimes a tendency to treat pre-European contact America as separate from the post-contact period. In Chapter 2, we attempt to counter this inclination by including a document—"Dudley and Ruth Patterson See Their History in Places"—in which late-20th-century Western Apaches explain how ancient stories continued to guide them, and an essay—"The Old World and the Modern World: A Hopi View," by Dennis Wall and Virgil Masayesva—in which contemporary Hopis discuss the continuing relevance of pre-contact traditions about corn. That document and essay, in fact, are also two examples of another continuing emphasis of this edition: the use and acknowledgment of not only written texts but also oral sources. Additionally, we highlight those Indigenous people who continue to live east of the Mississippi River in the 21st century. In Chapter 15, the document "Eddie Tullis (Poarch Band of Creek Indians) Outlines the Benefits of Bingo and Gaming, 1985" addresses the ways in which eastern Indians have fought for sovereignty and defied racism since 1900.

We have also made some more subtle changes. Like the second edition, this edition foregrounds the topic of gender with even more essays that make it central to their study. The second edition strived to increase Indian voices—female as well as male—throughout. That this edition again managed to increase both female and Indian representation among the essay authors—with the additions of, for example, Donna Akers' (Choctaw) essay "An Eastern Nation's Removal:

Choctaws Leave the Homeland" in Chapter 8 and Malinda Maynor Lowery's (Lumbee) essay "Creating Community and a Native Identity in Jim Crow Georgia, 1890–1920" in Chapter 11—is a positive testament to the growing number of scholars with those particular backgrounds. As with the second edition, we believe we have achieved a broad geographical coverage of North America. In this edition, we include two essays that focus on urban Indian communities in the twentieth century: Myla Vicenti Carpio's "Fighting Colonization in the Urban Southwest: Laguna Pueblos in Albuquerque" in Chapter 13, and Steve Amerman's "Making an Indian Place in Urban Schools" in Chapter 14. In the documents, we push the boundaries out to Native Hawaiians and Native Alaskans (Chapter 11's "Queen Lili'uokalani Protests the United States' Annexation of Hawai'i, 1905" and Chapter 14's "Emil Notti (Athabaskan) Describes Economic Changes in Alaska and Calls for Self-Determination, 1968"), and we also include an essay in Chapter 9 that looks at interactions between Native peoples and those Hawaiians who came to California during the Gold Rush ("Indigenous Families in the Borderlands," by David Chang). In the final chapter, we include documents and essays that address the most recent developments in American Indian history. New documents and essays in the chapter, such as Nicolas Rosenthal's "Dawn of a New Day? Indian Gaming in Southern California," and "Steve Russell (Cherokee) Argues for a Hemispheric Indigenous Identity, 2010," discuss gaming and Indigenous identity.

For all our attempts at expanding this new edition's coverage of topics, themes, places, peoples, authors, and recent scholarship, we do realize the difficulty in rendering a comprehensive American Indian history in a single volume of 15 chapters, designed for a semester-long course. In some sense, we believe that what we are presenting here is the proverbial tip of the iceberg, or perhaps even the tip of the tip of the iceberg. Our hope is that the essays and documents give you and your students plenty of important things to think and talk about, with the understanding that what they offer are mere starting points for longer and deeper conversations about American Indian history.

As with the other volumes in this series, our book brings together a set of primary source documents, with a collection of essays written by scholars in the field. We have chosen documents and essays that, as much as possible, speak to each other, allowing students to make connections and explore common questions. Each chapter begins with an introduction that sets the stage for the readings to follow, and suggests potential lines of inquiry for students to consider, on their own or through class discussions. In addition, we have composed brief contextual statements to precede both the documents sections and essays sections in each chapter. But, as valuable as the documents are in giving us eyewitness accounts of these pasts, and as helpful as the essays can be in interpreting them, neither need be accepted fully and unquestioningly. Indeed, it is incumbent upon students—with instructors as their guides—to question them, and to notice their potential limitations as well as their contributions.

We have included "further reading" sections at the end of each chapter. Of course, books are but one form of information for furthering one's education. There are now many excellent documentaries and websites devoted to Native

American history and culture. Scholars and students of American Indian history can investigate H-AmIndian, part of the H-Net (History-Internet) listserv program. Most tribes have their own websites. To get a sense of ongoing issues of importance to American Indians, students might check the online versions of newspapers such as *Indian Country Today* or *News from Indian Country*. Beyond the books, journal articles, films, and websites, there remains no substitute for the voices of the American Indian people themselves.

In any book about American Indians, a brief note on terminology is warranted. What is the proper term to use when describing the first inhabitants of the Western Hemisphere? There is no consensus among scholars. The word "Indian" comes from Columbus's errant belief and hope that, in 1492, he had reached India. "Native American" may then seem like a better term, until one realizes that the word "America" is not of indigenous origin, but rather is derived from the Italian explorer Amerigo Vespucci. Indigenous peoples themselves have different views about which term they prefer: "Indigenous peoples," "Native peoples," "First peoples," "Native Americans," or "American Indians." Though the latter two terms come from words of non-Indian origin, they have been around for so long that perhaps some Native people have, to a degree, taken ownership of them. In this book, mainly for the sake of variety—but with the understanding that, again, no single word is ideal—we use all the aforementioned terms.

Tribal names can also be problematic. Here, too, many come from the names Europeans used rather than the terms the people used to identify themselves. Whereas many tribes simply referred to themselves as "the people" in their language, Europeans often gravitated to misnomers, frequently borrowing a term—and not always a complimentary one—from a neighboring tribe. Hence, many people use the term "Sioux," an Ojibwe word for "snake people," rather than "Lakota," "Dakota," or "Nakota," translating to "the people." Today, some groups self-identify as "Sioux," some prefer "Lakota," "Dakota," or "Nakota," and some are content with any of those terms. As with the overarching terms, we tend to vary the terminology we use for tribal affiliations, balancing a tribe's own identification with terms with which beginning students might be more familiar, and deferring to the term that the speaker in a document or essay uses.

Issues of terminology are not unique to Indigenous peoples. Almost all names used to identify ethnic and racial groups are imprecise, masking greater internal diversity. Thus, we use various terms to refer to the people who came to the Western Hemisphere from Europe: "Europeans," "EuroAmericans," "whites," "Anglo Americans," "white Americans," "Americans," "non-Indians," etc. Again, as with "American Indians," no term is perfect; if one term seems better than another in a given situation, we have used it. Otherwise, we have opted for simple variety.

We have many people to thank for helping us produce this revised edition. We wish to thank our various editors: Jeff Greene, Thomas Paterson, Terri Wise, Ann West, and Pradhiba Kannaiyan for their excellent advice and assistance along the way. We thank also the following instructors who provided us with detailed and incisive suggestions for how we might keep the good qualities of the second edition, while still producing an improved version with this third edition: Rosanne Barker, Sam Houston State University; Frank J. Esposito, Kean University; William Hewitt, West Chester University of Pennsylvania; Robert Irvine, Eastern Oregon University; George Milne, Oakland University; James O'Donnell, Marietta College; Holly Rine, Le Moyne College; and Doug Rossinow, Metropolitan State University. William Bauer thanks Bridget Baumgarte (Alaska Native), David Christensen, and Margaret Huettl (Ojibwe) for serving as research assistants on this project; Brandi Hilton-Hagemann, Matt McIntosh, Karl Snyder, Julie Stidolph, and Skott Vigil (Ute and Yankton) for advice on topics, documents and essays for this book; and the University of Nevada, Las Vegas history department chair David Tanenhaus for securing research time to complete this project. Steve Amerman thanks his colleagues at Southern Connecticut State University, with special appreciation to Marie McDaniel, who helped point him toward materials addressing the 1492–1776 period in American Indian history, and to Resha Cardone, who assisted him in understanding some of the Spanish names in the documents. Whatever errors and flaws remain are the authors' responsibility.

All four of us wish to also thank our students, who have shaped our thinking about American Indian history and this book in numerous ways, whether by posing questions we had never before considered or by reminding us to bring greater clarity to concepts that may be particularly complex. Finally, all of us wish to thank our families for their constant support and encouragement, and, for those of us with young children still in the house (William and Steve), their always fascinating and always amusing distractions. If not for their companionship, support, and love, this project would not have been possible, nor would it have been as meaningful.

A.L.H.
P.I.
W.J.B.
S.K.A.

CHAPTER 1

Approaching American Indian History

It is perhaps customary to begin a book like this with a set of questions. What, if anything, does one need to know about American Indian history? Who should study American Indian history? How should they approach the subject? How should they write and talk about it? And, who is an "American Indian"? Such questions, it turns out, are not as simple as they might initially seem, and people have not—and still do not—always agree on their answers. With regard to the first question—"What does one need to know about American Indian history?"—the answer for too long and for too many was essentially "Not much," or even "Nothing." Until relatively recently, historians, history books, and college history departments ignored Native Americans. Or, if they did mention them, it was as the uncivilized, primitive obstacles to Anglo-American settlement. Usually, students and scholars viewed Native Americans' capitulation to European conquest as inevitable, though, at times, they might view Native resistance as noble, even if it was still ultimately futile. In either case, however, the approach was the same: Indians were important to American Indian history only so long as they put up a fight on the frontier. Once the English, and then the United States, subdued them, their significance ceased.

But, like people across the globe, Indigenous peoples themselves have long appreciated and maintained their histories, in their own ways. They continued to do so during the times in which they encountered, and resisted, European arrivals in their homelands. And, contrary to what Europeans may have long believed, they have persisted in keeping their histories beyond the era of conquest, up to the present day. In other words, Native peoples have always possessed a history, and they still do. Non-Natives have just been slow to hear it, to notice it, and to accept the different ways in which Indians have recorded it.

This chapter does not pretend to provide complete or definitive answers to the questions posed in the opening paragraph. But it does serve to briefly introduce you to at least some of the possible answers. As you make your way through the rest of this book, we encourage you to keep in mind the ideas expressed and discussed here.

◈ ESSAYS

The essays in this chapter present differing perspectives on how scholars and students have approached American Indian history in the past, how they approach it today, and how they should approach it in the future. Both essay authors, Devon Abbott Mihesuah and R. David Edmunds, have PhDs in history. Mihesuah (Choctaw Nation of Oklahoma) is a professor at the University of Kansas, while Edmunds (Cherokee) is a professor at the University of Texas at Dallas. As you read their essays, pay special attention to areas where they seem to agree, as well as places where they may appear to disagree. If you see examples of the latter, how far apart do those disagreements seem to be? To what extent could some of the differences be in style, as well as substance? Also consider how audience and "genre" may play a role in these pieces. Mihesuah's essay is from a chapter in an edited volume, published in 2004, entitled *Indigenizing the Academy: Transforming Scholarship and Empowering Communities*. Edmunds's essay, in contrast, is a version of a speech he gave as his presidential address to the 2007 meeting of the "Western History Association," an organization devoted to the history of the American West as a whole, and whose membership—though it includes some scholars of Native heritage—is predominantly non-Native. Beyond matters of genre, audience, style, disagreement, and agreement, both authors have important things to say. Consider their arguments here as well as in the chapters that follow. In fact, you might contemplate what Mihesuah and Edmunds would think of this book itself: Does it sufficiently "counter colonialism"? Does it effectively "practice inclusion"?

Countering Colonization

BY DEVON MIHESUAH (CHOCTAW)

Why do we write American Indian history? What is the point of attempting to reconstruct the past? Historians usually say they study and write Native history because they are curious about long-ago happenings. Something—a specific event, a person, a chain of happenings—has caught their interest. Perhaps they are interested in their ancestors, human nature, or discovering stories of those who are often ignored in U.S. history texts. These are among the reasons I entered graduate school in 1984.

Thousands of books and essays have been written about Native peoples and Indigenous-white relations, so obviously, there is a great deal of interest in historic Natives among scholars and readers. However, there is a great deal of difference between historians who are concerned about present-day realities Natives face and historians—both non-Native and Native—who pursue their armchair interests while vehemently supporting academic freedom and claiming

Reprinted from *Indigenizing the Academy: Transforming Scholarship and Empowering Communities*, edited by Devon Abbott Mihesuah and Angela Cavender Wilson by permission of the University of Nebraska Press. Copyright © 2004 by Devon Abbott Mihesuah and Angela Cavender Wilson.

to be inclusive in their writings, yet simultaneously appearing to have no concern for the people they write about.

Most humanities scholars argue that acquiring knowledge of the world's cultures and their histories is important to understanding ourselves and is the mark of an educated person. Even many individuals who are not formally educated watch *National Geographic Explorer*, The Discovery Channel, or read *Biography* because they are curious about humanity. While curiosity about Others is not a problem in itself, it becomes a moral problem when scholars write colonialist histories about Others for distribution only among themselves in the ivory tower and only for their benefit.

Grants, fellowships, and awards have been bestowed upon hundreds of historians who write about Natives, and there is no question that many historians of "Indian history" have prospered from creating versions of the past. Contrary to the lifestyles of historians in academia, conditions for many Natives remain stark. Standing Rock Sioux Vine Deloria Jr. stated in 1991 that "We need to eliminate useless or repetitive research and focus on actual community needs; it is both unethical and wasteful to plow familiar ground continually." Indeed, poverty, racism, disease, frustration, and depression are common throughout many tribal nations. How many works of history actually analyze the perpetrators of colonialism in an attempt to ascertain how we have arrived at this point? How many history books and essays have tried to find solutions to these problems? What can we say is the usefulness of all these history books that focus on Natives? If essays are going to continue to be reprinted in anthologies, then why can't we see more collections of papers devoted to the historical reasons why Natives are in their current situations, in addition to proposed solutions to the problems? Ironically, many of the "powerhouse" scholars have never met an Indian or visited tribal lands, illustrating the actuality that "highly educated" people can simultaneously be insulated from many of the realities of life. As a historian who has read hundreds of history works in my eighteen years of seriously studying "Indian history," and who also knows quite a few historians, I can think of only a few non-Native or Native historians who study past events truly with tribes' benefits in mind.

Native intellectual activists and our non-Native allies are growing in number, and most of us are concerned about this issue, much to the discomfort of established historians who have maintained their power base in Native history and in Native studies as a whole. Indigenous intellectuals are also becoming increasingly vocal in their objections to the way their ancestors have been portrayed or ignored in works of history and how those images and absences in stories about this country's past translate in the present. We are impatient with scholars who continue to profit from editing anthologies of essays focusing on familiar topics we've seen repeatedly and composing stories that are useless as tools of decolonization. Our impatience also stems from facing gatekeepers determined to keep Native intellectuals who have much to say out of the picture and from being denied tenure or promotion (or at least receiving it only after resorting to formal complaints or legal action) and funding for projects, in addition to receiving poor evaluations from patriotic students who don't want to hear about colonialism in the United States.

Many scholars understand that how history is written can directly impact modern Native people for good and bad. Like Wahpetunwan Dakota historian Angela Cavender Wilson asserts, "American Indian history is a field dominated by white, male historians who rarely ask or care what the Indians they study have to say about their work." Many Natives argue that they possess viable versions of their pasts, and Native scholars know that their theories and methodologies have been ignored, while the majority of works focusing on Natives do not contribute to tribes' well-being.

Kanien'kehaka scholar Taiaiake Alfred writes that "the state attempts to rewrite history in order to legitimize its exercise of power (sovereignty) over Indigenous peoples." Similarly [Michel] Foucault … states that writing history is often used for social and political reasons and that writing history can be an instrument of power; historian Alan Munslow argues that "written history is always more than innocent storytelling, precisely because it is the primary vehicle for the distribution and use of power." Although Natives can also invent versions of the past for their benefit, the reality is that Natives are rarely in authoritative positions, while many white historians have created history using their entrenched methodological standards to maintain and justify their power base and privileged positions.

History philosopher Hayden White asserts that "For any effort to comprehend that politics of interpretation in historical studies that instructs us to recognize 'the war is over' and to forgo the attractions of a desire for revenge, it seems obvious to me that such instruction is the kind that always emanates from centers of established political power and social authority and that this kind of tolerance is a luxury only devotees of dominant groups can afford."

I am not stating that all non-Native historians are bourgeois colonialists bent on keeping Natives in subservient positions. On the contrary, through my tumultuous years in academia some of my strongest supporters, good friends, and most knowledgeable mentors have been non-Natives.… [However], there are many historians, and some are Native, who have little interest in decolonization efforts, balanced narratives, and political activism. They are content to focus only on creating biased stories about the past and would be happy if modern Native people would stop dwelling on the transgressions committed by long-dead colonists and get on with life. And herein lies the problem: life today for many Natives is lived as colonized peoples who continue to be stereotyped, discriminated against and kept impoverished by subtle and blatant policies and behaviors that also occurred historically. To argue that everyone has equal shots at success is either ignorant or racist, and to continue to write similar history stories and to reprint the same stuff with no concern for the descendants of the ancestors we generate stories about is selfish.

[Friedrich] Nietzsche asserted that "the unhistorical and the historical are necessary in equal measure for the health of an individual, of a people, and of a culture." For Indigenous people, knowledge of the past is crucial for their identity growth and development, pride, problem-solving strategies, and cultural survival. Nietzsche also claims that being "unhistorical"—able to forget the past—is one way to find happiness. In some circumstances, the advice to "forget it and move on" is useful, especially for trivial day-to-day events and confrontations. But the strategy of becoming unhistorical is simply not possible for tribal people with complex histories and cultures and devastating past (and present) relations with non-Natives that have shaped their modern realities.

Without question, writing and teaching Indigenous history are political acts. There can be many versions created of the same historic event depending on the author's bias, political beliefs, social pressures, and major professors' and publishers' demands. Because of the growing number of concerned Indigenous scholars and their allies in the academy, all historians, Native and non-Native, are becoming more conscientious about presentation, whether they side with Native people or not. There are obvious strategies (apparent to Indigenous scholars and our allies, at least) that writers of Native history use in order to appear "politically correct," such as claiming in their book's introduction that they use "Indian voices," and do not, or thanking Native writers in the acknowledgments even though that person had nothing to do with the creation of the work, or claiming that he or she writes from the "Indian perspective." Many historians identify themselves as "ethnohistorians," another ploy they use to appear as if they are really doing thorough research. Although ethnohistory is supposed to be a melding of historical and anthropological methodologies (for example, archival research and oral accounts that would in theory be a more inclusive way of finding information), few ethnohistorians actually bother to talk with Natives and instead depend on theories formulated by white thinkers to create stories of what may have happened in the past.

Another example is asserting in their introductions that a Native scholar's theories provided inspiration for their work. In [Philip] Deloria and [Neal] Salisbury's *A Companion to American Indian History* (2000), for example, Angela Cavender Wilson is thanked in the introduction for helping to "form some of the understandings that underpin this book," but nowhere in the anthology do we see evidence of Wilson's influence, and only a brief discussion of her ideologies appear at the end of Deloria's essay "Historiography," which reveals Deloria's misunderstanding of what Wilson says.

Empiricist scholars argue that as long as one thoroughly scours the archives and remains objective while analyzing the data, then accurate history can be written. But consider the events in a day in the life of one modern person. Conversations take place all day. Phone calls are made, meals are consumed, goods are purchased, newspapers and chapters of books are read, television shows are watched and children are disciplined. Weights are lifted, miles are run, and appointments are kept. We drive back and forth across town, breathe thousands of breaths, listen to dozens of songs on the radio and try to tune out even more commercials. White lies, embellishments, gossip, and racist comments emerge as a result of wishful thinking, patriotism, blind faith, racism, and suspicion. Countless thoughts, visions, and nighttime dreams fill our consciousness and unconscious, all meshing together to form motivations and physical acts. Each day every person performs countless chores, thinks millions of thoughts, and makes decisions, and most of those actions and thoughts result in counteractions by either ourselves or someone else. The vast majority of everyday actions are not recorded or even remembered. And, we tend to forget the things we did the day before. If we don't document much of what happens today—and we have computers and dictaphones—how can anyone seriously state that we can reconstruct events of the long-ago past (populated by millions of people) with accuracy?

We can't. Even those Natives who argue the necessity of using oral testimonies agree with historian Norman J. Wilson's comment, "History is best defined as a continual, open-ended process of argument, which is constantly changing. No question is closed because any problem can be reopened by finding new evidence or by taking a new look at old evidence. Thus there are no final answers, only good, coherent arguments: history is not some irreducible list of 'the facts' but continually changing bodies of evidence."

Although we still try to do the best we can by including archival data along with oral testimonies, that is often not enough. It is usually a no-win situation for Native historians: we get hung up by gatekeepers who insist that the only "real Indians" lived in the past and therefore modern Natives possess only "mythological" stories. Real Natives (who, according to gatekeepers, aren't "really real") want to empower themselves and their tribes. They try to accomplish this by talking with elders in order to acquire traditional knowledge, but that information is not considered viable by influential gatekeepers such as Richard White, who refers to such data as "privileged information" that should not be used because it cannot be proved. It seems fair to say that work containing analysis based on oral stories is seen by many historians as inferior and not worthy of attention or citation.

Historians often create their historical stories in the same fashion as fiction writers, with imagination and creativity. A historian who wrote a Pulitzer Prize–nominated book once said to me that it took him days to compose the artful introductions to each chapter, paragraphs describing colorful sunrises, the weather, and emotions that he hoped had taken place in those days almost three hundred years ago. Was this fiction, or by coincidence, really real? It depends on how you define "fact." As Alan Munslow says, "The evidence is turned into 'facts' through the narrative interpretations of historians." Names, dates and places are only a part of the picture. The narrative (organization and creation of the story) gives the stories their substance and direction. Narrative is also the reflection of the author's bias, political agendas, and patriotic fervor. If one needs to prove a point, any history is possible. And if the history written agrees with and is accepted by the reader, then it is "fact," at least to that person.

Some historians argue that tribal stories are embellished and formulated to serve the purposes of the tribe, which may be true enough in some instances. But this brings up two important points about Native history. The first is that most Natives believe that the tribal stories held by those obligated to the task are more accurate than stories created by outsiders. This is a political, social, and religious statement that will not change just because some historians see Natives' interpretations as subjective. Second, mainstream historians are going to continue to write the way they do; therefore, Native historians and our allies should have the right to identify histories that are helpful to the tribes, accurate in their tribe's eyes, racist, or incomplete. Wilson proposed it first by entitling one of her essays "American Indian History or Non-Indian Perceptions of American Indian History?" and by suggesting that authors admit what they are attempting to accomplish.

A useful model in understanding why historians write the way they do is the "patterns" of history, … in which … writers analyze the past according to the standards and political and social climate of the generation in which the historians live. [Gerald N. Grob and George A. Billias write] "Every generation of American scholars seems to have reinterpreted the past in terms of its own age."… "Thus, each succeeding generation of Americans seems to have rewritten the history of the nation in such a way as to suit its own image." The late historian R. G. Collingwood concurs: "The historian … is not God, looking at the world from above and outside. He is a man, and a man of his own time and place. He looks at the past from the point of view of the present: he looks at other countries and civilizations from the point of view of his own."

Space does not allow exploring here the cycles of American Indian history beginning with Spanish missionaries or [James] Adair's *History of the American Indians* (1775) and moving through cycles of histories to the present. But what we can clearly see today in the realm of Native history are at least two distinct types of writing: one is a patriotic form that eschews Native voices and theories in favor of non-Native versions of the past, and the other emanates from the Indigenous intellectual camp and our allies who demand a more thorough story of the tribal past that tells the story of not just confrontation and resistance, but also of the colonialism that continues to the present and how Natives can recover traditional knowledge to empower themselves.

Numerous essays discuss specific periods of Native studies or the historiography of certain fields (such as military encounters, boarding schools, missionaries, or specific tribes), but many of those serve little purpose other than to make lists of what has been written. An exception … is Phil Deloria's essay …, in which he categorizes the periods of Native storytelling: "(1) an 'oral/traditional' period in which people used and recalled significant events as temporal markers imbued with historical and cultural significance; (2) a period shaped by Christianization, in which mergings of the ideologies and tropes of the Bible with those of oral traditions became relatively common, shaping the nature of historical discourse among Indian people; (3) a period shaped by academic and non-academic scholarship, in which detailed ethnographic and historical inquiry into Indian history helped reshape native conceptions and narrations of the past."

Deloria's grouping illustrates one of the problems with categorizing how "Indian history" has been written and how it is a misunderstanding of past and present tribal values. For example, this "oral/traditional period" is still in effect for many Indigenous peoples who depend on oral storytelling for cultural knowledge and identity. Second, not all indigenous peoples became Christians. They rejected the overtures of missionaries and would not have been influenced by the Bible; many still are not. Finally, the last listing does not actually exist because few scholars have reshaped anything, and, even if there is a revolution in academia, it will take quite a while before it affects tribal communities.

What good does all this historiographical listing serve? So far, none, really. We must be courageous enough to step on some toes and analyze the "important works" that are authored by the people who say hello to us in the hallways and at conferences (and who evaluate our promotion, merit, and grant applications). We must identify investigations of the past that can assist people in the present, and we must identify books that are not helpful. This does not mean students should not read the lesser studies; but they and their professors should be informed of the purposes their required readings serve. Awareness of Native history scholarship is crucial because the book list is growing and harm is done by many histories.

A common thread that runs through most stories of Natives' pasts is that authors tell stories in a vacuum and do not attempt to figure out how past events helped create the present. According to Natives who are concerned about their present-day situations, this is a critical methodological oversight. Some historians and philosophers, however, doubt that this should be done. Reconstructionist G. R. Elton, for example, dislikes this approach of "present-centered" history, which he argues is incomplete and "entails selecting from the past those details that seem to take the story along to today's concerns." This is not the methodology of Native intellectuals; they know from experience that the portrayal of peoples and events in the past directly impacts how their descendants are viewed and treated. Considering the dismal situation of many tribal people and their cultures, in addition to the privileged positions of descendants of the colonizers, most Native people would argue that an honest view of the past that is as thorough as we can muster does indeed tell the stories of how we arrived to where we are today. But what happens if inclusive stories are not told?

Since most Americans are ignorant of all things "Indian," they tend to believe what they see in movies, and most of what appears in movies came from information supplied from books. Historians who do not include Native voices and perspectives about their versions of the past tell readers that Native voices are not important or necessary. Many works on Native history attempt to justify colonialism, that it truly was (and continues to be) God's will that Natives are subsumed and inferior. And, on an ethical level that all of us can understand, the writers prosper while the objects of their writings often live in misery. Another problem is that many writers of history simply refuse to incorporate the perspectives of Native peoples about their past, which results in exclusive history and tragic perceptions of the present.

For example, many tribes, especially those of the Plains, are often portrayed as historic noble savages. Tribes that were victorious at the Battle of the Little Big Horn are usually described dramatically as organized and powerful adversaries. To Custer supporters (and modern Custer fans worldwide), they were without question strong, otherwise they could not have overwhelmed Hero Custer. Telling tales about Comanche Quanah Parker also serves this purpose. Parker was never chief of Comanches, yet historians continue to portray the war leader as "Chief" and Comanche men as monolithically warlike and aggressive in order to make U.S. victories over the powerful Comanche tribe appear more impressive.

Many Natives might say these descriptions are not problematic because they portray them heroically and in winning situations. But how do you suppose

Allen Lee Hamilton's [book] … comes across to my living, breathing full-blood Comanche father-in-law, in which Hamilton describes the "lurking" (p. 127) Comanches as living in "lairs" (p. 126), refers to Indian females as "squaws" (p. 132), and takes delight in describing Comanche atrocities without mentioning those committed by whites?

One obvious problem with these stories is stereotyping, and another is when storytellers and readers decide to turn against those "warlike" tribes because of fighting abilities that came into play while defending themselves. For example, even though countless Americans and Europeans adore the movie *Dances with Wolves* because it depicts Plains tribes exactly the way fans prefer to think of them—handsome, buffalo-hunting, and tipi-living (and didn't address the messier reservation period that makes them feel guilty)— many other reviewers feel the need to educate us about the "real" Lakotas, who were barbaric and committed to perpetrating atrocities upon hapless whites and powerless neighboring tribes. Much further south and even farther away in time, the Mexicas of Tenochtitlan engaged in behavior distasteful to many historians, and therefore, the same analytical strategy is used to evaluate them: they are often viewed as murderers who, in the words of historian Keith Windschuttle, "practiced incessant, ritualistic murder" because of "their whole bloodthirsty regime organized to gorge the appetites of their imaginary gods."

Not content to wail just about the Aztecs, Windschuttle asserts that "Human sacrifice was practiced by the Aztecs of Mexico, Mayas of Yucatan, Incas of Peru, the Tupinambas and the Caytes of Brazil, the natives of Guyana and the Pawnees and Huron tribes of North America." I know few Natives who will argue that some tribespeople were not violent and quite imaginative when it came to destroying their enemies and placating the Creator. But like those critics who refuse to consider the barbarism committed by European invaders who utterly devastated Native North and South America and are still doing it today, Windschuttle also is compelled to chastise those who sympathize with the Natives: "In taking the high moral ground on behalf of the indigenous dead of five centuries ago they are making a transparently insincere gesture." So what are they supposed to do? Unequivocally take the side of the colonizers because some Natives might display shocking behavior?

Considering the number of repetitive books that cite each other about historic Comanches, Sioux, and Iroquois tribes, non-Natives apparently find the dead ones more interesting than the live ones. Modern tribespeople are viewed much differently than those come and gone. Sadly, as my father-in-law can attest, Comanches in modern Oklahoma are often viewed with disdain by ignorant citizens. As with other plains tribes, the "military period" is quite popular, but intricacies of how and why they lost traditions (that is, the racism, policies, and subtle but effective behavior of neighboring whites) are usually skipped over. Now Comanches are collectively portrayed as pathetic drunks or freeloaders on welfare who are mere shadows of their former proud selves. One example of the latter interpretations of Plains tribes is the nonhistorian … Ian Frazier['s] … *On the Rez* (2000), which perpetuates the idea that the Sioux on Pine Ridge are all alcoholics wallowing in poverty and won't do anything about it. A cursory look through web listings that admire Frazier found a typical fan review: "If every textbook in every school were written with the style and grace—the sheer readability—of Ian Frazier's *On the Rez*, all the schoolchildren in America would clamor for more, anxious to read about our great land, eager to discuss what they have learned, and ready to move beyond folklore and stereotyping."

One cannot find many books more full of folklore and stereotyping than *On the Rez*, and to say that this book might inspire one to read more about the "great land" after learning the unfortunate situation on Pine Ridge is stunning to say the least. So, why do instructors prefer to use ... *On the Rez* instead of works about how tribes can empower themselves? Perhaps a look at Frederick Jackson Turner's stance can reveal part of the answer. Turner's thesis emphasizes this theme of Natives serving as obstacles for the intrepid migrating Americans to overcome, but after being confined to reservations the tribespeople became useless since they were no longer character-shaping obstacles. Maybe these stories are what many Americans need to read in order to maintain their sense of superiority and to justify the subjugation of Indigenous people.

Another example of how history storytelling impacts the present is that Indigenous women are invisible entities until they emerged in the past few decades, when historians began focusing on their important tribal roles. Until the 1960s and the advent of the women's movement, discussion of Native women was usually limited to Pocohontas and Sacajawea, who were exalted as heroines for assisting non-Native men in the westward movement. Despite the call from the 1960s onward for histories that include women and their tribal-stabilizing economic, religious, political, and social roles, a survey of the "Indian" section in any library reveals that the most prominent books about Natives (many authored by award-winning writers) do not mention women in their lengthy tribal narratives. Even authors, and some are Native, of recent publications who should know better also choose to exclude gender as topics in their works.

Their exclusions (which render their stories incomplete) would please G. R. Elton, who says that historians should not use modern standards of morality to assess the past and that "partial and uneven evidence must be read in the context of the day that produced it." Historians who ignore gender in their studies, or who place women in unimportant positions, apparently do not understand that women were excluded from historical documents for a reason: they were written by white men with no understanding of tribal gender roles, and who therefore produced biased, sexist, and incomplete diaries, letters, and reports. How do these incomplete stories impress young readers and scholars of Native histories who read these works and find that women did not exist? This does indeed impact Native women today, for unless students are cognizant of the powerful roles women held in their tribal societies and in their tribes' cosmologies (and that usually means being taught by sensitive professors concerned about women's issues, which, as we all know, makes a good many students and professors shudder), and unless Natives are taught of the important female tribal legacies, then women will continue to be abused and seen as second-class citizens, even among their own people.

There are numerous other examples of incomplete history: historians retain an intense interest in Andrew Jackson, although his Indian removal policy proved devastating to Natives and to their cultures. And Natives still feel the impact. Historians who prefer to focus on Jackson as a rugged individualist who epitomizes the American character either downplay or ignore the tragic results of his actions. In addition, Cherokees are also favorites of historians, and one cannot overestimate the influence historians of Cherokee history and culture have on modern Americans. Despite the large numbers of traditional, full-blood, and phenotypical-looking Cherokees in Oklahoma (at least), historians prefer to dwell on the mixed-blood, Christianized, "white Cherokees" who support colonialism, giving the impression to the modern U. S. public that all Cherokees look and act like their colonizers and they are an acceptable enough tribe to claim as part of their exotic, yet civilized, heritage.

With all these exclusions and biased histories on the shelves and in the works, why then, should "Indian history" continue to exist as a field of study? One answer is that if the works of Native historians are not respected or accepted because of the methodologies used to garner information, then neither should the work of historians who maintain the status quo. But that is not a pleasant response. There are some rationales that should allow the field to flourish, but they also mean that historians must reevaluate their motives for writing. Certainly, a lot of history written about Natives is useful because it supplies tribes with information such as names, dates, and places that may be missing in the tribal narratives. Sometimes scholars have the training and money to find information that has been lost to tribes. Some works are joint efforts, so both scholars and nonscholar Natives can learn and benefit. In fact, some of the scholars whom Native intellectuals take to task have uncovered much important information, and I, for one, am not hesitant to cite and credit useful data, regardless of who found it. The key word here is "some," however, and just because a publisher touts a work as "cutting edge" does not necessarily mean that the book or essay as a whole is useful.

A major reason for the field to continue is to revise stories that have already been told by not only including Native perspectives but also by honestly considering the impact of colonialism. Granted, many historians have already done much of the work, but what they omit is how these policies and ideologies have persisted to the present day and how the descendants of the Native people they discuss are alive and suffering the consequences of contact. Historians could spend the next few decades rewriting incomplete history.

Studying the Native past offers solutions to current problems. Taiaiake Alfred argues … that an understanding of traditional political processes and values will enable tribes to "restore pride in our traditions, achieve economic self-sufficiency, develop independence of mind, and display courage in defense of our lands and rights." Knowledge of the past is crucial for understanding treaty rights and land claims and ultimately is indispensable to keeping Native cultures alive. As noted elsewhere in this volume, the study of traditional diets and the correlations between diet change (especially the overuse of sugar, fats, carbohydrates, and alcohol) and health deterioration could motivate Natives to change their eating habits.

Abuse of women and children within tribal communities has escalated, and so have murder, rape and substance abuse. Many argue that among the reasons for self-destructive behavior and abuse of females is the poor self-esteem that stems from ignorance of tribal traditions. Learning tribal traditions, which includes women's respected places in tribal traditions, can help modern Natives cope with the impersonal world by offering them foundations to form their identities, self-confidence, and strategies for dealing with adversity. The academy is not the place for Natives to learn intimate tribal customs such as religion (that is the responsibility of the tribes), but the academy is an influential source of information for Native intellectuals who desire to work for their communities after graduation. Armed with tribal management, communication, and research skills, in addition to respect for Indigenous cultures, traditions, and concerns, the empowered academy-trained Native scholars can return to their families, communities, and tribes and hopefully inspire them to try to recover Indigenous knowledge from tribal elders who in many cases are waiting patiently for their descendants to engage them.

An inclusive view of the past can educate readers about the contributions of Natives to the world. Discovering their contributions to the world's diets, to the arts and sciences, and to the U.S. political system is empowering to Natives and can help establish pride and self-esteem. Because the portrayals of peoples and historical events directly impact how their descendants are viewed and treated today, more accurate presentations of the past help to counteract movies, television shows, literature, and cartoons that often portray Natives as savages, buffoons, teary environmentalists, or enthusiastic supporters of colonialism.

The key to this type of "contribution history" is to allow it to happen. All of these histories require Native perspectives, meaning that writers of history must talk with tribal people, not just rummage through archives, and they must respect tribes' privacy and not write about sensitive topics. Search, merit, and promotion committees, as well as publishing houses and hook reviewers, must be supportive of these types of histories that are actually stories with specific purpose and are often political and subjective, as are all histories.

We know this is a difficult task. "Successful" historians are not about to change what they are doing and give up their fan base. In fact, a recently formed group, The Historical Society, is bent on silencing those with political agendas. The Historical Society is a group that purports not to be conservative, but according to one of its supporters, who is concerned that not enough attention is devoted to political, economic, social, or military questions, "This is not to suggest that panels on race, ethnicity, or gender should be excluded. It is time, however, to address more serious concerns." It is interesting to note that race, ethnicity, and gender are relatively new historical topics, and the University of Arkansas' Evan B. Bukey's suggestion reveals the underlying agenda of the group that possesses a very strong, exclusive political agenda and hundreds of dues-paying members.

Native intellectual activists are interdisciplinary in their studies, meaning that they not only utilize a variety of methodologies to arrive at their conclusions, they also include Native voices and perspectives, question historians who do not appreciate Native versions of the past, and are concerned about their tribes and communities. Almost without exception, however, they face adversarial gatekeeping in their departments because of their nonmainstream approach to research and writing, in addition to their focus on what tribes need instead of what colleagues think they should write and how they must write it. Gatekeeping is a stark reality, and it is particularly stunning that Phil Deloria states that in regards to Indians and the Other, the "boundaries have disintegrated." He asserts that "one can see it in the most recent census data … in aesthetics … politics and the media … and in the telling of history." Indigenes suffering from racism, stereotyping, poverty, discrimination, and patronization, in addition to disrespect in academia for our ideologies, concerns, and work are pleased to read that. When, then, shall we expect to see respect and equality?

Considering that this is a country founded by colonizers whose policies and behaviors disrupted and almost destroyed Indigenous cultures, historians of the Indigenous past have a responsibility to examine critically the effects of their historical narratives on the well-being of Natives and to also examine their stories' influence on the retention and maintenance of the colonial power structure. Some historians feel so strongly about this ideology that we have shifted from being discipline-specific to interdisciplinary studies in order to write about a host of issues that concern Natives. Personally, I side with history philosopher Hayden White, who argues that "any science of society should be launched in the service of some conception of social justice, equity, freedom, and progress— that is to say, some idea of what a good society might be."

And what is wrong with that?

Practicing Inclusion

BY R. DAVID EDMUNDS (CHEROKEE)

AT THE 47TH ANNUAL CONFERENCE of the Western History Association, held at Oklahoma City in October 2007, twenty-seven of the fifty-nine formal sessions listed in the program were devoted entirely, or in part, to Native American history and culture. Indeed, papers focusing upon Native American history outnumbered any of the other popular topics (environmental history, the borderlands, religion, or gender) by a margin of over two to one. Obviously, this meeting was held in Oklahoma, whose license plates (even if they're not tribally issued) tout the state as "Native America," and the program committee was chaired by George Moses and Melissa Meyer, scholars who are, to say the least, receptive to Native American topics. But even after accounting for such a confluence of favorable factors, no other major historical association, with the exception of the American Society for Ethnohistory, has featured a program so devoted to Native American history.

For those of us who have spent our careers, or more accurately our lives, promoting, conducting research, publishing, and teaching in this field, nothing could be more heartening. Since 1970, the growth of Native American history as an academic field and its inclusion within the broader spectrum of American

R. David Edmunds, "Blazing New Trails or Burning Bridges: Native American History Comes of Age," *Western Historical Quarterly* 39 (Spring 2008): 4–15.

history has been steady, and its influence, if not always pervasive, still has markedly altered and improved the manner in which American history has been presented in most college or university classrooms. There are numerous examples that might be cited, but perhaps the best is the expanded coverage of the pre-Columbian period by college textbooks during these years.

In 1967, Samuel Eliot Morison's *The Oxford History of the American People*, a volume of over 1100 pages and the textbook used in many freshmen American history surveys during this decade contained only a precursory chapter of fifteen pages on the pre-Columbian period, and includes the complaint that "when we try to tell the story of man in America ..., the lack of data quickly brings us to a halt.... Thus, what we mean by the history of the American people is the history in America of immigrants from other continents." In 2007, as more modern survey texts, replete with special sections on Cahokia, the role of tribal people in the economic and political development of colonial America, Indian removal, and the defense of the western homelands illustrate, things have changed. Obviously, those of us who have championed this field would like to see more Native American history included within these texts, but we are encouraged by this increased coverage and look forward to its future growth and development.

Native American history, as a specialized field of study within the broader spectrum of American history emerged in the late 1960s. One can argue that it was a stepchild of the increased social and ethnic awareness of the 1960s, but it has antecedents in military history and the history of the American West. The first American Indian history position to be advertised in the AHA's "Professional Register" was listed in the February 1969 *AHA Newsletter*: a position in "colonial and/or American Indian" history at the University of Wisconsin at Stevens Point. During the 1970s demands for Native American history classes burgeoned and history departments across the country scrambled for historians qualified or willing to teach such courses. In 1972, the Newberry Library founded the D'Arcy McNickle Center for the History of the American Indian, and the center soon emerged as a focal point for what was then regarded as the "new" Indian history, an attempt to produce a scholarly history of Native American experiences from what hopefully would more accurately reflect Native American perspectives. Scholars can justifiably argue, from either side, over the success of this endeavor, but I think most historians would agree that the focus of Native American history has shifted away from its former emphasis on Native political and military responses to threats mounted by non-Indians toward historical inquiry that attempts to incorporate an understanding of the unique cultural adaptability of tribal people to a world in constant change. Cultural change has also been the focus of scholars who consider themselves to be ethno-historians, many of whom are members of the American Society for Ethnohistory, another professional organization that also has grown during these years. An essay of this length cannot provide a detailed description of the growth of Native American history over the past three decades, but by 2007, the field has become firmly established, has produced a second generation of publishing scholars, and seems to be an accepted part of the curriculum of academic institutions across the United States. Moreover, it is a field of inquiry that attracts a broad spectrum of students. Obviously, Native American students enroll in Native American history courses, but the classes also attract large numbers of non-Indians. Knowledgeable instructors in these courses understand that they have an obligation to provide Native American students in their classes with a broad or enlarged perspective of the Native American historical experience into which individual Native students can place their particular personal or tribal experiences; but instructors must also be aware that they have a responsibility to expose non-Indian students to patterns and events in the Native American past, and to help non-Indians understand how the Native American past has shaped both the Native American and non-Native present.

Native American Studies programs and/or departments also have emerged and blossomed during these years. Although some Native American scholars argue that these programs have roots as far back as the 1930s, formal programs of instruction in Native American or American Indian studies did not emerge until the late 1960s. The University of Minnesota, UCLA, U-Cal-Berkeley, and U-Cal-Davis, among others, established programs or departments in 1969, and by the mid-1970s over seventy-five similar programs had blossomed at institutions, large and small, across the United States and Canada. Many of these programs initially were fashioned piecemeal from a potpourri of departments, colleges, and student support services. Some had no formal administrative structure, but were a selection of courses from different academic departments or disciplines, that, when pieced together by a student, constituted a major or minor in Indian Studies. Others were led by part-time administrators who held tenure-track positions in more traditional departments, but served as program directors, and often as advisors to Native American students on campus. Some were organized around American Indian Studies centers, while others were served by faculty who held joint appointments in Native American Studies, and in traditional departments. The programs often were housed in Colleges of Arts and Sciences, but some were part of new colleges of Ethnic or Comparative Studies, or even formed part of the "College of Agriculture and Life Sciences."

In addition to Native American history, these programs featured courses in Native literature, political science (sovereignty, treaty-rights, and tribal government), art, anthropology, sociology, and education. Like many new academic programs, some of the Native American Studies programs experienced growing pains, but by the 1980s many were well-established parts of their institution's curriculum. Moreover, by the late 1980s many of the programs were led by a cadre of new Native American scholars: Indian academics trained in traditional disciplines, but whose research and writing focused on Native American subjects, and whose ties to particular tribal communities enabled them to approach these subjects from new or unique perspectives.

By the late 1980s many Native American academics and non-Indian faculty members serving in Native American Studies programs had been bloodied by the turf wars that both characterize and plague academic politics. Although champions of inter-disciplinarity argue that programs formed from several disciplines offer the best of all academic worlds, those of us familiar with these programs understand that sometimes they are neither fish nor fowl; they offer a cafeteria approach to a subject of interest, but often fail to provide a core or focus for the study of the subject. In addition, many faculty serving part-time in Native

American Studies programs, but housed and eventually tenured in more traditional departments found they could not serve two masters. Their tenure, promotions, and subsequent salary were more contingent upon appraisals of their performance within their home departments than their contributions to Native American Studies programs.

In response, many Native American scholars have argued adamantly for the establishment of Native American Studies *departments* equal in stature to more traditional departments within the university. Faculty in these departments would be tenured and promoted internally, not by other departments. In addition, they would design the department's curriculum, recommending to the university a course of study they believe would best serve the interests of their students, the university, and perhaps, more importantly, Native American people in general. Native American Studies departments, then, would become the vanguard in preparing a new generation of students, both undergraduate and graduate, to defend Native American communities, their land-base, and their sovereignty.

In 1970, shortly after I arrived at the University of Oklahoma, I was told by one faculty member (now retired and soon forgotten) not to waste my time pursuing Native American history. The field, according to this individual, was a passing fad. It had no real historiography, no revisionist texts, and no official schools of interpretation. It soon would be forgotten. His predictions could not have been more wrong, and thankfully, other historians such as Donald Berthrong and A. M. Gibson had advised me to ignore the man. In 2007, Native American history, First Nations' history, Indigenous People's history, or whatever a particular institution entitles it, flourishes in both traditional history departments and Native American Studies programs across the United States and Canada. Moreover, the field has a burgeoning historiography, multiple schools of interpretation, and has engendered considerable discussion over historical sources, methods of research, appropriate research topics, and audiences.

One focus of contention is the balance between more traditional documentary sources and oral history. As historians who have been trained in a traditional history department are aware, most historians believe that "real" history is written from documents. Although oral testimony, visual images, or even personal experiences can provide information regarding historical events, one only needs to examine the documentation (and in this case the very term illustrates the point) in scholarly books or essays to realize that written accounts (documents) provide the most commonly used sources in historical research and writing. In contrast, some members of Native American Studies programs or departments have championed the use of oral history as a preferred or privileged source in writing Native American history. They argue, often quite cogently, that by relying upon Native American oral accounts scholars can tap the memories and experiences of people who lived through many of the events they are attempting to analyze and understand, and that these accounts present a uniquely tribal perspective. Moreover, they point out that since many tribal communities have always relied upon the oral transmission of information and values as their primary means of communication, these accounts are valid cultural or historical sources. In addition, since many of these accounts have been shared by extended families of communities through several generations, they reflect a community's or tribe's general perception of what has happened and what is important about the past.

Of course some traditionally trained academic historians charge that such oral history is biased, lacks objectivity, and often suffers from a selected memory that ignores or even excludes extensive evidence that seems to refute the oral testimony. They point out that often there is very little or no written documentation to support claims or interpretations made in oral tradition, and that the inaccurate (or lack of) western chronology in the oral accounts compromises their validity. In response, the champions of oral tradition reply that written documents also reflect the biases of their authors and even if these biases are neutralized, the letters, accounts, or records usually were written by a single person and reflect only that individual's perspective. They are, to basely abuse a parable, like the detailed account of only one of the three blind men who encounter the elephant: there's much more to it than that. Moreover, as Native Americans point out, these written accounts were composed by non-Indians; they may present what contemporary Europeans believed took place, but the non-Indians were outsiders, not part of the communities about whom they were reporting.

So who's right and who's wrong in this argument? Well, both, so to speak. And since this is a presidential address [of the Western History Association], and I'm the president, I have no qualms about using my own experiences to illustrate this point. Quite frankly, I've used and continue to rely upon both; but I must admit I have used documents and oral history in different ways and as sources for different periods.

When writing about the history of Potawatomi, Shawnee, or Meskwaki people in the seventeenth, eighteenth, or early-nineteenth centuries, I have relied heavily upon documented sources. Admittedly, these documents have been composed by European or non-Indian authors, but they provide the chronological framework in which I have attempted to describe and discuss these tribal communities' activities during this period. It's not that contemporary oral history, or even oral histories transcribed in the early decades of the twentieth century have no memory of these earlier times. On the contrary, oral tradition from these tribal communities remember some events from these distant times quite well, but like all histories, they also seem to omit some parts of the story that place people and events within a broader context.

Yet even if an analysis or narrative is initially framed within a "documented" western chronology, the inclusion of materials from oral tradition can enrich and transform such an account and place tribal people as the focal point of a series of events. It also can assist in interpreting these events from a tribal perspective. For example, in 1730 a large party of Meskwaki people, enroute across Illinois, were intercepted on the prairie by a force of French and allied Indians. The Meskwakis sought refuge in a small grove of trees, fought off their besiegers for thirty-five days, fled during a midnight hailstorm, but most were tracked down and massacred on the prairie somewhere near modern Bloomington. The French accounts of these monumental (at least for the Meskwakis) events contain considerable details about the combatants, military tactics, and casualties. But it's the Meskwaki oral traditions, still held by tribal members and also recorded by some twentieth-century ethnologists that humanize this story and offer insights into the Meskwaki perception of these events. The Meskwakis did not flee from the siege in an ordinary hailstorm; they fled in a deluge sent by the Thunderers in response to a ceremonial plea in which the sacred wolfskin was accidently dropped into a small stream. But Wisaka, the Trickster, was also fickle, and the Meskwaki children cried, warning their besiegers of their passage. Moreover, the Meskwakis lost many kinsmen in the ensuing battle, but the Sacs gave them refuge, the people persisted, and they have continued to occupy their homeland.

The Meskwaki oral accounts of this battle, while not as detailed as reports by French officials, illustrate the impact of these events upon the Meskwaki people. They also enrich our understanding of these events, and are critical in providing a non-Indian audience with the emotional and cultural world-view of tribal people. In addition, it is oral history, more than any other factor, that illustrates the phenomenal perception of *place* that permeates most tribal people's sense of identity and beliefs about themselves. Indeed to study the history of tribal people is to study the land and surroundings that have shaped their lives, and there is no better medium for this inquiry than a people's oral tradition. The stories of the people are the very beating heart of a tribal nation; they strengthen the sense of community and offer continuity for the generations to come. From a tribal perspective, it doesn't matter when coyote brought the gift of bison to the people, only that he did it, for it helps to explain the surrounding world to a people inextricably tied to the landscape they inhabit. These insights are important for the continuity of tribal communities—but they also are important if non-Indians are to understand and appreciate the uniqueness and cultural values of Native American societies.

During the past quarter-century I have served as a consultant in support of several tribal governments in land claims or other legal action against state governments. In this litigation, I've also used both written documents and oral testimony. I would be less than honest if I did not admit that most attorneys, judges, and other officers of the court place far more credence on evidence gleaned from written documents than from oral accounts, and if academics, Native or otherwise, testify in these cases my advice is that they should be prepared to support their arguments with sufficient written documentation.

But oral tradition also has served me well in these legal proceedings. Several years ago, in support of an Otoe-Missouria claim to the Arkansas River bed that abutted their former reservation near Red Rock, Oklahoma, I assisted Browning [Pipestem], an Otoe-Missouria attorney in an attempt to prove that the river was navigable during the first decades of the twentieth century. Local newspapers contained no information regarding that "stretch" of the river, which today would hardly "float a shingle" due to the water that is diverted for irrigation upstream. Hoping for a positive answer, I met with a group of Otoe-Missouria elders and inquired if they could remember anyone traversing the Arkansas in a canoe or rowboat when they were children. I initially was disappointed when they replied they had never seen a small boat on the stream, but then Fannie Grant and Truman Dailey commented that of course they often had ridden the ferry across the river to visit relatives among the Osages. "What ferry?" I asked. (There was no mention of any ferry in any contemporary written sources.) "Oh," they all chimed in, "the one that used to carry teams and farm wagons across the river to Fairfax and Pawhuska." Needless to say, the Arkansas was navigable.

More recently, in testifying for the Seneca-Cayugas, I used oral tradition from a group of "relatively mature" Seneca-Cayuga women who described to me, in some detail, how members of the Seneca-Cayuga tribe of Oklahoma regularly journeyed to New York in the 1920s to participate in Cayuga tribal ceremonies, and how Seneca-Cayugas had often welcomed Cayugas from New York to festivals in Oklahoma. Since the claimants in this case earlier had argued that there had been no contact between Cayugas in New York and Oklahoma during these years, the opposing lawyer questioned the authenticity of the Seneca-Cayuga testimony by asking me how I could be sure these elderly women were old enough to remember those days. "Did you ask them their birthdates?" he inquired. I must admit I answered with some glee, that if he was brave enough to go into that room and ask six elderly Seneca-Cayuga women just how old they were, he was a better man than me. In response, the lawyer became angry, but the courtroom erupted in laughter, and the testimony moved on to other issues. But again, accounts of these visits between separate Cayuga communities, while critical to the Seneca-Cayuga case, were not the sort of information that academics glean from written documents.

So what does all this anecdotal material illustrate about Native American history, the tension between written and oral sources, and the agendas of traditional history departments and some Native American Studies programs? Quite a bit, I believe. About one year ago I was interviewed over the telephone, at some length, by a faculty member from a leading Native American Studies program who was conducting a survey of senior scholars ("old guys," according to my daughters), asking about their theoretical framework for Native American history. Was I a "colonialist," a "post-colonialist," a "post-modernist," or what? I confess to having some difficulty in consciously applying any of these theoretical frameworks to Native American history, so after thinking about this question for a short period, I answered that I guessed I probably was, for lack of a better term, some sort of "inclusionist." Although I had spent the past three decades focusing my efforts on the history of Native American people, I still believe that Native American history, while very important in itself, is critical to a larger history of all people in North America. Consequently, I would argue that meaningful Native American history should incorporate both documentary evidence and oral traditions. But on a grander scale, I also would argue that the study of Native American history should not be limited nor defined by narrow departmental boundaries nor by any single school of interpretation. At best, it incorporates a broad spectrum of analyses and approaches. It most certainly should be taught in Native American Studies programs, but it also should be offered in traditional history departments.

To whom should it be offered? Some faculty members in both Native American Studies programs and history departments have advocated that the target audience should be Native American students since knowledge of the past is critical for the defense of Native American communities. Surely all historians who focus on Native American people would agree with Philip Deloria that their research should be of use, in the broadest sense to tribal people, and I personally would urge any of you who have conducted research and written about particular tribal communities to share copies of your research materials with these tribes. Yet I hope our research and writing will transcend tribal lines and have a broader application to both indigenous people and non-Indians across the United States, and even throughout the world.

Creating a larger audience remains a critical part of our task. If we envision Native American history as an important tool in the defense of Native American people, lands, and culture, then we also must address a non-Native audience. Native American history should be taught to Native American students, but it also must be taught to non-Indians—otherwise we are preaching to the choir. Granted, some of the choir members could use a little fine-tuning and will benefit from the instruction, but the choir in this instance remains relatively small. In 2000, the Native American population of the United States, including enrolled members of federally recognized tribes, and people who self-identify as Native American on the census reports, numbered 4.1 million out of a total U.S. population of over 281 million. That's only about 1.5 percent. If we're going to defend our interests, we're going to need help. We need to educate non-Indians about what has happened. We need to cultivate their interest and support.

We also need the assistance of well-qualified scholars, regardless of their ethnicity. Historians such as Angie Debo, A. M. Gibson, Donald Berthrong, and Tom Hagan were writing Indian history long before it ever became fashionable, and many other non-Native scholars continue to explore the many facets of this subject. We should welcome their efforts. Obviously, tribal or Native American historians can add a unique perspective to the study of Native American history, and I'm aware that in the past some Native scholars have complained that their work has been rejected by "academic gatekeepers" who did not appreciate their tribal perspectives. If such is the case, if logical, sound historical interpretations or well-researched and well-written manuscripts have been unfairly rejected, then such actions should be condemned. Surely we all can agree that solid scholarship, regardless of its origins and/or point of view, should be presented and made available to the broadest possible audience. No single scholar or group of scholars should hold a monopoly on historical inquiry on any subject. We don't all need to agree—but we can learn from each others' endeavors. I know, for example, that the late Vine Deloria, Jr. did not share Father Paul Prucha's assessment of Andrew Jackson's Indian policies, but I have heard him praise *The Great Father*, Prucha's broad survey of federal Indian policy, as the best study of this subject in print.

Yet most gates swing two ways, and gatekeepers, like Janus, can look in more than one direction. Within the past decade, some Native academics have urged that scholarship conform to a new orthodoxy defined through the rhetoric of post-colonialism. A few individuals have gone so far as to demand that other scholars (including other Native Americans) first ask their permission before meeting with or initiating research upon the communities they believe they represent. I would hope that all responsible scholars would be sensitive to each tribal community's cultural boundaries. Obviously, some things, such as religious beliefs or personal relationships are privileged, should not be made public, and are not subjects for research or writing. But the same can be said of non-Native societies, although in these cases the cultural boundaries may have different parameters. Post-colonial theory can be a valuable tool in exploring the relationship between indigenous people and the federal government, but it should not be the only tool; it should not monopolize our analyses. We do not need a new cadre of self-appointed "gate-keepers."

And finally, before I leave you with the impression that the differences between dueling methodologies of Native American history are insurmountable, let me focus on our common interests. In May 2007, a steering committee of six leading scholars from Native American Studies or Indigenous Studies programs organized a meeting at the University of Oklahoma of academics and students interested in Native American Studies from across the United States and Canada. The focus of the meeting was not the rifts between scholars in Native American Studies programs and traditional academic departments, but rather our commonality of interests. The steering committee originally hoped to attract fifty scholars who shared their perspectives; instead they drew three hundred and fifty. As with most academic conferences, presentations at the meeting included a broad spectrum of opinions, but at the plenary session, held on Friday, 4 May, plans were made for a new Association for Native American and Indigenous Studies. The assembly of scholars agreed that the group's goals should be inclusion rather than exclusion and that the organization should be open to scholars from all departments, disciplines, programs, and ethnic identities. We will meet next spring at the University of Georgia.

So, in conclusion, where does all of this leave us? With considerable optimism, I hope. At the beginning of the twenty-first century, Native American history, while still experiencing some growing pains, obviously has come of age. We certainly have reputed the charges of early detractors who claimed that the field had/has no significant historiography or schools of interpretation. Indeed, these schools now have strong proponents, but we should, at least, be able to meet and openly discuss our different points of view. And finally, I would hope that our work would be of use and interest to indigenous communities, but I also would hope that it would expand our understanding of the broader American experience. The United States remains a collage of different, sometimes contesting, but also interlocking communities. But in the end, we're all in this together. We need to blaze new trails, not burn our bridges.

◈ FURTHER READING

Alfred, Taiaiake. *Peace, Power, Righteousness: An Indigenous Manifesto* (1999).

Bauer, William J., Jr. "Public Perceptions and the Importance of Community: Observations from a California Indian Who Has Lived, Learned, and Taught in Indiana, Oklahoma, and Wyoming." *American Indian Quarterly* 27 (Winter–Spring 2003): 62–66.

Blackhawk, N., ed. "Currents in North American Indian Historiography." *Western Historical Quarterly* 42 (Autumn 2011): 319–324.

Brown, Jennifer S. H., and Elizabeth Vibert, eds. *Reading Beyond Words: Contexts for Native History* (1996).

Cook-Lynn, Elizabeth. *New Indians, Old Wars* (2007).

Deloria, Philip, and Neal Salisbury. *A Companion to American Indian History* (2002).

———. "Commentary: Research, Redskins, and Reality." *American Indian Quarterly* 15 (Fall 1991): 457–468.

Deloria, Vine, Jr. *Custer Died for Your Sins: An Indian Manifesto* (1969).

Edmunds, R. David. "Blazing New Trails or Burning Bridges: Native American History Comes of Age." *Western Historical Quarterly* 39 (Spring 2008): 4–15.

———. "Native Americans, New Voices: American Indian History, 1895–1995." *American Historical Review* 100, no. 3 (1995): 717–740.

Fisher, Andrew. " 'This I Know from the Old People': Yakama Indian Treaty Rights in Oral Tradition." *Montana, the Magazine of Western History* 49 (Spring 1999): 2–17.

Fixico, Donald L. "Ethics and Responsibilities in Writing American Indian History." *American Indian Quarterly* 20 (Winter 1996): 29–39.

Harkin, Michael E., and David Rich Lewis, eds. *Native Americans and the Environment: Perspectives on the Ecological Indian* (2007).

Hauptman, Laurence M. *Tribes and Tribulations: Misconceptions About American Indians and Their Histories* (1995).

Hoxie, Frederick E. *Encyclopedia of North American Indians* (1996).

———. " 'Thinking Like an Indian': Exploring American Indian Views of American History." *Reviews in American History* 29 (March 2001): 1–14.

Hoxie, Frederick E., and Peter Iverson, eds. *Indians in American History: An Introduction* (1998).

Hoxie, Frederick E., Peter C. Mancall, and James H. Merrell, eds. *American Nations: Encounters in Indian Country, 1850 to the Present* (2nd ed., 2007).

Iverson, Peter. "The Road to Reappearance: American Indian History Since 1890." *Montana* 51, no. 4 (2001): 72–74.

Jacobs, Wilbur. *The Fatal Confrontation: Historical Studies of Indians, Environment, and Historians* (1996).

———. "The Indian and the Frontier in American History." *Western Historical Quarterly* 4 (January 1973): 43–56.

Klein, Laura F., and Lillian A. Ackerman, eds. *Women and Power in Native North America* (1995).

Krech, Shepherd, III. "The State of Ethnohistory." *Annual Review of Anthropology* 20 (1991): 345–375.

Kugel, Rebecca, and Lucy Eldersveld Murphy, eds. *Native Women's History in Eastern North America before 1900: A Guide to Research and Writing* (2007).

LaDuke, Winona. *All Our Relations: Native Struggles for Land and Life* (1999).

Lewis, David Rich. "Still Native: The Significance of Native Americans in the History of the Twentieth-Century American West." *Western Historical Quarterly* 24 (May 1993): 203–227.

Mancall, Peter C., and James H. Merrell, eds. *American Encounters: Natives and Newcomers from European Contact to Indian Removal, 1500–1850* (2nd ed., 2007).

Mankiller, Wilma. *Every Day Is a Good Day: Reflections by Contemporary Indigenous Women* (2004).

Martin, Calvin, ed. *The American Indian and the Problem of History* (1987).

Meyer, Melissa L., and Kerwin Lee Klein. "Native American Studies and the End of Ethnohistory." In *Studying Native America: Problems and Prospects,* ed. Russell Thornton (1998).

Mihesuah, Devon, ed. *Natives and Academics: Researching and Writing About American Indians* (1998).

Mihesuah, Devon Abbot, and Angela Cavender Wilson, eds. *Indigenizing the Academy: Transforming Scholarship and Empowering Communities* (2004).

Miles, George. "To Hear an Old Voice: Rediscovering Native Americans in American History." In *Under an Open Sky: Rethinking America's Western Past,* ed. William Cronon, George Miles, and Jay Gitlin. New York: W.W. Norton, 1992.

Ortiz, Alfonso. "Indian/White Relations: A View from the Other Side of the 'Frontier.'" In *Indians in American History: An Introduction,* ed. Frederick E. Hoxie and Peter Iverson (1988).

Parman, Donald L., and Catherine Price. "A 'Work in Progress': The Emergence of Indian History as a Professional Field." *Western Historical Quarterly* 20 (1989): 185–196.

Richter, Daniel K. "Whose Indian History?" *William and Mary Quarterly* 50 (April 1993): 379–393.

Sheridan, Thomas E. "How to Tell the Story of a 'People Without History.'" *Journal of the Southwest* 30 (1988): 168–189.

Sturtevant, William C., ed. *Handbook of North American Indians,* 20 vols. (1978).

White, Richard. "Indian Peoples and the Natural World: Asking the Right Questions." In *Rethinking American Indian History,* ed. Donald L.Fixico (1997).

CHAPTER 2

Early American History

For many Americans, the title of this chapter probably calls to mind images of men in powdered wigs, bearing muskets, penning declarations. Or, for some, it might conjure images of the Mayflower, coming to shore at Plymouth Rock. Others might push the timeline a bit earlier to consider the Spanish conquistadors and Columbus. But, that is probably as far back as most would go.

This chapter aims to challenge such assumptions. It asserts that "early American history" does not begin in 1492, or in 1620, or in 1776. Rather, the story begins thousands of years before the arrival of the Europeans, perhaps as far back as 40,000 years, to the time when the first people inhabited the "Americas." That people lived in the Western Hemisphere long before Columbus's journey is no longer in dispute. But, as recently as the 1950s, most Europeans and European Americans were reluctant to accept that Indigenous peoples in this pre-European era possessed what can properly be called a "history." They took as a given that history existed only if it was written down, and only if it focused on the development of "civilizations." Many, in fact, continue to hold this belief today. But, must there be writing for there to be history? And, was "civilization" absent from the Americas? Consider these questions as you read the documents and essays that follow. In addition, contemplate the question raised in Chapter 1: Why is this history worth studying? Why should we, non-Indians as well as Indians, seek to know something about early—that is, pre-Columbian—American history?

◈ DOCUMENTS

The first five documents in this chapter present excerpts and versions of five stories, from five distinct American Indian nations, from five different parts of the continent. The Skagit story (Document 1), from the Pacific Northwest, is placed first on purpose, to challenge the notion that American history must begin on the opposite end of the continent, in the Caribbean, with Columbus. Document 2 moves eastward from Skagit territory to the Arikiras of the northern Plains, whereas Documents 3 and 4 move further east still, to the Iroquois people of the

Northeast and the Cherokees of the Southeast, respectively. Document 5 returns to the west—or, to be more specific, the Southwest—with a version of a traditional Hopi story about their "Blue Corn Ear Maiden." This story, in fact, will connect particularly well with the second essay later in the chapter, which further discusses the enduring centrality of corn in Hopi culture. These documents derive from oral traditions, a historical source discussed in the essays in Chapter 1. They have been influenced by multiple potential factors: the teller, the translator, the transcriber, various possible editors, the particular version of the story, the intended audience, and even the time of year when the story was initially told. Given those considerations, are such stories "reliable" historical records? Are they "histories" at all? In whatever manner one might answer such questions, what do these stories teach us?

Oral traditions and written accounts are only two possible ways to transmit and maintain the past. With the final three documents in this chapter, the subject of American Indian history helps us further widen our sense of how history can be conveyed. In Document 6, the Pueblos sing their history. In Document 7, a Plains tribe records its history through pictographs. In this case, a Kiowa man named Dohasan presents his calendar, in which he has inscribed, for each year, a pictograph of an important event in the history of his people. Since Kiowas and other Plains Indians usually decided upon and composed pictographs in the winter, they often referred to such calendars as "winter counts." In Document 8, Dudley and Ruth Patterson, Western Apaches, try to explain to Keith Basso, a white anthropologist, that the land itself teaches them their history. Note that Patterson and Basso are having this conversation about "early American history" in modern, or at least recent, times—the 1970s and 1980s. What might that tell us? The map in the final document, Document 9, depicts some of the ancient sites mentioned in this chapter's essays on pre-Columbian history.

1. The Skagit Describe Their Origins, n.d.

In the beginning, Raven and Mink and Coyote helped the Creator plan the world. They were in on all the arguments. They helped the Creator decide to have all the rivers flow only one way; they first thought that the water should flow up one side of the river and down on the other. They decided that there should be bends in the rivers, so that there would be eddies where the fish could stop and rest. They decided that beasts should be placed in the forests. Human beings would have to keep out of their way.

Human beings will not live on this earth forever, agreed Raven and Mink, Coyote, and Old Creator. They will stay only for a short time. Then the body will go back to the earth and the spirit back to the spirit world. All living things, they said, will be male and female—animals and plants, fish and birds. And everything will get its food from the earth, the soil.

The Creator gave four names for the earth. He said that only a few people should know the names; those few should have special preparation for that knowledge, to receive that special spirit power. If many people should know the names, the world would change too soon and too suddenly. One of the names is for the sun, which rises in the east and brings warmth and light. Another is for the rivers, streams, and salt water. The third is for the soil; our bodies go back to it. The fourth is for the forest; the forest is older than human beings, and is for everyone on the earth.

After the world had been created for a while, everyone learned the four names for the earth. Everyone and everything spoke the Skagit language. When the people began to talk to the trees, then the change came. The change was a flood. Water covered everything but two high mountains—Kobah and Takobah. Those two mountains—Mount Baker and Mount Rainier—did not go under.

When the people saw the flood coming, they made a great big canoe. They loaded it with two of everything living on earth, with the male and female of every animal and plant. When the flood was over, the canoe landed on the prairie in the Skagit country. Five people were in the canoe. After the flood, when the land was dry again, they made their way back here.

A child was born to the man and his wife who had been in the canoe. He became Doquebuth, the new Creator. He created after the flood, after the world changed.

When he was old enough, Doquebuth was told to go to the lake—Lake Campbell it is called now—to swim and fast and get his spirit power. But the boy played around and did not obey orders. Coyote fed him, and the boy did not try to get his spirit power. So his family deserted him. When he came home, no one was there. His family had gone and had taken everything with them except what belonged to the boy. They left his dog behind and the hides of the chipmunks and squirrels the boy had shot when hunting. His grandmother left fire for him in a clamshell. From the skins which he had dried, the boy made a blanket.

When he found that his family had deserted him, he realized that he had done wrong. So he began to swim and to fast. For many, many days he swam and fasted. No one can get spirit power unless he is clean and unless his stomach is empty.

One day the boy dreamed that Old Creator came.

"Take my blanket," said Old Creator. "It is the blanket of the whole earth. Wave it over the waters, and name the four names of the earth. Then there will be food for everyone."

That is how the boy got his spirit power from Old Creator. He waved the blanket over the water and over the forest. Then there was food for everyone. But there were no people yet. The boy swam some more and kept on fasting.

Old Creator came to him again in a dream.

"Gather together all the bones of the people who lived here before the flood. Gather the bones and pile them into a big pile. Then wave my blanket over them, and name the four names of the earth."

The young man did as he was told in his dream, and people were created from the bones. But they could not talk. They moved about but were not quite completed.

The young Creator swam some more. A third time Old Creator came to him in a dream. This time he told the young man that he should make brains for the new people. So he waved the blanket over the earth and named the four names of the earth. That is how brains were made—from the soil of the earth.

Then the people could talk. They spoke many different languages. But where they should live the young Creator did not know. So he swam some more. In his dream, Old Creator told him to stop over the big island, from ocean to ocean, and blow the people back where they belonged. So Doquebuth blew the people back to the place where they had lived before the flood. Some he placed in the buffalo country, some by the salt water, some by fresh water, some in the forests. That is why the people in the different places speak different languages.

The people created after the flood prophesied that a new language would be introduced into our country. It will be the only language spoken, when the next change comes. When we can understand animals, we will know that the change is halfway. When we can talk to the forest, we will know that the change has come.

The flood was one change. Another is yet to come. The world will change again. When it will change, we do not know.

2. The Arikira Tell of Their Creation, n.d.

A long time ago, the Arikara lived under the ground. There were four animals who looked with pity upon the people, and these animals agreed to take the people up on top of the earth. These animals were the long-nosed Mouse, the Mole, the Badger, and the Fox. The Fox was the messenger to the people to tell them of what the animals were doing. The Mole was the first to dig. He ran back, for he was blinded by the brightness of the sun. The animals went out. The people came out of the earth, the Fox being in the lead. As the people were coming out there was an earthquake. The Arikara came out. The other people were again held fast by the earth.

These people who came out from the ground then journeyed west. They came to a place where the earth shook, so that there was a chasm or a steep bank. The people waited and cried. The Badger stepped forward and began digging, so that it made a pathway for the people.... After all the people had passed the first obstacles they sat down and gave thanks and made offerings to the gods.

Again they went upon their journey, and it stormed. In front of them was a river. They could not cross it, for it was very deep; but a Loon was sent by the gods. The Loon came to the people, and said: "Your mother is traveling in the heavens to help you. I was sent by the gods to open up this river, so you could cross and go on your journey." The Loon flew across the river, flew back, then dived and came out on the other side of the river. The river was opened; it banked up on each side; the people crossed over and the waters came together again. Some people were left on the other side.

The Arikaras Describe Their Origins, from "The Origin of the Arikara," in George A. Dorsey, ed., *Traditions of the Arikara* (Washington, D.C., 1904).

Again they journeyed, and they came to a place where Mother-Corn stopped and said: "The big Black-Wind is angry, for we did not ask it to come with us, neither did we make it one of the gods to receive smoke. But," said Mother-Corn, "the Black-Meteoric-Star understands this storm; it will help us." Mother-Corn went on, and said: "Here we are. We must hurry for the big Black-Wind is coming, taking everything it meets. There is a cedar tree. Get under that cedar tree. Get under that cedar tree," said Mother-Corn. "The Black-Meteoric-Star placed it there. The Star stands solid, for its right leg is cedar; its left leg is stone. It can not be blown away. Get under its branches." So the people crawled under its branches. The Black-Wind came and took many people, notwithstanding.

The people came out, and they went on. They came to another difficulty— a steep mountain bank, and they stopped. The Bear came forth, and said, "I will go through this place first." So the Bear went to digging steps for the people. Steps were made on both sides and the people went across.

After they had been gone for some time, a Dog came up, and said: "Why did you people leave me behind? I shall be the one that you shall kill, and my meat shall be offered to the gods. I shall also fix it so that all animals shall make great medicine-men of you. My father is the Sun. He has given me all this power. I will give my power to all animals, then I will stay with the people, so they will not forget my promise to them." The people were thankful to the Dog.

3. The Iroquois Depict the World on the Turtle's Back, n.d.

In the beginning there was no world, no land, no creatures of the kind that are around us now, and there were no men. But there was a great ocean which occupied space as far as anyone could see. Above the ocean was a great void of air. And in the air there lived the birds of the sea; in the ocean lived the fish and the creatures of the deep. Far above this unpeopled world, there was a Sky-World. Here lived gods who were like people—like Iroquois.

In the Sky-World there was a man who had a wife, and the wife was expecting a child. The woman became hungry for all kinds of strange delicacies, as women do when they are with child. She kept her husband busy almost to distraction finding delicious things for her to eat.

In the middle of the Sky-World there grew a Great Tree which was not like any of the trees that we know. It was tremendous; it had grown there forever. It had enormous roots that spread out from the floor of the Sky-World. And on its branches there were many different kinds of leaves and different kinds of fruits and flowers. The tree was not supposed to be marked or mutilated by any of the beings who dwelt in the Sky-World. It was a sacred tree that stood at the center of the universe.

The woman decided that she wanted some bark from one of the roots of the Great Tree—perhaps as a food or as a medicine, we don't know. She told her husband this. He didn't like the idea. He knew it was wrong. But she insisted,

The Iroquois Depict the World on the Turtle's Back, n.d., from *The Great Tree and the Longhouse: The Culture of the Iroquois* by Hazel W. Hertzberg. Published by the American Anthropological Association.

and he gave in. So he dug a hole among the roots of this great sky tree, and he bared some of its roots. But the floor of the Sky-World wasn't very thick, and he broke a hole through it. He was terrified, for he had never expected to find empty space underneath the world.

But his wife was filled with curiosity. He wouldn't get any of the roots for her, so she set out to do it herself. She bent over and she looked down, and she saw the ocean far below. She leaned down and stuck her head through the hole and looked all around. No one knows just what happened next. Some say she slipped. Some say that her husband, fed up with all the demands she had made on him, pushed her.

So she fell through the hole. As she fell, she frantically grabbed at its edges, but her hands slipped. However, between her fingers there clung bits of things that were growing on the floor of the Sky-World and bits of the root tips of the Great Tree. And so she began to fall toward the great ocean far below.

The birds of the sea saw the woman falling, and they immediately consulted with each other as to what they could do to help her. Flying wingtip to wingtip they made a great feathery raft in the sky to support her, and thus they broke her fall. But of course it was not possible for them to carry the woman very long. Some of the other birds of the sky flew down to the surface of the ocean and called up the ocean creatures to see what they could do to help. The great sea turtle came and agreed to receive her on his back. The birds placed her gently on the shell of the turtle, and now the turtle floated about on the huge ocean with the woman safely on his back.

The beings up in the Sky-World paid no attention to this. They knew what was happening, but they chose to ignore it.

When the woman recovered from her shock and terror, she looked around her. All that she could see were the birds and the sea creatures and the sky and the ocean.

And the woman said to herself that she would die. But the creatures of the sea came to her and said that they would try to help her and asked her what they could do. She told them that if they could get some soil, she could plant the roots stuck between her fingers, and from them plants would grow. The sea animals said perhaps there was dirt at the bottom of the ocean, but no one had ever been down there so they could not be sure.

If there was dirt at the bottom of the ocean, it was far, far below the surface in the cold deeps. But the animals said they would try to get some. One by one the diving birds and animals tried and failed. They went to the limits of their endurance, but they could not get to the bottom of the ocean. Finally, the muskrat said he would try. He dived and disappeared. All the creatures waited, holding their breath, but he did not return. After a long time, this little body floated up to the surface of the ocean, a tiny crumb of earth clutched in his paw. He seemed to be dead. They pulled him up on the turtle's back and they sang and prayed over him and breathed air into his mouth, and finally, he stirred. Thus it was the muskrat, the Earth-Diver, who brought from the bottom of the ocean the soil from which the earth was to grow.

The woman took the tiny clod of dirt and placed it on the middle of the great sea turtle's back. Then the woman began to walk in a circle around it, moving in the direction that the sun goes. The earth began to grow. When the earth was big enough, she planted the roots she had clutched between her fingers when she fell from the Sky-World. Thus the plants grew on the earth.

To keep the earth growing, the woman walked as the sun goes, moving in the direction that the people still move in the dance rituals. She gathered roots and plants to eat and built herself a little hut. After a while, the woman's time came, and she was delivered of a daughter. The woman and her daughter kept walking in a circle around the earth, so that the earth and plants would continue to grow. They lived on the plants and roots they gathered. The girl grew up with her mother, cut off forever from the Sky-World above, knowing only the birds and the creatures of the sea, seeing no other beings like herself.

One day, when the girl had grown to womanhood, a man appeared. No one knows for sure who this man was. He had something to do with the gods above. Perhaps he was the West Wind. As the girl looked at him, she was filled with terror, and amazement, and warmth, and she fainted dead away. As she lay on the ground, the man reached into his quiver, and he took out two arrows, one sharp and one blunt, and he laid them across the body of the girl, and quietly went away.

When the girl awoke from her faint, she and her mother continued to walk around the earth. After a while, they knew that the girl was to bear a child. They did not know it, but the girl was to bear twins.

Within the girl's body, the twins began to argue and quarrel with one another. There could be no peace between them. As the time approached for them to be born, the twins fought about their birth. The right-handed twin wanted to be born in the normal way, as all children are born. But the left-handed twin said no. He said he saw light in another direction, and said he would be born that way. The right-handed twin beseeched him not to, saying that he would kill their mother. But the left-handed twin was stubborn. He went in the direction where he saw light. But he could not be born through his mother's mouth or her nose. He was born through her left armpit, and killed her. And meanwhile, the right-handed twin was born in the normal way, as all children are born.

The twins met in the world outside, and the right-handed twin accused his brother of murdering their mother. But the grandmother told them to stop their quarreling. They buried their mother. And from her grave grew the plants which the people still use. From her head grew the corn, the beans, and the squash—"our supporters, the three sisters." And from her heart grew the sacred tobacco, which the people still use in the ceremonies and by whose upward-floating smoke they send thanks. The women call her "our mother," and they dance and sing in the rituals so that the corn, the beans, and the squash may grow to feed the people.

But the conflict of the twins did not end at the grave of their mother. And, strangely enough, the grandmother favored the left-handed twin.

The right-handed twin was angry, and he grew more angry as he thought how his brother had killed their mother. The right-handed twin was the one who did everything just as he should. He said what he meant, and he meant what he said. He always told the truth, and he always tried to accomplish what seemed to be right and reasonable. The left-handed twin never said what he meant or meant what he said. He always lied, and he always did things backward. You could never tell what he was trying to do because he always made it look as if he were doing the opposite. He was the devious one.

These two brothers, as they grew up, represented two ways of the world which are in all people. The Indians did not call these the right and the wrong.

They called them the straight mind and the crooked mind, the upright man and the devious man, the right and the left.

The twins had creative powers. They took clay and modeled it into animals, and they gave these animals life. And in this they contended with one another. The right-handed twin made the deer, and the left-handed twin made the mountain lion which kills the deer. But the right-handed twin knew there would always be more deer than mountain lions. And he made another animal. He made the ground squirrel. The left-handed twin saw that the mountain lion could not get to the ground squirrel, who digs a hole, so he made the weasel. And although the weasel can go into the ground squirrel's hole and kill him, there are lots of ground squirrels and not so many weasels. Next the right-handed twin decided he would make an animal that the weasel could not kill, so he made the porcupine. But the left-handed twin made the bear, who flips the porcupine over on his back and tears out his belly.

And the right-handed twin made berries and fruits of other kinds for his creatures to live on. The left-handed twin made briars and poison ivy, and the poisonous plants like the baneberry and the dogberry, and the suicide root with which people kill themselves when they go out of their minds. And the left-handed twin made medicines, for good and for evil, for doctoring and for witchcraft.

And finally, the right-handed twin made man. The people do not know just how much the left-handed twin had to do with making man. Man was made of clay, like pottery, and baked in the fire.

The world the twins made was a balanced and orderly world, and this was good. The plant-eating animals created by the right-handed twin would eat up all the vegetation if their number was not kept down by the meat-eating animals which the left-handed twin created. But if these carnivorous animals ate too many other animals, then they would starve, for they would run out of meat. So the right- and the left-handed twins built balance into the world.

These two beings rule the world and keep an eye on the affairs of men. The right-handed twin, the Master of Life, lives in the Sky-World. He is content with the world he helped to create and with his favorite creatures, the humans. The scent of sacred tobacco rising from the earth comes gloriously to his nostrils.

In the world below lives the left-handed twin. He knows the world of men, and he finds contentment in it. He hears the sounds of warfare and torture, and he finds them good.

In the daytime, the people have rituals which honor the right-handed twin. Through the daytime rituals they thank the Master of Life. In the nighttime, the people dance and sing for the left-handed twin.

4. The Cherokees Narrate Their Beginnings, n.d.

The earth is a great island floating in a sea of water, and suspended at each of the four cardinal points by a cord hanging down from the sky vault, which is of solid rock. When the world grows old and worn out, the people will die and the

James Mooney, *Myths of the Cherokee*, Nineteenth Annual Report, Bureau of Ethnology (Washington, D.C.: Government Printing Office, 1900).

cords will break and let the earth sink down into the ocean, and all will be water again. The Indians are afraid of this.

When all was water, the animals were above in Gălûñ'lătĭ, beyond the arch; but it was very much crowded, and they were wanting more room. They wondered what was below the water, and at last Dâyuni'sĭ, "Beaver's Grandchild," the little Water-beetle, offered to go and see if it could learn. It darted in every direction over the surface of the water, but could find no firm place to rest. Then it dived to the bottom and came up with some soft mud, which began to grow and spread on every side until it became the island which we call the earth. It was afterward fastened to the sky with four cords, but no one remembers who did this.

At first the earth was flat and very soft and wet. The animals were anxious to get down, and sent out different birds to see if it was yet dry, but they found no place to alight and came back again to Gălûñ'lătĭ. At last it seemed to be time, and they sent out the Buzzard and told him to go and make ready for them. This was the Great Buzzard, the father of all the buzzards we see now. He flew all over the earth, low down near the ground, and it was still soft. When he reached the Cherokee country, he was very tired, and his wings began to flap and strike the ground, and wherever they struck the earth there was a valley, and where they turned up again there was a mountain. When the animals above saw this, they were afraid that the whole world would be mountains, so they called him back, but the Cherokee country remains full of mountains to this day.

When the earth was dry and the animals came down, it was still dark, so they got the sun and set it in a track to go every day across the island from east to west, just overhead. It was too hot this way, and Tsiska'gĭlĭ', the Red Crawfish, had his shell scorched a bright red, so that his meat was spoiled; and the Cherokee do not eat it. The conjurers put the sun another hand-breadth higher in the air, but it was still too hot. They raised it another time, and another, until it was seven handbreadths high and just under the sky arch. Then it was right, and they left it so. This is why the conjurers call the highest place Gûlkwâ'gine Di'gălûñ'lătiyûñ', "the seventh height," because it is seven hand-breadths above the earth. Every day the sun goes along under this arch, and returns at night on the upper side to the starting place.

There is another world under this, and it is like ours in everything—animals, plants, and people—save that the seasons are different. The streams that come down from the mountains are the trails by which we reach this underworld, and the springs at their heads are the doorways by which we enter it, but to do this one must fast and go to water and have one of the underground people for a guide. We know that the seasons in the underworld are different from ours, because the water in the springs is always warmer in winter and cooler in summer than the outer air.

When the animals and plants were first made—we do not know by whom—they were told to watch and keep awake for seven nights, just as young men now fast and keep awake when they pray to their medicine. They tried to do this, and nearly all were awake through the first night, but the next night several dropped off to sleep, and the third night others were asleep, and then others, until, on the seventh night, of all the animals only the owl, the panther, and one or two more were still awake. To these were given the power to see and to go about in the dark, and to make prey of the birds and animals which must sleep at night. Of the trees only the cedar, the pine, the spruce, the holly, and the laurel were awake to the end, and to them it was given to be always green and to be greatest for medicine, but to the others it was said: "Because you have not endured to the end you shall lose your hair every winter."

Men came after the animals and plants. At first there were only a brother and sister until he struck her with a fish and told her to multiply, and so it was. In seven days a child was born to her, and thereafter every seven days another, and they increased very fast until there was danger that the world could not keep them. Then it was made that a woman should have only one child in a year, and it has been so ever since.

5. The Hopis Describe Blue Corn Ear Maiden's Revenge, n.d.

A long time ago, two maidens lived in Oraibi. They were close friends and often ground corn at one another's houses. Their friendship ended abruptly, however, when they both fell in love with the same young man. One of them, Yellow Corn Ear Maiden, had supernatural powers, and she made up her mind to destroy her rival, Blue Corn Ear Maiden. Early one morning the two girls carried their jugs to get water from Spider Spring, northeast of the village. On the way back they came to a sand hill, and Yellow Corn Ear Maiden said, "Let's sit down and rest for a while."

After a time she said: "Let's play catch. You run down the hill, and I'll throw something at you, and you throw it back." She drew from her bosom a pretty little wheel that gleamed with all the colors of the rainbow. When her friend reached the foot of the hill, Yellow Corn Ear Maiden threw the wheel at her, but it was so heavy that Blue Corn Ear Maiden collapsed on the ground when she caught it. When she stood up again, she was a coyote. Yellow Corn Ear Maiden laughed and said, "That's what you get for quarreling with me!" She shooed the coyote away, took her own jug, and went back to the village.

Sadly the coyote climbed the hill and tried to pick up her jug, but without hands she couldn't. She sat down and cried until evening. After dark she tried to enter the village, but the dogs drove her away. She made a large circuit around the village and tried to go in from another side, but she was again driven away by the dogs. By this time she was getting very hungry, so she went off to the west hoping to find something to eat.

It was the fall of the year, and the people were busy in the fields working on their crops. Carefully she crept up to one of the homemade shelters in which the farmers lived, found two roasted ears of corn that had been left on top, and ate them right up. She tried a third time to enter the village, but when the dogs smelled her and drove her away, she knew she wouldn't be able to get home as long as she looked and smelled like a coyote.

She wandered through the entire night, until she arrived at a place which belonged to two Qooqoqlom Kachinas who were hunting in that region. In their hut she found plenty of baked rabbit meat and entrails, and lots of rabbit

Henry Voth, *The Traditions of the Hopi*, Field Columbian Museum Publications in Anthropology, vol. 8 (Chicago: The Museum, 1905), as excerpted in Richard Erdoes and Alfonso Ortiz, American Indian Myths and Legends (New York: Pantheon Books, 1984), 409–412.

skins. Starving but also exhausted, she ate a little meat and a bit of entrail (which she did not like very much). Since the two hunters had already eaten and left for the hunt, she decided to stay in their hut and rest all day.

In the evening the two Qooqoqlom hunters returned. With their keen eyes and ears, they knew even as they approached that something was wrong. One of them peeked in and whispered, "There is a coyote in our hut and he's eaten some of our meat." He got his bow and arrows and was aiming at the intruder, when the other one said, "No, let's try to capture him alive and take him home to our grandmother, Spider Woman." So they went in but, much to their surprise, they heard the coyote sob and saw tears trickling from its eyes. Even they were touched by the sight, and one of them took a large piece of meat from his pouch, broke it in two, and gave a portion to the visitor, who ate it with relish. They then decided to go back home that evening. They tied up the meat and the skins, and also tied the feet of the coyote. Loading everything upon their backs, they returned to Kachina Gap, a short distance northwest of Oraibi.

As soon as they arrived, they called to Spider Woman, "Grandmother, we have brought you an animal. Come and help us lift it off our backs." She was delighted with her present, and placed the coyote with the rabbit meat near the fireplace. Then the woman looked closely at the wretched animal and exclaimed, "Alas! That poor one! This is no coyote. Thankfully you have not killed it. Where did you find it?" They told her how they had found and captured it in their hunting hut. She sent one of the men into the village after some *tomóala* a potent plant; the other one she sent to the woods to fetch a few juniper branches.

While they were gone she boiled some water, and when the man with the *tomóala* returned, she poured the water into a vessel and hooked one *tomóala* pod into the coyote's neck and another one into her back. She then plunged the animal into the water and covered her with a piece of native cloth. Placing her hand upon the cover, Spider Woman took hold of the two hooks and kept twisting and turning them until she had pulled off the skin of the coyote. When she threw aside the cloth, there was Blue Corn Ear Maiden, still in her original clothes, her hair tied in whorls just as it had been when she left the village. The woman asked how she had met this fate, and the maiden told her the whole story. Spider Woman comforted her, saying, "That Yellow Corn Ear Maiden is bad, but you will have your revenge."

At this point, the other hunter returned with the juniper branches. She took the maiden, together with the branches and the water, into another room and there bathed her, then gave her some corn, which the maiden ground into meal. The maiden stayed there for several days, until Spider Woman told her that her mother was very sick with worry and that she should go home. But first Spider Woman called together a number of Kachinas who lived nearby and told them all that had happened. "I want you to return her to her house," she said, and they were willing. She dressed the maiden in wonderful finery, put her hair into fresh whorls, and placed over her shoulders a new *atoo*. She instructed her to have her father make *bahos*, prayer sticks, and a number of *nakwakwosis* as prayer offerings to the leader of the Kachinas and the leader of the singing. Lastly, she gave her a plan to deal with Yellow Corn Ear Maiden. So off they set, the maiden walking in the rear of the line of Kachinas.

At early dawn, the so-called white dawn, they arrived near the house of the village chief, where the Pongowe kiva is at present situated; there they performed their first dance, singing while they danced. Those already stirring in the village rushed out to see the Kachinas dancing. Soon the news was whispered around through the whole village that the Kachinas had brought a maiden with them, and some soon recognized Blue Corn Ear Maiden and ran to the house of her parents. The latter refused to believe the news, and four messengers had to be sent to convince them. When they finally went to the Kachinas, the procession had arrived at the dancing plaza in the center of the village. "So you have come," the mother said, and began to cry. She wanted to take her daughter with her then, but the girl said, "Wait a little," and gave her father Spider Woman's instructions. The Kachinas continued their dancing, with the *mana*, [actually men dressed up like women] the female Kachinas waiting by their side. When finally the father brought the prayer offerings, he gave one *baho* to the leader, the other to his daughter. After the dancing was over, the daughter gave her prayer stick to the leader of the singing. The *nakwakosis* were distributed among the other Kachinas, and after the happy father had thanked them for bringing his child, they returned to their own homes.

Blue Corn Ear Maiden rested at her parents' for a day and a night, but early the next morning she went to grind corn, and as she did, she sang a little song about her adventures. When Yellow Corn Ear Maiden heard her voice, she came rushing out to proclaim how delighted she was at her friend's return. Blue Corn Ear Maiden treated her cordially, just as Spider Woman had told her to. They ground corn together all day, just as they had done before. In the evening they went after water again, to the same spring where they had gotten water before. While they were filling their jugs, Yellow Corn Ear Maiden noticed that her friend was dipping her water with a peculiar little vessel (which Spider Woman had given her) and that the water, which ran into the jug, was very beautiful, glistening with the colors of the rainbow. She said to her friend: "What have you there? Let me see that little cup." Yes," her friend said, "that is a very fine cup, and the water tastes good from it, too." Thereupon she drank from it and handed it to her friend, who also drank. Immediately she fell down and was turned into a bull snake. "There! You will remain on the ground forever," Blue Corn Ear Maiden said. "You tried once to destroy me, but it didn't work. No one will help restore you, though." She laughed, picked up her jug, and returned to the village.

So the bull snake slithered away to begin its lifelong wandering. It was often hungry, but as it couldn't move very fast, it had to capture its prey by luring little rabbits and birds with its powerful intoxicating breath.

Yellow Corn Ear Maiden tried finally to return to her village, where she was killed by her own parents. They, of course, didn't know the snake they had killed was their own daughter. But her soul was liberated to go to the Skeleton House.

Ever since then some dead sorcerers will take the form of bull snakes and leave their graves, still wound in the yucca leaves with which the corpse was tied up when laid away. If such a bull snake is killed, the soul of the sorcerer living in it is set free and can go to the Skeleton House, just as Yellow Corn Ear Maiden did at last.

6. The Pueblos Sing of the Sky Loom, n.d.

Oh our Mother the Earth oh our Father the Sky
Your children are we
    with tired backs we bring you the gifts you love

So weave for us a garment of brightness

May the warp be the white light of morning
May the weft be the red light of evening
May the fringes be the falling rain
May the border be the standing rainbow

Weave for us this bright garment
that we may walk where birds sing
    where grass is green

Oh our Mother the Earth oh our Father the Sky

7. Dohasan (Kiowa) Records History as a "Winter Count," 1832–1892

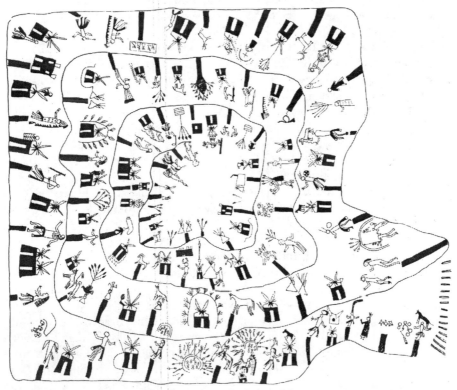

Phoebe A. Hearst Museum of Anthropology, Berkeley, CA.

8. Dudley and Ruth Patterson (Western Apache)
See Their History in Places, ca. 1979–1984

Back at his house in Cibecue, Dudley Patterson drains his cup of coffee and leans forward in his chair. On the ground near his feet a band of red ants is dismantling the corpse of a large grasshopper, and within seconds the intricate patterns of their furious activity have captured his attention. This does not surprise me. I have known Dudley for twelve years and on other occasions have seen him withdraw from social encounters to keep counsel with himself. I also know that he is mightily interested in red ants and holds them in high esteem. I would like to ask him a few more questions, but unless he invites me to do so (and by now, I suspect, he may have had enough) it would be rude to disturb him. He has made it clear that he wants to be left alone.

We sit quietly together for more than ten minutes, smoking cigarettes and enjoying the morning air, and I try to picture the cotton-wood tree that towers beside the stream at Trail Goes Down Between Two Hills. I am keenly aware that my perception of the tree has changed. The stories of Old Man Owl make its impressive size seem decidedly less important, and what strikes me as never before is its standing in the Cibecue community as a visible embodiment of myth, a leafy monument to Apache ancestral wisdom. I am also aware that the place-name identifying the tree's location—Gizhyaa'itiné—has taken on a vibrant new dimension. Formerly nothing more than a nicely descriptive toponym, it has acquired the stamp of human events, of consequential happenings, of memorable times in the life of a people. As a result, the name seems suddenly fuller, somehow larger, endowed with added force. Because now, besides evoking images of a piece of local countryside, it calls up thoughts of fabled deeds and the singular cast of actors who there played them out. Gizhyaa'itiné. Repeating the place-name silently to myself, I decide that Dudley Patterson's narratives have transformed its referent from a geographical site into something resembling a theater, a natural stage upon the land (vacant now but with props still fully intact) where significant moral dramas unfolded in the past. Gizhyaa'itiné. In my mind's eye, I can almost see the beautiful Apache sisters … really laughing at Old Man Owl.

Still engrossed in his ants, Dudley remains oblivious to the sights and sounds around him—a pair of ravens perched on his tool shed, the distant wailing of a distressed child, a vicious dogfight that erupts without warning in the tall grass behind his house. It is only when his older sister arrives on foot with a dishpan filled with freshly made tortillas that he glances up and sets his thoughts aside. He explains to Ruth Patterson that he has been talking to me about the land and how it can make people wise. "Wisdom," Ruth says firmly in Apache. "It's difficult!" And then, after inviting me to stay and eat with them, she enters Dudley's house to prepare a simple meal.

Ruth's remark prompts a surge of ethnographic gloom, forcing me to acknowledge that I know next to nothing about Apache conceptions of wisdom. In what is wisdom thought to consist? How does one detect its presence or absence? How is it acquired? Do persons receive instruction in wisdom or is it something they arrive at, or fail to arrive at, entirely on their own? And why is it, as Ruth had said, that wisdom is "difficult"? If I am to understand something of how places work to make people wise, an arresting idea I find instantly compelling, these are matters I must try to explore.

And who better to explore them with than Dudley Patterson? He is known to be wise—many people have said so—and I have to begin somewhere. So without further ado I put the question to him: "What is wisdom?" Dudley greets my query with a faintly startled look that recedes into a quizzical expression I have not seen before. "It's in these places," he says. "Wisdom sits in places." Hesitant but unenlightened, I present the query again. "Yes, but what is it?" Now it is Dudley's turn to hesitate. Removing his hat, he rests it on his lap and gazes into the distance. As he continues to look away, the suspicion grows that I have offended him, that my question about wisdom has exceeded the limits of propriety and taste. Increasingly apprehensive, I feel all thumbs, clumsy and embarrassed, an impulsive dolt who acted without thinking. What Dudley is feeling I cannot tell, but in less than a minute he rescues the situation and I am much relieved. "Wisdom sits in places," he says again. And then, unbidden, he begins to tell me why.

> Long ago, the people moved around all the time. They went everywhere looking for food and watching out for enemies. It was hard for them. They were poor. They were often hungry. The women went out with their daughters to gather acorns, maybe walnuts. They went in search of all kinds of plants. Some man with a rifle and bullets always went with them. He looked out for danger.
>
> Then they got to a good place and camped there. All day they gathered acorns. The women showed their daughters how to do it. Now they stopped working for a little while to eat and drink.
>
> Then one of the women talked to the girls. "Do you see that mountain over there? I want you to look at it. Its name is Dził Ndeezé (Long Mountain). Remember it! Do you know what happened long ago close to that mountain? Well, now I'm going to tell you about it." Then she told them a story about what happened there. After she had finished she said, "Well, now you know what happened at Long Mountain. What I have told you is true. I didn't make it up. I learned it from my grandmother. Look at that mountain and think about it! It will help make you wise."
>
> Then she pointed to another place and did the same way again. "Do you see that spring over there? Look at it! Its name is Dǫ' Bigowąné (Fly's Camp)." Now she told them a story about that place, too. "Think about it," she said. "Someday, after you have grown up, you will be wise," she said. Everywhere they went they did like that. They gave their daughters place-names and stories. "You should think about this," they said.

The same was done with boys. They went hunting for deer with their fathers and uncles. They didn't come home until they had killed many deer. Everyone was happy when they came back. Now they had meat to eat.

Then, when they were out hunting, one of the men would talk to the boys. "Do you see where the trail crosses the wash? Look at it! Its name is Ma' Téhilizhé (Coyote Pisses In The Water). Something happened there long ago. I'm going to tell you about it." Now he told the story to them. "Don't forget it," he said. "I want you to think about it. Someday it's going to make you wise."

Then they would stop at some other place. "This place is named Tséé Deeschii' Ts'ǫsé (Slender Red Rock Ridge). Something happened here, also," he said. He told them that story. "Remember what I have told you," he said.

It was like that. The people who went many places were wise. They knew all about them. They thought about them. I've been all over this country. I went with my grandfather when I was a boy. I also traveled with my uncles. They taught me the names of all these places. They told me stories about all of them. I've thought about all of them for a long time. I still remember everything.

Sitting with my back to Dudley's house, I cannot see that Ruth Patterson has come to the door and is listening to her brother as he speaks of places and wisdom. I sense her presence, however, and when I turn around she is looking at me, her comely face arranged in what I interpret as a sympathetic smile. "It's true," she says in a bright tone of voice. "Everything he says is true. It happened that way to me."

One time—I was a young girl then—I went with my mother to Nadah Nch'íí'é (Bitter Agave). That was in 1931. We went there to roast agave. There were other people with us, quite a few of them. They were all my relatives.

Then we made camp, right below that point at the north end of the mountain. We camped by the spring there. My mother was in charge of everything. She told us what to do.

Then we dug up a lot of agave and brought it back to camp. It was hard work. It was hot. We were young girls then. We weren't yet strong and got tired easily. We really wanted to rest.

Then my mother talked to us. "You should only rest a little while. Don't be lazy. Don't think about getting tired. If you do, you'll get careless and something might happen to you."

Then she told a story. "Maybe you've heard this story before but I'm going to tell it to you anyway." She pointed to that mountain named Túzhi' Yaahigaiyé (Whiteness Spreads Out Descending To Water). "It happened over there," she said to us.

"Long ago, on the east side of that mountain, there were lots of dead oak trees. There was a woman living with her family not far away. 'We're almost out of firewood,' she said to one of her daughters. 'Go up there and bring back some of that oak.'

"Then that girl went up there. She started to gather firewood. It was very hot and she got tired fast. 'I'm getting tired,' she thought. 'I've already got enough firewood. I'll go back home.'

"Then she picked up as much firewood as she could carry. She started walking down to her camp. She got careless. She stepped on a thin flat rock. It looked strong but she forgot she was carrying all that heavy oak. The rock broke when she stepped on it. She stumbled and fell down. She hit her head on the ground. For a while she was unconscious.

"Then she came to and noticed that she was bleeding from cuts on her cheek and chin. She walked unsteadily back to her camp. She told her mother what had happened.

"Then her mother talked to her. 'You acted foolishly but you're going to be all right. You failed to see danger before it happened. You could have fallen off the trail and gotten killed on those sharp rocks below it. You were thinking only of yourself. That's why this happened to you.'"

That's the end of the story. After my mother told it to us, she spoke to us again. "Well, now you know what happened over there at Whiteness Spreads Out Descending To Water. That careless girl almost lost her life. Each of you should try to remember this. Don't forget it. If you remember what happened over there, it will help make you wise."

Then we went back to work, digging up more of agave. I got tired again—it was still very hot—but this time I didn't think about it. I just tried not to be careless.

Nowadays, hardly anyone goes out to get agave. Very few of us do that anymore. The younger ones are afraid of hard work. Even so, I've told that story to all my children. I've told them to remember it.

I thank Ruth for telling me her story. She smiles but her eyes have filled with tears. Unable to stem the rush of her emotion, she turns away and goes back inside the house. Dudley is not visibly concerned. He explains that Ruth is recalling her youth. That was during the 1920s and 1930s when Ruth and her sisters were still unmarried and worked almost daily under the close supervision of their mother and two maternal aunts. Back then, Dudley says, Cibecue was different. There were fewer people and life was less centered on the village itself. Whole Apache families, including Dudley's own, spent weeks and months away upon the land—tending cornfields, roasting agave, hunting deer, and journeying to remote cattle camps where they helped the horsemen build fences and corrals. The families traveled long distances—old people and children alike, on foot and horseback, through all kinds of weather, carrying their possessions in heavy canvas packs over narrow trails that now have all but vanished. It was a hard way to live—there were times when it got very hard—but the people were strong and hardly ever complained. They had able leaders who told them what to do, and despite the hardships involved they took pleasure in their journeys. And wherever they went they gave place-names and stories to their children. They wanted their children to know about the ancestors. They wanted their children to be wise. Ruth is remembering all of this, Dudley reports, and it makes her a little sad.

9. Selected Native American Centers in North America, ca. 1250

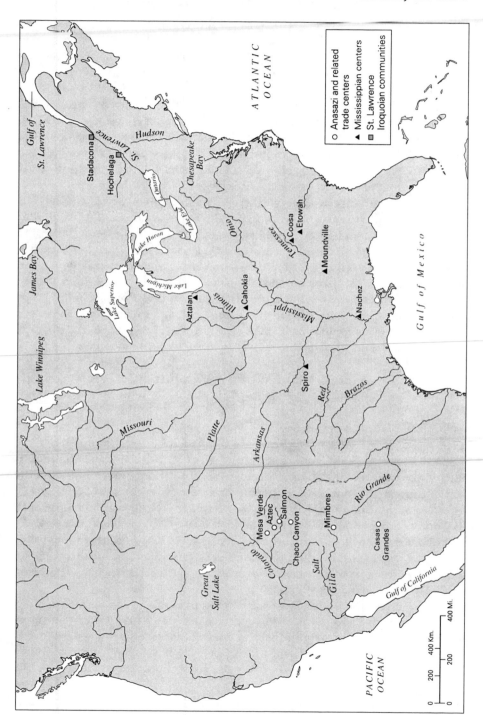

Map 2.1   Selected Native American Centers in North America, ca. 1250

◈ ESSAYS

The first essay in this chapter, "The Indians' Old World: A Continental View" by Neal Salisbury, continues to play with the words we commonly use to think about early American history. Many today still automatically use the adjective "new" to describe the Western Hemisphere. But, scientists assert that people have lived in the "Americas" for at least 12,000 years, and possibly as long as 40,000 years. Many Native peoples themselves maintain that they have always lived here. "New," then, is a relative term: new to whom? Salisbury, a professor emeritus at Smith College, provides us with a broad survey of North America in the years before European contact. What themes characterize his descriptions of this "old world"? Was it changeless? Monolithic? Simple? Were all Native peoples nomadic hunters? Was it somehow "uncivilized," and what might "civilized" actually mean?

The second essay considers whether the Indians' "old" world is completely detached from their present world. Whereas the first essay takes a wide continental view, this one adopts a focused perspective, limiting its scope to the Hopi Tribe. The authors, Virgil Masayesva, a Hopi, and Dennis Wall, a freelance writer-photographer, both worked for the Institute for Tribal Environmental Professionals (ITEP), an organization housed at Northern Arizona University in Flagstaff, Arizona. In their essay, they describe the thousand-year-long, intertwined, mutually sustaining history of the Hopi tribe and corn. Corn permeates their diet, labor, knowledge of nature, gender, stories, spirituality, and, ultimately, their very identity. For them, do the stories of their old world seem separate from their existence in the modern world?

The Indians' Old World: A Continental View

BY NEAL SALISBURY

Scholars in history, anthropology, archaeology, and other disciplines have turned increasingly over the past two decades to the study of native peoples during the colonial period of North American history. The new work in Indian history has altered the way we think about the beginning of American history and about the era of European colonization. Historians now recognize that Europeans arrived, not in a virgin land, but in one that was teeming with several million people. Beyond filling in some of the vast blanks left by previous generations' overlooking of Indians, much of this scholarship makes clear that Indians are integral to the history of colonial North America. In short, surveys of recent textbooks and of scholarly titles suggest that Native Americans are well on their way to being "mainstreamed" by colonial historians.

Substantive as this reorientation is, it remains limited. Beyond the problems inherent in representing Indian/non–Indian interactions during the colonial era lies the challenge of contextualizing the era itself. Despite opening chapters and lectures that survey the continent's native peoples and cultures, most historians continue to represent American history as having been set in motion by the

Neal Salisbury, "The Indians' Old World: Native Americans and the Coming of the Europeans," from *William and Mary Quarterly*, 53 (July 1996).

arrival of European explorers and colonizers. They have yet to recognize the existence of a North American—as opposed to English or European—background for colonial history, much less to consider the implications of such a background for understanding the three centuries following Columbus's landfall. Yet a growing body of scholarship by archaeologists, linguists, and students of Native American expressive traditions recognizes 1492 not as a beginning but as a single moment in a long history utterly detached from that of Europe. These findings call into question historians' synchronic maps and verbal descriptions of precontact Indians—their cultures, their communities, their ethnic and political designations and affiliations, and their relations with one another. Do these really describe enduring entities or do they represent epiphenomena of arbitrary moments in time? If the latter should prove to be the case, how will readings of Indian history in the colonial period be affected?

Far from being definitive, this article is intended as a stimulus to debate on these questions. It begins by drawing on recent work in archaeology, where most of the relevant scholarship has originated, to suggest one way of thinking about pre-Columbian North America in historical terms. The essay then looks at developments in several areas of the continent during the centuries preceding the arrival of Europeans. The purpose is to show how certain patterns and processes originating before the beginnings of contact continued to shape the continent's history thereafter and how an understanding of the colonial period requires an understanding of its American background as well as of its European context.

In a formidable critique of European and Euro-American thinking about native North Americans, Robert F. Berkhofer, Jr., demonstrates that the idea of "Indians" as a single, discrete people was an invention of Columbus and his European contemporaries that has been perpetuated into our own time without foundation in historical, cultural, or ethnographic reality. On the contrary, Berkhofer asserts,

> The first residents of the Americas were by modern estimates divided into at least two thousand cultures and more societies, practiced a multiplicity of customs and lifestyles, held an enormous variety of values and beliefs, spoke numerous languages mutually unintelligible to the many speakers, and did not conceive of themselves as a single people—if they knew about each other at all.

While there is literal truth in portions of Berkhofer's statement, his implication that Indians inhabited thousands of tiny, isolated communities in ignorance of one another flies in the face of a substantial body of archaeological and linguistic scholarship on North America and of a wealth of relevant anthropological literature on nonstate polities, nonmarket economies, and noninstitutionalized religions. To be sure, indigenous North Americans exhibited a remarkable range of languages, economies, political systems, beliefs, and material cultures. But this range was less the result of their isolation from one another than of the widely varying natural and social environments with which Indians had interacted over millennia. What recent scholars of precolonial North America have found even more striking, given this diversity, is the extent to which native peoples' histories intersected one another.

At the heart of these intersections was exchange. By exchange is meant not only the trading of material goods but also exchanges across community lines of marriage partners, resources, labor, ideas, techniques, and religious practices. Longer-distance exchanges frequently crossed cultural and linguistic boundaries as well and ranged from casual encounters to widespread alliances and networks that were economic, political, and religious. For both individuals and communities, exchanges sealed social and political relationships. Rather than accumulate material wealth endlessly, those who acquired it gave it away, thereby earning prestige and placing obligations on others to reciprocate appropriately. And as we shall see, many goods were not given away to others in this world but were buried with individuals to accompany them to another.

Archaeologists have found evidence of ongoing exchange relations among even the earliest known Paleo-Indian inhabitants of North America. Ten thousand years before Columbus, in the wake of the last Ice Age, bands of two or three dozen persons regularly traveled hundreds of miles to hunt and trade with one another at favored campsites such as Lindenmeier in northern Colorado, dating to ca. 8800 B.C. At the Lindenmeier site, differences in the flaking and shaping of stone points distinguished regular occupants in two parts of the camp, and the obsidian each used came from about 350 miles north and south of Lindenmeier, respectively. Evidence from a wide range of settlement sites makes clear that, as the postglacial warming trend continued, so-called Archaic peoples in much of the continent developed wider ranges of food sources, more sedentary settlement patterns, and larger populations. They also expanded their exchanges with one another and conducted them over greater distances. Highly valued materials such as Great Lakes copper, Rocky Mountain obsidian, and marine shells from the Gulf and Atlantic coasts have been found in substantial quantities at sites hundreds and even thousands of miles from their points of origin. In many cases, goods fashioned from these materials were buried with human beings, indicating both their religious significance and, by their uneven distribution, their role as markers of social or political rank.

While the Archaic pattern of autonomous bands persisted in most of North America until the arrival of Europeans, the complexity of exchange relationships in some parts of the continent produced the earliest evidence of concentrated political power. This was especially so for peoples who, after the first century A.D., developed food economies that permitted them to inhabit permanent, year-round villages. In California, for example, competition among communities for coveted acorn groves generated sharply defined political territories and elevated the role of chiefs who oversaw trade, diplomacy, and warfare for clusters of villages. Similar competition for prime fishing and trading locations strengthened the authority of certain village chiefs on the Northwest Coast. Exchange rather than competition for resources appears to have driven centralization in the Ohio and Illinois valleys. There the Hopewell peoples imported copper, mica, shell, and other raw materials over vast distances to their village centers, where specialists fashioned them into intricately crafted ornaments, tools, and other objects. They deposited massive quantities of these goods with the dead in large mounds and exported more to communities scattered throughout the

Mississippi Valley. Hopewell burials differentiate between commoners and elites by the quantity and quality of grave goods accompanying each. In the Southwest, meanwhile, a culture known as Hohokam emerged in the Gila River and Salt River valleys among some of the first societies based primarily on agriculture. Hohokam peoples lived in permanent villages and maintained elaborate irrigation systems that enabled them to harvest two crops per year.

By the twelfth century, agricultural production had spread over much of the Eastern Woodlands as well as to more of the Southwest. In both regions, even more complex societies were emerging to dominate widespread exchange networks. In the Mississippi Valley and the Southeast, the sudden primacy of maize horticulture is marked archaeologically in a variety of ways—food remains, pollen profiles, studies of human bone (showing that maize accounted for 50 percent of people's diets), and in material culture by a proliferation of chert hoes, shell-tempered pottery for storing and cooking, and pits for storing surplus crops. These developments were accompanied by the rise of what archaeologists term "Mississippian" societies, consisting of fortified political and ceremonial centers and outlying villages. The centers were built around open plazas featuring platform burial mounds, temples, and elaborate residences for elite families. Evidence from burials makes clear the wide social gulf that separated commoners from elites. Whereas the former were buried in simple graves with a few personal possessions, the latter were interred in the temples or plazas along with many more, and more elaborate, goods such as copper ornaments, massive sheets of shell, and ceremonial weapons. Skeletal evidence indicates that elites ate more meat, were taller, performed less strenuous physical activity, and were less prone to illness and accident than commoners. Although most archaeologists' conclusions are informed at least in part by models developed by political anthropologists, they also draw heavily from Spanish and French observations of some of the last Mississippian societies. These observations confirm that political leaders, or chiefs, from elite families mobilized labor, collected tribute, redistributed agricultural surpluses, coordinated trade, diplomacy, and military activity, and were worshipped as deities.

The largest, most complex Mississippian center was Cahokia, located not far from the confluence of the Mississippi and Missouri rivers, near modern East St. Louis, Illinois, in the rich floodplain known as American Bottoms. By the twelfth century, Cahokia probably numbered 20,000 people and contained over 120 mounds within a five-square-mile area. One key to Cahokia's rise was its combination of rich soil and nearby wooded uplands, enabling inhabitants to produce surplus crops while providing an abundance and diversity of wild food sources along with ample supplies of wood for fuel and construction. A second key was its location, affording access to the great river systems of the North American interior.

Cahokia had the most elaborate social structure yet seen in North America. Laborers used stone and wooden spades to dig soil from "borrow pits" (at least nineteen have been identified by archaeologists), which they carried in wooden buckets to mounds and palisades often more than half a mile away. The volume and concentration of craft activity in shell, copper, clay, and other materials, both local and imported, suggests that specialized artisans provided the material foundation for Cahokia's exchange ties with other peoples. Although most Cahokians were buried in mass graves outside the palisades, their rulers were given special treatment. At a prominent location in Mound 72, the largest of Cahokia's platform mounds, a man had been buried atop a platform of shell beads. Accompanying him were several group burials: fifty young women, aged 18 to 23, four men, and three men and three women, all encased in uncommonly large amounts of exotic materials. As with the Natchez Indians observed by the French in Louisiana, Cahokians appear to have sacrificed individuals to accompany their leaders in the afterlife. Cahokia was surrounded by nine smaller mound centers and several dozen villages from which it obtained much of its food and through which it conducted its waterborne commerce with other Mississippian centers in the Midwest and Southeast.

At the outset of the twelfth century, the center of production and exchange in the Southwest was in the basin of the San Juan River at Chaco Canyon in New Mexico, where Anasazi culture achieved its most elaborate expression. A twelve-mile stretch of the canyon and its rim held twelve large planned towns on the north side and 200 to 350 apparently unplanned villages on the south. The total population was probably about 15,000. The towns consisted of 200 or more contiguous, multistoried rooms, along with numerous kivas (underground ceremonial areas), constructed of veneered masonary walls and log beams imported from upland areas nearly fifty miles distant. The rooms surrounded a central plaza with a great kiva. Villages typically had ten to twenty rooms that were decidedly smaller than those in the towns. Nearly all of Chaco Canyon's turquoise, shell, and other ornaments and virtually everything imported from Mesoamerica are found in the towns rather than the villages. Whether the goods were considered communal property or were the possessions of elites is uncertain, but either way the towns clearly had primacy. Villagers buried their dead near their residences, whereas town burial grounds were apparently located at greater distances, although only a very few of what must have been thousands of town burials have been located by archaeologists. Finally, and of particular importance in the arid environment of the region, the towns were located at the mouths of side canyons where they controlled the collection and distribution of water run-off.

The canyon was the core of an extensive network of at least seventy towns or "outliers," as they are termed in the archaeological literature, and 5,300 villages located as far as sixty miles from the canyon. Facilitating the movement of people and goods through this network was a system of roads radiating outward from the canyon in perfectly straight lines, turning into stairways or footholds rather than circumventing cliffs and other obstacles.

What archaeologists call the "Chaco phenomenon" was a multifaceted network. Within the canyon, the towns controlled the distribution of precious water. The abundance of rooms reinforces the supposition that they stored agricultural surpluses for redistribution, not only within the canyon but to the outliers. The architectural uniformity of towns throughout the system, the straight roads that linked them, and the proliferation of great kivas point to a complex of shared beliefs and rituals. Lithic remains indicate that the canyon imported most of the raw materials used for manufacturing utilitarian goods and ornamental objects from elsewhere in the Southwest. Particularly critical in this respect was turquoise, beads of which were traded to Mexico in return for copper bells and macaws and to the Gulf of California for marine shells. The Chaco phenomenon thus entailed the mobilization of labor for public works projects and food production, the control and distribution of water, the distribution of prestige goods of both local and exotic origin, and the control of exchange and redistribution both within and outside the network. In distinct contrast to Cahokia and other Mississippian societies, no evidence exists for the primacy of any single canyon town or for the primacy of certain individuals as paramount leaders.

Given the archaeological record, North American "prehistory" can hardly be characterized as a multiplicity of discrete microhistories. Fundamental to the social and economic patterns of even the earliest Paleo-Indian bands were exchanges that linked people across geographic, cultural, and linguistic boundaries. The effects of these links are apparent in the spread of raw materials and finished goods, of beliefs and ceremonies, and of techniques for food production and for manufacturing. By the twelfth century, some exchange networks had become highly formalized and centralized. Exchange constitutes an important key to conceptualizing American history before Columbus.

Although it departs from our familiar image of North American Indians, the historical pattern sketched so far is recognizable in the way it portrays societies "progressing" from small, egalitarian, autonomous communities to larger, more hierarchical, and centralized political aggregations with more complex economies. That image is likewise subverted when we examine the three centuries immediately preceding the arrival of Europeans. In both American Bottoms and the San Juan River basin, where twelfth-century populations were most concentrated, agriculture most productive, exchange most varied and voluminous, and political systems most complex and extensive, there were scarcely any inhabitants by the end of the fifteenth century. What happened and why?

Cahokia and other Mississippian societies in the Upper Midwest peaked during the late twelfth and early thirteenth centuries. Data from soil traces indicate that even then laborers were fortifying Cahokia's major earthworks against attack. At the same time, archaeologists surmise, Cahokia was headed toward an ecological crisis: expanded settlement, accompanied by especially hot dry summers, exhausted the soil, depleted the supply of timber for building and fuel, and reduced the habitat of the game that supplemented their diet. By the end of the fourteenth century, Cahokia's inhabitants had dispersed over the surrounding countryside into small farming villages.

Cahokia's abandonment reverberated among other Mississippian societies in the Midwest. Fortified centers on the Mississippi River from the Arkansas River northward and on the Ohio River appear to have been strengthened by influxes of people from nearby villages but then abandoned, and signs from burials indicate a period of chronic, deadly warfare in the Upper Midwest. One archaeologist refers to the middle Mississippi Valley and environs during the fifteenth century as "the vacant quarter." A combination of ecological pressures and upheavals within the alliance that linked them appears to have doomed Cahokia and other midwestern Mississippian centers, leading the inhabitants to transform themselves into the village dwellers of the surrounding prairies and plains observed by French explorers three centuries later.

The upheavals may even have extended beyond the range of direct Mississippian influence to affect Iroquois and Hurons and other Iroquoian speakers of the lower Great Lakes region. These people had been moving from dispersed, riverside settlements to fortified, bluff-top villages over the course of several centuries; the process appears to have intensified in the fourteenth century, when it also led to the formation of the Iroquois and Huron confederacies. The Hurons developed fruitful relations with hunter-gatherers to the north, with whom they exchanged agricultural produce for meat and skins, and Iroquois ties with outsiders appear to have diminished except for small-scale interactions with coastal peoples to the south and east. Across the Northeast, political life was characterized by violence and other manifestations of intense competition. Whether the upheavals in exchange ties occasioned by the collapse of Cahokia were directly linked to the formation of the Iroquois and Huron confederacies, as Dena Dincauze and Robert Hasenstab have suggested for the Iroquois, or were simply part of a larger process generated by the advent of farming and consequent demographic and political changes, the repercussions were still evident when Europeans began to frequent the region during the sixteenth century.

Violence and instability were also apparent across the Southeast. Unlike in the Midwest, where enormous power had been concentrated in a single center, southeastern Mississippian societies were characterized by more frequently shifting alliances and rivalries that prevented any one center from becoming as powerful as Cahokia was from the tenth to thirteenth centuries. A pattern of instability prevailed that archaeologist David Anderson terms "cycling," in which certain centers emerged for a century or two to dominate regional alliances consisting of several chiefdoms and their tributary communities and then declined. Whole communities periodically shifted their locations in response to ecological or political pressures. Thus, for example, the great mound center at Etowah, in northwestern Georgia, lost its preeminence after 1400 and by the time of Hernando de Soto's arrival in 1540 had become a tributary of the nearby upstart chiefdom of Coosa.

From the mid-twelfth century through the fourteenth, the demographic map of the Southwest was also transformed as Chaco Canyon and other Anasazi and Hohokam centers were abandoned. Although southwesterners had made a practice of shifting their settlements when facing shortages of water and arable land and other consequences of climatic or demographic change, they had never done so on such a massive scale. Most archaeologists agree that the abandonments followed changes in the regional cycle of rainfall and drought, so that agricultural surpluses probably proved inadequate. They point to signs that the centralized systems lost their ability to mobilize labor, redistribute goods, and coordinate religious ceremonies and that such loss was followed by outmigration to surrounding and upland areas where people farmed less intensively while increasing their hunting and gathering. Trade between the Southwest and

Mesoamerica was disrupted at the same time, though whether as a cause or an effect of the abandonments is unclear.

Most Anasazi peoples dispersed in small groups, joining others to form new communities in locations with sufficient rainfall. These communities are what we know today as the southwestern pueblos, extending from Hopi villages in Arizona to those on the Rio Grande. These dispersals and convergences of peoples reinforced an emerging complex of beliefs, art, and ceremonies relating to kachinas—spirits believed to have influence in both bringing rain and fostering cooperation among villagers. Given their effort to forge new communities under conditions of severe drought, it is not surprising that southwestern farmers placed great emphasis on kachinas. The eastward shift of much of the southwestern population also led to new patterns of trade in which recently arrived Athapaskan speakers (later known as Apaches and Navajos) brought bison meat and hides and other products from the southern Great Plains to semiannual trade fairs at Taos, Pecos, and Picuris pueblos in exchange for maize, cotton blankets, obsidian, turquoise, and ceramics as well as shells from the Gulf of California. By the time of Francisco Vásquez de Coronado's *entrada* in 1540, new ties of exchange and interdependency bound eastern Pueblos, Athapaskans, and Caddoan speaker on the Plains.

When Europeans reached North America, then, the continent's demographic and political map was in a state of profound flux. A major factor was the collapse of the great centers at Cahokia and Chaco Canyon and elsewhere in the Midwest and Southwest. Although there were significant differences between these highly centralized societies, each ran up against the capacity of the land or other resources to sustain it. This is not to argue for a simple ecological determinism for, although environmental fluctuations played a role, the severe strains in each region resulted above all from a series of human choices that had brought about unprecedented concentrations of people and power. Having repudiated those choices and dispersed, midwestern Mississippians and Anasazis formed new communities in which they retained kinship, ceremonial, and other traditions antedating these complex societies. At the same time, these new communities and neighboring ones sought to flourish in their new political and environmental settings by establishing, and in some cases endeavoring to control, new exchange networks.

Such combinations of continuity and change, persistence and adaptability, arose from concrete historical experiences rather than a timeless tradition.

The Old World and the Modern World: A Hopi View

BY DENNIS WALL AND VIRGIL MASAYESVA (HOPI)

This article describes aspects of a unique relationship between an ancient agricultural practice and the culture that it sustains. Hopi agriculture, known as "dry

"People of the Corn: Teachings in Hopi Traditional Agriculture, Spirituality, and Sustainability," by Dennis Wall and Virgil Masayesva, is reproduced from *American Indian Quarterly* with permission from the University of Nebraska Press. Copyright 2005 by the University of Nebraska Press.

farming" because it relies strictly on precipitation and runoff water (along with hard work and prayer), has kept the Hopi culture intact for nearly a thousand years. But aside from the sustenance it provides the people of the high desert of northern Arizona, corn enters into nearly every aspect of traditional Hopi life, contributing to values development, the sharing and passing on of tradition, and the celebration and connection with the Great Mystery.

The authors of this article are members of the staff of the Institute for Tribal Environmental Professionals (ITEP), a tribal training and support organization based at Northern Arizona University in Flagstaff. ITEP's work involves helping tribes to build capacity in their environmental management programs. The institute's work centers on air quality management training but also addresses other media, including drinking water, wastewater, and solid waste, as well as challenges that tribes face with environmental toxins such as nuclear waste and heavy-metal deposition. Virgil Masayesva, director of ITEP is a member of the Hopi Tribe and was raised in the village of Hotevilla on Third Mesa on his family's farm (mentioned below), located in a valley that his family calls *Hopaq*. Dennis Wall, an Arizona native, is an author, longtime freelance writer-photographer, and ITEP's editor.

After their Emergence into the Fourth World, the clans that would one day comprise the Hopi people approached the Guardian Spirit, Masaw, in the region that is now northwest Arizona and asked his permission to settle there. Masaw recognized that the clan people's former life, which they knew was not bringing them happiness, had been given over to ambition, greed, and social competition. He looked into their hearts and saw that these qualities remained, and so he had his doubts that the people could follow his way. "Whether you can stay here is up to you," he told them.

Masaw warned the clan people that the life he had to offer them was very different from what they had before. To show them that life, Masaw gave the people a planting stick, a bag of seeds, and a gourd of water. He handed them a small ear of blue corn and told them, "Here is my life and my spirit. This is what I have to give you."

There is a distinction between the one true Hopi, Masaw, and the people who follow his way. Masaw is the true embodiment of a Hopi; the people who follow his way are merely Hopi *Senom*, or People of the Hopi. Following common tradition, however, members of the Hopi Tribe discussed in this article will be referred to as "Hopi."

To be Hopi is to embrace peace and cooperation, to care for the Earth and all of its inhabitants, to live within the sacred balance. It is a life of reverence shared by all the good people of Earth, all those in tune with their world. This manner of living lies beneath the complexities of *wimi*, or specialized knowledge, which can provide stability and wisdom but when misused can also foster division and strife.

Deeper still in the lives of traditional Hopi people lies the way of Masaw, a way of humility and simplicity, of forging a sacred bond between themselves and the land that sustains them. Masaw's way is embodied in corn. At the time of the Emergence, Masaw offered the clan people a manner of living that would not be easy. Dry-farming in the high desert of northern Arizona, relying only on precipitation and runoff water, requires an almost miraculous level of faith and is sustained by hard work, prayer, and an attitude of deep humility. Following the way of Masaw, the Hopi people have tended to their corn for nearly a millennium, and the corn has kept them whole.

For traditional Hopis corn is the central bond. Its essence, physically, spiritually, and symbolically, pervades their existence. For the people of the mesas corn is sustenance, ceremonial object, prayer offering, symbol, and sentient being unto itself. Corn is the Mother in the truest sense—the people take in the corn and the corn becomes their flesh, as mother's milk becomes the flesh of the child. Corn is also regarded as the child, as when the wife of a farmer tends to the seeds and newly received harvest, blessing and ritually washing the corn, talking and singing to the seeds and ears. The connection between the people and the corn is pervasive and deeply sacred. In a remarkable symbiosis between the physical and the spiritual, the Hopi people sustain the corn and the corn sustains Hopi culture.

Victor Masayesva Sr. remembers as a young man in the 1920s and 1930s working just after dawn in his family's cornfields north of the village of Kykotsmovi. He could hear other farmers up and down the valley, a place his family calls *Hopaq*, as they sang to their corn plants. "That's how you take care of the plants," he says. "You sing to them, because they're just like humans, they have their own lives, and they like to hear you singing to them."

The Hopis' intimate relationship with corn is a bond that reaches back for centuries (terraced fields near the village of *Paaqavi* have been farmed since at least AD 1200). That bond reflects their profound reliance on the plant to sustain them in both good and difficult times. Even in this century, says Masayesva, there have been winters when corn, dried and carefully stored, was essentially the only food available to the Hopi people.

In the early 1940s, when his two brothers were drafted into World War II, Masayesva considered moving to Phoenix to continue his work in highway construction. He spoke with his father, who told him, "I'm getting old, and soon I won't be able to take care of our fields any longer. I want you to take over the farming. This is your decision. If you choose to be a farmer, you won't get rich, but you can sustain not only yourself but your family, and there are other benefits. It's going to take a lot of hard work. You have to be able to accept that responsibility."

Masayesva spoke with some of the elders at Hotevilla, his village on Third Mesa. They told him that to be a farmer would be a good thing—the fundamental Hopi way. After careful consideration he made his decision, and he has been tending his family's fields, probably the largest fields remaining at Hopi, ever since.

"One of the things that Masaw wanted the people to do was to plant, to be farmers," Masayesva says. "A long time ago I spoke with one of the last major chiefs in this village. He told me he wished he were in my place. He had certain religious responsibilities, obligations, and he and the other priests were concerned that they might not fulfill those obligations. He told me, 'You're like a child, you don't have these things weighing down on you.'" The priest told Masayesva that he was living the simple life that Masaw had offered the people, and in doing so, he was blessed.

Masayesva says that farming is a crucial element in a way of life that binds the people, the corn, and the sacred mystery. Hopi farmers believe that singing to the plants is much like photosynthesis, that the songs energize and rejuvenate the plants. "It's all tied together. When you first plant your seeds, you take very good care of them, and when the plants come up, you go and sing to the plants, and the plants dance in rhythm to the song. That's how we were taught, and it is a practice we continue."

To test the strength and character of the clans, Masaw instructed them to travel in the four directions, to make their way in a difficult world and face the hardships that would determine whether they might come back and follow the life he offered to them. He told the clan people that at some point he would signal them that it was time to return.

Thus began the Migration Period, marked now throughout the Southwest and beyond by stone ruins and other structures, by petroglyphs and pictographs, and on a more subtle level by the spirits of the people who lived and died along the way.

During their journeys the clan people relied on corn as a primary means of survival. The varieties of corn they carried and cultivated were uniquely suited to the harsh, unforgiving environment in which they would eventually settle. During their travels they learned how to plant, cultivate, and protect the corn, how to use carefully developed techniques to sustain the plants, to channel water and discourage pests. Along with these things they learned precise methods of prayer and ceremony to ensure a harvest that might mean the difference between survival and starvation. No one can fathom the hardships they faced or which clans were left behind; those who were unable to embrace Masaw's way probably did not survive.

Sometime later Masaw sent out his signal, and slowly the surviving clans began moving back toward the Hopi Mesas. First to return were the people of the Bear Clan, who were told that their land included all that lay between the Colorado and Rio Grande rivers—with three mesas forming the spiritual center point. Soon they had founded and settled the village of Oraibi on Third Mesa. More clans followed, and in time a new community, a new tribe called Hopi, was formed.

One by one, other clans came to the mesas and demonstrated their special skills and talents. Over time, through careful negotiation among the different groups, a covenant was established that they would reject the old practice of clan selfishness and instead contribute to the whole of the newly forming tribe.

The clans settled in their separate villages on the mesas. In doing so they became one, the People of the Hopi. They planted their fields in valleys and canyons with the small, resilient corn that Masaw had given them, corn as hardy and sturdy as the people, and the corn and the people were able to survive. The harshness of the land was indeed the reason that Masaw had provided this place for the clan people, for in such a place only a life of humility, balance, and hard work would ensure their survival. Their shared hardship was the prime bond that held them together.

The Hopi developed ceremonial and spiritual practices common to all the clans, though they also kept their unique clan ways. The villages grew in number, the people kept to Masaw's way, and the corn kept the people whole, sustaining for a thousand years a culture unique in its richness, diversity, and pervasive spirituality.

Hopi corn farming is an endless cycle; the very seeds used now to plant blue, red, white, and yellow Hopi corn arise from a lineage that reaches back for many centuries. The tough, smallish plants have been bred to provide sustenance in an unforgiving environment. Agricultural methods developed by the Hopi people—such as planting the seeds deep in the soil and tending to them carefully by hand throughout the growing season—have resulted in an agricultural efficiency known in few other places on Earth. Hopi farming endures strictly through the bounty of the universe. Known as "dry farming," it employs techniques that take advantage of drainage and runoff but relies primarily on whatever precipitation falls in a given season.

Prayer and supplication, embodied most publicly in the dances of the *katsinas*, are religious/cultural practices woven deep into the daily lives of traditional Hopis. Through ritual and ceremony the people entreat the spirits of the earth, the sky, the mountains, and the clouds to bring the rain, to tame the wind, to provide a bounty in the fields year after year. This all-embracing focus on sacred ceremony is a powerful cultural binder, guiding the people in common purpose as it sustains a rich cultural tapestry of spirituality, work, and tradition.

Winter and Early Spring

To choose an arbitrary "starting point" for a year's agricultural cycle at Hopi, one can look first to late winter when the *katsinas* descend from the San Francisco Peaks north of Flagstaff to enter the villages and dance for rain and regeneration. The *katsinas* dance for the vitality not only of the Hopi people and their crops but for the bird world, the insect world, the reptile and amphibian worlds, the world of plants and animals and humans everywhere on Earth. They dance so that the living world will continue.

In the *kivas* in late winter special ceremonies are performed, including the planting of bean sprouts. The *kiva* chief monitors the growth of the plants with a close eye, as the sprouts are harbingers of the level of success the people can expect in the fields during the coming year. The relationship between the bean sprouts and the fall harvest exists on many levels, some of which cannot be shared with those outside the societies. Perhaps the most understandable is the practical relationship between plants and tenders: If the sprouts grow strong and hardy, those responsible for cultivating them will probably exercise equal care in the fields. A duty of the *kiva* chief is to admonish those whose sprouts are allowed to dry out or come up weak and spindly.

In the home farmers ask their wives what will be needed in the coming year's harvest. The wives of Hopi farmers are responsible for drying and storing seed stock from the previous year, for securing the seeds and dried corn from rodents and deterioration, and for keeping track of each year's planting needs— for both food and ceremony. These are skills and knowledge they pass on to their grandchildren, daughters, and nieces. The contribution of Hopi women to the longevity of these hardy varieties of corn cannot be overstated; through their understanding and keen eyes and careful genetic selectivity, Hopi women have kept the corn extant for centuries.

Zetta Masayesva, who has resided in the Hopi village of Hotevilla for many decades, describes her intuitive approach to selecting seed stock: "When I choose the seed corn I don't care if the ear is long or short, as long as the kernels look hard. Those are the ones that will come up. You can tell which ones are weak. We pick the ones that are strong, that will germinate. We know how to pick the ones that are not so good."

A traditional Hopi farmer married to a Hopi woman does not plant for himself but for his wife's family. Each year before planting begins his wife advises him on the quantities and types of corn needed to provide for the food and ceremonial needs of her family and perhaps others as well. The man in turn tells his wife how many gunnysacks of each type of corn seed that he will need to plant his fields, and she prepares them.

The corn planted each year will be used for a variety of purposes: for food, for ceremonial use, to contribute to weddings and other social events, for use during prayer, and as material for rituals performed by Hopi secret societies that cannot be shared with outsiders or even with other Hopis who do not belong to those societies. A farmer's wife must have a clear sense of these varied needs and how best to satisfy them in the coming harvest. Her understanding of the differ- ent needs for corn requires intimate knowledge of Hopi culture and religious and ceremonial practice. A woman who can determine the quantities and types of corn needed for the coming year holds a bounty of general knowledge of the Hopi way. Over time she will pass that knowledge on to her sons and daughters, nieces, nephews, and grandchildren.

Before the seeds leave the home, the woman blesses them with prayer and a symbolic washing, a sprinkling of water. She talks to the corn seeds, wishing them good fortune as they grow into new plants. She tells them that she looks forward to seeing them again when they return at harvest time. Zetta Masayesva describes her relationship to the seed stock: "It's kind of like a mother taking care of a child. You take special care, you wash their hair, talk to them, prepare them—in this case, for planting."

Victor Masayesva visits his fields in March to study them and prepare for cultivation. How much moisture has been retained in the soil? Has erosion caused runoff that must be repaired? Are there worms present? Some farmers plant in March, gambling on a frostless early spring. Sometimes they are lucky; other times the seedlings are frost-burned and killed off, though most of the hardy plants will regenerate new seedlings within a few weeks. Masayesva generally plants in mid-May, pursuing a conservative, reliable method that has never failed him.

Spring is a time when the family comes to Hopi from all over to assist in the planting. It is a period for renewing family bonds, for sharing stories and experi- ences, for working together toward a common, important purpose. In earlier times only the men would plant. These days female family members assist in the fields as well. The women are also responsible for providing food for all dur- ing the laborious planting process.

Leigh Kuwanwisiwma, the Hopi Tribe's cultural preservation officer and resident of Bacavi (*Paaqavi*) village on Third Mesa, recalls when he was a boy in the 1950s, around the end of the horse-drawn plow era of Hopi farming. He says farm work creates good children and responsible adults.

> Back when agriculture was widespread—and unfortunately that is
> declining these days—part of a boy's role was to get out there farming,
> learning the hardships, dealing with the environment, listening to his
> grandfather and father and uncles. I remember watching my grandfather
> saddling up the burro early in the morning. If my grandmother was
> packing a noon snack, we knew we would be out all day. At that
> moment my heart sank. It was hard work, and there were times when
> I hated it. But if grandmother was just packing water, I would be so
> happy because we would be home by noon and I could play!

The hardships of his youthful farming days, Kuwanwisiwma says, may have
seemed like heavy burdens then, but they have come to shape his adulthood,
instilling in him an appreciation for hard work, for patience and faith, and
for being able to put off the rewards of success in favor of duty and
responsibility.

In the fields of his youth, as he prepared the soil and repaired drainage channels, as he planted the corn seeds and offered them their first small taste of water,
Kuwanwisiwma was developing a fundamental connection with the earth. His
labor involved hoeing the soil, checking for and removing worms, thinning the
plants, channeling runoff, helping to erect windbreaks, and building stick shelters
around the plants to keep crows and coyotes away. As he performed these tasks,
he learned about farming, nature, the animal world, weather and wind, the
rhythms of life. Now he teaches the same knowledge and skills and, he hopes,
the deeper lessons they hold, to his young son.

Late Spring and Summer

After planting, a traditional Hopi farmer spends much of his time in the fields,
tending each plant with loving care. It is a labor-intensive way of farming. Often
family members work alongside him; in these days of outside jobs and distant
residences, their times together on the farm are perhaps more important for family cohesion than ever before.

There are numerous concerns in spring and summer: Worms are a constant
threat and must be removed by hand from individual plants; ravens and other
animals must be discouraged through various means; and if the field lies in a runoff path, the shaping of channels and dikes is ongoing, especially in a wet year
(the current multiyear drought has presented its own challenges). In the fields the
farmer relies on knowledge, faith, and prayer. In the villages the *katsinas* dance to
bring rain that will allow the plants to germinate and grow to fruition.

During late summer and early fall sweet corn is sometimes harvested and
roasted in stone-lined, underground steaming ovens. Victor Masayesva's oven is
located on the edge of one of his fields alongside a shallow arroyo. The oven is
primed with a wood fire and the corn is heaped inside and sealed off at the top.
The steaming process takes all night. Masayesva arises from bed several times
during the night to check that the oven remains completely sealed, ensuring a
well-steamed batch of corn which, when ready, will be shared heartily by family
members or dried for later use.

Autumn and the Harvest

When the corn plants have grown to four or five feet tall, when the ears are filling out and their husks have begun to crack with dryness, harvesting begins. This is another time in which the family gathers. Plants are knocked down and ears are harvested and tossed into truck beds to be carried home to the women of the family.

In Hopi tradition it is never proper for a man to simply bring the corn into the home, lay it down somewhere and tell the woman, "There you are." Instead corn is presented directly by the man, and the woman steps forward to receive it. Her receiving is a way of honoring him, as his personal, respectful presentation honors her.

When the corn harvest arrives Zetta Masayesva welcomes the ears into her home, thanking them for growing well and providing food for her family. Her long-held tradition, common for traditional Hopi women, is to handle each ear separately, greeting each one and talking to it as she examines it for quality and firmness.

There is another reason why the woman spends so much time touching and examining the harvest: She is searching for a small number of perfect ears, which she will set aside for ceremonial and ritual use. The ears she seeks are generally small and always elegant in form: large at the bottom, tapering smoothly to narrow tops, the end kernels arranged in perfect symmetry. These "Corn Mothers" will serve a variety of ceremonial needs—and not merely as "symbols," for to the Hopi people, corn is the Mother in a very real sense.

Drying and storage of corn are the domain of Hopi women. Ears are sorted and placed in their respective stacks. The Hopi tradition is to stack the ears neatly in the home in overlapping form. Some use boxes these days to store their corn; Zetta Masayesva frowns on that practice, but modern ways have crept into Hopi agricultural practices and many have shifted to more labor-efficient methods.

Winter and the Varieties of Corn-Based Food

Soon after the harvest is separated, dried, and stored, winter sets in. During the winter season, which can be bitterly cold on the mesas, and throughout the year, corn is a basic dietary component for the Hopi people.

A staple for Hopi meals is *piki*, a paper-thin, layered bread made most often from ground blue corn, water, and ashes, cooked by hand on a special flat stone (other varieties of corn are also used for piki including a delicious red-corn piki mixed with chili peppers). Zetta Masayesva says she, like most Hopi females, has been making piki since childhood. "I pat it down with my palms onto the hot stone. I've done it all my life, like most Hopi women, so we don't feel the heat of the stone on our hands."

Corn is steamed and dried or simply allowed to dry. It is used to make hominy, often eaten directly off the cob; for pudding (red corn is generally the variety used), heaped into a bowl and taken in pinches by the diners; for *somiviki*, small balls of cooked cornmeal wrapped and tied into husks; and eaten in various other forms, including steamed and roasted sweet corn.

For centuries corn grinding has been a formative social experience for Hopi girls. The work, performed by hand using grinding stones sometimes referred to by the Spanish terms *mano* and *metate,* is grueling, akin to the difficult labor that boys face in the fields. Grinding is a social bonding event for girls; as they work side by side they talk, joke, tell stories, and share cultural knowledge. Most important in terms of Hopi culture, it is a time when young girls learn to take their traditional place in the family, to accept their gender-based role as provider and nurturer in the home, and to learn the value and necessity of hard work.

Ceremonial Uses of Corn

The sacred nature of corn is reflected in its pervasive use in Hopi society not only for food but as ritual and ceremonial material. Secret Hopi societies use corn in a variety of ways, but outsiders are not privy to those uses. Across the many clans that make up the Hopi people, however, corn has universal uses related to celebrating, praying, and maintaining the people's connection to the Infinite.

In ground form white corn is the variety most commonly used for ceremony and ritual. White cornmeal and seeds are used in *kiva* rituals throughout the villages, and cornmeal is employed as an offering to each clan's guardian deity, represented by an icon in the home. White corn powder, or *homa*, is carried in a pouch by traditional Hopis, to be used for a variety of prayer offerings.

During *Powamu* (winter solstice) *pahos*, or prayer feathers, are given to people throughout the villages. Pahos serve multiple purposes, but most typically they are a way in which the people offer prayers for good health, a long life, and goodwill and happiness for all living creatures. In the hours before sunrise, pahos are deposited in special places and individual prayers are made, followed by the scattering of homa on the paho. This is followed by offerings to the rising sun.

Homa is used during the katsina ceremonies. It is used to "feed" and bless the katsinas as prayers are made that the katsinas will reward the people with an abundance of rain and a strong harvest of crops for the benefit of all people. As the katsinas begin their song, the katsina chief sprinkles homa on the dancing spirits with deliberate and passionate instructions that the dance be performed in harmony with the Earth and with vibrancy and a good heart. Some katsinas wear garb that is adorned with parts or symbols of the corn plant.

Childbirth and the Naming Ceremony

Corn is used ceremonially to mark significant milestones in the lives of the Hopi people. The ceremonial significance of corn is demonstrated from the moment a child is born, when a Corn Mother is placed beside the child, to remain with him or her for the first twenty days after birth.

White corn is used in infant naming ceremonies twenty-one days after a child is born. The ceremony is a combination of festivity, prayer, and family unity. Most importantly it is a time to give a name to the child that will stay with him or her for the remainder of life.

Mothers, grandmothers, and aunts gather on this special occasion, each prepared to offer a name that somehow reflects their clan lineage. Before the rising of the sun the newborn is first given a bath, and then the hair is washed, usually by the maternal grandmother. She is the first in line to begin the naming ceremony, followed by other grandmothers and a succession of aunts.

The white corn is gently brushed over the baby's naked chest, with words spoken from the heart, eternal words that are offered to the child: "Your name shall be (name). You shall carry this name through the rest of your life, in sickness and in health. You shall carry this name through your adulthood until the day that you shall sleep in peace." After the naming ceremony, at the breaking of dawn, the newborn is taken outdoors to face the rising sun, and the identification of a new child has begun.

Initiation

As in many cultures worldwide, an initiation ceremony is held to mark the transition point when a child begins moving into adulthood. At about the age of twelve it is time for Hopi boys and girls to take their place in one of two Hopi societies. Before their initiation begins, each child is given a Corn Mother. The ear of white corn is never large; clutching to the largest ears would be contrary to the Hopi way of humility. The initiate will hold the ear of white corn close throughout the long initiation ceremony. Afterwards parents sometimes plant the kernels, bringing forth new plants that hold special meaning for those involved.

End of Life

On the third day after death—the day before the spirit of the departed is released from the physical body—relatives take food to the burial place. At that time cornmeal is laid down along a ceremonial path to help guide the departing spirit on its way to the Grand Canyon, which the Hopi people consider their spiritual home. And so a life that has been linked to corn on every level from the very moment of birth now follows a trail of cornmeal to the final spiritual resting place.

When the clans accepted Masaw's way, they asked him to lead them. Masaw told them that would not be possible because, he said, he recognized that they carried a lot of knowledge and that they would eventually be controlled again by their own ambition—perhaps to some finality. "At that time," Masaw told them, "I will return to you." To that, the people of the clans assured Masaw, "We will remember our past and try not to repeat it, and we will continue to learn from experience."

In this era of heightened mobility and pervasive mass communication, the remoteness of the Hopi villages, which cushioned them for centuries from the impacts of Spanish colonialism and Euroamerican incursions, no longer represents the barrier it once was. Times are changing, and Hopi culture is stressed today as never before.

Kuwanwisiwma says that Masaw's spirit still abides at Hopi. The question now, he says, is whether the people can continue to hold to the old ways, to remain people of the corn. "The generation of Hopis today," says Kuwanwisiwma,

> lives in the real world. No longer can we say this is a "white man's world" and we're up here separate from that world on these mesas. We're part of the dominant culture. We too have become influenced materialistically through the cash economy, with different kinds of value systems that have become our way of life. That is, I suppose, good to some extent: You work hard for something and you gain materially. But at the same time it's impacted our culture; we now rely on other forms of survivability.
>
> The ceremonial cycle may be ongoing—though much has been lost already—but the strength of the culture is under strain because the corn, and the way of the farm, have slowly been impacted. When I got married in the early 1970s, my father gave me a piece of his cornfield, and he said, "You take care of it, grow your corn for your family and in-laws." That's how I assumed responsibility as a husband and father. And I think that kind of social responsibility to family can be strengthened if younger people can appreciate what it means to be part of the Hopi way through farming.
>
> Participation in the ceremonies, as we see now with younger kids being initiated and participating, is important. They need to be told in the kivas, in the homes, that the corn is the way the Hopis have chosen; it goes back to our Emergence. As Hopi people, we are fortunate to have survived this long. It is a privilege to be a part of this complex Hopi community of clans living under this one philosophy of corn, of humility. I think if we can continue to teach that, we'll strengthen the culture as it stands.

◈ FURTHER READING

Basso, Keith H. *Wisdom Sits in Places: Landscape and Language Among the Western Apache* (1996).

Calloway, Colin G. *One Vast Winter Count: The Native American West Before Lewis and Clark* (2003).

Clark, Ella E., ed. *Indian Legends of the Pacific Northwest* (1953).

Deloria, Vine, Jr. *Red Earth, White Lies: Native Americans and the Myth of Scientific Fact* (1997).

Dillehay, Thomas D. *The Settlement of the Americas: A New Prehistory* (2000).

Driver, Harold E. *Indians of North America* (2nd ed., 1969).

Echo-Hawk, Roger. "Ancient History in the New World: Integrating Oral Traditions and the Archaeological Record in Deep Time," *American Antiquity* 65 (April 2000): 267–290.

Erdoes, Richard, and Alfonso Ortiz. *American Indian Myths and Legends* (1984).

Fagan, Brian. *Ancient North America: The Archaeology of a Continent* (4th ed., 2005).

Hodge, Frederick Webb, ed. *Handbook of the American Indian North of Mexico*, 2 vols. (1907–1910).

Jennings, Francis. *The Founders of America* (1993).

Josephy, Alvin M, Jr., ed. *America in 1492: The World of Indian People Before the Arrival of Columbus* (1992).

Kehoe, Alice B. *North American Indians: A Comprehensive Account* (1981).

Lekson, Stephen. *A History of the Ancient Southwest* (2008).

Mann, Charles C. *1491: New Revelations of the Americas Before Columbus* (2005).

Martin, Joel W. *The Land Looks After Us: A History of Native American Religion* (2001).

Milner, George R. *The Moundbuilders: Ancient Peoples of Eastern North America* (2004).

Noble, David Grant, ed. *The Mesa Verde World: Exploration in Ancestral Pueblo Archaeology* (2006).

Oswalt, Wendell H. *This Land Was Theirs: A Study of North American Indians* (4th ed., 1988).

Pauketat, Timothy R. *Cahokia: Ancient America's Great City on the Mississippi* (2009).

Plog, Stephen. *Ancient Peoples of the American Southwest* (1997).

Russell, Howard S. *Indian New England Before the Mayflower* (1980).

Thomas, David Hurst. *Skull Wars: Kennewick Man, Archaeology, and the Battle for Native American Identity* (2000).

Waters, Frank. *Book of the Hopi* (1977).

Young, Biloine Whiting, and Melvin L. Fowler. *Cahokia: The Great Native American Metropolis* (2000).

Zolbrod, Paul G. *Diné bahane': The Navajo Creation Story* (1984).

CHAPTER 3

Strangers on the Shores, 1492–1600

Most Americans have been inclined to view the story of Christopher Columbus, as well as the stories of the later European explorers, from the perspectives of the sailors on the ships. In this chapter, we encourage you to instead consider, as much as possible, the point of view of the people on the shores. To the Native inhabitants of the Americas, the Europeans were strangers. Or, as the historian Daniel Richter has put it, rather than "facing west" and adopting the perspective of the Europeans coming to America, we must try to "face east" and seek to understand the process of encounter through Native eyes.

Encountering strangers was not, in fact, a new experience for Native peoples in 1492. As we noted in Chapter 2, the Western Hemisphere was not a static world of isolated communities before European contact. On the contrary, people frequently moved to new locales, or had new groups move in next to them, producing new interactions with new "strangers." In many ways, the people who began arriving in 1492 were not so different from those who had lived here before. They were, after all, people. But these newcomers came with different world views, agendas, tools, animals, plants, and—of particular importance—germs.

And yet, not all Native Americans actually met Europeans between 1492 and 1600. Direct contact in this period tended to occur, as the chapter title suggests, on the shores—of oceans, seas, and major rivers. Some people in the interior of the continent did not see a European until as late as the 1800s. And, among those communities who did meet Europeans early on, the nature and extent of the encounters varied significantly.

As you read the documents and essays in this chapter, strive to "face east," viewing this era from Native perspectives. What challenges did the new strangers pose? What possible opportunities did they present? How should they be dealt with? And, what of those who had yet to make direct contact with Europeans? What stories do they have to tell us, and what can we learn from them?

◈ DOCUMENTS

The documents in this chapter are the written records of Europeans as they "faced west" into a world that was, to them, "new." Document 1 is an excerpt from the journal of the person who, inadvertently, established the first sustained connection between the western and eastern hemispheres: Christopher Columbus. In Columbus, and with most of the strangers from the east, Indians found themselves dealing with people who possessed a pronounced—sometimes even extreme—confidence in the superiority of their own culture, coupled with a professed unwillingness to tolerate any challenges to that view. Few sources demonstrate this better than Spain's "requerimiento"—or "requirement," which is excerpted in Document 2. Yet, not all of the strangers behaved according to the dictates of the requerimiento. Indian people in what is now Texas and northern Mexico encountered the four survivors of an ill-fated 1528 Spanish expedition, among them an African slave, Estebanico. The Indians at first enslaved the survivors, but later came to regard them as healers worthy of respect. Finally, after eight years, the survivors stumbled into a group of other Spaniards in northwestern Mexico. Document 3 contains the translated words of one of those survivors, Álvar Núñez Cabeza de Vaca, as he describes this reunion and the Indians' reaction to it. Meanwhile, on the opposite side of the continent, Indians in Florida and the Southeast encountered a stranger who was quite different from de Vaca, and much more in line with the requerimiento: Hernándo de Soto. Native peoples responded to de Soto and his soldiers as best they could, as hinted at in Document 4, a Spanish record of the de Soto expedition.

Far to the north, indigenous peoples were beginning to make contact with Europeans other than the Spanish. In Document 5, Jacques Cartier records his version of an early French encounter with the Micmac people of the Gulf of St. Lawrence region in what is now Canada. Between Canada and Florida, another group of strangers also began showing up on Native shores. This group called themselves the "English." Document 6 tells of a late sixteenth-century Indian encounter with the English, taking place in what is now North Carolina.

What should we make of the various descriptions of Native peoples in this era? Should we accept all of the accounts in these documents at face value? To what extent is it possible to somehow still "face east" through these documents, to somehow partially glimpse Native views through the writings of these European observers? Do they give us the full story of American Indian history, from 1492 to 1600? On the other hand, do they tell us nothing of the story?

1. Columbus Describes the Caribs, 1492

"I [Columbus wrote], in ordei that they might feel great amity towards us, because I knew that they were a people to be delivered and converted to our holy faith rather by love than by force, gave to some among them some red caps and some glass beads, which they hung round their necks, and many other things of little value. At this they were greatly pleased and became so entirely our friends that it was a wonder to see. Afterwards they came swimming to the ships' boats, where we were, and brought us parrots and cotton thread in balls, and spears and many other things, and we exchanged for them other things, such as

L.A. Vigernas, ed., *The Journal of Christopher Columbus* (London: Anthony Blond & The Orion Press, 1960), 23–24.

small glass beads and hawks' bells, which we gave to them. In fact, they took all and gave all, such as they had, with good will, but it seemed to me that they were a people very deficient in everything. They all go naked as their mothers bore them, and the women also, although I saw only one very young girl. And all those whom I did see were youths, so that I did not see one who was over thirty years of age; they were very well built, with very handsome bodies and very good faces. Their hair is coarse almost like the hairs of a horse's tail and short; they wear their hair down over their eyebrows, except for a few strands behind, which they wear long and never cut. Some of them are painted black, and they are the colour of the people of the Canaries, neither black nor white, and some of them are painted white and some red and some in any colour that they find. Some of them paint their faces, some their whole bodies, some only the eyes, and some only the nose. They do not bear arms or know them, for I showed to them swords and they took them by the blade and cut themselves through ignorance. They have no iron. Their spears are certain reeds, without iron, and some of these have a fish tooth at the end, while others are pointed in various ways. They are all generally fairly tall, good looking and well proportioned. I saw some who bore marks of wounds on their bodies, and I made signs to them to ask how this came about, and they indicated to me that people came from other islands, which are near, and wished to capture them, and they defended themselves. And I believed and still believe that they come here from the mainland to take them for slaves. They should be good servants and of quick intelligence, since I see that they very soon say all that is said to them, and I believe that they would easily be made Christians, for it appeared to me that they had no creed. Our Lord willing, at the time of my departure I will bring back six of them to Your Highnesses, that they may learn to talk. I saw no beast of any kind in this island, except parrots."…

2. Spain Requires the Indians to Submit to Spanish Authority, 1513

On the part of the King, don Fernando [Ferdinand], and of doña Juana, his daughter, Queen of Castile and Léon, subduers of the barbarous nations, we their servants notify and make known to you, as best we can, that the Lord our God, Living and Eternal, created the Heaven and the Earth, and one man and one woman, of whom you and I, and all the men of the world, were and are descendants, and all those who come after us. But, on account of the multitude which has sprung from this man and woman in the five thousand years since the world was created, it was necessary that some men should go one way and some another, and that they should be divided into many kingdoms and provinces, for in one alone they could not be sustained.

This document can be found in Arthur Helps, *The Spanish Conquest in America and Its Relation to the History of Slavery and to the Government of the Colonies* (London: J.W. Parker & Sons, 1855–1861), Vol. I, pp. 264–267. This document can also be found in Marvin Lunenfeld, ed., *1492: Discovery, Invasion, Encounter* (Lexington, MA: D.C. Heath, 1991).

Of all these nations God our Lord gave charge to one man, called St. Peter, that he should be Lord and Superior of all the men in the world, that all should obey him, and that he should be head of the whole human race, wherever men should live, and under whatever law, sect, or belief they should be; and he gave him the world for his kingdom and jurisdiction.

And he commanded him to place his seat in Rome, as the spot most fitting to rule the world from; but also he permitted him to have his seat in any other part of the world, and to judge and govern all Christians, Moors, Jews, Gentiles, and all other sects. This man was called Pope, as if to say, Admirable Great Father and Governor of men. The men who lived in that time obeyed that St. Peter, and took him for Lord, King, and Superior of the universe; so also have they regarded the others who after him have been elected to the Pontificate, and so it has been continued even until now, and will continue until the end of the world.

One of these Pontiffs, who succeeded that St. Peter as Lord of the world, in the dignity and seat which I have before mentioned, made donation of these isles and *terra firme* [mainland] to the aforesaid King and Queen and to their successors, our lords, with all that there are in these territories, as is contained in certain writings which passed upon the subject as aforesaid, which you can see if you wish.

So their Highnesses are kings and lords of these islands and land of *terra firme* by virtue of this donation; and some islands, and indeed almost all those to whom this has been notified, have received and served their Highnesses, as lords and kings, in the way that subjects ought to do, with good will, without any resistance, immediately, without delay, when they were informed of the aforesaid facts. And also they received and obeyed the priests whom their Highnesses sent to preach to them and to teach them our Holy Faith; and all these, of their own free will, without any reward or condition, have become Christians, and are so, and their Highnesses have joyfully and benignantly received them, and also have commanded them to be treated as their subjects and vassals; and you too are held and obliged to do the same. Wherefore as best we can, we ask and require you that you consider what we have said to you, and that you take the time that shall be necessary to understand and deliberate upon it, and that you acknowledge the Church as the Ruler and Superior of the whole world and the high priest called Pope, and in his name the King and Queen doña Juana our lords, in his place, as superiors and lords and kings of these islands and this *terra firme* by virtue of the said donation, and that you consent and give place that these religious fathers should declare and preach to you the aforesaid.

If you do so, you will do well ... and we ... shall receive you in all love and charity, and shall leave you your wives, and your children, and your lands, free without servitude, that you may do with them and with yourselves freely that which you like and think best, and they shall not compel you to turn Christians, unless you yourselves, when informed of the truth, should wish to be converted to our Holy Catholic Faith, as almost all the inhabitants of the rest of the islands have done. And besides this, their Highnesses award you many privileges and exceptions and will grant you many benefits.

But if you do not do this, and wickedly and intentionally delay to do so, I certify to you that, with the help of God, we shall forcibly enter into your country and shall make war against you in all ways and manners that we can, and shall subject you to the yoke and obedience of the Church and of their Highnesses; we shall take you and your wives and your children, and shall make slaves of them, and as such shall sell and dispose of them as their Highnesses may command; and we shall take away your goods, and shall do all the harm and damage that we can, as to vassals who do not obey, and refuse to receive their lord, and resist and contradict him; and we protest that the deaths and losses which shall accrue from this are your fault, and not that of their Highnesses, or ours, nor of these gentlemen who come with us. And that we have said this to you and made this Requirement, we request the notary here present to give us his testimony in writing, and we ask the rest who are present that they should be witnesses of the Requirement.

3. Cabeza de Vaca Recounts His Experiences with the Indians of Mexico, 1536

After we saw clear traces of Christians and understood that we were so near them, we gave many thanks to God our Lord for wanting to take us out of such sad and miserable captivity, and the pleasure we felt [let] each one judge when he thinks about the time we spent in that land and the dangers and hardships through which we passed.

That night I asked one of my companions to go after the Christians, who were going through where we were leaving [the people] reassured, and it was three days' journey. This struck them [my companions] badly, they excusing themselves on grounds of fatigue and hardship, and although each of them could do it better than I, through being stronger and younger. But seeing their choice, the next day in the morning I took with me the black and eleven Indians. And along that trail that I found the Christians to be following I passed by three places where they had slept, and on this day I [we] walked ten leagues.

On the next day in the morning I [we] reached four Christians on horseback who registered great surprise at seeing me so strangely dressed and in the company of Indians. They remained looking at me for a long time, so astonished that they neither spoke to me nor dared to ask me anything. I told them to take me where their captain was, and so we went half a league from there where Diego de Alcaráz was, who was the captain, and after I talked to him he told me he was much at a loss because for many days he had not been able to take [capture] any Indians and that there was no other place to go [to look for them?], and among them [the Spaniards?] there was to be want and hunger. I told him Dorantes and Castillo remained behind, that they were ten leagues from there with many people who had brought [guided] us there.

From *We Came Naked and Barefoot: The Journey of Cabeza De Vaca Across North America* by Alex D. Krieger; edited by Margery H. Krieger, Copyright © 2002. By permission of the University of Texas Press.

He at once sent three horsemen and fifty Indians of those that they were leading [to get Dorantes and Castillo] and the black returned with them to guide them and I remained there and asked that they give me in testimony the year and the month and the day that he [Cabeza de Vaca] had arrived and the manner in which he [Cabeza de Vaca] had come, and so they did. From this river to the village of the Christians, which is called San Miguel, which is of the government of the province that they call New Galicia, there are thirty leagues....

After five days had passed Andrés Dorantes and Alonso del Castillo arrived with those who had gone after them and they brought with them more than six hundred persons who were of that town that the Christians [slave hunters] had forced to go up into the *monte* [thickly forested slopes] and were hiding throughout the land. And those who had come thus far with us brought them out from the *montes* and delivered them to the Christians, and they released all the other people they had brought up to there. And on arriving where I was, Alcaráz begged me to send [messengers] to call out the people from the towns that are along the river edge, who were wandering [and] hiding through the *montes* of that land, and to order them to bring us some food, although this was not necessary because they always took care to bring us everything they could. Soon we sent our messengers to call them [from the *montes*] and six hundred persons [from the towns] who brought all the maize they could collect and carried it in some vessels covered with clay in which they had buried and hidden [the maize]. And they brought us everything else they had, but we did not want to take all except the food, and we gave the rest to the Christians to divide among themselves.

After this we endured many and very great quarrels with them [the slave hunters] because they wanted to take as slaves the Indians we had with us, and because of this trouble we left leaving many Turkish bows [?] that we were carrying and many quivers [*çurrones*] and arrows and among them the five emeralds, for it was not agreed among us concerning them, and so we lost them. We gave the other Christians many bison robes and other things we carried.

We found ourselves in great trouble with the Indians [in making] them return to their homes and to feel assured and to plant maize. They did not want anything except to go with us until they might leave us, as they were accustomed, with other Indians, because if they should turn back without doing this they were afraid they would die. Because going with us they feared neither the [other] Christians nor their lances.

The Christians were sorry [to hear this] and said that their interpreter would tell them that we were of their own [people] and that we had been lost long before and were people of bad luck and little value, and that they were the lords of that land, whom they [the Indians] must obey and serve. But [the Indians] held all this to be worth very little or nothing. Among themselves they would comment that the Christians lied because we came from where the sun rises and they [the slavers] came from where the sun sets, and that we cured the sick and they killed those who were healthy, and that we came naked and barefoot and they were clothed and on horseback and with lances, and that we were not greedy for anything [but] rather everything that was given to us we in turn gave to others and kept nothing, and the others had no other purpose but to steal everything they found and never give anything to anyone. And in this manner they narrated all our deeds and praised them; on the contrary with regard to the others.

So they answered the interpreter of the Christians and let the others know by means of a language that they have among them, with which we understood them, and those who used it we called *Primahaitu*, which is like saying Basque, which we found to be [known] through more than four hundred leagues among these [people] through whom we traveled and there was no other [common language] through all those lands. Finally, he [the interpreter] could never prevail on the Indians to believe that we were of [like] the other Christians and with much difficulty and importunity we made them return to their houses and commanded them to be reassured and to settle their villages and to plant and till the land, which being deserted was already full of brush.

[This land] is without doubt the best of all that there are in the Indies and most fertile and abounding in supplies, and they plant three times a year. They have many fruits and very beautiful rivers and many other very fine waters. There are large indications and signs of mines of gold and silver; the people of it are well off; they serve the Christians (those that are friends) very willingly. They are very ready, much more than those of Mexico. And finally it is a land that lacks nothing to be very good.

Taking leave of us the Indians told us that they would do what we were commanding and would settle their villages if the Christians would let them, and thus I tell it and affirm as very certain, that if they should not do so it will be through the fault of the Christians.

After we sent the Indians away in peace and thanking them for the trouble they had endured with us, the Christians sent to us, with cunning deceit, a certain Zebreros, an *alcalde*, and with him two others. These took us through the brush forests [*montes*] and uninhabited places to get us away from contact with the Indians and so that we should not see or understand what in fact they [the slave hunters] would do. From which it appears how greatly the thoughts of men deceive, for we were going about to seek freedom for them and when we were thinking that we had it just the contrary took place, for they had agreed to go to attack the Indians that we were sending away reassured and in peace. And just as they intended they did. They took us through these brush forests [for] two days, without water, lost and without a road, and we all thought to die of thirst and of it there suffocated seven of our men. And many friends that the Christians were taking with them did not manage to reach until noon the following day the place where we ourselves found water that night. We journeyed with them twenty-five leagues, a little more or less, and at the end of them we arrived at a village of peaceful Indians and the *alcalde* who was leading us left us there and went on ahead another three leagues to a village that is called Culiacán, where was Melchior Diaz, the *alcalde mayor* and captain of that province....

4. Rangel and Oviedo Tell of De Soto's Invasion of Florida, 1539

Friday, which they reckoned to be the thirtieth of May, they began to unload the horses on land. The land where they disembarked is due north of the island of [Dry] Tortuga, which is in the mouth of the Bahama channel; and the cacique and lord of that land was named Oçita, and it is ten leagues to the west of the bay of Juan Ponce [on the east coast of Florida].

As soon as some horses went on land, General Vasco Porcallo de Figueroa and Juan de Añasco and Francisco Osorio went riding to see something of the land, and they found ten Indians with bows and arrows, who also came, as warriors, to reconnoiter these Christian guests and learn what people they were; and they wounded two horses, and the Spaniards killed two of those Indians, and the rest fled.

Two hundred and forty-three horses went in that armada, and of those, nineteen or twenty died on the sea, and all the rest came ashore; and having disembarked, the General and several foot soldiers went with the brigantines to see the town, and a gentleman, called Gómez Arias, returned in one and gave good news of the land and said also that the [native] people were hidden....

The next day, Wednesday, the Governor sent Captain Baltasar de Gallegos, with the Indian that remained, to look for some people or a town or house. At the time that the sun was setting, going off road, because the Indian who was the guide led them wandering and confused, thanks to God they saw from afar as many as twenty Indians painted red (which is a certain red ointment that the Indians put on when they go to war or wish to make a fine appearance), and they wore many plumes and carried their bows and arrows. And as the Christians ran forth against them, the Indians, fleeing, plunged into a forest [*monte*], and one of them came forth to the road shouting and saying: "Sirs, for the love of God and of St. Mary do not kill me: I am Christian, like you, and I am a native of Seville, and my name is Juan Ortiz." The pleasure that the Christians felt was very great, in that God gave them an interpreter and guide at such a time, of which they had great necessity. Delighted with this pleasure, Baltasar de Gallegos and all the Indians that came with him returned that night, very late, to the camp, and the Spaniards of the army became very agitated, believing it was something else and taking up arms; but having recognized who it was, the joy that all had was great, because they estimated that by means of that interpreter they would perform their tasks better.

Without losing time, the following Saturday the Governor determined to go with that interpreter Juan Ortiz to the cacique who had held him, who was called Mocoço, in order to make peace and bring him to the friendship of the Christians. He [Mocoço] waited in his town with his Indians and wives and children, lacking no one, and complained to the Governor about the caciques

In Lawrence A. Clayton, Vernon James Knight Jr., and Edward C. Moore, eds., *The De Soto Chronicles: The Expedition of Hernando de Soto to North America in 1539–1543*, 2 vols. (Tuscaloosa: University of Alabama Press, 1993). Reprinted with permission.

Orriygua, Neguarete, Çapaloey and Eçita, all four of whom are caciques on that coast, saying that they menaced him because he took our friendship and was willing to give that Christian interpreter to the Christians. Using the same interpreter, the Governor told him that he should not be afraid of those caciques or of others, because he would help him, and all the Christians and many more who would come soon would be his friends and would help him against his enemies.

This same day Captain Juan Ruiz Lobillo set out with as many as forty soldiers, on foot, for the interior, and he attacked some settlements [*ranchos*] though could not take but two Indian women; and in order to rescue them, nine Indians followed him for three leagues shooting arrows at him, and they killed one Christian and wounded three or four without his being able to do them damage, although he had arquebusiers and crossbowmen, because those Indians are so agile and such fine warriors that in any nation of the world they would be seen as men....

This Governor was very given to hunting and killing Indians, from the time that he served in the army of Governor Pedrarias Dávila in the provinces of Castilla del Oro and Nicaragua, and he also found himself in Peru and took part in the imprisonment of Atabaliba, where he became rich, and he was one of those who returned to Spain richer, because he carried and put in a safe place in Seville about one hundred thousand pesos of gold; and he decided to return to the Indies only to lose them along with his life, and to continue the bloody tactics of times past, which had been his practice in the aforementioned places. Therefore, continuing his conquest, he commanded that General Vasco Porcallo de Figueroa should go to Oçita, because it was said that there was a gathering of people there. And this Captain having gone there, he found the people gone, and he burned the town, and he set the dogs on [*aperrear*] an Indian he brought as guide. The reader must understand that to set the dogs on [an Indian] is to make the dogs eat them or kill them, tearing the Indian to pieces. The conquistadors in the Indies have always used greyhounds or fierce and valiant dogs in war; and this is why hunting Indians was mentioned above. Therefore, that guide was killed in that way, because he lied and guided poorly.

While Vasco Porcallo did what has been said, the Governor sent another Indian as messenger to the cacique Orriparacogi. [The messenger] did not return because an Indian woman told him that he should not, and for that she was thrown to the dogs....

The Governor departed from the town and port of Spiritu Sancto (called thus for the day that the Governor and his armada arrived there), and this departure was on a Tuesday, the fifteenth of July of the same year of fifteen thirty-nine. And that day they spent the night at the river [*río*] of Mocoço, bringing behind them many pigs that had been brought over in the armada for food in an emergency. And they made two bridges on which this army crossed the river. The next day they went to the lake [*laguna*] of the Rabbit, and that name was given to it because a rabbit which appeared in the camp frightened all the horses, and they broke loose, fleeing back more than a league, leaving not one behind, and all the Christians scattered in order to go after the horses, unarmed. If Indians had attacked them, although they [the Indians] might be few, the Spaniards would have got what they deserved....

These people and their Governor arrived at the first town of Ocale, which was called Uqueten, where they captured two Indians: and then he provided that some on horseback and the mules that they had carried from Cuba should go with corn to aid those who were coming behind, since there they had found abundance; and it did not arrive at a bad time, because they found them in that swamp eating herbs and their roots, some roasted and others stewed, without having salt and, what was worse, without knowing what they were. They were glad for the arrival of provisions, and the great hunger and necessity that they had gave them a refreshment and very acceptable flavor, and of such savor that it revived their diligence and brought forth strength from weakness, and the last of the rear guard arrived the following Tuesday where Governor Hernando de Soto was. But they [the Indians] had already wounded some soldiers who strayed and had killed a crossbowman who was named Mendoza. Having joined the army, they went to Ocale, a town in a good region of corn; and there, going to Acuera for supplies, the Indians, on two occasions, killed three soldiers of the guard of the Governor and wounded others and killed a horse, and all that was due to poor order, since those Indians, although they are archers and have very strong bows and are very skillful and accurate marksmen, their arrows do not have poison [*hierba*] nor do they know what it is.

5. Cartier Records His Meeting with the Micmacs, 1534

... The Cape of the said South land was called The Cape of Hope, through the hope that there we had to finde some passage. The fourth of July we went along the coast of the said land on the Northerly side to finde some harborough, where wee entered into a creeke altogether open toward the South, where there is no succour against the wind: we thought good to name it S. Martines Creeke. There we stayed from the fourth of July until the twelfth: while we were there, on Munday being the sixth of the moneth, Service being done, wee with one of our boates went to discover a Cape and point of land that on the Westerne side was about seven or eight leagues from us, to see which way it did bend, and being within halfe a league of it, wee sawe two companies of boates of wilde men going from one land to the other: their boates were in number about fourtie or fiftie. One part of the which came to the said point, and a great number of the men went on shore making a great noise, beckening unto us that wee should come on land, shewing us certaine skinnes upon pieces of wood, but because we had but one onely boat, wee would not goe to them, but went to the other side lying in the Sea: they seeing us flee, prepared two of their boats to follow us, with which came also five more of them that were comming from the Sea side,

---

Jacques Cartier on the Micmacs Meeting the French, 1534. This document can be found in Henry S. Burrage, ed., *Early English and French Voyages, Chiefly from Hakluyt, 1534–1608*, Original Narratives of Early American History Series (New York: Charles Scribner's Sons, 1906), 24–26.

all which approched neere unto our boate, dancing, and making many signes of joy and mirth, as it were desiring our friendship, saying in their tongue Napeu tondamen assurtah, with many other words that we understood not. But because (as we have said) we had but one boat, wee would not stand to their courtesie, but made signes unto them that they should turne back, which they would not do, but with great furie came toward us: and suddenly with their boates compassed us about: and because they would not away from us by any signes that we could make, we shot off two pieces among them, which did so terrifie them, that they put themselves to flight toward the sayde point, making a great noise: and having staid a while, they began anew, even as at the first to come to us againe, and being come neere out wee strucke at them with two lances, which thing was so great a terrour unto them, that with great hast they beganne to flee, and would no more follow us.

The next day part of the saide wilde men with nine of their boates came to the point and entrance of the Creeke, where we with our ships were at road. We being advertised of their comming, went to the point where they were with our boates: but so soone as they saw us, they began to flee, making signes that they came to trafique with us, shewing us, such skinnes as they cloth themselves withall, which are of small value. We likewise made signes unto them, that we wished them no evill: and in signe thereof two of our men ventured to go on land to them, and cary them knives with other Iron wares, and a red hat to give unto their Captaine. Which when they saw, they also came on land, and brought some of their skinnes, and so began to deale with us, seeming to be very glad to have our iron wares and other things, stil dancing with many other ceremonies, as with their hands to cast Sea water on their heads. They gave us whatsoever they had, not keeping any thing, so that they were constrained to goe backe againe naked, and made us signes that the next day the would come againe, and bring more skinnes with them....

6. An Englishman Discusses Trading with Indians on the Atlantic Coast, 1584

After thankes given to God for our safe arrivall thither, we manned our boats, and went to view the land next adjoyning, and "to take possession of the same, in the right of the Queenes most excellent Majestie, as rightfull Queene, and Princesse of the same, and after delivered the same over to your use, according to her Majesties grant, and letters patents, under her Highnesse great Seale....

We remained by the side of this Island two whole dayes before we saw any people of the Countrey: the third day we espied one small boate rowing towardes us having in it three persons: this boat came to the Island side, foure harquebuz-shot from our shippes, and there two of the people remaining, the third came along the shoreside towards us, and wee being then all within boord, he walked up and downe upon the point of the land next unto us:

Richard Hakluyt, *The Portable Hakluyt's Voyages: The Principal Navigations, Voyages, Traffiques, and Discoveries of the English Nation* (New York: Viking, [1967, 1965]).

then the Master and the Pilot of the Admirall, Simon Ferdinando, and the Captaine Philip Amadas, my selfe, and others rowed to the land, whose comming this fellow attended, never making any shewe of feare or doubt. And after he had spoken of many things not understood by us, we brought him with his owne good liking, aboord the ships, and gave him a shirt, a hat & some other things, and made him taste of our wine, and our meat, which he liked very wel: and after having viewed both barks, he departed, and went to his owne boat againe, which hee had left in a little Cove or Creeke adjoyning: assoone as hee was two bow shoot into the water, he fell to fishing, and in lesse then halfe an houre, he had laden his boate as deepe, as it could swimme, with which hee came againe to the point of the lande, and there he devided his fish into two parts, pointing one part to the ship, and the other to the pinnesse: which, after he had (as much as he might) requited the former benefites received, departed out of our sight.

The next day there came unto us divers boates, and in one of them the Kings brother, accompanied with fortie or fiftie men, very handsome and goodly people, and in their behaviour as mannerly and civill as any of Europe. His name was Granganimeo, and the king is called Wingina, the countrey Wingandacoa, and now by her Majestie Virginia.... When he came to the place, his servants spread a long matte upon the ground, on which he sate downe, and at the other ende of the matte foure others of his companie did the like, the rest of his men stood round about him, somewhat a farre off: when we came to the shore to him with our weapons, hee never mooved from his place, nor any of the other foure, nor never mistrusted any harme to be offred from us, but sitting still he beckoned us to come and sit by him, which we performed: and being set hee made all signes of joy and welcome, striking on his head and his breast and afterwardes on ours, to shewe wee were all one, smiling and making shewe the best he could of all love, and familiaritie. After hee had made a long speech unto us, wee presented him with divers things, which hee received very joyfully, and thankefully. None of the company durst speake one worde all the time: onely the foure which were at the other ende, spake one in the others eare very softly.

The King is greatly obeyed, and his brothers and children reverenced: the King himselfe in person was at our being there, sore wounded in a fight which hee had with the King of the next countrey, called Wingina, and was shot in two places through the body, and once cleane through the thigh, but yet he recovered: by reason whereof and for that hee lay at the chiefe towne of the countrey, being six dayes journey off, we saw him not at all.

After we had presented this his brother with such things as we thought he liked, wee likewise gave somewhat to the other that sat with him on the matte: but presently he arose and tooke all from them and put it into his owne basket, making signes and tokens, that all things ought to bee delivered unto him, and the rest were but his servants, and followers. A day or two after this, we fell to trading with them, exchanging some things that we had, for Chamoys, Buffe, and Deere skinnes: when we shewed him all our packet of merchandize, of all things that he sawe, a bright tinne dish most pleased him, which hee presently tooke up and clapt it before his breast, and after made a hole in the brimme thereof and hung it about his necke, making signes that it would defende him against his enemies arrowes: for those people maintaine a deadly and terrible warre, with the people and King adjoyning. We exchanged our tinne dish for twentie skinnes, woorth twentie Crownes, or twentie Nobles: and a copper kettle for fiftie skins woorth fifty Crownes. They offered us good exchange for our hatchets, and axes, and for knives, and would have given any thing for swordes: but we would not depart with any. After two or three dayes the Kings brother came aboord the shippes, and dranke wine, and eat of our meat and of our bread, and liked exceedingly thereof: and after a few dayes over-passed, he brought his wife with him to the ships, his daughter and two or three children: his wife was very well favoured, of meane stature, and very bash-full: shee had on her backe a long cloake of leather, with the furre side next to her body, and before her a piece of the same: about her forehead shee had a bande of white Corall, and so had her husband many times: in her eares shee had bracelets of pearles hanging downe to her middle, (whereof we delivered your worship a little bracelet) and those were of the bignes of good pease. The rest of her women of the better sort had pendants of copper hanging in either eare, and some of the children of the kings brother and other noble men, have five or sixe in either eare: he himselfe had upon his head a broad plate of golde, or copper, for being unpolished we knew not what mettal it should be, neither would he by any meanes suffer us to take it off his head, but feeling it, it would bow very easily. His apparell was as his wives, onely the women weare their haire long on both sides, and the men but on one. They are of colour yellowish, and their haire black for the most part, and yet we saw children that had very fine aburne, and chestnut coloured haire....

He was very just of his promise: for many times we delivered him merchandize upon his word, but ever he came within the day and performed his promise. He sent us every day a brase or two of fat Bucks, Conies, Hares, Fish the best of the world. He sent us divers kindes of fruites, Melons, Walnuts, Cucumbers, Gourdes, Pease, and divers rootes, and fruites very excellent good, and of their Countrey corne, which is very white, faire and well tasted, and groweth three times in five moneths: in May they sow, in July they reape, in June they sow, in August they reape: in July they sow, in September they reape: onely they cast the corne into the ground, breaking a little of the soft turfe with a wodden mattock, or pickeaxe: our selves prooved the soile, and put some of our Pease in the ground, and in tenne dayes they were of fourteene ynches high: they have also Beanes very faire of divers colours and wonderfull plentie: some growing naturally, and some in their gardens, and so have they both wheat and oates....

We were entertained with all love and kindnesse, and with as much bountie (after their maner) as they could possibly devise. We found the people most gen-tle, loving, and faithful, voide of all guile and treason, and such as live after the maner of the golden age. The people onely care howe to defend themselves from the cold in their short winter, and to feed themselves with such meat as the soile affoordeth: there meate is very well sodden and they make broth very sweet and savorie: their vessels are earthen pots, very large, white and sweete, their dishes are wodden platters of sweet timber: within the place where they feede was their lodging, and within that their Idoll, which they worship, of whome they speake incredible things....

They wondred marvelously when we were amongst them at the whitenes of our skins, ever coveting to touch our breasts, and to view the same. Besides they had our ships in marvelous admiration, & all things els were so strange unto them, as it appeared that none of them had ever seene the like. When we discharged any piece, were it but an hargubuz, they would tremble thereat for very feare, and for the strangenesse of the same: for the weapons which themselves use are bowes and arrowes: the arrowes are but of small canes, headed with a sharpe shell or tooth of a fish sufficient ynough to kill a naked man. Their swordes be of wood hardened: likewise they use wooden breast-plates for their defence. They have besides a kinde of club, in the end whereof they fasten the sharpe hornes of a stagge, or other beast. When they goe to warres they cary about with them their idol, of whom they aske counsel, as the Romans were woont of the Oracle of Apollo. They sing songs as they march towardes the battell in stead of drummes and trumpets: their warres are very cruell and bloody, by reason whereof, and of their civill dissentions which have happened of late yeeres amongst them, the people are marvelously wasted, and in some places the countrey left desolate....

And so contenting our selves with this service at this time, which wee hope hereafter to inlarge, as occasion and assistance shalbe given, we resolved to leave the countrey, and to apply our selves to returne for England, which we did accordingly, and arrived safely in the West of England about the middest of September.

We brought home also two of the Savages being lustie men, whose names were Wanchese and Manteo.

◈ ESSAYS

Neither of the essays in this chapter is written by a "historian"—if one takes that to mean a person whose graduate training is specifically in the field of history—but both offer valuable insights into the past, affirming that the study of history is open to contributions from a variety of disciplines. The first essay is by Bruce Trigger, a professor of archaeology at McGill University in Montreal, Canada, from 1964 until his death in 2006. Trigger provides a useful overview of Indian contacts with Europeans in the sixteenth and seventeenth centuries, from the Caribbean, to Central and South America, and then into North America. He offers several important glimpses into how the newcomers—and the changes they brought—may have looked from Native perspectives, and also sheds light on some of the ways in which Indians actively responded to the European challenge.

Whereas the first essay is authored by a scholar at the peak of his long career, and generally takes the North American shores as its geographical focus, the second is by a scholar at the start of his career, and adopts a specific community in the continental interior—the Comanche of the Great Plains—as its vantage point. The author of this essay, Cody Newton, was, as of 2012, a graduate student in anthropology at the University of Colorado at Boulder. As Newton notes, the Comanches may not have had their first direct contact with Europeans until 1706, more than 200 years after the Tainos sighted Columbus's ships in the Caribbean. To recall our discussion from the previous chapter, did this mean that the Comanches had no history before that year? If they did, what factors drove that history? Although they may not have made direct contact with European people until the 1700s, were they completely unaffected by the arrival of these strangers in the 1500s and 1600s? Read what Newton has to say in response to these questions, and pay additional attention to his research methods. How does Newton know what he knows? How confident can he be about his interpretations?

The Shores: Native Responses to Early European Contact

BY BRUCE TRIGGER

In this paper, I will attempt to assess the relative value of romantic and rationalist approaches for explaining the behavior of native North Americans in their earliest encounters with Europeans. In encountering Europeans after 1492, native Americans experienced novel challenges of both a practical and a cognitive sort. They clearly had well-established traditions of intertribal diplomacy, which guided their relations with neighboring groups. These traditions combined rationalistic calculations with culturally influenced objectives. At the same time, each culture possessed beliefs about the creation and nature of the universe that, while having adaptive significance, were far more independently determined by cultural traditions than were aspects of culture that were subjected to practical application on a regular basis. With the exception of sporadic contacts with the Norse in Newfoundland and the eastern Arctic, none of the native Americans had ever previously had to deal with anything like the bearded, white-skinned beings who began haunting their seacoasts. The latter's huge ships, abundant metal goods, brightly colored clothes, and thundering guns and cannons placed them in a different category from any known or imaginable native group. So too did the extreme self-confidence and arrogance with which the Europeans frequently conducted themselves. How were native peoples to interpret such strangers as they appeared with increasing frequency along their coasts, giving away trinkets, carrying off native people, and leaving behind unknown diseases, before coming into closer contact as shipwrecked sailors, traders, would-be conquerors, and finally settlers?

Trigger, Bruce. "Early Native North American Response to European Contact: Romantic Versus Rationalistic Interpretations," from the March 1991 issue of the *Journal of American History*. By permission of Oxford University Press on behalf of the *Journal of American History*.

First Perceptions

Indian folk traditions, often recorded generations after the events occurred, suggest that native North Americans believed the first European ships they saw to be floating islands inhabited by supernatural spirits and sometimes covered by white clouds (sails) from which lightning and thunder (cannons) were discharged, or else the mobile dwelling places of powerful spirits whom they prepared to welcome with sacrifices, food, and entertainment. These stories indicate that there was much about Europeans that offered itself to supernatural interpretation in terms of native religious concepts.

European records of early contacts with native Americans appear to corroborate the claim that in numerous instances native people interpreted the newcomers as supernatural. The Spanish who explored the settled Caribbean islands in the late fifteenth century were convinced that native beliefs in their divinity were a source of power that they could use to control these people. In 1492 Christopher Columbus concluded that the inhabitants of the Bahamas believed that he had come from the sky. The Spanish recounted natives holding prisoners under water to determine whether Europeans were immortal. Accounts derived from Spanish and Aztec sources provide detailed descriptions of how native religious beliefs played a major role in the subjugation of one of the most populous and complex societies in the New World by a handful of European intruders. The Aztec ruler Moctezuma Xocoyotzin's fears that Hernán Cortés might be the god Quetzalcoatl returning to rule Mexico caused him not to resist the Spanish invasion directly. This in turn facilitated the collapse of the Aztec tributary system and the eventual conquest of their city-state and all of Mexico. It is also clear that Cortés surmised the general nature of Moctezuma's fears and exploited them to his own advantage.

The accounts of the explorations of Jacques Cartier, Álvar Núñez Cabeza de Vaca, and Hernando de Soto described isolated instances when the Indians brought the sick of their communities to them and requested that they heal them. This suggests that these leaders were regarded as powerful shamans, if not as divinities, by native peoples in widely separated parts of North America. Native people are also reported to have worshiped and brought offerings to crosses erected by Francisco Vázquez de Coronado in what was to be the southwestern United States and to a large stone column put up by Jean Ribault in Florida, although it is possible that at least in the Southwest such behavior was motivated more by political than by religious considerations. The account of Francis Drake's voyage to California in 1579 describes the Coast Miwoks as offering sacrifices and lacerating their faces in the presence of the English visitors, despite the latter's efforts to make them stop. In 1587 English colonists in Virginia reported that because Indians had died of illness in each town they had passed through while they themselves had not become sick, they were viewed as the spirits of the dead returning to human society.

Similar incidents continued to be reported on the frontiers of European exploration in North America. Kenneth Morrison believes that early in their encounters the Abenakis (of what is now northern New England) inferred from European behavioral patterns that the Europeans might be the cannibal giants of their mythology. Jean Nicollet was said to have struck terror into the Winnebagos (or some other tribe of the upper Great Lakes region), who believed him to be a thunder spirit when he visited them in 1634. In 1670 Father Claude Allouez was treated as a *manitou* (spirit) when he visited the Mascoutens and Miamis on the shores of the Wolf River in Wisconsin. They made an offering of tobacco and appealed to him for relief from famine and disease. It is recorded that the Ojibwas of Red Lake, Minnesota, thought the first airplane they saw to be a thunderbird, or storm spirit, and rushed to the shore of the lake when it landed in order to throw tobacco offerings on the water.

Europeans were prepared to exploit North American Indian beliefs in their supernatural powers. Sometimes the deaths of early European explorers and settlers were concealed in the hope that Indians might continue to believe that they were immortal. In the course of their *entrada* into what is now the south-eastern United States, de Soto and his followers, drawing upon their experiences in Mexico and Peru, claimed that he was the Child of the Sun and in that capacity had a claim upon the obedience of local chiefs.

Many cultural relativists assume that these scattered pieces of evidence provide insights into how native North Americans generally perceived Europeans in the early stages of their encounter. They take it for granted that similar culturally conditioned beliefs determined native responses in many other instances of early contact, but that such beliefs either were less obvious or failed to be recorded by less sensitive or less interested European observers. This is a highly suppositious conclusion. Moreover, most of the native accounts of what happened were recorded long after the event, and many are clearly influenced by European values and religious concepts. While detailed ethnographic analysis has revealed undeniably traditional elements in some of these tales, it is dangerous to overgeneralize from them about how native peoples first perceived Europeans, especially when we consider the great variability in specific beliefs from one culture to another.

The total corpus of documentary evidence that religious beliefs played an important and widespread role in influencing native behavior is in fact very limited. For the most part, native American relations with Europeans are portrayed as having been governed by relatively straightforward concerns with exchange and defense. While some of the survivors of the Pánfilo de Narváez expedition found roles for themselves as shamans and traders among the hunter-gatherers of Texas, perhaps because they were not equipped to play an effective part in subsistence activities, hundreds of shipwrecked Spanish sailors were enslaved by chiefs in Florida. Did this plethora of prosaic accounts result from many European recorders failing to understand Indian behavior? The written historical evidence is inadequate to supply a definitive answer. In those cases where religious behavior is specifically ascribed to native people in sixteenth-century accounts, there is the equally difficult problem of the extent to which European observers uncritically ascribed their own ethnocentric views about non-Christian religious beliefs to native people, thereby either misinterpreting their actions or ascribing religious motives to them in situations where those did not apply.

Fortunately, evidence concerning those native beliefs is not limited to historical records. In recent years George Hamell has carried out an extensive analysis of the basic concepts underlying the traditional religious beliefs of the Algonquian-, Iroquoian-, and Siouan-speaking peoples of northeastern North America, using ethnographic data recorded from earliest European contact to the present day. He concludes that the cosmologies of these peoples equated certain natural materials with physical, spiritual, and social well-being, both during this life and after death. These substances included marine shell, white and red metals (native silver and copper), and white, green, and red crystals and other kinds of stones. Such substances, which came from beneath the earth and water, were associated with such supernatural beings as the horned serpent, panther, and dragon, who were the guardian spirits and patrons of animal medicine societies.

These concepts appear to explain the inclusion of objects made from marine shell, native copper, and rock crystal in native burials of the Eastern Woodlands in prehistoric times. Archaeological evidence of the continuity of these burial practices from the Archaic period to the historical era suggests a persistence of these beliefs for over six thousand years, although intertribal exchanges of shell, copper, and other materials had been at one of their periodic low ebbs in the centuries preceding European contact. Hamell further suggests that the Indians equated European copper, brass, and tin with native copper and silver and equated glass beads with crystals and colored rocks. Because the Europeans possessed such extraordinarily large amounts of metalware and glass beads and came from across the ocean, where in Indian cosmology mythical time and space converged, they were regarded as supernatural beings or the returning spirits of the dead.

Hamell's ideas may account for the historically attested interest of native groups in European copper, brass, and tin objects and in glass beads. They would also explain why copper and brass kettles were cut into tiny fragments and dispersed by exchange among the tribes of the Northern Woodlands during the sixteenth century and why most of these goods are found in burials rather than in abandoned living sites during this period. The renewed emphasis on securing objects made of ritually important substances and burying them with the dead would also account for the increasing intertribal exchange of marine shell during this period. Although marine shell was a North American product, it was as important as copper or crystals in native religious beliefs, and Europeans never provided a satisfactory substitute for it.

In the course of the sixteenth century, the increasing availability of European goods led to greater emphasis in much of eastern North America on east–west exchange patterns, which in some areas superseded the predominantly north–south ones of earlier periods. European goods may also have brought about major changes in native life. The final expansion of the Huron confederacy and the coming together of all the Huron tribes in a small area at the southeastern corner of Georgian Bay (of Lake Huron) by the end of the sixteenth century seems to have been motivated primarily by a desire to have access to the secure trade routes leading by way of Lake Nipissing and the Ottawa River to the St. Lawrence Valley, rather than simply by a need to place more distance between themselves and hostile Iroquoian groups to the south and east. Before Hamell began his research, I had observed that "in the Indian history of [the northeastern Woodlands], trading in exotic goods has often played a role that was out of all proportion to its utilitarian significance" and that "what appears in the archaeological record as a few scraps of metal seems in fact to have been a sufficient catalyst to realize certain potentials for development that were inherent in prehistoric Huron society, but which otherwise might never have come to fruition."

Hamell's research, while neither finished nor free from controversy, suggests that a combination of ethnographic and archaeological data may provide significant insights into how native people perceived Europeans and European goods in the early stages of their interaction. This in turn may assist in interpreting the limited historical texts that are available concerning contact in the sixteenth century. While there may have been considerable variability in the manner in which different native groups interpreted the first Europeans they encountered, the archaeological and ethnographic evidence that Hamell has assembled also suggests that throughout eastern North America there were numerous culturally shared religious beliefs that encouraged native peoples to attribute various supernatural powers to the Europeans.

Seventeenth-Century Pragmatism

In any discussion of how native peoples perceived Europeans, the far more abundant data from the seventeenth century are of vital importance. If native beliefs continued to play a preponderant role in determining native reactions to Europeans so long after first contact, it would reinforce the assumption that they had done so during the previous century. Recent historical and ethnographic research has challenged established rationalistic interpretations of native dealings with Europeans during the seventeenth century. In particular, a growing commitment to romantic and cultural relativist explanations of human behavior has led an increasing number of historians and anthropologists to reject the proposition that European goods had more than symbolic value to native peoples so long as their societies maintained any semblance of independence from European control. Hamell states that he looks to "Northeastern Woodland Indian myth for an explanation of ... their history during the two centuries following European contact." Calvin Martin has attracted a wide audience with his thinly documented claim that the fur trade developed, not as a result of native peoples' needing or especially desiring European goods, but as a by-product of their declaring war on fur-bearing animals and seeking to exterminate them because they held animal spirits to be responsible for the epidemics of European diseases that had begun in the sixteenth century. William Eccles portrays native cultures as economically independent, resilient, and able to determine their own destinies at least until the British conquest of New France in 1760. Conrad Heidenreich argues more specifically that "it is doubtful ... that the Huron maintained their relations with the French because they had become economically dependent on European goods." He claims that they had instead become militarily dependent on the French for protection against the Iroquois.

These arguments ignore a solid body of evidence that by the beginning of the seventeenth century the bulk of trade between Europeans and Indians was not in glass beads, other ornaments, and liquor. The first Indians who traded with Europeans may have hung metal axes and hoes on their chests as ornaments and used stockings as tobacco pouches. Yet, by the 1620s, the Montagnais at Tadoussac, near the mouth of the St. Lawrence River, were using large quantities of clothing, hatchets, iron arrowheads, needles, sword blades, ice picks, knives, kettles, and preserved foods that they purchased from the French. For some purposes, especially in wet weather, woolen clothing proved superior to their traditional skin garments. They had also ceased to manufacture birchbark baskets and stone axes. In the 1630s, the Mohawks, who lived close to the Dutch traders at Fort Orange (now Albany), continued to produce their own food but were purchasing a wide range of clothing and metalware from Europeans. By the early 1640s, they owned more than three hundred guns, which had been paid for partly with skins they had seized from neighboring tribes. The Hurons, who lived much farther inland and had considerable transportation problems, were more selective in their purchases of European goods. They were primarily interested in obtaining metal cutting tools. In particular they wanted knives of all sizes, axes, and iron arrowheads. They also purchased guns, when the French were willing to sell them, and copper and brass kettles. The latter were easier to transport than their heavy and fragile clay cooking pots, and when they were worn out, they could be cut up and used as raw material to manufacture metal arrowheads and cutting tools as well as ornaments. In addition, Huron traders carried home glass beads and metal bracelets, which weighed relatively little. They do not appear to have purchased much cloth or many items of clothing, and unlike the coastal tribes, they did not seek alcoholic beverages when they came to trade. In selecting European goods, the Hurons showed a marked preference for tools with cutting edges that were superior to their own and that replaced native implements such as stone axes that took a long time to manufacture.

Among the Huron, Iroquois, and other Iroquoian-speaking peoples, a stone- and bone-based technology did not completely disappear until the late seventeenth century, which is later than G. T. Hunt and some archaeologists have believed. They also continued to manufacture pottery vessels until then, and the arrival of metal cutting tools seems to have resulted in a florescence of bone working. Yet, well before 1650, there was a marked decline in the frequency of stone tools among these groups. This suggests that by 1636 the Hurons were sufficiently dependent on the French for metal cutting tools that one of their chiefs, Aenons, was not exaggerating when he said that if his people "should remain two years without going down to Quebec to trade, they would find themselves reduced to such extremities that they might consider themselves fortunate to join with the Algonquins and to embark in their canoes." It is clear from the context of this report that Aenons was referring to the necessity of securing European goods, not to maintaining a military alliance against the Iroquois.

From the first arrival of the Jesuit missionaries in the 1620s, the Hurons and their neighbors regarded them as shamans. Beginning in the late 1630s, many Indians concluded that these priests were sorcerers or malevolent spirits, who were responsible for the great epidemics of European diseases that afflicted the native people of the region at that time. The Indians probably also continued to believe that the French, who were able to manufacture such large quantities of metal goods, must possess great supernatural power. Yet in their eyes this did not make Europeans intrinsically different from the Indians, who were also able to practice witchcraft and whose amulets and relations with appropriate spirits enabled them to hunt, fish, and move about on snowshoes and in canoes more effectively than Europeans did. Ordinary Frenchmen who traded, traveled, lived with Indian families, and even intermarried with them were viewed as regular human beings. They had been observed to become ill and die, and a few of them had even been killed by the Indians. The slowness of most Europeans to master native languages and skills led many Indians to conclude that on the whole Europeans were slow-witted, which accorded with the traditional Iroquoian belief that hairy people were unintelligent.

The Indians were also appalled by what they saw as the greed, violence, and bad manners of the French, which all were recognizable, if negatively valued, patterns of human behavior. Huron chiefs felt confident of their ability to outwit and manipulate French traders and officials, even when they were becoming politically and economically reliant on them. All of this suggests that by the seventeenth century the fur-trading peoples of the northern Woodlands regarded most, if not all, Europeans as human beings who were different from themselves and in some respects more powerful, but with whom they could interact on a normal basis.

Cognitive Reorganization

It is thus evident that at some point those native groups that initially reacted to Europeans primarily on the basis of their traditional religious beliefs came to regard Europeans as human beings with whom, while continuing to take account of their special customs and sensibilities, they could do business as they did with any other foreign group. The Indians' increasing familiarity with Europeans led to a "cognitive reorganization" in which the rational component inherent in the mental processes of every human being began to play the dominant role in guiding native relations with Europeans, while religious beliefs ceased to play the important part that in many cases they had done in the early stages of the encounter. The key factor in bringing about this transformation was the Indians' observation and rational evaluation of European behavior. This development accords with the general principle that whenever culturally transmitted beliefs are employed to guide human behavior, they are subject to rational scrutiny on the basis of the resulting performance; where those beliefs encourage counterproductive behavior, the evaluation may result in their being rejected, revised, or judged inapplicable. In the case of early encounters between Indians and Europeans, the question remains: Under what circumstances did this cognitive reorganization occur?

Some answers are provided by historical data from the early sixteenth century. When Giovanni da Verrazzano visited the relatively sheltered Narragansetts of southern New England in 1524, he found them anxious to obtain blue beads as well as bells and other trinkets made of copper. They were not interested in steel or iron objects, mirrors, or cloth. This suggests that these Indians were interested only in objects that had precise counterparts in their traditional system of belief and exchange. By contrast, Indians living farther north along the coast of Maine, who presumably had more contact with European fishermen and their goods (they were wearing European copper beads in their ears), were far less trustful of Verrazzano and his crew and would take in exchange for their goods only "knives, fish-hooks, and sharp metal." Likewise, the Micmacs that Jacques Cartier encountered in Chaleur Bay in 1534 not only indicated very clearly that they wished to barter their furs with the French but also sought hatchets, knives, and other ironware, as well as beads, in exchange. The following year the Iroquoians of Hochelaga, on Montreal Island, seemed pleased with any European goods that Cartier gave them, while those who lived at Stadacona, within the limits of modern Quebec City, and who appear already to have had limited access to European goods being traded by Breton fishermen at the Strait of Belle Isle, sought hatchets, knives, and awls from the French, as well as beads and other trinkets.

While the more isolated Hochelagans brought their sick to Cartier for him to heal, the Stadaconans, on being informed by two of their boys (whom Cartier had kidnapped and taken to France the previous year) that the goods he was trading were of little value in his own country, demanded more of those goods in exchange from the French. At the same time it was the Stadaconans who cured Cartier's crew of the scurvy that was afflicting them. Cartier had attempted to conceal their sickness and deaths among his men, not because he believed the Stadaconans thought the French to be immortal, but because he feared they might attack if they realized how defenseless these intruders were. Soon after Cartier's visit, a large quantity of ironware was reported being taken to the Strait of Belle Isle to trade for furs.

These data indicate that while groups such as the Narragansetts of Rhode Island and the Hochelagans of the upper St. Lawrence (who were remote from European fishermen at Cape Breton and the Strait of Belle Isle) were pleased to secure glass beads and copper and tin trinkets, bands that lived closer to these trading areas were anxious to obtain metal cutting tools as early as the 1520s and 1530s. The latter groups also appear to have already adopted a naturalistic view of Europeans. This suggests that if many Indian groups initially viewed Europeans as supernatural beings, upon closer contact this interpretation was replaced by the conclusion that Europeans were human beings like themselves. At the same time, European metal cutting tools came to be universally valued for their utilitarian advantages. While iron knives may have performed no more efficiently than did stone hide scrapers, they cut better and were more durable and easier to keep sharp than were stone tools. Metal tools also performed better as perforators, needles, and projectile points than did the stone and bone tools the Indians had used theretofore. It was for practical reasons that coastal peoples soon were putting iron tools at the top of their shopping lists. Glass beads and scraps of copper continued to dominate the indirect trade with the interior, but by the beginning of the seventeenth century native groups living as far inland as the lower Great Lakes were seeking metal cutting tools in preference to all other European goods....

These observations may help to interpret the records of other major encounters between Europeans and native North Americans in the early sixteenth century. The native rulers who lived in the path of de Soto's pillaging expedition through what is now the southeastern United States adopted various strategies to placate, deflect, defeat, or speed him on his way. Yet overwhelmingly they conducted their relations with him in terms of what must have been the normal idiom of intergroup diplomacy in that region of hierarchical societies. De Soto was treated as a powerful chief with whom an alliance might be desirable or submission inevitable, but only rarely was he recorded as having been approached as a shaman and asked to cure the sick. Moreover, on at least two occasions rulers pointedly rejected claims that he possessed supernatural powers, including the panic-stricken assertion by his successor Luis de Moscoso that de Soto had not died but gone to the sky for a few days to visit the gods. The Indian ruler of Guachoya, mocking the latter tale, promised to offer two human sacrifices in honor of de Soto—a tradition in that area at the burial of neighboring chiefs. It would appear that previous contacts with shipwrecked Spanish sailors, would-be conquerors such as Juan Ponce de León and Pánfilo de Narváez, and colonists such as Lucas Vázquez de Ayllón had provided the native people living on the periphery of this densely settled region with an opportunity to assess Europeans and that the results of their observations were transmitted inland through the diplomatic networks linking adjacent tribes and chiefdoms. Despite the devastating effects of the Spanish plundering and burning of their settlements, the Indians of what is now the southeastern United States quickly took advantage of new resources that were presented to them; hogs, for example, were soon being eaten.

The accounts of Coronado's *entrada* into the Southwest also describe a naturalistic evaluation of Europeans by native people, who at first ineffectually opposed the Spanish invaders and then resorted to accommodative responses until Spanish exactions provoked them to renewed overt and clandestine resistance. Trading contacts with the Indians of northern Mexico possibly provided them with the information necessary to understand in advance what kind of beings the Spanish and their horses were and how they were likely to behave. Echoes of perceptions surrounding the original encounter between the Spanish and Aztecs in central Mexico may have been heard in an allegedly fifty-year-old prophecy of the Pueblo Indians that strangers would come from the south and conquer them, although this prophecy did not stifle resistance as more deeply rooted cultural traditions had done with Moctezuma.

The available evidence for the sixteenth century suggests that, whatever the initial Indian understanding of Europeans, a relatively short period of direct contact between the two groups resulted in a naturalistic interpretation of the newcomers. It also led to a growing demand for some European tools, which were seen as allowing tasks to be performed more effectively than did traditional stone and bone tools. These shifts involved the Indians' rationally assessing the performance of persons and goods and a desire to adopt a technology that would reduce their expenditure of energy on some routine tasks and improve the quality of their products. This technology was adopted as soon as it became available on a regular basis, even though it rendered native groups reliant on European suppliers.

The first impressions that native peoples had of Europeans and the initial strategies that these peoples devised for dealing with them seem to have been strongly influenced by their traditional beliefs. In some situations these strategies crucially shaped relations between the two groups. Where contact remained limited or indirect, initial interpretations persisted without significant modification for long periods. As relations became more direct and intense, it appears that these interpretations were rapidly modified by rational assessments of what Europeans were like and what they had to offer. In at least some areas, these assessments spread inland ahead of European exploration. This appears to have happened more quickly in densely settled regions than in more thinly populated ones.

This utilitarian assessment of European technology does not mean that native people did not continue to assign their own social meanings to European goods or that native belief systems did not play a major role in determining how native people viewed Europeans or how European goods were used in religious contexts such as burials. On the contrary, there is evidence that basic native belief systems remained intact for long periods. This does not, however, rule out the importance of a rationalist perspective for understanding major aspects of native behavior, contrary to what more extreme relativists seek to maintain.

Conclusion

It is impossible to understand native American responses to their contact with Europeans in the early sixteenth century without a detailed knowledge of native cultures. Amerindian world views appear to have played an important role in structuring their initial understanding of these encounters, and this in turn influenced how native people behaved in these situations. The little that we know about these world views suggests that they varied from one region or ethnic group to another and that even adjacent, highly similar world views could, depending on historically contingent situations, structure native interpretations of contact in different ways. From the beginning some interpretations of Europeans were probably more "rational" than others.

Nevertheless, in areas where contact became frequent, it does not appear to have been long before all native perceptions and behavior were significantly influenced by rational appraisals of Europeans and what they had to offer. The long-term evidence indicates that economic determinists were not mistaken when they claimed that native people appreciated the material benefits to be derived from many items of European technology and that they sought to utilize this technology even at the cost of growing dependence upon their European trading partners. Native leaders also learned from observation to understand the motivations of the different European groups with whom they interacted and to devise strategies for coping with their demands. Native people were not constrained by their traditional beliefs to the extent that a rational assessment of the dangers and opportunities of the novel situations in which they found themselves was precluded. In general these assessments appear to have been strong enough to survive the psychological disruptions that must have accompanied the unprecedented epidemics of European diseases that afflicted native North Americans in the course of the sixteenth and seventeenth centuries.

If, in the long run, native people failed to devise strategies that could halt European aggression, it was not because they were unable to understand European behavior from a rational point of view. They failed because they were overwhelmed by European technological superiority, by growing numbers of European settlers as their own populations declined because of European diseases, and by increasing dependence upon European technology. They also failed because they were unable to modify their social organizations and values quickly enough to compete with the more disciplined European societies that were seeking to dominate and exploit North America. In North American Indian societies, decision making depended upon a slow process of achieving consensus, while European ones had evolved complex hierarchies of authority and command. Native groups therefore had less political maneuverability and less potential for concerted action when competing with Europeans. The creation of such structures, involving as it did the formation of new institutions and new patterns of behavior, was a slow process, even when the need for change was clearly perceived. Native societies became increasingly dependent upon European ones and were dominated by them because they lacked time to develop the human and material resources required to compete with them, not because of their incapacity to understand in rational terms what was happening to them.

Although the examples in this paper have been drawn from North America, these conclusions should apply equally to relations between European colonists and native groups elsewhere in the Americas and around the world. Giving due importance to a rationalist approach explains why in the course of the expansion of the European world system there has not been more variation in the basic patterns of relations between Europeans and native peoples, and why world systems formulations ... are possible. Had relations between Europeans and native peoples been determined mainly by their respective ideologies, much more variation could be expected.

While cultural relativists have expanded our understanding of how in the beginning native reactions to Europeans were conditioned by their cultural beliefs, this approach must not undermine our appreciation of the ability of native people to monitor new situations and to devise strategies that allowed them to respond in a rational fashion to the opportunities as well as the disruptive challenges of a European presence. While the importance of native beliefs should never be underestimated, in the long run a rationalist and materialist analysis of cultural interaction seems to explain far more about what happened to native people following European contact than does an analysis that assigns primary explanatory power to their traditional beliefs.

The Interior: Comanche Mobility Before European Contact

BY CODY NEWTON

... On July 15, 1706, Juan de Ulibarri and his troops arrived at San Gerónimo de los Taos on their way to retrieve a group of repentant Picurí Indians living in El

Cody Newton, "Towards a Context for Late Precontact Culture Change: Comanche Movement Prior to Eighteenth Century Spanish Documentation," *Plains Anthropologist* 56 (February 2011): 53–69.

Cuartelejo. Upon arrival at Taos, Ulibarri was informed by the caciques that "they were very certain that the infidel enemies of the Ute and Comanche tribe were about to come to make an attack upon this pueblo." This news gave the Spaniards pause; however, the attack did not materialize and the expedition continued on after five days. This entry in Ulibarri's diary is remarkable in that it records the first European reference to the Comanche Indians and provides an initial characterization that followed this group through history: an aggressive society bent on raiding and attacking more sedentary groups.

The original territory of the proto-Comanche groups was the northwestern Plains where they emerged from Shoshonean peoples that were later known as the Eastern Shoshone. The Comanche speak a Central Numic language only moderately differentiated from Eastern (Wind River) Shoshone. The linguistic evidence leaves no doubt that the two groups are closely related, which along with current and documented social ties, is the basis for the determination of the original homeland of the Comanche. The interrelatedness of the Comanche and Shoshone dialects is linguistic evidence that the fissioning of the two groups occurred recently in history.

That the Comanche and Eastern Shoshone groups were socially and linguistically connected was recognized historically by both Europeans/Euroamericans and other Plains Indian groups. Both José Francisco Ruíz in 1828 and Jean Louis Berlandier in 1830 described a division of the Comanche in Texas they call the "Sonsores," whom Ruíz described as Comanche who "live further to the north." Prince Maximilian of Wied, who travelled throughout the Great Plains and Rocky Mountains in the 1830s, was aware that "[t]he Comanches, who call themselves Jamparicka, are said to speak practically the same language as the Snake [Eastern Shoshone] Indians." Another account indicates that when the Cheyenne first encountered Shoshones in the late 1700s they referred to them as "Mountain Comanches." And a Lakota chief told Rufus Sage in 1842 that the Shoshone had split

> into two tribes that ... long since sought home in other lands.... One crossed the snowhills towards the sun-setting.... The other journeyed far away towards the sun of winter.

Ethnographic documentation of Comanche history also reiterates this common origin for the two groups. Although the use of ethnographic data and oral tradition must be approached cautiously in its application to archaeological problems, these datasets can yield important information about the historical processes of the movements or events recounted. The published field notes from ethnographic work among the Comanche in Oklahoma during the 1930s contain numerous references to the Shoshone given by informants.

The Comanche Niyah indicates that she had never heard of the Shoshone until recently, but "[t]he old people knew of some people far to the west who talked their tongue." Tahsuda told the ethnographers the Shoshone

> had no horses, and dogs were used for pack horses. They would come down to visit. They were very poor, and would sell their children for

horses. They spoke the same language, but so fast that no one could understand it.

This passage highlights a trading and economic relationship via horse exchange that the Comanche maintained with the Shoshone, one that gave the Shoshone power on the northwestern Plains in the eighteenth century, as they were the first group in the region to obtain horses in sufficient numbers. It also supports the notion that return migration, and the continuation of ties with the origin group was an important aspect of the Comanche movement.

The ethnographers recorded an origin story told to them by different informants whereby the death of a boy in a kicking game caused the division of a large Comanche camp with a faction moving west to mix with Pueblo groups, as well as a group migrating north that became the Shoshone. Ella Clark recounts a Shoshone legend recorded by George Ruxton in the first half of the nineteenth century that takes place near Pike's Peak (likely Manitou Springs). Summarized, the legend states that long ago when all plains buffalo hunters spoke the same language, two hunters met at the spring—one with game and the other not. The unsuccessful hunter (a Comanche chief) is frustrated and insults the other hunter, who is a Shoshone chief, as belonging to a people who are subservient and "only a tribe of the Comanches," among other insults. In a fit of rage, the Comanche chief kills the Shoshone and thereafter is accosted and killed by Wankanaga, the father of both Shoshone and Comanche, for having "broken the bond between two of the mightiest peoples in the world."

This oral tradition is interesting for a couple of reasons: it talks of a location on the Front Range intermediate between the ultimate territory of both groups and indicates that there was a time that both were bison hunting groups on the Plains. A Shoshone told W.P. Clark in the late nineteenth century that the Comanche left them and "went South in search of game and ponies." While this statement does imply a movement to gain access to horses, the other reason given for the movement should be considered as well: they moved to gain better access to bison or good bison hunting territory. Ethnohistoric evidence documents that the Comanche maintained strong contact with Shoshone despite being separated by increasingly long distances and rival Indian groups (e.g., Ute, Cheyenne, and Arapaho) after the move to the southern Plains.

The oral tradition told to Ruxton and that told to W.P. Clark both imply that the divergence of the Comanche was poignant in the memory of the Shoshone. The Ruxton account indicates that animosity was a forcing factor in the split. Arguments causing groups to split occur in other cases as well, such as the story relating the schism of the Crow and Hidatsa, who, already split into two factions headed by ambitious chiefs, finally separated due to an argument over the disposal of a buffalo paunch. Yet despite the contentiousness of these stories, the Shoshone and Comanche, as well as the Crow and Hidatsa, maintained ties after their separation. Difficult to pin down in time and space, these schism stories do indicate a split occurred and that there were political reasons behind the separation, but despite these factors, the split was ultimately spatial not social.

Beginning in the late precontact period (ostensibly the fifteenth and sixteenth centuries), the Comanche-Shoshone join the Crow-Hidatsa and Arapaho-Gros Ventre as ethnohistorically recognizable cases of group ethnogenesis. The movement of the migrating group west and/or south and the maintenance of ties characterize these schisms. In all three cases the divergent group eventually became bison hunters on the western Great Plains. This implies that economic factors underlie the political and social overprint of the schism stories.

The Comanche, as they first appear in the historic accounts, appear to have been a plains bison hunting adapted society. In his analysis of the archaeological evidence from Idaho and Wyoming, Wright concludes that Shoshonean groups did not reach the Wyoming Basin until the fifteenth century. The evidence of a Shoshonean presence on the northwestern Plains and an association with bison kill sites begins to appear after the beginning of the sixteenth century and suggests the Shoshone-Comanche split occurred sometime following this expansion. Contemporaneous historic maps noting their presence suggest that the Shoshone ranged and/or raided as far east as the western Dakotas up into the late eighteenth century. Having established a presence on the northwestern Plains in the late seventeenth and early eighteenth century, the Shoshone acquisition of horses by about 1740 facilitated the expansion north and east.

Archaeological Context

Currently, the study of Comanche migration is hampered by a lack of known material cultural markers that distinguish Comanche occupation in the late precontact archaeological record. The Comanche, as we know them, are essentially a postcontact manifestation and any stone tools, ceramics, or other types of material culture they possessed prior are virtually unknown. Particularly, Comanche ceramics are unknown, which is an issue that has been only nominally addressed for many historically known northern and western Plains Indians. However, based on the close linguistic (and social) relationship between the Shoshone and the Comanche, along with the relatively recent separation of the two groups, it is reasonable to assume that diagnostic artifacts recognized as Shoshonean may also track Comanche groups.

Shoshonean expansion into the northwestern Plains can be traced by the occurrence of Intermountain Ware which is a distinctive type of coil and scrape (or molded) quartz tempered, gray-to-brown pottery. The most distinctive attribute of this pottery is the flat-bottomed or flowerpot-shaped vessel form. Intermountain Ware is found in the northwestern Plains beginning after A.D. 1400 and reaches the upper Yellowstone drainage by A.D. 1500–1600. Shoshonean diagnostics may also include a distinctively eared tri-notched arrowpoint.... Other sites, particularly kill (e.g., Glenrock) and rock art sites that may lack a strong Shoshonean association, are included in the sample because they are part of the following argument for Comanche movement. The occurrence of the two aforementioned artifact types is used in this study to mark Shoshonean movements or territory. It is acknowledged that steatite vessels and the distinctive leaf-shaped chipped stone bifaces known as Shoshone knives are also considered reliable markers for late Shoshonean occupations but these are not considered in the present study due to certain search parameters used in the data gathering.

The use of pottery types in archaeology to trace past human group movements is an important part of migration studies as ceramics, often more so than other classes of artifacts, can derivate group identity in the archaeological record. The attributes of style and manufacture imbued in pottery can signal different enculturative backgrounds and settlement histories. However, the overall paucity of pottery on the western Great Plains and general lack of a comprehensive analytic approach employing concepts such as technical style militates against a more fine-grained approach in this region. Therefore, basic pottery types are used to delineate and define group movements in this analysis. The use of Intermountain Ware to trace the movements of the Shoshone is based on the determination of researchers in the area who have used historic and ethnographic reports to tie this distinctive pottery to Shoshonean groups. This argument is also used to demonstrate a proto-Ute or Ute presence in the Western Slope through the occurrence of Uncompahgre Brown pottery which has a greater time depth in the region and can be differentiated from Intermountain Ware on the basis of form and surface finish....

The distribution of these sites indicates that there is clear separation between Shoshone/Comanche and Ute groups. There are abundant sites in the southern half of Wyoming that were occupied by Shoshonean groups from the fifteenth century into postcontact times which shows an expansion that ended in present-day northern Colorado before contact. The trickling of sites down the Front Range with Intermountain Ware may track the Comanche migration, but it is unclear given the lack of temporal control. Of particular interest are the sites that have been found in northern Colorado along the Front Range that contain Intermountain Ware, the primary sites being the Roberts Buffalo Jump, Graeber Cave, T-W Diamond, and Old Man Mountain. These Front Range sites contain some of the southernmost evidence of Shoshonean expansion and are found in the likely region where the Comanche-Shoshone schism occurred, a fact suggested by the later dates of the Colorado sites containing Intermountain Ware. A lack of sites with Shoshonean diagnostics in the Upper Arkansas River Basin may imply that the Comanche were not in this region for any substantial length of time prior to Spanish contact.

Intermountain Ware and tri-notched projectile points from bison kill sites such as Piney Creek, Big Goose Creek, and Vore, along with temporal data indicate that by late precontact to pericontact times (the sixteenth and seventeenth centuries) there is a definite Shoshonean signature on the eastern margins of the region. Although George Frison argues that Piney Creek and Big Goose Creek were Crow bison kills rather than Shoshone kills, the occurrence of Intermountain Ware at these sites indicates interaction with the latter in the region. Furthermore, Shoshone use of the Vore site is suggested by diagnostic tri-notched arrowpoints. A radiocarbon assay ([Beta 273950] 410 ± 40 B.P.) of bone collagen from the Glenrock bison kill site places the lower kill solidly in the fifteenth century....

Postcontact archaeological evidence of Comanche territory can also provide evidence that can be used to infer and understand the precontact

migration. Armored horse rock art images are obvious postcontact manifestations and these images show the early weaponry and warfare technology in
the post-horse/pre-gun era of the eighteenth century. In some cases, armored
horses are attributed to Comanche artists. Ascription of the central Plains
images to the Comanche is inferred based on stylistic differences with Apachean
or Puebloan motifs, similarities with northern Plains rock art styles, and the sharing
of attributes associated with Shoshonean motifs. As such, these images may not
only be indicative of territory inhabited or visited by the Comanche, but also
track their early southward movement. The rock art sites in southeastern Colorado
track the known occupation of Comanchería, and Comanche rock art sites in
southern Wyoming and northern Colorado indicate return and ties to a Shoshonean homeland that was revisited to maintain social and economic ties.

The initial appearance of the Comanche in Taos with the Ute whom they
were closely allied suggests movement down the Western Slope as another possible migration route. However, the Ute and Shoshone, at least in postcontact
times, maintained separate territories roughly delineated by the Yampa River.
This demarcation is evident in the archaeological distribution of the two pottery
types. There is little evidence of Shoshonean pottery (evidence of occupation
and movement through this region) on the Western Slope. A generalized intermountain hunter-gatherer subsistence strategy does not fit with what is known
about the Comanche at contact as their subsequent expansion into the southern
Plains points to a previously developed bison-based subsistence.

Paleoenvironmental Context

Any discussion of the possible push and/or pull factors for hunter-gatherer
migration in the western Great Plains and central Rocky Mountains has to
include a consideration of environmental and ecological factors. Fortunately,
the region that Shoshonean or Comanche groups moved through and inhabited
benefits from a robust paleoenvironmental database that is temporally synchro-
nized by tree-ring chronologies. These data include reconstructed summer
Palmer Drought Severity Indices (PDSI) and annual streamflow rates (in acre-
feet). PDSI data are an accurate proxy for vegetation growth and streamflow
data can indicate mountain snowpack.

The Great Plains region is susceptible to intraregional droughts that can
marginalize areas in terms of human habitability, particularly if game such as
bison move to other areas. As plains bison hunters and later pastoralists, range conditions were of crucial importance to the Comanche. Drought conditions in the
past have caused the depopulation of areas and are likely a factor in hunter-
gatherer movements throughout the prehistory of the region. For example, during
the middle Holocene, it is argued that Altithermal drought conditions caused the
movement of prehistoric populations from areas of the central and northern Plains
to the better-watered and ecologically richer refugia of the foothills and Front
Range of the Rocky Mountains.

Drought reconstruction from tree-ring data indicates that severe episodes,
termed megadroughts, happened in the fourteenth, fifteenth, and sixteenth centuries in the western United States. It is reasonable to infer that the patterning of

population movement argued for the Altithermal drought occurred at some scale during these later megadroughts. Along with the push out of areas that these megadroughts would have initiated, it is important to consider that these decadal-scale events waned after the return of more normal precipitation and that formerly depopulated areas would have become attractive again. The movement back into these regions following drought-related depopulation could explain the movements of bison hunters such as the Shoshone and later Comanche. In the Comanche case, the sixteenth century megadrought could have resulted in their southward movement to occupy areas devoid of other groups. This is speculative barring further evidence, but the location of the kill sites in mountain foothills does point to a plains periphery occupation, which may have been influenced by drought.

The initial expansion of bison hunters into the northwestern Plains has been characterized as a human response to the increased bison numbers brought about by the favorable climate of the Little Ice Age (beginning ca. A.D. 1450) that increased forage in the region. There is evidence that bison numbers on the central Plains did increase after the fifteenth century. However, the increase in annual precipitation that is postulated throughout the Little Ice Age is largely unsupported by reconstructed climatic data. Furthermore, temporally fine-grained paloeclimatic reconstructions indicate that there is considerable variability in precipitation on an annual or decadal level that is not always consistent with the first-order trends....

The three megadroughts are clearly demonstrated in the data from this region. As a possible factor in the Comanche migration, the megadroughts could have catalyzed movements in the region. The return to a wetter climate after the sixteenth century megadrought could have precipitated the movement of proto-Comanche groups down the Front Range into areas previously depopulated.

Different areal PDSI trends (as five-year moving averages) were largely the same during the initial time postulated for the Comanche movement.... The lack of substantial differences in the intraregional PDSI trends fails to demonstrate that climate was an obvious factor in any Comanche movements between the plains and mountains at that time. As well, the lack of discrepancies among these areas that would have either pushed or pulled Comanche groups could point to other social or economic factors that precipitated the movement.

The initial movement of the Comanche into the southern Plains in the early eighteenth century from the foothills or mountains of the Sangre de Cristo Range is considered in light of streamflow data from the major rivers that drain the area. As with the intraregional PDSI data, the streamflow volumes between the rivers flowing east and those flowing west and south do not differ substantially. However, streamflow volumes for the last fifteen years of the eighteenth century were largely above average, especially the Rio Grande/Colorado numbers. In a specific sense, the snowpack (reflected by the streamflow numbers) indicates that this region was not subject to any severe droughts that would have pushed the Comanche out of the mountains and foothills.

A look at the more fine-grained paleoclimatic data for causes of the initial phase of the migration via regional comparisons of the summer PDSI data and the streamflow data does not show any great discrepancies among the areas analyzed that would have pushed or pulled the Comanche groups within the region. This supports an argument that this movement was due to other factors. However, articulating the particular movements of the Shoshonean and Comanche groups with climatic events is almost impossible given that the reversal and plateaus of the radiocarbon calibration curve of the last five hundred years precludes discrete calendric dates. If the movement into vacated or depopulated areas is to be considered a possible pull factor in the Comanche movement, then the role of non-native disease must be considered as well. In the Great Plains, depopulation of the region is the first-order trend after the beginning of the fifteenth century. The impacts of epidemic contact with Europeans could have been felt in the region as early as the 1520s. In areas of the Great Plains this trend has been attributed to these epidemic diseases. Disease related depopulation of the region would have opened up areas for resettlement in the following centuries and, although difficult to truth in the archaeological record, must certainly have been a causal factor in the postcontact group movements on the western Great Plains.

Population estimates for eastern Colorado indicate that by the mid-fifteenth century the Platte River and Arkansas River basins were at their lowest points in 2500 years and 1500 years respectively. The populations continued to decline in the Arkansas River basin until the beginning of the eighteenth century. Gilmore suggests that proto-Apachean groups entered the Arkansas River basin beginning in the fifteenth century and resided in the mountains and high plains until "[i]ncreasing effective moisture after A.D. 1500 allowed highly mobile, mountain adapted people [the proto-Apache] who had established trade relationships with horticulturalists and who perhaps had some experience growing corn to move out onto the Plains, adopt an economy much more reliant on food production, and become more sedentary." The Comanche encountered these established Apachean groups when they entered the region which may have thwarted initial Comanche movement onto the plains.

Initially, entrance into the southern Plains was made difficult by groups such as the Plains Apache and other groups like the Jumanos, Pawnee, and Wichita with their established trading networks and many decades worth of interaction with Europeans and European materials. This economic and geographical configuration was disrupted by waves of disease, especially smallpox, that struck the Rio Grande valley and western southern Plains beginning in the 1670s and peaking in 1706–1707. The peripheral location of the Comanche groups at contact expanded as the depopulation, social and economic disruption wrought by these pathogens, along with the concurrently increasing Comanche access to horses and other goods/resources, facilitated movement into the southern Plains.

Discussion and Conclusions

… As an established bison hunting presence on the northwestern Plains prior to the acquisition of horses, it is not difficult to envision a scenario where the Shoshone-Comanche split occurred on the plains due to the directed push to obtain horses, which first came to be known to Shoshonean groups in the late seventeenth century. The recovery of Shoshonean artifacts from kill sites such as

Roberts, the timing of more northerly bison kill sites, and the presence of other Front Range sites generally support the timing and movement along the bison-hunter route. It was only upon encountering the more numerous and established Plains Apache on the southern and central Plains, who had been obtaining horses since at least the early seventeenth century, that Comanche groups retreated to the mountains and foothills where they allied with Ute groups.

Fray Silvestre Vélez de Escalante of the 1776 Domínguez-Escalante expedition that traveled through the southern Rockies references a 1686 Spanish document written by Fray Alonso de Posada that relates the Green River "separated the Yuta nation from the Comanche." If taken at face value this reference, albeit secondary, would be the earliest known to the Comanche and likely the earliest to a Shoshonean group located north of the Ute. Regardless of referent, this indicates that in the late seventeenth century the Spanish were aware of a territorial demarcation rather than any alliance between me Ute and a Shoshonean group. Subsequent alliance with the Ute, contingent upon a mutual focus on acquiring horses and trade goods, began to deteriorate in the 1730s once the Comanche came to dominate the plains northeast of the Spanish frontier with its rich grazing and access to trade from both Spanish and eastern (French/English) sources. On the other hand, the Comanche retained strong ties with the Shoshone throughout the postcontact and historic periods despite considerable geographic separation. The Comanche traded horses and captives north to the Shoshone and visited a fur trade rendezvous on the Green River.

The movement of the Comanche south as bison hunters along the Front Range, possibly into territories vacated during megadroughts in the fifteenth and sixteenth centuries, was an expansion initially slowed by established groups such as the Plains Apache groups in the Arkansas River basin. Earlier access to horses and European trade goods facilitated the Plains Apache hegemony on the region and their subsequent expansion to the plains east and north may have forced the Comanche into the Sangre de Cristo Mountains. Here, they allied with the Ute who were obtaining horses in limited numbers during the seventeenth century. The Pueblo Revolt of 1680 removed the Spanish from the upper Rio Grande and Pecos river valleys, liberated the Spanish horses and enabled the Puebloans to handle and breed them. This was a watershed event for bison hunters like the Comanche as they were able to obtain horses in the numbers that they required through both trading and/or raiding. Horses became the vehicle through which the Comanche expanded and maintained Comanchería.

More sedentary part-time horticulturalists, like the Plains Apache, were at a disadvantage once the Comanche began to campaign against them. By the end of the 1720s, the Comanche had driven the Apache from the Arkansas River valley completing the first phase of their territorial conquest that would reach its full expression by the middle of the eighteenth century. It was initially the access to bison hunting grounds and pasture that catalyzed the Comanche movement onto the southern Plains, and their subsequent development of a semi-pastoral economy that incorporated raiding and trade evolved from recognition of the strategic position that they had gained with the territory.

Understanding the timing and process of the Comanche migration prior to Spanish contact is obviously complicated by a lack of archaeology tracing the group from the northwestern Plains to the southern Plains. At this point, development of a model of Comanche migration is constrained by the lack of these empirical underpinnings. However, there is considerable potential to develop a more robust understanding of this middle movement because both the precursors in the archaeological record exist and there is a known postcontact homeland.

Continued research and reinvestigation of existing sites and assemblages along the proposed migration path, especially reanalysis of the pottery assemblages for Intermountain Ware, or its possible derivatives, would be an important step in addressing this issue. Also important, ... would be working from the known of Comanche occupied areas, especially those early postcontact sites (e.g., sites with armored horse rock art) which potentially contain material culture correlates that can be traced back into the late precontact archaeological record.

In time, with a more directed approach, the archaeological record will certainly yield the data crucial to understanding late precontact Comanche (and other western Plains Indian groups) lifeways and writing Native histories where contact need not be the beginning (or the end) of the narrative.

◈ FURTHER READING

Anderson, Gary Clayton. *The Indian Southwest, 1580–1830* (1999).

Axtell, James. *After Columbus: Essays in the Ethnohistory of Colonial North America* (1989).

———. *Beyond 1492: Encounters in Colonial North America* (1992).

———. *The Invasion Within: The Contest of Cultures in Colonial North America* (1985).

———. *Natives and Newcomers: The Cultural Origins of North America* (2000).

Binnema, Theodore. *Common and Contested Ground: A Human and Environmental History of the Northwestern Plains* (2001).

Blackhawk, N., ed. *Violence Over the Land: Indians and Empires in the Early American West* (2006).

Calloway, Colin G. *New Worlds for All: Indians, Europeans, and the Remaking of Early America* (1997).

Crosby, Alfred. *The Columbian Exchange: Biological and Cultural Consequences of 1492* (1972).

———. *Ecological Imperialism: The Biological Expansion of Europe, 900-1900* (1986).

———. "Virgin Soil Epidemics as a Factor in Aboriginal Depopulation in America." *William and Mary Quarterly* 33 (1976): 289–299.

Denevan, William M. *The Native Population of the Americas in 1492* (1976).

Dobyns, Henry F. *Their Numbers Became Thinned: Native American Population Dynamics in Eastern North America* (1983).

Duncan, David Ewing. *Hernando de Soto: A Savage Quest in the Americas* (1995).

DuVal, Kathleen. *The Native Ground: Indians and Colonists in the Heart of the Continent* (2006).

Ethridge, Robbie. *From Chicaza to Chickasaw: The European Invasion and the Transformation of the Mississippian World, 1540–1715* (2010).

Fischer, David Hackett. *Champlain's Dream: The European Founding of North America* (2008).

Flint, Richard. *No Settlement, No Conquest: A History of the Coronado Entrada* (2008).

Galloway, Patricia, ed. *The Hernando de Soto Expedition: History, Historiography, and "Discovery" in the Southeast* (1997).

Hämäläinen, Pekka. *The Comanche Empire* (2008).

Hassig, Ross. *Mexico and the Spanish Conquest*. Norman: University of Oklahoma Press, 1994.

Horn, James. *A Kingdom Strange: The Brief and Tragic History of the Lost Colony of Roanoke* (2010).

Hudson, Charles M. *Knights of Spain, Warriors of the Sun: Hernando de Soto and the South's Ancient Chiefdoms* (1997).

Jennings, Francis. *The Invasion of America: Indians, Colonialism, and the Cant of Conquest* (1976).

John, Elizabeth A. H. *Storms Brewed in Other Men's Worlds: The Confrontation of Indians, Spanish, and French in the Southwest, 1540–1795* (1996).

King, Jonathan H. C. *First Peoples, First Contacts: Native Peoples of North America* (1999).

Kupperman, Karen Ordahl. *Roanoke: The Abandoned Colony* (2007).

Mancall, Peter. *Deadly Medicine: Indians and Alcohol in Early America* (1995).

Merrell, James. *The Indians' New World: Catawbas and Their Neighbors from European Contact Through the Era of Removal* (1989).

Milanich, Jerald T. *Florida Indians and the Invasion from Europe* (1995).

Reséndez, Andrés. *A Land So Strange: The Epic Journey of Cabeza de Vaca* (2007).

Richter, Daniel K. *Facing East from Indian Country: A Native History of Early America* (2001).

Salisbury, Neal. *Manitou and Providence: Indians, Europeans, and the Making of New England, 1500–1643* (1982).

Schlesier, Karl H., ed. *Plains Indians, A.D. 500–1500: The Archaeological Past of Historic Groups* (1995).

Stannard, David E. *American Holocaust: The Conquest of the New World* (1992).

Steele, Ian K. *Warpaths: Invasions of North America* (1994).

Symcox, Geoffrey, and Blair Sullivan. *Christopher Columbus and the Enterprise of the Indies: A Brief History with Documents* (2005).

Thornton, Russell. *American Indian Holocaust and Survival* (1987).

Trigger, Bruce G. *The Children of Aataentsic: A History of the Huron People to 1660* (1972).

White, Richard. *The Roots of Dependency: Subsistence, Environment, and Social Change Among the Choctaws, Pawnees, and Navajos* (1983).

◈

CHAPTER 4

Southern and Northern Encounters, 1600–1700

For a growing number of Native peoples in North America in the seventeenth century, Europeans became an increasing and unavoidable presence in their lives. But, while many may know something of Indian encounters with the English along the Atlantic Coast in these years, few know much about the additionally important stories of Native contacts with the Spanish in the continent's southern regions, or with the French—and Dutch—in its northern reaches. This chapter addresses this imbalance, complicating the usual east-to-west trajectory upon which most Americans tend to view their history. In the materials that follow, continue to consider this history from indigenous perspectives. What did American Indians do about the Spanish, the French, and the Dutch? Did they all merely succumb—and quickly—to European conquest? Or, did they all take up arms against the invaders? If the latter, was such military resistance simply futile, always ending in Indian defeat and failure? Or, were there yet other possible responses, beyond capitulation and combat? Keep the themes in this chapter in mind, too, as you read the following chapter, which will turn to the stories of Native encounters with that seemingly more familiar group, the English. How were those interactions similar to, but also different from, the interactions with invaders from the north and south?

◈ DOCUMENTS

Indians in present-day "New Mexico" encountered the Spanish as early as the 1540s, when Francisco Vasquez de Coronado and his entourage came looking for the mythical "seven cities of gold." Coronado did not find the cities (they did not exist), but other Spaniards returned around the year 1600 to convert Native peoples to Christianity and establish agricultural colonies. Most "Pueblo" Indian villages—named by the Spanish for the word "town"—had to eventually yield to the Spanish imposition of forts, missions, and power. But, in 1680, after decades of oppression, enslavement, and forced Christianization, the Pueblos launched a coordinated revolt against Spanish rule. The rebellion was successful, and remains one of the most striking examples of an indigenous military victory against Europeans in the history of the Western Hemisphere. More than ten years passed before Spanish authorities could reassert some control over the region. Documents 1 and 2 are depositions, taken one year after the uprising, that provide Pueblo explanations of the revolt's causes and leaders.

The Pueblo Revolt temporarily stalled Spanish activity in New Mexico, but not elsewhere in the present-day American Southwest. Document 3, a letter from a Spanish priest to the Viceroy of Mexico in 1691, shows that Indians along the present-day Texas/Louisiana border were continuing to deal with the incursions of Spanish missionaries, soldiers, and settlers. It offers a description of the local "Caddo" Indian culture, but, as with all European documents from this period, the views are still noticeably colored by the observer's background and agenda.

While Indians of the seventeenth-century Southwest were contending with the growing presence of the Spanish, Indians in the Northeast were simultaneously adjusting to the increasing arrivals of the French, Dutch, and British. In Document 4, a Dutchman recounts his 1634–1635 trek into present-day upstate New York to check on their partners in the fur trade, the Mohawks and Oneidas, both member nations of the formidable Iroquois Confederacy. Competing with the Dutch (and the British) for the lucrative fur trade were the French. In Document 5, dated 1659–1660, a French Jesuit priest discusses French appreciation for, and general resentment of, Iroquois power in the region, a power— they claimed—that the Dutch had enhanced. And, just as Pedro Naranjo and Juan offered glimpses of Native views of Europeans in the Southwest, Document 6 provides a look at Indian views of Europeans in the Northeast. It is a record of a speech, translated and transcribed by a French missionary, that a Micmac elder gave to a group of French settlers around 1677. Document 7 maps selected American Indian communities as they existed in the seventeenth century, several of which are noted in the other documents and essays in this chapter.

1. Pedro Naranjo (Keresan Pueblo) Provides His Explanation for the Pueblo Revolt, 1681

In the ... plaza de armas on [December 19, 1681], for the prosecution of the judicial proceedings of this case his lordship caused to appear before him an Indian prisoner named Pedro Naranjo, a native of the pueblo of San Felipe, ... who was captured in the advance and attack upon the pueblo of La Isleta. He makes himself understood very well in the Castilian language and speaks his mother tongue and the Tegua. He took the oath in due legal form in the name of God, our

Pedro Naranjo's (Keresan Pueblo) Explanation of the 1680 Pueblo Revolt, 1681, from Charles W. Hackett, ed., *Revolt of the Pueblo Indians of New Mexico and the Otermin's Attempted Reconquest, 1680–1682*, translated by Charmion C. Shelby, pp. 245–249.

Lord, and a sign of the cross, under charge of which he promised to tell the truth concerning what he knows. . . .

Asked whether he knows the reason or motives which the Indians of this kingdom had for rebelling, forsaking the law of God and obedience to his Majesty, and committing such grave and atrocious crimes, and who were the leaders and principal movers, and by whom and how it was ordered; and why they burned the images, temples, crosses, rosaries, and things of divine worship, committing such atrocities as killing priests, Spaniards, women, and children, the rest that he might know touching the question, he said that since the government of Señor General Hernando Ugarte y la Concha they have planned to rebel on various occasions through conspiracies of the Indian sorcerers, and that although in some pueblos the messages were accepted, in other parts they would not agree to it; and that it is true that during the government of the said señor general seven or eight Indians were hanged for this same cause, whereupon the unrest subsided. Some time thereafter they [the conspirators] sent from the pueblo of Los Taos ... two deerskins with some pictures on them signifying conspiracy after their manner, in order to convoke the people to a new rebellion, and the said deerskins passed to the province of Moqui [the Hopi pueblos], where they refused to accept them. The pact which they had been forming ceased for the time being, but they always kept in their hearts the desire to carry it out, so as to live as they are living to-day. Finally, in the past years, at the summons of an Indian named Popé who is said to have communication with the devil, it happened that in an estufa [kiva] of the pueblo of Los Taos there appeared to the said Popé three figures of Indians who never came out of the estufa. They gave the said Popé to understand that they were going underground to the lake of Copala. He saw these figures emit fire from all the extremities of their bodies, and that one of them was called Caudi, another Tilini, and the other Tleume; and these three beings spoke to the said Popé, who was in hiding from the secretary, Francisco Xavier, who wished to punish him as a sorcerer. They told him to make a cord of maguey fiber and tie some knots in it which would signify the number of days that they must wait before the rebellion. He said that the cord was passed through all the pueblos of the kingdom so that the ones which agreed to it [the rebellion] might untie one knot in sign of obedience, and by the other knots they would know the days which were lacking; and this was to be done on pain of death to those who refused to agree to it. As a sign of agreement and notice of having concurred in the treason and perfidy they were to send up smoke signals to that effect in each one of the pueblos singly. The said cord was taken from pueblo to pueblo by the swiftest youths under the penalty of death if they revealed the secret. Everything being thus arranged, two days before the time set for its execution, because his lordship had learned of it and had imprisoned two Indian accomplices from the pueblo of Tesuque, it was carried out prematurely that night, because it seemed to them that they were now discovered; and they killed religious, Spaniards, women, and children. This being done, it was proclaimed in all the pueblos that everyone in common should obey the commands of their father whom they did not know, which would be given through El Caydi or El Popé. This was heard by Alonso Catití, who came to the pueblo of this declarant to say that everyone must unite to go to the villa to kill the governor and the Spaniards who had remained with him, and that he who did not obey would, on their return, be beheaded; and in fear of this they agreed to it. Finally the señor governor and those who were with him escaped from the siege, and later this declarant saw that as soon as the Spaniards had left the kingdom an order came from the said Indian, Popé, in which he commanded all the Indians to break the lands and enlarge their cultivated fields, saying that now they were as they had been in ancient times, free from the labor they had performed for the religious and the Spaniards, who could not now be alive. He said that this is the legitimate cause and the reason they had for rebelling, because they had always desired to live as they had when they came out of the lake of Copala. Thus he replies to the question....

Asked for what reason they so blindly burned the images, temples, crosses, and other things of divine worship, he stated that the said Indian, Popé, came down in person, and with him El Saca and El Chato from the pueblo of Los Taos, and other captains and leaders and many people who were in his train, and he ordered in all the pueblos through which he passed that they instantly break up and burn the images of the holy Christ, the Virgin Mary and the other saints, the crosses, and everything pertaining to Christianity, and that they burn the temples, break up the bells, and separate from the wives whom God had given them in marriage and take those whom they desired. In order to take away their baptismal names, the water, and the holy oils, they were to plunge into the rivers and wash themselves with amole, which is a root native to the country, washing even their clothing, with the understanding that there would thus be taken from them the character of the holy sacraments. They did this, and also many other things which he does not recall, given to understand that this mandate had come from the Caydi and the other two who emitted fire from their extremities in the said estufa of Taos, and that they thereby returned to the state of their antiquity, as when they came from the lake of Copala; that this was the better life and the one they desired, because the God of the Spaniards was worth nothing and theirs was very strong, the Spaniards' God being rotten wood. These things were observed and obeyed by all except some who, moved by the zeal of Christians, opposed it, and such persons the said Popé caused to be killed immediately. He saw to it that they at once erected and rebuilt their houses of idolatry which they call estufas, and made very ugly masks in imitation of the devil in order to dance the dance of the cacina [kachina, or spirit]; and he said likewise that the devil had given them to understand that living thus in accordance with the law of their ancestors, they would harvest a great deal of maize, many beans, a great abundance of cotton, calabashes, and very large watermelons and cantaloupes; and that they could erect their houses and enjoy abundant health and leisure. As he has said, the people were very much pleased, living at their ease in this life of their antiquity, which was the chief cause of their falling into such laxity. Following what has already been stated, in order to terrorize them further and cause them to observe the diabolical commands, there came to them a pronouncement from the three demons already described, and from El Popé, to the effect that he who might still keep in his heart a regard for the priests, the governor, and the Spaniards would be known from his unclean face and clothes, and would be punished. And he stated that the said four persons stopped at nothing to have their commands obeyed. Thus he replies to the question....

2. Juan (Tiwa Pueblo) Offers His Account of the Pueblo Revolt, 1681

... [H]e had brought into his presence another Indian who said his name is Juan, and in his language Vnsuti, that he is a native of the pueblo of Alameda, a widower, and that he did not know his age. Apparently he is more than a hundred years old because he declares that he remembers distinctly, as if it were yesterday, when the Spaniards entered this kingdom, and that when he was baptized he was able to stand on his own feet. His lordship received the oath from him in due legal form before God, our Lord, and a sign of the cross, under charge of which he promised to tell the truth as he might be questioned and might know it, the seriousness of the oath having been explained to him by the said interpreter. Being asked if he knows why he is arrested, he said that he judges it was because some Spaniards caught him in the pueblo of Alameda on the occasion when, finding himself alone and without any relative and having kin among the Spaniards, he had gone in search of them; and that before he arrived the Spaniards caught him and brought him to this camp. He did not hide himself or do anything whatever; rather, he is rejoiced to find himself among Christians, and although he is a prisoner, he is well content. Asked to state truly what he knows or has heard of the discussions and juntas which the rebellious Indians are holding, he says what he has heard in general is that they are saying they must die from hardships of cold and want; that they have gone to the sierras, leaving the sick in caves among the rocks; and that although it is true that many have desired to go down to their pueblos peacefully, because the señor governor and captain-general has sent to find them, and because the Spaniards who went to Cochití also summoned them, granting them the said peace to which many of them agreed so that they might go to the quiet of their houses, the chief captains who governed them took them away from their pueblos, carrying them to the sierras, and being unwilling to agree to anything; and the rest of the people do what they order out of fear. This is what he knows and has heard, and this is why they say that they want to die. He has heard nothing else about this matter. Asked to state and declare truthfully what reasons or motives the natives of this kingdom had for rebelling, he said that he does not know, nor has he heard any reason given. Asked why they killed religious and Spaniards and burned the church and all the houses, which they did after living so long a time among the Spaniards, protected from the enemy Apaches, being Christians and living quietly in their pueblos and under the law of God, he said that to him, he being so old, they never communicated anything; that the most he knew, which is common knowledge, was that when they committed this destruction it was by order of an Indian from San Juan

Juan (Tiwa Pueblo) explains the Pueblo Revolt, 1681, from Charles W. Hackett, ed., *Revolt of the Pueblo Indians of New Mexico and the Otermin's Attempted Reconquest, 1680–1682*, translated by Charmion C. Shelby, vol. II, pp. 344–46. Copyright © 1942 University of New Mexico Press.

whom he does not know, who came down through all the pueblos in company with the captains and many other people, ordering them to burn the churches, convents, holy crosses, and every object pertaining to Christianity; and that they separate from the wives the religious had given them in marriage and take those whom they wished; and other things that he does not remember. He said that this Indian of San Juan told and gave all the people to understand in the pueblos where he went that they should do as he said because they would thereby be assured of harvesting much maize, cotton, and an abundance of all crops, and better ones than ever, and that they would live in great ease. The people have remained very well content and pleased with all this until now, when they have experienced the contrary, and have seen that they deceived them, for as a matter of fact they have had very small harvests, there has been no rain, and everyone is perishing.

3. Casañas Assesses the Native Peoples of Texas, 1691

Fray Francisco Casanas De Jesus Maria to the Viceroy of Mexico

August 15, 1691.

Most Excellent Sir,

Because of the many reports I have received of the zeal that warms your Excellency's Christian and Catholic heart, I am induced to write these few lines—as, owing to my duties, I have had no time in which to finish a long report which I am engaged in writing—in order that your Excellency may learn in detail the few things I have seen, experienced, and learned during this year. I am also induced to write this letter and this brief report on account of the information which certain chiefs of the Province of the Cadodachos and certain chiefs of this Province of Texas—known also by the name of Asinai—have given me. I am likewise moved to write you this letter and to send you this brief report of the things I have thought most necessary to call to your attention at this time for the encouragement of the conversion of these souls of the Lord in order that His Most Holy Name and that of His Blessed Mother may be praised among all nations. . . .

The ordinary food which these poor wretches have for their sustenance is corn, beans, and the other articles mentioned above. Of meat they never have more than two kinds, one boiled and the other roasted. They eat while seated on benches of wood, all of one piece and not very high from the ground. The ground, or their knees, serve as a table. For table cloths and napkins, they make use of the very first things they can lay their hands upon. They wipe their fingers on whatever they find in this way, no matter

Fray Francisco Casañas de Jesús María, in Mattie Austin Hatcher, trans., "Descriptions of the Tejas and Asinai Indians, 1691–1722, 1," *Southwestern Historical Quarterly* Online 30 (January 1927): 206–218, and Mattie Austin Hatcher, trans., "Descriptions of the Tejas and Asinai Indians, 1691–1722, II," *Southwestern Historical Quarterly* Online 30 (April 1927): 283–304. Reprinted with permission from Texas State Historical Association.

whether it be a piece of wood or something else; while those who are not so nice will use their feet. But, in spite of all this, they lick their spoons—using for this purpose the two fingers of the right hands. The plates they use are round earthen pans; and, as the Indians always eat their meat boiled or roasted and without broth, they put it on very pretty little platters which the women make of reeds. When they are in the part of the country where they have none, they use leaves or the ground itself. While those who are not very polite use their own feet. The usual way of sitting is with one knee raised. The way they give thanks is to take a pipe with tobacco. Of the first four whiffs they take, they blow one into the air, one toward the ground, and the other towards the two sides. It seems that whenever they eat they try to finish up everything set before them. They take a long time to eat and while they are eating, they sing and talk, and, from time to time, whistle. Those who eat everything placed before them consider themselves great men.... Before the meal, however, they take nothing until a portion of everything is first sent to the *caddí* [chief] ... while all the others form ready to dance, he [the *caddí*] speaks—first to the corn, asking that it allow itself to be eaten. In the same way he talks to the other things they use. He tells the snakes not to bite, the deer not to be bitten. He then consecrates the whole harvest of the house to God and ends by declaring that God has said that they may now eat and that if they do not they ought to die of hunger. Everybody falls to and they eat until they are gorged—for their way of eating always comes to this....

For clothes these poor creatures usually wear only buffalo skins and very carefully dressed deer skins. During the very hot season, the men generally go about the house naked; but the women, even when very young, are always covered from the waist down. Neither the men nor the women lack articles of adornment for their festivities, such as collars, ornaments, and pendants like the Mexican Indians wore when they were heathens. These Indians knew neither gold nor silver. Many of their ornaments they have secured from other nations, such as glass beads, bells, and other things of a similar nature which are not to be found in this country. At their festivities some of the guests pride themselves on coming out as gallants, while others are of so hideous a form that they look like demons. They even go so far as to put deer horns on their heads, each conducting himself according to his own notion.

Their custom of painting themselves for their *mitotes* is ridiculous. They use paints of various colors and all gather together in one place whenever they are ready to set out on a war expedition. They claim that the paint serves to keep their enemies from recognizing them. They do the same thing for the same reason whenever they know that visitors are coming from some other tribe....

The nature and inclination of all these heathen tribes—so far as I have learned on many occasions—is very good in many respects. They are quite willing to work to secure supplies for their sustenance during certain seasons of the year; since there are times of cold rainy weather when the Indians can not leave their houses. They are likewise handicapped by the lack of clothing, since ordinarily they have only a deer skin or a buffalo robe. During this season they entertain themselves around the fire by making handwork. The men make arrows, moccasins, and such other little things as are needed by those who till the soil. The women make reed mats, pots, earthen pans, and other clay utensils for domestic use. They also busy themselves in dressing deerskins and buffalo hides—the women as well as the men; for all of them know how to do this, as well as how to make many other little things that are needed around the house....

The custom they follow when a man takes a wife is not very commendable. In some ways the arrangement seems a good one; but I have found that it is not very binding. If a man wants a certain woman for his wife who he knows is a maiden, he takes her some of the very best things he has; and if her father and mother give their permission for her to receive the gift, the answer is that they consent to the marriage. But they do not allow him to take her away with him until they have first given notice to the *caddí*. If the woman is not a maiden, there is no other agreement necessary than for the man to say to the woman that if she is willing to be his friend he will give her something. Sometimes this agreement is made for only a few days. At other times they declare the arrangement binding forever. There are but few of them who keep their word, because they soon separate from each other—especially if the woman finds a man who gives her things she likes better than those the first man gave her.... The thing I approve is that they never have but one wife at a time. If a man wants to take a new wife, he makes a difference between them, never living with them both at the same time.... As soon as they [the Catholic missionaries] learn the language, it will be easy for them to free these barbarians from their evil ways by their own good example, their religious zeal, and their fatherly advice and council. Therefore, we are trusting in the Lord that, by leading them to the true knowledge, we will free them from their false ideas....

At this juncture I think that it would be wise for the sake of stability for a good *presidio* to be built and this country round about settled by families, distributed at the points where the missions may be located. In this manner, I have no doubt that it will be easy to settle the Indians in the *pueblos* adjacent to the Spaniards who are to live near the missions. It is already understood that the soldiers will bring their wives, and that wherever the *presidio* may be placed, whether in this province or as far north as the *Caudaudachos*, the location should be a good one.... I add, also, that it would not be a bad idea—since the corrective of your Excellency's protection is lacking—for some evangelical minister to be given the power to punish such things as he may think ought to be punished and to expel from this region any person who, by his example, incites a revolution. In this way the unconverted would be aware of the punishment, and they would all realize that the punishment was for something done against God's will. They are not ignorant of God. Indeed, all of them know there is only one God whom they call in their language *Ayo-Caddi-Aymay*. They try, in all their affairs, to keep him in a good humor in every way possible. They never in any manner venture to speak of him in jest, because they say that, when he punishes them for anything, he does it well and that whatever he does is best. They also believe that he punishes those who are angry with him....

They tell me that I must write to Your Excellency, their great captain, and tell you in this missive that they want to be friends, but if the Spaniards want to live among them it must be under such conditions that no harm will be done the Indians by the Spaniards if they do come without their wives; but, if the Spaniards bring their wives, the Indians will be satisfied.

I must say that the demand of these Indians is just and reasonable.... And do not send criminals taken from the prisons, or bachelors, or vagabonds, who, when they are here, away from home where there are no Christians, would commit great atrocities, and, by their depraved lives and bad example, counteract the efforts of the ministers, depriving them of the fruit of these souls of the Indians....

The demon put it into their heads that we had brought [an] epidemic into the country; and, when they saw that during the scourge which the Lord sent upon them in the year 1691 some three or four hundred persons—more or less—had died in that province during the month of March, they maintained their superstition even more firmly, saying that we had killed them. Some of them tried to kill us....

Another gross superstition they have, in which all of them believe implicitly, is that the old men made Heaven and that a woman, who sprang from an acorn, first gave them its outlines; and that it was done by placing timbers in the form of a circle and that Heaven was formed in this way. They further declare that the woman is in Heaven and that she is the one who daily gives birth to the sun, the moon, the water when it rains, the frost, the snow, the corn, the thunder, and the lightning; and many other similar absurdities, such as when one of the leading men dies they go through many ceremonies....

The Lord knows that in this whole matter I am inspired only by the desire I have that not a single soul shall be lost and that these poor miserable people may die only after receiving the holy baptism....

They are an industrious people and apply themselves to all kind of work. Indeed, if during the year and three months I have been among them if I had had some bells, some small clasp knives, some glass beads, and some blue cloth—which they greatly prize,—some blankets, and other little things to exchange with these Indians, I could have started a convent with the articles it would have been possible to make from the best materials that are abundant here. I, therefore, declare that it will be well for the ministers to have some of these things—not that one person only should have them—because the Indians are of such a nature that they have no love save for the person who gives them something. So strong is this characteristic that only the person who gives them something is good while all others are bad. They do not even want to receive the holy sacrament of baptism except from some person who has given them a great many things....

I have information that the *Cadaudacho* have hopes that the French will return, because they promised when leaving the country that they would return when the cold season again set in, and that a great many of them would have to come in order to occupy the country completely. This is nothing but Indian gossip, though for several reasons it is to be feared that they speak as they are instructed to speak. The French may also be compelled to return on account of their companions whom they left here. I know nothing more of this matter than that in the month of February there were nine or ten Frenchmen at a feast which the Indians had in a neighboring province, about thirty leagues from us called the province of *Nacaos*....

May Your Excellency receive this short summary; and, with the greatest submission, I implore Your Excellency to be its protector. May Your Excellency be favored with a long life and may our Lord make it happy is the wish of your chaplain of the Mission of Santíssima Nombre de María, to-day, the 15th of the month of August of this most happy year of 1691.

Your most humble chaplain, who loves you even more dearly through the love of Jesus Christ, kisses Your Excellency's feet.

Fray Francisco de Jesús María....

4. Van den Bogaert Journeys into Mohawk and Oneida Country, 1634–1635

Praise God above all. At Fort Orange [Albany, New York] 1634

11 December. Report of the most important things that happened to me while traveling to the Maquasen [Mohawk] and Sinnekens [Oneidas]. First of all, the reasons why we went were that the Maquasen and Sinnekens had often come to our Commissary Martin Gerritsen and me, saying that there were French Indians in their country, and that they had called a truce with them, so that they, namely, the Maquasen, would trade furs with them there, because the Maquase wanted as much for their furs as did the French Indians. Therefore, I asked Sr. Martin Gerritsen's permission to go there and learn the truth of the matter in order to report to their High Mightinesses as soon as possible, because trade was going very badly. So for these reasons I went with Jeromus la Croex and Willem Tomassen. May the Lord bless our journey.

Between nine and ten o'clock we left with five Maquasen Indians mostly toward the northwest, and at one half hour into the evening, after eight miles, we came to a hunter's cabin where we spent the night by the waterway that runs into their country, and is named Oÿoge. The Indians here fed us venison. The country is mostly covered with pine trees and there is much flat land. This waterway flows past their castle in their country, but we were unable to travel on it because of the heavy flooding....

13 ditto. In the morning we went together to the castle over the ice that had frozen in the waterway during the night. When we had gone one half mile, we came into their first castle that stood on a high hill. There were only 36 houses, row on row in the manner of streets, so that we easily could pass through. These houses are constructed and covered with the bark of trees, and are mostly flat above. Some are 100, 90, or 80 steps long; 22 or 23 feet high. There were also some interior doors made of split planks furnished with iron hinges. In some houses we also saw ironwork: iron chains, bolts, harrow teeth, iron hoops, spikes, which they steal when they are away from here. Most of the people were out hunting for bear and deer. These houses were full of grain that they

Harmen Meyndertsz van den Bogaert, "A Journey into Mohawk and Oneida Country, 1634–1635," in *In Mohawk Country: Early Narratives about a Native People*, ed. Dean R. Snow, Charles T. Gehring, and William A. Starna (Syracuse, NY: Syracuse University Press, 1996), 2–4.

call ONESTI and we corn; indeed, some held 300 or 400 skipples. They make boats and barrels of tree-bark and sew with it. We ate here many baked and boiled pumpkins which they call ANONSIRA. None of the chiefs was at home, except for the most principal one called ADRIOCHTEN, who was living one quarter mile from the fort in a small cabin because many Indians here in the castle had died of smallpox. I invited him to come visit with me, which he did. He came and bid me welcome, and said that he wanted us to come with him very much. We would have gone but we were called by another chief when we were already on the path, and turned back toward the castle. He had a large fire started at once, and a fat haunch of venison cooked, from which we ate; and he also gave us two bearskins to sleep on, and presented me with three beaver pelts. In the evening I made some cuts with a knife in Willem Tomassen's leg, which had swollen from walking, and then smeared it with bear's grease. We slept here in this house, and ate large quantities of pumpkin, beans, and venison so that we suffered of no hunger here but fared as well as it is possible in their country. I hope that everything shall succeed.

14 ditto. Jeronimus wrote a letter to the commissary, Marten Gerritsen, asking for paper, salt, and ATSOCHWAT, i.e., Indian tobacco. We went out with the chief to see if we could shoot some turkeys, but got none. However, in the evening I bought a very fat turkey for 2 hands of sewant [wampum], which the chief cooked for us; and the grease that cooked from it he put in our beans and corn. This chief let me see his idol which was a marten's head with protruding teeth, covered with red duffel-cloth. Others keep a snake, a turtle, a swan, a crane, a pigeon, and such similar objects for idols or telling fortunes; they think that they will then always have luck. Two Indians left from here for Fort Orange with skins....

16 ditto. In the afternoon a good hunter named SICKARIS came here who wanted us to go with him very much and carry our goods to his castle. He offered to let us sleep in his house and stay there as long as we pleased. Because he offered us so much, I presented him with a knife and two awls; and to the chief in whose home we had stayed I presented a knife and a scissors....

18 ditto. Three women came here from the Sinnekens with some dried and fresh salmon, but they smelled very bad. They sold each salmon for one guilder or two hands of sewant. They also brought much green tobacco to sell, and had been six days underway. They could not sell all their salmon here, but went with it to the first castle....

5. A French Missionary Describes the Iroquois, 1659–1660

... The Ocean which separates us from France sees, on its eastern side, only rejoicing, splendor, and bonfires; but, on its western, nothing but war, slaughter, and conflagrations....

[Author unknown], "The Jesuit Relations and Allied Documents, 1610–1791," Vol. 45, Relation of 1659–1660, ed. Reuben Gold Thwaites, from http://puffin.creighton.edu/jesuit/relations/relations_45.html (accessed 7/23/13).

What consoles us is our full assurance that people do not regard us merely as do those who, being themselves in port or on the shore, contemplate with some compassion the wreck of a poor vessel shattered by the storm, and even shed some tears over it. But we promise ourselves much more, knowing the vows, the prayers, the penances, and all sorts of good works, which are being performed almost everywhere for the conversion of our Savages; and learning of the good purposes with which God has inspired many persons of merit, for accomplishing the destruction of the Iroquois. That means, to open a door, high and wide, for proclaiming the Faith and giving the Preachers of the Gospel access to peoples of great extent, in regard to both the territories which they occupy, and the diversity of Nations composing them—all of whom are four or five hundred leagues distant from us in the forests, shunning the common enemy. Were it not for the latter, they would come and enrich this country with their furs, and we should visit them to enrich Heaven with the glorious spoils that we should wrest from the powers of Hell....

We know—and we will state the facts more fully in the third chapter—that there are tribes of the same language, both stationary and wandering, as far as the North sea, on whose shores these nations border; and that there are others, very recently discovered, extending as far as the South sea. They stretch out their arms to us, and we ours to them, but on both sides they are too short to unite across such a distance; and when, finally, we are on the point of embracing each other, the Iroquois steps in between and showers blows upon both of us.

We know that very far beyond the great Lake of the Hurons,—among whom the Faith was so flourishing some years ago, when the Iroquois did not molest our Missions, and before he had expelled us from them by the murder of our Fathers and the pillage of those nascent Churches,—we know that some remnants of the wreck of that Nation rallied in considerable numbers beyond the lakes and mountains frequented by their enemies, and that but recently they sent a deputation hither to ask back again their dear old Pastors. But these good Pastors are slain on the way by the Iroquois, their guides are captured and burned, and all the roads are rendered impassable.

We even know that among the Iroquois the Faith is in a vigorous condition, although they do not possess it in their own persons, but in those of numerous captives. These only long to have us with them, or to be themselves with us....

Finally, we know that, whithersoever we go in our forests, we find some fugitive Church, or else some infant one; everywhere we find children to send to Heaven, everywhere sick people to baptize, and adults to instruct, But everywhere, too, we find the Iroquois, who, like an obtrusive phantom, besets us in all places....

They prevent the tribes from five or six hundred leagues about us, from coming down hither, laden with furs that would make this country overflow with immense riches—as was done in a single journey which some of those Nations undertook this year—although secretly, and, as it were, by stealth, from fear of their foes....

What gives the enemy this advantage over us is, that all the rural settlements outside of Québec are without defense, and are distant from one another as much as eight or ten leagues on the banks of the great River. In each house there are only two, three, or four men, and often only one, alone with his wife and a number of children, who may all be killed or carried off without any one's knowing aught about it in the nearest house.

I say nothing of the losses that France would suffer if these vast regions should pass from her control. The foreigner would reap, a great advantage, to the detriment of French navigation." ...

They come like foxes through the woods, ... They attack like lions ... They take flight like birds, disappearing before they have really appeared. ...

Of the five tribes constituting the entire Iroquois nation, that which we call the Agnieronnons has been so many times at both the top and the bottom of the wheel, within less than sixty years, that we find in history few examples of similar revolutions. ... We cannot go back very far in our researches in their past history, as they have no Libraries other than the memory of their old men; and perhaps we should find nothing worthy of publication. What we learn then from these living books is that, toward the end of the last century, the Agnieronnons were reduced so low by the Algonkins that there seemed to be scarcely any more of them left on the earth. Nevertheless, this scanty remnant, like a noble germ, so increased in a few years as to reduce the Algonquins in turn to the same condition as its own. But this condition did not last long; for the Andastogehronnons waged such energetic warfare against them during ten years that they were overthrown for the second time and their nation rendered almost extinct, or at least so humiliated that the mere name Algonkin made them tremble, and his shadow seemed to pursue them to their very firesides.

That was at the time when the Dutch took possession of these regions and conceived a fondness for the beavers of the natives, some thirty years ago; and in order to secure them in greater number they furnished those people with firearms, with which it was easy for them to conquer their conquerors, whom they put to rout, and filled with terror at the mere sound of their guns. And that is what has rendered them formidable everywhere, and victorious over all the N'ations with whom they have been at war; it has also put into their heads that idea of sovereign sway to which they aspire, mere barbarians although they are, with an ambition so lofty that they think and say that their own destruction cannot occur without bringing in its train the downfall of the whole earth.

But what is more astonishing is, that they actually hold dominion for five hundred leagues around, although their numbers are very small; for, of the five Nations constituting the Iroquois, the Agnieronnons do not exceed five hundred men able to bear arms, who occupy three or four wretched Villages.

... [I]t is beyond doubt that, if the Agnieronnons were defeated by the French, the other Iroquois Nations would be glad to compromise with us, and give us their children as hostages of their good faith. Then those fair Missions would be revived at Onnontagué, at Oiogoen, and in all the other remaining Iroquois Nations, among whom we have already sown the first seeds of the faith. These have been so well received by the common people that we may not, without distrusting the divine Providence, despair of one day reaping therefrom very abundant fruits. Moreover, the great door would be open for so many old and new missions toward the tribes of the North, and toward those newly discovered ones of the West, all of whom we embrace under the general name of Algonquins. But it is a subject of too wide a scope and demands a separate Chapter.

6. A Micmac Responds to the French, 1677

I am greatly astonished that the French have so little cleverness, as they seem to exhibit in the matter of which thou hast just told me on their behalf, in the effort to persuade us to convert our poles, our barks, and our wigwams into those houses of stone and of wood which are tall and lofty, according to their account, as these trees.

Very well! But why now, ... do men of five to six feet in height need houses which are sixty to eighty? For, in fact, as thou knowest very well thyself, Patriarch—do we not find in our own all the conveniences and the advantages that you have with yours, such as reposing, drinking, sleeping, eating, and amusing ourselves with our friends when we wish? This is not all, ... my brother, hast thou as much ingenuity and cleverness as the Indians, who carry their houses and their wigwams with them so that they may lodge wheresoever they please, independently of any seignior whatsoever? Thou art not as bold nor as stout as we, because when thou goest on a voyage thou canst not carry upon thy shoulders thy buildings and thy edifices. Therefore it is necessary that thou preparest as many lodgings as thou makest changes of residence, or else thou lodgest in a hired house which does not belong to thee. As for us, we find ourselves secure from all these inconveniences, and we can always say, more truly than thou, that we are at home everywhere, because we set up our wigwams with ease wheresoever we go, and without asking permission of anybody. Thou reproachest us, very inappropriately, that our country is a little hell in contrast with France, which thou comparest to a terrestrial paradise, inasmuch as it yields thee, so thou sayest, every kind of provision in abundance. Thou sayest of us also that we are the most miserable and most unhappy of all men, living without religion, without manners, without honour, without social order, and, in a word, without any rules, like the beasts in our woods and our forests, lacking bread, wine, and a thousand other comforts which thou hast in superfluity in Europe. Well, my brother, if thou dost not yet know the real feelings which our Indians have towards thy country and towards all thy nation, it is proper that I inform thee at once. I beg

---

This document can be found in William F. Ganong, trans. and ed., *New Relation of Gaspesia, with the Customs and Religion of the Gaspesian Indians,* by Chrestien LeClerq (Toronto: Champlain Society, 1910), pp. 104–106. It can also be found in Colin Calloway, ed. *The World Turned Upside Down: Indian Voices from Early America* (Boston: Bedford Books, 1994), 50–52.

thee now to believe that, all miserable as we seem in thine eyes, we consider ourselves nevertheless much happier than thou in this, that we are very content with the little that we have; and believe also once for all, I pray, that thou deceivest thyself greatly if thou thinkest to persuade us that thy country is better than ours. For if France, as thou sayest, is a little terrestrial paradise, art thou sensible to leave it? And why abandon wives, children, relatives, and friends? Why risk thy life and thy property every year, and why venture thyself with such risk, in any season whatsoever, to the storms and tempests of the sea in order to come to a strange and barbarous country which thou considerest the poorest and least fortunate of the world? Besides, since we are wholly convinced of the contrary, we scarcely take the trouble to go to France, because we fear, with good reason, lest we find little satisfaction there, seeing, in our own experience, that those who are natives thereof leave it every year in order to enrich themselves on our shores. We believe, further, that you are also incomparably poorer than we, and that you are only simple journeymen, valets, servants, and slaves, all masters and grand captains though you may appear, seeing that you glory in our old rags and in our miserable suits of beaver which can no longer be of use to us, and that you find among us, in the fishery for cod which you make in these parts, the wherewithal to comfort your misery and the poverty which oppresses you. As to us, we find all our riches and all our conveniences among ourselves, without trouble and without exposing our lives to the dangers in which you find yourselves constantly through your long voyages. And, whilst feeling compassion for you in the sweetness of our repose, we wonder at the anxieties and cares which you give yourselves night and day in order to load your ship. We see also that all your people live, as a rule, only upon cod which you catch among us. It is everlastingly nothing but cod—cod in the morning, cod at midday, cod at evening, and always cod, until things come to such a pass that if you wish some good morsels, it is at our expense; and you are obliged to have recourse to the Indians, whom you despise so much, and to beg them to go a-hunting that you may be regaled. Now tell me this one little thing, if thou hast any sense: Which of these two is the wisest and happiest—he who labours without ceasing and only obtains, and that with great trouble, enough to live on, or he who rests in comfort and finds all that he needs in the pleasure of hunting and fishing? It is true, ... that we have not always had the use of bread and of wine which your France produces; but, in fact, before the arrival of the French in these parts, did not the Gaspesians live much longer than now? And if we have not any longer among us any of those old men of a hundred and thirty to forty years, it is only because we are gradually adopting your manner of living, for experience is making it very plain than those of us live longest who, despising your bread, your wine, and your brandy, are content with their natural food of beaver, of moose, of waterfowl, and fish, in accord with the custom of our ancestors and of all the Gaspesian nation. Learn now, my brother, once for all, because I must open to thee my heart: there is no Indian who does not consider himself infinitely more happy and more powerful than the French.

7. Selected Native American Centers in North America, ca. 1645

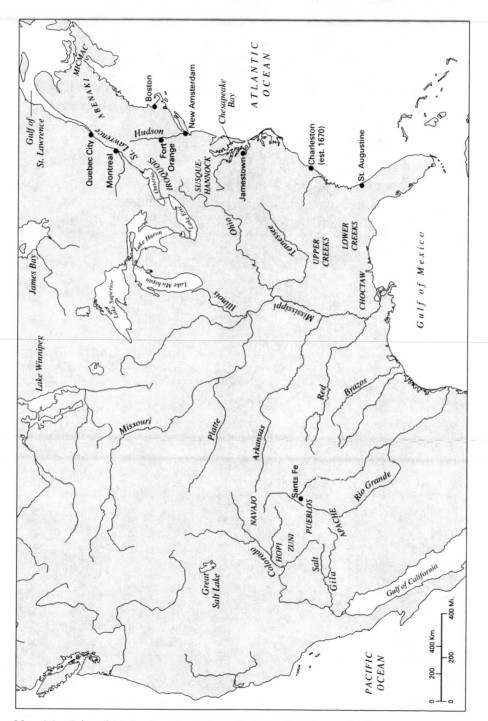

Map 4.1   Selected Native American Centers in North America, ca. 1645

◈ ESSAYS

Like the documents in the preceding section, the essays in this chapter disrupt the prevailing sense that seventeenth-century American Indian history occurred only along the eastern seaboard and only with the English. The first essay is by Stefanie Beninato, a longtime resident of New Mexico who holds a PhD in history as well as a J.D. in law. In her detailed analysis of the complex story of the Pueblo Revolt, she attempts to better understand which person—or persons—provided the main leadership for this campaign to expel the Spanish. Where Beninato's essay tends to highlight the political maneuverings of Indian men in the Southwest, the second essay emphasizes the economic activities of Indian women in the Northeast. Rather than addressing military resistance (though that certainly occurred here), this second essay concentrates on trade relations. Were Indians helpless in these situations? And, were Indian women only background figures in this business— passive, compliant, and silent? With her essay focusing on Iroquois (also known as "Haudenosaunee") women, Jan Noel, a historian at the University of Toronto, provides us with some insights into these questions.

Southern Encounters: Indian Leaders in the Pueblo Revolt of 1680

BY STEFANIE BENINATO

Although the Pueblo Revolt of 1680 was one of the most successful rebellions against Spanish authority anywhere in the world, historians have largely ignored its tactical aspects, including the question of native leadership in the revolt. In a controversial article published in 1967, Fray Angelico Chavez, however, looked at the long-ignored role of "hybrid" leaders. Believing that the Pueblos were too passive and too disunited to form the alliance, Chavez postulated that a mulatto of Mexican-Indian ancestry, taking on the role of the god Pose-yemu, secretly directed the revolt from a kiva at Taos. Documentary evidence does support Chavez' assertion that a Naranjo was a leader of the revolt. A cultural analysis, however, undermines his assumption that Naranjo was an adult non-Pueblo or even from the first generation of a Pueblo/non-Pueblo marriage. To take on the revered role of Pose-yemu, the sun god and savior, one would have had to achieve an esteemed status. Given the apprentice-like system within the Pueblo sociopolitical structure, it would be nearly impossible for an adult non-Pueblo to achieve this status and very difficult even for for a first generation of a mixed marriage to do so.

The Revolt of 1680 marked the high point in the Pueblos' long struggle against Spanish economic, political, and religious domination. For the eight decades prior to the revolt, tensions had mounted steadily throughout the region as Spanish civil and religious authorities as well as settlers exploited the Pueblo

Stephanie Beninato, "Popé, Pose-yemu, and Naranjo: A New Look at Leadership in the Pueblo Revolt of 1680," *New Mexico Historical Review* 65 (October 1990), pp. 417–35. Reprinted with permission.

Indians. Respect for Spanish authority was also eroded among the Pueblos by the continuous struggle between church and state in colonial New Spain.

The Pueblo people populated dozens of autonomous villages and spoke several distinct languages. There had been a number of unsuccessful attempts to expel the Spaniards, but there had never been a sufficient degree of unity among the various pueblos. By 1680, however, the situation had reached crisis proportions. Death and devastation, brought on by a long period of drought beginning in 1667 and by disease in the following decade, fertilized the seeds of rebellion already planted in the Pueblo region. The Spaniards forbade kachina dances; they raided kivas and destroyed masks and other ceremonial items. They arrested native leaders and humiliated and even killed them. As the Franciscan missionaries became more and more determined to suppress and abolish the native religions, a unified resistance formed among the priestly elite of the pueblos.

Most historians and writers, using the scattered testimonies in the Antonio de Otermín journals of 1680–1682, point to Popé as the moving force ("*motor*") behind the revolt. Even though the seminal documents list other leaders, there is nothing in the commentaries accompanying these documents to suggest that scholars seriously entertained the idea that anyone else shared the principal leadership with Popé. For many, Popé has become the symbol of "uncompromising hostility to the conquerors" and the unquestioned leader.

What little is known of this Tewa medicineman from San Juan lends weight to this point of view. Popé was deeply involved in native religion, probably through leadership in one of the moieties or societies of the pueblo. Refusing to take a Christian name, he had long resisted the Spanish religion and struggled with a fierce and bitter energy to keep alive the traditional beliefs and rituals among his people. Popé was one of the many medicinemen whom the Spaniards labeled a troublemaker and kept under constant surveillance because of their continuing defiance in conducting kachina dances and other rituals. In 1675, with the coming of the drought, Popé's religious activities began to take on political colorings. He told the people that the gods were displeased with the people's acceptance of the Spanish religion and that the Spaniards must be made to leave their land. He was among the forty-seven religious leaders that Governor Juan Francisco Treviño arrested and tried for witchcraft in that year in an attempt to control the restlessness of the Pueblo population. Four of the leaders were hanged; the rest were whipped and publicly humiliated before a group of Tewas secured their release. After this, Popé became more determined to drive the Spaniards out of the region. Returning to San Juan for a short time, he began to hold secret organizational meetings. Eventually Popé moved his base of operation to the remote pueblo of Taos, in order to escape Spanish surveillance and the concern of his relatives for themselves. In contemporary sources, Popé was described as a leader who possessed extraordinary talents and the ability to communicate with spiritual beings. Later, he was repeatedly named as the principal leader of the revolt.

In his "Pohé-yemo" article, Chavez asserted that a mulatto named Naranjo from Santa Clara secretly led the revolt, using Popé as his principal spokesperson. He concluded that Naranjo, as the *teniente* of Pose-yemu, was the sole tactical leader of the revolt. His theory challenged the long-held assumption that Popé was the primary leader of the revolt. Like the commentaries, however, Chavez' article failed to address the existence of multiple leadership in Pueblo culture.

Chavez focused on unraveling the mystery of the identity of Pose-yemu's representative ("*teniente*") described by the Indians caught during the first days of the Pueblo Revolt. Chavez first suspected that a real person was the representative of Pose-yemu when he studied the records of a controversy which took place in Santa Fe in 1766 involving the Naranjo family of the Santa Clara/Santa Cruz valley. By tracing back what he believed were five generations of this family, Chavez discovered that not only were the ancestors Negroid, but also that they were accused of having fomented Indian insurrections in the past....

Chavez also used the testimony given by Pedro Naranjo before Otermín on December 1681 in a rather circumspect way to confirm that another leader was present. Naranjo was the only one of five Indians interrogated at that time to testify that the "command of the father whom they did not know ... would be given through El Caydi, one of the three spirits or El Popé" and that the mandate came "from Caydi and the two other spirits." Chavez merely stated that even though Naranjo wanted to steer away from the "dangerously close" description of the tall, black representative of Pose-yemu, he was unwilling to let Popé take full credit. Chavez felt that this impression based on circumstantial evidence was further bolstered by Naranjo's leadership role, which presumably gave him more knowledge.

Chavez relied most heavily on the third body of records, that is, the genealogy contained in the documents surrounding the 1766 controversy to establish the identity of this other leader. (He also used supplementary documentation, which he later incorporated into his book on the genealogy of New Mexico families.)

The following is a brief history of the relevant members of the Naranjo family pieced together by Chavez: the original ancestor was a very black mulatto from Puebla, New Spain, named Mateo who was freed at twenty years of age by his master Mateo Montero on the condition that he settle in New Mexico. He served a soldier named Alonso Martin Naranjo and married an Indian woman servant, whom Chavez believed was from New Spain. Mateo was the only male Negroid servant mentioned in the Juan de Oñate papers of 1597–1600.

The second generation included Diego, Pedro, and Domingo. In 1632, Diego was arrested by Capitán Bartolomé Romero for participating in a kachina dance inside a kiva at the Alameda Pueblo. According to Chavez, nothing more was heard of him. Pedro was the eighty-year-old sorcerer caught by Otermín's forces near Isleta. He had been sent from the upper pueblos to teach the "old ways." Domingo, according to Chavez, was identified by Spanish officers of the colonial militia as the forebearer ("*tronco*") of the rebellious Naranjos of Santa Clara. These officers declared that he was a son of a very black Negro ("*Negro atezado*") and an Indian servant ("*india criada*"). Chavez stated that Domingo "cast his lot with the Taos Indians in 1680 and seems to have died by the time of Diego de Vargas's return to Taos in 1692. (It is important to note that Chavez believed that Domingo was the tactical genius of the revolt in his "Pohé-yemu" article; although in an earlier study, he had postulated that Diego was the leader.)

The third generation included Lucas and Joseph, sons of Domingo. Lucas was referred to as "el mulato Naranjo del pueblo de Santa Clara." Chavez believed Lucas was one of the five Indians interrogated by Otermín in December 1681. At that time, Lucas claimed he was a Piro Indian. He participated in the revolt of the Tewas in 1696 and was killed by his brother Joseph, who shifted alliances frequently. Chavez believed that Joseph, too, was one of the four other Indians interrogated with Pedro Naranjo in December 1681. At that time he was referred to only as Joseph and he gave no tribal affiliation. He could, however, speak fluent Castilian. According to Chavez, Joseph went to live at Taos, after escaping from Otermín. Twelve years later, he was sent with another Indian to parley with Diego de Vargas when Vargas approached the deserted Taos Pueblo. At that time, he referred to himself as Josephillo and was called "el espanol" by the Taos Indians because of his language proficiency. Later, Joseph went over to the Spaniards, killing Lucas to expiate his own role as an apostate. This marked Joseph's rise in the Spanish society to become the first Chief War Captain of the Pueblo auxiliaries. In the testimony of 1766, those who claimed to know Joseph described him as a black-complected person using such sobriquets of "*el Negro*" and "*el Mulato.*"

In developing the mythological bases for his argument, Chavez examined Pedro Naranjo's testimony in detail to show that this was "no mere Pueblo speaking in Pueblo terms and concepts." Chavez viewed his testimony as an Hispanic-Indian concoction from New Spain grafted onto Pueblo mythology and expressed in terms the Spaniards could understand, e.g. "communication with the devil." He looked at three elements in Naranjo's testimony in detail: his use of the mythological lake of Copala as an equivalent to the Pueblos' point of emergence, Shipapu; his use of the names of the three guiding spirits in the Taos kiva; and his use of the Pueblo god Pose-yemu. Chavez believed on the whole, that these three mythological elements demonstrated that not only was there a mulatto leader of Mexican-Indian ancestry, but also that he had a grasp of both Spanish and Pueblo psychology. In particular, Chavez asserted that the first two elements established Naranjo's Mexican-Indian ancestry and the third element demonstrated his superior intelligence, which Chavez attributed to his non-Pueblo ancestry.

Pedro Naranjo repeatedly stated that the three spirits in the kiva were going to the lake of Copala. Chavez focused on this to point out that Pedro Naranjo confused Pueblo and Aztec myths. According to Chavez, the word "Copala" had no connection with New Mexico Pueblo mythology. In a very detailed note, Chavez traced the origins of this word and outlined the genesis of the legend. It has a long history of confused associations starting with the "Tale of Seven Cities" told by Amadis of Gaul in the beginning of the sixteenth century. It was associated with the Aztec and Toltec origin myths of the seven caves and later became interchangeable with New Mexico. To show Naranjo's confusion between Copala and Shipapu, Chavez created a composite sketch of the Pueblo emergence myths, using reports by such outstanding ethnologists as Adolph

Bandelier, Elsie Clews Parsons and Leslie A. White. According to Chavez' reading of the myths, the ancestors lived underground under the lake; but they emerged through a hole in the ground.

The second element Chavez looked at in the mythology was the connection of the three spirits—especially their names—to Aztec religious lore. Chavez relied heavily on the *Florentine Codex,* which was a compilation by Fray Bernardino de Sahagún in the sixteenth century with an English translation done in the 1950s. It is a series of volumes with the Nahuatl and English texts side-by-side.

El Caudi, Tilini and Tleume were the three fire-emitting gods in the Taos kiva. The names, Chavez said in a note, have the sound and look of Nahuatl (the Aztec language) rather than of any of the Pueblo tongues. More specifically, they suggest the names of two Aztec gods of Fire and War and one of the names of the high priest of Tlascala, i.e. Achcautli.

Chavez concluded that this mélange of mythological figures could only have come from Mexican-Indians in general and more specifically, from ones that were familiar with Spanish culture and who were second generation or who had been removed from their original culture.

As for the third element, Chavez merely stated that the myth of Pose-yemu was known in one linguistic form or another in all the pueblos. He believed that the use of the myth as a unifying device showed Naranjo's understanding and knowledge of native mythology's effects on Indian behavior; as a subterfuge, it showed his grasp of Spanish psychology. Naranjo correctly assumed that by becoming Pose-yemu's teniente, his existence as a person would be obscured because the Spaniards looked upon the "ancient ones" as evil spirits.

By concentrating on establishing the ancestry and physical description of Domingo Naranjo, Chavez' theory failed to make use of significant information in the documents. It also ignored certain cultural factors that militate against any adult non-Pueblo being a Pueblo leader at the time of the revolt.

The documentary evidence supports Chavez' assertion of a leadership role for the Naranjo family and of their ancestry. An analysis of the evidence in a cultural framework, however, contradicts the following two elements: that an adult non-Pueblo could assume a leadership position at that time in Pueblo society and that there was a single leader of the revolt. My hypothesis is that the mother of Domingo (and presumably of Diego and Pedro) was a Pueblo Indian and that there was a generation between Domingo and Joseph from which came the teniente of Pose-yemu. (I think it is also possible that Domingo and Diego were the same person.)

An understanding of the religion and social organization of the Pueblos, therefore, is essential in order to evaluate my alternative. The Pueblos' way of life was based on spiritual worship and religious ceremony. Every phase of Pueblo life had its religious aspects. The people saw themselves as inextricably woven into an eternal cycle of life, where the welfare of the individual was indivisible from the welfare of his people. The *caciques,* the religious leaders, were responsible for the total well-being of the entire village. They directed not only spiritual affairs, but also the political and secular activities within the pueblo.

Because of its religious base, therefore, Pueblo society in its religious, political and social aspects tended to be a centralized theocracy with a complicated, and often overlapping, hierarchical system controlled by an elite of older men. There were a number of organizations within the hierarchical structure. Each had its own priest and each priest played a special role in the religious life. In Tewa society, there were moieties, that is, a system of dual leadership. Other pueblos had clans which served similar functions. The top echelon of these theocracies was the managing group or the "keepers of the gateway of the lake" as they are known in Tewa. They dominated the political arena and planned and executed many of the ceremonial rituals. Each cacique had subordinates (called the right and left arms) who implemented decisions. There was also an outside chief, known as the war captain. He served as a defensive military leader and as an internal law enforcement officer. He and his second-in-command would act together in an official capacity when a decision for the whole pueblo had to be rendered by someone. Moreover, there is evidence to suggest that there were interpueblo structural links, especially for religious ceremonies such as initiation.

Membership in the moiety or the clan was a normal part of the growth and development of the Pueblo child; it allowed the child to assume a legal identity in the eyes of the society. In Keres society, clan membership was matrilineal; while in Tewa society, moiety membership generally followed a patrilineal pattern, although there was no rigid adherence to this rule. Young men who showed aptitude and interest were groomed for positions of leadership within the religious and political structure—much like an apprenticeship. It is obvious from the documents of the revolt that offspring of mixed blood marriages, such as Alonso Catiti of Santo Domingo Pueblo and Francisco El Ollita of San Ildefonso, did attain leadership positions in each pueblo's ruling hierarchy. According to Alfonso Ortiz, however, the acceptance of an outsider by marriage into the Pueblo social structure was markedly different from the acceptance of a child of a mixed marriage. The order of prestige given to a marriage to a member of a different Pueblo or to a non-Pueblo depended on the degree of intercultural amicability. For such an outsider to be accepted into the religious hierarchy in the seventeenth century would have been highly unlikely because of Spanish persecution of native religions and the fear of informers. In any event, such a person would have been treated as a child in terms of the initiation process.

Candidates for leadership positions, therefore, were gradually acquainted with the necessary esoteric knowledge through stages of initiation, similar in concept to an apprentice system. Years of training were necessary before such a person became familiar with the enormous amount of ritual and administrative details that these roles required. The ability "to talk like an Indian," that is, the acquisition of an advanced level of esoteric knowledge, necessitated not only membership in a religious society but also an intensive preoccupation with matters of a religious nature. Usually there were not more than three or four men in any pueblo who had acquired this level of knowledge. To achieve an esteemed status, a man had to have above average success in at least a few mandatory roles and to give unstintingly of his time in religious or secular affairs. Members of the priestly hierarchy who achieved esteemed status wielded tremendous power in the pueblo. Not only were they guardians of traditional cultural values, but they also were liaisons between the supernatural and secular worlds. In his study of Santa Clara Pueblo, W. W. Hill found that the attitude toward persons of this status generally was ambivalent: they were praised and feared at the same time.

This discussion of Pueblo culture, therefore, highlights several important elements that form the basis for an ethnographic analysis of the issue of leadership in the Pueblo Revolt: First, the ruling system was autocratic and its members had distinct, but complementary, functions. Moreover, there is some indication that an interlocking of the religious system on an intervillage basis was not foreign to the Pueblos. Participation in the religious system was an incremental learning process defined by initiation rites; a person with an eteemed status signified the achievement of an upper echelon position after a long rise through the hierarchy. Although a Pueblo's status and position are not hereditary, a family's position did influence a child's attitudes and experiences.

These cultural elements, therefore, strongly suggest the following: the need to rise through the religious hierarchy militates against any adult non-Pueblo from becoming a leader of the revolt since the basis for such authority was religious. In addition, there are several instances in the Otermín documents in which Popé and the teniente are described as "greatly feared." This may, in fact, be a watchword indicating an esteemed status—which required a long initiatory process. It would seem, therefore, that such status would not normally be achieved by the offspring of a mixed marriage—and certainly not by an adult non-Pueblo. Finally, the inter-Pueblo ritual experience gives a strong historical basis for discounting the possibility of a single leader and indicates a pattern of shared authority among several pueblos.

The documentary basis of Chavez' theory is narrow and selective in its use of information. Using evidence taken from a few Indians during and immediately after the revolt, Chavez' article focused only on establishing the existence and description of another leader besides Popé. These statements could have been connected to testimonies taken from Spaniards during this period. This would have strengthened the idea that someone other than Popé was the tactical leader by negating the possibility that the Indians' declarations were merely reflections of Popé's interpretation of the gods' message. For instance, the statement of an Indian that Popé "had the mandate of an Indian who lives very far away from this kingdom toward the north … who is the representative of Pose-yemu" could have been tied to the report made by Fray Francisco de Ayeta, the *visitador general* of the Franciscans, to Otermín in which he declared that "other heretics and sectarians" ordered the Indians to wash at the river with herbs to "cleanse themselves of the stain … of the holy sacrament of baptism."

This wider use of the documents, however, raises the question of multiple leadership—an issue the article does not address. Besides Ayeta's report, there are other contemporary testimonies that would confirm the historical model of intertribal leadership. Don Pedro Nanboa, a native of the pueblo of Alameda, for example, declared that the "nations of the Teguas, Taos, Percuris, Pecos, and Jemez had long been plotting to overthrow the Spaniards." This implication of multiple leadership was also corroborated in the information given by several Spaniards immediately after the revolt.

Moreover, Chavez' thesis would be strengthened by connecting the impression of another leader in the testimonies made in 1680 with that given by Pedro Naranjo in 1681, who stated that "the command of the father whom they did not [know] … would be given through El Caydi, one of the three spirits or El Popé" and that "the mandate came from Caydi and the other spirits." The article did not note the fact that two of the other Indians interrogated in December 1681 also mentioned other leaders. Juan of Tesuque indicated that Saca of Taos had a leadership role. Joseph, whom Chavez believed was a Naranjo, stated that there were four primary leaders including El Taque from San Juan, whom other sources did not mention. In addition, the article failed to pick up what might be a significant clue as to the identity of the leader and his mulatto ancestry in Pedro's statement that Popé came down in person with El Saca and *El Chato* (my emphasis) from the Pueblo of Taos. In Spanish, "*chato*" means "flatnosed," suggesting negroid features.

Instead of making these connections, however, Chavez' article focused on Pedro Naranjo's testimony (that is the use of certain terms) to show the latter's familiarity with Spanish civil and religious practices in order to establish his ancestry. In terms of the records of the Naranjo family history, Chavez was able to document thoroughly the third to the fifth generation of the family. The interconnections between the first two generations and the later ones, however, were fragmentary. Chavez has worked extensively with these documents in genealogical studies and the basis of many of his interconnections were, by his own admission, "educated guesses." …

In terms of the mythological aspects of his theory, Chavez demonstrated the Mexican–Indian ancestry of Domingo by concentrating on the Aztec and Spanish elements in Pedro Naranjo's testimony. In particular, Chavez focused on Naranjo's use of the lake of Copala and the names of the three gods in the kiva to show his familiarity with Spanish and Aztec culture. This point seems well taken. As Chavez has shown, both elements have strong links to Spanish and/or Mexican lore. The names of the gods are very similar to those of two of the Aztec gods of fire and war and that of the high priest of Tlascala, Achcautli. The only comparable name of a Pueblo god is the Tewa god Tinini Povi (Olivella Flower Shell Youth) for the spirit Tilini. This god appears to be an unlikely identity for a person to assume who is seeking power. Although Ortiz calls him a revered god, he appears to be a Mercury-like figure. He definitely lacks the powerful and universal significance of Pose-yemu.

I think that Chavez' argument that Naranjo's use of the lake of Copala showed confusion with the Pueblos' origin myths, however, is unwarranted. First of all, Chavez' interpretation of the Pueblo myths, that is, having the first people emerge from a hole in the ground, seems questionable. Many of the emergence myths are recorded as having the ancestors "come out of the lake." Tewa and Zuñi myths, in particular, clearly state that the people came out of the lake, and in fact, have actual geographic locations for Shipapu. For Tewas, it is natural for the spirits to relate their entrance and exit to a lake, since they believe that lakes and ponds are used exclusively by deities as entrances to the underworld. It is quite possible that Pedro Naranjo was using mythological devices that Spaniards could relate to. The Aztec war gods would create a strong visual image. Like the myth of the lake of Copala, it was an image with which the Spaniards had previous experience. These concepts would have meaning for the Spaniards.

The greatest deficiency in the mythological basis of Chavez' argument was his failure to develop the importance of Pose-yemu in Pueblo culture. Not only was the myth a common one in Pueblo culture, and thus acted as a unifying device; but its functional aspect was highly significant during the time of the revolt, which, in fact, marked a crisis in Pueblo religion and culture. In addition, an analysis of the interrelations between Pose-yemu and the three Aztec gods show a remarkable understanding of the interworkings of the mythological elements of these three cultures.

The general outline of the Pose-yemu myth is as follows: Pose-yemu was begot magically by World Man using a piñon nut. As a youth, Pose-yemu was badly treated by his people, even after he was recognized by his father, the Sun, and given a name. Eventually he became a great wizard and the village prospered. He predicted coming events. Pose-yemu left his people and traveled to the south, promising to return at a later date.

Not only is the myth of Pose-yemu known in one linguistic form or another in all the pueblos; but the legend is highly developed, especially among the Rio Grande Tewas. A loose translation of "Pose-yemu" is "he who strews morning dew." The Pueblo people find Pose-yemu rising in the mist of a lake on a warm summer's day, which, at least, indirectly correlates to Pedro Naranjo's testimony on the lake of Copala. Pose-yemu is also known as the sun-youth and is popular as a religious figure and as a culture hero.

Besides the ideological power of this mythological device in the Pueblo Revolt due to its universal appearance in Pueblo religion, the legend contains several important themes relating to Pueblo social structure. Perhaps the most important ones to the offspring of a mixed-blood marriage would be the idea of non-acceptance during youth and that of testing through adversity, which is an important factor in gaining esteem in Pueblo society.

More important than its mythological elements, however, are the functional aspects of Pose-yemu in Pueblo culture. Pose-yemu is a savior. He will "return to restore his people to their proper place" and "rule over them and be father to them all"; in other words, he provided for the general well-being of the pueblo. More important, during the Spanish contact period, Pose-yemu played the role of ritual leader and teacher. He served as an "early warning system" for the preservation of native religious ceremonies. For instance, he ordered kachina dances to be held underground. According to Ralph Emerson Twitchell, representing Pose-yemu was an office of great responsibility. It required an outstanding knowledge of ritual lore, wisdom, and prudence, which would discredit the idea that an adult non-Pueblo or even a child of a mixed marriage could fill this office. As noted before, the taking on of this role of kachina corresponds to the meaning of "teniente" as used in the documents of the Pueblo Revolt. It expresses the double function of "taking the place of" and "assuming the person of" (Pose-yemu, in this case).

Another important factor is the close association of Pose-yemu with the Twin War gods. These three figures share many similar characteristics and many of the same mythological elements; however, the Twin War gods stayed in the pueblos and established institutions. They were the patrons of the Zuni Bow priests, which correspond closely to the Tewa War Society. In earlier times, the head of the Warrior Society and the caciques shared responsibility. If a Naranjo was Pose-yemu, this might point to a role as a leader in the Warrior Society, indicating a fighting function which would not be incompatible with Popé's function as cacique. This interpretation is supported by the designation of both Domingo and Joseph as capitán mayor.

The interrelation of Pose-yemu with the Aztec gods and the interrelation of the role of Pose-yemu's teniente and that of the Caydi strongly bolster Chavez' theory that a mulatto individual of Mexican-Indian ancestry was a leader in the revolt. In the kachina dances, the mask of the sun is used to portray Pose-yemu. The insignia of the Aztec god Tlaltatecuini (the spirit Tilini in the kiva) is the sun, which appears on the god's flag, shield, shoes, and paper vestments. It is also significant that the representatives of these Aztec gods would smear their faces with black pigment during rituals. Although the fact that the Aztec priests painted their faces black may be coincidental, it would certainly heighten the authority of a black mulatto who played the role. With Pose-yemu's connection with the Twin War gods, there is not only a close association of symbols, but also an indirect association of functions (that is, war) among these Aztec and Pueblo gods.

In Pedro Naranjo's testimony, there is a change from the three spirits giving orders to the "commands of the father ..." being given through "El Caydi or El Popé" to the "mandate being given by Caydi" before he and the other two spirits "return to their state of antiquity." In a note, Chavez suggested that El Caydi is the name of a high priest in Aztec culture. There was a transformation, therefore, from god to high priest.

These similarities associated with the gods and with the roles of Caydi and the teniente suggest a desire for consistency, which is understandable if these mythological figures were represented by a real person who wanted to maintain his authority, and yet, camouflage his identity from Spanish officials. More important, however, Pedro Naranjo's testimony indicates the giving up of the role of kachina and the return to the role of priest. This transition would allow one to hide his identity but to maintain the same role as intermediary between the gods and the people. It also suggests the assumption of a more active role outside the kiva. If the representative of Pose-yemu was a medicineman of war, then he, unlike a cacique, could carry a weapon and fight. This transition also seems to point to the larger role the person played in Pueblo society and to indicate that he was a highly esteemed leader, who had been well integrated into the culture.

In conclusion, I feel that analysis of the mythology, ancestry and other information in the documents in a cultural framework supports Chavez' contention that there was a mulatto who was a tactical leader. By concentrating on establishing genealogical lines instead of analyzing the evidence in the contemporary sources in the context of Pueblo culture, however, Chavez' theory overlooked significant information in the documents as well as certain cultural factors that militate against an adult non-Pueblo from being a Pueblo leader in the revolt. It suggests that such a person would have to be at least from the first generation of a marriage between a Pueblo and non-Pueblo. More probably, it indicates an offspring from the second generation of such a marriage because of the necessity of achieving an esteemed status so one could take on the revered role of Pose-yemu. Moreover, cultural analysis indicates that the concept of a single leader is not viable in the theocratic social structure of the Pueblo world. In addition, the mythological aspects indicate that the teniente of Pose-yemu occupied the position of tactical leader as the head of a warrior society. Such a role was not incompatible with the functions of the caciques.

Northern Encounters: Haudenosaunee Women and the Fur Trade

BY JAN NOEL

During the American Revolution two genteel women, Abigail Adams of Massachusetts and Konwatsi'tsiaenni of the Mohawk Valley, spoke about their own desired outcomes of the great struggle. Adams exhorted her husband to think about the rights of all and to "Remember the Ladies" as he and his countrymen debated questions of political representation in Philadelphia in 1776. As a wife under the laws of coverture, Mrs. Adams could not control property; nor could she vote or count on a supportive political network. It is not surprising then that her request was shunted aside as a joke. At the same time Konwatsi'tsiaenni (also known as Molly Brant), who was both an Iroquois (or, to use their own name for themselves, Haudenosaunee) clan mother and the widow of a powerful Indian agent, Colonel William Johnson, exhorted warriors to support the British cause, speaking in council in the Mohawk Valley and later in exile north of the border. Indian agent Daniel Claus asserted "one word from her goes farther than a thousand from any white Man without Exception," and British officer Alexander Fraser declared, "Molly Brant's Influence over them ... is far superior to all of their chiefs put together." Political prestige within her clan, enhanced by a strategic marriage, enabled Konwatsi'tsiaenni to influence public events in the colonial world.

Compared to Konwatsi'tsiaenni, even the most privileged women of the day in England and New England had little political influence. If in earlier times things had perhaps been otherwise, by the eighteenth century these women had received some effective schooling in how to hold their tongues.... Abigail Adams had

Jan Noel, "Fertile with Fine Talk': Ungoverned Tongues Among Haudenosaunee Women and Their Neighbors," in *Ethnohistory*, Volume 57, no. 2, pp. 657–687. Copyright, 2010, the American Society for Ethnohistory. All rights reserved. Republished by permission of the copyrightholder, and the present publisher, Duke University Press. www.dukeupress.edu.

difficulty influencing policy in a culture where to be ladylike rather than "whorish" required staying out of the public arena and guarding one's tongue.

Things were, of course, quite different among the Haudenosaunee. Konwatsi'tsiaenni was a member of a group anthropologists have long singled out for endowing its women, and above all its matrons or clan mothers, with unusually high status. Although the power of clan mothers to select and depose chiefs is well accepted, there has been less consensus over the centuries (among early observers and the ethnologists who came in their wake) about the degree to which they possessed an active voice in councils and other forms of political decision making. Some found evidence to support the claims of eighteenth-century Jesuit Father Joseph-François Lafitau that women held "all real authority" and were "the souls of the Councils, the arbiters of peace and war" and controllers of the "public treasury." Others tended toward the conservative views of his contemporary, Father Pierre F. X. de Charlevoix, who responded to such claims that "they have indeed assured me that the women deliberate first on what will be proposed to Council, and that they then give their conclusions to the Chiefs ... but it certainly looks as though all that is for the sake of form and with restrictions." His view that there was little substance to claims about extraordinary powers was echoed in the widely reprinted views of ethnographer Elisabeth Tooker, who believed the longhouses and tools women controlled were of little value, and that "Council meetings were the work of men.... Women could, of course, and did attempt to influence the opinion of men.... Women have always and everywhere tried to defend their own interests in ways that they could."

At the beginning of the twenty-first century, the authors of two new monographs weighed in on the side of Father Lafitau's rather astonishing claims about female social, political, and economic authority. Barbara Alice Mann's *Iroquoian Women: The Gantowisas*, which combines aboriginal sources and viewpoints with close analysis of conventional scholarship, argues that various European observers who saw women staying in the background made the incorrect assumption that they were politically passive. They failed to understand that Haudenosaunee "etiquette" required a woman's council to delegate a male speaker to address men, just as men's councils would delegate a female speaker to address women. Since the European delegates were always male, matrons never addressed them directly but either advised Haudenosaunee negotiators behind the scenes or employed the more formal process of a male Woman's Speaker, who dressed in a skirt and carried a corn pounder, to convey the wishes of the Women's Council. In a similar vein, a second twenty-first-century monograph on the subject, Université de Montréal anthropologist Roland Viau's *Femmes de personne: Sexes, genres et pouvoirs en Iroquoisie ancienne*, points out how the language of politics, and the language of faith, too, acknowledged the importance of Haudenosaunee women. Viau identifies some eleven terms used by seventeenth- and eighteeth-century European observers to indicate female leaders, such as *femme considérable, matrone, captainesse, dame du conseil*, and *femme de qualité*. In the religious cycle, Grandmother Moon, Sky Woman, and the Three Sisters were luminaries, and females served on an equal basis with men as Keepers of the Faith. Viau asserts that the culture was "strongly feminine" and that males did not assume authority over women. He also gives new life to the notion that women's position in fact expanded in the period after 1650 and remained strong until about 1850. Male absences and fatalities relating to colonial warfare and trade concentrated governance increasingly in the hands of women. This would mean their voices were growing more influential in precisely the period that Anglo-American women's voices were becoming muted. Whatever the particular timing and extent of these feminine powers, the new monographs reconfirm long-standing views about Iroquoia as that rarest of entities: a well-documented society in history that was actually nonpatriarchal.

We turn next to listen for any faint hint that the singular gender arrangements in Iroquoia touched colonists in any way. One would not, of course, expect centuries-old European patriarchal traditions to crumble merely through contact with a more egalitarian culture. But since the groups interacted daily at a time when the Haudenosaunee were quite powerful, was there any effect at all on the gender practices of their neighbors? We can turn to business and travel accounts, court records, and government correspondence for interchanges between Haudenosaunee from the Mohawk and St. Lawrence River valleys with their Dutch, English, and French neighbors. Because colonial authorities were unwilling or unable to enforce fur trade regulations on powerful First Nations, they focused on tracking down non-native malefactors among their own citizenry. Sometimes the trail ended at a woman's door, and it seems more than coincidental that the majority of nonnative women known to have been involved in illicit trade were either northern French or Dutch.

Women from these European cultures had more autonomy than was common in the Anglo-American tradition. When they arrived in the first half of the seventeenth century, the French and Dutch settlers bordering Iroquoia brought with them European legal codes that were relatively respectful of female property rights. In both cultures, daughters as well as sons were expected to inherit equal or significant shares of the family property. Within marriages, although husbands had managerial powers, there existed a "community of goods" regarded as joint property of spouses rather than property of the husband; and a widow inherited half of these assets for use during her lifetime. A French wife could legally engage in business if she secured her husband's written permission; in the Dutch system, simple verbal permission sufficed. While scholars of Dutch New York view traditions there as refreshingly egalitarian, scholars of New France have not reached a consensus on the extent to which the formal protections created favorable conditions in practice. Still, no one questions that both of these continental systems compared favorably with Anglo-American common law, under which wives lost their legal personality and widows were "among the least protected anywhere in the world." The more equitable codes survived regime changes in both regions, persisting for a generation or more after the English takeovers of New Netherland in 1664 and New France in 1760.

Possessing significant claims to family assets helped a number of women in French Canada and Dutch New York take the helm as merchants, estate managers, and small manufacturers. Dutch businesswomen were typically married or widowed, figures such as ship owner Margaret Hardenbrook of New Amsterdam, who crossed the Atlantic a number of times on business, and Maria Van Rensselaer, who served as *patroonesse* of a vast rural estate for decades after her husband's death. Seventeenth-century missionary Jasper Danckaerts offered insight into another upcountry "tradress" whom he roundly condemned as "a truly worldly woman, proud and conceited, and sharp in trading [with Indians and others].... She has a husband ... who remains at home quietly, while she travels over the country to carry on the trading. In fine she is one of those Dutch female traders who understand business so well." She displayed two attributes that were typical of our subjects here: she moved around quite a bit, and she was evidently more the captain of her own fate than someone's "deputy husband." She shipped wheat down the Hudson and, over the captain of the vessel's objections, mixed substandard wheat with a good load, then traveled down to the Catskills before returning to Albany. In New France, female traders included not only wives and widows but single women such as the aristocratic Louise de Ramezay, daughter of a Montreal governor, who traveled between Montreal and the Richelieu Valley supervising her tanning, milling, and export lumber operations. These entrepreneurs were accepted figures among the Dutch and French of North America—a minority to be sure, but not an insignificant one. In vastly larger numbers, ordinary women traded their produce and handiworks at local markets....

Trafficking across Borders

Examining speech in the trade in peltries, the region's leading export, befits a preindustrial society in which both sexes were economic producers. In the fur trade, the spoken word was especially important, since many bargains were made verbally rather than in writing. For one thing, people had no desire to leave a paper trail of what was often illicit activity, with illegal fur trade estimated to have comprised at times as much as two-thirds of the French total and four-fifths of New York exports of beaver. Then too, many participants could not write. More so than in England and New England, the broad swath of the Canadian population lived in a predominantly oral culture. Not a single newspaper was published in the colony, and the few books found in prosperous homes were usually devotional ones. The rate of literacy (a bare 25 percent) lagged far behind that of New England. Even officers at the fur posts sometimes lacked "the first elements of history or geography" and wrote embarrassingly misspelled letters. Their Indian trading partners seldom wielded the pen either.

For the Haudenosaunee, smuggling furs out of Canada through northern New York and down to Albany was a lucrative operation. At Fort Orange/Albany, merchants paid better prices for peltries than did the monopoly French West Indies Company. They supplied goods cheaply, including luxuries such as oysters, white sugar, ribbons, lace, and colored stockings; and valuable trade supplies such as wampum and the prized English woolens known as strouds. Spiriting those goods between New York and Canada brought commissions to carriers, some of whom have been traced to the Sault St. Louis mission. At the southerly end of the route, Haudenosaunee traders of both sexes interacted with the Dutch from the 1630s onward.

As with most illicit activities, the records do not tell us all we wish to know. Fortunately we now have three detailed sources to help us piece together the story. Decades ago Canadian scholar Jean Lunn used the mid-eighteenth-century account book of Albany merchant Robert Sanders to uncover some of the secrets of this trade. Correspondence of Canadian officials to the French court has been another source of information. We can now piece together more of the story with the help of a newly translated and annotated version of a second, much earlier Albany account book kept by Evert Wendell and his family. Some 325 Indians were recorded to have opened accounts with siblings Evert, Harmonius, and Hester Wendell during the period 1695–1726. About 70 percent of them were Haudenosaunee, usually Mohawk or Seneca, along with some Onondaga and Cayuga.

The transactions were questionable on several grounds. First of all, rum was the Wendells' second-largest item of trade (after cloth goods), and it violated Albany trade regulations to sell alcohol. In that context a trade item sold by the dozens almost exclusively to Canadians, on credit, is intriguing: *tonties* translate from Dutch as "small kegs or casks." Though one might expect bigger containers for transnational shipments of rum, was it perhaps easier to whisk it undetected past authorities this way? In any case, English goods of any sort were not supposed to enter Canada except in small quantities sold for use of individual trappers, though over the years there were substantial shipments of trade items. Lastly, customers who took away goods on credit frequently failed to live up to their part of the bargain, leaving some two-thirds of the Wendell accounts unsettled. The Albany merchants took the losses in stride but must have factored them into their prices.

After the Wendells' day, transborder smuggling apparently grew more elaborate. Jean Lunn's scholarly detective work matched up events mentioned in Canadian officials' complaints about smuggling with events noted in the 1750s account book of Albany merchant Robert Sanders. The New Yorker protected his French Canadian trading partners by sending them parcels using coded symbols such as pipes and roosters. The French records revealed the way the aboriginal traders spirited the contraband past French forts in the St. Lawrence and Richelieu valleys. They would sometimes stop and divert officials with the paltry pack in their canoe while their friends hustled a much heavier pack through nearby woods. They were also known to send the same lightly loaded canoe past a fort many times, fooling the commander into thinking a big haul was just a series of small permissible bundles of fur trapped by individual Indians. At other times they got through by brandishing weapons or extracting a pass from the governor himself under threat of resettling in the English colonies.

Revisiting the account books of Albany merchants and the French colonial correspondence allows us to piece together information about women involved in this long-distance trade. In the Wendell records of 1695–1726 female traders were virtually as common as males (having an active role in 49.6 percent of accounts) and assumed similar responsibilities, such as bringing in comrades to meet the Wendells or standing as surety for such newcomers. About 10 percent of the aboriginal traders were from Canada, including the women Ohon-saioenthaa, Okaajthie, Anna, and Quanakaraghto. Most commonly females were identified simply as wives, sisters, or mothers of a named male, or by some personal characteristic. For example, a pockmarked "female Mohawk … from Canada" arrived to trade just after Christmas in 1705, bearing "greetings from the priest." She purchased red duffel stockings and nine bars of lead, promising to return later with five martens to pay for them. Her boy bought a coat. She reappeared to pawn an ax in March, then came again with beaver pelts to settle her account in May. She, her son, and various other family members traded with the Wendells for several years, exchanging their martens and beavers for items such as stockings, blue blankets and coats, and a red stroud blanket. She introduced another trader, an elderly Oneida woman, to the Wendells. The relationship continued on a happy note with Evert Wendell noting in 1706 "the boy and his mother have paid everything" and, perhaps in gratitude, he had "given for her son for free a piece of strouds."

In another case, "a limping female savage" first came down from Canada in 1697. Over the years Evert Wendell sold her a kettle, shirts, and rum in exchange for hides of bear, deer, elk, and martens; at one point she served as a guarantor for another woman trader. Limp or no limp, in 1700 she pledged the merchant eight beavers "for a French canoe … with which she went to Canada." She returned to Albany again, beavers in hand, in 1701. She and her husband and daughter were still trading with the Wendells in 1709.

Among six regular carriers Robert Sanders employed were four men—Togaira, Caingoton, Joseph Harris, and Conaquasse—and two women, Agnesse and Marie-Magdeleine (whom Sanders described as having an impediment in one eye). Clearly not confined to the village clearings, these women, like those in the earlier Wendell account, made a business of traveling the 210–mile route between Montreal and Albany. Agnesse did it at least three times between May and July of 1753. Canoes loaded with barrels of oysters or 130–pound shipments of beaver were typical. Marie-Magdeleine's remarks to Sanders that she knew one Montreal merchant whom she was supplying "perfectly well" and another one "well" suggest these women were integrated into the French network, too. The carriers had some control over their terms, helping themselves to a commission from the goods. Colonial women were also part of the network. Sanders explained to one of his French clients that he was sending her cloth in exchange for her furs and would have included some beautiful lace, but because the carrier siphoned lace off for sale to friends Sanders dared send no more.

Smuggling Sisters

The most spectacular smuggling operation linking such carriers with colonists that has yet come to light revolves around the Haudenosaunee mission near Montreal and three local spinsters. Hiding furs in the baskets that shoppers carried to markets were Haudenosaunee women from Sault St. Louis. The colony's highest officials sent a series of letters to the French minister of marine in the 1740s as they pieced together the particulars. Intendant Gilles Hocquart wrote on 11 October 1743, "My suspicions would fall on the Demoiselles Desauniers, although I have not been able to ascertain proof or catch them in *flagrante delicto*." That same year his co-ruler, Governor-General Beauharnois, asked the minister of marine himself for permission to remove those individuals if suspicions were confirmed. Marguerite, Marie-Anne, and Mageleine Desauniers, the correspondence revealed, had begun modestly enough, merely supplying clothing (*hardes*) to the Indians. Though they came from a fur-trading family, they were not under the authority of father or husband but operated on their own as "filles majeures, non-mariées." Comfortable members of the bourgeoisie, they owned what authorities described as a "beautiful big house" in Montreal, though they chose not to live there. Instead they amassed a wide variety of merchandise at their store across the river at the mission. Later, this establishment was found to contain stockpiles of supplies used for the western fur trade. A functionary of the French West Indies Company alerted government officials that the sisters should naturally have received some furs from the Indians in payment for all those goods. Why did they never bring any into the company's office, through which all peltries were required to pass? The sisters protested they had nothing to do with clandestine furs. Incredulous, the officials ordered them to close shop. But why did they nonetheless opt to stay at the mission without any visible means of support, instead of returning to the comforts of Montreal? Officials registered suspicions that they were trading still.

Some fur trade cultural intermediaries, as Richard White has demonstrated, "went native" in the fashion of the buckskinned frontiersman; but our female "Middle Ground" figures kept a foot in the worlds of the council fire *and* the drawing room. Their sex may have been an advantage. At the mission, according to Father Lafitau, Haudenosaunee women were largely in charge, the men usually away on war parties or in pursuit of furs. The Desauniers were said to be charitable to the sick and poor, a practice that dovetailed with native custom and may have further ingratiated them with the women there. Another important advantage was their ability to speak Haudenosaunee fluently.

They communicated well with fellow colonists too. Their French network included their many relatives among Montreal merchants. They could claim credit with the French military for feeding war parties. When the governor and intendant finally mustered the resolve to eject the Desauniers from the mission, army officers, clergymen, and prominent traders all sent petitions on their behalf. Fellow traders attested that the sisters had done business in Montreal and the village of Sault St. Louis for about twenty-four years "with all the rectitude and probity suitable to merchants, and they have always conducted themselves with honor and distinction in their business." Upon receiving this petition at Versailles, how could the minister of marine know that one of the signatories, Alexis Lemoine Monière, had the same name that appeared in Albany merchant Robert Sanders's letter-book as one of the leading Montreal smugglers? Merchant, commander, and priest leapt to exonerate those distinguished sisters who had obviously been saying the right things to all those men who rushed to their defense. Perhaps such fine-talking ladies also made the genteel governor reluctant to strike.

While rumors swirled around them, Marguerite, Marie-Anne, and Magde-
leine Desauniers and the Haudenosaunee women with their fur-filled baskets
continued to pursue the business at hand. The ever-inventive Desauniers came
up with an explanation for the rumors: they had discovered the secret for curing
the valuable ginseng the Indians found in the woods, and the people maligning
them must be doing it out of sheer envy. The authorities, however, continued to
see the principal issue as pelts, not plants. In 1750, some native informants admitted to the governor that besides trading with the enemy via Orange (Albany) and
Chouaguen (Oswego) posts, members of the ring proceeded with canoe-loads of ill-
gotten goods to the upper country posts. Having heard enough, Governor-General
Jacques-Pierre Taffanel de La Jonquière ordered eight soldiers to physically eject the
Desauniers from the mission. When La Jonquière died, though, the sisters took
advantage of the naïveté of his interim successor to secure permission to go to the
mission one last time, for twenty-four hours, to collect debts the Indians purportedly owed them. Months later, a newly arrived governor-general found them
still there. Yet another order went out for their removal. Intendant Hocquart,
who had already informed the court what shrewd dealers colonial women
were, declared the Desauniers had outdone them all. He explained to his superior
at Versailles in 1751 that the sisters were "very adroit, very fertile with fine talk,
unparalleled in presenting lies and truth with equal conviction." When he at last
forced them out of business, they took sail for France to make their case at the
French court. They arrived back in the colony with the glad tidings that the king
himself had given them permission to resume business. But why, when asked,
could they produce no document to prove it?

Not until 1752 did the Desauniers and their Haudenosaunee suppliers finally
wind down their operation. Or did they? The following year, the Sanders letter-
book mentions sending contraband to a Madame Desmurseaux/de Mousseaux,
evidently the wife of Monsieur de Merceau/Desmurceaux, the commander at
Fort Sault St. Louis, who lived just a stone's throw away from the Desauniers'
now-shuttered storehouse. Had Madame simply taken over the sisters' traffic
without—or perhaps *with*—their blessing?

The Desauniers thus eluded the grasp of the highest officials in New France for
many years, largely because they were trading partners of the formidable "praying
Iroquois" who had moved north to settle at the Jesuit mission at Sault St. Louis.
This group was deemed "the most warlike in North America" in 1735. They were
worrisome allies because they tended to put solidarity with other Haudenosaunee
ahead of any European alliances. There was concern that they might even turn on
the French colonists and attack them. The colonial powers dared not alienate them
by clamping down too hard on smuggling; yet for the sake of their own trading
companies and national interests, they had to keep it within limits.

Officials thought the Desauniers sisters themselves were stirring up the most
dangerous kind of trouble: "I am only too certain," Governor-General La
Jonquière wrote, "of the sway they have gained over the Iroquois of the Sault,
the sentiments of independence, even rebellion, they hasten to suggest to them."
It seems they knew how to play on French fear of the settlement in the heart of
their colony which was, one official wrote, practically "an independent republic."

As war approached in the 1750s, another allegation of the sisters' power came from military engineer Louis Franquet, who said they had dissuaded the Indians from letting the government build fortifications around the mission.

If the allegations had any degree of truth, then the Desauniers' influence went well beyond matters of profit and loss. Is it possible one or more of them gained a voice of authority in any way resembling that of clan mothers or women councillors? Adopted Europeans occasionally did so. Longtime New York trader Sarah McGinnis, for example, worked as a Tory agent during the American Revolution just as Molly Brant did. Based within the Mohawk encampment, McGinnis used her position to prevent a wampum belt bearing demoralizing news of a British defeat from going farther than her village. At Sault St. Louis, too, it may have helped that outsider-insider distinctions were blurred in a village that included a number of different First Nations, people of mixed blood, European adoptees, and friends. We are unlikely to ever know precisely what position the Desauniers held among the Haudenosaunee; we know only that colonial commanders were alarmed. Clearly the sisters made use of their fluency in the Haudenosaunee tongue, just as they made use of their "unparalleled" persuasiveness in French. These were womanly words with economic implications; and, according to French officials, military implications as well.

Other Malefactors

For more run-of-the-mill activity, there is plenty of evidence that the woods and posts resounded with commercial bargaining by women of all sorts....

Dutch New York, like French Canada, resisted generalizations about the stigmatizing and silencing of female speech. The actors in these commercial dramas included not just hardscrabble settlers but "ladies" drawn from families of commanders, burghers, and merchants, driving bargains with no apparent concern for loss of status.

If women of all these cultures traded as often as all this evidence suggests, how could anything so commonplace escape notice? One of the most interesting findings Kees-Jan Waterman made in his analysis of the Wendell records is that although nearly 50 percent of the accounts they opened involved women, these were typically identified only as the sister, wife, or mother of their male relatives, while men were almost always named. Indeed, 93 percent of the native traders who could not be identified by name were women. Waterman's newly translated, richly annotated edition of a New York Dutch account book allows us to see, for the first time, how aboriginal women were written out of the record at the trade counter itself. Also written out was trade known to have been conducted by one or more female members of the Wendell family, accounts either unsigned or subsequently lost. It is no wonder historians have subsequently failed to perceive their presence. White or indigenous, the fur trader entered the cultural imagination as a masculine figure: the trapper in buckskins, the muscular voyageur, or the managerial gentleman in a top hat. Their female relatives carrying furs, commissioning canoes, settling accounts, hoodwinking officials, and escorting other women to meet the dealer, fell into oblivion.

Conclusion

As Waterman observed, "In general, participation by women in the fur trade in the Northeast has not been described in the literature," even though his scholarship suggests they were just about as active as males. Discovering the public activities of Haudenosaunee and colonial women along the New York-Canada borderlands requires a close, often oblique reading of records that were written by male officials and later analyzed by scholars who assumed women were mainly confined to private places. Abandoning that trope, new scholarship on the New York fur trade by Waterman and on Iroquoia by Barbara Alice Mann and Roland Viau confirms the very active public presence not only of Haudenosaunee matrons but of many ordinary women of that nation. They provide new support for long-standing claims that there flourished in the Mohawk Valley and the mission near Montreal that rarest of entities: a nonpatriarchal people. Situated at a crossroads of economic, military, and missionary activity, its attributes can be found in the historical record.

We know less about that culture's interaction with colonial women. Although we will never recapture the entire context and meaning of centuries-old encounters around council fires or inside cabins, scholars from different standpoints might agree on the value of considering more carefully female dealers from several cultures who make shadowy appearances in the records of lawmen and merchants in Canada and New York. Colonial neighbors of the New York Haudenosaunee, living long amid "barbarism," forgot to ask nicely for somebody in charge to "remember the ladies." They rather hoped the lawmakers would not notice them at all. Their stories warrant incorporation in the ethnographic record, in the canons of fur trade, perhaps even in "national" history, if we are to transcend timeworn biases that have, of late, become less tenable than ever.

Scholarship does evolve with the times, and our own times make womanly "words with power" more conceivable than they used to be, as we see in the twenty-first-century works we have discussed. They clear the way for reconceiving the fur trade in the colonial Northeast. Years ago, Richard White's *The Middle Ground* showed how European and native cultures met and melded in highly creative ways in the Upper Great Lakes country, though it told us little about women's economic agency. Sylvia Van Kirk, Susan Sleeper-Smith, Bruce White, and others have labored to uncover that agency in the fur trade, but their work dealt mainly with later periods in the West. The cases we have reviewed here suggest that looking at the Mohawk corridor between Montreal and Albany in colonial times will yield new findings about the essential role of women in transnational trade. When women from other cultures operated in Haudenosaunee villages, did they ever assume any of the authority that matrons possessed? A closer look at the mores governing these situations will be fascinating. The autonomy and unconventionality of some of the colonists reviewed here may reveal a degree of "going native" sufficient to justify what Natalie Davis called "an enquiry about the history of European women that ... [makes] use of Iroquois tropes and frames."

The history of fur traders on those eastern frontiers is full of mysteries, including smokescreens they themselves created. Forgotten pre-Victorian realities beckon us to search more carefully for a range of female activities that tended to escape the purview of historians, even though they clearly exercised colonial governors, commanders, and sheriffs, and were even discussed at the French court. Whether we consider prevaricating Dutch wives and French spinsters, or their Haudenosaunee accomplices who paddled long distances to barter contraband, they all drew strength from laws or customs that allowed women to control assets and to engage in trade and unchaperoned travel (all the safer since among the Haudenosaunee rape was extremely rare). As female voices lost authority on both sides of the early modern Atlantic, the New York-Canada borderlands were home to three cultures in which women continued to speak up. Verbal exchanges are the very essence of commerce, especially in the oral cultures that still enveloped the Haudenosaunee and many of their neighbors. Some three centuries after the deals were made, their exuberant speech—salty, rebellious, dripping with lies—unsettles the narrative of domestic angels with well-governed tongues.

◈ FURTHER READING

Anderson, Gary Clayton. *The Indian Southwest, 1580–1830* (1999).

Anderson, Karen. *Chain Her by One Foot: The Subjugation of Native Women in Seventeenth-Century New France* (1991).

Axtell, James. *The Invasion Within: The Contest of Cultures in Colonial North America* (1985).

Barr, Juliana. *Peace Came in the Form of a Woman: Indians and Spaniards in the Texas Borderlands* (2007).

Blackburn, Carole. *Harvest of Souls: The Jesuit Missions and Colonialism in North America, 1632–1650* (2000).

Brooks, James F. *Captives and Cousins: Slavery, Kinship, and Community in the Southwest Borderlands* (2002).

Burke, Thomas. *Mohawk Frontier: The Dutch County of Schenectady, New York, 1661–1710* (1991).

Cushner, Nicholas P. *Why Have You Come Here? The Jesuits and the First Evangelization of Native America* (2006).

Dickason, Olive P. *Canada's First Nations: A History of Founding Peoples from Earliest Times* (1992).

Dolin, Eric Jay. *Fur, Fortune, and Empire: The Epic History of the Fur Trade in America* (2010).

Edmunds, R. David, and Joseph L. Peyser. *The Fox Wars: The Mesquakie Challenge to New France* (1993).

Fenton, William N. *The Great Law and the Longhouse: A Political History of the Iroquois Confederacy* (1998).

Foster, William C. *Spanish Expeditions into Texas, 1689–1768* (1995).

Greer, Allan. *Mohawk Saint: Catherine Tekakwitha and the Jesuits* (2005).

Gutiérrez, Ramon A. *When Jesus Came, the Corn Mothers Went Away: Marriage, Sexuality, and Power in New Mexico, 1500–1846* (1991).

Jennings, Francis. *The Invasion of America: Indians, Colonialism, and the Cant of Conquest* (1976).

John, Elizabeth A. H. *Storms Brewed in Other Men's Worlds: The Confrontation of Indians, Spanish, and French in the Southwest, 1540–1795* (1996).

Kessell, John L. *Pueblos, Spaniards, and the Kingdom of New Mexico* (2008).

Knaut, Andrew K. *The Pueblo Revolt of 1680: Conquest and Resistance in Seventeenth-Century New Mexico* (1995).

Mann, Barbara Alice. *Iroquoian Women: The Gantowisas* (2000).

Martin, Calvin. *Keepers of the Game: Indian-Animal Relationships and the Fur Trade* (1978).

Merwick, Donna. *The Shame and the Sorrow: Dutch-Amerindian Encounters in New Netherland* (2006).

Nichols, Roger L. *Indians in the United States and Canada: A Comparative History* (1998).

Parmenter, Jon. *The Edge of the Woods: Iroquoia, 1534–1701* (2010).

Peterson, Jacqueline, and Jennifer S. H. Brown, eds. *The New Peoples: Being and Becoming Métis in North America* (1985).

Richter, Daniel K. *The Ordeal of the Longhouse: The Peoples of the Iroquois League in the Era of European Colonization* (1992).

Richter, Daniel K., and James H. Merrell, eds. *Beyond the Covenant Chain: The Iroquois and Their Neighbors in Indian North America, 1600–1800* (1987).

Riley, Caroll L. *The Kachina and the Cross: Indians and Spaniards in the Early Southwest* (1999).

Rushforth, Brett. *Bonds of Alliance: Indians and the Making of Racial Slavery in French North America* (2012).

Sando, Joe S. *Pueblo Nations: Eight Centuries of Pueblo Indian History* (1992).

Sleeper-Smith, Susan. *Indian Women and French Men* (2001).

———, ed. *Rethinking the Fur Trade: Cultures of Exchange in an Atlantic World* (2009).

Spicer, Edward H. *Cycles of Conquest: The Impact of Spain, Mexico, and the United States on the Indians of the Southwest, 1533–1960* (1962).

Szasz, Margaret Connell, ed. *Between Indian and White Worlds: The Cultural Broker* (1994).

Trigger, Bruce G. *The Children of Aataentsic: A History of the Huron People to 1660* (1972).

Trimble, Stephen. *The People: Indians of the American Southwest* (1993).

Usner, Daniel H., Jr. *Indians, Settlers, and Slaves in a Frontier Exchange Economy: The Lower Mississippi Valley Before 1783* (1992).

Van Kirk, Sylvia. *Many Tender Ties: Women in Fur-Trade Society, 1670–1870* (1980).

Wallace, Anthony F. C. *The Death and Rebirth of the Seneca* (1970).

Weber, David J. *The Spanish Frontier in North America* (1992).

———, ed. *What Caused the Pueblo Revolt of 1680?* (1999).

White, Richard. *The Middle Ground: Indians, Empires, and Republics in the Great Lakes Region, 1650–1815* (1991).

CHAPTER 5

Eastern Encounters, 1600–1700

Virtually everyone has heard some version of the Pocahontas and Thanksgiving stories, two tales of seventeenth-century Indian encounters with the English along the eastern shores of North America. However, relatively few people have a good understanding of the historical basis for these popular stories, in large part because the stories are usually presented without important chronological context. Few get a chance to learn much about Pocahontas's people before the arrival of John Smith, or of Native New England cultures on the eve of the Pilgrims' quest for a "Promised Land." Likewise, few have an opportunity to think much about what happened after Pocahontas's alleged romance with Smith, or after the famous turkey feast in Massachusetts. This chapter starts from these stories, which should be familiar on at least a basic level, and pushes us into less familiar terrain. What happened before these encounters? What happened after? And, how might this broadened view and added context enhance our understanding of these stories of encounter, and of American Indian history on the Atlantic Coast in general?

◈ DOCUMENTS

The first three documents offer us views of American Indian history in the place the English would name "Virginia." In Document 1, John Smith, a leader of the English colonists, describes the Powhatan people, also known as the "Renápe," meaning "human beings." The excerpts here pay particular attention to the differing roles, as Smith saw them at least, for Renápe men as opposed to women. Document 2 is a version of a speech that Powhatan, a leader of the Renápe, evidently gave to Smith in 1609, two years after the English had first set up their colony at Jamestown. In the speech, Powhatan—who was also Pocahontas's father—articulates his ideas about what the desired political relations between his people and the newcomers should be. Powhatan presided over a large and powerful confederacy in the area, and initially, when the English were small in number and weak, he simply sought to make them subordinate members of his people's domain. It is not entirely clear who translated and recorded the speech, and the translation is obviously in the Shakespearian English of the time, but it may still convey some of the authentic viewpoints of this Native leader. In any event, despite Powahatan's attempts at diplomacy, the rapidly increasing numbers of English pushed ever further into Renápe lands, and conflict came to mark much of the Native-English encounters in seventeenth-century Virginia. Document 3 provides an English perspective on one such violent episode from 1622 when Powhatan's brother, Opechancanough, led an offensive to drive out the English invaders. Opechancanough's strategy ultimately failed; English expansions only continued.

Even though the English arrived in Virginia a full thirteen years before they landed in "New England," most still see the latter story as the "real" beginning of American history. The other documents in this chapter look at Native encounters with the English in this region. Like Virginia, New England was populated by dozens of separate Indian nations. The Wampanoags, Massachusetts, Narragansetts, Pequots, Mohegans, Nipmucs, and many other tribes would meet English newcomers who differed from those in Virginia. Whereas the English went to Virginia mainly for economic reasons—they hoped to be latter-day English versions of the gold-seeking Spanish conquistadors—their migration to New England was motivated largely by religious factors. The Pilgrims and Puritans sought a "Promised Land" where they would be free from the religious persecution they experienced in their native England, and where they could establish a morally exceptional "city on a hill." As in Virginia, some Indians sought diplomatic political relations with the newcomers. In Document 4 English Pilgrim leader William Bradford writes of the peace treaty they made with the local Wampanoag Indians in 1620. Indeed, this would be the basis for the famous "Thanksgiving" feast to seal the Wampanoag-Pilgrim alliance. While human generosity was present in this story, political and economic calculations were at work as well. The Wampanoags, hard hit by diseases that arrived in 1616 when European fishermen came to shore, needed an ally against other local Indian nations, and the Pilgrims, small in number and barely surviving in the foreign environment, needed whatever assistance they could get. Document 5, written more than a decade after the Mayflower's arrival, gives an additional English view of the Native peoples of the region, including the Pequots and Narragansetts. Of special note here is that the observer, William Wood, conveys some fairly positive opinions of the Indians, reminding us perhaps that not all Europeans always viewed all Indians in a purely negative light. Still, most of the English remained wary of those they often referred to as "savages," and, by the 1630s, many began to see the Pequots in particular as a godless enemy that needed to be conquered, if not exterminated completely. As in Virginia to the south, violent conflict ensued. In the final document, Captain John Underhill describes his interpretation of the English massacre of a Pequot village in 1637.

1. Captain John Smith Describes Powhatan Women and Men, 1624

The greatest labour they take, is in planting their corne, for the Country naturally is overgrowne with wood. To prepare the ground they bruise the barke of the trees neare the root, then doe they scortch the roots with fire that they grow no more. The next yeare with a crooked peece of wood they beat up the weeds by the rootes, and in that mould they plant their Corne. Their manner is this. They make a hole in the earth with a sticke, and into it they put foure graines of wheate and two of beanes. These holes they make foure foote one from another; Their women and children do continually keepe it with weeding, and when it is growne middle high, they hill it about like a hop-yard....

Their corne they rost in the eare greene, and bruising it in a morter of wood with a Polt, lap it in rowles in the leaves of their corne, and so boyle it for a daintie. They also reserve that corne late planted that will not ripe, by roasting it in hot ashes, the heat thereof drying it. In winter they esteeme it being boyled with beanes for a rare dish, they call *Pausarowmena*. Their old wheat they first steepe a night in hot water, in the morning pounding it in a morter.

They use a small basket for their Temmes [sieve], then pound againe the great, and so separating by dashing their hand in the basket, receive the flower in a platter made of wood, scraped to that forme with burning and shels. Tempering this flower with water, they make it either in cakes, covering them with ashes till they be baked, and then washing them in faire water, they drie presently with their owne heat: or else boyle them in water, eating the broth with the bread which they call *Ponap*. The groutes and peeces of the cornes remaining, by fanning in a Platter or in the wind, away, the branne they boyle 3 or 4 houres with water, which is an ordinary food they call *Ustatahamen*. But some more thriftie then cleanly, doe burne the core of the eare to powder, which they call *Pungnough*, mingling that in their meale, but it never tasted well in bread, nor broth....

They [the Indians] are very strong, of an able body and full of agilitie, able to endure to lie in the woods under a tree by the fire, in the worst of winter, or in the weedes and grasse, in Ambuscado in the Sommer. They are inconstant in every thing, but what feare constraineth them to keepe. Craftie, timerous, quicke of apprehension, and very ingenuous. Some are of disposition fearefull, some bold, most cautelous, all Savage. Generally covetous of Copper, Beads, and such like trash. They are soone moved to anger, and so malicious, that they seldome forget an injury: they seldome steale one from another, least their conjurers should reveale it, and so they be pursued and punished. That they are thus feared is certaine, but that any can reveale their offences by conjuration I am doubtfull. Their women are carefull not to be suspected of dishonestie without the leave of their husbands. Each houshold knoweth their owne lands, and

---

John Smith, The Generall [sic] Historie [sic] of Virginia, the Summer Isles, and New England... (1624), in *The Complete Works of John Smith*, ed. Philip Barbour (Chapel Hill: University of North Carolina Press, 1986), 2: 112–116.

gardens, and most live of their owne labours. For their apparell, they are some-time covered with the skinnes of wilde beasts, which in Winter are dressed with the hayre, but in Sommer without. The better sort use large mantels of Deare skins, not much differing in fashion from the Irish mantels. Some imbrodered with white beads, some with Copper, other painted after their manner. But the common sort have scarce to cover their nakednesse, but with grasse, the leaves of trees, or such like. We have seene some use mantels made of Turky feathers, so prettily wrought and woven with threads that nothing could be discerned but the feathers. That was exceeding warme and very handsome. But the women are alwayes covered about their middles with a skin, and very shamefast to be seene bare. They adorne themselves most with copper beads and paintings. Their women, some have their legs, hands, breasts and face cunningly imbro-dered with divers workes, as beasts, serpents, artificially wrought into their flesh with blacke spots. In each eare commonly they have 3 great holes, whereat they hang chaines, bracelets, or copper....

Men, women, and children have their severall names according to the sever-all humor of their Parents. Their women (they say) are easily delivered of childe, yet doe they love children very dearely. To make them hardie, in the coldest mornings they wash them in the rivers, and by painting and oyntments so tanne their skinnes, that after a yeare or two, no weather will hurt them.

The men bestow their times in fishing, hunting, warres, and such manlike exercises, scorning to be seene in any woman-like exercise, which is the cause that the women be very painefull, and the men often idle. The women and children doe the rest of the worke. They make mats, baskets, pots, morters, pound their corne, make their bread, prepare their victuals, plant their corne, gather their corne, beare all kind of burdens, and such like....

2. Powhatan (Chief of Powhatan Confederacy) Speaks to Captain John Smith, 1609

Captaine Smith, you may understand that I having seene the death of all my people thrice, and not any one living of these three generations but my selfe; I know the difference of Peace and Warre better than any in my Country. But now I am old and ere long must die, my brethren, namely Opitchapam, Opechancanough, and Kekataugh, my two sisters, and their two daughters, are distinctly each others successors. I wish their experience no lesse then mine, and your love to them no lesse then mine to you. But this bruit from Nandsamund, that you are come to destroy my Country, so much affrighteth all my people as they dare not visit you. What will it availe you to take that by force you may quickly have by love, or to destroy them that provide you food. What can you get by warre, when we can hide our provisions and fly to the woods? Whereby you must famish by wronging us your friends. And why are you thus jealous of our loves seeing us unarmed, and both doe, and are willing still to feede you,

This document can be found in Philip L. Barbour, ed., *The Complete Works of Captain John Smith* (Chapel Hill: University of North Carolina Press, 1986), 1: 247.

with that you cannot get but by our labours? Thinke you I am so simple, not to know it is better to eate good meate, lye well, and sleepe quietly with my women and children, laugh and be merry with you, have copper, hatchets, or what I want being your friend: then be forced to flie from all, to lie cold in the woods, feede upon Acornes, rootes, and such trash, and be so hunted by you, that I can neither rest, eate, nor sleepe; but my tyred men must watch, and if a twig but breake, every one cryeth there commeth Captaine Smith: then must I fly I know not whether: and thus with miserable feare, end my miserable life, leaving my pleasures to such youths as you, which through your rash unadvisednesse may quickly as miserably end, for want of that, you never know where to finde. Let this therefore assure you of our loves, and every yeare our friendly trade shall furnish you with Corne; and now also, if you would come in friendly manner to see us, and not thus with your guns and swords as to invade your foes.

3. An Englishman Reports on Violence in Virginia, 1622

These small and scattered Companies [of Indians] had warning given from one another in all their habitations to meete at the day and houre appointed for our destruction, at all our severall Townes and places seated upon the River; some were directed to goe to one place, some to another, all to be done at the same day and time, which they did accordingly: some entering their Houses under colour of trucking [trading], and so taking advantage, others drawing our men abroad upon faire pretences, and the rest suddenly falling upon those that were at their labours.

... Thus have you seen the particulars of this massacre, out of Letters from thence written, wherein treachery and cruelty have done their worst to us, or rather to themselves; for whose understanding is so shallow, as not to perceive that this must needs bee for the good of the Plantation after, and the losse of this blood to make the body more healthfull, as by these reasons may be manifest.

First, Because betraying of innocency never rests unpunished: And therefore *Agesilaus*, when his enemies (upon whose oath of being faithfull hee rested) had deceived him, he sent them thankes, for that by their perjury, they had made God his friend, and their enemy.

Secondly, Because our hands which before were tied with gentlenesse and faire usage, are now set at liberty by the treacherous violence of the Savages, not untying the Knot, but cutting it: So that we, who hitherto have had possession of no more ground then their waste, and our purchasse at a valuable consideration to their owne contentment, gained; may now by right of Warre, and law of Nations, invade the Country and destroy them who sought to destroy us: whereby wee shall enjoy their cultivated places, turning the laborious Mattocke

Edward Waterhouse, "A Declaration of the State of the Colony and Affaires in Virginia...", 1622, in Susan Myra Kingsbury, ed., *The Records of the Virginia Company of London*, vol. 3 (Washington: Government Printing Office, 1933). This document is also available in Camilla Townsend, ed., *American Indian History: A Documentary Reader* (Chichester, UK: Wiley-Blackwell, 2009), 46–48.

into the Victorious Sword (wherein there is more both ease, benefit, and glory) and possessing the fruits of others labours. Now their cleared grounds in all their villages (which are situate in the fruitfullest places of the land) shall be inhabited by us, whereas heretofore the grubbing [clearing] of woods was the greatest labour.

Thirdly, Because those commodities which the Indians enjoyed as much or rather more than we, shall now also be entirely possessed by us. The Deere and other beasts will be in safety, and finitely increase, which heretofore not onely in the generall huntings of the King (whereat foure or five hundred Deere were usually slaine) but by each particular Indian were destroied at all times of the yeare, without any difference of Male, Damme, or Young ...

Fourthly, Because the way of conquering them is much more easie then of civilizing them by faire meanes, for they are a rude, barbarous, and naked people, scattered in small companies, which are helps to Victories, but hinderances to Civilitie: Besides that, a conquest may be of many, and at once, but civility is in particular, and slow, the effect of long time, and great industry. Moreover, victorie of them may bee gained many waies; by force, by surprise, by famine in burning their Corne, by destroying and burning their Boats, Canoes and Houses, by breaking their fishing Weares, by assailing them in their huntings, whereby they get the greatest part of their sustenance in Winter, by pursuing and chasing them with our horses, and blood-Hounds to draw after them, and Mastives to teare them, which take this naked, tanned, deformed Savages, for no other then wilde beasts, and are so fierce and fell upon them, that they feare them worse then their old Devill which they worship, supposing them to be a new and worse kind of Devils then their owne. By these and sundry other wayes, as by driving them (when they flye) upon theire enemies, who are round about them, and by animating and abetting their enemies against them, may their ruine or subjection be soone effected ...

Fiftly [sic], Because the Indians, who before were used as friends, may now most justly be compelled to servitude and drudgery, and supply the roome of men that labour, whereby even the meanest [poorest] of the Plantation may imploy themselves more entirely in their Arts and Occupations, which are more generous, whilest Savages performe their inferiour workes of digging in mynes, and the like, of whom also some may be sent for the service of the Sommer Ilands [in the Caribbean].

Sixtly, This will for ever hereafter make us more cautelous [cautious] and circumspect, as never to bee deceived more by any other treacheries, but will serve for a great instruction to all posterities there, to teach them that *Trust is the mother of Deceipt*, and to learne them that of the Italian, *Chi no fida, non s'ingannu*, Hee that trusts not is not deceived; and make them know that kindnesses are misspent upon rude natures, so long as they continue rude; as also, that Savages and Pagans are above all other for matter of Justice ever to be suspected. Thus upon this Anvile shall wee now beate out to our selves an armour of proofe, which shall for ever after defend us from barbarous Incursions, and from greater dangers that otherwise might happen. And so we may truly say according to the French Proverb, *Aquelq chose Malheur est bon*, Ill lucke is good for something.

4. William Bradford Tells of Samoset, Squanto, and Massasoit, 1620

... All this while the Indians came skulking about them, and would sometimes show them selves aloofe of, but when any approached near them, they would rune away. And once they stoale away their tools wher they had been at worke, & were gone to diner. But about the 16. *of March* a certaine Indian came bouldly amongst them, and spoke to them in broken English, which they could well understand, but marvelled at it. At length they understood by discourse with him, that he was not of these parts, but belonged to the eastrene parts, wher some English-ships came to fhish, with whom he was aquainted, & could name sundrie of them by their names, amongst whom he had gott his language. He became profitable to them in aquainting them with many things concerning the state of the cuntry in the east-parts wher he lived, which was afterwards profitable unto them; as also of the people hear, of their names, number, & strength; of their situation & distance from this place, and who was cheefe amongst them. His name was *Samaset*; he tould them also of another Indian whos name was *Squanto*, a native of this place, who had been in England & could speake better English then him selfe. Being, after some time of entertainmente & gifts, dismist, a while after he came againe, & 5. more with him, & they brought againe all the tooles that were stolen away before, and made way for the coming of their great Sachem, called *Massosoyt*; who, about 4. or 5. *days after*, came with the cheefe of his friends & other attendance, with the aforesaid *Squanto*. With whom, after frendly entertainment, & some gifts given him, they made a peace with him (which hath now continued this 24. years) in these terms.

1. That neither he nor any of his, should injurie or doe hurte to any of their peopl.
2. That if any of his did any hurte to any of theirs, he should send the offender, that they might punish him.
3. That if any thing were taken away from any of theirs, he should cause it to be restored; and they should doe the like to his.
4. If any did unjustly warr against him, they would aide him; if any did warr against them, he should aide them.
5. He should send to his neighbours confederats, to certifie them of this, that they might not wrong them, but might be likewise comprised in the conditions of peace.
6. That when ther men came to them, they should leave their bows & arrows behind them.

After these things he returned to his place caled *Sowams*, some 40. mile from this place, but *Squanto* continued with them, and was their interpreter,

---

This document can be found in William Bradford, *Of Plymouth Plantation: The Pilgrims in America*, edited by Harvey Wish (New York: Capricorn Books, 1962), pp. 72–73.

and was a spetiall instrument sent of God for their good beyond their expectation. He directed them how to set their corne, wher to take fish, and to procure other commodities, and was also their pilott to bring them to unknowne places for their profitt, and never left them till he dyed. He was a *native of this place,* & scarce any left alive besids him self. He was caried away with diverce others by one *Hunt,* a Mr. of a ship, who thought to sell them for slaves in Spaine; but he got away for England, and was entertained by a marchante in London, & imployed to New-found-land & other parts, & lastly brought hither into these parts by one Mr. *Dermer,* a gentle-man imployed by Sr. Ferdinando Gorges & others, for discovery, & other designes in these parts....

5. William Wood Records His Impressions of the Indigenous Peoples of New England, 1634

Of the Pequots and Narragansetts,

Indians Inhabiting Southward.

The Pequots be a stately, warlike people, of whom I never heard any misdemeanor, but that they were just and equal in their dealings, not treacherous either to their countrymen or English, requiters of courtesies, affable towards the English.

Their next neighbors, the Narragansetts, be at this present the most numerous people in those parts, the most rich also, and the most industrious, being the storehouse of all such kind of wild merchandise as is amongst them. These men are the most curious minters of their wam-pompeag and mowhacheis, which they form out of the inmost wreaths of periwinkle shells. The northern, eastern, and western Indians fetch all their coin from these southern mintmasters. From hence they have most of their curious pendants and bracelets. From hence they have their great stone pipes, which will hold a quarter of an ounce of tobacco, which they make with steel drills and other instruments. Such is their ingenuity and dexterity that they can imitate the English mold so accurately that were it not for matter and color it were hard to distinguish them. They make them of green and sometimes of black stone; they be much desired of our English tobacconists for their rarity, strength, handsomeness, and coolness. Hence likewise our Indians had their pots, wherein they used to seethe their victuals before they knew the use of brass. Since the English came, they have employed most of their time in catching of beavers, otters, and musquashes, which they bring down into the bay, returning back loaded with English commodities, of which they make a double profit by selling them to more remote Indians who are ignorant at what cheap rates they obtain them in comparison of what they make them pay, so making their neighbors' ignorance their enrichment. Although these be populous, yet I never heard they were

William Wood, *New England's Prospect,* ed. Alden T. Vaughan (1634; Amherst: University of Massachusetts Press, 1977), 75–89.

desirous to take in hand any martial enterprise or expose themselves to the uncertain events of war, wherefore the Pequots call them women-like men. But being uncapable of a jeer, they rest secure under the conceit of their popularity and seek rather to grow rich by industry than famous by deeds of chivalry....

Of Their Dispositions and Good Qualifications, as Friendship, Constancy, Truth, and Affability.

To enter into a serious discourse concerning the natural conditions of these Indians might procure admiration from the people of any civilized nations, in regard of their civility and good natures. If a tree may be judged by his fruit, and dispositions calculated by exterior actions, then may it be concluded that these Indians are of affable, courteous, and well-disposed natures, ready to communicate the best of their wealth to the mutual good of one another; and the less abundance they have to manifest their entire friendship, so much the more perspicuous is their love in that they are as willing to part with their mite in poverty as treasure in plenty. As he that kills a deer sends for his friends and eats it merrily, so he that receives but a piece of bread from an English hand parts it equally between himself and his comrades, and eats it lovingly. In a word, a friend can command his friend his house and whatsoever is his (saving his wife), and have it freely. And as they are love-linked thus in common courtesy, so are they no way sooner disjointed than by ingratitude, accounting an ungrateful person a double robber of a man, not only of his courtesy but of his thanks which he might receive of another for the same proffered or received kindness. Such is their love to one another that they cannot endure to see their countrymen wronged, but will stand stiffly in their defense, plead strongly in their behalf, and justify one another's integrities in any warrantable action.

If it were possible to recount the courtesies they have showed the English since their first arrival in those parts, it would not only steady belief that they are a loving people, but also win the love of those that never saw them, and wipe off that needless fear that is too deeply rooted in the conceits of many who think them envious and of such rancorous and inhumane dispositions that they will one day make an end of their English inmates. The worst indeed may be surmised, but the English hitherto have had little cause to suspect them but rather to be convinced of their trustiness, seeing they have as yet been the disclosers of all such treacheries as have been practised by other Indians. And whereas once there was a proffer of an universal league amongst all the Indians in those parts, to the intent that they might all join in one united force to extirpate the English, our Indians refused the motion, replying they had rather be servants to the English, of whom they were confident to receive no harm and from whom they had received so many favors and assured good testimonies of their love, than equals with them who would cut their throats upon the least offence and make them the shambles of their cruelty. Furthermore, if any roving ships be upon the coasts and chance to harbor either eastward, northward, or southward in any unusual port, they will give us certain intelligence of her burthen and forces, describing their men either by language or features, which is a great privilege and no small advantage. Many ways hath their advice and endeavor been advantageous unto us, they being our first instructors for the planting of their Indian corn, by teaching us to cull out the finest seed, to observe the fittest season, to keep distance for holes and fit measure for hills, to worm it and weed it, to prune it and dress it as occasion shall require.

These Indians be very hospitable, insomuch that when the English have traveled forty, fifty, or threescore miles into the country, they have entertained them into their houses, quartered them by themselves in the best rooms, providing the best victuals they could, expressing their welcome in as good terms as could be expected from their slender breeding; showing more love than compliment, not grumbling for a fortnight's or three weeks' tarrying but rather caring to provide accommodation correspondent to their English custom. The doubtful traveler hath oftentimes been much beholding to them for their guidance through the unbeaten wilderness....

6. Captain John Underhill Describes the Pequot War, 1638

.... Captaine *Mason* and my selfe entring into the Wigwams, hee was shot, and received many Arrowes against his head-peece, God preserved him from any wounds; my selfe received a shotte in the left hippe, through a sufficient Buffe coate, that if I had not beene supplyed with such a garment, the Arrow would have pierced through me; another I received betweene necke and shoulders, hanging in the linnen of my Head-peece, others of our souldiers were shot some through the shoulders, some in the face, some in the head, some in the legs: Captaine *Mason* and my selfe losing each of us a man, and had neere twentie wounded: most couragiously these *Pequeats* behaved themselves: but seeing the Fort was to hotte for us, wee devised a way how wee might save our selves and prejudice them, Captaine *Mason* entring into a Wigwam, brought out a fire-brand, after hee had wounded many in the house, then hee set fire on the West-side where he entred, my selfe set fire on the South end with a traine of Powder, the fires of both meeting in the center of the Fort blazed most terribly, and burnt all in the space of halfe an houre; many couragious fellowes were unwilling to come out, and fought most desperately through the Palisadoes, so as they were scorched and burnt with the very flame, and were deprived of their armes, in regard the fire burnt their very bowstrings, and so perished valiantly: mercy they did deserve for their valour, could we have had opportunitie to have bestowed it; many were burnt in the Fort, both men, women, and children, others forced out, and came in troopes to the *Indians*, twentie, and thirtie at a time, which our souldiers received and entertained with the point of the sword; downe fell men, women, and children, those that scaped us, fell into the hands of the *Indians*, that were in the reere of us; it is reported by themselves, that there were about foure hundred soules in this Fort, and not above five of them

John Underhill (with Paul Royster, ed.), "Newes from America; Or, A New and Experimental Discoverie of New England...," *Electronic Texts in American Studies*, Paper 37, http://digitalcommons.unl.edu/etas/37 (accessed 1/18/12).

escaped out of our hands. Great and dolefull was the bloudy sight to the view of young souldiers that never had beene in Warre, to see so many soules lie gasping on the ground so thicke in some places, that you could hardly passe along. It may bee demanded, Why should you be so furious (as some have said) should not Christians have more mercy and compassion? But I would referre you to *Davids* warre, when a people is growne to such a height of bloud, and sinne against God and man, and all confederates in the action, there hee hath no respect to persons, but harrowes them, and sawes them, and puts them to the sword, and the most terriblest death that may bee: sometimes the Scripture declareth women and children must perish with their parents; sometime the case alters: but we will not dispute it now. We had sufficient light from the word of God for our proceedings....

◈ ESSAYS

The English people who began arriving on the Atlantic Coast in the seventeenth century brought with them a certain set of plans, cultural views, material items, animals, plants, and—unknowingly—germs. Their backgrounds affected their interpretations of Indian cultures, including, for example, Indian gender roles (as you may have noticed in some of the preceding documents). The English commonly assumed that Indian men, who spent much of their time hunting, were "free and lazy," while the women, who remained near the villages tending the agricultural fields, were "submissive drudges." In her essay, Helen C. Rountree, Professor Emerita of Anthropology at Old Dominion University, examines this view by recreating a day in the life of women in a Renápe hamlet, as it would have been in the spring of 1607. In doing so, she not only reveals Renápe gender roles, but also casts a light on Indian society on the eve of English settlement.

Native peoples on the eastern seaboard sometimes succeeded in making the newcomers into trading partners and even political allies. But, at other times, native groups were drawn into violent clashes with them. In her essay, Katherine Grandjean, an assistant professor of history at Wellesley College, assesses the war that the Pequots fought with the English from 1636 to 1637. Explaining the cause—or, most always, causes—of any war is challenging and often contentious. This war, fought in what is now Connecticut, is no different. To the interpretations that historians have already put forth about this conflict, Grandjean adds her own, focusing in particular on environmental factors.

The documents and essays in this chapter, taken together, provide perspectives on the earlier part of the seventeenth century. Compared to Indians' encounters with Europeans in the southern and northern parts of North America (the focus of Chapter 4), Indians in Virginia and New England experienced the influx of larger groups of strangers who hungered for more land. Those trends would only continue and accelerate in the latter part of the 1600s, making Indian history in this region distinct, and distinctly challenging. Indeed, around the same time the Pueblos were winning against the Spanish in 1680, Indians along the Atlantic Coast lost two pivotal wars in 1676: Bacon's Rebellion in Virginia and King Philip's War in New England. In the seventeenth century, the Virginia and New England stories may have begun with hopeful stirrings of cooperation and coexistence, whether through the (mythical) tale of a Pocahontas–John Smith romance or through the celebration of Thanksgiving, but they ended in conflict and military conquest.

The "Virginia" Encounter:
Powhatan Women and the English

BY HELEN C. ROUNTREE

In my writings on the Powhatan Indians up to now, I have played it fairly safe and close to the documents, which regrettably has meant writing mainly about the men's world. In this essay I want to start trying to bring the women of A.D. 1607 to life, which means going out onto limbs, occasionally onto twigs. I will, at least, distinguish between what we can safely know and what must be inferred, and I will give evidence for that knowledge or inference as I go.

The eyewitness accounts of the Powhatan Indians of 1607 were all written by people who had several severe disabilities as ethnographers. They were males who found themselves describing a society in which men and women were probably not accustomed to talking with each other freely. I will elaborate on the reticence issue at the end of the essay, for it would have been an outcome of several things I must establish first. But for now, we must face the likelihood that even a deeply curious Englishman like William Strachey would not have elicited detailed responses from the few Powhatan women he could have interviewed. In addition, the early writers were Elizabethan Englishmen, so they saw Powhatan lifeways through a very cloudy lens. Aside from their own strongly patriarchal cultural background, which colored their views of all women, including Powhatan ones, they were in the New World to establish a colony for their own people, at the expense of the "wild" native people if necessary. From the very beginning of Jamestown, the invaders were braced for Indian resistance and prepared (they hoped!) to take military action if that resistance materialized. John Smith, Strachey, and Henry Spelman observed the natives for purposes of surveillance, not "pure" knowledge. The result in the early accounts of the Powhatan Indians is therefore an almost myopic emphasis on men's activities: war, politics, and religion. It was, after all, those activities in concert that could seriously threaten the English enterprise. Women mattered only insofar as they raised corn, a commodity the colonists had to purchase whenever their own supplies were inadequate.

Thus if we want to reconstruct more fully what Powhatan women's lives were like, we must go far beyond milking the limited historical sources for all they are worth. In this essay I will use three additional kinds of information on

Helen Rountree, "Powhatan Indian Women: The People Captain John Smith Barely Saw," in *Ethnohistory*, Volume 53, no. 4, pp. 1–29. Copyright, 2006, the American Society for Ethnohistory. All rights reserved. Republished by permission of the copyrightholder, and the present publisher, Duke University Press. www.dukeupress.edu

which to base inferences. All three may make document-clinging historians uncomfortable, but that is too bad. I am a cultural anthropologist, and it is time I returned to my spreading roots.

First, I will use ethnographic analogy, an anthropological technique based on the premise that two or more cultures that have some basic similarities, especially ecological and economic ones, may have other similarities in related areas of life, such as the status of women compared to men. This technique is a valid basis for making inferences if it is used carefully; I will use other Eastern Woodland farming cultures and cite accounts of them dated as closely as possible to first contact with Europeans, keeping in mind that those accounts often show considerable myopia of their own.

Second, since Smith and Strachey do say something, however minimal, about the wild plants that Powhatan women used, I have been doing for several years now what I call "reconstructive ethnobotany" for the Powhatans: compiling a list of the edible, utilitarian, and medicinal plants in eastern Virginia that are both native and wild and that the Powhatans either were recorded as using or *could have used*. Such a list sheds light not only on possible nutritional matters but also on people's seasonal movements within their territories. The plants grow in certain habitats, most of which are away from the Indian town sites, and are useful at certain seasons, so women gathering them would have had to visit those habitats at the relevant times. Before I began the list, I had the usual Euro-American view of Indian women as stay-at-homes; now I know better.

Third, I have turned to "living history"—and have pushed its local practitioners at Jamestown Settlement to begin expanding the museum-centered way it is usually done—to tell me what some of the "quality of life" was like for Powhatan women. The settlement's Indian Village staff could tell me in detail about doing hands-on crafts that could be practiced in town, while talking to tourists. But my idea of living history further involves my identifying plants and their locations and then our collecting and preparing them—and noticing which muscles hurt afterward. For instance, digging tuckahoe for bread making was women's work, since the English writers do not include it in the men's list of tasks. It can be very hard work in itself, as we have discovered; it also involved travel to and working in marshes at frequent intervals in the late spring and early summer, which in turn required women to have regular access to dugout canoes and strong bodies to paddle them. Before I tried any foraging or canoe paddling, I thought of Indian women as hardworking but not as "fitness nuts." Now, having tried it—and having heard a physical anthropologist (Donna Boyd, who analyzes skeletal remains from protohistoric and early contact Virginia sites) say that the women's skeletons she sees are more robust than those of most modern males—and then having reread Smith and Strachey, I know better.

The present essay does not deal with Powhatan women in their "public" appearances, which were the occasions on which English visitors, treated as VIPS, would have seen them. We already know from Smith's, Strachey's, and Spelman's accounts that women could inherit or be assigned chiefly power and that their raising of corn was considered important in the Powhatan world, as it was among other coastal Algonquians. Nor does this essay deal much with how women got married and divorced, for I have described that elsewhere. Instead I want to look at women's daily work to try to get at the texture that underlay and helped explain their other, seemingly contradictory appearances in the English records. Powhatan females were supposedly semiservants doing a "painefull" number of support jobs for their huntin' and fishin' husbands, whose apparent "idleness" caused everybody to live "from hand to mouth" much of the year. Yet simultaneously these women had considerable sexual autonomy; they were able to turn down suitors (few English maidens of that time were given such a choice) and to take lovers later on with their husbands' permission. Hardworking drudges with freedom? As we shall see, the word *drudge* is the part that does not fit.

In the following pages there are four points that I will emphasize about the daily lives of Powhatan females: (a) Women had to schedule their work, sometimes well ahead, although they did not do it on English clock time; Smith was wrong to think that life at any time of year was opportunistically lived "from hand to mouth." (b) Women worked in groups, most often same-sex ones, sometimes because they had to and at other times because sociability lightens any load. (c) Powhatan women had to be physically strong and energetic to do their work, just as the men did. No Virginia source says so, but the nature of the work, if we try it ourselves, demands toughness. And English writers in other colonies agree: John Lawson says the Carolina Indian women were "of a very hale Constitution"; Roger Williams, writing of the southern New England Algonquians of 1643, mentions "the hardness of their constitution," while David Zeisberger describes the women as "strong" among the Delawares, Miamis, Shawnees, and Munsis of his day. (d) Women's work in the Powhatan world was at least as varied as men's work. True, it did not have the excitement and tremendous though temporary exertions characteristic of warfare and the chase, tempered by periods of resting up and politicking. But continuous and carefully paced as it was, women's work appears to have taken place in a number of different settings each day and to have required a considerable variety of skills. People who do work that they themselves plan and that is socially exclusive, demanding of skill and energy, and interestingly varied are unlikely to be drudges, in their own eyes or in the eyes of knowledgeable others. I submit that that was the case with Powhatan women.

Let us take a Powhatan hamlet through a day, focusing on the women who live there. I will set the scene in a real but unnamed hamlet that has been excavated archaeologically. The community, dated to just before and after the arrival of the English seven miles away at Jamestown, was within the Paspahegh chiefdom, a small political group subject to the paramount chief Powhatan and located on both sides of the mouth of the Chickahominy River.... Open vistas along the rivers were the kind that the Powhatans, ever alert for enemies, preferred.

The trees ... are bald cypresses, which grow along the margins of both rivers there and are more rot resistant than any other species. Prime canoe-making materials are right at hand.... other resource-rich ecological zones are also fairly close by for women to exploit. Besides the river itself, there are extensive freshwater marshes (sources of edible roots and house-building materials) bordering the tributary creeks and considerable expanses of deciduous woodland (sources of nuts and fuel) between the waterways. Below the fifty-foot contour, the land is gently rolling or, at the village site itself, nearly flat and well suited for horticulture. In fact, the soil at the site contains the largest single parch of Pamunkey loam, the region's best corn-growing soil, to be found along the Chickahominy. This was truly a hamlet that had everything. It also had neighbors: Out of the scope of the map, there were other Paspahegh villages and the chief's town within a few miles up and down the James. The female and male denizens of our hamlet would have been continually meeting their friends and relatives from those other settlements, both in planned visits and in chance encounters as they went about the work that took them away from home.

... Peering over a tree branch, we are looking at the randomly oriented layout of several reed-mat-covered houses (Strachey says that bark coverings were for rich people), though neither I nor the archaeologists can be sure that all the houses shown existed simultaneously. The hamlet had small groves of trees between the scattered houses, according to Strachey, to protect them in storms and to give the people shade....

We are doing our spying on the first of May 1607. It is an ordinary day. There is no priestly curing ceremony going on, nor are any boys being starred on the *huskanaw* (initiation) process. There is no ripe corn as yet, so no thanksgiving celebrations are in the offing. Wowinchopunck, the Paspahegh chief, is not visiting, and the great Powhatan is staying up on the York River, where he belongs. The English ships bringing colonists will not get this far up the James for three more days. (Everybody knows they are coming, of course, and gossip about them is rife.) The shad and herring are finishing their spring runs, so that nets and traps are still bringing in a lot of food. The women are weeding the fields they planted last month and planting second fields now. Last year's supply of corn, beans, and gathered nuts has run out. It is a time both for farming and for heavy foraging in the women's world—the very time that women's work would be most "painefull."

People wake up in the early dawn, since (according to George Percy) they will finish their ablutions before the sun rises. The houses in which they have slept are barrel-vaulted affairs whose smoke holes and low doors ensure that the interiors are easily filled with smoke; reconstructions of such houses always smell of wood smoke. On the authority of Strachey we know that fires are always going in the houses, for letting them go out would be bad luck. They also repel insects during the warm months (mosquitoes, that is—the only escape from fleas is to move house) and provide heat in the cold months. Like us, the Powhatans believe in heating sleeping rooms rather than using lots of bedding; what little bedding they do use consists of mats and skins that are rolled up and stored during the day. So during the past night, someone in each household has agreed to feed the fire at intervals. As the Indian Village staff at Jamestown Settlement can attest, a moderate-sized fire can fill an Indian house with a layer of smoke that reaches down to about two feet above the floor. Perhaps that is another reason why the "beds" lining the walls of Powhatan houses are only, according to Strachey's description, sitting distance high ("a foote highe and somwhat more"): sleepers do not have to inhale thick smoke all night. The beds are rather narrow, and couples have slept head to foot ("heades and points one by the other"). Such beds allow no privacy unless mat partitions are put up around them. And mats, in single or multiple layers, and also the outer bark walls of chief's houses, are far from soundproof. If Powhatan women and their husbands procreate on those beds, rather than out in the fields or woods (English sources are silent on the matter), then there can be visual but not sonic privacy for lovemaking. Corroboration comes from Lawson, who indicated in 1709 that among the Carolina Indians, people considered it enough not to be actively watched.

Everybody, even babes in arms, goes to the river to bathe before dawn. Cleanliness is the main reason during the warm months; when the water is cold, then hardiness also comes into play. It is not only infants, mentioned by Smith, who need endurance. Children and adults of both sexes spend the daylight hours outdoors, weather permitting, since houses built in the Powhatan fashion are rather dark to try to work in. Moreover, people do active jobs that make nontailored clothing a hindrance (think of trying to dig roots while wearing an "Indian blanket" of deerskins). So everybody makes a virtue of necessity and, wearing few clothes, strives to be "hardy." Bathing every morning in all weathers helps. After the bath, as the sun rises, people make tobacco offerings and pray to the sun. They have reason to want supernatural help: the day will bring real hazards (see below), and everyone needs a good crop of corn this year.

The next order of business is breakfast, which is informal. Powhatan people eat freely when food is available and they are hungry, except for the boys, whose mothers make them shoot a tossed bit of moss before they can have their breakfast. Not much food is ready yet, though. Whatever stew was left over from supper has been kept simmering, probably on the house's fire that had to be kept going anyway, but it has been raided all night as people woke up feeling peckish. There is no leftover roast meat, for people were careful to eat it all up last night (the alternative would be either spoiled meat or, if it was left over the fire, mummified roasted flesh). So now some of the hamlet's women and girls start pounding dried tuckahoe into flour for bread, talking volubly as they work and possibly singing work songs to keep up the pounding rhythm. Others fetch springwater to start the day's stew. Men and boys will go out to get meat at intervals all day long: boys gather mussels, men and boys alike try their luck in hunting, and anyone can dip into the fish trap if the tide is right. The first things to come in will probably be quickly roasted and eaten along with the newly baked bread; later contributions will go into the family stewpots.

With breakfast goes a final discussion of the day's work, most of the plans having been made the previous evening. Work parties need to be agreed on for various of the women's jobs, the number of women in the hamlet being limited, and also for any clearing of new fields by men. The work of both sexes today will also involve traveling in canoes; the women are as dextrous and almost as strong in handling them as the men. So allocation must be made of the available dugouts.

I cannot reconstruct the specific composition of the work parties among the hamlet's women, beyond saying that it was surely kin-based. The women living in the hamlet would have been connected through the men, in patrilocal Powhatan society, and they would have included men's mothers, unmarried sisters, and wives and cowives (young wives married for affection and older wives married by contract for their experience). The women working together might be members of an extended family, or they might cooperate because of sameness of age or personal congeniality. There is nothing at all to tell us. But work together they did: Powhatan women were probably almost never alone. Group effort lightened the load in land-based work. On the water it was a necessity, for a dugout canoe, even a small one, is heavy and cumbersome to maneuver. To make any speed at all in one requires at least two people paddling or poling, while keeping it on course is best done with yet another person using a paddle as a rudder astern. Thus we shall see several parties of women working actively away from the hamlet on this day and returning to do more work sociably back in town. Any one woman would have engaged in all the kinds of work over a period of several days, there being no occupational specialization in Powhatan society.

Work Party No. 1 goes out to the fields, probably in the morning before the sun gets too hot; May in eastern Virginia is hot but not baking hot. The field in the drawing is very near the houses, which is the women's preference; other fields are farther away and require a trudge. The women are planting one field and weeding another that was planted a month ago; yet another field will be planted in a month's time. The planting process probably involves some sort of "medicine" or prayer to ensure a good crop, though the English accounts say nothing whatever about this. It will not work this year: The summer of 1607 will be a dry one.

The planting tools the women use, crooked sticks scraped smooth on both sides, are simple and lightweight, but the work involves a lot of bending over and reaching. It is a good thing that each field is less than an acre, even with multiple women doing the work. Some women carry babies to the fields in their cradleboards, which can be conveniently hung from a tree nearby. Powhatan women, like other Woodland Indian women, probably nurse their babies for well over a year after birth, so it would make sense to keep baby and food source together. Each family (or possibly extended family) has several fields of varying age (one to three years) to care for, each with a different spring planting time; later, when all of the fields are under cultivation, some of the men may help their busy wives. They will also work with their women to produce a field of corn for the chief, as well as start the clearing process on a new field to replace a three-year-old field that is nearly exhausted. As the years go by and fields are cleared, cultivated, and allowed to go back to woods, the areas under cultivation move up and down the riverside on the fairly level ground. So do the houses, which are so biodegradable that it is simpler to build a new one "closer to work" than to resheathe an old one completely in a location now distant from the current fields.

When the women finish their weeding, they leave a boy or two behind to act as a scarecrow (a "scarecrow hut" is shown in a John White painting from Carolina, and Williams wrote about children sitting in "little watch-houses" to scare off birds). Powhatan boys, young as they are, are already under pressure to become marksmen and contribute to the stewpot, so logically they will not only scare off birds but also sit quietly and allow corn-eating animals like raccoons, opossums, and even deer to enter the field and get close enough to shoot.

Corn is food that confers high status on its owners. Any unravaged corn that the fields produce will be harvested and processed by the women; also allocated for cooking by the women; and apparently owned by the women. Strachey's description of people hiding their valuables (including corn) from one another indicates that Powhatan couples did not have community property, nor did men own things "in right of" their wives. Further, Spelman writes that shovels ranked high among the English goods bought by the Powhatans in the early years of the Jamestown colony; they replaced the women's crooked sticks and were apparently purchased by the women themselves. The women in our hamlet produce several things that English traders will soon want: corn, beans, and "tryed [rendered] deares suyt [suet] made up handsomely in Cakes." And when the hungry English try to buy corn from men in the Indian towns, they may be dickering with the wrong people.

Work Party No. 2 may have the same personnel as No. 1 for it consists of women gathering the berries and greens that are ready to eat on this May day. The best places for such gathering are recently abandoned fields (for the greens) and older fallow fields and woodland edges that have thicketlike growth in them (for the berries). The sensible time to do the gathering is on the way home from the current cornfields, if one is to heed the adage "Never return empty-handed." Women do this kind of foraging daily; men who are courting women also collect berries rather than flowers on the way home from the hunt. Berry and greens picking can be surprisingly physical work; so is the job of humping home the proceeds, especially with a child in a cradleboard on one's back. There are also real dangers involved in coming and going to fields that are not always next door to one's house. There is always the possibility that warriors from enemy tribes (and even rival tribes within the Powhatan paramount chiefdom) will try to abduct a woman or girl, though late fall is a more likely time for it to happen. Snakes are less likely to lurk and bite when a group of women comes along talking animatedly. But twisted ankles away from home and brier scratches that become easily infected are misfortunes that can happen at any time and that sensible people, male and female, avert by making offerings to various kinds of *okeus* (minor deities) before setting out from town....

One of the women belonging to the hamlet is staying out of my drawing altogether because she is menstruating. When their periods come, Powhatan women seclude themselves in a house out of people's way for fear of endangering the men and ruining their hunting. It is something of a vacation, quite pleasant if a woman does not suffer from cramps. Other women bring her food, possibly already cooked, and they and her female children can visit her freely.

Still another woman, moving freely about the hamlet, is very pregnant. She does not slacken in her work, however, so she stays fit. That fitness and her remaining well nourished even in spring, because she lives where tuckahoe and runs of spawning fish are plentiful, will help her carry her fetus to term and deliver it "easily," to use Smith's term. Other Woodland Indian women had similarly easy deliveries. According to Lawson, "The *Indian* Women will run up and down the Plantation, the same day, very briskly, and without any sign of Pain or Sickness; yet they look very meager and thin." Williams makes a specific connection between physical fitness and quick recovery from childbirth: Southern New England Indian women had easy deliveries because of the seasonal farming and clamming and daily corn-pounding labors they performed. He adds that he had "often knowne in one Quarter of an houre a Woman merry in the House, and delivered and merry again; and within two dayes abroad, and after foure or five dayes at worke, &c." Daniel Gookin, writing of the same region, makes claims for an even shorter recovery time: The women "many times are so strong, that within a few hours after the child's birth, they will go about their ordinary occasions."

[Some of the Powhatan] would have been doing their jobs in the comfort of sapling-and-mat shades. These open-sided affairs have lofts on which they put "their Corne, and fish to dry," and people also visit and "eate, sleepe and [cook] their meate" there when they want a place that is both cool and well lit. Shades of this sort are ideal for men resting from the hunt or women resting from digging tuckahoe (but still twining cordage, grating deer bones into needles, etc., "on automatic pilot"). One can be refreshed without missing anything that is going on in the hamlet.

Everyone is home by late afternoon. Depleted as they may be, the stewpots' contents are at their most varied, considering all the different food-getting activities that have gone on today; fish and animal carcasses are roasting, and more fish has been laid up to dry. The thumping of pestles in mortars sounds all over the hamlet as women pound more tuckahoe to make bread for the evening meal. As the sun goes down, people make offerings to okeus in thanks for a day of safety and success in getting food. They are free to eat before and after the ritual, if they are hungry, and most of them are. No roasted meat will be left over, nor will much stew.

In the evening, after a typically long, strenuous day, women and men alike will sing and dance! The dancing is "coed," though the dancers do not touch one another, and it is active enough to burn up most of the energy left over from the day's tasks. It probably also burns away the frustrations that some people feel in having to work closely on a daily basis with people who may irritate them. Further, it is a chance for both sexes to attract premarital or extramarital partners, through dancing well and by singing what Strachey calls "amorous dittyes" (how I wish he had given details). As the evening grows late, people will disappear from the dance ground into their houses (or other people's if they have an assignation). There many of them, with or without much privacy, embrace their partners, for as Strachey observes, these strong, active people, male and female, are "most voluptious ... uncredible yt is, with what heat both Sexes of them are given over to those Intemperances." Even the lustiest individuals, however, will eventually fall asleep.

Powhatan women were active, productive, and in many ways autonomous components of the Virginia Indian population. Far from being unwilling victims who were made to do the farming by lazy males, they knew their work, made doing it a social occasion, and reaped a reward of power in the family for their efforts. They foraged for a wide variety of plants, which would have been impossible to do randomly with any success. They had to know which things were appropriate to what uses, where they grew, and in what season they were worth collecting. That required a very good memory. I have found that just the native wild *edible* plants in eastern Virginia number about eleven hundred species. The differing habitats that had to be visited at the same time, and the wide variety of other jobs that I have shown women tackling, meant that they had to do some careful scheduling to get everything done.

Women did work that could vary greatly in a day, as I have shown; their work varied even more if we consider the annual round. The word *drudgery*, with its implication of being tied to the eternal repetition of unpleasant labor, simply does not apply to their lives. Not only did Powhatan women's work vary, but it also had the women moving in and out of town continually. Further, it was not necessarily unpleasant, because women could pace themselves and visit with one another as they went about their business.

All of the different kinds of women's tasks could be done in company, and certain of the jobs, like house building and anything that involved canoe travel, required group effort if they were to be done at all. Living and working constantly in close proximity to other women, even congenial ones, probably created several other traits in Powhatan culture that are poorly documented in the surviving English accounts. Neither the women nor anyone else except the priests could afford to value privacy and solitude. The intensely cooperative life, lived mostly outside the house walls even when people were "at home," would have precluded such things. As a corollary, one of the most effective ways to punish someone in that society would be ostracism, not only painful to people reared in such an environment but also economically detrimental. As another corollary, it is likely that the early-seventeenth-century Powhatans resembled the mid-eighteenth-century Delawares, Munsis, and others so vividly described by Zeisberger: They kept up a peaceful, cooperative front, while their aggressions went underground, taking the form of gossip and even witchcraft. Even the great Powhatan's daughter Pocahontas was afraid of witchcraft. Until she converted to Anglicanism and received a new name, Rebecca, she would not reveal her personal name, Matoaka, "in a superstitious feare of hurte by the English if her name were knowne."

Women who grew up working together in groups at tasks in which men participated little or not at all would also grow up having relatively little in common with those men and expecting little psychological intimacy with them. The men, for their part, were so focused in on performing as great hunters and daring warriors that they could probably spare little emotional energy for understanding a sex whose life experiences were so different from theirs. People sought emotional intimacy within their own sex, for only there could one find real understanding. Powhatan men would also have lacked Europeans' ideas about men's "needing" to supervise or "take care of" members of the "weaker" sex. The physical robustness of the women and the amount of time they spent working geographically apart from men would have made such ideas irrelevant. Powhatan men and women, like those in other Eastern Woodland tribes, would have valued each other as economic partners and sought one another out as sexual partners, kinship distance permitting. But most men and women appreciated and respected one another without feeling very close, except for the affection allowed between close blood relatives. Zeisberger describes the situation vividly, albeit for the Delawares of a later century: "It is a common saying among them, 'My wife is not my friend,' that is, she is not related to me and I am not concerned about her, she is only my wife."

Having the two sexes belong to two different but moderately overlapping worlds allowed Powhatan men and women to live more comfortably with some facts of their marital lives that English writers like Strachey describe explicitly. Polygyny works better, with less strife between cowives as well as husband and wives, if husband and wives do not expect a great deal of each other's time and attention. Affairs, permitted to women with husbands' permission (apparently often given) and seemingly free for men to engage in, were less likely to cause jealousy if husband and wife were not even supposed to be emotionally close. Chiefly marriages, which required a separation after the birth of one child, were also easier for the parties to bear when little intimacy developed between them. Temporary marriage by contract, with the time period stated and renewable by mutual agreement, was less likely to inflict pain on less involved participants when one partner wanted to continue the relationship while the other one contemplated ending it.

As the customs just described show, Powhatan women had a great deal of autonomy from men in the sexual realm as well as in the economic one. Their making few public appearances as political or religious leaders misled visiting English colonists into assuming that they were dominated by and considered far inferior to men. Yet, as I hope my description of their economic lives has shown, the women's hard and varied physical work was done with little input from men. And since it contributed many highly valued things that men's labors did not, women's economic autonomy was related to, if not a contributing cause of, their sexual freedom in marriage. Both argue strongly that on an everyday basis, women were considered—by men as well as by themselves—an esteemed and vital half of Powhatan society.

The "New England" Encounter: The Pequot War

BY KATHERINE A. GRANDJEAN

In the earliest English colonies, hunger and violence often traveled in lockstep. Across the fledgling empire, quite a lot of men and women felt "the sharpe pricke

Grandjean, Katherine A. "New World Tempests: Environment, Scarcity, and the Coming of the Pequot War." *William and Mary Quarterly* 68 (January 2011): 75–100.

of hunger" and, as George Percy explained in writing about early Virginia, quite a lot of "miseries ensewed." The "Crewell hunger," whose punishments "noe man [can] trewly descrybe butt he w[hi]ch hathe Tasted the bitternesse thereof," was a nasty character that pushed Englishmen to do nasty things. Colonists went hungry, it seems, not simply because they failed to cultivate food but because they suffered the wrath of the American environment. Early English colonization, historians are now learning, was frustrated by some profound environmental challenges. Though the Little Ice Age has long been a part of the colonial narrative, scholars are just now beginning to map shorter cold spells, droughts, and storms that wrought particular havoc on English planting. All these things had rather poisonous effects on English encounters with Indians. To a degree not yet grasped, food scarcity directly preceded much of the violence that characterized English colonization. In telling the story of English encounters with New World natives, historians have not fully accounted for the roles hunger and scarcity played in thwarting peaceful relationships. Across the colonies, in different times and places, the pattern repeated: competition for food sparked violence. This pattern even lurks in the background of some unexpected scenes of early American history. An illustrative case is the Pequot War.

In the 1630s an "ocean of Troubles" engulfed New England. It crested with a war waged by English colonists and their native allies on the Pequot Indians. The Pequot War—named for its eventual losers—lasted roughly from 1636 to 1638. War is, in fact, a lofty word for what occurred during these years; the conflict is better understood as a series of bloody raids and surprise attacks: traders killed, corn burned, and captives taken. Eventually, the violence escalated toward a wholesale assault on the Pequot people. The war reached its gruesome apex with the burning of Mystic Fort, where, in May 1637, hundreds of Pequots perished in a single morning. This attack was the bloodiest episode that the newly planted New England colonies had yet known. Despite a rich documentary record, historians have long had difficulty explaining the coming of this war. In unraveling the mystery of what sent the English colonies barreling into war with the Pequots, scholars have pointed to a complex array of factors. Some have stressed Puritan religious fervor, which predisposed colonists to read Indian actions as Satan's test of the very project of New England's city on a hill; others highlight economic competition between the English and the Pequots, who had long enjoyed control of the Long Island Sound trading market. Many have faulted a rapacious colonial appetite for Indian land. In recent years a rough consensus has formed around the notion that the war was driven largely by the belligerent English "determined to extend their authority" into the Pequots' domain. What most studies miss is that, among the factors pushing New England over the brink, a different sort of hunger was also at work.

The Pequot War arrived in a season of want. In the mid-1630s New England was experiencing widespread scarcity brought about largely by environmental distress. A great hurricane blasted through the colonies in 1635, destroying much of that year's harvest; harsh cold followed. Yet in the same moment, the colonies were also expanding wildly. Thousands were pouring into the northeast, in a great migration that stretched English provisions thin. Crops failed and cattle died just as waves of new immigrants put sudden stresses on New England's ability to provide for itself. Scholars tend to imagine early New England as a steady bastion of English strength, better fed and more orderly, for instance, than its chaotic stepsibling, the Chesapeake. But if one scratches beneath the bluster of contemporary accounts, the Pequot War somewhat complicates that image. The truth is that, in some regards, New England may not have been so markedly different. As in Virginia, combat over resources—in particular that humble staple, Indian corn—drove English colonists to blows with their native neighbors. Here, too, it pushed them to do unspeakably brutal things. Though it has been broadly overlooked, this is the Pequot War's proper context: a time of dearth and desperation for perhaps both the English and native people. No historian has yet examined the Pequot War in light of these environmental realities, but the glaring backdrop against which the war broke out was this struggle with hunger and scarcity.

Nothing can justify the war's injustices. No explanation, despite historians' compulsion to somehow explain the inexplicable, satisfies entirely. But, with scarcity and hunger in view, certain things about the war that have consistently nettled scholars become more comprehensible. The environmental context is critical to understanding why English colonists behaved as they did, eventually precipitating war with the Pequots....

The hunger bearing down on New England might not have spiraled into war had it not been for John Oldham's murder. In July 1636, a thick heat hovering over Long Island Sound, the English trader's corpse was discovered entangled in the netting of his pinnace, afloat off Block Island.... When the boat was discovered, Indians were still aboard, apparently cutting off his hands and feet....

Though Oldham's death became the most notorious incident, it was not the first. It recalled other attacks, including one that had happened two years earlier, in 1634. That summer another English trader—Captain John Stone—had been slain, apparently by Pequot tributaries....

Why a few such episodes escalated into Indian war remains one of the riddles of early American history. If the English reaction to Stone's and Oldham's deaths was extreme, it seems difficult to believe that it had anything to do with the particular people killed. Stone had been something of a ne'er-do-well, a "freebooter" and a rascal. Oldham, too, had a colorful past. Though he had lately become somewhat respected in elite circles, he had gained a reputation as a troublemaker years earlier in Plymouth. That these men were hardly eminent citizens has left some historians doubtful that English leaders would provoke a war simply to avenge their deaths. It is easier to imagine that Englishmen conveniently seized on these "relatively minor incidents" to justify attacking one of the more formidable native groups nearby. The Pequots were indeed powerful. Situated along the northern shore of Long Island Sound, mostly to the east of the Pequot (later Thames) River, they had recently enjoyed a period of great power coinciding with the advent of native-European trade. The waters that eventually claimed Oldham's body lay at the nexus of complex trading spheres, where Dutch, English, and native interests overlapped. Though they had recently fallen out with Dutch traders, the Pequots largely dictated trade terms in the region. Living along a coast whose shores brimmed with quahog shells, they enjoyed a great measure of control over the making and trading of wampum the white and purple beads so prized by Dutch and Indian traders. The Pequots' relative power in this trading world undoubtedly made them special targets for English economic jealousy. It seems possible, then, that the English-driven esca-lation of violence was attributable to plainly economic motives, a bold and trans-parent grab at Pequot wealth and territory. Certainly the Pequot War was, in some respects, an "economic contest." But to read the war's origins as so much high-level jousting over trade overlooks the more fundamentally troubling les-sons that its prelude held for the English.

The overblown English reaction to these traders' deaths becomes far less surprising when one reconstructs the role such men played in knitting together the English northeast, especially in light of the scarcity of circulating provisions. Consider the region's social geography. Early New England was little more than a spotty patchwork of settlements. In the late 1630s, it was perhaps at its spottiest. The English settlements had just begun to expand: in a few short, recent years, the near-bursting Massachusetts Bay had spun off several new plantations, none particularly nearby. Connecticut was settled in mid-1635, not long before the great hurricane; Providence and Springfield, in 1636. By water these places were separated by long, arduous boat trips; by land, lengthy and unfamiliar woodland stretches. Between English settlements lay huge pockets of uncertain-ties, deterring all but the most intrepid travelers. Even dauntless Englishmen had only a tenuous command of the great, yawning spaces between colonies. In 1648 Roger Williams hinted at how the English felt about this geography when he described his fellow colonists as "poore grashoppers, hopping and skipping from branch to twig in [a] vale of teares." Herein lay the fundamental importance of early New England's watermen: in the 1630s, traders such as Oldham were among New England's few grasshoppers. In a time when provisions were precar-iously short, Oldham was one of the only traders transporting goods to the northeast's scattered English settlements.

Much about the communications landscape in the seventeenth century remains murky, but English letters permit something of a reconstruction. They make plain that in the 1630s communications were fragile and waterborne and rested on the backs of just a few seamen. We can glimpse the role that men such as Oldham played in connecting the English colonies in Pequot War–era corre-spondence. Those carrying letters between Massachusetts and Connecticut, for instance, were a select few English shipmasters and traders: Gallop, John Hodges, Oldham, John Throckmorton, and Joseph Tilly. Bostonian John Winthrop relied on these important figures to send messages to his son, John Winthrop Jr., isolated in the fort at the mouth of the Connecticut River, and his letters reflect that the exchange was almost wholly water-bound. Ships and seamen sail through Winthrop's script, looping back and forth along the coast: "Sonne, I wrote vnto you by the Rebecka," he noted, before taking another opportunity to send "by mr. Oldhams Pinace." The "Blessing," the "Wrenne," the "Bacheler" all came and went. All these voyages were not easy. Even under the best of circumstances, navigating New England's coastal geography could be tricky. Early on, travel and communications between Connecticut and Massachusetts Bay proved nettlesome, as frequent shipwrecks and other calamities vexed intercolonial carriers. Weather took its toll on boats, much as it did on crops and cattle. In October 1635 two shallops "goeinge laden with goodes to Conectec[o]t" were dashed against Brown's Island; all aboard drowned. The following month a pinnace returning from Connecticut to the Massachusetts Bay was "cast awaye in manemett Baye." Its crew wandered for ten lonely days through "extreame Colde, & deepe snowe." In October 1637 another furious storm claimed one more coasting vessel. "The Wren, a small pinnace, coming from Connecticut," Winthrop recorded, "was taken in a N.E. storm, and ... wrecked." Her crew survived, if only to see pieces of the pinnace pulled out to sea. Land travel was little better. It was also far less common. Though traces of those traveling the one hundred miles between Massachusetts Bay and Connecticut are meager, for these years, it is clear that few did. Not until 1633 is there a record of any Englishman attempting that trek, and then it was the infamous Oldham.

The wheel of New England's economy turned on these men, but the colonies depended on them in more basic ways. Even in bountiful times, coastal traders were often the ones to procure and supply food. Newer settlements often looked to add to their own meager harvests by trading with more established English towns or with Indians. Men such as Oldham, therefore, had a special role to play in transporting precious goods to places in need. Plymouth and Massachusetts had relied on purchases of Indian corn, the latter using Oldham as an intermediary. As a trader he had brokered for corn when necessary from Indian neighbors. On at least one occasion, he had helped feed Massachusetts Bay, where, in 1634, the *Rebecka* unloaded "500: bz. of Corne given to mr Io: Oldham" by the Narragansetts. And after his death, the Connecticut government's first concern was with Oldham's stock of corn. Even as they dealt with escalating tensions with the Pequots, magistrates carefully appointed men to "looke to & prserue the Corne of Mr. Olda & ... bringe an Accompt the next Cort what quantitie there is of it." Another trader's downfall is perhaps more revealing than Oldham's. Though less remembered, Hammond's fate also hints at traders' crucial role, especially in times of crisis. Only a month before Oldham was found, Hammond, on his way to Virginia, had shipwrecked in the sound. He and a companion had "escaped on shore" but were subsequently "killed by the Indians." What made Hammond's fate so grievous was that it scuttled a crucial voyage. when he died the coaster had been on his way to Virginia—his boat loaded with everything he could "make and borrowe"—to trade for "Corne." He had been engaged in an important journey seeking food for the hungry northern English. Historians rarely, if ever, cast Hammond's death as a factor in the coming of the Pequot War, yet Massachusetts Bay considered it a serious grievance against the Pequots. With English hunger restored to view, the fearful meaning of these deaths becomes easier to grasp. These men were the ones who brought letters, news, provisions, and food. The lesson English observers surely drew, in watching such events unfold, was this one: because the violence threatened those who carried goods between English colonies, it threatened all.

Some were more vulnerable than others, especially the two hundred or so colonists huddled along the Connecticut River. These souls were at pains to communicate with other English, from whom they were separated by a chancy overland trek or a week-long boat trip. The lonely predicament of Connecticut settlements goes far in explaining how the murders of a few traders—even traders with arguably sordid pasts—could have triggered such a tremendous overreaction. Begun barely a year before Oldham's death, the Connecticut plantations were in a precarious position in 1636. They had endured the ferocious weather and hunger pangs afflicting most of New England, though not well. Conditions at Saybrook, downriver from the Connecticut plantations, were no better. Servants in the fort lodged a written complaint that they were insufficiently clothed and fed. Bread, breakfast, and beer had all been "taken away," they protested, leaving them nothing to eat but "peass porig." The hunger extended beyond the fort's lower ranks. When a shipmaster failed to bring him corn in May 1636, John Winthrop Jr. pleaded to his father in writing to be "supplied by the first shipping that arrive with any store of provisions." He complained, "I see noe meanes to be supplied heere." Only two months later, Oldham was discovered dead. And here was the problem: scarcity was amplified by even small hiccups in English shipping. These fledgling villages relied on ties to markets in Massachusetts Bay for survival. Particularly for Connecticut colonists, Oldham's loss made the possibility of being cut off from other Englishmen real. Oldham's killing was offensive not merely because it was at the hands of Indians; it also literally robbed grain from English colonists' mouths.

One wonders whether robbing food from colonists was precisely the point. Though the evidence will likely never be conclusive, the timing and context of Oldham's death are telling: he died in July, just about the time when local native groups would have been readying themselves for the green corn feasts, an annual celebration of immature summer corn. It was also a moment in which the English colonies were experiencing the height of scarcity. Those circumstances raise the possibility that Oldham had tried to bully some Block Islanders into sparing some corn, thus inviting retaliation, or even that they had looked to remedy their own hardships with a rash grab at Oldham's goods. Plunder, in some sense, was a factor: when Oldham's pinnace was discovered, a canoe "full of Indians and goodes" was hastily departing. But even if the tug-of-war over food had little to do with Oldham's fate, it had everything to do with what followed, not least because the episode presented new reasons and opportunities for the hungry English to seize food from natives. In what followed Oldham's downfall, it became clear just how desperate a few lonely men in Connecticut were to lay their hands on a bit of Indian corn.

CORN WAS CENTRAL to waging the Pequot War. Some English clamored for Indian corn, whereas others burned and destroyed it with abandon. Corn was everywhere stolen, fired, or dug up. In the records surrounding the war, English interest in corn is palpable. War narratives show almost a bald obsession with it. To witness Englishmen razing Indian cornfields may not seem especially notable; it was a favorite strategy for crippling native enemies throughout early American history. But, once one comprehends the environmental difficulties that had plagued New England in these years, the records that capture the Pequot War's unfolding assume a somewhat different countenance. The recurrent mentions of corn that are threaded into these tales begin to appear in telling relief. When the English and their Mohegan and Narragansett allies finally crushed the Pequots in 1637, it is worth pausing to remember that among the principal spoils they shared was corn taken from the Pequots. Corn may not have been merely coincidental to the fighting of the Pequot War. Eagerness for provisions pushed some English into a desperate and belligerent stance; it led them to make hasty decisions that contributed to the coming of the war.

That corn should take center stage in the march toward war is perhaps unsurprising; it was a prized commodity both among the English and Indians. Corn was the one food on which both peoples depended. In early modern England, the word "corn" would have referred to virtually any grain; by "corn," what New Englanders truly meant was Indian corn, or maize, which was not a part of the English diet prior to colonization but was embraced almost instantly by English colonists. Indian corn was hearty and easy to grow, whereas English grains required more coaxing and labor before they would thrive. When efforts to plant wheat and other traditional English crops faltered, colonists converted quickly, and maize soon became a staple food for people and livestock. Corn consumption fueled the settlement of English colonies. Maize was also fundamental to native culture. Indians ate corn in many ways: dried, ground, boiled, baked into bread, or "whole like beans, eating three or four corns with a mouthful of fish or flesh," as William Wood reported in 1633. On hunts, while traveling, or during war, Indian men ate *nókehick*, parched corn mixed with water for a quick and easy meal. The staple was also celebrated in a variety of rituals and ceremonies, including the green corn feasts that many native groups staged around the mid- to late-summer growth of immature, new corn. Corn was such a precious resource in early New England that it sometimes functioned as a kind of currency; colonists were occasionally allowed to pay taxes in bushels of corn, and native and English alike used it to pay off debts.

The English military reaction to John Oldham's death revolved around Indian corn. Early actions taken against the Block Islanders and the Pequots— the assaults that finally provoked full-scale warfare—essentially amounted to corn raids. To avenge Oldham's death, in August 1636 Massachusetts dispatched a force of men under John Endecott to Block Island to raid and punish its inhabitants, who were Oldham's reputed killers. Endecott's men, to their disappointment, met with few Indians on the island. What they found were "great heaps of pleasant corn ready shelled," which, only after realizing they were "not able to bring it away," they burned. Failing to find many people, Endecott's men took out their frustrations on the Block Islanders' crops. The wanton destruction they unleashed on the island was extensive; John Underhill, a party to the expedition, remembered spending nearly two days pillaging the island. When they discovered a village "where was much corn," the soldiers took out their weapons and cut it all down, as if doing battle with the stiff, defenseless stalks. If English colonists did not have enough to eat, the soldiers ensured that neither would the island's Indians.

Not all Englishmen were ready to engage in such rampant waste, no matter how fervently they resented the great heaps of corn the Indians possessed. If Massachusetts men had the luxury of punishing Block Island by devastating its food supply, those in Connecticut did not. Unsurprisingly, given their need for provisions, some in Connecticut disagreed with Endecott's tactics. Perhaps revealing how ill fed colonists in Connecticut were versus those in Massachusetts, military men differed over how to handle Indian corn stores. Bay militiamen were rather quick with flame, whereas those garrisoned at Fort Saybrook hoped to salvage the corn for themselves. The man in charge at Saybrook, Lion Gardiner, was not pleased with Massachusetts Bay's reckless instigation of Indian war. Saybrook was "famished" even in peace, he warned, and war would be disastrous, sure to divorce Saybrook from access to its meager corn-fields. Thus, when he heard that Endecott's force also planned to visit Pequot territory and to demand answer for John Stone's still-unresolved killing, Gardiner—at least according to his own claims—objected strenuously.

But it was Gardiner's own empty belly that helped ignite the Pequot War. The best evidence that English desire for corn tipped the colonies toward war comes from his pen. Gardiner had been concerned about the specter of hunger well before the war. Preparing to build Fort Saybrook in 1636, he had warned Massachusetts magistrates of the danger in attending to fortifications before provisions. "I said it was Capt. Hunger that threatened them most," Gardiner later wrote. When it was clear that his protests against Endecott's expedition would do nothing, he decided to be pragmatic. Gardiner saw in the escalating tensions with the Pequots an opportunity to secure some much-needed sustenance. He thought of the Pequots' piles of corn, "gathered" and "ready to put into their barns," and suggested the English soldiers raid the harvested grain. "Sirs, Seeing you will go," he begged Endecott's men, "I pray you, if you don't load your Barks with Pequits, load them with corn, for … both you and we have need of it." Gardiner's haste to procure Pequot corn even extended to supplying vessels and bags in which to carry it ("I will send my shallop … to go with you, [and] you may load your barks with corn," he offered. "But they said they had no bags to load them with, then said I, here is three dozen of new bags, you shall have thirty of them, and my shallop to carry them"). Gardiner even suggested an elaborate system for guarding the corn and carrying it to the waterside.

It was the resulting rampage at Pequot that ultimately provoked war. Even if they had not endured quite the same hardships, Pequot men and women were surely in no mood to share. Imagine their horror when English soldiers arrived in August 1636 and began plundering. When Endecott's men disembarked at Pequot after raiding Block Island, they threatened to "march through the country, and spoil your corn" if given no explanation for Stone's murder. Satisfaction eluding them (a short, perhaps perfunctory, parley went nowhere), Endecott's soldiers went about laying waste to Pequot much as they had to Block Island. When they spied Pequots hurriedly burying corn and other items, the English made it their mission to dig up even these hidden stores. Gardiner's men, in the meantime, rushed to scoop as much corn as possible into their sacks (though they were attacked as they scurried back to their boats). Burned, trampled, or stolen, much corn was destroyed. Corn raiding was not the sole offense committed by the English, nor was it the only explanation for Pequot anger. But the decision to plunder ruthlessly helped set New England on the course to war with the Pequots. The Indians could not sit idly by as Gardiner's henchmen snatched grain by the sackful. That they understood Gardiner's men to be key offenders during the raid is clear from their immediate reaction. Pequot vengeance came to Fort Saybrook in the form of a siege: supplies were cut off as the Indians harassed the fort and pilfered its livestock. They also retaliated in kind for what Gardiner's men had done: they attacked Saybrook's pitiable cornfield.

Unfortunately for the English, stealing Indian corn solved very little. After the raids on Block Island and Pequot, Gardiner's men had returned to Fort Saybrook with a "pretty quantity of corn." ("I was glad of the corn," Gardiner remembered.) But whatever relief Gardiner felt that August was short lived. As the calendar turned again toward winter, cattle and corn were once more costly and scarce. "Cattle were grown to high rates;—[and] Corn was now at 5s. the bushel," John Winthrop recorded before adding, "Things went not well at Connecticut. Their cattle did, many of them, cast their young, as they had done the year before." By November Saybrook was once again desperate for "victualls." When a ketch passed by, carrying corn from the nearby Narragansetts, Gardiner hurriedly commandeered some of its booty. "I haue tacken one hondard buchils of it," he explained, "becaus I do not know whethar we shall haue anie relief or not." Connecticut's hunger problem still had not abated when Pequot retaliation reached the river towns in an attack on Wethersfield in April 1637. Even as Connecticut soldiers prepared to march on Pequot in response, John Mason felt the gnawing in his empty stomach. "Our Commons were very short," he wrote, "there being a general scarcity throughout the Colony of all sorts of Provision." As they boarded the boat for Pequot, the Reverend Thomas Hooker said a few words to the soldiers. Hooker prayed that the Pequots *should be Bread for us*. And thus when the Lord turned the Captivity of his People, and turned the Wheel upon their Enemies ... then was our Mouth filled with Laughter, and our Tongues with Singing."

No surviving account of the war casts the conflict as having been fought for corn. Nowhere, in ink, did any Englishman admit any such thing. But given the scarcity of provisions vexing New England, raiding native corn as well as punishing Indians was clearly all too tempting to English leaders as well as ordinary souls in 1636. Perhaps Oldham's death was, after all, merely an excuse for what terrors came later. Yet in the matrix of causality, in the calculus that unfolded in English minds, hunger certainly played a role. Never underestimate the yearning, particularly on the part of Connecticut colonists, for food. Reading English provocation of the war as having simply been about trade, then, misses some of the desperation—and contingency—that lay behind colonists' belligerence. It misses the privation that pushed Gardiner's hand in 1636. The Pequot War thus illuminates a pattern of events that extends far beyond New England. This story unfurled itself countless times in many other dark corners of the English Empire. When in 1625 George Percy wrote his

"Trewe Relacyon" of Jamestown's now-famous Starving Time, he prefaced it with a feeble reminder that "if we Trewly Consider the diversety of miseries mutenies and famishmentts w[hi]ch have attended upon discoveries and plantacyons in theis our moderne Tymes, we shall nott fynde our plantacyon in Virginia to have Suffered aloane." He may have been more right than historians have yet understood.

The hardships New England experienced in the 1630s were not unique. They paled next to the horrors endured by English colonists in other places and times. Early Virginia, Roanoke, and even Plymouth, during its infancy years earlier, all weathered much more severe periods of deprivation, ordeals that resulted in innumerable deaths and famously inspired Englishmen to procure corn from Indians by whatever means necessary....

The pattern extends beyond the English colonies. During Kieft's War, the first Indian war weathered by New Netherland, "desire for food and other plunder" contributed to "Dutch hostility to the Indians around New Amsterdam." Kieft's War may or may not have had a climatic dimension (though, perhaps not coincidentally, it followed almost immediately on the heels of the Pequot War). But New Spain's most famous Indian rebellion clearly did. The 1680 Pueblo Revolt was preceded by years of drought, paltry harvests, and famine. When hungry Apaches and Navajos "began attacking the kingdom's settlements ... and carrying off whatever food they found," Puebloans were thus easily inspired to vent years of bitterness toward the Spanish in a devastatingly successful uprising. Though historians have studied all these episodes in some depth, they have rarely considered them collectively. Yet together they suggest a pattern of interaction that cut across colonies and even empires. If European powers dealt differently with Indians, attention to the backdrop of the early American environment nonetheless suggests some commonalities. The equation, in fact, seems tragically simple: the contest for food resources that was triggered by European colonization and exacerbated by environmental stressors all too frequently set encounters off on the wrong foot. Oddly, perhaps because scholars have not fully noted the Pequot War's context of environmental and demographic distress, they have not read it as a similar story. But in many ways, it was.

To those living in New England in the 1630s, the parallel would not have been nearly so hidden. New Englanders had the benefit of knowing what had happened in some of those other places. They knew what calamities Virginians had undergone, which raises nagging questions: why did they not know better? Did New Englanders not know what might issue from a too-hasty decision to steal, burn, or otherwise destroy Indian corn? They did, but perhaps Virginia's example was not so much a deterrent as an accelerant. Perhaps northern colonists were all too eager to escape the fates of their southern compatriots. At least one narrative of the Pequot War (though written by one whose role in the war is unclear) hinted that the knowledge of what had happened in Virginia may have prompted New England settlers to act with greater severity toward the Pequots. Virginia's colonists had done too much to placate the Indians, went this lesson, and had thus invited destruction: "Too much lenity of the English towards the Virginian salvages," Philip Vincent wrote, "had like to have been the destruction of the whole plantation." New Englanders, by contrast, had "assured [themselves] of their peace, by killing the barbarians, better than our English Virginians were by being killed by them. The harsh culmination of the Pequot War turned Virginia's story on its head. Virginia's Indian problems had peaked with the 1622 attack in which hundreds of English died in a single day; the Pequot War neatly reversed this outcome. It was a similar story with the opposite end: victory came, instead, with an English assault that claimed hundreds of Pequot lives.

In May 1637 the war reached its climax in a grisly spectacle of fire and death. At dawn on May 26, 1637, English soldiers surprised the Pequots slumbering at Mystic Fort. John Mason's forces—fresh from praying that the Pequots might be "bread for us"—had with them "little refreshment"; some on the march had fainted and were given sips of liquor to revive them. The plan, Mason later wrote, had been to kill the Pequots and then raid their supplies. "We had formerly concluded to destroy them by the Sword and save the Plunder," he remembered. But when it became clear that this tactic would not work, Mason arrived at a new plan: "We must Burn them." He acted quickly. Mohegan and Narragansett allies to the English formed a loop around the fort, preventing escape, as Mason and other English soldiers took burning wood from within the Pequots' own wigwams and set fire to all inside. Hundreds of Pequots burned alive. The enormity of this event is almost blinding. So numerous were the deaths that morning that John Underhill, present at the burning, later empathized with the English militiamen who were unaccustomed to seeing such carnage. "Great and doleful was the bloody sight," he wrote, "to the view of young soldiers that never had been in war, to see so many souls lie gasping on the ground." Trying to grasp the whole of the war's story while looking backward through the Fort Mystic massacre is not unlike gazing downward, through water, at the bottom of a pond: much is distorted. After this one morning, the Pequots were all but broken. Captivity, slavery, and death followed for most that had survived. The gravity of English actions on May 26 thus makes it difficult to avoid viewing the Pequot War as a great and brutal display of English strength. It was not. What happened in the war was as much the result of English desperation.

As the war drew to a close in 1637, some English looked eagerly toward a brighter, less hungry future. In his account of the conflict, Vincent grafted an impossibly happy ending onto the narrative, complete with corn aplenty. "Corn and cattle are wonderfully increased," he reported buoyantly, so much so that colonists sometimes even had enough "to spare to new comers." Lush fields of planted grain now greeted these new arrivals, gushed Vincent: indeed they "never saw such a field of four hundred acres of all sorts of English grain, as they saw at Winter-towne." His descriptions may not have been entirely fanciful. There was some relief: in July 1637 the English shared Pequot corn stores with their Narragansett allies. And though 1638 greeted New Englanders with a notably severe winter and a spring so cold that the corn seed "rotted in the ground" (not to mention an April snowstorm featuring "flakes as great as shillings"), John Winthrop reported that the year's harvest happily yielded "corn beyond expectation" in Massachusetts. Things were not quite as hopeful in Connecticut. Dearth struck again in 1638, forcing colonists to beg corn from the Pocumtucks to their north. It is probably not a coincidence, furthermore, that harvest-time found Mason making yet another visit to Pequot, ostensibly to punish the Pequots who had begun to resettle there. In effect it was another corn raid: the Connecticut militia planned to "supplant them, by burning their Wigwams, and *bringing away their Corn*." While there the English spent the day filling their bark with corn, "whereof there was Plenty, it being their time of Harvest." At last, and once more at Pequots' expense, Connecticut filled its rumbling belly. Its colonists ate well that year.

◈ FURTHER READING

Axtell, James. *The Indians' New South: Cultural Change in the Colonial Southeast* (1997).

Bragdon, Kathleen J. *Native People of Southern New England, 1500–1650* (1996).

————. *Native People of Southern New England, 1650–1775* (2009).

Cave, Alfred A. *The Pequot War* (1996).

Cronon, William. *Changes in the Land: Indians, Colonists, and the Ecology of New England* (1983).

Drake, James D. *King Philip's War: Civil War in New England, 1675–1676* (1999).

Fur, Gunlög. *A Nation of Women: Gender and Colonial Encounters Among the Delaware Indians* (2009).

Gallay, Alan. *The Indian Slave Trade: The Rise of the English Empire in the American South, 1670–1717* (2002).

————, ed. *Indian Slavery in Colonial America* (2009).

Galloway, Patricia. *Choctaw Genesis, 1500–1700* (1996).

Gleach, Frederic. *Powhatan's World and Colonial Virginia: A Conflict of Cultures* (1997).

Hauptman, Laurence M., and James D. Wherry, eds. *The Pequots in Southern New England: The Fall and Rise of an American Indian Nation* (1990).

Hudson, Charles M., and Carmen Chaves Tesser, eds. *The Forgotten Centuries: Indians and Europeans in the American South, 1521–1704* (1994).

Jennings, Francis. *The Invasion of America: Indians, Colonialism, and the Cant of Conquest* (1976).

Katz, Steven T. "The Pequot War Reconsidered." *New England Quarterly* 64 (June 1991): 206–24.

Kelton, Paul. *Epidemics and Enslavement: Biological Catastrophe in the Native Southeast, 1492–1715* (2007).

Kupperman, Karen Ordahl. *Indians and English: Facing Off in Early America* (2000).

————. *The Jamestown Project* (2007).

Lepore, Jill. *The Name of War: King Philip's War and the Origins of American Identity* (1998).

Mandell, Daniel R. *King Philip's War: Colonial Expansion, Native Resistance, and the End of Indian Sovereignty* (2010).

Martin, Joel W. *Sacred Revolt: The Muskogees' Struggle for a New World* (1991).

Merrell, James. *The Indians' New World: Catawbas and Their Neighbors from European Contact Through the Era of Removal* (1989).

Oberg, Michael Leroy. *Uncas: First of the Mohegans* (2003).

Plane, Ann Marie. *Colonial Intimacies: Indian Marriage in Early New England* (2000).

Pulsipher, Jenny Hale. *Subjects unto the Same King: Indians, English, and the Contest for Authority in Colonial New England* (2005).

Richter, Daniel K. *Before the Revolution: America's Ancient Pasts* (2011).

Rountree, Helen C. *Pocahontas, Powhatan, Opechancanough: Three Indian Lives Changed by Jamestown* (2005).

————. *Pocahontas's People: The Powhatan Indians of Virginia Through Four Centuries* (1990).

————. *The Powhatan Indians of Virginia: Their Traditional Culture* (1989).

Salisbury, Neal. *Manitou and Providence: Indians, Europeans, and the Making of New England, 1500–1643* (1982).

Szasz, Margaret Connell. *Indian Education in the American Colonies, 1607–1783* (1988).

Townsend, Camilla. *Pocahontas and the Powhatan Dilemma* (2004).

Vaughan, Alden T. *New England Frontier: Puritans and Indians, 1620–1675* (1995).

CHAPTER 6

◈

War and Survival, 1700–1763

Wars between Indians and the English closed out the seventeenth century along the Atlantic Coast, and wars would continue to dominate Native experiences further inland—into and beyond the Appalachians—in the following century. But, as wrenching and as devastating as such conflicts were, they do not fully describe Indigenous peoples' existence east of the Mississippi in the eighteenth century. People went on living during and in between wars. And, even when the military defeats were particularly decisive—as they had been in 1676 with Bacon's Rebellion and King Philip's War, and as they would be again with the end of the Seven Years' War in 1763—Indian communities somehow managed to survive and carry on. As historian Daniel Mandell has said, even as Anglo-Americans pushed ever westward, Native American societies endured "behind the frontier." Accordingly, this chapter presents documents and essays that seek to give the subject of war its proper due, but balances them with readings that simultaneously acknowledge the significance of Native survival, a persistence that continues into the present day. Both themes—war and survival—contain underlying complexities. Was war always a simple matter of a single Indian entity fighting a single European entity? Did survival mean keeping your tribe's culture and community perfectly intact, preserving it in a pure precontact form?

◈ DOCUMENTS

The first three documents in this chapter address the theme of war in eastern North America, while the latter four reveal the simultaneous reality of survival. Document 1 concerns the Seven Years' War, waged in North America from 1756 to 1763. The Seven Years' War is also known as the French and Indian War, and, indeed, it pitted the French and their Native allies on one side, and the British and their Indian allies on the other. In the document, a Moravian ambassador for Pennsylvania records the perspectives of Lenapes (referred to by the English as "Delawares") with regard to the conflict and their position in it. The Seven Years' War was only the latest in a series of wars, dating back to the 1600s, fought in North America between the British and the French. It stands out, however, in its decisiveness. The British won, and their victory was great enough that they were able to force France to relinquish virtually all of its North American land claims. While this was cause for celebration for the British—and for their colonists—and an unfortunate defeat for the French, it produced profound chaos and insecurity for Indian tribes between the Appalachians and the Mississippi. With no French to enlist as occasional allies to stem the tide of British settlement into their territories or to otherwise stave off the imposition of British power, many Indian peoples quickly found themselves in a particularly desperate situation. At the war's official conclusion in 1763, Native peoples wondered what to do. Some believed their only hope lay in adjusting to the new order of things, but others believed that the times called for further armed retaliation. Document 2, taken from a French soldier's journal, conveys the words of a main advocate of the latter path, an Ottawa man named Pontiac. The soldier, probably a man named Robert Navarre, begins by translating a speech given by Neolin (who he also refers to as "The Wolf"), and then relates a speech from Pontiac himself. Document 3 is an excerpt from the journal of William Trent, a militia captain at Fort Pitt in western Pennsylvania. Native warriors laid siege to the fort in the late Spring and Summer of 1763, until, on June 24, 1763, two Indian leaders were allowed into the fort to speak. As Trent writes it, the British then attempted to employ a particularly chilling method of continuing the war against the Indians. Although historians debate the actual extent and impact of that method, that it was even considered is an indication of the virulence of the hatred that existed among some in these times.

As wars raged just to their west, Indians east of the Appalachians continued their existence "behind the frontier." To be sure, they were not unaffected by the wars; many of the men of these tribes were actually called into service by the British. But, they also dealt with other aspects of life: economics, politics, and religion, for example. Still, was Indian survival here only physical, or was it cultural as well? Were Indians merely "assimilating," with their cultures on the way toward eventual disappearance? The final four documents offer some subtle clues. In Document 4, a Wampanoag woman named Naomai Omaush issues her last will and testament in 1749. While it contains Christian terms and ideas, it was originally written in the Massachusett dialect of the Algonquian language. Some of those original Algonquin terms are preserved in this translation. Document 5 is also from the Wampanoags, in this case the Mashpee band, and records a petition they made to the government of the Massachusetts colony in 1752. In Document 6, an English missionary named Joseph Fish tells of his efforts to Christianize the Narragansett Indians, who resided primarily in Rhode Island. How much success did he seem to feel he was having? In the seventh and final document, a Mohegan man named Samson Occom gives an account of his life in the mid-1700s. In much of his writing, Occom defends Indian rights and Indian culture. The passage presented here is but a small snapshot of Occom's life and ideas at a particular time, but it provides hints about the degree of cultural continuity versus cultural change among his Mohegan people in the eighteenth century.

1. Delaware Indians Discuss the French and Indian War, 1758

The land is ours, and not theirs; therefore, we say, if you will be at peace with us, we will send the *French* home. It is you that have begun the war, and it is necessary that you hold fast, and be not discouraged, in the work of peace. We love you more than you love us; for when we take any prisoners from you, we treat them as our own children. We are poor, and yet we clothe them as well as we can, though you see our children are as naked as at the first. By this you may see that our hearts are better than yours. It is plain that you white people are the cause of this war; why do not you and the *French* fight in the old country, and on the sea? Why do you come to fight on our land? This makes every body believe, you want to take the land from us by force, and settle it....

Brother, your heart is good, you speak always sincerely; but we know there are always a great number of people that want to get rich; they never have enough; look, we do not want to be rich, and take away that which others have. God has given you the tame creatures; we do not want to take them from you. God has given to us the deer, and other wild creatures, which we must feed on; and we rejoice in that which springs out of the ground, and thank God for it. Look now, my brother, the white people think we have no brains in our heads; but that they are great and big, and that makes them make war with us: we are but a little handful to what you are; but remember, when you look for a wild turkey you cannot always find it, it is so little it hides itself under the bushes: and when you hunt for a rattle-snake, you cannot find it; and perhaps it will bite you before you see it. However, since you are so great and big, and we so little, do you use your greatness and strength in compleating this work of peace. This is the [first] time that we saw or heard of you, since the war begun, and we have great reason to think about it, since such a great body of you comes into our lands. It is told us, that you and the *French* contrived the war, to waste the *Indians* between you; and that you and the *French* intended to divide the land between you: this was told us by the chief of the *Indian* traders; and they said further, brothers, this is the last time we shall come among you; for the *French* and the *English* intend to kill all the *Indians*, and then divide the land among themselves....

Brother, I suppose you know something about it; or has the Governor stopped your mouth, that you cannot tell us?

2. Neolin (Delaware) and Pontiac (Ottawa) Urge Tribes to Fight the British, 1763

After the Indian [Neolin] was seated the Lord said to him: "I am the Master of Life, and since I know what thou desirest to know, and to whom thou wishest to speak, listen well to what I am going to say to thee and to all the Indians:

Reuben G. Thwaites, ed., *Early Western Travels* (Cleveland: Arthur H. Clark, 1904), 1: 214–16.

M. Agnes Burton, ed., *Journal of Pontiac's Conspiracy, 1763* (Detroit: Published by Clarence Monroe Burton under the auspices of the Michgan Society of the Colonial Wars, 1912). As excerpted in Pekka Hamalainen and Benjamin H. Johnson, eds., *Major Problems in the History of North American Borderlands* (Boston: Wadsworth, 2012), 174–176.

"I am He who hath created the heavens and the earth, the trees, lakes, rivers, all men, and all that thou seest and hast seen upon the earth. Because I love you, ye must do what I say and love, and not do what I hate. I do not love that ye should drink to the point of madness, as ye do; and I do not like that ye should fight one another. Ye take two wives, or run after the wives of others; ye do not well, and I hate that. Ye ought to have but one wife, and keep her till death. When ye wish to go to war, ye conjure and resort to the medicine dance, believing that ye speak to me; ye are mistaken,—it is to Manitou that ye speak, an evil spirit who prompts you to nothing but wrong, and who listens to you out of ignorance of me.

"This land where ye dwell I have made for you and not for others. Whence comes it that ye permit the Whites upon your lands? Can ye not live without them? I know that those whom ye call the children of your Great Father supply your needs, but if ye were not evil, as ye are, ye could surely do without them. Ye could live as ye did live before knowing them,—before those whom ye call your brothers had come upon your lands. Did ye not live by the bow and arrow? Ye had no need of gun or powder, or anything else, and nevertheless ye caught animals to live upon and to dress yourselves with their skins. But when I saw that ye were given up to evil, I led the wild animals to the depths of the forests so that ye had to depend upon your brothers to feed and shelter you. Ye have only to become good again and do what I wish, and I will send back the animals for your food. I do not forbid you to permit among you the children of your Father; I love them. They know me and pray to me, and I supply their wants and all they give you. But as to those who come to trouble your lands,—drive them out, make war upon them. I do not love them at all; they know me not, and are my enemies, and the enemies of your brothers. Send them back to the lands which I have created for them and let them stay there. Here is a prayer which I give thee in writing to learn by heart and to teach to the Indians and their children."

The Wolf [Neolin] replied that he did not know how to read. He was told that when he should have returned to earth he would have only to give the prayer to the chief of his village who would read it and teach him and all the Indians to know it by heart; and he must say it night and morning without fail, and do what he has just been told to do; and he was to tell all the Indians for and in the name of the Master of Life:

"Do not drink more than once, or at most twice in a day; have only one wife and do not run after the wives of others nor after the girls; do not fight among yourselves; do not 'make medicine,' but pray, because in 'making medicine' one talks with the evil spirit; drive off your lands those dogs clothed in red who will do you nothing but harm. And when ye shall have need of anything address yourselves to me; and as to your brothers, I shall give to you as to them; do not sell to your brothers what I have put on earth for food. In short, become good and ye shall receive your needs. When ye meet one another exchange greeting and proffer the left hand which is nearest the heart.

"In all things I command thee to repeat every morning and night the prayer which I have given thee."

The Wolf promised to do faithfully what the Master of Life told him, and that he would recommend it well to the Indians, and that the Master of Life would be pleased with them. Then the same man who had led him by the hand came to get him and conducted him to the foot of the mountain where he told him to take his outfit again and return to his village. The Wolf did this, and upon his arrival the members of his tribe and village were greatly surprised, for they did not know what had become of him, and they asked where he had been. As he was enjoined not to speak to anybody before he had talked with the chief of his village, he made a sign with his hand that he had come from on high. Upon entering the village he went straight to the cabin of the chief to whom he gave what had been given to him,—namely, the prayer and the law which the Master of Life had given him.

This adventure was soon noised about among the people of the whole village who came to hear the message of the Master of Life, and then went to carry it to the neighboring villages. The members of these villages came to see the pretended traveler, and the news was spread from village to village and finally reached Pontiac. He believed all this, as we believe an article of faith, and instilled it into the minds of all those in his council. They listened to him as to an oracle, and told him that he had only to speak and they were all ready to do what he demanded of them.

Pontiac ... sent runners the following day, Monday, the 2nd of May, to each of the Huron and Pottawattamy villages to discover the real feeling of each of these two nations, for he feared to be crossed in his plans. These emissaries had orders to notify these nations for him that Thursday, the 5th of May, at mid-day, a grand council would be held in the Pottawattamy village which was situated between two and three miles below the Fort toward the southwest, and that the three nations should meet there and that no woman should be allowed to attend for fear of betraying their plans.

Pontiac ordered sentinels to be placed around the village in order not to be disturbed in their council. When all these precautions had been taken each Indian seated himself in the circle according to rank, and Pontiac at the head, as great chief of all, began to speak. He said:

"It is important for us, my brothers, that we exterminate from our lands this nation which seeks only to destroy us. You see as well as I that we can no longer supply our needs, as we have done, from our brothers, the French.

The English sell us goods twice as dear as the French do, and their goods do not last. Scarcely have we bought a blanket or something else to cover ourselves with before we must think of getting another; and when we wish to set out for our winter camps they do not want to give us any credit as our brothers, the French, do.

"When I go to see the English commander and say to him that some of our comrades are dead, instead of bewailing their death, as our French brothers do, he laughs at me and at you. If I ask anything for our sick, he refuses with the reply that he has no use for us. From all this you can well see that they are seeking our ruin. Therefore, my brothers, we must all swear their destruction and wait no longer. Nothing prevents us; they are few in numbers, and we can accomplish it. All the nations who are our brothers attack them,—why should we not attack? Are we not men like them? Have I not shown you the wampum belts which I received from our Great Father, the Frenchman? He tells us to strike them,—why do we not listen to his words? What do we fear? It is time.

Do we fear that our brothers, the French, who are here among us will prevent us? They do not know our plans, and they could not hinder anyway, if they would. You all know as well as I that when the English came upon our lands to drive out our Father, [François Marie Picotè de] Belestre [the last French commander at Detroit], they took away all the Frenchmen's guns and that they now have no arms to protect themselves with. Therefore, it is time for us to strike. If there are any French who side with them, let us strike them as well as the English. Remember what the Master of Life told our brother, the Wolf, to do. That concerns us all as well as others. I have sent wampum belts and messengers to our brothers, the Chippewas of Saginaw, and to our brothers, the Ottawas of Michillimackinac, and to those of the Thames River to join us. They will not be slow in coming, but while we wait let us strike anyway. There is no more time to lose. When the English are defeated we shall then see what there is left to do, and we shall stop up the ways hither so that they may never come again upon our lands."

3. William Trent Describes Pontiac's Uprising, 1763

June 17th The same Indians came and called again and desired Mr. McKee would come over, he refused; they then recommended it to him to set [off] for the Inhabitants in the Night, or to come over to them and they would take care of him at their Towns till the War was over, they acquainted him all Nations had taken up the Hatchett against us, and that they intended to attack this Post with a great Body in a few days; that Venango and all the other Posts that way were already cut off that they were afraid to refuse taking up the Hatchet against us as so many Nations had done it before it came to them.

About 12 o'Clock at Night two Expresses came in from Ligonier with Letters from the General.

18th The Enemy set fire to another House up the Ohio.

One o'Clock in the Morning the 2 Expresses that came last set [off] for Ligonier again with Letters.

June 19th Two Indians crep along the Bank of the Mono[ngahela. A] Centinel ... was posted on the Bank of the River.... Soon after a number of Indians were seen ... taking ... some Horses, and the Garrison was turning out one Stuart a Soldiers Gun went [off] by accident and mortaly wounded him of which he dyed the next day.

20th Nothing extrodinary

21st About 11 o'Clock at Night the Indians on the opposite side of the Mongehela repeated all's well after our Centinels.

22 Between 9 and 10 o'Clock in the Morning a smoke was seen rising on the Back of Grants Hill where the Indians had made a fire and about 2 o'Clock several of them appeared in the Spelts field moving of the Horses and Cattle. About 5 o'Clock one James Thompson who it was supposed was gone after a Horse was killed and scalped in sight of the Fort on this a great number of Inds

William Trent (with editing by A.T. Volwiler), "William Trent's Journal at Fort Pitt, 1763," *Mississippi Valley Historical Review* 11 (December 1924): 390–413 (see esp. p. 400).

appeared on each River and on Grants Hill shooting down the Cattle and Horses. A Shell was thron amongst a number of them from a Hauwitz which burst just as it fell among them. About an Hour after they fired on the Fort from Grant's Hill and the other side of the Ohio, a shot from the opposite side of the Ohio wounded a Man in the Mongehela Bastion. About 7 o'Clock three Indians were seen about 150 yards from the Fort on the Monongehela Bank Mr. McKee and two others fired on them and killed one of them.

23 about 12 o'Clock at Night Two Delawares called for Mr. McKee and told him they wanted to speak to him in the Morning.

24th The Turtles Heart a principal Warrior of the Delawares and Mamaltee a Chief came within a small distance of the Fort Mr. McKee went out to them and they made a Speech letting us know … [Fort] Ligonier was destroyed, that great numbers of Indians [were coming and] that out of regard to us, they had prevailed on 6 Nations [not to] attack us but give us time to go down the Country and they desired we would set of immediately. The Commanding Officer thanked them, let them know that we had everything we wanted, that we could defend it against all the Indians in the Woods, that we had three large Armys marching to Chastise those Indians that had struck us, told them to take care of their Women and Children, but not to tell any other Natives, they said they would go and speak to their Chiefs and come and tell us what they said, they returned and said they would hold fast of the Chain of friendship. Out of our regard to them we gave them two Blankets and an Handkerchief out of the Small Pox Hospital. I hope it will have the desired effect.

4. Naomai Omaush (Wampanoag) Records Her Will, 1749

Know ye this all Christian people of God. I Naomai Ommaush of Gayhead know that very soon I go the way of all the earth, whence I shall not be able to return again. And now I hope, if I should die this year, I would have my sins be forgiven by the blood of my Lord, the Lord Jesus Christ.

And again I know that although my body dies and has rotted (?), it shall rise again on the last day, and also my soul shall also enter where he is, on the great day of resurrection, to go to meet the Lord in heaven. And then we shall dwell with the lord forever.

And I Naomai Omaush say this before God: I willingly bequeath this property of mine to my kin. Each one shall take, after I die, what I have not yet used.

To Zachary Hossueit, the minister, I bequeath one *ohquoh*—it is straight-looking (?) (and) large—and also six pewter dishes, and also seventeen pewter spoons. [[And this]]* And also to his wife Butthiah Hossueit I bequeath one of

---

*Historian Colin G. Calloway notes that the letters in brackets indicate deletions by the writer of the document and that the words in parentheses are the original Massachusett terms.

In Ives Goddard and Kathleen J. Bragdon, eds., *Native Writings in Massachusett*, 2 vols. (Philadelphia: American Philosophical Society, 1988), 1: 55. This document is also available in Colin G. Galloway, *The World Turned Upside Down: Indian Voices from Early America* (Boston: Bedford Books, 1994), 52–53.

my dresses—whichever one she pleases she shall choose when I have died. And I say at this time, no one shall have the authority to defraud them out of the things I bequeath to them. And, witnesses, see [[m[y m]ark (and) m[y sea]l]] my mark and also my seal.

Naomai Omaush, her (X) mark and Seal (S)

Witnesses:
Jude Hossueit, his mark (X).
Buthiah Accomus, her mark (X). On July 8, 1749.
On July 8, 1749, on that date (?) I also say I bequeath to [[my broth]] my kinsman (*nuttauwatueonk*) Calab Elisha one blanket.

On July 8, 1749, on that date (?) I say that I bequeath to my kinswoman (*nuttauwatueonk*) Jeanohumun one *ohquohkoome kaskepessue* and also one of my dresses.

On July 8, 1749, on that date (?) also I bequeath to my kinsman (*nuttauwam*) Henry Amos (some of) that cloth of mine that I may then have; of the red he shall have one *penchens* because of how kind he has been to me.

On July 8, 1749, on that date (?) I bequeath to my kinswoman (*nuttauwaeh*) Ezther Henry one dress of mine of blue (?) calico; I bought it from her late mother, and she shall have it.

On July 8, 1749, on that day I bequeath to my kinswoman (*nuttauwam*) Marcy Noah one petticoat. And those other things more that I have of household goods, those I shall use as long as I live. And then if I do not use them all, you shall divide them up when I have died.

My bequeathing of all this to my kin (*nuttauwamoog*) was done; I willingly do it on this date (?) before my G[o]d, the Lord Jesus Christ.

[Se]e my mark and also my seal.

Naomai Omaush, her (X) mark and seal (S)

[Wi]tnesses:
[Jude] Hossueit, his mark (X).
[Buth]i[a]h Accomus, her mark (X).

5. The Mashpee Wampanoags Petition the Massachusetts General Court, 1752

Barnstable, June 11, 1752

Oh! Our honorable gentlemen and kind gentlemen in Boston in Massachusetts Bay, here in New England, the great ones who oversee the colony in Boston, gentlemen. Oh!, Oh!, gentlemen, hear us now, Oh! ye, us poor Indians. We do

---

In Ives Goddard and Kathleen J. Bragdon, eds., *Native Writings in Massachusett*, 2 vols. (Philadelphia: American Philosophical Society, 1988), 1: 373. This document is also available in Colin G. Galloway, *The World Turned Upside Down: Indian Voices from Early America* (Boston: Bedford Books, 1994), 105–106.

not clearly have thorough understanding and wisdom. Therefore we now beseech you, Oh!, Boston gentlemen. Oh! Hear our weeping, and hear our beseeching of you, Oh!, and answer this beseeching of you by us, Oh!, gentlemen of Boston, us poor Indians in Mashpee *in Barnstable County.*

Now we beseech you, what can we do with regard to our land, which was conveyed to you by these former sachems of ours. What they conveyed to you(?) was this piece of land. This was conveyed to us by Indian sachems. Our former Indian sachems were called Sachem Wuttammohkin and Sachem Quettatsett, in Barnstable County, the Mashpee Indian place. This Indian land, this was conveyed to us by these former sachems of ours. We shall not give it away, nor shall it be sold, nor shall it be lent, but we shall always use it as long as we live, we together with all our children, and our children's children, and our descendants, and together with all their descendants. They shall always use it as long as Christian Indians live. We shall use it forever and ever. Unless we all peacefully agree to give it away or to sell it. But as of now not one of all of us Indians has yet agreed to give away, or sell, or lend this Indian land, or marsh, or wood. Fairly, then, it is this: we state frankly we have never conveyed them away.

But now clearly we Indians say this to all you gentlemen of ours in Boston: We poor Indians in Mashpee, *in Barnstable County*, we truly are much troubled by these English neighbors of ours being on this land of ours, and in our marsh and trees. Against our will these Englishmen take away from us [these] what was our land. They parcel it out to each other, and the marsh along with it, against our will. And as for our streams, they do not allow us peacefully to be when we peacefully go fishing. They beat us greatly, and they have houses on our land against our will. Truly we think it is this: We poor Indians soon shall not have any place to reside, together with our poor children, because these Englishmen trouble us very much in this place of ours in Mashpee, Barnstable County.

Therefore now, Oh! you kind gentlemen in Boston, in Massachusetts Bay, now we beseech you: defend us, and they would not trouble us any more on our land.

6. Joseph Fish Preaches to the Narragansett Indians, 1768

June 20. 1768 … Found the School kept us as Usual, and more Schollars, of late, attending: about 15 Children, pretty Steadily come to School. Nothing Materially differing in Indians Circumstances Since last there: but Mr. Deake's Situation very difficult and distressing, on Account of his Debts. Tells me he Owes about £20–£Money, and all of it, to divers persons, now due, by Notes of hand or Obligations on Demand. His Creditors Patience no longer to be expected. Two Notes already committed to hands of Authority, to be heard. He expects a *Writ* or Two, before this Week is out: And can't See Any Way to avoid being taken out of his Business; which must break up the School. The Consequence he Apprehends will be, That the Indians, From their great Regard to Mr. *Greaves* N. Londo., Will Make

William S. Simmons, ed., "Joseph Fish Preaches to the Narragansett Indians," from *Old Light on Separate ways: The Narragansett Diary of Joseph Fish* © 1982 by the University Press of New England, reprinted by permission.

Application to *Him*, or to the *Church* of England for a Schoolmaster and *Support*. On Consulting his Case, I promised him to write the Commissioners in his Behalf.

A[t] about Two, Preachd at Indian Meeting house, to 20 Indians, (They having heard that I would not Come today, and Numbers of them, through Carelessness, having forgot the Lecture.) From Matth: 22–39. *Thou Shalt love thy Neighbour as Thy Self*—A grace and Duty much Wanting and greatly Neglected Among these Indians. In the Fore part of My Discourse, Indians Seemd Sleepy and Careless—Digressed and rousd them, by Awakening Touches. Towards the Close of my Discourse, A Molatto (Amnon,) a Lusty Man, having for Some time discovered Something Singular in his Countenance, fell into great distress, manifested by Crying out bitterly, which continued through the Remainder of Sermon. Finishd off with a fervent Prayer, trembling as he Spoke. Found upon Speaking to him after Sermon, that the Word reachd his Conscience, Wakd up a Sense of his Guilt, in late evil Conduct, having been long reputed a Christian, but of late Years or Months, walkd unbecoming his Profession. Several other Indians, manifested Some deep Impressions from the *Word*.

After Lecture, Visited Two Families. Wm. Sachem (of the Sachems Party and his Uncle,) who never heard me preach Save once. Found him Serious and Attentive, while I talkd to him on the Affairs of his Soul. Has got a hope of Grace, in Former times but for Years past lives poorly. I endeavourd to Awake him to a Sense of his Duty and Danger. Here found about a Dozen Indians, Men and Women, who had been *Hoeing* for Will. I gave *Them* an Exhortation, and proceeded to find *Toby*.

The Indians commonly Fence their Fields with thick *Hedges*—No *Barrs*, I was obligd to break through their Hedges, with my Horse, and repair them, Well as I could. After travelling through the Thickets, many times no path, and passing deep valleys and Steep Hills, over Which I could but just climb, with my Horse in hand, for near 3/4 hour, (Mr. Deake in company my Guide) I found Sqr. *Tobys* (as Calld,) living much retird and then Alone. He's the Oldest Indian Man, in the Tribe. In his 86th Year. Entirely (or Near it) *blind*. Reckoned (not without good reason,) a pious Man. Talkd familiarly of *Death* and *Heaven*. Said he longd to go Home to his Fathers house, which he hopd for, in a little time. Twas now Night. Took leave of the Old Man....

Tuesday, June 21. Returnd to the Indian houses, in the Morning. Visitted Four Indian Families. Discoursed with a Christian Indian Woman, (*Henry Harrys* Wife,) Under Soul Trouble, declining Health and many Afflictions. Her Daughter (a Widow) A bed with a Bastard Child—I endeavourd to awake the poor thoughtless, unconcernd Creature to a Sense of her Guilt and Danger. Calld at [?*Sachs*] Daughters—Dropped a Word of encouragement to a poor Creature in Travail.

Visited old Robins. His Daughter an Impudent Secure, Lewd person—Two Bastard Children with her. I endeavourd to Alarm her Conscience, by Shewing the certain Destruction of *Fornicators* etc.

Visited John *Shattock*, And, among other things, Reprovd him for not reading the *Bible* (as he Says he Can read it Well,) in his Family daily. Owns he has not read it for a long time. I endeavourd to Convince him of his Sinfull neglect, and excite him to his Duty. Left the Indians between Ten and Eleven o'Clock, and returnd home by post Road....

Monday July 18. 1768 ... Very hot and I much unwell; but reachd the School house about *One*. The School kept up, and about the Number of Schollars as before (15, or more). Mr. Deake Somewhat relievd of the pressures mentiond in Journal of last Visit. He approved of my Proposal to Commissioners for advancing half a years pay—Said twould much relieve him.

Many people at the Indian Meeting, Yesterday (Lords day,) English and Indians. Numbers behavd very wickedly, in time of the Indians Worship. In the day time or Evening Some of Them got drunk and Two Squaws fell upon another Squaw, that was heavy with Child, and beat, kickd and abusd her, So that her Life was much doubted of.

Preachd at Indian Meeting house to 30 Indians, Chiefly Women and young persons, from Matth. 5.4. Nothing Special Appeard in the Audience.

After Lecture Visited Samel. *Niles*, (about 1 1/2 Mile North East from Meeting house) intending, to have Spent the Remainder of the Day and Next Day Forenoon, in Visiting Indians: but Mr. Deake and Niles told me there was (likely,) Scarce An Indian to be found at home; As the Busy Season calld them Abroad. So thought it pity to Spend my time, in Visiting Empty Houses. Concluded to deferr my intended Visits to the Next Journey....

7. Samson Occom (Mohegan) Gives a Short Narrative of His Life, 1768

From my Birth till I received the Christian Religion

I was Born a Heathen and Brought up In Heathenism, till I was between 16 & 17 years of age, at a Place Calld Mohegan, in New London, Connecticut, in New England. My Parents Livd a wandering life, for did all the Indians at Mohegan, they Chiefly Depended upon Hunting, Fishing, & Fowling for their Living and had no Connection with the English, excepting to Traffic with them in their small Trifles; and they Strictly maintained and followed their Heathenish Ways, Customs & Religion, though there was Some Preaching among them. Once a Fortnight, in ye Summer Season, a Minister from New London used to come up, and the Indians to attend; not that they regarded the Christian Religion, but they had Blankets given to them every Fall of the Year and for these things they would attend and there was a Sort of School kept, when I was quite young, but I believe there never was one that ever Learnt to read any thing,—and when I was about 10 Years of age there was a man who went about among the Indian Wigwams, and wherever he Could find the Indian Children, would make them read; but the Children Used to take Care to keep out of his way;—and he used to Catch me Some times and make me Say over my Letters; and I believe I learnt Some of them. But this was Soon over too; and all this Time there was not one amongst us, that made a Profession of Christianity— — Neither did we Cultivate our Land, nor

This document can be found typescript in Baker Library Special Collections, Dartmouth College, Hanover, N.H. It can also be found in Colin G. Calloway, ed., *The World Turned Upside Down: Indian Voices from Early America* (Boston: Bedford Books, 1994).

kept any Sort of Creatures except Dogs, which we used in Hunting; and we Dwelt in Wigwams. These are a Sort of Tents, Covered with Matts, made of Flags. And to this Time we were unaquainted with the English Tongue in general though there were a few, who understood a little of it.

From the Time of our Reformation till I left Mr. Wheelocks

When I was 16 years of age, we heard a Strange Rumor among the English, that there were Extraordinary Ministers Preaching from Place to Place and a Strange Concern among the White People. This was in the Spring of the Year. But we Saw nothing of these things, till Some Time in the Summer, when Some Ministers began to visit us and Preach the Word of God; and the Common People all Came frequently and exhorted us to the things of God, which it pleased the Lord, as I humbly hope, to Bless and accompany with Divine Influence to the Conviction and Saving Conversion of a Number of us; amongst whom I was one that was Imprest with the things we had heard. These Preachers did not only come to us, but we frequently went to their meetings and Churches. After I was awakened & converted, I went to all the meetings, I could come at; & Continued under Trouble of Mind about 6 months; at which time I began to Learn the English Letters; got me a Primer, and used to go to my English Neighbours frequently for Assistance in Reading, but went to no School. And when I was 17 years of age, I had, as I trust, a Discovery of the way of Salvation through Jesus Christ, and was enabl'd to put my trust in him alone for Life & Salvation. From this Time the Distress and Burden of my mind was removed, and I found Serenity and Pleasure of Soul, in Serving God. By this time I just began to Read in the New Testament without Spelling,—and I had a Stronger Desire Still to Learn to read the Word of God, and at the Same Time had an uncommon Pity and Compassion to my Poor Brethren According to the Flesh. I used to wish I was capable of Instructing my poor Kindred. I used to think, if I Could once Learn to Read I would Instruct the poor Children in Reading,—and used frequently to talk with our Indians Concerning Religion. This continued till I was in my 19th year: by this Time I Could Read a little in the Bible. At this Time my Poor Mother was going to Lebanon, and having had Some Knowledge of Mr. Wheelock and hearing he had a Number of English youth under his Tuition, I had a great Inclination to go to him and be with him a week or a Fortnight, and Desired my Mother to Ask Mr. Wheelock whether he would take me a little while to Instruct me in Reading. Mother did so; and when She Came Back, She Said Mr. Wheelock wanted to See me as Soon as possible. So I went up, thinking I Should be back again in a Few Days; when I got up there, he received me With kindness and Compassion and in Stead of Staying a Fortnight or 3 Weeks, I Spent 4 Years with him.—After I had been with him Some Time, he began to acquaint his Friends of my being with him, and of his Intentions of Educating me, and my Circumstances. And the good People began to give Some Assistance to Mr. Wheelock, and gave me Some old and Some New Clothes. Then he represented the Case to the Honorable Commissioners at Boston, who were Commission'd by the Honorable Society in London for Propagating the gospel among the Indians in New England and parts adjacent, and they allowed him 60 £ in old Tender, which was about 6 £ Sterling, and they Continu'd it 2 or 3 years, I can't tell exactly.—While I was at Mr. Wheelock's, I was very weakly and my Health much impaired, and at the End of 4 Years, I over Strained my Eyes to such a Degree, I Could not peruse my Studies any Longer; and out of these 4 years I Lost Just about one year;—And was obliged to quit my Studies.

❖ ESSAYS

The essays that follow continue to treat the twin themes of war and survival in the eighteenth century. The British were quick to pin the blame for the Seven Years' War, the largest war of the century before the American War for Independence, on the French and the Indians, and to further look upon the Indians as mere pawns of the French. Was this, in fact, the case? In the first essay, Ian Steele, an emeritus professor of history at the University of Western Ontario, delves into this question, focusing on the story of the Shawnee nation in this era. Why, according to Steele, did the Shawnees end up going to war with the British? The second essay returns again to the topic of survival behind the frontier. In the essay, Jean O'Brien, an Ojibwe woman and a professor of history at the University of Minnesota, explores the lives of Native women in New England. While these women may not have found themselves on the front lines of wars between the French, the English, and other Indian tribes, they nevertheless faced the vital challenges of maintaining their Native cultures and communities within a society that increasingly sought to render them invisible. Indeed, women played a particularly important role in protecting these cultures, as many Native New England men went off to fight in the wars further west in these years. As O'Brien tells it, to what degree were these women successful in their efforts to "win the battle" for their peoples' identities?

War: The Shawnees and the Seven Years' War

BY IAN STEELE

News that Ohio Shawnee had proclaimed a "perpetual war" against the English came as a pleasant surprise, on New Year's Day 1755, to Canadian lieutenant Joseph-Gaspard Chaussegros de Léry, a sixteen-year veteran of frontier war and diplomacy who was then serving at the Lake Erie outpost of Chatakoin. Over a drink, Huron courier Le Glorieux attempted to explain to Léry that the Shawnee were furious with the English for imprisoning several of their warriors in Charles Town, South Carolina. Léry was puzzled at this reversal of the recent trend in Shawnee-English relations and, like historians subsequently, could not believe

Ian Steele, "Shawnee Origins of Their Seven Years' War," in *Ethnohistory*, 53 (Fall 2006): pp. 657–687. Copyright, 2006, the American Society for Ethnohistory. All rights reserved. Republished by permission of the copyrightholder, and the present publisher, Duke University Press. www.dukeupress.edu

that imprisonment of a few warriors in distant Charles Town could ignite a major war in the Ohio country.

Could such an incident prompt repudiation of a flourishing new economic and diplomatic relationship and spark a wider and more sustained conflict than relatives seeking private revenge might be expected to launch? Historians of the Seven Years' War, including myself, have too readily presumed that the Shawnee needed no specific provocation to join French and Delaware allies; the systemic injustice of the Anglo-colonial invasion seemed reason enough to believe French claims that most Ohio Amerindians, including the Shawnee, were easily recruited. The most recent scholarly overview of the war's causes has pointedly sought Amerindian agency, emphasizing Mingo (Ohio Six Nations) chief Tanighrisson's role in the "murder" of Canadian ensign Joseph Coulon de Villiers de Jumonville in May 1754. That killing, or the resulting counterattack at Fort Necessity, has long been regarded as central in moving the Europeans to war. However, Ohio Amerindians, including the Shawnee, the Delaware, and most of the Mingo, overwhelmingly rejected Tanighrisson's choice of enemy and of ally, and instead joined the French in the ensuing war.... Present understandings of the origins of the Seven Years' War too readily ignore the role of the Shawnee and implicitly misconstrue them as disgruntled opportunists easily drawn into a French-led alliance against the Allegheny frontiers of the encroaching British Empire.

Eighteenth-century Amerindians are now knowable primarily as distorted shadows cast by the far from neutral light of other peoples' records, and the scattered and migratory Shawnee are even more elusive. Therefore there is special value in examining a significant incident in which the records nearly allow the Shawnee to speak, through translators, for themselves. To understand how the Ohio Shawnee came to launch their own war against the British in 1754, it is helpful first to review what can be known of Shawnee-British relations in the previous decade and then to examine the Charles Town captivity and its impact in some detail. Equally interesting is the exceptionally well-recorded Amerindian insistence that this captivity was the sole cause of Shawnee hostility, evidence that has been overlooked, discounted, or dismissed by historians of this war and of the Shawnee.

The 1754 Ohio Shawnee declaration of war abruptly ended a trend toward diplomatic harmony and increasing trade with the British, though that trend itself could not have been predicted before 1747. The Shawnee had long resented the British-allied Six Nations of Iroquois, who had dispersed the Shawnee from their ancestral homes on the lower Wabash and Ohio rivers in the 1670s. The Shawnee then scattered throughout eastern North America, reinforcing the variety inherent in their five patrilineal "divisions" and dozen clans. They usually surfaced before 1765 only as supporting actors in the history of others. However, the Shawnee sustained their language and identity despite cooperating and competing with a wide variety of hosts and neighbors.... By 1731 some were trading with Canadians, visiting Montreal to seek help against their Mingo rivals, and flying a French flag at the Allegheny River settlement that Pennsylvanians called Chartier's Town. Attempts by Pennsylvania and the Six Nations to assert control, by "recalling" the Shawnee from the Ohio, failed completely. When an Anglo-French war began in

1744, the disparate Shawnee were regarded suspiciously by the Pennsylvania government's frontier diplomat, Conrad Weiser, as "the most restless and mischievous of all the Indians," and some were certainly tending to support the French....

Within two years, however, a number of Ohio Shawnee were clearly displaying friendliness toward English traders. French gifts and trade goods had become scarce with the fall of Louisbourg and with British maritime blockades. Equally important, the pro-French Shawnee faction in the region was greatly weakened when 185 Shawnee warriors, including Chartier, and their families moved south to settle with the Creek nation in what would later be called Alabama. Some Ohio Shawnee became openly anti-French: some were involved in the widespread anti-French "Conspiracy of 1747" and, two years later at Lower Shawnee Town, Shawnees fired on and briefly captured the heralds of Céloron de Blainville's famous expedition to plant lead plates and otherwise assert French claims in the Ohio Valley. The French later retaliated for their hostile reception by killing one Shawnee and holding three others captive in Fort des Miami for several months. When a prominent Canadian/Seneca party came to Logstown in 1751 to arrest all English traders and to confiscate and distribute their goods to the inhabitants as presents, these would-be enforcer-benefactors were thwarted by the local Mingos and Shawnees, who protected Pennsylvania traders, including Andrew Montour and George Croghan. At his next conference with the Six Nations, New France's governor complained about their "nourishing vipers" by allowing English traders in the Ohio country. The next year the governor of French Louisiana urged increased caution in dealing with the Shawnee, hoping that their general hostility toward all Europeans could be directed more toward the English. Pennsylvania's frontier-oriented secretary, Richard Peters, later remembered this as an ideal time when Pennsylvania traders "had Store houses on the Lake Erie all along ye Miami River, & up & down all the fine Country waterd by ye Branches of ye Miamis, Sioto, & Muskingham Rivers & upon the Ohio from Buckaloons an Indian Town near its head to below ye Mouth of ye Miami River an Extent of 500 miles on one of ye most beautiful Rivers in ye world."

Conrad Weiser led Pennsylvania's concurrent diplomatic initiatives to the Ohio Shawnee, Mingo, Delaware, and Miami, bypassing Six Nations influence symbolized by his ailing Oneida friend, Shickellamy. Yet Weiser attempted to re-create a version of the familiar "covenant chain" strategy by working exclusively through Tanighrisson and Scarouyady, Mingo leaders who had formal, if very frayed, links to the Six Nations Council at Onondaga. Weiser's overtures were themselves an admission that Pennsylvanian traders, who were displacing both Six Nations and French traders on the Ohio, could not expect effective Six Nations protection in Ohio country. Overtures of 1747 were confirmed by a Shawnee-Pennsylvania alliance at Lancaster and at the new council fire at Logstown in September 1748. By early 1752, several Ohio Shawnee chiefs, including a leading Chillicothe headman, Itawachcomequa, assured an embarrassed Pennsylvanian governor that they were counting on English friendship and advice as they planned an attack on the French Fort des Miami. This raid was to be in conjunction with pro-English dissidents among the Piankashaw and Miami, gathered at their new trading town of Pickawillany; like their pro-English Shawnee neighbors, the people of Pickawillany had recently become formal allies of Pennsylvania. The four Shawnee chiefs had doubtlessly been coached in their letter-writing by self-interested Pennsylvanian traders who, together with Lieutenant Governor James Hamilton, knew very well that the colony's Quaker-controlled assembly would never support such aggression, especially in peacetime. Virginians interested in Ohio lands soon proved willing, though not able, to challenge the French.

In June 1752 the Ohio diplomatic landscape began to shift from under the Shawnee-English connection. Negotiators at a Logstown conference publicly revealed the Virginian and Pennsylvanian agendas to the Mingo leaders, with Shawnees, Delawares, Miamis, and Wyandots as concerned, if reportedly silent, witnesses. Expansive Virginian claims to the Ohio, agreed to by the Six Nations at Lancaster back in 1744, were finally exposed, and Tanighrisson even succumbed to colonial pressure to accept a Virginian "store house" on the Ohio as well. Iroquoians were again failing the Shawnee, who were also told to stop raiding south against the British-allied Cherokee, though it should be noted that the Catawba were not specifically mentioned. Within eight days of these revealing negotiations, the pro-English Shawnee received a greater shock: a large Ottawa/Canadian raiding party completely destroyed the Pickawillany post of their new Miami allies. This raid certainly preempted any Shawnee-Miami attack on Fort des Miami and gradually revealed, by the lack of British colonial retaliation, the hollowness of the Pennsylvanian and Virginian agreements to support their new Ohio Amerindian allies.

When thirteen Shawnee warriors set out from the new village of Wakatomika (also known as Waketummaky or Lapitchuna) on the Muskingum River in April of 1753, to raid the distant Catawba for prisoners and scalps, they could not have imagined the consequences. These attacks were traditional for various Eastern Woodland peoples and were intended to weaken and humiliate a worthy enemy, replace specific war casualties, and advance the martial reputations of the raiders. Such raids can now be traced only when there were encounters with European settlers, and the venture of 1753 is the only Shawnee raid for which adequate records exist. According to Shawnee tradition, the Catawba had been their enemies since creation and had, within living memory, traitorously deserted the Amerindian alliance against South Carolina in the Yamasee War (1715–17). The resulting defeat had forced the Savannah branch of the Shawnee to abandon the river that still bears their name, and some of these had migrated north to Pennsylvania, passing memories on to their children, who were now among the Ohio Shawnee. According to one eminent Shawnee of the next generation, a Shawnee warrior intent on becoming a war chief needed to participate in twelve raids into enemy territory and lead four of them successfully. A raid was considered successful only if the entire raiding party returned unhurt, and if it brought back at least one scalp or prisoner. The ability to distribute gifts of scalps, prisoners, or prize goods was a mark of status and honor among the Shawnee and their neighbors. This view of martial valor, widely shared among eastern Amerindians, helps explain the aftermath of this raid, as well as the social, military, and diplomatic history of this period.

Although not aimed at the English, the 1753 Shawnee raid was certainly meant to defy the Six Nations Iroquois. The Six Nations and the Catawba had made a tentative peace in 1751, finally ending a century of war and small-scale raiding....

This well-equipped Shawnee raid became a bizarre, yet consequential and uniquely revealing fiasco. After "a pipe dance" that included ample liquor, the party set off with horses and several rifled guns, evidence of adaptability, status, and prosperity. The expedition was also armed with a medicine bundle, which featured a belt of black wampum and prized buffalo-hair "prisoner ties" for expected captives. The bundle included silver bracelets and a silver cross that could be construed, by suspicious English interrogators, as marks of French influence. The leader was Itawachcomequa, or The Pride, from the prestigious *Calaka* (Chillicothe) Shawnee division and also related to Munsee Delaware chief Custaloga; Itawachcomequa had been prominent in Chartier's attack on Pennsylvanian traders in 1745. By early 1752, however, Itawachcomequa had become one of the four pro-English Shawnee chiefs who requested Pennsylvanian assistance as the chiefs prepared to attack the French. Hamilton later called Itawachcomequa's war party "the Flower of their Nation for Courage and Activity" and said that they were leaders of the pro-English faction who were sorely needed in the Ohio country during the rapidly developing confrontation with the French. A Shawnee spokesman would later refer to Itawachcomequa as "a noted Man among the Shawonese, a great Warrior and a true Friend to the English."

After a few days' travel, some of the Shawnees had sober second thoughts. They encountered Thomas Burney, a Pennsylvanian acquaintance who told them of his own narrow escape in the unavenged destruction of Pickawillany the previous June. Burney warned that Iroquoian warriors had recently killed white people along the main Warrior's Path southward, making that preferred route much too dangerous at the moment. Likely leaving their horses with Burney, the Shawnees proceeded "out of the Way, and by the Heads of the Rivers." The group lost its way in the Appalachians, or at least some lost enthusiasm, and seven of them turned back, including two who reportedly had become lame and others who agreed to see them safely home.

The remaining six persevered in their quest, reaching South Carolina in about six weeks. "After we had marched a very long Way, not knowing the Path, we found ourselves in the white People's Country. The white People told us that if we should be taken, we should be carried Prisoners to Charles Town." Responding to reports of suspicious strangers in quest of local Catawba, thirty South Carolina militiamen surrounded the six Ohio Shawnees in a farmhouse near the Salkehatchie River in the southeastern corner of the colony. The Shawnees agreed to surrender their weapons and be conducted to the governor "under the Care and Protection of a Party of our Militia, rather than as Prisoners of War, that they may go without Fear," as a sympathetic Lieutenant Governor William Bull explained in sending them on to Governor James Glen in Charles Town. Bull added, "I have treated them kindly, for which they seem very thankful, and told them they are a going to hear your Excellency's Talk."

This "capture" can usefully be regarded as a negotiation, with Itawachcomequa and his party taking up Bull's invitation to meet with Glen. Amerindian warriors did not surrender to whites, were very seldom taken as captives, and some are known to have regarded incarceration as much worse than death. In the wars between 1754 and 1765, only one severely wounded Ohio Shawnee is known to have been captured, while twenty were killed by the British army, colonial regiments, or militia. These six Shawnee warriors were confident that they would be recognized and treated as English allies.

What these Shawnees later said indicates that although they understood English quite well, they did not know enough about the situation in which they found themselves. South Carolinians were very fearful of Amerindian attacks in 1753, in the backcountry and near the capital. There had been a rumor-fed panic in 1751 among South Carolinians and Cherokee, prompting some migration and fortification on both sides in anticipation of war. The 1751 peace between the Catawba and the Six Nations Iroquois had theoretically ended attacks between these rival allies of the British colonies, but inadequately identified "northern Indians" intensified their raids on the Catawba, encouraged by the increasingly belligerent French. In addition, private revenge raiding by small parties was bound to continue despite the best efforts of British governors, intercultural brokers, and the most sincere and accommodating of chiefs.

After "a gang of Northern Indians" had killed a white settler within thirty-five miles of Charles Town in April 1753, veteran governor Glen had issued a proclamation offering £100 to anyone who captured or killed any of those involved and promising £50 to those who captured or killed any "other Northern Indians who shall come into our Settlements after the Expiration of Three Months, unless such Indians shall have in their Company some white Man, and be coming down on any Business or Message to this Government." It is significant that the nervous South Carolina government was offering identical rewards for unknown Amerindians, whether dead or alive. This was a clear invitation for militia, settlers, and bounty hunters to summarily kill Amerindian strangers and avoid any danger posed by live captives or forfeiture of reward caused by their plausible explanations. Amid these incidents, word arrived of the major French military initiative into the Ohio Valley, where they were urging Amerindians to turn against the English. If the six Shawnees had done anything suspicious after giving up their weapons, their chances of reaching Charles Town alive would have been slim. Itawachcomequa and his companions had entered very dangerous country.

Would Amerindian captives fare better because they understood some English, clearly regarded themselves as British allies, surrendered their weapons without inflicting any casualties, were supported by a lieutenant governor's sympathetic letter, and were escorted to a diplomatic meeting during Governor Glen's declared three-month grace period? The initial reception in Charles Town was certainly not encouraging. In an item widely reprinted in the British colonies, the South Carolina Gazette of 18 June described "some Northern Indians, lately taken and brought to Town by Capt. David Godin's Company of Militia," hoping other militias would act similarly and "soon clear the Country of these French and Northern Indians that have for some Years past infested this Province." Glen immediately ordered the Shawnees to prison and then, together with his Council, questioned them individually, accusing them of murder and of contradicting each other. Once an adequate translator was found, the Council heard Itawachcomequa, who was still willing to declare, "I am a Friend to all the People here. I am a Shavanah and loyal to the English." If Itawachcomequa actually described himself a Savannah Shawnee, his hearers might well have been skeptical; the Savannah fought the South Carolinians in 1715–18, then left. If the translator or transcriber merely used the local term for the Shawnee, this statement was credible. Although many Shawnees had grievances, and their opinion of Europeans was neither high nor uniform, they were described in a 1755 report by Edmond Atkin, a former South Carolina councillor and soon to become superintendent of Indian affairs for the southern frontier, as reliable allies of the British in the early 1750s.

The frankest statement of the warriors' purpose was offered by the youngest Shawnee, a teen captured with his father and initially interrogated with him. The youth later admitted that they came to capture Catawba prisoners but had taken none and that the buffalo hair cords and the black wampum belt were intended to be put around the necks of captives. He also said that white people had promised the Shawnees freedom if they went to talk with the governor; this supports the view that the Shawnees understood they were meeting with the governor, and therefore were willing to surrender their weapons. Another Shawnee prisoner said that the entire war party had been drunk when they set out and some had turned back when they sobered. Other prisoners' explanations less wisely included an intended visit to "Shartier's people" living among the Creeks.

Strangers, even those captured by chance during peacetime, seemed easier to exploit than to set free. In deciding to hold the Shawnees in prison, Glen was violating Amerindian understandings of hospitality, diplomacy, and dignity. Hospitality between allies, who were regarded as fictive kin, was presumed to be a fair sharing of resources and conditions and might extend for weeks or months. Diplomacy presumed that those invited to hear the governor talk, and displaying good faith in surrendering weapons, had even more reason to expect good treatment; even enemy diplomats were to be respected, and violations prompted war, like that between the Creek and Cherokee in 1715. Amerindian dignity was so violated by close confinement as to be considered worse than death; incarceration was the most humiliating outcome possible for warriors who had traveled so far to confirm and enhance their status. The governor and council, admitting that "there are not any positive Proof that they had actually killed any of our People," kept the Shawnees in jail for nearly a month before deciding what to do with them. When a Catawba chief gloated about the sickly look of his jailed Shawnee enemies, the governor revealed his complete misunderstanding of the situation. More than once he insisted that the prisoners were being well treated in jail. Although apparently ignorant of the degradation he was inflicting, Glen did voice concern to the Commons House of Assembly two weeks later: "I should be sorry that any of them should die in Prison, [and] I think the sooner we get rid of them, the better."

Glen and his council proposed sending two of the Shawnees home, accompanied by letters to the lieutenant governors of Virginia and Pennsylvania making clear that the other four Shawnees would be released when headmen of their tribe came to Charles Town and gave assurances for the future good behavior of their people. However, the South Carolina Commons House balked at sending even two back, "till the People of the Nation to whom they shall belong shall restore such Slaves as they have taken in this Province and carried away Captives into their Country." Early in October, after the six Shawnees had been imprisoned for nearly four months, Glen finally acted on his own, writing Pennsylvania's lieutenant governor Hamilton that, though he remained suspicious of these Shawnee and concerned for the safety of South Carolina's Amerindian allies, he was sending along two of the captives. Hamilton was asked to invite Ohio Shawnee headmen down to Philadelphia or to send "some proper Person" home with the two returnees to explain the terms under which the other four would be released. Glen's calculations now included his assembly's idea of having the Shawnee return all "our friendly Indians or Mustee Slaves," noting that northern raiders were carrying off "such of our Slaves as had the least Tincture of Indian Blood in them." It is noteworthy that Glen said nothing about having the return orchestrated through Iroquoian intermediaries. Six Shawnees had become prisoners without being charged; four of them were now held hostage by a British colonial government willing to act on the widely shared assumption that one alien could be punished for the behavior of inadequately identified others.

Within two months, news of their brethren's capture had reached the Ohio Shawnee. While there is no record of Shawnee efforts to recover captured warriors, the Shawnee regarded this entrapment and incarceration in peacetime as outrageous. Two years earlier, the Shawnee had threatened the pro-French Miami with war following the capture of a Shawnee woman and a boy. In September of 1753, at conferences with uninformed and evasive Virginians and Pennsylvanians in Winchester and Carlisle respectively, the Shawnee and their Delaware neighbors both asked those governments to intervene to secure the release of the Shawnee captives. The Mingo leader Scarouyady, who regarded the Shawnee raid, the imprisonments, and these diplomatic petitions as disturbing violations of the Iroquois diplomatic overlordship that he and Tanighrisson were trying to embody, threatened to go to Charles Town himself to retrieve those he regarded as errant Shawnee subordinates. Perhaps Scarouyady should have been allowed to proceed, but he was persuaded not to leave the Ohio at this critical time. By the end of October, Robert Dinwiddie and Hamilton had dutifully written Glen inquiring about the Shawnee captives.

Before the ship carrying the two returning Shawnees left for Philadelphia, three of the four remaining Shawnee hostages escaped from the Charles Town Watch House "by cutting out one of the Iron Barrs of a Window, and bending two others." Outside assistance, perhaps even help from the Ohio Valley, was never identified; inside connivance to be rid of a problem that now included at least one very sick prisoner, was never reported. As the South Carolina council curtly explained to Dinwiddie, "Through the Negligence of the Centinel [they] escaped out of the Prison, and as they have not been retaken, have[,] as we suppose, bent their Course to their own Country." At least publicly, Governor Glen did not give up so easily, offering a few more details when he sought the help of Creek chiefs in recovering the hostages. Glen claimed that the Shawnees had initially been suspected of several attacks, even including the murder of the son of Creek chief Red Coat King. The Shawnees had been held "till the Matter was cleared up" and two were sent home to report that the others would be released on the return of "such ... Indians or Slaves as they had stollen from us." Again Glen offered a European perspective on imprisonment as a legitimate and unexceptional precaution, and emphasized that the prisoners had been well treated, given good beef and corn or bread every day and rum "very often." Despite these kindnesses, Glen complained, three had decided to escape and one of these died in the woods soon afterward. The casualty was Itawachcomequa, who died either in the woods or in jail. Glen asked the Creek to inquire about the escapees, especially among Chartier's transplanted Shawnee community, and to return the fugitives to him. He likely projected his own values on the lone Shawnee hostage who remained in custody and may still have been ill, claiming that he "thought it dishon[o]urable to go and still continues here."....

The capture and return of the Shawnees had proven a diplomatic disaster for the English. Governor Glen received neither captives nor assurances from the Shawnee; the remaining hostages had been exploited to support bold demands that lost all force when most of the hostages escaped. Glen, supported by his assembly, evidently sent the last remaining Shawnee hostage home via Virginia the following spring; he was reportedly with George Washington's doomed force near Fort Necessity in June 1754. Once again a hostage was apparently being used in an unsuccessful attempt to lure the Shawnee to a conference. Neither Lieutenant Governor Hamilton nor Pennsylvania seems to have gained much from involvement in this affair, though we do not know what Patten reported. Hamilton's diplomatic emissaries and Mingo intermediaries met strong interference. The two returned Shawnees were, in effect, exchanged for Croghan and Montour, and there was no immediate sign of Shawnee gratitude or reciprocity. English attempts to exploit the detainees had created a Shawnee grievance at a particularly dangerous time, a grievance of honor that could not easily be addressed diplomatically.

Although this bungled hostage-taking triggered anti-English violence that began six decades of intermittent war between the Ohio Shawnee and "the long knives," the Shawnee did not launch their war for another seven months. Only one of the numerous reports of the victory over George Washington's forces at Fort Necessity in July 1754 claimed that any Shawnees had been attacking with the French, Canadians, and mission Indians. Even in September 1754, when Itawachcomequa's brother and brother-in-law attended a meeting to receive condolence gifts, a Shawnee orator belatedly thanked Hamilton for "procuring the Discharge of some of the Shawanese, who had been Prisoners in Carolina, and our kind Treatment of them in their Return, and Goodness in sending them back to their Nation." There was no mention here of the complete Pennsylvanian failure to keep faith with the neighboring pro-English Miami killed in the destruction of Pickawillany. There was no complaint about the sudden absence of English trade goods in the Ohio country in 1753, though Shawnees who were considering which Europeans were the lesser evil in this crisis still needed to ensure their own access to guns, gunpowder, and ammunition. These considerations were leading many Shawnees to a different conclusion than that voiced by this orator who, in accepting the condolence gifts, told Hamilton that Itawachcomequa's death would not cause a breach with the English, though he was much lamented "and the most High knows how he came to his End."

While one Shawnee was reassuring the English that September, others were attacking them at Buffalo Creek on South Carolina's Broad River. The Shawnees who had escaped alive from the Charles Town jail had made their way home. Their confinement and escape turned them and their influential kin against the English, and others would have been convinced to join them either out of anger or in recognition of the sudden French strength and English weakness in the region. Marquis Duquesne, New France's governor, claimed that it was persistent French chiding that had eventually prompted the cautious Shawnee to seek revenge, and they had finally raided the English and sent prisoners, scalps, and an invitational war belt to neighboring tribes, including the Huron. This was the news that La Glorieux was passing on to Léry as 1755 began.

The Shawnees who had attacked the Buffalo Creek settlement in September 1754 returned without casualties and with trophies to distribute; they had killed and scalped sixteen recently established frontier settlers and thirteen others were reported missing and presumed captured. While the Carolinians could not identify the attackers in what they considered the unprovoked "Buffalo Creek Massacre," the Cherokee reported that the raiders had been Shawnee. It was likely the same avenging raiding party that, on its way home through the Cumberland Gap, killed three men at Holston's River, on land contested by the Shawnee, other tribes, and Virginians.

The Ohio Shawnee quickly came to focus on Virginia, not the more distant Carolinas, in their ensuing wars with the "long knives." Perhaps the particular score had been settled with Carolina, but it had been delayed because it was recognized as a declaration of a more general war against all the English. Land grievances, intrusions from Virginia into Ohio country, and military practicalities may all have convinced angry Shawnees to target the Virginians as their primary English enemy....

The Shawnee killed or captured more Virginians than other colonials between 1754 and 1765, and the Shawnee cooperated with the French most fully when the French targets were Virginian. Compared to other Indian attackers on the Allegheny frontiers during this period, including their very close Delaware allies, the Shawnee seem to have captured more, and killed fewer. Such apparent differences could be due to relatively poor English identification of Shawnee attackers or to the survival of detailed lists of captives still held by the Shawnee late in 1765, including some who may not have been captured by them initially. The Shawnee also tended to limit their participation in extended campaigns organized by the French. In such sustained operations, more characteristic of European than Amerindian war, a warrior could not take prisoners until the final action of the campaign, because each captor needed to guard and sustain his own captives. In these circumstances it was easier and safer to take scalps until the last strikes, though campaigns could also suddenly terminate if suitable prisoners had been captured. In contrast, the separate and parallel Ohio Shawnee war of revenge against the English lasted much longer than any

Shawnee contribution to French-backed multiracial expeditions. Shawnee attacks were usually single-strike surprise raids, with terrifying beginnings that quickly shifted to the very different tactics needed to take and keep healthy captives.

Whether or not the Shawnee were deliberately seeking multiracial demographic growth, they captured those less likely to resist with guns and more likely to adjust to life in the Shawnee communities. In clearly identified Shawnee attacks, very few children under sixteen were killed compared to the number captured (2:42), despite the fact that crying children could assist pursuers in locating war parties hurrying their captives westward. Five times as many women over sixteen were captured by the Shawnee as were killed (27:5), but there is no evidence that Virginia's Scots-Irish borderers regarded this as creating kin, like the all-but-extinct "bride-stealing" of their homelands. Women made attractive captives because they could produce more food than they consumed, even when they did not become fully integrated members of the Shawnee villages. Because adult men predominated in the armies, militias, and as laborers on Euro-American frontiers, it should be remembered that men were nearly twice as likely as women to be victims of Shawnee attacks. Nor is it surprising that adult men were eight times more likely to be killed (39:5) than were women. The Shawnee choice of captives also suggests that they regarded the capture and adoption of prisoners as a mercy to victims, and nothing like the "fate worse than death" of Amerindians in colonial jails. There are no surviving reports that the Shawnee saw the taking of captives as particularly appropriate revenge for the Charles Town captivities. Not all captives were adopted, and those who were not lived harder lives, but there is evidence of full acceptance and even eventual prominence for numerous captives taken into Shawnee society. It is particularly revealing that the Shawnee propensity to take captives was not eroded by years of war in which their English-speaking enemies took no Shawnee prisoners at all. The endless English rhetoric about exchanging prisoners with the Shawnee therefore would have been seen as entirely empty.

With justification, the Shawnee came to be compared to Spartans, the first to make war and the last to make peace. The major sticking point in Anglo-Shawnee peace negotiations between 1758 and 1765 was, invariably, the return of captives. When the British needed the neutrality of Ohio Amerindians, the return of captives could be ignored completely. After the British had defeated the French, the return of all adopted captives and even their children became a British precondition for negotiating peace. The painful return of adopted captives was, for the British, the most convincing indication that the will to peace reached beyond the Shawnee negotiators, and beyond the return of those captives who had become part of the negotiators' own families. Between 1760 and 1763 the Shawnee did not return captives in any numbers, though their raids on the British colonies were suspended. The climax of the British campaign in the Ohio in "Pontiac's War" was aimed directly at Wakatomika, where Colonel Henry Bouquet's expedition extracted some captives, a promise of the return of the remaining captives, and six hostages to support that promise. The six Shawnee hostages taken here all escaped from Pittsburgh within a month, aborting this demand for the return of captives as effectively as had the Charles Town escape a dozen years earlier.

The Shawnee captivity in Charles Town never became part of French or English descriptions of the origins of the Seven Years' War....

Early British and American histories of this world war were determined to blame the French and had no room for the embarrassing and implausible story of their own mistreatment of Shawnee captives and its consequences....

For Amerindians justifying the Shawnee war against the English, and fixing the blame on the latter, the captivity in Charles Town was their consistent explanation. In 1764, a Shawnee negotiator embroidered a little in reminding the British, "We the Shawanese never intended to be at Variance wth our Brs the English, That it is altogether yr own Faults, formerly when a Number of our Nations were going to War agt our Enemies the Catabas and was oblig'd to travel through your Country, then you laid Violence on some of our Warriors & killed them."

At the very least, these Amerindian diplomats thought the Charles Town captivities were a serious grievance to be used for diplomatic advantage when the English needed Amerindian cooperation in approaching Fort Duquesne. A claim that the British started the war, in unprovoked and undeniable violation of the kinship implied by treaty, was intended to affect the terms of a negotiated truce or peace. Admittedly, such an Amerindian argument was much more useful than admitting the attraction of visible French military strength and trading supplies during 1753, when Pennsylvania failed to avenge the destruction of Pickawillany, and English traders withdrew. Even in translation and transcription by their opponents, these diplomats sound convinced or at least they expected to be convincing; the captivity was emphasized by spokesmen who had no intention of appearing inept. They regarded the captivity as a major and undeniable grievance and used it expecting to embarrass their English counterparts and reduce their demands. It was a charge against which the British made no reply, because they had none....

There is special value in remembering that the Shawnee launched their own war against the English 250 years ago, with Delaware and Mingo allies who had their own grievances, and with Canadian allies who had a very different agenda. The Shawnee did not join a French war as bloodthirsty opportunists, as has been too easily presumed by those unaware of the Charles Town captivities, and the Shawnee disappointed the French when asked to participate in ventures not seen as part of their own war. Although not quite a "perpetual war," the Shawnee did not make peace before their Seven Years' War lengthened to eleven years. Peace, or at least a truce, came in 1765 only after the British tacitly accepted the Shawnee refusal to meet a central precondition, the return of all captives. By the next year, some Ohio Shawnees were again planning a multitribal war against the English. The Shawnee went on to fight the "long knives" of Virginia and Kentucky for another generation, between Dunmore's War of 1774 and Tecumseh's death in 1813. This long and bloodied path was continually hardened by new grievances and mutual atrocities, but it was first cut by the outrageous Charles Town imprisonments of 1753.

Survival: Indian Women in Eighteenth Century New England

BY JEAN M. O'BRIEN (OJIBWE)

In 1624, Edward Winslow, Governor of Plymouth colony, observed about Native Americans that "[t]he women live a most slavish life; they carry all their burdens, set and dress their corn, gather it in, and seek out for much of their food, beat and make ready the corn to eat and have all household care lying upon them." Winslow's use of the term "slavish" in this passage is instructive. The portrayal of the Native American woman as "squaw drudge" who toiled endlessly for her "lazie husband" was both a common English analysis of Native American division of labor in the northeastern woodlands and a commentary upon English expectations about gender roles. Observers viewed Indian women as "slaves" because, unlike English women, they performed virtually all of the agricultural labor in their societies. In fact, most labor the English would have regarded as male work was performed by Indian women.

The "squaw drudge" permeated early observations of Native Americans in the northeast. Two centuries later, different kinds of images of Indian women could be found in local accounts. Consider the following: "The last Indian here was 'Hannah Shiner,' a full-blood who lived with 'Old Toney,' a noble-souled mulatto man ... Hannah was kind-hearted, a faithful friend, a sharp enemy, a judge of herbs, a weaver of baskets, and a lover of rum." This description, taken from a nineteenth-century history of Medford, Massachusetts, reflects not just the passage of time but also the extent to which relations, roles, and expectations had changed on both sides of a sustained cultural encounter.

The juxtaposition of these two fundamentally different portrayals reveals crucial changes in the circumstances of Indian women in New England. Four key structural changes differentiate the historical eras from which the images come. First, Indian societies that were "tribal" and politically independent prior to intensive colonization became effectively "detribalized" and politically encompassed by the late seventeenth century. By this time, most Indian individuals and families were incorporated into English communities, mostly in small clusters that rendered Indians virtually invisible within the context of the now-dominant New English society. Second, the prosperity of Indian societies, based on diversified agricultural economies and intensive use of seasonally available plant and game resources, was undermined as the English gained possession of nearly all Indian land by the end of the seventeenth century. The central element of the Indian economy was thus eliminated, requiring fundamental changes that resulted in the recasting of Native gender roles. Third, Indian societies that stressed communal values, sharing, and reciprocity were thrust into a market economy with the advent of colonization. Immersion in the market left Indians at the mercy of English legal institutions and affected the shape of Native social welfare practices. And fourth, Indians were quickly rendered a minority

Jean O'Brien, "*Divorced from the Land: Resistance and Survival of Indian Women in Eighteenth-Century New England,*" in Gender, Kinship, Power: A Comparative and Interdisciplinary Study, Mary Jo Maynes, et al. (New York: Routledge Press, 1996), 319–44.

population within their own homelands by the astounding success of the English demographic regime, which was coupled with Indian struggles caused by imported diseases and military encounters. These structural changes compelled Indians to see the landscape in a different way, requiring them to make massive adjustments, and eliciting myriad and contradictory responses.

As they successfully dispossessed and displaced Indians, the heirs of English colonialism seized the power to define the rules governing the social order, and they constructed surviving New England Indians as peculiar and marginal. Local historians underscored the "disappearance" of the Indian population by singling out individuals such as Hannah Shiner as representing the "last survivor" of their "tribe." Even so, historians used their representations of Indians as peculiar and marginal, as hopelessly "other," to continue to constitute and affirm an English identity. They presented Indians such as Hannah Shiner as the complement to "Englishness," thereby reminding themselves of the persistent difference between Indian survivors and themselves. But more than just reinforcing the difference between Indians and themselves, the ways in which they used this binary operated to emphasize English dominance.

The English colonial regime imposed a different landscape, one requiring Indians to transform their relationship to the land. Gender figured prominently in this transformation. The English aimed to "divorce" Indians from their possession of the land in order to establish themselves and English culture in their place. New England Indians' agricultural, hunting, fishing, and gathering economy was interpreted as wasteful, and the sedentary agriculture pursued by English men was seen as the only proper pursuit for Native men. Yet even as they pursued the larger project of English colonialism (replacing Indians and Indian ways of using the land with English people using the land in English ways), colonists also aimed to convert surviving Indians to English culture. As they separated Indians from possession of virtually all their land, colonists also sought to "divorce" Indian women from their role as agriculturalists, replacing them with male Indians working drastically reduced plots of land to the exclusion of hunting and other older economic pursuits. From the perspective of the English, "divorce" from the land would fulfill the biblical directive to "subdue the earth and multiply" by bringing land into agricultural production to sustain a growing English Christian population. And it would also place Indian women and men in a "proper" relationship to the land. In the most crucial sense, however, the English failed to "divorce" either Indian women or Indian men from the land. Although in narrow legal terms, the English succeeded in imposing their own rules for possessing the land, New England Indians did not monolithically embrace English gender ways. They remained crucially connected to the land that sustained their kinship and visiting networks and their own sense of proper place.

In addressing the transformations accompanying the cultural conflicts between Indians and English colonists, I will focus on the issue of "gendered division of labor" rather than on the important problem of lineality in the northeastern woodlands, which also involved different conceptions of how gender ought to operate. Use of the dichotomous construction of matrilineal/patrilineal obscures much diversity in the ordering of families, reckoning of descent, ordering of power relations, and much more. Because of the paucity of early sources that provide detailed information on social organization, combined with the early occurrence of devastating epidemics throughout the region, there is much we will never know about the "precontact" shape of social organization in the northeastern woodlands. Indian peoples in early New England were concerned overwhelmingly with resisting and surviving English incursions, and the disruptions of epidemics that accompanied early contact certainly must have obscured their previous shape at least to some extent. About all that is evident is that, by the eighteenth century, patrilineal naming practices predominated among Indians; whether this was the case because it had always been so, or because the English imposed these forms on Indians in bureaucratic transactions, is not so clear.

About a gendered division of labor, much more seems to be apparent. Most scholars agree that women performed most agricultural labor (except growing tobacco), built and transported bark or mat wigwams from place to place, manufactured baskets and pottery, gathered shellfish and wild foodstuff, processed hides, made clothing, and raised children. Men also made some household tools and were the principal woodworkers, making canoes and fortifications, for example.

By 1700, Native American groups in New England had a long history of encounters with Europeans. Indians reeled from the impact of imported epidemic diseases, with many groups suffering demographic declines on the order of 90 percent. Military conquest followed quickly on the heels of the epidemiological disasters. The last major war in southeastern New England ended in 1676, terminating the political independence of those Native groups who had hitherto avoided encompassment by the English. These events effectively ended the autonomy of Indian groups in that region and rendered many aspects of the aboriginal economy obsolete through massive displacement and dispossession. Under the cumulative impact of the colonial experience, a great many New England Indians found themselves landless, a diasporic population vulnerable to the institutions of English colonialism.

Missionary sponsorship had secured land bases for several Indian groups in the seventeenth century as part of English efforts to transform Indian cultures. Here, the English expected Indians to alter their gender roles in conformity with English cultural prerogatives. Indian groups were allowed to retain small plots of land provided they would express responsiveness to missionary messages about cultural change. The English expected Indians to erect compact, English-style towns in order to fix them in particular places, directed men to forego hunting in favor of agricultural duties, and trained women in "household skills," especially spinning and weaving. Indians were encouraged to adopt English work habits, individual ownership of land, English tastes in material culture, and values structured by a market economy. Some Indians experimented with cultural transformations along these lines, but success in the market economy did not follow so easily. Many Indians were landless at the beginning of the eighteenth century, and, as their land was transformed into a commodity, Indian landowners continued to lose land. Many were encompassed within the flourishing English settlements, finding niches in colonial economies, performing agricultural and nonagricultural labor.

Although some Indians steadfastly resisted English influences on their lifeways, and others struggled within the market economy, still others borrowed extensively from English culture as a means of accommodating to English colonialism. In some senses, Jacob and Leah Chalcom symbolized Indian transformation as conceptualized by the English. Chalcom purchased land, established an English-style farm, and built a frame house in Natick, Massachusetts, an important mission town established seventeen miles southwest of Boston. He was involved actively in the local land market, buying and selling small parcels from time to time as he strove to upgrade his farm. The cultural priorities of this family are visible in their childrearing practices. The Chalcom children were literate, and the daughters were given dowries upon their marriages to local Indian men. After his death, Chalcom's estate included a thirty-acre homelot and "Buildings thereon," plus other lands, an assortment of household goods and husbandry tools, a horse, a cow, and books. After debts against his estate were discharged, fifty-two acres of land remained to be divided among his heirs.

The women in Chalcom's family had made corresponding changes in their life-ways, including their separation from agricultural tasks. Leah Chalcom and her widowed daughters, Esther Sooduck and Hepzibeth Peegun, inherited land from their husband and father respectively. Finding themselves without husbands, they pondered what to do with their inheritance. In 1759 they petitioned the Massachusetts General Court to sell their forty-six acres, arguing that "as your Petitioners [have been] brought up to Household business, [we are] incapable of improving said lands." They requested that their lands be sold and the money be put out to earn interest for their income and support, a strategy adopted by a number of women. The implication here is quite clear: These women were no longer farmers and were thus unable to "improve" the land except insofar as it represented a monetary resource. The mother and daughters recognized that English financial strategies could sustain them and prolong the nurturing functions of land from which they were effectively torn loose. Putting money "at interest" constituted one strategy for women who had maintained clear "legal" connections to the land. Their decision not to use the land for gardening, as English women often did, in part reflected their perception that if they chose to keep the land it would "speedily be exhausted by frequent Law-Suits."

The "Household business" to which Leah Chalcom and her daughters referred reflects the efforts of English missionaries to realign Native American gender roles. Biblical imperatives motivated missionaries who aimed to train Indian women in English skills for structuring a household, and to integrate Indian families into the market economy. In 1648, missionary John Eliot wrote that: "[t]he women are desirous to learn to spin, and I have procured Wheels for sundry of them, and they can spin pretty well. They begin to grow industrious, and find something to sell at Market all the yeer long[.] Some Indian women continued to pursue these tasks that missionaries had pushed so vigorously in the early years of intensive English-Indian contact. Fifteen percent of inventories of Indian estates from Natick filed between 1741 and 1763 listed spinning wheels. Ruth Thomas, who died in 1758, was described in her probate docket as a weaver; Esther Freeborn and Hannah Lawrence, sisters who both left wills, were described as spinsters.

Esther Sooduck, also a weaver, died in 1778. Her probate documents vividly evoke the kinds of changes Indian women confronted even though very few accumulated and held onto material goods as successfully as Esther had. Her house, described as "much out of repair," nonetheless contained an impressive array of furnishings and sat upon thirty acres of land. Included among her belongings were a bed and bedstead, a chest, a trunk, a rug, a table and two chairs, plus knives, forks, and pewter. She read her two old Bibles with "speticals." She owned two spinning wheels, as well as baskets and "Baskets Stuf." Apparently merged in her economic pursuits were English skills (spinning and weaving) and Native American artisanal production (basket-making).

Native American women displayed transformations in their work habits, material life, aesthetic emphases, and even their physical appearance. Hannah Lawrence owned several articles of clothing when she died in the 1770s, including several gowns and aprons (one of them linen) as well as quilted petticoats and a pair of shoes with buckles. Cloth replaced animal skins, petticoats and gowns were substituted for skirts and leggings. These accommodations were rooted in more than a century of profound cultural change. And in many ways, they represent an *uprooting*, a broken connection: English-style clothing signified the distance women had moved from their former way of life. Eighteenth-century economic adaptations no longer produced the materials for older ways of clothing production, and adopting English styles probably reflected not just this reality but also newer Indian tastes.

There were many ways in which Native American women in eighteenth-century New England *were* divorced from the land: the colonial experience reoriented their relationship to the land in tangible and not so tangible ways. English ideals for cultural change aimed to realign the Indians' gendered economy and make room for English people to subdue the land in English ways. For Indian women, this meant a stark separation: once the principal producers of the crucial agricultural element of subsistence economies, women were expected to sever the vital connection they had to the soil as its principal cultivators and nurturers. Though the English who wanted to accomplish these changes may not have noticed, their models for transformation went well beyond a simple shift in the gendered organization of labor. On the practical level, knowledge and skills were altered drastically, and the content of material life was dramatically recast. On the ideological level, less visible reverberations can only be imagined in individual and corporate identity, belief systems, and other deeply rooted cultural values. The tensions accompanying these transformations can be glimpsed in one possible explanation for the ultimate failure of Indian men as farmers in a market economy, which suggests that their reluctance to tend crops stemmed from their view that these "effeminate" pursuits properly remained women's work. In refusing English gender ideals, many Indian men resisted this foundational concept of English colonialism.

Leah Chalcom, Esther Sooduck, Hannah Lawrence—all of these women came from one kind of Indian community. They all lived in Indian-dominated towns, their land ownership sanctioned by the English, who conferred "possession" of these reduced plots of land according to English legal principals. At least in this nominal sense, they were beneficiaries of missionary endeavors. Although they were relatively successful in emulating English ways, as the eighteenth century unfolded, the slow but steady dispossession of Indian landowners allowed fewer Indians to replicate earlier successes. Other Indians were uprooted utterly almost from the beginning of their contact with the English. They adjusted to English invasion differently, mapping out alternative kinds of lifeways. After the 1660s, for example:

> The remnant of the Pocumtuck Confederacy, adopting in part the
> English costume, had gathered about the English in the valley
> towns ... Here they lived a vagabond life, eking out, as they could, a
> miserable existence on the outskirts of civilization ... So hampered,
> their stock of venison or beaver, with which to traffic for English
> comforts, was small, and the baskets and birch brooms made by the
> squaws ill supplied their place.

This is a stark outline of the principal difficulties Indians faced in making the transition to landlessness within a society emphasizing the market. With the possibilities for hunting gone, and no land—what remained? Production of Indian crafts constituted one possibility for women, who remained important in the economy and maintained this earlier economic role, which was possible even when landless. In their artisanal production, women continued to cultivate the specialized knowledge required to gather materials for fashioning baskets and other crafts. Their craftwork represented a revealing accommodation to dispossession: reaping basket stuff did not require "possession" of the land. At the same time, in marketing Indian goods, they earned an income and reinforced their "Indianness" in the popular perception.

Craft production by Indian women constituted one of the crucial threads that ran through the seventeenth, eighteenth, and nineteenth centuries in New England. Indian women in the eighteenth century were engaged especially in basket making as an economic activity, but other artisanal skills were added as well. In 1764, Abigail Moheag attested that she was "64 years of Age and ... a widow [for] more than fifteen years and hath ... by her Industry in the business of making Brooms Baskets and horse Collars; Supported her Self till about two years ago She was taken sick." The inventory from Hannah Speen's estate listed "baskets and barkes, brombs and brombsticks." Craftwork, including the production of "new" items like horse collars, moved from the periphery of women's economic activities to the center as Indian women became enmeshed in the market and were no longer engaged in farming. For some women, craft production was fundamentally redefined. No longer one activity in an integrated economy, performed seasonally and for purposes largely internal to the household, artisanal activities became specialized and divorced from seasonal rhythms, and a principal means to get a living....

Banding together just to survive, these women struggled within a radically changing world. Often their situation was complicated by the dramatic transformations accompanying their dispossession, which stretched Indian communities thinly across the landscape to form a network of small clusters of families throughout southeastern New England. One response was to move constantly in search of a niche. As landlessness accelerated throughout the eighteenth century, a pattern of Indian vagrancy emerged: this pattern, accepted by the dominant society as natural, was also an accommodation strategy. Indian women, especially, were described as wandering from place to place, a characteristic that was associated in the pubic mind particularly with Indians. An Englishman of Dorchester petitioned the General Court in 1753 as follows:

> An Indian Woman called Mercy Amerquit, I think Born Somewhere about Cape-Cod, but had no settled Dwellingplace any where,...
> Strolled about from one Town & Place to another, & sometimes she wrought for persons that wanted her work[. She] came to my House... and desired liberty to tarry a little while, and your Petr condescended, expecting that she would go some other place in a little time (as their manner is) and what work she did for your Petr she was paid for as she earned it.

It is clear from this passage that English observers expected Indians to "wander." Their semisedentary lifeways had always been regarded most simplistically as nomadism. In the eighteenth century this translated into constant movement, "from one Town & Place to another ... as their manner is." In this case, an arrangement seems to have been negotiated that involved Mercy Amerquit performing labor for wages as well as for her temporary residence with the narrator. He expected her to "go [to] some other place in a little time," and the arrangement was regarded as rather unexceptional. The only reason this relationship was documented at all was because Amerquit died while in the petitioner's residence and he sought to recover money he expended for her burial.

The story of Mercy Amerquit was by no means unique. An Englishman from Roxbury reported to the General Court about sixty-year-old Hannah Comsett, who became ill at his house: "She informs that her Mother was born at Barnstable, she at Scituate, and that for 30 years past she has been [strolling] about from Town to Town getting her living where she could but never lived During that time the space of one year at any Town at any time." Though Hannah Comsett's mobility seems rather astounding, there are so many similar stories available that it is certain it was not an aberration.

The mechanisms behind Indian vagrancy were complex. Prior to the arrival of the English, Indian societies in New England reaped abundance from economies that depended upon knowledge about and extensive use of resources and a semi-sedentary lifeway. Scheduled mobility lay at the center of this system. In the eighteenth century, Indian migrations may have been scheduled, but if so, they were motivated by very different priorities since they could no longer rely on movements governed by independently composed Indian communities to and from places that "belonged" to them in the strict legal sense. Probably kinship ties and some knowledge of labor markets entered into movements, but for women like Mercy and Hannah, there seemed to be nothing particularly patterned about their shifting about. Perhaps it was setting about to track the occasional charitable English colonist that spurred on the solitary and needy

Indian women, from whom a different kind of resource might be procured. One important element that differentiated earlier migratory practices from new patterns was their largely individual nature; this new "vagrancy" drew upon older patterns and places, but was not necessarily kin-group sponsored movement with planned, deliberate ends in mind. At the heart of the problem lay landlessness, whether it had resulted from military conquest in the seventeenth century or from failure in the market economy in the eighteenth. "Divorced" from the land initially when their economic role was redefined along English lines, a much more literal separation had been accomplished for most by the middle of the eighteenth century.

The situation of these women hints at two recurrent themes regarding Indian women in eighteenth-century New England. First, transiency is graphically described in a manner consistent with the emerging problem of landless poverty in New England more generally. The "wandering Indian" had much in common with the "strolling poor," although the fact that the English categorically distinguished between the two offers testimony for their separatist views about race. The problem of Indian women seems to have been compounded, however. The extent to which these are stories of women alone, or mostly alone, is the second theme and it is most striking.

Where were the men? The evidence suggests that, despite the missionary model of settled agriculture performed by men within nuclear families on family farms, transiency also remained characteristic even of landowning Indian men. Most Indian landowners lost what they had over time, and the tendency for Indian men to enter service in two areas (military service and the emerging whaling industry) contributed to a grossly distorted sort of transiency. As a result of their participation in these activities, Indian men were absent for extended periods of time, engaged in dangerous pursuits that seriously jeopardized their lives and well-being and compromised their ability to function effectively within the English-dominated society. Whaling, in fact, fostered the same sort of debt peonage that proved so devastating in fur trade relationships. These orientations contributed to uncertainty and instability for Indian families and also reduced the number of Indian men available as desirable spouses. Interpretations of the involvement of Indian men in the military and labor at sea have stressed the continuity in skills and culturally determined priorities they offered them. But some men also abandoned their families to escape their predicaments; evidence may be found in scattered narratives of Indian men "absconding" as difficult circumstances evolved into insurmountable economic and legal problems. Such was the case for Eunice Spywood's husband, who "Some Years Ago Absconded and left her in very distressing Circumstances, and he ... never returned."

An important cumulative effect of English colonialism was to reconfigure the relationships among Indian mobility, a gendered division of labor, and household structures. The semisedentary Indian economy entailed a gendered mobility that assumed that women and men would be apart for periods of time: Men departed central villages for hunting and fishing, leaving women to tend crops and gather wild plant resources near their villages, for example. But these periods of separation were scheduled, part of the seasonal rhythm of life, and as such they rendered neither women nor men helpless. Newer patterns of male mobility (such as participation in the whaling industry and the military) that drew upon older Indian life-ways frequently left women alone to experience harsher circumstances than before, when kin-based social welfare and flexible marriages had provided them with the means to alleviate their wants. At least for women like Mercy Amerquit and Hannah Comsett, mobility was circumscribed by virtue of their being separated from men. And whereas whaling and military service may have reformulated earlier patterns of Indian male mobility, allowing men to resist the redefinition of gender in economic and social roles, the wives of these men—women like Eunice Spywood—were defined as "responsibilities" in new ways and experienced far greater hardship as a result of their men's flight. The English nuclear family model thus reconfigured kin responsibilities and marriage, leaving Indian women newly vulnerable to "divorce" in dramatically different ways.

Whatever the underlying motivations, Indians of both sexes experienced hardship as a direct result of participation of Indian men in military service, especially. The social and demographic impact of the Seven Years' War on Indian enclaves in New England was enormous. In 1756, a cluster of Indians at Mattakesett in Pembroke, Massachusetts, pleaded to the General Court "that Several of us [have] in the late Warrs, lost our husbands & Sons, & Some of our Sons [are] yet in Sd Service, & that some of us are old, blind, & bed rid & helpless poor Creatures, Many of us [are] old Women & want help." Indians of Eastham and Harwich in Barnstable County, Massachusetts, complained that many of their men "Have Died in ye Service & left their Squa & Children in Distressing Circumstances." In 1761 Ezra Stiles reported that in Portsmouth, Rhode Island, "4 Ind. Boys [had] enlisted in the service ... only one Boy more in Town, & he [is] about 10 y. old. I can't find ... any Ind. Men in Town, ... but several Squaws, perhaps 8 or 10." At Milford, Connecticut, there were twenty male Indians in 1755, at the beginning of the Seven Years' War, but in 1761 "not one: but 3 or 4 Squaws."

Even when they did return, many Indian men were rendered incapable of working to support themselves or their families as a result of war-related disabilities. Thomas Awassamug complained to the Massachusetts General Court in 1761 that "he having been engaged ... as a Soldier ... for more than thirty years past, has indured inexpressible hardships, and fatigues and thereby brought on him the Gout, and many other ailments ... And [he has] no means of support." Awassamug sought to stir compassion by describing in detail his "deplorable Circumstances," and to clarify his own relationship with the colony by reminding the magistrates that he had "jeopardized his life in so many ... very dangerous Enterprizes against those of his nation who remain Savage, and in behalf of his friends, the English." The General Court allowed a small sum to be paid out of the public treasury for his temporary relief.

No comprehensive evidence is available to investigate the precise dynamics of demographic change for Indians in eighteenth-century New England. Several censuses gathered by Stiles in his journeys through the region are suggestive, however. In addition to his more random observations, Stiles compiled detailed lists of residents by household from three Indian communities he visited in 1761 and 1762. In these communities, widows constituted heads of households in proportions ranging from 29 percent (Mashantucket Pequot in Groton, Connecticut) to 52 percent (the "Potenummekuk" Indians in Eastham and Nauset, Massachusetts). These figures suggest that the tribulations outlined above were not idle and unconnected complaints.

One solution to the apparently growing problem of unbalanced sex ratios and insufficient numbers of Indian men was for Indian women to find spouses among free or enslaved African Americans, who occupied similarly marginal positions in New England. The dynamics of intermarriage between Indians and African Americans are difficult to map precisely from the surviving documentary record. Impressionistic evidence does exist. Stiles observed in 1761 that "At Grafton [Massachusetts] ... I saw the Burying place & Graves of 60 or more Indians. Now not a Male Ind. in the Town, & perh. 5 Squaws who marry Negroes." A nineteenth-century history of Needham, Massachusetts, noted that there was "a colony of negroes, with more or less Indian blood, dwelling along the south shore of Bullard's Pond (Lake Waban)." Clearly, intermarriage did occur, as yet another kind of accommodation on the part of Indian women, representing an important demographic shift for Native populations of the northeast.

Equating "Indianness" with "blood quantum" (the perceived importance of "pure" blood lines) in rigid ways, English observers failed to understand the demographic and cultural changes that were reconfiguring "race" in New England. Intermarriage, which blurred the picture for those who looked for racial "purity," helped the Native population of New England to survive the devastating consequences of English colonization. Most colonists who noticed Indians just lamented what they saw as an inevitable process of extinction. Some vaguely grasped the complex process of vagrancy and intermarriage that was so central to eighteenth-century accommodations, even if their cultural blinders rendered them incapable of analyzing the changes. In 1797, the minister at Natick observed that

> It is difficult to ascertain the complete number of those that are now
> here, or that belong to this place, as they are so frequently shifting
> their place of residence, and are intermarried with blacks, and some
> with whites; and the various shades between these, and those that are
> descended from them, make it almost impossible to come to any
> determination about them.

Indians became, like other groups displaced by the colonizing impulse of the English, a diasporic population defined by the complex transformations and dislocations brought about by English colonialism. In the end, the migratory pattern and complexities of intermarriage created an erroneous impression in the minds of English observers that the Native population was simply and inevitably melting away.

In truth, monumental Indian adjustments spanned the entire colonial period and stretched into the nineteenth century. Both precontact Native American societies in the northeast and early modern European societies were organized according to particular expectations about gender roles. In New England, Indian women were responsible for most agricultural tasks, for gathering wild foods, building houses, most craft production, and childrearing. Men were warriors, diplomats, hunters, and fishermen, and they aided women in agricultural production by clearing fields. This way of organizing society came into direct conflict with English expectations, and the ability to maintain an economy that perfectly reflected older Native gender roles ran into the hard realities of changing circumstances. The loss of political independence and the massive displacement of Indians within their homelands brought tremendous changes that affected Indian women and men in different ways. Hunting and fishing became marginal, diplomacy became obsolete, and military involvement was transformed into economic activity. Agriculture was enormously altered in technique and organization: it became predominantly if not exclusively a male activity for Indian landowners, and it became a diminishing element of the Indian economy as Indians continued to lose land throughout the eighteenth century.

Although English expectations for change within Indian culture (encapsulated most fully in missionary platforms) called for altering the gendered Indian division of labor, the English did not fully succeed in "divorcing" Indian women (or men) from the land. Even though they quite successfully dispossessed Indians, Indians remained in the homelands that continued to sustain their kin, community, and sense of place. Indian women and men found creative solutions for resisting displacement and surviving as Indian people in a milieu theoretically designed to erase their difference completely.

How does all of this connect to Hannah Shiner? The manner in which she is portrayed in the nineteenth-century account that I began with, compared to how she might have been characterized in the seventeenth century, speaks volumes. This Indian woman is not described generically, as most Indian women were when regarded as members of a tribal unit, but as an individual with an Anglicized name. Her categorization as an Indian is based on the observer's judgment of her (pure) genealogy. And her husband is seen as a "mulatto," a mate who probably could trace some African American heritage. Hannah Shiner was assigned several traits, including two ("judge of herbs" and "weaver of baskets") that were associated in the public imagination with "Indianness," and especially with Indian women. They also suggest trades, or means of support, that had always been female activities. Hannah Shiner symbolizes the tumultuous changes experienced by Native peoples in seventeenth- and eighteenth-century New England. Indian peoples survived the catastrophe of English colonization, and they resisted the erasure of their Indianness. Men and women experienced the fundamental transformations in their life-ways differently. "Divorced" from the land in some respects but, crucially, not in others, many women displayed the characteristics that are visible in this brief description of Hannah Shiner. Apparently accepted and incorporated as an individual member of the community of Medford, Massachusetts, Hannah Shiner represents a particular kind of transformation, though not of the sort English missionaries had in mind. "Marginal" and a bit "exotic," she was portrayed as a bit of "local color," a tangible tie to what seemed to be (but was not) an increasingly distant Indian past. Her configuration by a local historian as such was precisely what Anglo-Americans needed for her to continue to represent the "otherness" necessary for the ongoing construction of their own difference.

◈ FURTHER READING

Anderson, Fred. *Crucible of War: The Seven Years' War and the Fate of Empire in British North America, 1754–1766* (2000).

Bragdon, Kathleen J. *Native People of Southern New England, 1650–1775* (2009).

Brooks, Joanna, ed. *The Collected Writings of Samson Occom, Mohegan: Leadership and Literature in Eighteenth-Century Native America* (2006).

Brooks, Lisa. *The Common Pot: The Recovery of Native Space in the Northeast* (2008).

Calloway, Colin G., ed. *After King Philip's War: Presence and Persistence in Indian New England* (1997).

———. *The Scratch of a Pen: 1763 and the Transformation of North America* (2006).

———. *The Shawnees and the War for America* (2007).

———. *The Western Abenakis of Vermont, 1600–1800: War, Migration, and the Survival of an Indian People* (1990).

———. *The World Turned Upside Down: Indian Voices from Early America* (1994).

———, and Neal Salisbury, eds. *Reinterpreting New England Indians and the Colonial Experience* (2004).

Dixon, David. *Never to Come to Peace Again: Pontiac's Uprising and the Fate of the British Empire in North America* (2005).

Fenn, Elizabeth A. "Biological Warfare in Eighteenth-Century North America: Beyond Jeffery Amherst." *Journal of American History* 86 (March 2000): 1552–1580.

Haefeli, Evan, and Kevin Sweeney. *Captors and Captives: The 1704 French and Indian Raid on Deerfield* (2003).

Harper, Stephen Craig. *Promised Land: Penn's Holy Experiment, the Walking Purchase, and the Dispossession of the Delawares, 1600–1763* (2006).

Hinderaker, Eric. *Elusive Empires: Constructing Colonialism in the Ohio Valley, 1673–1800* (1997).

Jennings, Francis. *Empire of Fortune: Crowns, Colonies, and Tribes in the Seven Years' War in America* (1988).

Juricek, John T. *Colonial Georgia and the Creeks: Anglo-Indian Diplomacy on the Southern Frontier, 1733–1763* (2010).

Kalter, Susan, ed. *Benjamin Franklin, Pennsylvania, and the First Nations: The Treaties of 1736–62* (2006).

Kenny, Kevin. *Peaceable Kingdom Lost: The Paxton Boys and the Destruction of William Penn's Holy Experiment* (2009).

Mandell, Daniel R. *Behind the Frontier: Indians in Eighteenth-Century Eastern Massachusetts* (1996).

Merrell, James H. *The Indians' New World: Catawbas and Their Neighbors from European Contact Through the Era of Removal* (1989).

————. *Into the Woods: Negotiators on the Pennsylvania Frontier* (2000).

Merritt, Jane. *At the Crossroads: Indians and Empires on a Mid-Atlantic Frontier, 1700–1763* (2003).

Middleton, Richard. *Pontiac's War: Its Causes, Course and Consequences* (2007).

O'Brien, Jean M. *Dispossession by Degrees: Indian Land and Identity in Natick, Massachusetts, 1650–1790* (1997).

Oliphant, John. *Peace and War on the Anglo-Cherokee Frontier, 1756–1763* (2001).

Perdue, Theda. *Cherokee Women: Gender and Culture Change, 1700–1835* (1998).

Piker, Joshua. *Okfuskee: A Creek Indian Town in Colonial America* (2004).

Ranlet, Philip. "The British, the Indians, and Smallpox: What Actually Happened at Fort Pitt in 1763?" *Pennsylvania History* 67 (Summer 2000): 427–441.

Richter, Daniel K. *Before the Revolution: America's Ancient Pasts* (2011).

Silver, Peter. *Our Savage Neighbors: How Indian War Transformed Early America* (2008).

Silverman, David J. *Faith and Boundaries: Colonists, Christianity, and Community Among the Wampanoag Indians of Martha's Vineyard, 1600–1871* (2005).

Snyder, Christina. *Slavery in Indian Country: The Changing Face of Captivity in Early America* (2010).

Stevens, Laura M. *Poor Indians: British Missionaries, Native Americans, and Colonial Sensibility* (2004).

Sugden, John. *Blue Jacket: Warrior of the Shawnees* (2000).

Szasz, Margaret Connell. *Scottish Highlanders and Native Americans: Indigenous Education in the Eighteenth-Century Atlantic World* (2007).

Ward, Matthew. *Breaking the Backcountry: The Seven Years' War in Virginia and Pennsylvania, 1754–1765* (2003).

Wheeler, Rachel. *To Live Upon Hope: Mohicans and Missionaries in the Eighteenth-Century Northeast* (2008).

White, Richard. *The Middle Ground: Indians, Empires, and Republics in the Great Lakes Region, 1650–1815* (1991).

CHAPTER 7

Continental Transformations,

1763–1815

The Native peoples of North America witnessed tremendous changes in the late 1700s and early 1800s. In much of the eastern half of the continent, Indigenous communities found themselves swept up in yet another European conflict that was not of their making. In this case, European colonists, now increasingly calling themselves "Americans," rebelled against their mother country, Great Britain. Meanwhile, Native peoples far to the west confronted their own notable European challenge, in this case from the Spanish. After more than two centuries' worth of activity elsewhere in the Western Hemisphere, including parts of the American Southwest, the Spanish had now turned their attention north up the Pacific Coast to present-day California. In 1769, while British troops made rebellious Boston into an occupied city, Native Californians watched as Franciscan priests initiated an occupation of their own.

Thus, as the eighteenth century drew to a close and the nineteenth century began, American Indians on both sides of the continent experienced momentous transformations. How were the transformations similar, and how did they differ? In what ways did they echo previous Indian histories, and in what ways did they depart from them? How did Native peoples respond to the changes? And to what extent did the Spanish period prepare, or not prepare, Native Californians for the challenge that was yet to come, this one emanating from the nation born of that eastern war: the United States of America?

◈ DOCUMENTS

In the eastern half of the continent between 1763 and 1815, no event was more transformative than the American Revolution. It brought obvious changes for the former English colonists, but it also altered the lives of Native peoples in far-reaching ways. Documents 1 through 5 give us a variety of looks at the Revolutionary War through Native eyes. As Document 1 reveals, in the summer of 1776, a delegation of Iroquois leaders, on the invitation of the American revolutionary government, travelled to Philadelphia. There, they received presents and a message from the Congress of the new United States. The Iroquois Confederacy would have to consider their position in the colonists' war, as would Indians up and down the east coast. The Cherokees, under the leadership of Dragging Canoe, decided to join the British and fight the Americans. By the spring of 1777, American forces had made the Cherokees suffer for their decision, and most were ready to make peace. Document 2 is a message that Colonel Nathaniel Gist, whose wife was a Cherokee, sent to the Cherokees to offer them peace, and to warn of what might happen should they refuse. In Document 3, Dragging Canoe presents a Cherokee response to Gist's words. Mary Jemison gives an Iroquois (Seneca) account of the war in Document 4. Jemison happened to be English; she had been captured by the Senecas while a teenager, and was eventually adopted into the tribe. Document 5 further tells the story of the Iroquois, in this case through the treaty they had to sign with the now fully independent United States following the war, in 1784.

The last two documents shift our attention chronologically and geographically. They offer glimpses of California Indian history in the early 1800s. In Document 6, Pablo Tac, a Luiseño who was reared in the Mission of San Luis Rey de Francia and who later studied for the priesthood in Rome, gives an account of his early life in the California missions. In Document 7, Lorenzo Asisara, a Costanoan, provides an alternate view of the California mission experience in a story about how one group of mission Indians responded to the rule of a particular friar, Father Quintana.

1. The United States Speaks to the Iroquois, 1776

[June 11, 1776]

The presents being provided for the Indians, they were called in, and the speech agreed to, was delivered as follows:

BROTHERS,

We hope the friendship that is between us and you will be firm, and continue as long as the sun shall shine, and the waters run; that we and you may be as one people, and have but one heart, and be kind to one another like brethren.

BROTHERS,

The king of Great Britain, hearkening to the evil counsel of some of his foolish young men, is angry with us, because we will not let him take away from us our land, and all that we have, and give it to them, and because we will not do everything that he bids us; and hath hindered his people from bringing goods to us; but, we have made provision for getting such a quantity of them, that we hope we shall be able to supply your wants as formerly.

This document can be found in Colin Calloway, ed., *Early American Indian Documents: Treaties and Laws*, Vol. 18 Revolution and Confederation (Bethesda, MD: University Publications of America, 1994), pg. 39.

BROTHERS,

We shall order all our warriors and young men not to hurt your or any of your kindred, and we hope you will not suffer any of your young men to join with our enemies, or to do any wrong to us, that nothing may happen to make any quarrel between us.

BROTHERS,

We desire you to accept a few necessaries, which we present you with, as tokens of our good will towards you.

The presents being delivered, the Indians begged leave to give a name to the president; the same being granted, the Onondago chief gave the president the name of Karanduawn, or the Great Tree, by which name he informed him the president will be known among the Six nations.

||After which the Indians took their leave and withdrew.||

2. Colonel Gist of Virginia Addresses the Cherokee Chiefs, 1777

[March 28, 1777]

Brothers, Occunastotah, Raven, Dragging Canoe, and old Tassel.

When I parted with you I promised to be back before cold Weather was done, and according to your desire, have spoke to the great Warriours of the American states for Peace for you, and now send by your own People some of the Talks they gave me and have several more good Talks to give when you come to this Place to treat. I also now send you two strings of Wampum that was delivered me by the Delawares and Shawnees, for the Cherokees, desiring that they would no more listen to the Lying bad Talks carried you by some of their foolish People and the Mingoes.

You know all, particularly the Dragging Canoe, that what I advised last year, before you went to War, was for your good, and would have saved the Lives of many of your People, and saved your Towns from being destroyed. Now I tell you again, this Year, it will be much worse than last, unless you now make Peace, when the good Time is come As it is the last offer of Peace you will get from Virginia. So dont blame me when hard time comes again among you. As I have now told you the Truth, advised you for your good, and now offer to shake hands with all my Brothers the Cherokees in behalf of Virginia. The Bearer hereof or Runner sent from you with a white Flag, must come to me here in twenty days, that I may know whether you are coming for Peace or not; they shall be kindly treated and kept from harm.

Great Island Fort 28 March 1777

Nathal. Gist.

This document can be found in Colin Calloway, ed., *Early American Indian Documents: Treaties and Laws, Vol. 18 Revolution and Confederation* (Bethesda, MD: University Publications of America, 1994), pg. 216.

3. Dragging Canoe (Cherokee) Replies to Colonel Gist, 1777

[April 1777]

At a Treaty held at this place last April the Commissioners sent a Talk by Col. Gist to the Dragging Canoe who returned Colo. Gist the following answer.

Brother

Though your messenger is not come to me yet I have heard your Talks and hold them fast as long as I live, for they have opened my Eyes and made me see clear, that Cameron and Stewart have been telling me lies, when we had any Talks with the Virginians he was always mad with us, and told us that all that the Virginians wanted was to get our Land and kill us, and that he had often told us we would not hear him till the Virginians would come and kill us all. Now Brother I plainly see that he made me quarrel with the greatest friends that we ever had, who took pity on us even in the greatest distress, when my old men, women and children is perishing for something to live on, this makes it more plain to me that he cared not how many of us were killed on both sides so that we were dead, killed in Battle, or perrished with hunger, any way so we were dead.

Brother, I heard you were taken prisoner and confined, my heart was sorry as tho you had been my born Brother, when I thought of their bad treatment to you I expected never to see you. I thought they had killed you or sent you away as that I should never see you more. That made my heart very cross and I went to war more for revenge for you than any other reason. But now Brother I am sorry for it, since I see that the great being above has sent you back to save me and my people. Now Brother the great Warrior and your beloved men are sitting together, I am determined that I nor my people shall never spoil their good talks while I live, when I am dead there will be annother man to take my place.

Brother I am going to see the man that told me all those lieing Talks and return him his meddle and Beds and tell him for the future to keep all his lieing talks to himself. He sends me word that he is coming from Mobile with a great many Scotsmen and intends to offer you a peace; if you wont accept it he intends to kill and force you to it. Brother I shall make no stop on the road, but shall be back soon and come straight to you and tell you all the news. If I should not come in soon pray excuse me to the beloved men as you are better acquainted with me than they are, and you can talk better than I can, and you know Brother I will not do anything that will make you ashamed of me among your people.

This document can be found in Colin Calloway, ed., *Early American Indian Documents: Treaties and Laws*, Vol. 18 Revolution and Confederation (Bethesda, MD: University Publications of America, 1994), pp. 217–18.

4. Mary Jemison Remembers the American Revolution, 1775–1779

Thus, at peace amongst themselves, and with the neighboring whites, though there were none at that time very near, our Indians lived quietly and peaceably at home, till a little before the breaking out of the revolutionary war, when they were sent for, together with the Chiefs and members of the Six Nations generally, by the people of the States, to go to the German Flats, and there hold a general council, in order that the people of the states might ascertain, in good season, who they should esteem and treat as enemies, and who as friends, in the great war which was then upon the point of breaking out between them and the King of England.

Our Indians obeyed the call, and the council was holden, at which the pipe of peace was smoked, and a treaty made, in which the Six Nations solemnly agreed that if a war should eventually break out, they would not take up arms on either side; but that they would observe a strict neutrality. With that the people of the states were satisfied, as they had not asked their assistance, nor did not wish it. The Indians returned to their homes well pleased that they could live on neutral ground, surrounded by the din of war, without being engaged in it.

About a year passed off, and we, as usual, were enjoying ourselves in the employments of peaceable times, when a messenger arrived from the British Commissioners, requesting all the Indians of our tribe to attend a general council which was soon to be held at Oswego. The council convened, and being opened, the British Commissioners informed the Chiefs that the object of calling a council of the Six Nations, was, to engage their assistance in subduing the rebels, the people of the states, who had risen up against the good King, their master, and were about to rob him of a great part of his possessions and wealth, and added that they would amply reward them for all their services.

The Chiefs then arose, and informed the Commissioners of the nature and extent of the treaty which they had entered into with the people of the states, the year before, and that they should not violate it by taking up the hatchet against them.

The Commissioners continued their entreaties without success, till they addressed their avarice, by telling our people that the people of the states were few in number, and easily subdued; and that on the account of their disobedience to the King, they justly merited all the punishment that it was possible for white men and Indians to inflict upon them; and added, that the King was rich and powerful, both in money and subjects: That his rum was as plenty as the water in lake Ontario: that his men were as numerous as the sands upon the lake shore:— and that the Indians, if they would assist in the war, and persevere in their friendship to the King, till it was closed, should never want for money or goods. Upon this the Chiefs concluded a treaty with the British Commissioners, in which they agreed to take up arms against the rebels, and continue in the service of his Majesty till they were subdued, in consideration of certain conditions which were stipulated in the treaty to be performed by the British government and its agents.

This document can be found in James Seaver, ed., *The Narrative of the Life of Mary Jemison.* Copyright © 1824.

As soon as the treaty was finished, the Commissioners made a present to each Indian of a suit of clothes, a brass kettle, a gun and tomahawk, a scalping knife, a quantity of powder and lead, a piece of gold, and promised a bounty on every scalp that should be brought in. Thus richly clad and equipped, they returned home, after an absence of about two weeks, full of the fire of war, and anxious to encounter their enemies. Many of the kettles which the Indians received at that time are now in use on the Genesee Flats....

Previous to the battle at Fort Stanwix, the British sent for the Indians to come and see them whip the rebels; and, at the same time stated that they did not wish to have them fight, but wanted to have them just sit down, smoke their pipes, and look on. Our Indians went, to a man; but contrary to their expectation, instead of smoking and looking on, they were obliged to fight for their lives, and in the end of the battle were completely beaten, with a great loss in killed and wounded. Our Indians alone had thirty-six killed, and a great number wounded. Our town exhibited a scene of real sorrow and distress, when our warriors returned and recounted their misfortunes, and stated the real loss they had sustained in the engagement. The mourning was excessive, and was expressed by the most doleful yells, shrieks, and howlings, and by inimitable gesticulations.

During the revolution, my house was the home of Col's Butler and Brandt, whenever they chanced to come into our neighborhood as they passed to and from Fort Niagara, which was the seat of their military operations. Many and many a night I have pounded samp for them from sun-set till sun-rise, and furnished them with necessary provision and clean clothing for their journey....

At that time I had three children who went with me on foot, one who rode on horse back, and one whom I carried on my back.

Our corn was good that year; a part of which we had gathered and secured for winter.

In one or two days after the skirmish at Connissius lake, Sullivan and his army arrived at Genesee river, where they destroyed every article of the food kind that they could lay their hands on. A part of our corn they burnt, and threw the remainder into the river. They burnt our houses, killed what few cattle and horses they could find, destroyed our fruit trees, and left nothing but the bare soil and timber. But the Indians had eloped and were not to be found.

Having crossed and recrossed the river, and finished the work of destruction, the army marched off to the east. Our Indians saw them move off, but suspecting that it was Sullivan's intention to watch our return, and then to take us by surprize, resolved that the main body of our tribe should hunt where we then were, till Sullivan had gone so far that there would be no danger of his returning to molest us.

This being agreed to, we hunted continually till the Indians concluded that there could be no risk in our once more taking possession of our lands. Accordingly we all returned; but what were our feelings when we found that there was not a mouthful of any kind of sustenance left, not even enough to keep a child one day from perishing with hunger.

The weather by this time had become cold and stormy; and as we were destitute of houses and food too, I immediately resolved to take my children and look out for myself, without delay. With this intention I took two of my little ones on my back, bade the other three follow, and the same night arrived on the Gardow flats, where I have ever since resided....

... The snow fell about five feet deep, and remained so for a long time, and the weather was extremely cold; so much so indeed, that almost all the game upon which the Indians depended for subsistence, perished, and reduced them almost to a state of starvation through that and three or four succeeding years. When the snow melted in the spring, deer were found dead upon the ground in vast numbers; and other animals, of every description, perished from the cold also, and were found dead, in multitudes. Many of our people barely escaped with their lives, and some actually died of hunger and freezing.

5. The Iroquois and the U.S. Make the Treaty of Fort Stanwix, 1784

Articles

Concluded at Fort Stanwix, on the twenty-second day of October, one thousand seven hundred and eighty-four, between Oliver Wolcott, Richard Butler, and Arthur Lee, Commissioners Plenipotentiary from the United States, in Congress assembled, on the one Part, and the Sachems and Warriors of the Six Nations, on the other.

The United States of America give peace to the Senecas, Mohawks, Onondagas and Cayugas, and receive them into their protection upon the following conditions:

Article I.   Six hostages shall be immediately delivered to the commissioners by the said nations, to remain in possession of the United States, till all the prisoners, white and black, which were taken by the said Senecas, Mohawks, Onondagas and Cayugas, or by any of them, in the late war, from among the people of the United States, shall be delivered up.

Article II.   The Oneida and Tuscarora nations shall be secured in the possession of the lands on which they are settled.

Article III.   A line shall be drawn, beginning at the mouth of a creek about four miles east of Niagara, called Oyonwayea, or Johnston's Landing-Place, upon the lake named by the Indians Oswego, and by us Ontario; from thence southerly in a direction always four miles east of the carrying-path, between Lake Erie and Ontario, to the mouth of Tehoseroron or Buffaloe Creek on Lake Erie; thence south to the north boundary of the state of Pennsylvania; thence west to the end of the said north boundary; thence south along the west boundary

---

This document can be found in Wilcomb E. Washington, comp., *The American Indian and the United States: A Documentary History*, 4 Volumes (Westport, CT: Greenwood Press, 1973), Vol. IV, pp. 2267–2271.

of the said state, to the river Ohio; the said line from the mouth of the Oyonwayea to the Ohio, shall be the western boundary of the lands of the Six Nations, so that the Six Nations shall and do yield to the United States, all claims to the country west of the said boundary, and then they shall be secured in the peaceful possession of the lands they inhabit east and north of the same, reserving only six miles square round the fort of Oswego, to the United States, for the support of the same.

Article IV. The Commissioners of the United States, in consideration of the present circumstances of the Six Nations, and in execution of the humane and liberal views of the United States upon the signing of the above articles, will order goods to be delivered to the said Six Nations for their use and comfort.

Oliver Wolcott	Oneidas.
Richard Butler,	Otyadonenghti,
Arthur Lee.	Dagaheari.
Mohawks.	Cayuga.
Onogwendahonji,	Oraghgoanendagen.
Towighnatogon.	
Onondagas.	Tuscarora.
Oheadarighton,	Ononghsawenghti,
Kendarindgon.	Tharondawagen.
Senecas.	Seneca Abeal.
Tayagonendagighti,	Kayenthoghke.
Tehonwaeaghriyagi.	

Witnesses: Sam. Jo. Atlee, Wm. Maclay, Fras. Johnston, Pennsylvania Commissioners. Aaron Hill, Alexander Campbell, Saml. Kirkland. Miss'y. James Dean, Saml. Montgomery, Derick Lane, Capt. John Mercer, Lieut. William Pennington, Lieut. Mahlon Ford, Ensign. Hugh Peebles.

6. Pablo Tac (Luiseño) Recalls His Life in a California Mission, 1835

... The Fernandino Father, as he was alone and very accustomed to the usages of the Spanish soldiers, seeing that it would be very difficult for him alone to give orders to that people, and, moreover, people that had left the woods just a few years before, therefore appointed alcaldes from the people themselves that knew how to speak Spanish more than the others and were better than the others in their customs. There were seven of these alcaldes, with rods as a symbol that they could judge the others. The captain dressed like the Spanish, always remaining

This document can be found in Pablo Tac, *Indian Life and Customs at the Mission San Luis Rey: A Record of California Mission Life by Pablo Tac, An Indian Neophyte*, edited by Minna Hewes and Gordon Hewes (San Luis Rey, CA, 1958), pp. 12–13, 19–21.

captain, but not ordering his people about as of old, when they were still gentiles. The chief of the alcaldes was called the general. He knew the name of each one…. In the afternoon, the alcaldes gather at the house of the missionary. They bring the news of that day, and if the missionary tells them something that all the people of the country ought to know, they return to the villages shouting, "Tomorrow morning…."

Returning to the villages, each one of the alcaldes wherever he goes cries out what the missionary has told them, in his language, and all the country hears it. "Tomorrow the sowing begins and so the laborers go to the chicken yard and assemble there." And again he goes saying these same words until he reaches his own village to eat something and then to sleep. In the morning you will see the laborers appear in the chicken yard and assemble there according to what they heard last night.

    With the laborers goes a Spanish majordomo and others, neophyte alcaldes, to see how the work is done, to hurry them if they are lazy, so that they will soon finish what was ordered, and to punish the guilty or lazy one who leaves his plow and quits the field keeping on with his laziness. They work all day, but not always. At noon they leave work, and then they bring them *posole*. (*Posole* is what the Spaniards of California call maize in hot water.) They eat it with gusto, and they remain sated until afternoon when they return to their villages. The shoemakers work making chairs, leather knapsacks, reins and shoes for the cowboys, neophytes, majordomos and Spanish soldiers, and when they have finished, they bring and deliver them to the missionary to give to the cowboys. The blacksmiths make bridle bits, keys, bosses for bridles, nails for the church and all work for all….

In the Mission of San Luis Rey de Francia the Fernandino Father is like a king. He has his pages, alcaldes, majordomos, musicians, soldiers, gardens, ranchos, livestock, horses by the thousand, cows, bulls by the thousand, oxen, mules, asses, 12,000 lambs, 200 goats, etc. The pages are for him and for the Spanish and Mexican, English and Anglo-American travelers. The alcaldes to help him govern all the people of the Mission of San Luis Rey de Francia. The majordomos are in the distant districts, almost all Spaniards. The musicians of the Mission for the holy days and all the Sundays and holidays of the year, with them the singers, all Indian neophytes. Soldiers so that nobody does injury to Spaniard or to Indian; there are ten of them and they go on horseback. There are five gardens that are for all, very large. The Fernandino Father drinks little, and as almost all the gardens produce wine, he who knows the customs of the neophytes well does not wish to give any wine to any of them, but sells it to the English or Anglo-Americans, not for money, but for clothing for the neophytes, linen for the church, hats, muskets, plates, coffee, tea, sugar and other things. The products of the Mission are butter, tallow, hides, chamois leather, bear skins, wine, white wine, brandy, oil, maize, wheat, beans and also bull horns which the English take by the thousand to Boston.

[Daily life in a mission Indian household begins] when the sun rises and the stars and the moon go down, then the old man of the house wakens everyone and begins with breakfast which is to eat *juinis* heated and meat and tortillas, for we do not have bread. This done, he takes his bow and arrows and leaves the house with vigorous and quick step. (This is if he is going to hunt.) He goes off to the distant woods which are full of bears and hares, deer and thousands of birds. He is here all day, killing as many as he can, following them, hiding himself behind trees, climbing them, and then loaded with hares he returns home happy. But when he needs wood, then he leaves the house in the morning with his tump-line [carrying strap] on his shoulders and his ax, with companions who can help him when the load is very heavy, and in the afternoon he returns home. His old woman staying at home makes the meal. The son, if he is man, works with the men. His daughter stays with the women making shirts, and if these also have sons and daughters, they stay in the mission, the sons at school to learn the alpha-bet, and if they already know it, to learn the catechism, and if this also, to the choir of singers, and if he was a singer, to work, because all the musical singers work the day of work and Sunday to the choir to sing, but without a book, because the teacher teaches them by memory, holding the book. The daughter joins with the single girls who all spin for blankets for the San Luiseños and for the robe of the Fernandino Father. At twelve o'clock they eat together and leave the old man his share, their cups of clay, their vessels of well-woven fiber which water cannot leak out of, except when it is held before the face of the sun, their frying pans of clay, their grills of wood made for that day, and their pitchers for water also of clay. Seated around the fire they are talking and eating. Too bad for them if at that time they close the door. Then the smoke rising, being much, and the opening which serves as a window being small, it turns below, trying to go out by the door, remains in the middle of the house, and they eat, then speaking, laughing and weeping without wishing to. The meal finished they return to their work. The father leaves his son, the son leaves his sister, the sister the brother, the brother the mother, the mother her husband with cheer, until the afternoon. Before going to bed again they eat what the old woman and old man have made in that time, and then they sleep....

7. Lorenzo Asisara (Costanoan) Tells of an Indian Response to a Priest's Authority, 1812

Lorenzo's Narrative: "The Death of Padre Andrés Quintana"

The following story which I shall convey was told to me by my dear father in 1818. He was a neophyte of the Mission of Santa Cruz. He was one of the original founders of that mission. He was an Indian from the rancheria of *Asar* on the *Jarro* coast, up beyond Santa Cruz. He was one of the first neophytes baptized at the founding, being about 20 years of age. He was called Venancio Asar, and was the gardener of the Mission of Santa Cruz.

My father was a witness to the happenings which follow. He was one of the conspirators who planned to kill Father Quintana. When the conspirators were

From Edward D. Castillo, trans. and ed., "The Assassination of Padre Andrés Quintana by the Indians of Mission Santa Cruz in 1812: The Narrative of Lorenzo Asisara," *California History* 68 (Fall 1989), 117–25. Reprinted by permission of the California Historical Society.

planning to kill Father Quintana, they gathered in the house of Julian the gardener (the one who made the pretense of being ill). The man who worked inside the plaza of the mission, named Donato, was punished by Father Quintana with a whip with wire. With each blow it cut his buttocks. Then the same man, Donato, wanted vengeance. He was the one who organized a gathering of 14 men, among them were the cook and the pages serving the Father. The cook was named Antonio, the eldest page named Lino, the others named Vicente and Miguel Antonio. All of them gathered in the house of Julian to plan how they could avoid the cruel punishments of Father Quintana. One man present, Lino, who was more capable and wiser than the others, said, "The first thing we should do today is to see that the Padre no longer punishes the people in that manner. We aren't animals. He [Quintana] says in his sermons that God does not command these [punishments]—but only examples and doctrine. Tell me now, what shall we do with the Padre? We cannot chase him away, nor accuse him before the judge, because we do not know who commands him to do with us as he does." To this, Andrés, father of Lino the page, answered, "Let's kill the Padre without anyone being aware, not the servants, nor anyone, except us that are here present." (This Lino was pureblooded Indian, but as white as a Spaniard and man of natural abilities.) And then Julian the gardener said, "What shall we do in order to kill him?" His wife responded, "You, who are always getting sick—only this way can it be possible—think if it is good this way." Lino approved the plan and asked that all present also approve it. "In that case, we shall do it tomorrow night." That was Saturday. It should be noted that the Padre wished all the people to gather in the plaza on the following Sunday in order to test the whip that he had made with pieces of wire to see if it was to his liking.

All of the conspirators present at the meeting concurred that it should be done as Lino had recommended.

On the evening of Saturday at about six o'clock [October 12] of 1812, they went to tell the Padre that the gardener was dying. The Indians were already posted between two trees on both sides so that they could grab Father when he passed. The Padre arrived at the house of Julian, who pretended to be in agony. The Padre helped him, thinking that he was really sick and about to die. When the Padre was returning to his house, he passed close to where the Indians were posted. They didn't have the courage to grab him and they allowed him to pass. The moribund gardener was behind him, but the Padre arrived at his house. Within an hour the wife of Julian arrived [again] to tell him [the Father] that her husband was dying. With this news the Padre returned to the orchard, the woman following behind crying and lamenting. He saw that the sick man was dying. The Padre took the man's hand in order to take his pulse. He felt the pulse and could find nothing amiss. The pulse showed there was nothing wrong with Julian. Not knowing what it could be, the Padre returned to pray for him. It was night when the Padre left. Julian arose and washed away the sacraments [oil] that he [the Padre] had administered, and he followed behind to join the others and see what his companions had done. Upon arriving at the place where they were stationed, Lino lifted his head and looked in all directions to see if they were coming out to grab the Father. The Father passed and they didn't take him. The Father arrived at his house.

Later, when the Father was at his table dining, the conspirators had already gathered at the house of the alleged sick man to ascertain why they hadn't seized Father Quintana. Julian complained that the Padre had placed herbs on his ears, and because of them, now he was really going to die. Then the wife of Julian said, "Yes, you all did not carry through with your promised plans; I am going to accuse you all, and I will not go back to the house." They all answered her, "All right, now, in this trip go and speak to the Father." The woman again left to fetch Father Quintana, who was at supper. He got up immediately and went where he found the supposedly sick man. This time he took with him three pages, two who walked ahead lighting his way with lanterns and behind him followed his Mayordomo Lino. The other two were Vincente and Miguel Antonio. The Father arrived at the gardener's house and found him unconscious. He couldn't speak. The Father prayed the last orations without administering the oils, and said to the wife, "Now your husband is prepared to live or die. Don't come to look for me again." Then the Father left with his pages to return to his house. Julian followed them. Arriving at the place where the two trees were (since the Father was not paying attention to his surroundings, but only in the path in front of him), Lino grabbed him from behind saying these words, "Stop here, Father, you must speak for a moment." When the other two pages who carried the lanterns turned around and saw the other men come out to attack the Father, they fled with their lanterns. The Father said to Lino, "Oh, my Son, what are you going to do to me?" Lino answered, "Your assassins will tell you."

"What have I done to you children, for which you would kill me?"

"Because you have made a *cuarta de hierro* [a horse whip tipped with iron] ... ," Andrés answered him. Then the Father retorted, "Oh, children, leave me, so that I can go from here now, at this moment." Andrés asked him why he had made this *cuarta de hierro*. Quintana said that it was only for transgressors. Then someone shouted, "Well, you are in the hands of those evil ones, make your peace with God." Many of those present (seeing the Father in his affliction) cried and pitied his fate, but could do nothing to help him because they were themselves compromised. He pleaded much, promising to leave the mission immediately if they would only let him.

"Now you won't be going to any part of the earth from here, Father, you are going to heaven." This was the last plea of the Father. Some of them, not having been able to lay hands on Father, reprimanded the others because they talked too much, demanding that they kill him immediately. They then covered the Father's mouth with his own cape to strangle him. They had his arms tightly secured. After the Father had been strangled, they took a testicle [*grano de los companonez*] so that it would not be suspected that he had been beaten, and in a moment Padre expired. Then Lino and the others took him to his house and put him in his bed.

When the two little pages, Vincente and Miguel Antonio, arrived at the house, the former wanted to tell the guard, but the other dissuaded him by saying, "No, they, the soldiers, will also kill your mother, father, all of the others and you yourself and me. Let them, the conspirators, do what they want." The two hid themselves. After the Indians had put the Father in his bed, Lino looked for the two pages, and he found them hidden. They undressed the body of Father Quintana and placed him in the bed as if he were going to sleep. All of the conspirators, including Julian's wife, were present. Andrés asked Lino for the keys to the store-room. He handed them over saying, "What do you want?" And they said silver and beads. Among the group there were three Indians from the Santa Clara mission. These proposed that they investigate to see how much money there was. Lino opened the box and showed them the accumulated gold and silver. The three Indians from Santa Clara took as much as they could carry to their mission. (I don't know what they have done with that money.) The others took their portions as they saw fit.

Then they asked for the keys to the convent or the nunnery. Lino gave the keys to the *jayunte*, or barracks of the single men, to one of them in order to free them and gather them together below in the orchard with the unmarried women. They gathered in the orchard so that neither the people in the plaza nor in the rancheria nor in the guard-house would hear them. The single men left and without a sound gathered in the orchard at the same place where the Father was assassinated. There was a man there cautioning them not to make any noise, that they were going to have a good time. After a short time the young unmarried women arrived in order to spend the night there. The young people of both sexes got together and had their pleasure. At midnight Lino, being in the Padre's living room with one of the girls from the single women's dormitory, entered the Father's room in order to see if he was really dead. He found him reviving. He was already on the point of arising. Lino went to look for his accomplices to tell them that the Padre was coming to. The Indians returned and they crushed the Father's other testicle. This last act put an end to the life of Father Quintana. Donato, the one who had been whipped, walked around the room with the plural results of his operation in hand saying, "I shall bury these in the outdoor privy."

Donato told Lino that they should close the treasure chest with these words, "Close the trunk with the colored silver (that is the name that the Indians gave to gold) and let's see where we shall bury it." The eight men carried it down to the orchard and buried it secretly without the others knowing.

At about two o'clock in the morning, the young girls returned to their convent and the single men to their *jayunte* without making any noise. The assassins gathered once more after everything had occurred in order to hear the plans of Lino and Donato. Some wanted to flee, and others asked, "What for? No one except us knows." Lino asked them what they wanted to take to their houses, sugar, *panocha* [a sugar loaf], honey, or any other things, and suggested that they lay down to sleep for a while. Finally everything was ready. Donato proposed to return to where the Father was to check on him. They found him not only lifeless, but completely cold and stiff. Lino then showed them the new whip that the Padre was planning to use for the first time the next day, assuring them that he [Father Quintana] would not use it. He sent them to their houses to rest, remaining in the house with the keys. He asked them to be very careful. He arranged the room and the Bible in the manner in which the Father was accustomed to doing before retiring, telling them that he was not going to toll the bells in the morning until the Mayordomo and Corporal of the guard came and he had talked to them. All went through the orchard very silently.

This same morning (Sunday) the bells should have been rung at about eight o'clock. At that hour the people from the villa de Branciforte began to arrive in order to attend the mass. The Mayordomo, Carlos Castro, saw that the bells were not being rung and went to ask Lino, who was the first assistant to the Father, in order to ask why the Padre had not ordered him [to toll the bells]. Lino was in the outer room feigning innocence and answered the Mayordomo that he couldn't tell him anything about the Father because he was still inside sleeping or praying, and that the Mayordomo should wait until he should speak to him first. The Mayordomo returned home. Soon the Corporal of the guard arrived and Lino told him the same as to the Mayordomo. The Mayordomo returned to join in the conservation. They decided to wait a little while longer. Finally Lino told them that in their presence he would knock on the door of the room, observing, "If he is angry with me, you will stand up for me." And so he did, calling to the Father. As he didn't hear noise inside, the Mayordomo and Corporal asked Lino to knock again, but he refused. They then left, encharging him to call the Father again because the hour was growing late. All of the servants were busy at their jobs as always, in order not to cause any suspicion. The Mayordomo returned after ten o'clock and asked Lino to call the Padre to see what was wrong. Lino, with the keys in his pocket, knocked at the door. Finally the Mayordomo insisted that Lino enter the room, but Lino refused. At this moment, the Corporal, who was old Nazario Galindo, arrived. Lino (although he had the key to the door in his pocket) said, "Well, I am going to see if I can get the door open," and he pretended to look for a key to open the door. He returned with a ring of keys but he didn't find one that opened the lock. The Mayordomo and Corporal left to talk to some men who were there. Later, Lino took the key that opened the door, saying that it was for the kitchen. He opened another door that opened into the plaza (the key opened three doors), and through there he entered. Then he opened the main door from inside in front of which the others waited. Lino came out screaming and crying, and carrying on in an uncontrolled manner and saying that the Padre was dead. They asked him if he was certain and he responded, "As this light that illuminates us. By God, I'm going to toll the bells." The three entered, the Corporal, the Mayordomo, and Lino. He didn't allow anyone else to enter. The Corporal and the Mayordomo and the other people wrote to the other missions and to Monterey to Father Marcelino Marquinez. (This Marquinez was an expert horseman and a good friend.) The poor elderly neophytes, and many other Indians who never suspected that the Father was killed, thought that he had died suddenly. They cried bitterly. Lino was roaring inside the Father's house like a bear.

The Fathers from Santa Clara and from other missions came and they held the Father's funeral, all believing that he had died a natural death, but not before examining the corpse in the entrance room, and had opened the stomach in order to be certain that the Padre had not been poisoned. Officials, sergeants, and many others participated in these acts but nothing was discovered. Finally, by chance, one of those present noted that the testicles were missing, and they were convinced that this had been the cause of death. Through modesty they did not reveal the fact and buried the body with everyone convinced that the death had been a natural one....

◈ ESSAYS

The American Revolution is a story that most of us think we know quite well: Colonists cast off the tyrannical rule of the British in their pursuit of freedom, equality, and democracy. But simply including American Indians in the story revises—significantly if not completely—our understanding of this seminal event in United States history. In the first essay below, Colin G. Galloway, Professor of History and Native American Studies at Dartmouth College, does just that, paying particular attention to Indian experiences in the years following the Revolution. While Native peoples in the east were contending with the political upheavals that the Revolutionary War generated, Indians in California were dealing with the cultural disruptions brought on by the Spanish missions. Indigenous Californians found Spanish cultural attitudes toward sexuality, for example, to be not only strange, but also troublesome, since Spanish priests insisted on forcibly imposing their beliefs upon them. In the second essay, Albert L. Hurtado, emeritus professor of history at the University of Oklahoma, details the dissonance between the two cultures, and relates some of the problems that ensued from it.

Eastern Transformations: The Aftermath of the American Revolution in Indian Country, 1783–1800

BY COLIN G. CALLOWAY

For all the devastation the American Revolution brought to Indian country, Indians remained a force to be reckoned with at the war's end. In reading the reports of American invasions of Indian country, it is easy to assume, as did some American commanders, that burning Indian villages and destroying crops constituted a knockout blow. But burning homes, razing fields, and killing noncombatants does not necessarily destroy people's will to fight or even their ability to win. Geoffrey Parker's observation about the resilience of peasant communities victimized by European wars—"as in Vietnam, what was easily burnt could also be easily rebuilt"—sometimes held true for Indian communities during the Revolution. Many survived the destruction of their villages. George Rogers Clark recognized the limitations of the American

Colin Calloway, *The American Revolution in Indian Country* (Cambridge, UK: Cambridge University Press, 1995). Reprinted with the permission of Cambridge University Press.

search-and-destroy missions, and an officer on Sullivan's campaign agreed that burning crops and villages was not the same as killing Indians: "The nests are destroyed but the birds are still on the wing." A British officer reviewing the American campaigns against the Iroquois and the Cherokees agreed that such a system of warfare was "shocking to humanity," and as sound military strategy was "at best but problematical." The Indians in the West were holding their own in 1782. The real disaster of the American Revolution for Indian peoples lay in its outcome.

Speaking on a war belt in council with the British in Detroit in December 1781, the Delaware war chief Buckongahelas declared that his warriors had been making blood "fly" on the American frontier for five years. The next year, 1782 the last of the war, witnessed even bloodier conflict. Indians routed American forces at Blue Licks and Sandusky. Americans slaughtered Moravian Delawares at Gnadenhütten and burned Shawnee villages. Delawares ritually tortured Colonel William Crawford and, as atrocities mounted, they and the Shawnees pushed "their retaliation to great length by putting all their prisoners to death."

Then the British and Americans made peace. The Peace of Paris recognized the independence of the thirteen colonies and transferred to the new United States all land east of the Mississippi, south of the Great Lakes, and north of the Floridas. Wyandot chiefs, who had heard rumors of peace, told Major De Peyster "we hope your children [i.e., the Indians] will be remembered in the Treaty," but the peace terms made no mention of the Indian people who had fought and died in the Revolution and who inhabited the territory to be transferred. The Peace of Paris brought a temporary lull in hostilities, but it brought no peace to Indian country. Rather, by ending open conflict between non-Indian powers, it deprived Indians of allies and diplomatic opportunities as they continued their struggle for independence against Americans who claimed their lands as the fruits of victory.

If a speech that John Heckewelder attributed to Captain Pipe is accurately dated and recorded, Indians were apprehensive of British betrayal even as they carried war to the Americans in 1781. "Think not that I lack *sufficient sense to convince me*," the Delaware chief told Major De Peyster at Detroit, "that altho' You *now* pretend to keep up a perpetual enmity to the Long Knives (American People), you may, e'er long, conclude a Peace with them!" The British, he said, had set him on their enemy like a hunter setting his dogs on his quarry, but he suspected that if he glanced back, "I shall probably see my Father shaking hands with the Long Knives." Pipe's worst fears were now realized. As news of the peace terms filtered into Indian country, Indian speakers in council after council expressed their anger and disbelief that their British allies had betrayed them and handed their lands over to their American and Spanish enemies. The head warrior of the Eufalees refused to believe that the English would abandon the Indians; another Creek chief dismissed reports of the treaty as "a Virginia Lie." The Iroquois were "thunderstruck" when they heard that British diplomats had sold them out to the Americans without so much as a reference to the tribes. Little Turkey of the Overhill Cherokees concluded, "The peacemakers and our Enemies have talked away our Lands at a Rum Drinking." Okaegige of the Flint River Seminoles reminded the British that the Indians took up the hatchet for the king "at a time we could scarce distinguish our Friends from our Foes," and asked if the king now intended to sell them into slavery. Fine Bones, speaking for his Cowetas and other Upper Creeks, said they could not now turn around and take the Spaniards and Virginians by the hand; if the English intended to evacuate, the Indians would accompany them.

Alexander McGillivray told the British he could no longer keep his people in the dark. After nine years of faithful service, "at the Close of it to find ourselves & Country betrayed to our Enemies & divided between the Spaniards & Americans is Cruel & Ungenerous." The Indians had done nothing to permit the king to give away their lands, "unless ... Spilling our blood in the Service of his Nation can be deemed so." The Indians had been "most Shamefully deserted." Turning to the Spaniards, McGillivray reiterated that Britain had no right to give up what it did not own, and that the Creeks as a free nation had the right to choose what allies they thought most appropriate. "The protection of a great Monarch is to be preferred to that of a distracted Republic," he said, courting Governor Estevan Miró, but making it clear he would turn to the Americans for trade if necessary. Spanish officials referred patronizingly to McGillivray as "nuestro mestizo," but McGillivray deftly pursued Creek, not Spanish, interests in the decade after the Revolution.

Many southern Indians—"having made all the world their Enemies by their attachment to us"—expressed their determination to evacuate along with the British rather than stay and come to terms with the Americans and Spaniards, but the British discouraged them. William Augustus Bowles, masquerading as a Creek chief in London eight years later, summed up the situation: "The British Soldier, when he left the shore of America, on the proclamation of peace, had peace indeed, and returned to a Country where Peace could be enjoyed; But to the Creek & Cherokee Indians was left, to drain to the dregs the remainder of the bitter cup of War, unassisted & alone." McGillivray asked the British army at least to leave the Creeks military stores so that they could defend themselves against the Americans.

Indian people farther from the center of revolutionary conflict felt the betrayal equally hard. The Chippewa chief, Matchekwis, visited Michilimackinac in September 1784, and when Captain Daniel Robertson refused his requests for presents, the Indian

> abused me in a very particular manner, as all our great men below, saying we were all Lyers, Impostures &c. that had encouraged him and others to go to Canada &c. to fight and loose their Brothers and Children, now despise them, and let them starve, and that they, the Indians ought to chasse us and our connections out of the country.

British officers and Indian agents scrambled to save face and reconcile the Indians to "this unfortunate event," fearing that their former allies might with good reason turn and vent their rage on the people who had betrayed them. British traders prepared to leave Indian villages even as British officers stressed the need to maintain the usual supplies to the Indians although the war was over. Sir John Johnson's speech to the Iroquois, in which he naively or cynically reassured them that he could not believe the United States intended to deprive them of their land on pretext of having conquered it, was relayed to other tribes. The Indians were advised to bear their losses with fortitude, forget what was past, and look forward to the blessings of peace. Not too sure themselves about the peaceful intentions of the new republic, and determined to protect their interests among the Indians, the British resolved to hold on to the frontier posts that were supposed to be handed over to the United States "with all convenient speed" under the peace terms. Retention of these posts, which stretched from Lake Champlain to Michilimackinac, conveyed the impression that the British were on hand to support the tribes in continuing resistance to the United States, even though Britain carefully avoided renewed war with the United States. Spain operated a similar policy to check American expansion in the south: Spanish officials encouraged McGillivray "by word of mouth" and did their best to "help the Indians without the Americans being able to prove that we have done so."

Meanwhile, Americans made the most of British perfidy. They told the Shawnees that Britain had cast them aside "like Bastards." Virginian emissary John Dodge told the Chickasaws that the English had been forced to withdraw from the country and "their Poor foolish Indians which refused to make Peace with us, is miserable on the Earth, Crying & begging for mercy Every Day." General Philip Schuyler told the Six Nations Indians that the British deceived them if they told them they were included in the peace; "the treaty does not contain a single stipulation for the Indians, they are not even so much as mentioned." At the beginning of the war, Schuyler said, he had asked the Six Nations to sit still and they had not listened. Now, like the Loyalists, they had forfeited their lands. "We are now Masters of this Island, and can dispose of the Lands as we think proper or most convenient to ourselves," the general declared. Six Nations delegates listened in bewilderment. From what he heard from his messengers, Joseph Brant thought Schuyler "as Saucy as [the] very devil," and thought the Iroquois delegates behaved shamefully. "After our friends the English left us in the lurch, still our own chiefs should make the matter worse," he wrote to Major Robert Mathews. "I do assure you I begin to prepare my death song for vexation will lead one to rashness."

The peace signed in Paris did little to change things in the backcountry world inhabited by Indians and American frontiersmen. Frontier vendettas continued and old scores remained unsettled. Some people on the eastern seaboard were appalled by the massacre of the Moravian Delawares in 1782, but William Irvne, commanding at Fort Pitt, knew that people who lived closer to the Indians and had lost relatives in the war felt very differently. He warned his wife to keep her opinions about the massacre to herself, as he would: "No man knows whether I approve or disapprove of killing the Moravians." The Indian-hating that produced and sanctioned the Moravian massacre paid no regard to words of peace exchanged in Paris and made real peace impossible in Indian country. Commander De Peyster at Detroit warned his superiors in the fall of 1782 that the backcountry settlers would continue to make war on the Delawares, Shawnees, and Wyandots even after Britain and her revolted colonists made peace. Allan MacLean at Niagara feared that while he was busy preventing the Indians from going to war in the spring of 1783, the rebels "were preparing to cut the throats of the Indians.

Nor were all Indian people eager to embrace the peace. Warriors with relatives to avenge paid little attention to formal peace terms worked out by men far from the bloodletting. A Potawatomi, singing the war song, told Major De Peyster he was eager for action in 1781 because "you see me here in mourning and I am ashamed to remain so." Another asked De Peyster "for means to enable him to revenge himself" for the loss of his kinsman. John Montour, a mixed-blood Delaware who flits in and out of the records, "was one of Seven Brothers, all of them reckoned able good Warriors at the Commencement of the Rebellion, five of them have been Since killed in the service." While the war drew to a close and the British tried to keep their allies at peace, John and his surviving brother were out in Indian country, anxious for revenge. In November 1782, they came into Fort Niagara with four scalps and three young female prisoners, saying they knew nothing about the suspension of hostilities.

The end of the Revolution produced a new phase of conflict between Indians and Americans in the Ohio country. Murders, horse thefts, raids, and counterraids continued with little abatement. "While empires and states went about making peace," explains Richard White, "the villages continued to act on their own." Like the British after 1763, American policymakers could no more control their citizens than Indian chiefs could control their young men. A flood of backcountry settlers invaded Indian country, broke down what remained of the "middle ground" arrangements of coexistence that had been built up over generations, and knocked the heart out of federal attempts to regulate the frontier. Many of these people, reported a congressional committee, had no more desire for peace with the Indians than the British had for peace between Indians and Americans. As revolutionary violence gave way to postwar peace and a future of prosperity in some other areas of the country, vengeance and strife continued to be a way of life and of getting things done in Indian country, even in relations between whites. Tension between frontier settlers and eastern elites resulted in western demands for autonomy, separatist movements, violent confrontations, and the breakdown of normal means of redress.

During the war, American soldiers had returned from expeditions into Indian country with stories of the rich lands awaiting them once independence was won. With the Peace of Paris under their belts, Americans now set about taking over Indian lands as the spoils of victory. Peace initiated a new era of land speculation and unleashed a new land rush into Indian country.... A delegation of 260 Iroquois, Shawnee, Cherokee, Chickasaw, Choctaw, and "Loup" Indians visiting the Spanish governor of Saint Louis in the summer of 1784 already felt the effects of the American victory:

> The Americans, a great deal more ambitious and numerous than the
> English, put us out of our lands, forming therein great settlements,
> extending themselves like a plague of locusts in the territories of the
> Ohio River which we inhabit. They treat us as their cruelest enemies

are treated, so that today hunger and the impetuous torrent of war
which they impose upon us with other terrible calamities, have
brought our villages to a struggle with death.

Faced with an empty treasury and no means of replenishing it except by
selling off Indian lands, the United States government focused its attention on
the Old Northwest, where individual states relinquished their claims to western
lands to the national government. A congressional committee, reporting in
October 1783, noted that the Indian tribes of the northwest and the Ohio Valley
seriously desired peace, but cautioned that "they are not in a temper to relinquish their territorial claims, without further struggles." Nevertheless, the report
continued, the Indians were the aggressors in the recent war. They had ignored
American warnings to remain neutral and "had wantonly desolated our villages
and destroyed our citizens." The United States had been obliged, at great
expense, to carry the war into Indian country "to stop the progress of their
outrages." The Indians should make atonement and pay compensation, "and
they possess no other means to do this act of justice than by compliance with
the proposed boundaries." Rather than continue a costly war, the report recommended that the United States make peace with the tribes and negotiate boundaries that could then be renegotiated as Indians retired west before the inevitable
press of settlement.

Acting on the assumption of Indian war guilt and eager for the spoils
of victory, American commissioners demanded lands from the Iroquois at Fort
Stanwix in 1784; from the Delawares, Wyandots, and their neighbors at Fort
McIntosh in 1785; and from the Shawnees at Fort Finney in 1786. They brushed
aside Indian objections in arrogant confidence that Indian lands were theirs for the
taking by right of conquest. In 1775, Congress had instructed its treaty commissioners to "speak and act in such a manner as they shall think most likely to obtain
the friendship or at least the neutrality of the Indians." Times had changed. James
Duane, chairman of the Committee on Indian Affairs in the Continental Congress
and mayor of New York City from 1784 to 1789, urged the United States not to
continue the British practice of cultivating relations with the Indians as if they
were nations of equal standing. The Six Nations should be treated as dependents
of the State of New York. They should adopt American diplomatic protocol, not
vice versa. Unless the United States seized the opportunity to implement this new
hardline approach, said Duane, "this Revolution in my Eyes will have lost more
than half its' [sic] Value." American treaty commissioners followed Duane's advice
and dispensed with wampum belts and elaborate speeches. "In their place," writes
James Merrell, they "substituted blunt talk and a habit of driving each article home
by pointing a finger at the assembled natives." Moreover, the federal government
was just one player in the competition, as individual states, land companies, and
speculators scrambled for Indian lands.

Iroquois delegates at Fort Stanwix tried to argue for the Ohio River as the
boundary to Indian lands, but the American commissioners would have none
of it. "You are a subdued people," they lectured the delegates. "We are at
peace with all but *you; you* now stand out *alone* against our *whole* force." Lest

the Indians miss the point, American troops backed up the commissioners. At Fort McIntosh, when chiefs of the Wyandots, Chippewas, Delawares, and Ottawas said they regarded the lands transferred by Britain to the United States as still rightfully belonging to them, the American commissioners answered them "in a high tone," and reminded them they were a defeated people. At Fort Finney, when Shawnees balked at the American terms and refused to provide hostages, one of the American commissioners picked up the wampum belt they gave him, "dashed it on the table," and told them to accept the terms or face the consequences.

Indian representation at these treaties was partial at best, and the Americans exploited and aggravated intratribal divisions. Six Nations delegates who returned home from Fort Stanwix were denounced by their own people, and the Six Nations in council at Buffalo Creek refused to ratify a treaty made under such duress.... The British had provided them with gifts as allies seeking their support, but the Americans demanded land in return for the few gifts they offered. Some chiefs signed treaties knowing that others would do so if they refused.

"If ever a peace failed to pacify, it was the peace of 1783," observed historian Arthur Whitaker in reference to the South. The end of the Revolution marked the beginning of years of turmoil as the region became an arena of competing national, state, and tribal interests, international intrigues, land speculation, and personal ambitions. The principal result of the war in the southern backcountry was to transfer control of a vast frontier from the Indians and their British allies and associates to the Whigs and the new men who emerged to lead them in the course of the Revolution. Until the southern states yielded their claims to western lands, the federal government had no lands to sell in the South and simply hoped to prevent full-scale Indian war. North Carolina did not cede its western land claims to Congress until 1789; Georgia not until 1802. These states, plus the "state" of Franklin, made their own treaties with the Indians, generally refused to cooperate with the federal government in its attempts to implement a coherent Indian policy in the region, and sometimes tried to sabotage federal treaty-making efforts. Meanwhile, the aggressions of Carolinian and Georgian backcountry settlers threatened to embroil the whole frontier in conflict. The United States negotiated the Treaties of Hopewell, with the Cherokees in late 1785 and with the Choctaws and Chickasaws in January 1786. The treaties confirmed tribal boundaries but did little to preserve them. Cherokee leaders appealed for assistance to Patrick Henry of Virginia in 1789· "We are so Distrest by the No. Carolina People that it seems Like we sho'ld soon become no People. They have got all our Land from us. We have hardly as much as we can stand on, and they seem to want that little worse than the Rest."

The Creeks emerged from the Revolution with their lands relatively intact, but Georgia demanded all the lands between the Oconee and Ocmulgee rivers as war damages. At the Treaty of Augusta in November 1783, a handful of compliant Creek chiefs, primarily from the neutral and pro-American groups in the nation, led by Hopoithle Mico (the Tame King) of Tallassee and Cussita Mico (the Fat King) of Cussita ceded roughly eight hundred square miles to

Georgia. McGillivray and the rest of the Creeks condemned the treaty, and in June 1784 signed the Treaty of Pensacola, placing themselves under Spanish protection. The Creeks entered the postrevolutionary era further divided into bitter factions. Factionalism had helped them avoid exclusive dependence on one ally throughout much of the eighteenth century and had secured them multiple outlets for trade. But as European allies began to fall away after the Revolution, McGillivray recognized that without Spanish support, "we may be forced to purchase a Shameful peace & barter our Country for a precarious Security." Now factionalism became dangerously dysfunctional, and the conflict between McGillivray and Hopoithle Mico augured the civil strife of 1813.

Treaties made over the opposition of the majority of the tribes left boundaries in dispute. Indians punished intruders whom the United States government failed to keep off their lands, and settlers retaliated. Even where there was no conflict, the fiction that all Indians had fought for the British in the Revolution justified massive dispossession of Native Americans in the early republic, whatever their role in the war. Catawbas derived maximum mileage from their revolutionary services, and by wrapping themselves in the flag used their record of service in the patriot cause "to carve a niche for themselves in the social landscape of the Carolina piedmont." However, they were an exception. Whereas other revolutionary veterans were granted land bounties, Indian veterans lost land. The Mashantucket Pequots served and suffered in the patriot cause, but in 1785 they were complaining to the government of Connecticut that "our Tribe find ourselves Interrupted in the Possession of our Lands by your People round about Cutting & Destroying our Timber & Crowding their Improvements in upon our Lands." Neighboring Mohegans found that both "white strangers & foreign Indians" encroached on their land and sold their timber from under them in defiance of state laws. In Massachusetts, Indians had fought and bled alongside the colonists in their struggle for liberty, but in 1788 the state reinstituted its guardian system for Indians, and deprived Mashpee of its right of self-government by establishing an all-white board of overseers. The Penobscots and Passamaquoddies found their Maine hunting territories invaded by their former allies.... The state stripped the Penobscots and Passamaquoddies of most of their land in a series of post-Revolution treaties. New England Indians who had moved to Oneida country only to be driven back by the war, and "who for their Fidelity and Attachment to the American Cause, have suffered the Loss of all things," petitioned the Connecticut Assembly for relief at the war's end.

The Oneidas had suffered mightily in the American cause during the war. General Philip Schuyler had assured them during the Revolution that "sooner should a fond mother forget her only son than we shall forget you." Once they had helped the Americans win independence, the Oneidas would "then partake of every Blessing we enjoy and united with a free people your Liberty and prosperity will be safe." But the Oneidas fared little better than their New England friends or their Cayuga and Seneca relatives in the postrevolutionary land grabbing conducted by the federal government, New York State, and individual land companies.... The State of New York meanwhile negotiated a string of treaties, illegal under the Indian Trade and Non-Intercourse Act of 1790, that by 1838 had robbed the Oneidas of their entire homeland. The bitter divisions the Revolution produced within the Oneidas were "not yet forgotten" by 1796.

As many Revolutionary War veterans, often illiterate, signed away their land grants for a pittance to more powerful and prosperous citizens of the new nation, so too Indian veterans, who had fought to win the United States's independence, often found themselves reduced to selling off land simply to survive. Simon Joy Jay, or Choychoy, a Mohegan who was wounded in the Revolution, "fighting for the Country," had to sell his land to support himself in old age and infirmity. The widow of Indian Daniel Cyrus, a white woman named Sarah, who lost two sons in the war, likewise had to sell her land to support herself in old age. Abenaki Indian patriots in Vermont fell on equally hard times.

The widows of men from Mashpee who had given their lives in the struggle for independence were forced to look outside their communities for husbands. By 1793, Indian towns like Mashpee included not only Africans and Anglo-Americans, but also Germans who had served in the war as mercenaries and had since married into the community and were raising families.

Many Indian peoples clung to their ancestral lands, even where those lands had been in the middle of war zones. Some Mohawk families returned and remained in their Fort Hunter and Canajoharie homes until the 1790s. But most Mohawks found new homes at Grand River or the Bay of Quinté. The peace that ended the Revolution did not end the vast movement of people that scattered Loyalists and African Americans across the globe and displaced Indian populations throughout North America. The war's end found Indian refugees at Niagara, Schenectady, Detroit, Saint Louis, Saint Augustine, and Pensacola, and the peace continued to dislocate thousands of Indians. Indian peoples pressured by Anglo-American expansion continued, as they had in the past and would in the future, to seek refuge in Canada.... Stockbridge Indians, unable to secure relief from their former allies after the Revolution, joined other Christian Indians from New England in moving to lands set aside for them by the Oneidas in New York, joining "People of many Nations" at New Stockbridge. Hundreds of refugee Indians drifted west of the Mississippi and requested permission to settle in Spanish territory. Abenaki Indians, dispersed by previous wars from northern New England into the Ohio Valley, turned up in Arkansas and Missouri in the decade after the Revolution, testimony to the continuing dislocation of Indian communities that the conflict occasioned in eastern North America. The migrations of Indian peoples across the Mississippi generated repercussions on the plains and threatened to disturb "the tranquility of the Interior Provinces of New Spain."

For American Indians, the new republic was still very much a revolutionary world in which their struggles continued with little abatement. For many Indian peoples, the Revolution was one phase of a "Twenty Years' War" that continued at least until the Treaty of Greenville in 1795. Before it was over, a whole generation had grown up knowing little but war. The Indians' war of independence went on until 1795, 1815, and beyond, and it took many forms, as Indians mounted "spirited resistance" and "sacred revolts." Confronted with renewed pressures and aggressions, spurred on by the murder of mediation chiefs like Moluntha and Old Tassel, and encouraged by the presence of Britons and Spaniards waiting in the wings for the experiment in republicanism to fail, many of the tribes renewed their confederacies. Shawnees, Chickamaugas, and Creeks carried war belts throughout the eastern woodlands; Indian ambassadors traveled from Detroit to Saint Augustine and back, urging united resistance. Warriors from a host of tribes continued a war of independence that was multitribal in character. In a council held at the mouth of the Detroit River in November and December 1786, delegates from the Five Nations, as well as Hurons, Delawares, Shawnees, Ottawas, Chippewas, Potawatomis, Miamis, Cherokees, and Wabash allies, sent a speech to the United States from the "United Indian Nations," declaring invalid all treaties made without the unanimous consent of the tribes. Led by capable chiefs who had risen to prominence during the Revolution—Joseph Brant, Little Turtle, Buckongahelas, Blue Jacket, Dragging Canoe, and McGillivray—revived Indian confederacies continued the wars for their lands and cultures into the 1790s and exposed the American theory of conquest for the fiction it was.

Americans in the new republic, like their British and Spanish rivals, were often hard-pressed to keep up with the political changes the Revolution generated in Indian country, as new communities emerged, new power blocs developed, and new players called different tunes. "Tribes" ceased to be the functioning unit of Indian politics and diplomacy, if they ever had been....

Not until the mid-1790s did the Indian war for independence as waged by these warriors come to an end. General Josiah Harmar and General Arthur St. Clair met with defeat and disaster in their campaigns against the northwestern confederacy. Only in 1794 did the Americans inflict a telling victory on the tribes at Fallen Timbers and get at the extensive cornfields on the Auglaize and Maumee rivers, which had sustained the Indian war effort for years....

By 1795 the war for Ohio was lost. Little Turtle and others who had been on the forefront of resistance joined the old chiefs in making peace at the Treaty of Greenville, and ceded most of Ohio to the United States. That same year, the Treaty of San Lorenzo effectively deprived southern Indians of Spanish support in their resistance to American expansion.

In the Northwest Ordinance of 1787, the United States had committed itself to expansion while simultaneously treating Indian people with "the utmost good faith." Men like Henry Knox and Thomas Jefferson wrestled with the dilemma of how to take Indian lands and still act with "justice and humanity." With their victory finally secured and Indians no longer a major military threat, Americans finally resolved the dilemma inherent in their belief that United States Indian policy could combine "expansion with honor." Since too much land encouraged idleness and presented an obstacle to "civilization," and Indian people could survive in the new nation only by becoming "civilized," the United States would deprive them of their lands for their own good. Not surprisingly, the good intentions of a few men became lost amid the pressure to rid the Indians of their lands.

Burned villages and crops, murdered chiefs, divided councils and civil wars, migrations, towns and forts choked with refugees, economic disruption, breaking of ancient traditions, losses in battle and to disease and hunger, betrayal to their enemies, all made the American Revolution one of the darkest periods in American Indian history. The emergence of the independent United States as the ultimate victor from a long contest of imperial powers reduced Indians to further dependence and pushed them into further dark ages. Two Mohegans, Henry Quaduaquid and Robert Ashpo, petitioning the Connecticut Assembly for relief in 1789, expressed the sentiments and experiences of many Native Americans as the new nation came into being: "The Times are Exceedingly Altr'd, Yea the Times have turn'd everything Upside down." Seneca communities, in Anthony Wallace's words, became "slums in the wilderness," characterized by poverty, loss of confidence in traditional certainties, social pathology, violence, alcoholism, witch fear, and disunity. Cherokees, reeling from the shock of defeat and dispossession, seemed to have lost their place in the world, and the very fabric of their society seemed to be crumbling around them.

And yet, in the kaleidoscopic, "all-change" world of the revolutionary era, there were exceptions and variations. Despite new colors on the map of Florida, political change in Seminole country reflected not new dependence on a foreign power so much as increasing independence from the parent Creek confederacy. While Alexander McGillivray continued traditional Creek policies of playing off competing nations with considerable skill, the Seminoles emerged by the new century as a new player and an unknown quantity in the Indian and international diplomacy of the southeast. Many Indian communities succumbed and some disappeared in the new world produced during the Revolution, but others were in process of formation and asserting their separate identity.

Like the Shawnees who built and rebuilt Chillicothe, Indians adjusted and endured. Contrary to predictions of extinction and assumptions of stasis, Indian communities survived, changed, and were reborn. The Revolutionary War destroyed many Indian communities, but new, increasingly multiethnic, communities—at Niagara, Grand River, Chickamauga, and the Glaize—grew out of the turmoil and played a leading role in the Indian history of the new republic. The black years following the Revolution saw powerful forces of social and religious rejuvenation in Handsome Lake's Longhouse religion among the Iroquois, far-reaching stirrings of cultural assertiveness, political movements like the northwestern Indian confederacy of the 1780s and 1790s, a renascence in Cherokee country, and pan-Indian unity under the leadership of Tecumseh and the Shawnee Prophet in the early years of the new century.

The American Revolution was a disaster for most American Indians, and the turmoil it generated in Indian country continued long after 1783. But by the end of the eighteenth century, Indian peoples had had plenty of experience suffering and surviving disasters. They responded to this one as they had to others and set about rebuilding what they could of their world. But now they were rebuilding on quicksand, for the new America had no room for Indians and their world.

Western Transformations: Indians, Sexuality, and the California Missions, 1760–1840

BY ALBERT L. HURTADO

For a long time now, the Franciscan missions have figured prominently in the popular history of California and in the palmy brochures of the tourist industry. In the twentieth century, there has grown a powerful myth that is known to every school child and traveler to the Golden State: In 1769, good Father Junípero Serra led to California a band of pious missionaries who Christianized the awed Indians, peacefully recruited them to the missions, and made the grateful neophytes into useful citizens of the Spanish empire. The kindly friars worked selflessly to make life— and the afterlife—better for the Indians. When Mexico broke from Spain and took over California, jealous private citizens broke up the missions, took the land, and abused the mission Indians, thus undoing the religious work of half a century. The mission ruins remained, the story concludes, as crumbling and quaint reminders of California's humane and idealistic beginnings.

Like all good myths, there is some truth in this tale. Its main shortcoming, however, is that it pays so little attention to the Indians who were the objects of the missionaries' attention. Few historians have looked carefully at the impact of the missions on native people. Fewer still have examined the motives and responses of Indians who chose to enter or remain outside the mission. These scholars have, however, unearthed the alarming population history of the missions that challenges the California mission myth. In 1769, there were about three hundred thousand Indians in California, with perhaps sixty thousand living between San Francisco Bay and San Diego, where the missions were located. By the end of the mission era in the 1830s, there were perhaps one hundred fifty thousand Indians left in the entire state. Disease was the principal cause of this appalling destruction, for Indians had little resistance to the maladies that Spaniards brought to California. Evidently the missions facilitated the spread of illnesses because they concentrated native populations that had formerly been dispersed. This tragic outcome, of course, was not what the fathers had intended. Nevertheless, missions became agencies of native destruction, even as they held out the promise of eternal salvation.

This essay will examine an aspect of the mission experience that has not received much attention—Indian sexuality and Franciscans' attempts to control it. Sexuality is only one aspect of Spanish-Indian relations, but it is important for several reasons. First, sexual relations are a universal feature of human existence that not only replicate life, but society as well. Second, anything that affects fertility is of particular importance in the study of a population like the California Indians, who were in rapid, prolonged decline. Third, because sexual relations are intensely personal human experiences, knowledge of sexuality provides insight into the historical life of the individual. Finally, an analysis of this

Hurtado, Albert L. "Sexuality in California's Franciscan Missions: Cultural Perception and Sad Realities," in *California History*, vol. 71, no. 3, Fall 1992. © 1992 by the California Historical Society Published by the University of California Press.

one aspect of Spanish-Indian interaction provides a way to better understand population dynamics that advance beyond ungovernable environmental factors—such as disease—and delves into the realm of human choice.

Before Father Junípero Serra founded California's Franciscan missions, he led a religious revival in Mexico's Oaxaca region. Francisco Palóu, Serra's companion and biographer, approvingly reported that Serra's religious work produced concrete results. He reformed an adultress who at the tender age of fourteen had begun to cohabit with a married man whose wife lived in Spain. This sinful arrangement had lasted for fourteen years, but upon Serra's order the woman left the house of her lover. The man was desolate. He threatened and begged her to return, but to no avail. Then "one night in desperation," Palóu related, "he got a halter, took it with him to the house where she was staying, and hung himself on an iron gate, giving over his soul to the demons." At the same moment a great earthquake shook the town whose inhabitants trembled with fear. Thereafter, the woman donned haircloth and penitential garb and walked the streets begging forgiveness for her shameful past. "All were edified and touched at seeing such an unusual conversion and subsequent penance," the friar wrote. "Nor were they less fearful of divine Justice," he added, "recalling the chastisement of that unfortunate man." Thus, Palóu believed, the tragedy brought "innumerable conversions … and great spiritual fruit" to Serra's Oaxaca mission.

This story was a kind of parable that prefaced Palóu's glowing account of Serra's missionary work in California. It demonstrated not only the presence of sexual sin in Spain's American colonies—which is not especially surprising—but that priestly intervention could break perverse habits, and that public exposure and sincere repentance could save souls. This incident is especially important to us because, on the eve of his expedition to California, Palóu linked Serra's Mexican missionary triumph with the rectification of sexual behavior. Thus, a discussion of sexuality in the California missions is not merely a prurient exercise, but goes to the heart of missionaries' intentions. While errant sexuality was not the only concern of priests, the reformation of Indian sexual behavior was an important part of their endeavor to Christianize and Hispanicize native Californians. Their task was fraught with difficulty, peril, and tragedy for Indians and Spaniards alike.

Changing Indian behavior was difficult because native people already behaved according to sexual norms that, from their point of view, worked perfectly well. From north of San Francisco Bay to the present Mexican border, tribespeople regulated sexual life so as to promote productive family relationships that varied by tribe and locality. Everywhere, the conjugal couple and their children formed the basic household unit, which was sometimes augmented by aged relatives and unmarried siblings. Indian families, however, were not merely a series of nuclear units, but were knit into a complex set of associations that comprised native society. Kinship defined the individual's place within the cultural community, and family associations suffused every aspect of life.

Indian marriages were usually confined within economic and social ranks and tended to stabilize economic and power relationships. Chiefs (who were occasionally women) were usually from wealthy families and inherited their positions. Since secure links with other groups provided insurance against occasional food shortages, chiefs frequently married several elite women from other tribelets (small, local groups that were largely sovereign and autonomous). Diplomatic polygyny provided kinship links that maintained prosperity and limited warfare that could result from poaching or blood feuds. In the event of war, kinship considerations helped to determine who would be attacked, as well as the duration and intensity of conflict.

Given the significance and complexity of kinship, marriage was an extremely important institution, governed according to strict rules. Parents or respected tribelet elders often arranged marriages of young people and even infants. California Indians regarded incest—defined according to strict consanguinial and affinal rules—as a bar that prohibited marriage if a couple was related within three to five generations, depending on tribal affiliation. Consequently men had to look for eligible wives outside their tribelets. Since most groups had patrilocal residence customs, women usually left their home communities, thus strengthening the system of reciprocity among independent local groups that girded native California.

The bride price—a payment by a prospective husband to the bride's family—symbolized women's place in this scheme. The groom gave his parents-in-law a gift to recognize the status of the bride's family, demonstrate the groom's worth, and compensate her family for the loss of her labor. The bride price did not signify that the wife was a chattel. No husband could sell his spouse, and an unhappy wife could divorce her husband. Even so, men were considered to be family heads and descent was often through the male line and the couple's new residence was usually in the groom's *ranchería*.

California's native household economy was based on hunting and gathering according to a gendered division of labor. Men hunted and fished, and—after the advent of white settlement—raided livestock herds. Women gathered the plant foods that comprised the bulk of the Indian diet—acorns, seeds, roots, pine nuts, berries, and other staples. All California tribes prized hard-working, productive women. Women's material and subsistence production was of basic importance to Indian society, but women made another crucial contribution as well. They bore children, thus creating the human resources needed to sustain native communities. When populations suffered significant reductions, the lack of fertile women meant that the capacity to recover was limited.

Recreating the sexual behavior of any historic people is difficult, but it is especially difficult in societies that lacked a written record. Still, modern anthropology and historical testimony make possible a plausible—if partial—reconstruction of intimate native life. California Indians regulated sexual behavior both in and out of marriage. Premarital sex does not seem to have been regarded with disapproval, so virginity was not a precondition for selecting a respectable mate. After marriage, spouses expected fidelity from their husbands and wives, possibly because of the importance of status inheritance. Consequently, adultery was a legitimate cause for divorce, and husbands could sometimes exact other punishments for sexual misbehavior by their wives. Chumash husbands sometimes whipped errant wives. An [Esselen] man could repudiate his wandering wife, or turn her over to her new lover, who had to pay the cuckold an indemnity, usually the cost of acquiring a new bride. A wronged Gabrielino husband could retaliate by claiming the wife of his wife's lover, and could even go so far as to kill an adulterous spouse, but such executions were probably rare.

Women were not altogether at the mercy of jealous and sadistic husbands, for they could divorce husbands who mistreated them, a circumstance that probably meant they could leave if their husbands committed sexual indiscretions. Chumash oral narratives reveal that women often initiated sex and ridiculed inadequate partners. When it suited them, some women killed their husbands. It is impossible to know how frequently adulterous liaisons and subsequent divorces took place, but anthropologists characterize the common Gabrielino marital pattern as serial monogamy with occasional polygyny, indicating that separations were common. It is not unreasonable to suppose that, because so many marriages were arranged in youth, some California Indians subsequently took lovers after meeting someone who struck deeper emotional chords than their initial partners had. Nor is it implausible to speculate that some grievances were overlooked completely in the interest of maintaining family harmony and to keep intact the economic and diplomatic advantages that marriage ties were meant to bind. Prostitution was extremely rare in California, and before the arrival of the Spaniards, was noted only among the Salinan Indians. The lack of a flesh trade may indicate that such outlets were simply not needed because marriage, premarital, and extramarital associations provided sufficient sexual opportunities.

Another sexual practice recorded among a few California Indian groups was male homosexual transvestism, or the so-called berdache tradition, which was evident in some other North American tribes. The berdache dressed like women and generally assumed many female gender roles, but they were not thought of as homosexuals. Instead, it appears that some Indian groups believed that they belonged to a third gender that combined both male and female aspects. In sex, they took the female role, and they often married men who were regarded as heterosexual males. Sometimes a chief took a berdache for a "second wife" because it was believed that such a person worked harder.

Horrified by existing social and marital patterns among the Indians they encountered, Serra and the secular colonizers of Spain's northern frontier narrowly based their familial concepts on a Spanish model that was in some respects internally contradictory. The state regarded marriage as a contract that—among other things—transferred property and guaranteed rights to sexual service. On the other hand, the Church regarded marriage as a sacrament before God and sought to regulate alliances according to religious principles.

In theory, if not always in practice, Spanish society forbade premarital sex and required marital fidelity. Marriages were monogamous and lasted for life; the Church granted divorces only in the most extraordinary cases, although remarriage of widows and widowers was permitted. The Church regarded all sexual transgressions with a jaundiced eye, but held some acts in special horror. By medieval times Christian theologians had worked out a scheme of acceptable sexual behavior that also reflected their abhorrence of certain practices. Of course, fornication, adultery, incest, seduction, rape, and polygamy were sins, but far worse than any of these were the execrable "sins against nature," which included masturbation, bestiality, and homosexual copulation. The Church allowed married intercourse only in the missionary position; other postures were unnatural because they made the woman superior to her husband, thus thwarting God's universal plan. Procreation, not pleasure, was God's purpose in creating the human sexual apparatus in the first place. Therefore, to misuse the instruments of man's procreative destiny was to thwart the will of God. Medieval constraints on intimate behavior began to erode in the early modern period, but Catholic proscriptions against "unnatural" sexual behavior remained a part of canon law when Spain occupied California.

Such was the *formal* sexual ideology that Franciscans, soldiers, and *pobladores* brought to California. All unapproved sexual practices were considered sinful lust. Maintaining sexual orthodoxy in the remotest reaches of the empire, however, proved to be a greater task than Franciscan missionaries and secular officials could accomplish. Part of the problem was that Spaniards also brought to California an *informal* sexual ideology rooted in Mediterranean folkways that often ran counter to the teachings of the Church. In this informal scheme, honor was an important element in determining family and individual social ranking, and male status was linked to sexual prowess. To seduce a woman was to shame her and to dishonor her family, while it conferred honor on her consort and asserted his dominant place in the social hierarchy. This double standard arose, in part, because men viewed women as sexually powerful creatures who could lead them astray, and more importantly, dishonor their families. Spanish society controlled female sexual power by segregating women, sometimes going so far as to sequester them behind locked doors, to assure that they would not sully the family escutcheon with lewd conduct. Thus, Catholic priests labored to restrict sexual activity in a world of philanderers, concubines, prostitutes, lovers, and lawful spouses.

California's Spanish colonizers brought with them these formal and informal ideas about sexuality that were riven with contradictions. The conquest of the New World and its existing alien sexual conventions made matters even more complicated but did not keep Spaniards from intimate encounters with native women. From the time of Cortéz, the Crown and the Church encouraged intermarriage with native people, and informal sexual amalgamation occurred with great regularity. Throughout the Spanish empire, interracial sex resulted in a large mixed-race (*mestizo*) population. Ordinarily, the progeny of these meetings attached themselves firmly to the religion and society of their Spanish fathers. Thus, sexual amalgamation was an integral part of the Spanish colonial experience that served to disable native society and strengthen the Hispanic population, as it drew Indians and their mixed-race children into the colonial orbit. This was the world that Serra had tried to reform in Oaxaca; yet it was a world that he and fellow Spaniards would unwittingly replicate in California.

In 1775 Father Serra wrote thoughtfully to the Viceroy of New Spain about interracial marriages.... Serra's idealistic vision of colonization incorporated Spanish town building and Catholic marriages that tamed the sinful natures of Spaniards and Indians and harnessed them to Spanish imperial goals. If Serra had had his way, however, the only sexual activity in California would have occurred in the few sanctified marriage beds that were under the watchful eye of the friars.

But that was not to be. Serra recognized that Spanish and Indian sexual transgressions occurred, and they troubled him. Common Indian sexual behavior, viewed in light of Catholic mores, amounted to serious sins that merited the friars' solemn condemnation. Perhaps the worst cases were the berdache, who seemed to be ubiquitous in some parts of California....

Civil and Church officials agreed on the need to eradicate homosexuality as an affront to God and Spanish men alike. At Mission Santa Clara, the fathers noticed an unconverted Indian who, though dressed like a woman and working among women, seemed to have undeveloped breasts, an observation easily made because Indian women traditionally wore only necklaces above the waist. The curious friars conspired with the corporal of the guard to take this questionable person into custody, where he was completely disrobed, confirming that he was indeed a man. The poor fellow was "more embarrassed than if he had been a woman," said one friar. For three days the soldiers kept him nude—stripped of his gender identity—and made him sweep the plaza near the guard house. He remained "sad and ashamed" until he was released under orders to abjure feminine clothes and stay out of women's company. Instead, he fled from the mission and reestablished a berdache identity among gentiles.

The Spanish soldiers thoroughly misconstrued what they were seeing and what they had done. The soldiers no doubt thought they had exposed an impostor who was embarrassed because his ruse had been discovered. They did not realize that their captive himself—and his people—regarded him as a woman, and he reacted accordingly when stripped and tormented by men. Humiliated beyond endurance and required to renounce a sexual preference that had never raised an eyebrow in Indian society, the Santa Clara transvestite was forced to flee, but perhaps he was more fortunate than he knew. Father Francisco Palóu reported a similar incident at the Mission San Antonio, where a berdache and another man were discovered "in an unspeakably sinful act." A priest, a corporal, and a soldier "punished them," Palóu revealed, "although not as much as they deserved." When the horrified priest tried to explain how terrible this sin was, the puzzled Indians told him that it was all right because they were married. Palóu's reaction to this news was not recorded, but it is doubtful that he accepted it with equanimity. After receiving a severe scolding, the homosexual couple left the mission vicinity. Palóu hoped that "these accursed persons will decrease, and such an abominable vice will be eradicated," as the Catholic faith increased "for the greater Glory of God and the good of those pitiful, ignorant people."

The revulsion and violence that ordinary Indian sexual relations inspired in the newcomers must have puzzled and frightened native people. Formerly accepted by some Indian groups as an unremarkable part of social life, berdache faced persecution at the hands of friars and soldiers. To the Spaniards, homosexual behavior was loathsome, one of the many traits that marked California Indians as a backward race. In a word, they were "incomprehensible" to Father Geronimo Boscana. The "affirmative with them, is negative," he thought, "and the negative, the affirmative," a perversity that was clearly reflected in the open Indian practice of homosexuality. In frustration, Boscana compared the California Indians "to a species of monkey."

For Spaniards and California Indians alike, the early days of colonization created a confused sexual landscape, but Spanish intolerance of homosexuality was not the only cause of this. In order to convert the Indians, the Franciscans had to uproot other aspects of the normative social system that regulated Indian sexuality and marriage. At the very least, the missionaries meant to restructure Indian marriage to conform to orthodox Catholic standards of monogamy, permanence, and fidelity, changes in intimate conduct that engendered conflict on the California frontier....

Franciscans applied these Christian marriage rules to California. Records from seven missions in northern California show that between 1769 and 1834 the Church remarried 2,374 Indian couples. This practice was wise, for it permitted thousands of native couples to retain family and emotional attachments while taking up Catholic and Spanish life. The retention of conjugal connections eased the Indian transition to mission authority and no doubt encouraged some Indians to convert.

Not all Indian marriage customs were similarly admissible under Catholic scrutiny, however. Father Francisco Palóu, generally sympathetic to Indian marriage customs, found that the Chumash were inclined to wed "their sisters-in-law, and even their mothers-in-law," thus amplifying the sin of polygamy with incest. Chumash widows and widowers remarried within their deceased spouse's family, a practice that the Church prohibited. Indian spouses with such ties who wished to enter the mission had to abandon established marriages, lie about their relationships, or reject conversion.

In other ways the road to imposing a new sexual orthodoxy in California was a hard one. Christian ceremonies did not automatically eliminate older cultural meanings of Indian marriage, nor did they necessarily engender Catholic values in the Indian participants. Dissident neophyte runaways sometimes abandoned their old wives and took new ones according to tribal custom. When fathers forbade specific neophyte marriages, unhappy Indians found ways to insist on having the relationship that they preferred. In 1816, for example, an Indian man, probably Chumash, left Mission San Buenaventura to be with the woman he wanted at Santa Barbara. "This happens," Father José Señan revealed, "every time his shackles are removed." It is not clear if the missionaries had shackled the man for previously running off to his lover or for some other offense, but Señan allowed that it would be best to permit the couple to wed quietly. If, however, the Indian made mischief, "send him back to us."

All Christian marriages, of course, were not blissful, nor did they all reflect the wifely obedience that Hispanic society celebrated. Sometimes dissatisfied Indian wives used traditional kinship links to solve domestic problems. The inherent possibilities of such arrangements were revealed in 1795, after a skirmish between unconverted Chumash Indians near Mission San Buenaventura. Almost immediately after the fight—and perhaps related to it—the priests found a dead neophyte in the mission garden. His Christian wife, her traditional brother, and two neophytes had decapitated him. Their motives are not known, but it is clear that neophytes who wanted to violate Christian precepts—or observe Indian concepts of justice—could enlist traditional kin to do so.

Costanoans near Mission Santa Cruz became restive because of Spanish interference with Indian marriages. In 1794 a traditional Costanoan man organized some Christian and gentile Indians, who attacked the mission guards, wounded two soldiers, and burned two buildings. The motive for this assault, Father Lasuén explained, was that the soldiers had taken the Costanoan leader's wife, along with some other neophyte runaways, to the San Francisco presidio. Evidently the Spaniards ran risks when they separated Indian couples. A few years later, the Santa Cruz friars claimed that sexual restrictions caused Costanoan neophytes to flee from the mission. Indians who could not "entirely gratify their lust because of the vigilance of the missionaries," they reckoned, decamped "in order to give full sway to their carnal desires."

The missionaries simply could not understand or accept that Indians adhered to more inclusive sexual and kinship rules than did Spanish Catholics. Instead, Franciscans like Father Lasuén thought of California Indians as people utterly without "government, religion, or respect for authority," who "shamelessly pursue without restraint whatever their brutal appetites suggest to them." They were "people of vicious and ferocious habits who knew no law but force, no superior but their own free will, and no reason but their own caprice." Father Lasuén evidently believed that sex was high on the list of brutal native appetites, for he thought that Indians were inclined to "lewdness."

What is lewd in one culture, however, is not necessarily lewd in another. Conflicting Indian and missionary attitudes about the human body are a case in point. California Indian men were customarily nude, and the women wore only skirts of bark or skins. Missionaries wondered that nudity did not embarrass the Indians, who "showed not the least trace of shame" even though the natives saw that Spaniards wore clothes. A Spaniard who went about naked would not have been allowed to run loose in society for very long, and the Franciscans regarded undress as a mark of uncivility and paganism. Consequently, missionaries devoted much time and energy to clothing the neophytes. Indians and missionaries were caught in a classic case of cultural misunderstanding. The missionaries could not accept Indian sexual attitudes and practices because they contravened a sacred sexual ideology and Spanish cultural norms. Indians could not comprehend the need for punitive restrictions.

Caught in this conflict, missionaries demanded that Christian Indians adopt formal Spanish attitudes about sex and punished them when they did not. Within the mission they tried to achieve this goal by segregating the Indians by gender at night, a policy that—as we shall see—was not altogether successful. Neophytes who failed to live up to Catholic standards ran afoul of the missionaries, who imposed corporal punishment. When, for example, Chumash neophytes at Mission Santa Barbara reverted to polygyny—which the friars evidently regarded as concubinage after Christian conversion—Father Esteban Tapis first admonished the offenders. On the second offense,

Tapis laid on the whip, and when this did not convince the Indians of the error of their ways, he put them in shackles.

Franciscans believed they had a right to use corporal punishment to correct unruly Indians. Indeed, the lash was used as an instrument of discipline through- out Spanish society. Eighteenth-century Spanish parents whipped children; teachers whipped pupils; magistrates whipped civil offenders; pious Catholics whipped themselves as penance. Although many Indians appeared to have deeply resented corporal punishment, some neophytes accepted the lash as a fact of mission life when their sexual transgressions caught the watchful eyes of the friars, but the Spanish and Catholic understanding of the whip as an instrument of correction, teaching, mortification, and purification no doubt eluded them. In Indian society corporal punishment as a means of social control was rare. Some tribes permitted husbands to physically punish adulterous wives, who were judged not only to have violated moral codes but to have threatened the economic and diplomatic role of the family.

Indian sexuality was not the only carnal problem that the fathers had to contend with in California. Civilians and soldiers brought to California sexual attitudes and behavior that were at odds with both Catholic and Indian values. Rape was a special concern of friars, who persistently condemned Spanish deviant sexual behavior in California. As early as 1772, Father Luís Jayme com- plained about some of the soldiers, who deserved to be hanged for "continuous outrages" on the Kumeyaay women near Mission San Diego. "Many times," he asserted, the Indians were on the verge of attacking the mission because "some soldiers went there and raped their women." The situation was so bad that the Indians fled from the priests, even risking hunger "so the soldiers will not rape their women as they have already done so many times in the past." ...

In 1775 some eight hundred neophyte and non-Christian Kumeyaays, fed up with sexual assaults and chafing under missionary supervision, attacked Mission San Diego. They burned the mission and killed three Spaniards, includ- ing Father Jayme, beating his face beyond recognition. As Jayme and Serra had predicted, sexual abuse against Indians made California a perilous place. Still, the revolt did not dissuade some Spaniards from sexual involvement with Indian women. In 1779, Serra was still criticizing the government for "unconcern in the matter of shameful conduct between the soldiers and Indian women," a complaint that may have been directed at mutual as well as rapacious liaisons.

Serra's argument implied that without supervision, some Spaniards acted without sexual restraint. As we have seen, Spaniards believed in a code of honor that rewarded sexual conquest. Soldiers may have asserted their ideas about honor and status by seducing California Indian women, but there was no honor in rape. Honorable sexual conquest required a willing partner who was overcome by the man's sensuality, masculinity, and magnetism, not merely by his brute ability to overpower her. Recall the San Diego rapists, who tried to mitigate their actions by making a payment to their victim. Serra argued that these were men of bad character who could not control their urges.

Rape, however, is a violent, complex act that requires more than opportu- nity and a supposed super-heightened state of sexual tension. Recent research shows that rape is an act of domination carried out by men who despise their victims, in this case because of their race, as well as their gender. Stress, anger, and fear also motivate some rapists.

It should not be forgotten that Spaniards were fearful of California Indians. The soldiers were outnumbered and surrounded by Indians who seemed capable of overwhelming them at any moment. Frequent minor skirmishes, livestock thefts, and occasional murders reinforced the Spanish conception of the Indian enemy.... It is not difficult to imagine that some men, sent to a dangerous frontier outpost, violently used Indian women as objects to ward off fear and to express their domination over the numerous native people that the Spanish Crown and Catholic Church sought to subdue, colonize, and convert.

Sexuality, unsanctioned and perversely construed as a way to control native people, actually threatened Spain's weak hold on California by angering the Indians and insulting their ideas about sexuality, rectitude, and justice. It is impossible to know how many rapes occurred in Spanish California, but sexual assaults affected Indian society beyond their absolute numbers. Moreover, Indian rape victims likely displayed some of the somatic and emotional symptoms of rape trauma syndrome, including physical wounds, tension, sleeplessness, gastrointestinal irritations, and genitourinary disturbances. In our own time, rape victims are often stricken with fear, guilt, anger, and humiliation, and some women who have suffered rape develop a fear of normal sexual activity. There is no reason to believe that Indian women did not react to rape in similar ways. Fear of assault may also have affected many women who were not themselves victims, but who tried to help friends and relatives cope with the consequences of rape. Sexual assaults echoed in the Indian social world, even as they frightened friars who feared the consequences of an outraged Indian population.

It is impossible to know how many free-will assignations occurred in California during the mission period, but it is safe to assume that such cross-cultural trysts were fraught with misunderstanding. Indian women, accustomed to looking outside their communities for husbands, likely viewed Spaniards as potential mates who could bring them and their families increased power, wealth, and status. Some women may have hoped that sex would lead to marriage, but it seldom did.

Indians responded to Spanish sexual importunities in several ways. Physical resistance to missionization, as happened at San Diego and on the Colorado River, was one way to deal with rapists and other unwanted intruders. Marriage to a Spaniard was another strategy that could protect women, but evidently only some Indians, a small minority, were able to use this tactic. Other Indians withdrew from Spanish-controlled areas to avoid any infringement on their social life and values. On the other hand, some women might have entered the missions for the protection from sexual abuse that the mission setting provided.

There is also reason to believe that Indians altered their sexual practices as a result of meeting the Spanish. Prostitution, which had been rare among the Indians, became common. In 1780, Father Serra complained about Nicolas, a neophyte who procured women for the soldiers at San Gabriel. A few years later, a Spanish naturalist observed that the Chumash men had "become pimps, even for their own wives, for any miserable profit."

Nicolas and other Indians had several reasons to resort to prostitution. Spanish men seduced and raped their female kinfolk, but did not marry them. Perhaps Indians were recovering lost bride prices through prostitution. Perhaps, since some Hispanic men were willing to pay for sex, prostitution seemed a logical way to enhance the economic value of wives and daughters, who were expected to be productive. Perhaps, prostitution was simply a means of economic survival, taken out of desperation. How women felt about being so used is not known, but the missions would have been one avenue of escape for those who were unhappy with these new conditions. In the early years of colonization, Indian women outnumbered male neophytes, indicating that females found the mission especially attractive in a rapidly changing world.

Another California Indian reaction to a new sexual world was physiological: they contracted syphilis and other venereal diseases, maladies they had not previously been exposed to. So rapidly did syphilis spread among Indians that in 1792 a Spanish naturalist traveling in California believed the disease was endemic among the Chumash. Twenty years later, the friars recorded it as the most prevalent and destructive disease in the missions....

Despite the intentions of Serra and other friars, mission life did not necessarily provide neophytes with a respite from sexual activity. Friars declared almost unanimously that mission Indians committed a variety of sexual sins. Between 1813 and 1815, missionaries recorded that the neophytes were guilty of "impurity," "unchastity," "fornication," "lust," "immorality," "incontinence," and so forth, indicating that the mission experience had not fully inculcated Catholic sexual values in the neophytes.

How could the friars have known about the intimate lives of [mission] Indians? The Indians confessed their sins at least once a year, and suspicious priests questioned the neophytes closely about their sexual behavior. Franciscan *confesionarios*, with lists of questions in California Indian languages, provide some idea of the level of priests' interest in neophyte sex. Have you ever sinned with a woman, a man, an animal? Do you have carnal dreams? Did you think about the dream later? What is your relationship with the people with whom you sin? Have you given your wife or husband to someone else? Do you become aroused when you watch them or when you see animals having intercourse? What did you think? Do you play with yourself? Have you tried to prevent pregnancy? Have you ever *not* had sex with your wife when she wanted to? So the questions continued for many pages. The investigation of Indians' sexual lives was thorough and relentless. Thus missionaries knew that men and women fell short of ideal sexual behavior. The friars' frank words about Indian sexuality betray disappointment born of the unspoken realization that their best missionary efforts had not reformed Indian sexuality.

The combination of virulent endemic syphilis and sexual promiscuity created a fatal environment that killed thousands of mission Indians and inhibited the ability of survivors to recover population losses through reproduction. Franciscans—and some of their critics—believed that the carnal disintegration of the California missions occurred because the Indians simply continued to observe the sexual customs of their native society. According to the missionaries, the Indians were unrestrained libertines who had learned nothing of Catholic moral behavior in the missions, and were incapable of realizing that syphilis was killing them. This view is incomplete because it assumes that sexual behavior was unregulated in native society and that Indian sexual behavior was unchanged during sixty-five years of mission experience.

Perhaps mission Indian sexuality was a response to new conditions. Who would have understood disparate demographic conditions at the missions better than the neophytes themselves? Locked into a system that seemed to assure their ultimate destruction, dying rapidly from unheard-of diseases, perhaps neophytes chose procreation as a means of group survival. Sadly, they failed, but it was not for want of trying.

It should not be assumed that neophyte sexual behavior was monolithic. Rather, it was influenced by both ethnic and gender considerations. By the end of the mission period, missionaries had recruited substantial numbers of interior Indians to replace the coastal neophytes, who were rapidly dying. Many of the new inland converts formerly had fought against the coastal Indians. In the mission, long-standing inter-tribal animosities could have released inter-ethnic sexual aggression that was meant to assert dominance in this new setting. Priests reported that mission women who became pregnant resorted to abortion and infanticide, and these acts may have been based in Indian customs, especially in the case of the Chumash, who believed that, unless the first child died, the mother would not conceive again. Thus, Indian women who attempted to apply old norms to assure fertility contributed to the destruction of the Indian population. Women had other reasons to abort pregnancies. Unwed mothers would be subjected to close questioning and punishment by priests. What if the father were a soldier who did not want his identity revealed, what then?

Whatever the causes of mission sexuality, neophytes relied on old ways and new ones to solve difficult problems in a new setting. In the end, efficacious solutions eluded them, but it is not accurate to say that Indians were immoral, amoral, or incapable of assimilating the message that the missionaries brought them. The mission experience demonstrates that Indians were simultaneously resolute and unsure, conservative and radical, forward looking and bound to tradition. They exemplified, in other words, the human condition.

Ultimately, the history of California's missions is a sad story of human misunderstandings and failures and terrible unintended consequences. That Spaniards and Indians were often incapable of comprehending each other should hardly be surprising, because they came from radically different cultures. As was so often the case in the history of the Western Hemisphere, Indians and newcomers talked past each other, not with each other. This was true even of their most personal contacts in California. Sacred and profane, intimate, carnal, spiritual, ecstatic, bringing life and death—Indian and Spanish sexuality embodied the identity and paradox of their all-too-human encounter.

◈ FURTHER READING

Bouvier, Virginia M. *Women and the Conquest of California, 1542–1840: Codes of Silence* (2001).

Calloway, Colin. *The American Revolution in Indian Country: Crisis and Diversity in Native American Communities* (1995).

Campbell, William. *Speculators in Empire: Iroquoia and the 1768 Treaty of Fort Stanwix* (2012).

Campisi, Jack, and Laurence M. Hauptman, eds. *The Oneida Indian Experience: Two Perspectives* (1988).

Castillo, Edward D. "Gender Status and Decline, Resistance, and Accommodation Among Female Neophytes in the Missions of California: A San Gabriel Case Study." *American Indian Culture and Research Journal* 18:1 (1994): 67–94.

Cook, Sherburne F. *The Conflict Between the California Indian and White Civilization* (1976).

Costo, Rupert, and Jeannette Henry Costo, eds. *The Missions of California: A Legacy of Genocide* (1987).

Crosby, Harry W. *Antigua California: Mission and Colony on the Peninsular Frontier, 1697–1768* (1994).

Dowd, Gregory Evans. *A Spirited Resistance: The North American Indian Struggle for Unity, 1745–1815* (1992).

Gaff, Alan D. *Bayonets in the Wilderness: Anthony Wayne's Legion in the Old Northwest* (2004).

Glatthaar, Joseph T., and James Kirby Martin. *Forgotten Allies: The Oneida Indians and the American Revolution* (2006).

Griffin, Patrick. *American Leviathan: Empire, Nation, and Revolutionary Frontier* (2007).

Gutiérrez, Ramon A. *When Jesus Came, the Corn Mothers Went Away: Marriage, Sexuality, and Power in New Mexico, 1500–1846* (1991).

Hackel, Steven W. *Children of Coyote, Missionaries of Saint Francis: Indian-Spanish Relations in Colonial California, 1769–1850* (2005).

———."The Staff of Leadership: Indian Authority in the Missions of Alta California." *William and Mary Quarterly* 54 (1997): 347–376.

Hagan, William T. *Longhouse Diplomacy and Frontier Warfare: The Iroquois Confederacy in the American Revolution* (1976).

Hatley, Tom. *The Dividing Paths: Cherokees and South Carolinians through the Era of Revolution* (1993).

Herndon Ruth Wallis, and Ella Wilcox Sekatau. "The Right to a Name: The Narragansett People and Rhode Island Officials in the Revolutionary Era." *Ethnohistory* 44 (Summer 1997): 433–462.

Hinderaker, Eric. *Elusive Empires: Constructing Colonialism in the Ohio Valley, 1673–1800* (1997).

Hurt, R. Douglas. *The Indian Frontier, 1763–1846* (2002).

Hurtado, Albert L. *Intimate Frontiers: Sex, Gender, and Culture in Old California* (1999).

————."Sexuality in California's Franciscan Missions: Cultural Perceptions and Sad Realities," *California History* 71 (Fall 1992): 370–385.

Jackson, Robert H. *Indian Population Decline: The Missions of Northwestern New Spain, 1687–1840* (1994).

————, and Edward Castillo. *Indians, Franciscans, and Spanish Colonization: The Impact of the Mission System on California Indians* (1995).

Jennings, Francis. *The Ambiguous Iroquois Empire: The Covenant Chain Confederation of Indian Tribes with English Colonies from its Beginnings to the Lancaster Treaty of 1774* (1984).

Johansen, Bruce E. *Forgotten Founders: How the American Indian Helped Shape Democracy* (1982).

MacLeitch, Gail D. *Imperial Entanglements: Iroquois Change and Persistence on the Frontiers of Empire* (2011).

Mann, Barbara Alice. *George Washington's War on Native America* (2005).

Newell, Quincy D. *Constructing Lives at Mission San Francisco: Native Californians and Hispanic Colonists, 1776–1812* (2009).

Sadosky, Leonard J. *Revolutionary Negotiations: Indians, Empires, and Diplomats in the Founding of America* (2009).

Sandos, James A. *Converting California: Indians and Franciscans in the Missions* (2004).

Shannon, Timothy J. *Iroquois Diplomacy on the Early American Frontier* (2008).

Silverman, David J. *Red Brethren: The Brothertown and Stockbridge Indians and the Problem of Race in Early America* (2010).

Taylor, Alan. *The Divided Ground: Indians, Settlers, and the Northern Borderland of the American Revolution* (2006).

Tiro, Karim M. *People of the Turning Stone: The Oneida Indian Nation from Revolution through Removal* (2011).

Tuete, Fredrika J., and Andrew R.L. Cayton, eds. *Contact Points: American Frontiers from the Mohawk Valley to the Mississippi, 1750–1830* (1998).

◈◇◈

CHAPTER 8

A Tightening Circle, 1750–1840

By the early to mid-1800s, European encroachments and impositions were increasingly hemming in American Indians across the continent. While Chapter 7 cast our eyes primarily on the edges of North America, this chapter looks more at the middle, revealing that the areas where Indians retained full autonomy were becoming ever fewer. By the end of this period, Native nations on the Plains were beginning to feel the pressure posed by the upstart—but large and growing—nation to their east, the United States. Part of that pressure, in fact, came not from white Americans themselves, but from Indian tribes east of the Mississippi. These eastern tribes had been clinging to their existence amidst a swelling tide of American settlement and power, but the U.S. government decided that these remnant communities were blocking further development and began demanding that they move west to the newly designated "Indian Territory." Thus, by the mid-nineteenth century, Plains Indian nations faced not only an influx of European newcomers from the east, but a wave of "Native newcomers" as well.

Still, is Plains Indian history, from the time of their first European contact in the 1600s, merely a story of steady and inevitable decline? And what of the eastern tribes? Throughout history, human societies have sometimes experienced tough migrations to new lands. What was distinctive about the western migrations of eastern Indian tribes in the early 1800s? Whether tribes migrated or stayed (relatively) in place in these years, the circle of their existence—their lands, their cultural freedom—became smaller, and it would continue to shrink in the years to come. Yet, did it ever collapse into nothingness? To what extent were Indians able to "push back" against the closing circle? Keep these questions in mind, for they will be taken up more fully in many of the chapters that follow.

◈ DOCUMENTS

In Documents 1 and 2, Spaniards report on Comanche activities in central Texas in 1758. At this time, were the Comanches wilting under the European presence? Document 3, in which Chief Sharitarish of the Pawnee speaks to President James Monroe in 1822, offers a contrasting outlook. Sharitarish tells of challenges his people were already experiencing, even though the age of gold rushes, emigrants, railroads, white settlers, and other rapid, large transformations was still a few decades off. Meanwhile, Indians to the east had been experiencing accelerated, massive changes for several decades prior to Sharitarish's speech. Document 4, the Northwest Ordinance of 1787, outlines the distinctive, early U.S. approach to territorial expansion, with a pledge of "utmost good faith," but with an important "unless." Native peoples resisted this expansion, both subtly and directly. One of the more famous leaders of direct resistance against expansion was Tecumseh, whose 1810 speech is excerpted here in Document 5. Though other tribes, like the Cherokee and Choctaw, fought expansion—and removal—more through the courts than on the battlefields, the end result remained a forced move to the west. In Document 6, Commissioner of Indian Affairs Thomas L. McKenny expresses the U.S. government's rationale for removal in 1828. Documents 7 and 8 present two examples of Indian responses to that policy. Document 7 conveys the opinion of Cherokee newspaper editor Elias Boudinot. Boudinot, who was educated in New England schools and married an American woman, opposes removal here, but he later believed it was ultimately necessary to save the Cherokee nation. Many Cherokees remained firmly opposed. After the Cherokees had moved to their new home, opponents of removal killed Boudinot and other Indians who had signed the removal treaty. The final document, by a Choctaw man named George Harkins, articulates his people's feelings about being forced from their homeland.

1. A Spanish Soldier Describes the Comanche Destruction of the San Saba Mission in Texas, 1758

… The Sergeant was asked then why he had not tried to reach the Mission by some other route, instead of the one occupied by the hostile Indians. He said: There is a canyon between the hillsides and the river, and his party was caught in it when the enemy opened fire. The squadron became disorganized, and only one soldier, Joseph Vázquez, was able to slip through the barbarians to the shelter of the woods along the river bank, and he made his way as best he could by unobstructed paths. The witness declared that he and his soldiers would have put up a stronger resistance if the enemy had been armed only with bows and arrows, for the Spaniards were accustomed to fighting Indians armed with less powerful weapons [than muskets] and were able to protect themselves against arrows by means of their leather jerkins and shields, but they were helpless against the accurate musket fire of the Indian barbarians. The Sergeant expressed regret that there was no force in the Presidio able to prevail against a strong body of the enemy equipped with the same weapons as ours, and very cunning and treacherous besides.

He was asked whether, in his 30 years in the King's service, in the presidios and on the frontiers, he had ever before seen so many hostile Indians equipped with

This document can be found in Leslie Byrd Simpson, ed., *The San Saba Papers: A Documentary Account of the Founding and Destruction of the San Saba Mission* (San Francisco: John Howell Books, 1959), pp. 52–3.

firearms and so skilled in their use as those he encountered on his way to the Mission. He replied that he had never seen or heard of hostile Indians attacking our forces in such numbers and so fully armed. Formerly the barbarians had fought with arrows, pikes, hatchets, and similar weapons, against which the officers and soldiers of the presidios had held the advantage and had won many victories: at the Presidio of San Antonio del Río Grande, for example, and elsewhere. At the same time our forces had endured much suffering and many deaths at the hands of the savage barbarians, who did not spare the lives of the religious, or those of the women and children. Nor did they spare the buildings and workshops, which they burned to the ground.

2. A Spanish Official Assesses the Comanche, 1758

... [T]he new Presidio of San Luis [also known as San Sabá] as well as the Mission under its protection, was attacked by 2,000 Comanche Indians and other allied nations, equipped with firearms and apparently instigated by [French] foreign political agents. They have in fact destroyed the Mission, with the lamentable murder of the Reverend Father President, two other Missionaries, two of the soldiers of the guard, and four others whom Colonel Don Diego Ortiz Parrilla had sent to their relief. The rest then retreated.

This occurrence, your Excellency, besides the sorrow that such a disaster must bring us, ought to make us cautious on many points, for the Comanche Nation is warlike and well instructed in the use of firearms through frequent communication with the French. The San Sabá River, moreover, flows through the very middle of the Apache Nation, which is as unfriendly to the Spaniards as it is unfaithful and treacherous, and false to its promises. The Governor [of Coahuila], having learned by experience, has made this clear. Another circumstance (which deserves the closest attention) is that the invaders are directed by foreign political agents.

3. Chief Sharitarish (Pawnee) Voices Concern for His People, 1822

My Great Father:—I have travelled a great distance to see you—I have seen you and my heart rejoices. I have heard your words—they have entered one ear and shall not escape the other, and I will carry them to my people as pure as they came from your mouth.

My Great Father— ... If I am here now and have seen your people, your houses, your vessels on the big lake, and a great many wonderful things far beyond my comprehension, which appear to have been made by the Great Spirit and placed in your hands, I am indebted to my Father [Major Benjamin O'Fallon] here, who invited me from home, under whose wings I have been protected ... but there is still another Great Father to whom I am much

---

Leslie Byrd Simpson, ed., *The San Saba Papers: A Documentary Account of the Founding and Destruction of the San Saba Mission* (San Francisco: John Howell Books, 1959), 32–33.

This document can be found in James Buchanan, *Sketches of the History, Manners, and Customs of the North American Indians* (New York: W. Borradaile, 1824), pp. 38–42.

indebted—it is the Father of us all…. The Great Spirit made us all—he made my skin red, and yours white; he placed us on this earth, and intended that we should live differently from each other.

He made the whites to cultivate the earth, and feed on domestic animals; but he made us, red skins, to rove through the uncultivated woods and plains; to feed on wild animals; and to dress with their skins. He also intended that we should go to war—to take scalps—steal horses from and triumph over our enemies—cultivate peace at home, and promote the happiness of each other.

My Great Father:—Some of your good chiefs, as they are called [missionaries], have proposed to send some of their good people among us to change our habits, to make us work and live like the white people…. You love your country—you love your people—you love the manner in which they live, and you think your people brave. I am like you, my Great Father, I love my country—I love my people—I love the manner in which we live, and think myself and warriors brave. Spare me then, my Father; let me enjoy my country, and I will trade skins with your people. I have grown up, and lived thus long without work—I am in hopes you will suffer me to die without it. We have plenty of buffalo, beaver, deer, and other wild animals—we have an abundance of horses—we have everything we want—we have plenty of land, if you will keep your people off of it….

There was a time when we did not know the whites—our wants were then fewer than they are now. They were always within our control—we had then seen nothing which we could not get. Before our intercourse with the whites, who have caused such a destruction in our game, we could lie down to sleep, and when we awoke we would find the buffalo feeding around our camp—but now we are killing them for their skins, and feeding the wolves with their flesh, to make our children cry over their bones.

Here, my Great Father, is a pipe which I present you, as I am accustomed to present pipes to all the red skins in peace with us. It is filled with such tobacco as we were accustomed to smoke before we knew the white people. It is pleasant, and the spontaneous growth of the most remote parts of our country. I know that the robes, leggings, moccasins, bear claws, etc., are of little value to you, but we wish you to have them deposited and preserved in some conspicuous part of your lodge, so that when we are gone and the sod turned over our bones, if our children should visit this place, as we do now, they may see and recognize with pleasure the deposits of their fathers; and reflect on the times that are past.

4. The United States Issues the Northwest Ordinance, 1787

Article III

Religion, morality, and knowledge, being necessary to good government and the happiness of mankind, schools and the means of education shall forever be

---

This document can be found in Francis N. Thorpe, ed., *Federal and State Constitutions: Colonial Charters and Other Organic Laws of the States, Territories, and Colonies, Now or Heretofore, Forming the United States of America* (Washington, D.C.: Government Printing Office, 1909), Vol. II, pp. 957–964.

encouraged. The utmost good faith shall always be observed toward the Indians; their lands and property shall never be taken from them without their consent; and, in their property, rights, and liberty, they never shall be invaded or disturbed, unless in just and lawful wars authorized by Congress; but laws founded in justice and humanity shall, from time to time, be made, for preventing wrongs being done to them and for preserving peace and friendship with them.

5. Tecumseh (Shawnee) Speaks Out Against Land Cessions, 1810

... It is true I am a Shawnee. My forefathers were warriors. Their son is a warrior. From them I only take my existence; from my tribe I take nothing. I am the maker of my own fortune; and oh! that I could make that of my red people, and of my country, as great as the conceptions of my mind, when I think of the Spirit that rules the universe. I would not then come to Governor Harrison, to ask him to tear the treaty, and to obliterate the landmark; but I would say to him, Sir, you have liberty to return to your own country. The being within, communing with the past ages, tells me, that once, nor until lately, there was no white man on this continent. That it then all belonged to red men, children of the same parents, placed on it by the Great Spirit that made them, to keep it, to traverse it, to enjoy its production, and to fill it with the same race. Once a happy race. Since made miserable by the white people, who are never contented, but always encroaching. The way, and the only way to check and stop this evil, is, for all the red men to unite in claiming a common and equal right in the land, as it was at first, and should be yet; for it never was divided, but belongs to all, for the use of each. That no part has a right to sell, even to each other, much less to strangers; those who want all, and will not do with less. The white people have no right to take the land from the Indians, because they had it first; it is theirs. They may sell, but all must join. Any sale not made by all is not valid. The late sale is bad. It was made by a part only. Part do not know how to sell. It requires all to make a bargain for all. All red men have equal rights to the unoccupied land. The right of occupancy is as good in one place as in another. There cannot be two occupations in the same place. The first excludes all others. It is not so in hunting or travelling; for there the same ground will serve many, as they may follow each other all day; but the camp is stationary, and that is occupancy. It belongs to the first who sits down on his blanket or skins, which he has thrown upon the ground, and till he leaves it no other has a right.

This document can be found in Samuel Gardner Drake, *Biography and History of the Indians of North America* (Boston: Antiquarian Institute, 1837), 5: 21–22.

6. Indian Commissioner Thomas L. McKenney Explains Removal, 1828

... I forbear also to remark, except briefly, upon measures of general policy in regard to our Indians. The subject is growing in interest every day, and is surpassed only by the extreme delicacy of their situation, and of our relations with them. I refer especially to those whose territory is embraced by the limits of States. Every feeling of sympathy for their lot should be kept alive, and fostered; and no measures taken that could compromit [compromise] the humanity and justice of the nation; and none, I am sure, will be. But the question occurs—*What are humanity and justice in reference to this unfortunate race?* Are these found to lie in a policy that would leave them to linger out a wretched and degraded existence, within districts of country already surrounded and pressed upon by a population whose anxiety and efforts to get rid of them are not less restless and persevering, than is that law of nature immutable, which has decreed, that, under such circumstances, if continued in, *they must perish?* Or does it not rather consist in withdrawing them from this certain destruction, and placing them, though even at this late hour, in a situation where, by the adoption of a suitable system for their security, preservation, and improvement, and at no matter what cost, they may be saved and blest? What *the means* are which are best fitted to realize such a triumph of humanity, I leave to be determined upon by those who are more competent than I am to decide. But that something must be done, and done soon, to save these people, if saved at all, it requires no very deep research into the history of the past, or knowledge of their present condition, embracing especially their relation to the States, to see.

7. Elias Boudinot (Cherokee) Opposes Removal, 1828

... Our last Washington papers contain a debate which took place in the house of representatives, on the resolution, recommended by the Committee on Indian Affairs, published in the second Number of our paper. It appears that the advocates of this new system of civilizing the Indians are very strenuous in maintaining the novel opinion, that it is impossible to enlighten the Indians, surrounded as they are by the white population, and that they assuredly will become extinct, unless they are removed. It is a fact which we would not deny, that many tribes have perished away in consequence of white population, but we are yet to be convinced that this will always be the case, in spite of every measure taken to civilize them. We contend that suitable measures to a sufficient extent have never been employed. And how dare these men make an assertion without sufficient evidence? What proof have they that the system which they are now recommending, will succeed? Where have we an example in the whole

---

This document can be found in the Annual Report of the Commissioner of Indian Affairs, 1828.

This document can be found in Theda Perdue, ed., *Cherokee Editor: The Writings of Elias Boudinot* (Knoxville: University of Tennessee Press, 1983), pp. 95–96.

history of man, of a Nation or tribe, removing in a body, from a land of civil and religious means, to a perfect wilderness, *in order to be civilized*. We are fearful these men are building castles in the air, whose fall will crush those poor Indians who may be so blinded as to make the experiment. We are sorry to see that some of the advocates of this system speak so disrespectfully, if not contemptuously, of the present measures of improvement, now in successful operation among most of the Indians in the United Sates—the only measures too, which have been crowded with success, and bid fair to meliorate the condition of the Aborigines....

8. George Harkins (Choctaw) Laments His People's Forced Exile, 1832

To the American People.

It is with considerable diffidence that I attempt to address the American people, knowing and feeling sensibly my incompetency; and believing that your highly and well improved minds could not be well entertained by the address of a Choctaw. But having determined to emigrate west of the Mississippi river this fall, I have thought proper in bidding you farewell, to make a few remarks of my views and the feelings that actuate me on the subject of our removal....

We were hedged in by two evils, and we chose that which we thought least. Yet we could not recognize the right that the state of Mississippi had assumed to legislate for us. Although the legislature of the state were qualified to make laws for their own citizens, that did not qualify them to become law makers to a people who were so dissimilar in manners and customs as the Choctaws are to the Mississippians. Admitting that they understood the people, could they remove that mountain of prejudice that has ever obstructed the streams of justice, and prevented their salutary influence from reaching my devoted countrymen? We as Choctaws rather chose to suffer and be free, than live under the degrading influence of laws, where our voice could not be heard in their formation.

Much as the state of Mississippi has wronged us, I cannot find in my heart any other sentiment than an ardent wish for her prosperity and happiness.

I could cheerfully hope that those of another age and generation may not feel the effects of those oppressive measures that have been so illiberally dealt out to us; and that peace and happiness may be their reward. Amid the gloom and honors of the present separation, we are cheered with a hope that ere long we shall reach our destined home, and that nothing short of the basest acts of treachery will ever be able to wrest it from us, and that we may live free. Although your ancestors won freedom on the fields of danger and glory, our ancestors owned it as their birthright, and we have had to purchase it from you as the vilest slaves buy their freedom.

In *Great Documents in American Indian History*, ed. Wayne Moquin with Charles Van Doren (New York: Da Capo Press, 1995), 151–153.

Yet it is said that our present movements are our own voluntary acts—such is not the case. We found ourselves like a benighted stranger, following false guides, until he was surrounded on every side, with fire or water. The fire was certain destruction, and feeble hope was left him of escaping by water. A distant view of the opposite shore encourages the hope; to remain would be utter annihilation. Who would hesitate, or would say that his plunging into the water was his own voluntary act? Painful in the extreme is the mandate of our expulsion. We regret that it should proceed from the mouth of our professed friend, and for whom our blood was commingled with that of his bravest warriors, on the field of danger and death.

But such is the instability of professions. The man who said that he would plant a stake and draw a line around us, that never should be passed, was the first to say he could not guard the lines, and drew up the stake and wiped out all traces of the line. I will not conceal from you my fears, that the present grounds may be removed—I have my foreboding—who of us can tell after witnessing what has already been done, what the next force may be.

I ask you in the name of justice, for repose for myself and my injured people. Let us alone—we will not harm you, we want rest. We hope, in the name of justice, that another outrage may never be committed against us, and that we may for the future be cared for as children, and not driven about as beasts, which are benefitted by a change of pasture.

Taking an example from the American government, and knowing the happiness which its citizens enjoy, under the influence of mild republican institutions, it is the intention of our countrymen to form a government assimilated to that of our white [brethren] in the United States, as nearly as their condition will permit.

We know that in order to protect the rights and secure the liberties of the people, no government approximates so nearly to perfection as the one to which we have alluded. As east of the Mississippi we have been friends, so west we will cherish the same feelings with additional fervor; and although we may be removed to the desert, still we shall look with fine regard, upon those who have promised us their protection. Let that feeling be reciprocated.

Friends, my attachment to my native land is strong—that cord is now broken; and we must go forth as wanderers in a strange land! I must go—let me entreat you to regard us with feelings of kindness, and when the hand of oppression is stretched against us, let me hope that every part of the United States, filling the mountains and valleys, will echo and say stop, you have no power, we are the sovereign people, and our friends shall no more be disturbed. We ask you for nothing that is incompatible with your other duties.

We go forth sorrowful, knowing that wrong has been done. Will you extend to us your sympathizing regards until all traces of disagreeable oppositions are obliterated, and we again shall have confidence in the professions of our white brethren.

Here is the land of our progenitors, and here are their bones; they left them as a sacred deposit, and we have been compelled to venerate its trust; it is dear to us yet we cannot stay, my people are dear to me, with them I must go. Could I stay and forget them and leave them to struggle alone, unaided, unfriended, and forgotten by our great father? I should then be unworthy the name of a Choctaw, and be a disgrace to my blood. I must go with them; my destiny is cast among the Choctaw people. If they suffer, so will I; if they prosper, then I will rejoice. Let me again ask you to regard us with feelings of kindness.

◈ ESSAYS

In the first essay, Pekka Hämäläinen, Rhodes Professor of American History at Oxford University, continues the story of the Comanche Nation that the Cody Newton essay began in Chapter 3. Again, by peering back into the centuries before the United States entered the picture in the nineteenth century, Hämäläinen tells a story of this region that differs from many people's preconceptions. By the middle of the 1800s, the Comanches, along with other peoples of the southern Plains, would begin encountering displaced eastern tribes. Although the Cherokee case, with the landmark legal challenges and the "Trail of Tears" journey, is the most well-known story of removal in this era, the Cherokee are but one of many tribes who experienced exile. The story of the Choctaw—who inhabited parts of present-day Mississippi, Alabama, and Louisiana—is the subject of the second essay in this chapter, written by Donna L. Akers, Associate Professor of History and Ethnic Studies at the University of Nebraska. Akers, herself a member of the Choctaw Nation of Oklahoma, narrates her people's journey, infusing it with explanations of how the Choctaw endured expulsion, both culturally and physically. Note, for example, how Choctaw creation stories, much like the creation stories included in Chapter 2, factored into their views of removal. As you read these essays, reflect on the questions posed in the chapter introduction. Did 1840 mark the end of Comanche history? Of Choctaw history?

A Western Nation's Rise and Decline: Comanche Economy on the Southern Plains

BY PEKKA HÄMÄLÄINEN

Few works in Plains Indian scholarship have been as influential as John C. Ewers's 1954 portrayal of the Upper Missouri River trade center. In a compelling, tightly argued essay entitled "Indian Trade of the Upper Missouri before Lewis and Clark," Ewers demonstrated that in the eighteenth- and early nineteenth-centuries Mandans, Hidatsas, and Arikaras operated a thriving trade center at their earth lodge villages along the banks of the Upper Missouri River. This trade center was a great gathering point for peoples and goods alike. The corn, horses, manufactured goods, and luxuries of the villagers

Pekka Hämäläinen, "The Western Comanche Trade Center: Rethinking the Plains Indian Trade System," *Western Historical Quarterly* 29 (Winter 1998), 485–513. Copyright by Western History Association. Reprinted by permission.

attracted both Indians and Euro-Americans from all directions, creating one of the busiest trading hubs in Native North America. Since its publication, Ewers's classic article has inspired a plethora of studies, which have further elaborated on his model of a Missouri River-centered trade system. Perhaps the greatest contribution of these works is the insight that the Upper Missouri villagers were not only a major trading locale within the Plains region, but also a focal point in an extraordinarily complex Native American trade network that stretched from the Great Lakes in the East to the Pacific Ocean in the West.

Our enduring intellectual fascination with Mandan, Hidatsa, and Arikara commerce has greatly deepened our understanding of the dynamics of Plains Indian trade, but the focus on this system has also created problems. The elaborate Upper Missouri trade has captured the scholarly imagination so completely that the other Plains regions have received only meager coverage. There has been particularly little interest toward the eighteenth- and nineteenth-century Southern Plains hunters—Comanches, Kiowas, and Plains Apaches. Scholars have identified active trading points among Caddos, Wichitas, and other eastern horticulturists of the Southern Plains, and while the hunters appear in these studies as trading allies, the primary attention has clearly been on the villagers. A more balanced picture can be found from the recent studies on Plains-Pueblo interaction, but these works have concentrated solely on the precontact and early contact periods before 1700. Ignored as an object of specific studies, the eighteenth- and nineteenth-century southwestern Plains have been viewed as a mere hinterland for the adjacent, more sophisticated trade centers. Almost without exception, the Comanches, Kiowas, and Plains Apaches have been depicted as secluded and unspecified groups, whose only function was to procure commodities, mainly horses and bison products, for the bustling Mandan, Hidatsa, and Arikara markets, and to provide an outlet for the surplus goods of the Upper Missouri that villagers channeled to the south. On a map, a single arrow extending from the Upper Missouri villages to the southwestern Plains has usually sufficed to describe the hunters' participation in the Plains trade system.

Enveloped in the myth of independent, self-sufficient bison hunters and horse raiders, the Comanches, Kiowas, and Plains Apaches form a largely unwritten chapter of Plains Indian economic history. It has been only in the last few years that scholars have begun to fill in the details. Pivotal in this trend have been recent Comanche studies, which show that these people, especially Western Comanches who lived near New Mexico on the western flank of Comanchería, were much more active traders than has previously been thought. However, what kind of role the Comanches played in the Plains Indians trade system is still largely unclear. This essay attempts to answer that question by taking the new Comanche studies a step further: Western Comanches were not only active traders, but also operated a major trade center. This center existed from the 1740s to about 1830 on the Upper Arkansas River Valley and was the nexus point of an extensive trade network that stretched from the Rio Grande to the Mississippi River and from central Texas to the Missouri River. Describing the evolution, structure, and eventual collapse of this previously unrecognized

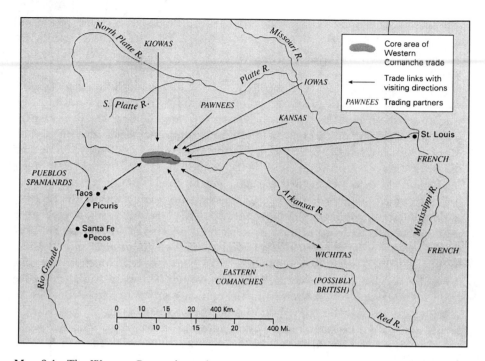

Map 8.1   The Western Comanche trade center in the mid- and late-eighteenth century.

trade center should dispel the traditional conceptualization of the Plains trade system that relegates to the southwestern Plains a mere backup role. Or, to put it another way, the Western Comanche center is the missing piece that allows us to abolish the old bias toward the Northern Plains and to form a picture of the Plains trade system that is more balanced geographically and more accurate and richer historically.

Before entering the Euro-American historical consciousness as the horse-mounted rulers of the Southern Plains, Comanches were members of the Eastern Shoshone people who hunted bison on foot along the northwestern margins of the Plains. Having left their traditional homelands in present-day Nevada, Utah, and Idaho around 1500, the Shoshones flourished as Plains hunters until the late seventeenth century, when a Siouan expansion from the east forced them to retreat to the Great Basin. While migrating toward the mountain deserts, the Shoshones apparently intersected the northward expanding horse frontier, which had been launched during the Pueblo Revolt in 1680, when the fleeing Spanish colonists left behind most of their livestock. Horse technology opened unforeseen hunting possibilities on the bison-rich Plains, thus encouraging some Shoshones to reenter the grasslands. This time taking a more southern route across the mountain ranges, these Shoshone bands moved onto the southwestern Plains around 1700. The southern route brought the Shoshones in contact with the Utes, who named them *komantcia*, and when the Spanish encountered them in 1706, they followed the Ute practice and called them Comanches.

When the Shoshone-Comanches reentered the Plains they were the aggressors. In 1700, most of the western shortgrass Plains were the domain of various Apache bands, which in the preceding centuries had gradually migrated southward from the Subarctic. The two groups were immediately drawn into intense warfare for the region's natural resources, markets, and trade routes. Even though the southwestern Plains encompassed a huge expanse, both groups depended on relatively small areas, the river valleys, for their survival. The Comanches needed the water, grass, cottonwoods, and shelter of the valleys for their growing horse herds, and the Apaches needed the same micro-environments for their mixed hunting and farming economy. The Comanches also tried to replace the Apaches as the preferred trading allies of New Mexico. This would have allowed them to monopolize the access to Spanish manufactured goods and Pueblo garden products that were an indispensable addition to their high protein and high fat, bison-based diet. Another allurement of the New Mexican markets was that Taos, Pecos, and other eastern Pueblos were attached to a complex Native trade network that covered most of the Southwest and thus provided access to distant luxuries, such as exotic pottery. On the broadest level, the wars can be seen as a rivalry over the crucial trading location between the Pueblos in the west and the Southern Plains villages in the east. East-west trade routes along the major waterways of the Southern Plains date back at least to the last centuries of the first millennium. Later, around the mid-fifteenth century, an elaborate exchange system with two geographically differentiated branches emerged between the Pueblos and the southeastern Plains. In the north, Apaches trafficked in meat, hides, and corn along the Arkansas River, while farther south, a semi-nomadic community called Jumanos built a flourishing trading culture along the Red, Brazos, and Colorado Rivers. The more numerous Apaches gradually replaced the Jumano middlemen, seizing total control of the east-west routes by 1700. But the dominance of the Apache traders was short-lived. As the Jumanos faded away, Comanche contenders emerged, touching off yet another chapter in the struggle over the lucrative Southern Plains trade.

Comanche-Apache rivalry continued into the nineteenth century, but all-out warring lasted only a few decades. The Apaches' semi-sedentary way of life made them vulnerable to Comanche cavalry attacks and guerrilla warfare. The well-mounted and mobile Comanches were also able to acquire firearms from French traders, while the Apaches' only access to European markets was through the Spanish, who refused to sell guns to Indians. Militarily beaten and economically marginalized, most Apache bands abandoned the Plains and fled westward to the Sangre de Cristo Mountains. By the early 1730s, Comanches controlled most of the major river valleys of the southwestern Plains as well as the trade with New Mexico. The stage was also open for them to seize the highly desired trading niche between the commercial and population clusters of the Southwest and southeastern Plains.

However, if the Comanches had expected their victory to yield immediate prosperity, their hopes soon vanished. The hard-won monopoly of New Mexico markets proved to be a disappointment. The Comanches traded rather extensively with the Pueblos, bartering hides, dried meat, and tallow for corn, beans, squash, tobacco, and pottery, but trade with the Spanish, who redirected much of Pueblo commerce into their own hands, was a constant source of frustration. The Spanish did trade axes, knives, hoes, bridles, horses, and mules for bison products, deerskins, Apache and Pawnee slaves, and salt, but the volume of the trade did not meet Comanche expectations. (The Comanches obtained salt, a highly demanded commodity, from the Salinas area in present-day New Mexico.) It is important to note that the problem had more to do with the limitations of Spanish supply than the magnitude of Comanche demands; the Comanches had relatively finite needs—they obeyed the nomadic maxim that favors mobility over material accumulation.

The Spanish failure to supply the Comanches stemmed from several factors, the principal of which was New Mexico's marginal position in the Spanish overseas empire. Lacking exploitable natural resources, New Mexico was regarded essentially as a buffer colony that served to protect the empire's more vital southern areas from foreign invasion. It received limited financial support from the Crown and consequently suffered from chronic economic stagnation and shortages of goods. These problems were aggravated by Spain's mercantilistic trade laws, which protected Spain's own manufacturers by forcing the colonies to rely on the mother country for their supply of manufactured commodities. The effects of these laws on New Mexico were disastrous. Remote from the sea, the colony had to ship its goods from Mexico City along a circuitous and extremely costly land route. New Mexican merchants also suffered from the bureaucratic inflexibility of the Spanish administrative system. In 1501, in order to guarantee the continuity of Spain's military hegemony in the Americas, the Crown had forbidden the distribution of firearms among Indians. Fearful of losing the Comanche trade to French gun traders, Spanish officials petitioned frequently for an exemption from the law, but the rigid bureaucracy did not react until the late 1780s. Similarly, the sale of livestock was also restricted by laws, again preventing New Mexicans from meeting Comanche demand. In the 1750s, for example, New Mexican governors repeatedly forbade the sale of mares, studs, and donkeys to Indians, thereby trying to prevent them from raising surplus animals for exchange with the French.

To compensate for their unfavorable trading position with New Mexico, the Comanches began to raid the colony for the goods they could not acquire by trade. This proved to be a perfect solution to their dilemma, for they could still carry on a limited exchange with the New Mexicans, whose options were restricted by a delicate play-off situation: the Spanish could not punish Comanche raiders by cutting off their trade completely, because that would have left the door wide open for French traders—and French colonialism—to filter in from the Mississippi Valley. Consequently, from about the late 1730s to the late 1770s, a peculiar pattern of alternating trade and warfare dominated Comanche-New Mexican relations. Governor Thomas Vélez Cachupín's notations at Taos in 1750 summarize the situation well:

> [T]he trade that the French are developing with the Cumanches
> [*sic*] ... will result in most serious injury to this province. Although

the Cumanche nation carries on a like trade with us, coming to the pueblo of Taos, where they hold their fairs and trade in furs and in Indian slaves whom they take from various nations in their wars, and in horses, mares, mules, knives, large knives [belduques], and other trifles, always, whenever the occasion offers for stealing horses or attacking the pueblos of Pecos and Galisteo, they do not fail to take advantage of it.

Also in reaction to the insufficiency of the New Mexican trade, the Comanches began to form other commercial ties, thereby initiating a process that eventually established them as the dominant trading group on the Southern Plains. The first logical step in this direction was to seek contact with French traders and unlicensed *coureurs de bois*, who in the early eighteenth century began to inch their way up the Arkansas River from their infant colonies in the Lower Mississippi Valley and the Illinois Country. Although the primary motive of the French was to open trade with New Mexico, which they erroneously imagined was rich in silver, they were also eager to trade with the Indians, whose products fueled their domestic consumption and external commerce. The first tentative Comanche-French contacts occurred in the 1720s, but it took more decades before Louisiana's slowly growing economy reached a level that allowed large-scale trading operations in the West. A final barrier to the trade was removed in the late 1740s, when the French unlocked the Upper Arkansas commerce by mediating an alliance between the Comanches and Wichitas....

Meanwhile, the Comanches also forged commercial ties with the various horticultural groups to the east and northeast. Such trade offered considerable benefits for both groups....

These mutual benefits laid the foundation for a rapid expansion of the Comanche trade network. This expansion began in the late 1740s, when the Comanches entered into an alliance with the Wichitas, who lived along the Lower Arkansas River and consisted of four subgroups: Taovayas, Tawakonis, Iscanis, and Wichita proper. The Wichitas formed the cornerstone of the Comanche trade system. They were the main importers of garden produce and tobacco to the Comanches, and they were the primary exporters of Comanche horses, mules, and products of the hunt. The Wichitas also served as middlemen between the Comanches and French, channeling horses, mules, bison products, and Apache slaves to the east and guns and other manufactured goods to the west. This lucrative tripartite trade continued to thrive even after Osage pressure forced the Wichitas to relocate to the Red River in the late 1750s.

The momentum of the Wichita accord also carried the Comanches into an alliance with the Pawnees, the Wichitas' close relatives, by the early 1750s. Trade with the Pawnees, who controlled an extensive territory from a core area of villages along the Loup and Platte Rivers, was an important addition to the Comanche commercial system. It provided the Comanches access to the guns and other manufactured goods the Pawnees acquired from their Arikara and Wichita relatives and French traders. The peace also decreased Pawnee horse raids, which had plagued the Comanches since the 1720s, although it did not make the new allies entirely immune to mutual aggressions. As with most Plains Indians, the Comanches and Pawnees viewed occasional raids on trading allies as a sanctioned way to rectify periodic imbalances in resource distribution.

During the latter part of the eighteenth century, the Comanches also managed to extend their trade zone among the Kansas, who lived near the junction of the Missouri and Kansas Rivers and who were engaged in the burgeoning fur trade the Spanish and French were developing from St. Louis and Louisiana....

... While the majority of Comanches were carving out a trade empire in the east and north, a part of the nation migrated in the 1740s and 1750s southeastward to Texas, where they put down new roots and began to raid Spanish horse ranches. The result was a division of the Comanches into two distinct branches, which Spanish officials labeled as Eastern (Texas) and Western (New Mexican) Comanches. The eastern division consisted mainly of Kotsotekas (*kuhtsutɄhka*, "buffalo eaters") who resided around the middle Red River Valley, while the more diverse western branch included Yamparikas (*yampatɄhka*, "root eaters"), Jupes (*hupenɄɄ*, "timber peoples"), and Kotsotekas who occupied a core region extending from the Upper Canadian Valley north of the Arkansas River. Although distinct units, the two branches continued to interact, as Domingo Cabello y Robles, governor of Texas, reported in 1786: "[T]he Eastern Cumans [Comanches] take the horses which they acquire in their wars and pillages to the rancherías of the Western Cumanches, who are known by the name Yambaricas, and barter them for guns, powder, bullets, lances, cloth, pots, knives, etc., which the Western Indians acquire from the Canse [Kansas] ... and Aguaés [Pawnees]."

This account is significant for several reasons. First of all, Cabello makes a clear distinction between the economic orientation of the divisions: he associates the Western Comanches more with trading and the Eastern Comanches more with raiding. Although overgeneralized—the eastern bands traded quite actively with the Wichitas and Euro-Americans—Cabello's distinction is valid in the sense that the Western Comanches qualify better as specialized traders. The Eastern Comanche commercial system never became as extensive as that of their western relatives, for they focused increasingly on raiding the wealthy but poorly protected Spanish ranches and missions in Texas and Northern Mexico. Cabello's account also shows that the two Comanche divisions had an established trade relationship, in which the western bands bartered a portion of their manufactured goods for the eastern bands' horses and mules. This trade channel was critical to the Western Comanches, who needed large numbers of animals to stock their trade with Wichitas, Pawnees, Kansas, Kiowas, Iowas, and French. The need for horses became even more acute in the 1760s, when the Western Comanches began to supply animals to the New Mexicans, the very same people they had stripped of horses through their incessant raids.

An often overlooked aspect of the Southern Plains trade system is the involvement of British traders. When the Treaty of Paris in 1763 established the Lower Mississippi Valley as a boundary between Spain and England, the British immediately secured their control of the eastern bank by lining it with a string of military and trading posts. During the following years, these posts became centers for a sizable British contraband trade to the Southern Plains....

Viceroy Antonio María de Bucareli lamented in 1772 that the Comanches, along with most Southern Plains groups, had obtained such quantities of British guns that they had begun to abandon their traditional weapons. In return for their firearms, the British probably received typical Western Comanche exports— horses, mules, and products of the hunt—as well as precious intelligence concerning the military conditions in Spain's northern frontier.

The Western Comanches were, therefore, consummate traders, who controlled an extensive commercial network on the Southern Plains. More than this, however, they also operated a trade center that was very similar to the other well-known major centers of Native North America. To sustain this argument it is necessary to define exactly what is meant by a major trade center. Although no systematic theoretical treatment of the concept in the Native North American context is available, most scholars agree that a major trade center meets most or all of the following criteria: 1) the center serves an extensive hinterland by being an axis of several trade routes, some of which involve long-distance trade; 2) commodities moving through the center are varied and preferably include both durable and non-durable goods; 3) the volume of commodities moving through the center is considerable; 4) the center is capable of producing surplus commodities for exchange; 5) the center serves as a collecting and redistribution point of commodities; and 6) the center has a precise geographical location.

The Western Comanche case fits this profile almost perfectly. To begin with, the Western Comanche traders were the main axis of a complex and multifaceted commercial network that spanned several environmental zones, linking together numerous groups and embracing a vast hinterland. Further, a great variety of both durable and non-durable commodities passed through their hands: guns, powder, ammunition, knives, axes, kettles, bridles, textiles, horses, mules, slaves, salt, bison products, deerskins, tobacco, corn, beans, squash, fruit, and other agricultural products.

Although lack of significant quantities of data prevents a detailed analysis of the amount of goods moving through the Western Comanche center, fragmented sources indicate that the volume was substantial....

When not interrupted by raiding, the Western Comanche–New Mexican trade was quite voluminous too. In 1774, for example, 60 Western Comanche households came to Taos and traded 140 horses, more than two per family. But horses were not the only staple exchanged in great quantities. The high demand for labor in the silver districts of Nueva Vizcaya and the *Recopilación* of 1681, which obliged Spanish to ransom Indian captives enslaved by other Native groups, stimulated the slave trade....

However, to understand the true significance of the Western Comanche trade, the questions of culture and meaning must also be considered. The value of trade goods is not a given; it is culturally determined, and when goods cross ethnic boundaries, culture intervenes and attaches new meanings to them. To Western Comanches, as to many other Native peoples of North America, the value of many Euro–American goods was less utilitarian than supernatural and symbolic; paints were not just simple mixtures of oil, water, and dye, but powerful symbols that helped the Western Comanches perform ceremonies, and medals were not just pieces of cheap silver, but important tokens of chiefly authority. This notion has far-reaching implications when estimating the extent of Western Comanche trade. Although an exchange of a few containers of paint may not seem to add much to the volume of exchange from an Euro-American perspective, it may have been a major transaction for Western Comanches, as they were purchasing something that was laden with symbolic value. A telling manifestation of the power of beads, mirrors, medals, and other non-utilitarian trade goods is that a large portion of them accompanied their owners to graves and the afterlife. It is, of course, impossible to give any exact measure to this non-material element of the Western Comanche trade, but it would be equally impossible to understand that trade without acknowledging its existence.

One of the most compelling factors supporting the view that the Western Comanches ran a major trade center is their massive surplus production. They were famous for their skillfully tanned bison and deer hides, but horses were clearly their primary export product. They were first reported to have large herds in 1740, and by the late 1770s and 1780s they had between two and one-half to three horses per capita. This number attests to the existence of a substantial surplus economy since hunting and transportation needs on the Plains required only a maximum of one horse per person. To understand just how heavily the Western Comanches were committed to surplus production, one has to realize that their horse wealth was not based exclusively on their access to the New Mexican ranches. Instead, they adopted an elaborate horse production system, which featured advanced herding strategies, extensive use of Indian and New Mexican captives as herders, and a dispersed settlement pattern that was geared to the demands of horse foraging rather than bison hunting. Through its vast capacity, this production system functioned as an engine that allowed the Western Comanches to build and operate their complex and far-flung trade network.

The Western Comanches also played an important redistributive role in the Plains commercial system. Besides purchasing horses from the Eastern Comanches with manufactured goods, they also passed on guns, powder, ammunition, and tools to New Mexicans, who suffered from a chronic shortage of manufactured items…. What makes these redistribution activities significant is that they contradict so strikingly the conventional view of the Southern Plains hunters as mere consumers of the manufactured goods that adjacent trade centers channeled to the interior. Like the Mandan, Hidatsa, and Arikara villages, whose status as a pivotal trade center was enhanced greatly by their strategic location at the intersection point of the expanding gun and horse frontiers, the Western Comanches too could profit from their position between the sources of these goods. Like their northern counterparts, the Western Comanches ran a major redistribution point, which absorbed and sent out various commodities to all directions.

The only difficulty in identifying the Western Comanches as operators of an important trade center is that their mobile lifestyle makes it difficult to visualize a geographically fixed center. A closer look reveals, however, that despite their migratory way of life, their trading activities were geographically focused. In his detailed discussion on Comanche foreign policies, Thomas W. Kavanagh has distinguished between two contrasting and spatially distinct Western Comanche strategies. The southern groups, primarily Kotsotekas living east of Pecos, specialized in raiding and were often hostile toward Europeans, while the Yamparika, Jupe, and Kotsoteka bands ranging northeast of Taos usually welcomed foreign traders. Kavanagh's analysis places the nucleus of Western Comanche commercial activities in the vicinity of the Upper Arkansas Basin, a view that is supported by direct evidence pertaining to Western Comanche trade. The eighteenth-century historical record contains several references to traders visiting the Western Comanches on the Upper Arkansas Valley. One of the most telling accounts comes from the Spaniard Felipe de Sandoval. While traveling to New Mexico in 1749, Sandoval encountered a huge Western Comanche trade fair of more than four hundred tipis on the Big Timbers of the Arkansas, a thick growth of cottonwood stretching from the Purgatoire River to the present-day Colorado-Kansas border, and the favorite campsite of the Western Comanches. During his sojourn at the camp, Sandoval witnessed visits from other Comanche, French, Wichita, and even German traders, who stayed several days among their hosts bartering firearms, powder, ammunition, hatchets, and glass beads for horses, slaves, and robes.

Situating the trade center on the Upper Arkansas River was founded on compelling strategic logic. The valley was separated from New Mexico only by the relatively passable Sangre de Cristo Range, and it was easily accessible to the Pawnees, Kansas, Iowas, and Kiowas from the north and northeast and to the Wichitas, French, British, and Eastern Comanches from the east and southeast. This central location freed the Western Comanches from the arduous and often treacherous task of traveling after the trade and allowed them to focus their commercial activities at their own camps. The French, who considered the Arkansas artery the key to the Southern Plains trade, frequented Western Comanche camps, but others came too…. José Francisco Ruíz, a knowledgeable Mexican frontier official, wrote in 1828 that the Pawnees went to trade with the Comanches, but the Comanches never visited them. Although there is no direct evidence, it is almost certain that this pattern dates back to the eighteenth century. Before 1800, the Pawnees traveled to the western shortgrass Plains to hunt bison twice a year and to Santa Fe to trade about once every three years, and it is likely that they conducted most of their trade with the Western Comanches during those hunting and trading expeditions. It is also probable that the Kansas and Iowas visited Western Comanche camps during their regular hunting excursions to the western Plains and Upper Arkansas country. Facilitating the Pawnee, Kansa, and Iowa trade journeys was an intricate web of established Indian trails that led from the Republican and Kansas Rivers to the Great Bend of the Arkansas, almost at the doorsteps of the Western Comanches.

The Western Comanches made trade journeys only to New Mexico and the Wichita villages, and even these routes were active in two directions….

The historical and archeological evidence does not allow locating specific sites of the Western Comanche trade center on the Upper Arkansas Basin. One

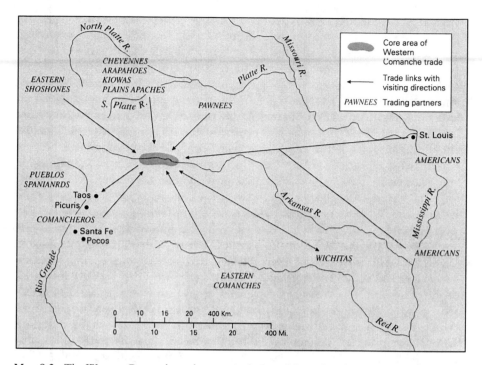

Map 8.2 The Western Comanche trade center in the late-eighteenth and early nineteenth centuries.

reason for this is that the late eighteenth- and nineteenth-century Comanches have received little attention from archeologists, who have focused their efforts on earlier periods and other areas. Moreover, the temporary camps of the nomadic Western Comanches do not yield enough diagnostic artifacts for systematic spatial analysis of their economic and commercial activities. On the other hand, even if the problem of evidence could be eliminated, it still would be impossible to determine an exact location. Although the Big Timbers was its focal point, the center constantly shifted up, down, and across the Arkansas corridor as the Western Comanches moved from one source of game, grass, and timber to another. This does not mean, however, that the Western Comanches did not operate a genuine trade center. Like the great Shoshone rendezvous on the Great Basin or the Dakota rendezvous on the James River, the Western Comanche center is best conceptualized, to use William R. Swagerty's terminology, as a significant impermanent center, a shifting trading point within a confined geographical region. This places the Western Comanche center below primary permanent centers, but above minor trading points, tertiary centers, and local trade hubs in Swagerty's finely-grained scale.

Because of their temporary nature, Swagerty ranked the Shoshone and Dakota rendezvous as secondary centers in order to distinguish them from the primary permanent centers in the Southwest, Pacific Northwest, and on the Upper Missouri. The Western Comanche center does not necessarily fit into this category, however. The fact that the center was more stable than the seasonal Shoshone and Dakota rendezvous suggests that it could be labeled as a primary impermanent center. This becomes even more emphatic when one considers how crucial a role the center played in the Southern Plains trade system. The traditional conceptualization is that the system revolved around the Pueblo towns and eastern farming villages, which can be viewed as gateway communities, crucial passage points into and out of distinct ecological and economic zones. However, between the two gateway communities lay the ideally located Western Comanche center, where numerous trade routes intersected, linking together different ecosystems and different economies. It was the vital nucleus, a great central place that incorporated the southwestern and southeastern gateways into a compact interregional commercial system.

After having dominated the Southern Plains commerce for over three decades, the Western Comanche traders suddenly faced a severe reversal. The reversal began in 1779, when Spain, tired of continuous raids, launched a full-scale war against the Western Comanches. For several years Juan Bautista de Anza, the gifted governor of New Mexico, waged a systematic and successful war against the Western Comanches, leaving no room for peaceful transactions. At the same time, the Western Comanches' ties with Louisiana started to deteriorate as well. Although the colony had been transferred to Spain in 1762, most French traders had stayed behind to continue their activities on the Southern Plains. During the 1770s, however, Spanish officials gradually took full control over the colony and enacted laws that suppressed the Comanche trade, which they accurately saw as a stimulus for continuing horse raids in New Mexico and Texas. Moreover, to protect Upper Louisiana against British encroachments from Canada and American expansion from the Ohio River Valley, Spanish officials redirected the colony's commercial power toward the strategically crucial Northern Plains. Finally, British traders were eliminated from the Southern Plains after 1779, when Spain joined the thirteen rebelling colonies against England and seized the eastern side of the Lower Mississippi River, thus making it difficult for British traders to slip into the Southern Plains. This situation was ratified in 1783 by the Treaty of Paris, which expelled England from the southeastern corner of North America. Although the Spanish granted a monopoly over the Indian trade in the Floridas to a Scottish company, they were careful not to allow the company to extend its operations across the Mississippi River onto the Southern Plains, which were regarded as a buffer zone for Northern New Spain.

As the Western Comanches' ties with colonial powers were quickly loosened, their relations with their Native trading allies began to unravel as well. Exchange with the Kansas and Iowas, whose trading power was impaired by overhunting and Osage expansion, seems to have faded in the late eighteenth century, for there is no trace of such trade in the nineteenth-century historical record. Interaction with the Kiowas was disrupted by hostilities, which were sparked by Kiowa and Plains Apache expansion toward Western Comanche territory in the late eighteenth century. But the most serious setback was an erosion of the Wichita alliance, which reflected a general decline of the Wichita trading culture. The downfall of Wichita traders began when Spain rechanneled the bulk of Louisiana's commercial resources to the Northern Plains, but an even more serious blow was their virtual elimination from the Mississippi Valley trade by the formidable Osages. The Western Comanches-Wichita trade did not end completely, but contacts were sporadic at best and strained by violence as the Comanches attempted to steal what they could not get through trade.

By the late eighteenth century, then, the Western Comanche trade center had become virtually paralyzed. Of earlier contacts, only the Pawnees and Eastern Comanches remained, while the ties with the other allies had been either badly frayed or completely cut off. To make matters worse, the Southern Plains were swept in 1780–1781 by a devastating smallpox epidemic, which killed thousands, further slowing the already sluggish pulse of the Western Comanche trading economy. The Western Comanche community curled inward to regroup itself economically and socially. However, this hiatus lasted only a short time. As the old trade contacts melted away, new ones were already being forged, and within a few years the Western Comanche trade center was as busy as ever.

This swing of the pendulum was triggered by the famous Comanche-Spanish accord in 1786. In this peace initiative, the Western Comanches and the Spanish agreed to refrain from all hostilities and to develop commercial relations with each other. For their part, the Spanish promised to establish regular trade fairs, to distribute presents to peaceful chiefs, and to regulate the fairs so that the shrewd New Mexican traders could not exploit their Native clients. In return, the Western Comanches agreed to stop raiding, to trade only with New Mexico, and to accompany Spain on joint military expeditions against the Apaches. These agreements gave rise to a thriving trade. Nine fairs were held at Taos, Pecos, and Picurís in 1787 alone, and during the following decades the Spanish sponsored regular fairs at the eastern Pueblos.

On the other hand, the peace also opened the southwestern Plains to New Mexican traders, who soon challenged the Pueblo fairs as the main link between the Western Comanches and the colony. Trade on the Plains became an official part of New Mexico's frontier policy in the late 1780s, when the Spanish, Pueblos, and *génizaros* (detribalized Plains Indians) were allowed to take their trade out to the grasslands. These traders, commonly known as Comancheros, made several annual visits to the Plains, bartering metal goods, fabrics, tobacco, and beads for Western Comanche horses, mules, bison hides, dried meat, tallow, deerskins, and captives. Reflecting their waning interaction with the Pueblo farmers, the Western Comanches also bought large amounts of bread, flour, corn meal, sugar, and other food-stuffs from the Comancheros. The fragmented record suggests a brisk exchange…. Perhaps the most striking feature of the New Mexican-Comanche trade was, however, the gun trade, which was legalized in 1786. Viceroy Bernando de Gálvez, the architect of the policy, justified the sale of guns by arguing that it would weaken the Indians' military force because the muzzle-loading musket was a less effective weapon than the bow, which "is always ready for use." Moreover, to ensure this, Gálvez specified that guns should have long barrels, to "make them awkward for long rides on horseback, resulting in continual damages and repeated need for mending or replacement." Nonetheless, the Western Comanches were eager to buy even these inferior guns because they did kill effectively in inter-tribal wars and thus made precious commodities in inter-tribal trade.

As to the geography of the trade, it was formerly believed that the Comancheros depended on chance meetings with their Native clients, but recent studies suggest that they relied more on fixed rendezvous. Significantly, one of the most important of these gatherings was held at the confluence of the Arkansas and Purgatoire Rivers, at the western edge of the Big Timbers of the Arkansas. When the members of the Stephen H. Long expedition explored the Upper Arkansas River in 1820, they found a well-marked Spanish trail leading from the valley toward Taos via the Purgatoire corridor.

At the same time the Western Comanches were enjoying their revitalized trade with New Mexico, they also managed to reactivate their eastern trade contacts. Enticed by the commercial vacuum left by French and British traders, the Americans began to infiltrate the Southern Plains in the 1790s from their bases at the Lower Mississippi watershed and Kentucky. The first recorded Western Comanche-American contact took place in 1796, when a group of Americans built a blockhouse among the Yamparikas. Spurred by the Louisiana Purchase and the opening of the Santa Fe Trail in 1821, the trickle of American traders gradually grew into a stream, and during the first third of the century several American trading parties visited the Upper Arkansas and Western Comanche countries. The dynamics of the American trade closely resembled those of the Comanchero trade: Americans took manufactured goods and foodstuffs among the Western Comanches and received in return horses, mules, and bison products. The only major difference was the absence of trade in captives, which played an important part in the Comanchero trade. Although the Comanche-American trade clearly violated the Comanche-Spanish treaty, there was little the Spanish could do. As was the case during the earlier Spanish–French competition, their options were limited by the dynamics of colonial rivalry: coercing the Western Comanches by cutting commercial ties with them would have only meant losing them permanently to the American orbit. Once again, the Western Comanches had managed to turn their strategic position between two colonial spheres into a commercial success.

A major chapter in the renaissance of the Western Comanche commerce was the revival of northern contacts. Between about 1790 and 1806, possibly through several truces, the Western Comanches, Kiowas, and Plains Apaches gradually forged a lasting peace. The three groups established a joint occupancy of the southwestern Plains.... Moreover, the three groups also traded with each other, taking advantage of variations in their resource domains: the experienced Western Comanche herders could offer more horses and mules, but the Kiowas and Plains Apaches had better access to the handy, high-quality British guns through their Upper Missouri contacts.

The ethnic composition of this northern trade branch changed in the early nineteenth century, when Cheyennes and Arapahoes, driven from their homelands near the Black Hills by the Lakotas, displaced the Kiowas and Plains Apaches as intermediaries between the Western Comanches and the Upper Missouri villages....

Already bustling with renewed trading activity, the Western Comanche trade center received a further boost when the Eastern Shoshones established a trade relationship with their relatives....

Besides incorporating new groups into their commercial system, the Western Comanches also continued to trade with some of their traditional allies. Although often interrupted by raiding and violence, the trade connection with Pawnees endured.... Yet the most important of the old, persisting trade contacts was the one with the Eastern Comanches....

So, as the eighteenth century drew to a close, the Western Comanches once again operated a major trade center, which fanned out to all directions to involve numerous groups. This new system differed from the earlier one in several ways. The volume of the trade was higher, reflecting matured and more regular trade links. Although the Western Comanches had engaged in systematic trade before, their commerce with Comancheros, Americans, and central Plains middleman tribes was even more institutionalized. The type of commodities moving through the center changed too. Trade in subsistence goods decreased, and horses and manufactured products became the primary items of trade. This shift can be attributed to a decline in trade with Pueblo and Wichita farmers, emergence of horse markets in the Northern Plains, and an increased southward flow of guns and other Euro-American goods through Cheyenne middlemen. Manufactured products poured in also from New Mexico, which was enjoying the blessings of Spain's Bourbon reforms—increased financial support from the Crown, refined administration, and resultant economic revitalization. Clearly, the Western Comanches were becoming dependent on Euro-American merchandise and technology.

Yet another, more internal, change was that the Upper Arkansas center became increasingly a Yamparika and Jupe enterprise....

Finally, the Western Comanches focused their commercial activities on their own camps almost exclusively, thereby etching their trade center in the cultural landscape of the Southern Plains even more firmly. Kiowas, Plains Apaches, Cheyennes, Arapahoes, Pawnees, Eastern Comanches, Eastern Shoshones, Comancheros, and Americans all gathered in the late eighteenth and early nineteenth centuries at the Yamparika and Jupe camps on the Upper Arkansas. The Yamparikas and Jupes made regular trade journeys only to the Taos, and even these visits became more infrequent as the Comancheros moved the trade from the Rio Grande Valley to the Plains. Although the Western Comanches were still nomadic bison hunters and as mobile as ever, their favorite campsites on the Upper Arkansas functioned as remarkably stable trading places. They spent the long winter months in the shelter of the Big Timbers and they often hunted and camped in the valley or its vicinity during other seasons, making it easy for their trading partners to find them on almost a year-round basis. Consequently, there was no contradiction in being both mobile hunters and operators of a geographically fixed trade center. Although the two activities required dissimilar settlement patterns, they were bound together by the central position of the Upper Arkansas Valley in the Western Comanche universe.

The trading success of the Western Comanches stemmed largely from their strategic location at the confluence of several highly contrasting ecological and economic zones. They occupied a superb hunting niche between two major agricultural spheres, the Southwest and southeastern Plains, which allowed them to engage in mutual exchanges in two directions. Furthermore, the mild winters and abundant shortgrasses made the southwestern Plains the most favorable region of the Plains for horse herding and put the Western Comanches in a strong trading position over other Plains tribes and Euro-Americans. On the other hand, many of their trading allies either came from or lived near colonial centers and consequently had better access to manufactured goods. Such marked differences in resource availability generally promote exchange and inter-dependence, but they can also foster hostilities by encouraging groups to level out the imbalances by force. This was especially true on the Plains, where fluctuating climatic and political conditions often caused short-term difficulties for Indians in producing enough surplus goods to maintain their trade at a desired level. When such difficulties arose, Plains groups recurrently relied on raiding to acquire the goods they needed. The Western Comanche trade system was no exception: Pawnees often stole horses from Western Comanches, who in turn raided Pawnees for slaves, Spanish for horses, and Pueblos for corn.

Due to this delicate balance between trading and raiding, the Western Comanches used a variety of social, ritual, and political mechanisms to maintain or reestablish peaceful relations within their trade network. The most famous of these sustaining mechanisms was the calumet ceremony, which created inter-social cohesion by establishing fictive kinship bonds between prominent members of two parties. The ceremony involved reciprocal gift-giving, ritual feasting, and dancing, and it climaxed with the handing of the calumet from the father to his adopted son. Although there are no direct references to the use of the calumet among the Western Comanches, it is almost certain that they were familiar with the ceremony, for all their key trading partners practiced it. A less formal variation of the calumet ceremony was the "peace of the market," a method that allows societies to engage in trade despite ongoing warfare between them. This strategy played a central role in structuring Western Comanche-Spanish interaction before the 1780s, when the relations vacillated between war and peace. The two groups regularly arranged a peace for a few days to allow trade to take place. After the fairs, the Comanches consistently resumed their raids, apparently at no surprise to the Spanish.

Yet another key institution that helped maintain stable intergroup relations was gift-giving. To establish or reaffirm friendship, the Western Comanches exchanged presents—usually such luxury items as tobacco, paints, and special clothing—with all their trading partners. Gifts not only bound strangers together in fictive kin relations, but also stimulated trade, for the Native cultural code obliged relatives to supply each other's needs. Thus, when American traders left for the Southern Plains to buy horses and bison products from the Comanches, they equipped themselves with large amounts of goods to be distributed before the actual trade. The most revealing example of the crucial importance of gifts comes, however, from New Mexico, where Spanish officials spent thousands of pesos annually to maintain peaceful relations with the Western Comanches.

To ease communication within their multifaceted and linguistically diverse trade system, the Western Comanches promoted the use of their own language among their trading allies. They seem to have been highly successful in this. By the late eighteenth century, they could conduct most of their commerce with the New Mexicans in their own language, and as their trading power continued to grow, Comanche became the Southern Plains Indians' other universal language along with the sign language. In a word, Comanche may have well been to the Southern Plains what the famous Chinook jargon was to the Pacific Northwest: a trade lingua franca. On the other hand, to further smooth interaction, the Comanches adopted many Euro-American, particularly Spanish, terms for key trade items. For example, the Comanche word for an iron bar is *póro*, which is a derivation from a Spanish word *barra*. Other telling examples include *pijura* (*frijole*; bean) and *supereyos* (*sombrero*; hat).

The efforts of Western Comanche chiefs also helped stabilize the trade system. It was the chiefs, particularly the political leaders, *paraibos*, who decided when, where, and how trading took place, what was exchanged, and at what prices. This chiefly control supported the trade system in several ways. By confining the exchange to their own tipis, chiefs provided a safe trading environment for visitors and thereby guaranteed the continuity of trade relations. Their control over price negotiations largely eliminated Euro-American attempts to push up their prices, which in turn could have undermined Western Comanche trading power. By regulating the commodity flows, chiefs also managed to curtail the distribution of alcohol, thus minimizing drinking-related social problems and the subsequent decline of commercial drive. Perhaps most importantly, chiefs acted as a filter against Euro-American attempts to turn the trade into a tool for political manipulation. For example, while seemingly yielding to colonists' attempts to elevate powerful but loyal Native leaders who could enforce trade agreements, Western Comanche chiefs seldom coerced those agreements, because they wanted to keep their followers' trading and raiding options open. Chiefs maintained their control over trade well into the nineteenth century, and in this way were a major factor behind Western Comanche commercial success.

This discussion of the sustaining mechanisms is important not only because it sheds light on the inner operations of the Southern Plains trade system, but because it reinforces the argument that the Western Comanches were a major trading group. They were astute traders who controlled a complex trade system through an active and skillful use of various social, ritual, and political mechanisms. In fact, the Western Comanches can be fittingly portrayed as specialized traders, who not only produced, collected, and redistributed commodities, but also nurtured a mature trading culture, complete with effective communication systems and elaborate trade etiquette.

This trading culture, together with an advantageous geographical location, allowed the Western Comanches to dominate the Southern Plains trade for almost a century. Despite massive geopolitical changes, diseases, and depopulation, their trade center flourished until about 1830, when a complex set of international, regional, and local changes finally resulted in its decline. Like its emergence, the disintegration of the Western Comanche center was a gradual process. The first trading connection to dissolve was the important northern one, which linked the Western Comanches to the Upper Missouri center via Cheyenne and Arapaho middlemen. Pushed by the Lakotas and drawn by the lush southern horse pastures, the Cheyennes and Arapahoes began in the late 1820s to gravitate toward the Arkansas Valley, which became in the 1830s a scene of bitter fighting between them and a Western Comanche, Kiowa, and Plains Apache alliance. The Western Comanche trade network shrank further when their New Mexican connection crumbled. The catalyst here was Mexico's acute financial troubles, which prevented the new republic from maintaining comparable commercial ties Spain had forged with the Western Comanches between 1786 and 1821. As New Mexico lost its commercial value, it once again became a target for raiding, and from the late 1820s on, war rather than trade dominated the Western Comanche–New Mexican relations.

The most serious blow to the Western Comanche traders was, however, the establishment of Bent's Fort on the Upper Arkansas River in the early 1830s. Boasting an annual trade of 15,000 hides and large quantities of horses, the lucrative post simultaneously opened new commercial opportunities for the Western Comanches and replaced them as the paramount traders of the Southern Plains. In the 1830s and 1840s, Southern Plains tribes, Santa Fe traders, and New Mexicans no longer gathered at Western Comanche camps but at Bent's Fort, which, in a sense, was an American sequel to the once flourishing Western Comanche trade center. The displacement of the Western Comanches was a calculated move by the Bent brothers, who were fully aware of the Big Timbers' history as a major commercial point.

Outmaneuvered by the Bents, the Western Comanche traders were relegated to secondary importance. They traded sporadically with the Osages in the 1830s and 1840s, and the Comancheros visited them until the 1870s, but Bent's Fort had put an end to their role as major traders. Edged out from commercial supremacy, the Western Comanches began to rely increasingly on raiding, inextricably linking themselves with that activity in the minds of the encroaching Americans as well as later historians.

The tumultuous 1830s also witnessed the collapse of the other Native trade centers of the Plains. The combined effects of smallpox and expansion of American fur companies up the Missouri River terminated the Mandan, Hidatsa, and Arikara villages as a major trade center. Similarly, increasing Osage aggression and the removal of tribes from the eastern United States in the 1830s delivered a fatal blow to the crumbling Wichita trading culture. The disintegration of the Western Comanche trade center should thus be seen as a part of the general collapse of the Plains Indians trade system. By the 1830s, there were no major Native trade centers left on the Plains, and for the next three or four decades commerce on the Great Plains was dominated by large Euro-American fur companies and their capitalistic production systems, which utilized the Indians only as a source of cheap labor in the expanding world economy.

An Eastern Nation's Removal: Choctaws Leave the Homeland

BY DONNA L. AKERS (CHOCTAW)

In 1830, the United States Congress passed the Indian Removal Act, effectively authorizing President Andrew Jackson to dispossess and forcibly remove thousands of Native people from their homelands in the American Southeast to lands west of the Mississippi River. The Removal Era has been explored by American historians over the years using classic historical methods and sources. They have recorded and analyzed the usual political and economic happenings and the prominent men with which these events are associated. White America's philosophical and cultural beliefs have been examined in an effort to understand the underpinnings of Manifest Destiny and America's insatiable drive for land and dominance. Various racial and political attitudes have been studied, along with economic factors such as the price of cotton on the world market. What has rarely been examined, however, is what Removal meant to Native people, from a Native point of view.

The archives and other written sources that are usually mined by modern scholars are almost exclusively written by non-Native people. Government and military records and accounts, even personal journals and diaries, reflect white authorship. Some of these sources include transcriptions of the speeches and other oral communications made by Native people. But these are, almost without exception, orations that were crafted and intended for white audiences—usually government personnel or national legislatures—and therefore conform to the Native perception of what would be important or meaningful to the larger American culture.

Sources that Native people trust to relate their experiences sometimes differ markedly from those considered valid or reliable by mainstream white historians. Most Native groups passed cultural and historical knowledge from generation to generation, not through written records but through oral accounts. Some mainstream scholars distrust oral sources, so often the information available from these records is omitted from the historical record, leaving a one-sided version of American history. Oral narratives contain an illimitable opportunity for Native cultural understanding and knowledge. Although they may evolve over the years, this makes them not less reliable than written records, but more so—*if* one is seeking information regarding the Native perception of events within their cultural context. To understand the historical experience of the Choctaws, it is essential to enter their world to the greatest extent possible. Without an understanding of the Choctaw world, historians only relate the experience of white America.

Sources written in Native languages also are largely excluded from the historical record—usually because of pedestrian difficulties inherent in translation. In addition, however, this is due to the racialist/colonialist thinking of the dominant majority, which discounts the value of Native sources. It would be

Reprinted from the *American Indian Culture and Research Journal*, volume 23, number 3, by permission of the American Indian Studies Center, UCLA. © 2012 Regents of the University of California.

unthinkable for a French historian not to have a working knowledge of the French language. Why is it acceptable for students of Native people not to be familiar with, or knowledgeable about, the language(s) of the people they are researching? To get at the historical experiences and perspectives of all participants during the Removal Era, therefore, it is necessary to consult the oral as well as the written record—and to examine records written in Native languages as well as European.

In 1830 the Choctaw Nation occupied some of the most fertile lands in North America. In the heart of what would become the Cotton Kingdom, the Choctaws' lands encompassed most of the Mississippi delta lands of Mississippi, as well as regions of Alabama and Louisiana. According to Choctaw traditions, these lands had been Choctaw lands forever, given to them by the Great Spirit, *Chitokaka*. The Choctaws resided in villages along rivers and streams, where they followed a primarily agricultural and sedentary lifestyle.

Choctaw society was based on matrilineal kinship. Clans provided the fundamental Choctaw identity, and heritage was reckoned through the mother's line. During the late eighteenth century, a few white men moved among the Choctaws as traders, adventurers, or outcasts of their own European or American homelands. Some married Choctaw women and spent their lives enveloped in Choctaw society. Since matrilineal kinship provided Choctaw identity, their offspring were fully accepted and reared as Choctaws. The children's first language was Choctaw, and their social training and identity was that of Choctaw children. Their paternal heritage sometimes contributed a rudimentary knowledge of the English language. Their father's occasional Euramerican visitors, as well as the tribe's participation in commerce among the white traders, brought exposure to the distant world of Americans on the east coast. But for the most part these influences were limited, and most of the so-called "mixed-blood" families lived lives dominated, on a day-to-day basis, by the Choctaw world.

In the early nineteenth century the Choctaws sought to appease American demands by ceding sections of land that, at first, seemed of negligible necessity to the Choctaws. However, the demands for land cessions continued and escalated, until during the mid-1810s, Choctaws leaders saw that they must halt further cessions altogether. Choctaw participation in the world market was limited primarily to trading deer hides in exchange for guns, ammunition, metal tools, and utensils. A few among the Choctaw had begun to sell crops and cattle to nearby Native or white communities, but as their land base shrank from cessions to the United States, so did the game supply within Choctaw territories. The Choctaw economy had incorporated the fur trade and the resulting acquisition of European manufactured goods into the core of Choctaw life. The sudden contraction of this market and the increased difficulty in obtaining European trade goods created a violent disruption and rapid disintegration of Choctaw society. Simultaneously, white traders smuggled enormous quantities of illegal liquor into the Choctaw Nation, promoting its consumption and hence the erosion of Choctaw life-ways. Real deprivation and economic hardship struck with a vengeance, as a whirlwind of change battered the Choctaws from every direction.

In order to understand the enormous psychological impact the Removal Era had on the Choctaws, one must examine the range of relationships between themselves and non-Choctaws. Relations with outsiders were a fundamental facet of Choctaw being. Reciprocity was at the heart of all relations, including those formed by kinship or clan. Relations with outsiders followed the precepts of kinship, and to Choctaws, these relations were not a parody of kinship relations, but were, in fact, actual kinship realized. White Americans and Europeans had long observed these facets of diplomacy and ritual friendship among the Choctaws and other Native peoples. However, they understood only vaguely that these rituals encompassed a fundamental concept central to Native belief systems.

To the Choctaw, fictive kinship relations with outsiders were essential to human coexistence and could not be avoided. The Choctaw Nation defined outsiders as either kin or foe. They believed that everything in life—the physical, mental, abstract, and concrete—was of one functional whole, one system that tied every being together in permanent yet ever dynamic relationships. If all were partners in an interconnected system, one could not act without affecting all others. Therefore, harmonious relationships with animal spirits, inanimate objects, and other human beings were essential. In this worldview, balance and harmony were fundamental to the community's and the individual's existence and well-being. If balance or harmonic relations were disturbed, dire consequences would follow, causing all to suffer.

In their earliest relations with the United States, the Choctaw Nation came from a powerful position. Allied with the Americans during the War of 1812, they provided essential assistance during the Battle of New Orleans, fighting under Andrew Jackson. Subsequently, they assisted Jackson in his assault on the Red Sticks, tipping the balance to the Americans during the Battle of Horseshoe Bend. Intense loyalty and fidelity to one's allies and kin permeated these relations. In the second decade of the nineteenth century, even as the relative balance of power shifted and Choctaws became weaker than the ever-strengthening Americans, the Choctaws believed that their relationship with the Americans would continue unchanged. Since all were part of a non-hierarchical system in the Choctaw worldview, each group would continue to recognize and act upon the bonds of kinship, even though their relative power or strength might change.

However, the American government conceptualized its relationship with the Choctaw within a hierarchical framework based on relative power. To Americans, it was natural for Choctaws to assume an inferior role. All their dealings with the Choctaws reflect an arrogance founded on their unquestioning belief in their own cultural superiority. Prior to 1800, and perhaps in the first decade of that century, the United States recognized the strength and military prowess of the Choctaws and sought to engage in a diplomatic relationship between equals. In the next two decades, however, Choctaw power declined precipitously, relative to that of the American nation. As a result, Americans began to view their relations with the Choctaws as one of superior to inferior—in both the military and political sense. Having always had a persistent belief in their unquestionable moral and cultural superiority, Americans married the changing relationship of power to their philo-sophical belief in their inherent superiority, creating a monster that consumed the lands and lives of thousands of Native people without compunction.

The 1820s saw the rise of Andrew Jackson to national prominence. He was extremely popular in the backwoods areas of the American South, where he consistently called for the expulsion of the resident Native nations. The momen-tum of expansionism escalated exponentially during this decade, as whites poured into the western reaches of the American South hungering for cheap land, and the constituents of American politicians demanded the expulsion, by force if necessary, of the Indians occupying lands they coveted. Whites began invading and squatting on Choctaw soil. The Choctaws thought that surely their "Father" in Washington would evict these interlopers, as promised in the treaties. The reciprocal relationships long recognized between the Choctaws and the American government demanded this much. The Choctaws were confident, because of their traditional expectations of the behavior of allies and friends, that the American government would stem the incursions into their lands, and would guarantee, as promised, their continued sovereignty and territorial integrity. Despite Jackson's long personal history with the Choctaws, however, he now formed the core of those calling for their dispossession and exile. This betrayal was met with disbelief and shock. As a traditional people, the Choctaws found the pace of events and the sudden shift in American policy from assimilation to dispossession incomprehensible. Even the most biculturally adapted Choctaws never believed that betrayal on such a scale actually would occur. The treachery of their old ally, Jackson, and his sponsorship of their expulsion and exile created a tremendous reaction among the Choctaws. But before we explore their reac-tion to this betrayal, one must examine what dispossession and exile meant to the Choctaw people.

Indian Removal, as the whites termed it, created moral and spiritual crises intimately linked to fundamental Choctaw beliefs about place, origin, and identity. Choctaws bad a deep spiritual and physical attachment to the earth. The earth was the source of all power, a "numinous presence of the divine, the sacred, the truly real by reference to which everything else found its orientation." Most Native people, including Choctaws, vested the earth with an overriding maternal quality: the earth mother gave life and sustained all living things. As siblings, all humans and animals intimately were connected, kindred in a literal sense. All had spirits and destinies irrevocably intertwined with the destiny of humankind.

Many traditional Choctaws believed that humans sprang from the earth from many primeval pairs scattered over the regions of the earth. They were each cre-ated separately from the different natural features and substances found in the region of the earth in which each people lived. For example, in a land of forests, the original humans came from the trees; in rugged, mountainous areas, they came from the rocks; on the plains, people emerged from the soil. "Mother earth" gave birth literally as well as spiritually to the Choctaw people.

After their arrival in the American Southeast, sometime back in the ancient mists of time, the Choctaws began to inter their dead in a great mound, built to honor the spirits of the dead. Taking three generations to construct, this sacred mound was called *Nanih Waiya*, known also as *Ishki Chito*, "the Great Mother." This pyramidal mound was located in the southern part of what is now Winston County, Mississippi. Years passed in peace, and then a devastating epidemic struck the people. Everyone died but the headman, who was immortal. When all but this one had perished, the great mound opened and swallowed him.

After the passage of many years, the Great Spirit created four infants, two of each sex, out of the ashes of the dead at the foot of *Nanih Waiya*. They were suckled by a panther, and when they were older and strong enough to leave, the prophet emerged from the Mother and gave them bows, arrows, and an earthen pot. Stretching out his arms, he said, "I give you these hunting grounds for your homes. When you leave them you die." With these words, he stamped his foot; *Nanih Waiya* opened, and, holding his arms above his head, he disappeared forever.

All Choctaw children learned these stories in childhood. They were taught as moral and historical lessons, intertwining the spiritual and literal as did the Choctaws in all areas of their lives. Through the oral traditions, Choctaws learned that they not only were part of the Earth, but also part of a specific legion of the earth. The gift of the Great Spirit was *this* land. They were never to leave it, or the nation would die.

The original migration tradition of the Choctaw people emphasizes their attachment to this particular spot of earth (a sacred reciprocal agreement with the dead also is tied to this specific place). This tradition relates how the Choctaw people traveled for forty-three years, everyone carrying the bones of their ancestors. Many of the people carried so many bones that they were unable to carry anything else. Some were so overloaded that they would carry one load forward a half day's journey, deposit it, and then return for the remainder, which they then would carry forward the next day. This task was considered a sacred duty. According to the spiritual teachers, the spirits of the dead "hovered around their bones to see that they were respectfully cared for, and that they would be offended and punished with bad luck, sickness, or even death for indignities, or neglect of their bones."

Each day, at the end of their travels, the people's leader—the *Isht Ahullo*—would plant the Sacred Pole in the ground. At dawn, the leader would rise and see the direction in which the Sacred Pole was leaning—the direction in which the people were to travel that day. One morning at dawn, the leader observed that the Pole "danced and punched itself deeper into the ground; and after some time settled in a perpendicular position, without having nodded or bowed in any direction." The Choctaws' long journey was at last at an end. The Choctaws arrived at the leaning hill—known to the people later as *Nanih Waiya*—in a "plentiful, fruitful land of tall trees and running waters" envisioned by the great Choctaw chiefs in a vision forty-three years before.

At the end of this journey, some of the younger Choctaws did not understand their sacred duty to the dead bones of their deceased kinsmen. The *Isht Ahullo* explained that the people always must take care of "the precious remains of the fathers and mothers," for the Choctaw people were charged by the spirits, who are hovering thick around us now, to take care of them; and carry them whithersoever the nation moves. And this we must not, we dare not fail to do. Were we to cast away the bones of our fathers, mothers, brothers, sisters, for the wild dogs to gnaw in the wilderness, our hunters could kill no more meat; hunger and disease would follow; then confusion and death would come; and the wild dogs would become fat on the unscaffolded carcasses of this unfeeling nation of forgetful people. The vengeance of the offended spirits would be poured out upon this foolish nation.

In historical times, the Choctaws continued to take their responsibility to the spirits of the dead very seriously. Every time they moved their villages, they transported the remains of those who had died. This duty was considered a sacred pact with the dead. In return for honoring the remains of the dead, living Choctaws would be watched over by the spirits of their ancestors. The spirits spoke to the living through dreams and visions, guiding and assisting the Choctaws in all things.

Traditional Choctaws literally believed that they emerged from the Great Mother Mound. In the mid-nineteenth century, the elderly Choctaws, when asked their place of birth, insisted that they emerged from *Nanih Waiya*. Thus, the forced exile from Mississippi separated the Choctaw people from their own mother. They had been warned by the prophets that the people would all die if they ever left their lands.

The Choctaws tried to convey the imperative reasons that they remain in the lands of their ancestors to the U.S. agents and government. They could not understand the whites' assertion that they took the Choctaws' well-being to heart as they forced them away from that which gave them life. One old man haltingly attempted to impart some understanding of their dilemma to an American agent. He said, "We wish to remain here where we have grown up as the herbs of the woods, and do not wish to be transplanted into another soil." The Choctaws saw themselves as part of the soil, an integral element of the ecosystem, tied inextricably to this specific part of the earth. Their world was a vast, complex system of life and spirits, all comprising an indivisible whole. Like the old man's herbs, the Choctaws believed they could not be separated from their mother, the land of which they were a part. The Choctaws could no more be separated from these lands and survive than could the pine forests of the Southeast be uprooted and transplanted hundreds of miles to the West. The Choctaws were *part* of their homelands. Separation from it meant their death.

Compounding the enormity of the thought of separation from their homelands was the Choctaw understanding of the west as the direction of death. West, both a direction and a place, held special meaning in Choctaw cosmology. The Choctaw afterworld was located on earth, somewhere in the west. According to Choctaw traditions, the *shilup*, or inside shadow, one of the two spirits that every person has, left the body after death and traveled low over the earth to the west, the Land of Death. Choctaw mortuary rituals had to be performed properly or the *shilup* could not make the journey to the after-world and instead would hover about the place of death, punishing the living kin who had failed him.

Once the *shilup* arrived in the west, it went to a place of happiness and delight, *shilup i yokni*. However, murderers were excluded from this happy ending. They were unable to find the path leading to the land of happiness and instead remained in view of, but unable to reach, that destination. This place of the murderous spirits was called *atuklant illi*, the Second Death. The horror this place conjured up in the minds of Choctaws cannot be overesti-mated. It was the land of the living dead, the place where the most horrible spirits roamed in unending despair and hopelessness. It was said that in this place, "the trees are all dead, and the waters are full of toads and lizards, and snakes—where the dead are always hungry, and have nothing to eat—are always sick and never die—where the sun never shines, and where the spirits climb up by the thousands on the sides of a high rock from which they can overlook the beautiful country of the good hunting-grounds ... but never can reach it." This was the destination the Americans reserved for the Choctaw people.

To the Choctaw, the west, then, was the Land of the Dead; it was the loca-tion of the Second Death, where spirits unable to reach the afterworld roamed forever. The west was the direction from which their ancestors fled in ancient times out of dire necessity. Leaving their homelands in the east meant breaking the covenant with the spirits of the ancestors. In the Choctaw world-view, the act of leaving would mean the nation's death. If they left behind the remains of the dead and abandoned their sacred duty, they would commit the most heinous crime in Choctaw cosmology.

The American arrangements for their physical removal left the Choctaws no choice. They had to abandon the bones of the dead. Under the best of circumstances, there was no way for them physically to disinter all the remains and transport them. In fact, the Choctaws had to abandon most of their mate-rial possessions since the United States government provided few conveyances for people, much less baggage. Most necessities remained behind, such as the hominy mortars which the women considered their most essential tool for food preparation.

Abandoning the bones of the dead was unthinkable to most Choctaws. Even the more acculturated Choctaws of mixed Native and white heritage found themselves unable to reconcile themselves to such an act. Many Choctaws, therefore, refused to leave. The Choctaws believed that every human had two souls. The *shilup* left the body and traveled west to the Land of Death. The *shilombish*, however, remained at the site of death guarding the remains of the body and its treatment by living Choctaws. One elderly Choctaw man explained this to the American agents: "In those pines you hear the ghosts of the departed. Their ashes are here, and we have been left to protect them. Our warriors are nearly all gone to the far country west but here are our dead. Shall we go, too, and give their bones to the wolves?" Women especially were reluctant to leave. Many families were split apart, as mothers and grandmothers adamantly refused to abandon the bones of their dead children and their *shilombish*, the outside shadow.

The Treaty of Dancing Rabbit Creek was the instrument used by the United States government to force the Choctaws from their homes. Under the guise of legality, this treaty was procured in 1830 by fraud and deception, against the consent of almost the entire Choctaw Nation. Over the subsequent protests of thousands of Native people and white missionaries, the U.S. Senate ratified the treaty, and the government informed the Choctaws that they had three years in which to leave.

This news produced the most profound reactions among the Choctaw. Chaos was the immediate result. The people quit planting crops, many simply gave up. The months of summer passed without a harvest, and when the winter came, the people began to starve. Alcoholic bingeing became the norm, and the children suffered. Drinking led to violence, as hopelessness engulfed the nation. Thirteen Choctaws died from alcohol poisoning in one month. One missionary reported that the entire nation was in utter disarray. The men stopped hunting, the women stopped planting, starvation and disease followed. Children wailed all night from hunger and inattention. Missionary Cyrus Kingsbury reported that the consequences of the treaty "almost beggars description. Loud exclamations are heard against the treaty in almost every part of the nation.... The nation is literally in mourning.... Multitudes are so distressed with their prospects as to sit down in a kind of sullen despair. They know not what to do."

In 1831 the first parties were assembled to leave at certain appointed gathering places throughout the nation. The night before one party departed, the women covered their heads with their skirts, keening the death songs all night long. The warriors sat stoically, facing away from the fires, into the woods. In the morning, as the soldiers stirred the reluctant Choctaws, men and women lovingly touched the leaves and branches of the trees as they departed. They left in autumn, as one of the worst winters in memory struck throughout the South. When they reached the Mississippi River, they were stopped indefinitely by ice floes obstructing passage. The ferries and steamboats stopped running, forcing parties of Choctaws to camp out night after night in freezing rain. The Choctaws seemed unsurprised by the suffering; they were forewarned by the oral prophecies.

The journey to the West was characterized by American ineptitude, incompetence, and fraud. Many Choctaws died or became seriously ill due to exposure, disease, and inhumane arrangements for their journey. Most of the nation was forced to walk the entire journey, which was more than five hundred miles. They traveled in kinship groups. Stories are still related of the suffering and death inflicted on the Choctaw people. One large group of emigrants was lost in a Mississippi swamp. The men, women, children, and elderly walked in chest deep swamp water for thirty miles. They went without food for nearly six days, and many began dying from exposure and starvation. They had given up and were singing their death songs when a rescue party reached them. One witness reported that among the bodies of the dead Choctaws were one hundred horses standing up in the mud, stiff from death.

The survivors were so disoriented that their rescuers had to lead them out of the swamp by their hands, like little children.

A Memphis citizen observed a group of exiled Choctaws on the road, completely unprepared for the harsh winter weather. They had no tents— nothing with which to shelter themselves. Not one in ten had even a moccasin on their feet and the great majority of them walked. This same man witnessed the travails of another Choctaw party who camped in the woods near his home. One night a hail storm began, followed by two days of heavy snowfall. The Choctaw party was stranded in the coldest winter weather the region ever had experienced. He reported that they lay in their camp for more than two weeks without shelter of any kind and with very few supplies. The second week, the weather averaged twelve degrees farenheit. The abrupt departure left many with little or no time to prepare or pack necessities, which they were told would be supplied by the United States government. The government failed to do so. Only one blanket was issued per family—and most families averaged six members.

Yet another party traveled through sleet and snow for twenty-four hours, most barefoot and nearly naked, in order to reach Vicksburg without exhausting their inadequate supplies. The disgusted U.S. Army captain who was their official escort, reported that "If I could have done it with propriety I would have given them shoes. I distributed all the tents and this party are entirely without." He complained about the inadequate provisions made for the Choctaws, and said that the sight of these people and their suffering would convince anyone of the need for an additional allowance for transportation.

As if the weather were not enough, the Choctaws were dogged by sickness on their exile west. Cholera, the most dreaded scourge of the times, struck again and again. A report of its presence in Memphis caused all the wagon drivers hired by the U.S. government to abandon their teams, leaving 150 wagons for the sick and aged standing with full teams of horses. Agent William Armstrong reported that these Choctaws suffered dreadfully from cholera, stating, "The woods are filled with the graves of the victims.... Death was hourly among us and road lined with the sick."

The Choctaws were forced to abandon traditional mourning rituals on the journey west. The bodies of the dead were not scaffolded. Typically lasting more than three months, the rituals were viewed as superstitious and heathen by the United States agents. The Choctaws sought to take their dead with them to the new lands, but the U.S. agents did not allow them to do so. One group's U.S. agent forced the Choctaws to bury their dead the morning after their death, according to Euramerican tradition. He expressed his satisfaction in his report to his superiors in Washington that the dead had been "decently interred." The Choctaws, of course, understood that the *shilup* of these people were unable to travel to the land of death without the proper ritual of scaffolding and funeral cries. They would be forced to wander the earth, and would punish those who had thus abandoned their sacred duty.

Nearly one-third of the Choctaw Nation died on the march west. Many of these were young children and elderly tribespeople, who disproportionately suffered from exposure, hunger, and disease. The enormous death toll produced social and political chaos. The council of elders that governed each town no longer existed when the Choctaws tried to rebuild in the West. The clans could not survive the death of so many of the elders. The elders were the leaders of each clan—they made the important clan decisions, and all those affecting the smaller kinship units. Since clans traveled together, some suffered death disproportionately, thus upsetting the checks and balances of power so carefully constructed over the centuries by the Choctaw. Their deaths also severely impacted the transmission and survival of cultural knowledge and ritual....

The Choctaws always have been survivors, and have shown themselves adept at meeting the challenges of a changing environment. Within a few years the majority had found kinsmen, erected shelters, and cleared fields. As early as 1833, several hundred Choctaw families had settled on the banks of the Arkansas River, planting crops in anticipation of the arrival later of many more emigrants, for whom they planned to provide corn. Perhaps these folks thought they had escaped the worst, for the spring planting had gone well and most of the people who survived the march were recovering. However, some saw the anger of the spirits raining down on the nation when in June 1833 the Arkansas River overflowed its banks in the greatest flood in its history. In astonishment at the damage done by the raging waters, the United States agent wrote that the Choctaw houses and fields were completely washed away, as though they had never existed. The cattle and horses some Choctaws had managed to bring with them drowned. Incessant rains continued all spring, flooding the entire river network in the new Choctaw Nation. Since the agrarian Choctaws always lived near rivers and streams, many, if not most, were ruined that year. Some families were completely stranded by the high waters, and many began to starve.

Terrible sickness followed the floods. Carcasses of dead animals lined the riverbanks and floated in the waters, making it unfit for human consumption. The U.S. agent wrote that many were starving—"more than they ever suffered before from hunger." ...

In fulfillment of the prophecies, the nation was dying. As soon as they departed from their beloved homelands in the east, the Choctaws succumbed to exposure, illness, accidents, depression, misery, and death. No one was left unscathed. Even the U.S. agents were appalled at the suffering of the Choctaw people. The official U.S. government reports indicated that some 20 percent of the Choctaw people had died on the journey, and a great number more— perhaps another 20 percent—died soon after their arrival. The elders died disproportionately, making reestablishment of social and political institutions problematic. Old living patterns, important to the cohesion of the nation, proved impossible to duplicate in the West. Many survivors of the journey did not move from their point of entry into the new lands. According to American observers, they were so depressed, they simply stayed put where they landed and did nothing. Some did not even build shelters or make any effort at all to clear fields or plant crops. Suicide became commonplace, whereas it was almost unknown in prior times.

Word traveled to and from the old nation in the Southeast and the new lands in the years of the Removal. Choctaw families in the West reported the great tragedy befalling the nation. Some of the newly arrived émigrés turned around and started back. Others wrote kin that they should not come west. Those who stayed behind in Mississippi, intending to come later, now decided not to make the journey at all. These people became the prey of invading whites, many of whom were unscrupulous and had no compassion for Native people in distress. The thousands of Choctaws still in Mississippi were forced off their lands and into the remote and worthless swamplands. From there they sometimes would return to look upon their former bountiful homes and farms, all now in the hands of white men.

The new lands of the Choctaws in the West became known among the Choctaw as the Land of Death. The misfortunes continued. On November 13, 1833, the Choctaws experienced a terrible omen. That night, an extraordinary meteor shower lit up the night sky as bright as day "with myriads of meteors darting about in the sky." Some of the women and children screamed and cried in terror, while others hid. All night long, the showers continued. The terror was not limited to the Choctaws. The Kiowas recorded this event, too, finding it so important that they named the season "the Winter that the Stars Fell." The Choctaws knew that the Great Spirit spoke through natural events such as this and that the unnatural event portended great misfortune. This celestial event coincided with the U.S. announcement that no more provisions would be provided for the people. The period covered by the Treaty for their emigration had expired. And despite the terrible floods and illness and death suffered in the past two years, the United States intended to do nothing more to assist the exiles.

The suffering of the Choctaw people intensified with the horror of a smallpox pandemic that struck Native people throughout the West from 1836 to 1840. More than 10,000 Native people died in the northern plains alone. Newly arrived emigrants in the Choctaw Nation brought the disease with them. More than 1,000 Choctaws died, including their renowned and beloved leader, Mingo Mushulatubbee. Some families were destroyed completely, all members succumbing within days of each other. Whooping cough decimated the population of babies and toddlers among the Choctaws. One observer reported that all of the small children for miles were killed by one whooping cough epidemic in the nations.

As the decade of the 1840s began, the Choctaw people struggled to survive and rebuild in their new lands. The nation had been decimated by Indian Removal. Some estimate that more than one-third of the nation died as a result of their forced exile west and as many as 4,000 Choctaws remained behind in the Southeast, to be dispossessed from their homes and relegated to wandering in the swamplands, working occasionally as stoop laborers on lands that had been their own. The social and political organization of the nation was in shambles. The clans so central to Choctaw identity and community barely survived the exile. Despite the terrors of the 1830s, however, the nation refused to die. The Choctaws began to rebuild, and in an uneven fashion social and political institutions began once again to function.

The story of the American policy of Indian Removal must be reexamined and retold. It was not merely an official, dry, legal instrument as it often is portrayed. Removal, as experienced by Native people, was an official U.S. policy of death and destruction that created untold human pain and misery. It was unjust, inhuman, and a product of the worst impulses of Western society. Indian Removal cannot be separated from the human suffering it evoked—from the toll on the human spirit of the Native people. It cannot be remembered by Americans as merely an official U.S. policy, but must be understood in terms of the human suffering it caused, and the thousands of deaths and lives it destroyed.

◈ FURTHER READING

Barr, Juliana. *Peace Came in the Form of a Woman: Indians and Spaniards in the Texas Borderlands* (2007).

Binnema, Theodore. *Common and Contested Ground: A Human and Environmental History of the Northwestern Plains* (2001).

Blackhawk, Ned. *Violence Over the Land: Indians and Empires in the Early American West* (2006).

Bowes, John P. *Exiles and Pioneers: Eastern Indians in the Trans-Mississippi West* (2007).

Boyd, Robert. *The Coming of the Spirit of Pestilence: Introduced Infectious Diseases and Population Decline Among the Northwest Coast Indians, 1774–1874* (1999).

Calloway, Colin G. *One Vast Winter Count: The Native American West Before Lewis and Clark* (2003).

———. *The Shawnees and the War for America.* New York: Viking, 2007.

Carson, James Taylor. *Searching for the Bright Path: The Mississippi Choctaw from Prehistory to Removal* (1999).

Debo, Angie. *The Rise and Fall of the Choctaw Republic* (2nd ed., 1961).

DeRosier, Arthur H., Jr. *The Removal of the Choctaw Indians* (1970).

Dowd, Gregory Evans. *A Spirited Resistance: The North American Indian Struggle for Unity, 1745–1815* (1992).

DuVal, Kathleen. *The Native Ground: Indians and Colonists in the Heart of the Continent* (2006).

Edmunds, R. David. *Tecumseh and the Quest for Indian Leadership* (1984).

Ewers, John C. *Indian Life on the Upper Missouri* (1968).

———. "Intertribal Warfare as the Precursor of Indian-White Warfare on the Northern Great Plains." *Western Historical Quarterly* 6 (1975): 397–410.

Galloway, Patricia. *Choctaw Genesis, 1500–1700* (1996).

Gibson, Arrell Morgan, ed. *America's Exiles: Indian Colonization in Oklahoma* (1976).

Gibson, James R. *Otter Skins, Boston Ships, and China Goods: The Maritime Fur Trade of the Northwest Coast, 1785–1841* (1992).

Green, Michael D. *The Politics of Removal: Creek Government and Society in Crisis* (1982).

Hämäläinen, Pekka. *The Comanche Empire* (2008).

Hauptman, Laurence M. *Oneida Indian Journey: From New York to Wisconsin, 1784–1860* (1999).

Heidler, David S., and Jeanne T. Heidler. *Indian Removal* (2007).

Hicks, Brian. *Toward the Setting Sun: John Ross, the Cherokees, and the Trail of Tears* (2011).

Horsman, Reginald. *Expansion and American Indian Policy, 1783–1812* (1992).

Hudson, Angela Pulley. *Creek Paths and Federal Roads: Indians, Settlers, and Slaves and the Making of the American South* (2010).

Jung, Patrick J. *The Black Hawk War of 1832* (2007).

Kavanaugh, Thomas W. *Comanche Political History: An Ethnohistorical Perspective, 1706–1875* (1996).

Kidwell, Clara Sue. *Choctaws and Missionaries in Mississippi, 1818–1918* (1995).

Mandell, Daniel R. *Tribe, Race, History: Native Americans in Southern New England, 1780–1880* (2008).

McKee, Jesse O., and Jon Al Schlenker. *The Choctaws: Cultural Evolution of a Native American Tribe* (1980).

McLoughlin, William G. *Cherokees and Missionaries, 1789–1839* (1984).

Miles, Tiya. *The House on Diamond Hill: A Cherokee Plantation Story* (2010).

———. *Ties That Bind: The Story of an Afro-Cherokee Family in Slavery and Freedom* (2005).

Mt. Pleasant, Alyssa. "Debating Missionary Presence at Buffalo Creek: Haudenosaunee Perspectives on Land Cessions, Government Relations, and Christianity." In *Ethnographies and Exchanges: Native Americans, Moravians, and Catholics in Early North America*, ed. A.G. Roeber (2008).

O'Brien, Greg. *Choctaws in a Revolutionary Age, 1750–1830* (2002).

O'Connell, Barry, ed. *On Our Own Ground: The Complete Writings of William Apess, a Pequot* (1992).

Perdue, Theda. *Cherokee Women: Gender and Culture Change, 1700–1835* (1998).

Preston, David L. *The Texture of Contact: European and Indian Settler Communities on the Frontier of Iroquoia, 1667–1783* (2009).

Prucha, Francis Paul. *American Indian Policy in the Formative Years: The Indian Trade and Intercourse Acts, 1790–1834* (1962).

———. *American Indian Treaties: The History of a Political Anomaly* (1994).

———. *The Great Father: The United States Government and the American Indians* (1984).

Rollings, Willard H. *The Osage: An Ethnohistorical Study of Hegemony on the Prairie-Plains* (1992).

Ronda, James P. *Finding the West: Explorations with Lewis and Clark* (2001).

———. *Lewis and Clark Among the Indians* (1984).

Saunt, Cladio. *Black, White, and Indian: Race and the Unmaking of an American Family* (2005).

Sugden, John. *Tecumseh: A Life* (1998).

Tayac, Gabrielle, ed. *IndiVisible: African-Native American Lives in the Americas* (2009).

Thorne, Tanis. *The Many Hands of My Relations: French and Indians on the Lower Missouri* (1996).

Weber, David J. *Bárbaros: Spaniards and Their Savages in the Age of Enlightenment* (2005).

West, Elliott. *The Contested Plains: Indians, Goldseekers, and the Rush to Colorado* (1998).

White, Richard. *Roots of Dependency: Subsistence, Environment, and Social Change among the Choctaws, Pawnees, and Navajos* (1983).

Wilkinson, Charles F. *American Indians, Time, and the Law* (1987).

Willig, Timothy D. *Restoring the Chain of Friendship: British Policy and the Indians of the Great Lakes, 1783–1815* (2008).

Wood, W. Raymond, and Thomas D. Thiessen, eds. *Early Fur Trade on the Northern Plains: Canadian Traders Among the Mandan and Hidatsa Indians, 1738–1818* (1985).

Yarbrough, Fay. *Race and the Cherokee Nation: Sovereignty in the Nineteenth Century* (2007).

Native People, Families, and Nations Confront American Western Expansion, 1840–1865

During the 1840s, people from across North America and around the world rushed into the American West. By the beginning of the decade, the last of the Choctaws, Cherokees, and other members of the so-called Five Civilized Nations from the southeast had taken up the exhausting process of making new lives in Indian Territory. American citizens left Independence, Missouri, for the West Coast, establishing Protestant missions in Oregon or securing lands under Mexican law in Texas and California. In the latter soon-to-be state, Spanish and Mexican settlements were limited to the Pacific Coast, south of the San Francisco Bay Area. The Anglos who settled in Mexican California clustered around John A. Sutter's fort in the Sacramento Valley. In 1848, the Treaty of Guadalupe Hidalgo ended the Mexican War and transferred California and the Great Basin to the United States. Additionally, in January 1848, Sutter's workers found gold in the Sierra Nevada foothills and set off a frenzied, worldwide rush for the precious metal. Tens of thousands of gold seekers, including Americans, African Americans, Chinese, Frenchmen, Chileans, and Indigenous people from Hawai'i and Mexico stampeded into California. Many of these men had little regard for Indian life or property. On the Plains, members of the powerful Lakota and Comanche nations expanded their territorial boundaries and forced neighboring Native nations to move into other areas. As in many regions and periods of history, the movement of people altered the social, political, and economic conditions of the American West.

Native peoples west of the Mississippi responded to these migrations in different ways. The region west of the Rocky Mountains was home to hundreds of thousands of Indians, many not well known to the average American. In California—the most heavily populated area—the majority of Indians lived in small communities, sometimes called rancherias, and subsisted on a diet of indigenous game and plants. In the Great Basin (Nevada and parts of Oregon, Utah, and Idaho), Paiutes and Shoshones hunted game and harvested plants in their arid homelands. In all of these areas, Native peoples practiced a gendered division of labor: men brought in game and fish, and women cultivated and harvested seeds, nuts, tubers, and acorns. The overland immigration of Americans and the California Gold Rush exposed these Native peoples to racism and violence. Americans who saw Native women at work derisively called California and Great Basin Indians "diggers," a slur against Indian gender roles as well as race. After the California Gold Rush began, miners and other Americans attacked California Indian rancherias, often with little or no provocation. As we shall see, California Indian men and women lived a precarious existence in the 1840s and 1850s.

Meanwhile, Americans frequently crossed over the Great Plains. Here, Lakotas, Dakotas, Cheyennes, Arapahos, Comanches, and other peoples relied on the bison herds that spread over the plains for food, clothing, and housing. They erected buffalo-skin tipis wherever the hunting was good and moved on when game retreated. In the popular imagination, this roving existence has come to be associated with all Indians. Americans used the stereotype of the Indian as a hunter/warrior/nomad to justify the dispossession of all Native people. This cliché, however, obscures the realities of Plains Indian life and history. In the middle of the nineteenth century, Plains Indians, such as the Dakotas, Lakotas, and Comanches, were expanding into new territories, much like citizens of the United States. Thus, on the Plains, there was not one expansionistic nation; there were several.

◈ DOCUMENTS

Between 1840 and 1865, the American invasion of the West and the mobility of Native nations unsettled social, political, and economic relations in the region. In Document 1, Paiute Sarah Winnemucca describes her grandfather's encounter with overland emigrants in the Great Basin. What motivated Winnemucca's grandfather's to meet with the immigrants? In Document 2, Nisenan William Joseph details the Gold Rush, and in Document 3, Lassik Lucy Young tells a non-Indian woman (who, unfortunately, transcribed the interview in stereotypical language) her family's efforts to evade soldiers in California's northwestern mountains. How did Indigenous people respond to and shape their experiences in the California Gold Rush? How did the Gold Rush affect Native men and women differently? The next trio of documents considers the period from the perspective of Great Plains Indians. In Document 4, Lakota leader Black Hawk asserts Lakota land claims at a treaty conference at Horse Creek, Nebraska, in 1851. What were the Lakota nation's boundaries in the 1850s? How did the Lakota claim those lands? In Document 5, Dakota leader Wabasha explains how traders took advantage of his people and provoked what historians call the Dakota War of 1862. After the Dakota War ended, Document 6 reveals, President Abraham Lincoln ordered the execution of 39 Dakota men. Why did the Dakota War begin? From a Dakota perspective, were these executions justified?

1. Sarah Winnemucca (Paiute) Recalls Her Father's Encounter with Overland Emigrants, c. 1845

I was a very small child when the first white people came into our country. They came like a lion, yes, like a roaring lion, and have continued so ever since, and I have never forgotten their first coming. My people were scattered at that time over nearly all the territory now known as Nevada. My grandfather was chief of the entire Piute nation, and was camped near Humboldt Lake, with a small portion of his tribe, when a party travelling eastward from California was seen coming. When the news was brought to my grandfather, he asked what they looked like? When told that they had hair on their faces, and were white, he jumped up and clasped his hands together, and cried aloud,

"My white brothers,—my long-looked for white brothers have come at last!"

He immediately gathered some of his leading men, and went to the place where the party had gone into camp. Arriving near them, he was commanded to halt in a manner that was readily understood without an interpreter. Grandpa at once made signs of friendship by throwing down his robe and throwing up his arms to show them he had no weapons; but in vain,—they kept him at a distance. He knew not what to do. He had expected so much pleasure in welcoming his white brothers to the best in the land, that after looking at them sorrowfully for a little while, he came away quite unhappy. But he would not give them up so easily. He took some of his most trustworthy men and followed them day after day, camping near them at night, and travelling in sight of them by day, hoping in this way to gain their confidence. But he was disappointed, poor dear old soul! ....

Seeing they would not trust him, my grandfather left them, saying, "Perhaps they will come again next year."...

The next year came a great emigration, and camped near Humboldt Lake. The name of the man in charge of the trains was Captain Johnson, and they stayed three days to rest their horses, as they had a long journey before them without water. During their stay my grandfather and some of his people called upon them, and they all shook hands, and when our white brothers were going away they gave my grandfather a white tin plate. Oh, what a time they had over that beautiful gift,—it was so bright! They say that after they left, my grandfather called for all his people to come together, and he then showed them the beautiful gift which he had received from his white brothers. Everybody was so pleased; nothing like it was ever seen in our country before. My grandfather thought so much of it that he bored holes in it and fastened it on his head, and wore it as his hat. He held it in as much admiration as my white sisters hold their diamond rings or a sealskin jacket. So that winter they talked of nothing but their white brothers. The following spring there came great news down the Humboldt River, saying that there were some more of the white brothers coming, and there was something among them that was burning all in a blaze. My grandfather

Sarah Winnemucca Hopkins, *Life Among the Piutes: Their Wrongs and Claims* (Reno: University of Nevada Press, 1994), 5–9.

asked them what it was like. They told him it looked like a man; it had legs and hands and a head, but the head had quit burning, and it was left quite black. There was the greatest excitement among my people everywhere about the men in a blazing fire. They were excited because they did not know there were any people in the world but the two,—that is, the Indians and the whites; they thought that was all of us in the beginning of the world, and, of course, we did not know where the others had come from, and we don't know yet.... What a laughable thing that was! It was two negroes wearing red shirts!

The third year more emigrants came, and that summer Captain Fremont, who is now General Fremont.

My grandfather met him, and they were soon friends. They met just where the railroad crosses Truckee River, now called Wadsworth, Nevada. Captain Fremont gave my grandfather the name of Captain Truckee, and he also called the river after him. Truckee is an Indian word, it means *all right*, or *very well*. A party of twelve of my people went to California with Captain Fremont....

During the time my grandfather was away in California, where he staid till after the Mexican war, there was a girl-baby born in our family. I can just remember it. It must have been in spring, because everything was green. I was away playing with some other children when my mother called me to come to her. So I ran to her. She then asked me to sit down, which I did. She then handed me some beautiful beads, and asked me if I would like to buy something with them. I said:

"Yes, mother, some pine nuts."

My mother said:

"Would you like something else you can love and play with? Would you like to have a little sister?" I said,

"Yes, dear mother, a little, little sister; not like my sister Mary, for she won't let me play with her. She leaves me and goes with big girls to play;" and then my mother wanted to know if I would give my pretty beads for the little sister.

Just then the baby let out such a cry it frightened me; and I jumped up and cried so that my mother took me in her arms, and said it was a little sister for me, and not to be afraid. This is all I can remember about it.

When my grandfather went to California he helped Captain Fremont fight the Mexicans. When he came back he told the people what a beautiful country California was. Only eleven returned home, one having died on the way back.

2. William Joseph (Nisenan) Describes the Gold Rush, c. 1849

Long ago the Indians had a camp on the north side of the oke·m mountain, the white people call that Mt. Oakum. The bluff by the river at the north side of that, (they) call that pu·lak' Bluff, and the white people call that Buck's Bar, in that river Indians and white men prospected for gold.

Hans Jorgen Uldall and William Shipley, Nisenan Texts and Dictionary, vol. 46 of the *University of California Publications in Linguistics* (Berkeley: University of California Press, 1966), 177–181. Copyright © 1966 The Regents of the University of California.

On the west side of Mt. Oakum two white men had their home in a small log cabin. From there they used to go to work at the river every day. The door of their house being left open, an Indian boy who was hunting around, felt hungry and went to that house to eat. When he had finished eating he saw two buckskin sacks full of gold, and silver money on that table. He took (it), put (it) in his pocket, and went off with (it).

When the two men came home from work they missed the gold and the money. They followed that Indian's tracks. They tracked (him) to the Indian's camp. They saw (him) playing cards and putting down sackfuls of gold. The white men took him right there. They took back all the money. But they took him all the same to a little valley on the west side of Mt. Oakum.

The white men gathered. From there, afterwards, they summoned all the Indian chiefs. They kept him there all day, waiting for one chief. When it was about three o'clock, they put a rope around (his) neck.

At length, that chief arrived. The Indians said, "(They) are waiting for you, they are going to hang the boy, go and prevent (it)!"

That chief went in the center (of the group of people). He talked, speaking white language, "Captain he says, Lowas he says, Hemas he says, 'Hang him up!'" he said.

(The white people) said to the mule, "Get up!" (The mule) pulled (him) up by the rope and hanged (him). All the Indians hollered and cried. When (he) was dead, (they) let (him) back down. They gave (him) to the Indians. The Indians took the body along and burned (it).

After that the Indians did not burgle or steal anything belonging to white people, "That is the way (they) will treat us if they catch (us)," they said. When the chiefs made speeches they said, "Do not take anything from (them), do not steal from (them), (they) will treat you that way if they catch (you)! Those white men are different men, they are not our relatives," they said, "(They) will hang you without mercy!" they said. All the chiefs preached that. They talked about that at every big time [celebration]. The Indians were very much afraid of the whites in the early days. That is what was done, the whites were bad in the old days, those who prospected for gold. Those who have come now brought women along, white women, those ones were good, they gave us all kinds of food when we went to their houses. That was bad whites in the early days, those who prospected for gold. Those who came next were good whites, married people, that was how it was in the old days.

About a year after that hanging (an Indian boy) found gold in a creek while he was hunting a deer, he killed the deer near that. He looked around for a tree to hang it on. He saw this gold. He took the deer along instead of hanging it up. When he brought (it) in to camp he told his relatives, "There is a lot of this gold, let us go tomorrow!" he said.

That morning at dawn they went, only the men, they left the women. They all brought a lot of gold. They took (it) to town to exchange (it), five or six times to that town, the same fellows.

The white men talked about (it), "Those Indians bring in a lot of gold from somewhere," said the storekeeper. Those white men talked about (it), those who worked on that river. "Let us watch those Indians, where is it they are always going?" they said. They saw those fellows go, the white men tracked (them) that way. From the hills they watched them at work. When the sun was in the west the Indians went back from work. (The white men) went past them in the opposite direction and found the gold.

The whites gathered and went there. When the Indians tried to go to work they found the whites there. They sneaked away, "That is those fellows, those who hanged that boy!" they said. That way those white men stole their prospecting place. The whites name that Indian Digging. The white men made a small town there and a ditch, and then they placer-mined with a lot of water and went twenty feet into the mountain.

This is over now, even the town is dead now, only one keeps a store there, a Chinaman. That is still called Indian Digging. That is what they did long ago, those fellows are dead and gone, there is not one of the Indians alive now. That is that.

3. Lucy Young (Lassik) Discusses the Dangers Native Women Faced in California, c. 1861

I never grow much. They call me "Li'l Shorty," but I know pretty near everything that time. My grandpa put his head on my head, smoove my hair, and hold his hand there.

"Long time you gonta live, my child," he say. "You live long time in this world."

Well, I live long enough. I guess 'bout ninety-five next summer, if I living till then....

First soldiers ever I see, my li'l sister 'bout three feet high. Took us to Fort Baker and down Van Duzen River. Mother run away, twice. Last time tookted us to lower country. I run off, too, many times.

It was in August. Soldiers had all Inyan together. Gonta takum to Hoopa.

Mother run away when we hit redwoods. Hide us all in hollow tree. Lay there all day. I had li'l cup and bucket soldier give me. Mother send me hunt water.

I 'fraid lost. Break bushes every li'l way. Offus dark in redwoods. Can't see nothing. Pretty soon come to big fern. I break it, lay in my track. Pretty soon hear waterfall, fill bucket. Turn back, find stick I broke. Find fern. Good thing I do that way. Might I lost. Too dark, them redwoods.

Two days we lay in hollow log. Hear soldier in camp, go li'l ways, listen. Go li'l further, listen.

Way down gulch, lotsa hazelnut, we eat. Travel on. 'Bout sundown come out open country....

We see horse track. Hide again. Somebody whistle. We drop in fern. Just see soldier hat go by. We watchum long ways. When dark come, we go way down open ridge.

Edith V.A. Murphey and Lucy Young, "Out of the Past: A True Indian Story Told by Lucy Young, of Round Valley Indian Reservation," *California Historical Society Quarterly* 20 (December 1941): 349–64.

Something rustle. I think dogs overtake us. We look back. Skunk family follow us—mother, five li'l ones.

We go down, find li'l flat, heavy timber. We lay down, sleep till sun-up. Mother never eat, just drink water. We got crackers, dried beef from soldiers.

There we stay till sundown. Mother begin get sick. If she die, she tell us go back to soldiers, not to no other white people. We go on. From top of mountain, we come to big pond. High mountain. I pack water for poor mother.

Poor li'l sister tired, can't hardly walk. I pack her by hand. Look all time for sarvice berry. Go way out around. See track. I think must be people. Nobody there. Look close, bear track, deer track, too.

Get pretty close our own country. Bunch grass country. We make li'l hole, so we lay down to sleep. Mother never sleep. I never sleep. Li'l sister sleep. Too tired li'l sister....

We go round behind Lassik Peak on top of ridge. Rocky. I want hunt water. I starve for water. I hunt for water like in redwoods, see li'l ferns, drink water, carry to mother, rest awhile, then go on. Too hungry we feel. I want go back on road, let soldiers catch us. Then we find sunflower, plenty. We gather head, seed dry 'nough to eat. We go down creek, catch crawfish. Mother can't eat hardtack, make it sick.

We had bedticking dresses, soldiers made us. I wear that. Mother holler: "Young ducks coming down in water." I stand in water, catch li'l ducky in my skirt. Two of 'em. Pretty good size. Can't fly yet. Run on top of water. We killum, club.

We had soldier matches. If didn't had, we could make fire with stick. Lotsa buckeye good for that in Soldier Basin. We swinge cotton [singe the down] off li'l ducks. Get lotsa maple leaf. Fill hole with coals. Wrap ducks in leaf, keep ashes off. Put in hole. Duck offus fat, taste good, smell good. I never eat. Want mother eat, get stronger. I eat dry beef, crackers, good enough. After we eat, I catch crawfish again that I lose outa dress skirt when duck come downstream.

We stay one night. That's all. Keep moving. Up hill here, all way to Kettenshaw. Got to that valley. White man been plant wheat, then go off, leave it. This wheat lotsa ripe. Moonlight. We all pick awhile, drop down sleep. I pick li'l longer. Drop down, sleep. Mother pick all night. Had basket pretty near full.

She wake us up: "Come, children. Big spring ahead of us. We make it tonight."

I 'fraid step on snake, I say. Mother got deerskin, make us high moccasin, up to knee. No moccasin for mother, hide ain't big enough.

We get to big spring, we stay all night, all day. Evening, mother want to go down to head of Soldier Creek. We stay there, gather brush, make basket, pounding basket, call it "Chesta-a." Pounding rock, call it "Bilt-sook."

Two days mother take make "Chesta-a," then pound wheat. Roast it first in old pan we find there. Make pinole.

Long time we stay there, get good basket roots along river. Kinda lonesome there. Talk 'bout move over li'l gulch, get hazelnut. Bear like hazelnut, too. I 'fraid bear get mother. She laugh, tell me if bear get it, take li'l sister to soldier. They gonta take care us both.

Then mother talk 'bout go Alder Point. No rain, no snow. I don't want go, I wanta stay where lotsa wood.

Mother gather hazelnut. Come back quick, 'mence crack all night by small firelight, take hazelnut out. Everytime I wake up, I hear cracking, cracking, so don't have to carry shell.

We move our camp back to Mad River. Don't stay long. Then go South Fork Mountain. There we stay 'bout month, eat hazelnut. Lotsa ketten (camas) bulb, too. Then come rain.

Poor mother, build bark house. He happy there.

One day, I see smoke over to Kettenchaw. Me'n li'l sister playing. We see big smoke raise over Kettenchaw. Mother come out, shade eyes with hand— look, look.

"Guess someum come back from Hoopa," he say.

Mother want go back, see who there. I 'fraid. I tell it: "You go there, someum kill us. I gonta take li'l sister, go to soldier, *now*."

We had thick black oak bark, we pack fire on it, save matches. Evening time, wind blow, 'way down ridge, I see big fire raise up where I drop coal.

Over Kettenchaw two women, one man, burn coals in grass for grasshopper. They see our smoke, know then we still alive.

"That's our cousin and li'l children," they say. "Them that run off from soldier." Lotsa Inyan die on road, starve.

Mother went down to river, stay all night. Morning come, we go way up ridge on top of Kettenchaw. Coming down, mother tell me: "Daughter, I dry for water." I get water. I ask it gonta flat down on Kettenchaw. He say "No, we get out on point see who is, if we know."

Had big load hazelnut to pack. "Push basket up for me, Daughter," mother say. He sit down, I lift strap, push basket up on back. Just then, I hear brush crack. Look quick, see soldier hat. I run back, way back, run in gulch. Mother call me: "Come back, don't run off." I lay there long time. After while, I come back.

Our cousins come there, dressed in soldier clothes. Man had mustache, too. Look strange. I ask it: "Where you woman?" "Coming slow," he say. "Sick, pack grasshopper, pack basket, nothing to eat but grasshopper."

Mother divide pinole and hazelnut. He feedum good. All us went back to Mad River. We had old uncle coming there. Lotsa fish in hole, deep hole. Can't catchum, so we get big root (soap root) poundum, put in hole. Lotsa fish come then top water ain't dead, ain't hurt, just float. If put in fresh water, gonta come alive again.

We eat that evening. They tell me go down river, look for old uncle. I run down quick, come back. Mother tell me: "Stay down li'l while. Might be pass us." I go out again, look all round, hear rock rattle. I watch, watch. See poor old fellow coming, pack big black basket.

I run to camp, say: "Old uncle coming now." "Go on," mother say, "go meetum." I do. He 'mence cry, hold my hand. He had to catch fish, like we did, too.

Fall time, then, acorns getting good. All want go back Alder Point, winter there. 'Mence rain hard. We camp, build bark house. Everybody tell li'l sister 'n me: "Go on outside, play." We get oak ball, playing, playing. We play pitch 'n catch.

White people come find us. Want take us all to Fort Seward. We all scared to dead. Inyan boy tell us: "Don't 'fraid, won't kill you."

Tookted us to Fort Seward, had Inyan women there, all man killed. Plenty house there; any Inyan escape from Hoopa, bring it to Fort Seward.

After while, Chief Lassik come in. White people went away to get grub, snowing. Find Inyan track way down some place on road. Three white men, two-three Inyan boys gonta hunt up who make track—find it.

"Don't run," Inyan boy tellum. "Gonta take you Fort Seward." They bringum, four Inyan men, five women, Fort Seward. Chief Lassik among them. He uncle-cousin my mother. They all stay there, kill deer, pack it in. Pack wood all time.

One white man come there, want take me South Fork Mountain. His woman got li'l baby. He want me stay his woman. He take me South Fork. He herd hogs, gonta takum to Weaver. I never stay long there. This Inyan woman whip me all time. Didden' talk my language. 'Bout week all I stay. Commence rain pretty hard. He tell me go get water. I go down, water muddy. I get it anyway. He ask me, make sign, "Where you get this water?" I showum down to river. He think I get water in hole near house. He throw out water, commence whip me, tell me go get water.

I go down river, pretty steep go down. I throw bucket in river. I run off. Never see bucket no more. I had soldier shoes, take off, tie around neck. Water knee deep. I just had thin dress, can run good. Come up big high bank. Keep look back see if that woman follow me....

That man what herd hogs, his Inyan boy speak my language. He say: "Why you come back?"

"That woman whip me every day," I say.

"What for she whip you?"

"Everything, little or big, she whip me."

Boy say: "White man say he gonta take all you folks over there, build you house."

That white man, same evening got me, took to his house. Then took me down South Fork again. I ride behind. He talk his women. He had cowhide rope. Short one. He upped that. Give woman good whipping with that. He stay all night, next morning go back Fort Seward. 'Nother Inyan boy where I was. I didden' know he spoke my language. When man come, that woman wash clothes down by the river. Want me stay take care baby. She go on, then this boy talk with me. He tell me: "Tomorrow, 'nother white man come, gonta take you off. Way down. Tomorrow, white man come."

So it did happen. He take me then. This boy say: "Better you stay white people, better for you. All your people killed. Nothing to come back for."

I didden' say nothing. Yes nor no.

He bring me back Alder Point, this white man did. From there he take me down low. I ride on packsaddle. Had big blanket over me. Winter time.

Get up on top of mountain, meet 'nother white man, got li'l Inyan boy with him. This boy talk my talk good. He ride packsaddle too. They take us way up to Blue Rock Mountain. White men live there. Dogs begin barking. We get there, ride up to gate. White man take me off. I can't walk. Ride all day. Take li'l boy off, too.

I see woman come out of door. I know that woman, one of my people. Bill Dobbins' mother. This one, her father's my aunt. She know me. I know her. She set down in chair, hug me, commence cry. I cry, too, cause think 'bout mother all time.

This woman live with old white man. He cook supper. This woman don't know how to cook. He come in, think I his daughter. "Your pappoose?" he say. She say: "No." Put hand on chest. "My Inyan," she say.

"Ah-hah," white say. He bring out li'l baby tumbler, give me li'l whisky, put sugar in it, cause riding in cold.

Then they took me to Long Valley. He had 'nother wife there. Next morning that other man was there, washing face. He come in, count my finger: "One, two, three, four, days you going down, close to ocean." That man washing was cutting wood there. I stay there and play with pups. I look back. Two small Inyan boys stand there. I look and feel afraid. Went in house.

That man cook supper. He go to bed overhead. I sleep in big blanket by chimney. He cook in kitchen in morning. "Get up," he say. "Breakfast ready."

Two Inyan women come in. Talk quick to me: "Poor my li'l sister, where you come from?" "I come from north. That bald-headed man bring me."

"He got wife and children," they say.

These women talk clipped my language. "That's way all Inyan children come here," they say. "He bringum all."

I half cry, all time for my mother. After while, bald-headed man come back, talk women long time. Gonta have big gamble over there, they say. Men got up and left. First, they give women grub, hog backbone, ribs.

These women say: "In four days you go stay old couple close by us." One um say: "I got white man, I come see you."

They leave for home. Little ridge, over hill. I hear Inyan talking, li'l way. I stand there and think. Only show for me to run off, now. Nobody there. I run in house. Match box on shelf. I put it in dress pocket. In kitchen, I find flour sacks. Take loaf bread, take boiling meat. Take big blanket from my bed.

I went out so quick, I never shut door. Then I went out to barn, open door, let all horses out.

All day I travel on edge of valley. I forgot I gonta have to swim Eel River. Then I see white man house, and lotta Inyan house, all smoke even—good sign. I go towards white man house. I go upstream, look for foot-log. Brush thick, too. I found big trail. 'Fraid then. Stop and listen, every li'l while. Pretty soon find footbridge. Just getting dark good. Star coming up. 'Nother big stream, Shallow water.

Lotsa people there. Lotsa bell. Talk. Laugh. Pack-train stop there. I cross above camp. Water knee-deep. Go up long hill. Pretty near daylight, come out on mountain. Come out in big open country where Billy Dobbins' mother lived.

Owl commence holler, coming daylight. Way this side, great big rock. Big live-oak. Hollow place. I lay blanket down. Sleep all day; dark, I wake up.

Night come. I pack shoes one shoulder, blanket, 'nother shoulder, pack grub in hand. Lotsa snow that time, Bell Springs Mountain. There I put on shoes. I come out in big opening, went down away from road.

Saw big mountain, went over it. I back-track li'l way. I see white man hunt for me on white horse. I lay still long time, travel all night.

Went down in canyon, find big log all dry underneath. I sleep right there all day. Had to cross two li'l creek, went barefoot there. When I cross those two li'l creek, I home to old stamping ground, not far from Alder Point.

Again I lay down in sun to sleep. Three days I stay there, 'fraid go down to Fort Seward. Good weather. Think 'bout mother all time. Half-time cry, once awhile. Two nights I stay alone, then I go to Fort Seward.

That white man told Inyan boys watch for me come home. Lotsa women there, man all killed.

I go where they get water, two-three places there where make buckeye soup. It ain't done yet. Nobody there. I taste buckeye, all bitter yet. I drink water, outa basket setting there. After awhile I see woman coming. I step behind brush. He never see me. He pour water in buckeye. Talk to self 'bout being bitter. It was my mother! Then I step in plain sight. He stir soup with hand, shake drops off. Look round. "Who's you," he say, "That you, my daughter?" I say: "Yes." He hug me and cry. Poor mother!

"Inyan boy watching," he whisper. "You come in 'bout morning, 'bout midnight?" "No," I told it. "Got grub, got blanket, I sleep down here, some place."

"Shall I bring buckeye soup tonight?" "No," I tell it. "Don't fetch grub out, might they follow you, find me."

Two night I hide out. I go way down creek down under big tree roots. Sleep dry. Then I go to house. All time I never leave no sign. Mother and li'l sister hunt me. Make believe gather wood, never find me.

My uncle hunt me the last night. I see him. Then I show up on open ground. He say: "Poor li'l thing, hunted, starving. 'Bout midnight I put you 'cross river in boat." I say: "Tell mother meet me out there."

He say them two li'l girl been take away from that 'nother woman. Cry all time.

Midnight, I go in, meetum. Watch stars for time. I eat. Mother give me 'nother blanket, food too. Them two men don't make no track—walk in leaves and river. Had big boat. Put my aunt and me 'cross river. If mother let li'l sister go, white men would kill mother.

We travel all night, sleep all day till sundown. Had lotsa dry meat. Left most of my white-man grub with mother. Found some of our people at Poison Rock, pretty near sundown. I see old man pack wood. He been on look-out. He go in big bark house. I look in door, big fire in middle of house.

Man say: "Li'l girl look in door." They get up, bring me in. Young girl lay there, sick, my half sister. That night she die. Snowing, raining hard. They dig hole right by house, put body in. All went out. Tore all house down, set it afire. Midnight, snow whirl, wind howl. Then we went over to 'nother house; all left there next day, went over to Soldier Basin.

We stay there awhile, went to Cottonwood. Some of our people there. We went to head of Mad River, next day to South Fork of Trinity River. We stay all night. Tired. No horses. Next day to Cottonwood.

My cousin, Ellen, Wylackie Tom's woman, was there. We found her right away. Then I stay at Cottonwood all summer. After awhile, my cousin living with white man, he want kill her, she leave him. I stay with her and li'l boy.

Ellen's cousin-brother say to me: "Take care my li'l boy, cause I gonta Hayfork. Maybe white folks kill me," he say. "Take care my boy, takum way off."

White man name Rogers come after this. Ellen my cousin's man, went to work for him. I go with her to Hayfork, and take li'l boy too.

Rogers, my white man, took me then to take care of, that summer. Marry me bimeby when get old enough, 'Bout size ten year girl, I guess, when first see soldier. I stay there at Hayfork long time. My mother come there, too. She die there after awhile at Hayfork.

My cousin, Ellen, younger than me but she got man first. We didn't neither one know much. Man told us cook beans. We cook green coffee for beans. Man cook long time for us.

Li'l sister, white man took her away. Never see her no more. If see it, maybe wouldn't know it. That's last young one tooken away. Mother lost her at Fort Seward.

I hear it, I went back, got mother, brought her to Hayfork. Lotsa Inyan there, lotsa different language, all different. Mother stay with me until she die.

You ask 'bout father. He got killed and brother in soldier war, before soldiers captured us. Three days fight. Three days running. Just blood, blood, blood. Young woman cousin, run from soldier, run into our camp. Three of us girls run. I lose buckskin blanket. Cousin run back, pick it up. I roll it up, put under arm—run more better that way....

Young woman been stole by white people, come back. Shot through lights and liver. Front skin hang down like apron. She tie up with cotton dress. Never die, neither. Little boy, knee-pan shot off. Young man shot through thigh. Only two man of all our tribe left—that battle.

White people want our land, want destroy us. Break and burn all our basket, break our pounding rock. Destroy our ropes. No snares, no deerskin, flint knife, nothing....

I hear people tell 'bout what Inyan do early days to white man. Nobody ever tell it what white man do to Inyan. That's reason I tell it. That's history. That's truth. I seen it myself.

4. Black Hawk (Oglala) Asserts Lakota Land Claims on the Plains, 1851

This morning, when the Council met, much difficulty was experienced in explaining to the Sioux the extent and effect of the boundary designated between them and the Cheyennes and Arrapahoes. The Platte was fixed as the boundary, but the Sioux asserted their claim to both sides of the river. They did not contend that the south side of the Platte belonged to them, but as they had always hunted on the south side, as far as the Republican Fork of the [Smoky River] and the waters of the Arkansas, they claimed the same right now, and therefore objected to the line. Speeches were made by Snake, and the Brave Bear, and others, only one of which is worth reporting.

Black Hawk (an Ogallahlah) said: "Father, if there is anything I do know, it is this country, for I was raised in it, with the interpreters and traders. You have split the country and I don't like it. What we live upon, we hunt for, and we hunt from the Platte to the Arkansas, and from here up to the Red Bute and the Sweet Water. The Cheyennes and Arapahoes agree to live together and be one people; that is very well, but they want to hunt on this side of the river. These lands once belonged to the Kiowas and the Crows, but we whipped those nations out of them, and in this we did what the white men do when they want the lands of the Indians. We met the Kiowas and the Crows and whipped them again, and the last time at Crow Creek. This last battle was fought by the Cheyennes, Arapahoes, and Ogallahlahs combined and the Ogallahlahs claim their share of the country."

Col. Mitchell finally succeeded in getting them to understand that in fixing a boundary to their country, he had no purpose of limiting them to that boundary in hunting, or to prohibit them from going into the territory of any other Nation, so long as they remained at peace.

5. Wabasha (Dakota) Explains How Nefarious Trading Practices Caused the 1862 Minnesota War, 1868

I went to Washington the first time as I have stated above [1837]. I went again a second time [1858] before our removal to Red Wood. I went for this purpose; I had then sold our lands from east to west, from sunrise to sunset; I went to secure a reservation for my people. The Great Father put a garrison of soldiers near our country at Red Wood [Fort Ridgely], and before going to Washington I collected the chief men of the tribe and took them to the fort; some of them failed to come. I spent half a day in hunting them up, and getting their signatures to a letter that they wished to write to the President [Franklin Pierce]. The

Daily Missouri Republican, November 9, 1851.

This document can be found in *Papers Relating to Talks and Councils Held with the Indians in Dakota and Montana Territories in the Years 1866–1869* (Washington, D.C.: Government Printing Office, 1910), pp. 90–1. It can also be found in Gary Clayton Anderson and Alan R. Woolworth, eds., *Through Dakota Eyes: Narrative Accounts of the Minnesota Indian War of 1862* (St. Paul: Minnesota Historical Society Press, 1988), pp. 28–31.

soldiers were put there to take good care of us and see that we were not inter-
fered with by the whites. I told the commandant at the fort that I wished him to
write a nice letter for us. I told him that I had always been brought up as an
Indian, had worn a blanket and feather, painted my face and carried a gun. I
wished him now to write to the Great Father that I had determined to leave
off these things. I said write that I am determined to leave the war path, and to
leave off drinking whisky, and give up plundering and thieving, and I want you
to give me your ways. I know that your ways are good, and that your people
obtain land and hold it, they plant corn and raise domestic animals. I wish you to
give my people land where we may do the same. If we are left without a country, we will be obliged to go out on the plains. We would be in danger of perishing by cold and starvation; and then there are other tribes that live there that
are likely to make war on us. I wish, therefore, the Great Father to give us land
on the Minnesota River, and to help us to live like whites. I took this letter and
carried it to Washington. After a few days I had an interview with the President.
He shook hands with me, and told me to tell him all that I wanted. I said, my
Father, all that I wish is written in this letter, and I handed him the letter. (Little
Crow and Little Six were the only chiefs that did not sign the letter.) A few days
afterwards, I was called to the Interior Department to attend to our business. I
was told that our request had been granted, and that a reservation had been
appropriated for us at Red Wood on the Minnesota River, and that each head
of a family should have assigned to him 100 acres of land; 80 of prairie and 20 of
timber. When I saw our Great Father, I spoke to him about what was my chief
desire, which was to have land. The traders were constantly following me for
other purposes, and opposing me bitterly; but I paid no attention to them—I
shut my ears against them. I only desired to get a title to lands and fix my people
so that they could live. I made a treaty at this time, and lands were given to us at
Red Wood, on both sides of the Minnesota River. I went home, and lived upon
the land, and built houses there. The Great Father told me, before leaving, that
he wished us to be well off, but that the whites would endeavor to get this land
from us, and that the traders were like rats; that they would use all their endeavors to steal our substance, and that if we were wise, we would never sign a
paper for anyone. If we did so, he said, we would never see 10 cents for all
our property. I remembered the words of our Great Father and I knew that
they were true. I was, consequently, always afraid of the traders.

Two years after this, when we had gathered our corn, we all went out on
the fall hunt for furs. After we had been out some time the traders, the most
active of whom was Mr. [Nathan?] Myrick, sent out for the chief to come in to
sign papers for him in reference to selling the land on the north side of the
Minnesota River [1858]. I refused to go in. The others, I am told, went
home and signed some papers and received for doing so, horses, guns, blankets,
and other articles. They told me this after I came home. I always refused to sign
papers for the traders, and they therefore hated me. By the result of this paper
signed without my consent or knowledge, the traders obtained possession of
all the money coming from the sale of the land on the north side of the
Minnesota River, and also half of our annuity for the year 1862. When this

became known to the young men of the tribe, they felt very angry. The tribe then assembled a council of soldiers near Wakutes' house, and invite me to attend. I did attend. In that council it was determined that they would not submit to having half of their annuity taken from them, and it was ordered that all Indians should draw their annuity in full from the disbursing officer, and refuse to pay the credits to the traders for that year. I made a speech in council and told the Indians that I thought it was proper that they should obtain their whole annuities and refuse to pay the traders, and that I did not want the half-breeds to be admitted to our councils; that they had always been the tools of the traders, and aided them to deceive the Indians. After this council I thought about this matter a great deal, but heard nothing about it further until early one morning, as I was making a fire, an Indian on horseback rode up to my house and said that the Indians were fighting the traders. I asked him the cause of this sudden outbreak. He said that some of Little Six's band had killed some whites in the big woods and had come back determined to kill all the traders, and that fighting had already commenced. I got on my horse and rode up to the store. I saw that the traders were already killed. I then went to Mr. [Philander] Prescott's house; he was an Indian farmer and a half breed. I told him to write me a letter to the fort, for that I would have no part in this matter. I was determined to fly to the whites. Mr. Prescott was very much frightened and did not write the letter well. I then went home and sent word to Wa ku ta [Wakute] and Hu sha sha [Red Legs], who had not yet heard of the outbreak. I then wished to go to the fort, but found it impossible for I was afraid of the Indians.

6. President Abraham Lincoln Orders the Execution of 39 Dakotas Involved in the Minnesota War, 1862

To Henry H. Sibley

Brigadier General H.H. Sibley Executive Mansion,
St. Paul Washington,
Minnesota. December 6th. 1862.

Ordered that of the Indians and Half-breeds sentenced to be hanged by the Military Commission, composed of Colonel [William] Crooks [of the Sixth Minnesota Volunteers], Lt. Colonel [William] Marshall [of the Seventh Minnesota Volunteers], Captain [Hiram] Grant, Captain [Hiram] Bailey [both of the Sixth Minnesota Volunteers] and Lieutenant [Rollin] Olin [assistant adjutant general on Sibley's staff] and lately sitting in Minnesota, you cause to be executed on Friday the nineteenth day of December, instant, the following named, towit

> "Te-he-hdo-ne-cha." No. 2. by the record.
>
> "Tazoo" alias "Plan-doo-ta." No. 4. by the record.

Abraham Lincoln to General Henry H. Sibley, December 6, 1862, *Collected Works of Abraham Lincoln, 1809-1865*, 8 volumes, (Ann Arbor: University of Michigan Digital Library Production Services, 2001), 5: 543–44.

"Wy–a–tah–to–wah" No. 5 by the record.

"Hin–han–shoon–ko–yag." No. 6 by the record.

"Muz–za–bom–a–du." No. 10. by the record.

"Wah–pay–du–ta." No. 11. by the record.

"Wa–he–hud." No. 12. by the record.

"Sna–ma–ni." No. 14. by the record.

"Ta–te–mi–na." No. 15. by the record.

"Rda–in–yan–kna." No. 19. by the record.

"Do–wan–sa." No. 22. by the record.

"Ha–pan." No. 24. by the record.

"Shoon–ka–ska." (White Dog). No. 35. by the record.

"Toon–kan–e–chah–tay–mane." No. 67. by the record.

"E–tay–hoo–tay." No. 68. by the record.

"Am–da–cha." No. 69. by the record.

"Hay–pee–don—or, Wamne–omne–ho–ta." No. 70. by the record.

"Mahpe–o–ke–na–ji." No. 96. by the record.

"Henry Milord"—a Half-breed. No. 115. by the record.

"Chaskay–don"—or Chaskayetay." No. 121. by the record.

"Baptiste Campbell" a Halfbreed. No. 138. by the record.

"Tah–ta–kay–gay." No. 155. by the record.

"Ha–pink–pa." No. 170 by the record.

"Hypolite Ange" a Half-breed. No. 175 by the record.

"Na–pay–Shue." No. 178. by the record.

"Wa–kan–tan–ka." No. 210. by the record.

"Toon–kan–ka–yag–e–na–jin." No. 225. by the record.

"Ma–kat–e–na–jin." No. 254. by the record.

"Pa–zee–koo–tay–ma–ne." No. 264. by the record.

"Ta–tay–hde–don." No. 279. by the record.

"Wa–She–choon," or "Toon-

kan–shkan shkan mene–hay." No. 318 by the record.

"A–e–cha–ga." No. 327. by the record.

"Ha–tan–in–koo." No. 333. by the record.

"Chay–ton–hoon–ka." No. 342. by the record.

"Chan–ka–hda." No. 359. by the record.

"Hda–hin–hday." No. 373. by the record.

"O–ya–tay–a–koo." No. 377. by the record.

"May–hoo–way–wa." No. 382. by the record.

"Wa-kin-yan-na." No. 383 by the record

The other condemned prisoners you will hold subject to further orders, taking care that they neither escape, nor are subjected to any unlawful violence. ABRAHAM LINCOLN,

President of the United States.

◈ ESSAYS

The American expansion into the West posed several problems for American Indian peoples. In the first essay, Professor Waziyatawin (Dakota), Indigenous Peoples Research Chair in Indigenous Governance at the University of Victoria, uses the oral histories passed down from grandmother to granddaughter to critically examine prevailing scholarly interpretations of the Dakota War of 1862. Wilson questions Anglo-American views used to justify Lincoln's decision to execute 39 Dakotas after the Dakota War of 1862. How did Indigenous kinship ties survive the wars of American expansion? How does Indigenous knowledge, which is passed orally between family members, challenge non-Indigenous interpretations of historical events, like the Dakota War of 1862? In the second essay, David Chang, professor of history at the University of Minnesota, explores how Indigenous peoples created families in a world on the move. During the Gold Rush, Kanaka Maolis (Indigenous Hawaiians) came to California, where they married Concow and other Native women. Chinese men, meanwhile, sought work in Hawai'i, where they married Kanaka Maoli women. Why did men and women seek spouses from different ethnic and cultural groups? What did the offspring of these unions experience in the mobile and turbulent American West?

Grandmother to Granddaughter: Remembering the Minnesota War of 1862

BY WAZIYATAWIN (DAKOTA)

The intimate hours I spent with my grandmother listening to her stories are reflections of more than a simple educational process. The stories handed down from grandmother to granddaughter are rooted in a deep sense of kinship responsibility, a responsibility that relays a culture, an identity, and a sense of belonging essential to my life. It is through the stories of my grandmother, my grandmother's grandmother, and my grandmother's grandmother's grandmother and their lives that I learned what it means to be a Dakota woman, and the responsibility, pain, and pride associated with such a role.

"Grandmother to Granddaughter: Generations of Oral History in a Dakota Family," by Angela Cavender Wilson, is reproduced from *American Indian Quarterly* with permission from the University of Nebraska Press. Copyright 1996 by the University of Nebraska Press.

These stories in our oral tradition, then, must be appreciated by historians not simply for the illumination they bring to the broader historical picture but also as an essential component in the survival of culture.

Maza Okiye Win (Woman Who Talks To Iron) was ten years old at the time of the United States–Dakota Conflict of 1862. She saw her father, Chief Mazomani (Walking Iron), die from wounds suffered in the Battle of Wood Lake. White soldiers wounded him while he was carrying a white flag of truce, She also witnessed the fatal stabbing of her grandmother by a soldier during the force marched to Fort Snelling in the first phase of the Dakota removal to Crow Creek, South Dakota. For three years Maza Okiye Win stayed in Crow Creek before she moved to Sisseton, South Dakota. Finally, after more than twenty-five years of banishment from Minnesota, she returned with her second husband, Inyangmani Hoksida (Running Walker Boy) to the ancient Dakota homeland of Mni-Sota Makoce, or Land Where The Waters Reflect The Heavens. By this time both she and her husband had become Christians and were known in English as John and Isabel Roberts. There they raised their children and three of their grandchildren.

Elsie Two Bear Cavender was born in Pezihuta zizi village in 1906 to Anna Roberts and Joseph Two Bear. She was raised by her grandparents, John and Isabel Roberts. Her Dakota name was Wiko (Beautiful), given to her by one of her great aunts when she was just a girl. Grandma always seemed embarrassed by that name—as though she didn't believe she was Beautiful enough to possess it and certainly too modest to introduce herself that way. But now that she is gone, I can use what I perceive to be a fitting name without embarrassing her. To me, she was always *Kunsi*, or Grandma. She had eight children, four of whom she buried in her lifetime. She was well known for her generosity, her wonderful pies and rolls, and her stories.

Grandma grew up in a rich oral tradition. Not only was she well acquainted with many of the myths and legends of our people, she also possessed an amazing comprehension of our history, and many of her stories revolved around the events of the United States–Dakota Conflict of 1862. Her grandmother, in particular, had carried vivid, painful memories of those traumatic times. Over time, those painful memories of my great-great-grandmother became the memories of my grandmother, and then, they became my memories.

Early on, when I first began thinking about these stories in an academic context, I realized my understanding of oral tradition and oral history were incompatible with those I was finding in other texts. This incompatibility was largely because of terminology. David Henige, in his book *Oral Historiography*, differentiates between oral history and oral tradition, conveying an understanding that seems to be representative of most scholars in the field, when he says, "As normally used nowadays, 'oral history' refers to the study of the recent past by means of life histories or personal recollections, where informants speak about their own experiences … oral tradition should be widely practiced or understood in a society and it must be handed down for at least a few generations." These definitions are applicable to Native American oral history and oral tradition only in a very limited way. Native peoples' life histories, for example, often incorporate the experiences of both human and non-human beings. In addition, this definition would not allow for the incorporation of new materials because it would then be outside the "tradition."

From a Native perspective, I would suggest instead that oral history is contained within oral tradition. For the Dakota, "oral tradition" refers to the way in which information is passed on rather than the length of time something has been told. Personal experiences, pieces of information, events, incidents, etc., can become a part of the oral tradition at the moment it happens or the moment it is told, as long as the person adopting the memory is part of an oral tradition.

Who belongs to an oral tradition? Charles Eastman, a Wahpetonwan Dakota reveals in his autobiography *Indian Boyhood* the distinct way in which the oral tradition was developed:

> Very early, the Indian boy assumed the task of preserving and transmitting the legends of his ancestors and his race. Almost every evening a myth, or a true story of some deed done in the past, was narrated by one of the parents or grandparents, while the boy listened with parted lips and glistening eyes. On the following evening, he was usually required to repeat it. If he was not an apt scholar, he struggled long with his task; but as a rule, the Indian boy is a good listener and has a good memory, so that his stories are tolerably well mastered. The household became his audience, by which he was alternately criticized and applauded.

This excerpt highlights the rigorous and extensive training required of young Dakota people. The Dakota oral tradition is based on the assumption that the ability to remember is an acquired skill—one that may be acutely developed or neglected. Eastman also describes the differentiation between myths and true stories, necessitating an understanding of history as being encompassed in oral tradition. However, few scholars working in oral history make any distinction between oral information collected from those belonging to a written culture and those belonging to an oral tradition. This is an area that is yet to be explored.

My grandmother, Elsie Cavender, received this type of training. She had much to tell about some of our more popular characters, stories starring our mythical trickster figure, Unktomi, as well as stories about Dakota men and women—mostly belonging to my lineage—who lived and died long before I was born.

In my own family, the importance of specific stories as interpreted by my grandmother was expressed by the frequency with which those were told. As a girl I was acquainted with an assortment of stories from these categories, and I remember having to request specifically those which were not in the historical realm. But I didn't have to request the stories we classify as "history." Those she offered freely and frequently. Especially in the last years of her life, on every visit she would tell stories about the Conflict of 1862, as if to reassure herself that she had fulfilled her obligations and that these stories would not be forgotten.

One of these stories has become particularly important to me since my grandmother's death because it deals with grandmothers and granddaughters, of which I am the seventh generation. Aspects of this story have helped shape my perception of what my responsibility is, as a mother and eventual grandmother, and as a Dakota. This particular story is an excerpt taken from an oral history project I began with my grandmother in 1990. This is an edited version with much of the repetition cut for the sake of clarity and conciseness in this presentation. However, under usual storytelling circumstances, the repetition is part of the storytelling procedure, often added for emphasis. Grandmother titled this portion of the United States–Dakota Conflict "Death March," consciously drawing on the similarities between the removal of Dakota from the Lower Sioux Agency, first to Fort Snelling and then on to Crow Creek, South Dakota, with the Bataan Death March in World War II. After one of our Dakota relatives who had participated in that march related to her his experiences she saw many parallels with 1862 and thought "Death March" a fitting title. This passage is in my grandmother's voice:

> Right after the 1862 Conflict, most of the Sioux people were driven out of Minnesota. A lot of our people left to other states. This must have been heartbreaking for them, as this valley had always been their home.
>
> My grandmother, Isabel Roberts (Maza Okiye Win is her Indian name), and her family were taken as captives down to Fort Snelling. On the way most of them [the people] walked, but some of the older ones and the children rode on a cart. In Indian the cart was called *canpahmihma-kawitkotkoka.* That means crazy cart in Indian. The reason they called the cart that is because it had one big wheel that didn't have any spokes. It was just one big round board. When they went they didn't grease it just right so it squeaked. You could just hear that noise about a mile away. The poor men, women, old people, and children who had to listen to it got sick from it. They would get headaches real bad. It carried the old people and the children so they wouldn't have to walk.
>
> They passed through a lot of towns and they went through some where the people were real hostile to them. They would throw rocks, cans, sticks, and everything they could think of: potatoes, even rotten tomatoes and eggs. New Ulm was one of the worst towns they had to go through.
>
> When they came through there they threw cans, potatoes, and sticks. They went on through the town anyway. The old people were in the cart. They were coming to the end of the town and they thought they were out of trouble. Then there was a big building at the end of the street. The windows were open. Someone threw hot, scalding water on them. The children were all burned and the old people too. As soon as they started to rub their arms the skin just peeled off. Their faces were like that, too. The children were all crying, even the old ladies started to cry, too. It was so hard it really hurt them but they went on.
>
> They would camp someplace at night. They would feed them, giving them meat, potatoes, or bread. But they brought the bread in on big lumber wagons with no wrapping on them. They had to eat food like that. So, they would just brush off the dust and eat it that way. The meat was the same way. They had to wash it and eat it. A lot of them

got sick. They would get dysentery and diarrhea and some had cases of whooping cough and small pox. This went on for several days. A lot of them were complaining that they drank the water and got sick. It was just like a nightmare going on this trip.

It was on this trip that my maternal grandmother's grandmother was killed by white soldiers. My grandmother, Maza Okiye Win, was ten years old at the time and she remembers everything that happened on this journey. The killing took place when they came to a bridge that had no guard rails. The horses or stock were getting restless and were very thirsty. So, when they saw water they wanted to get down to the water right away, and they couldn't hold them still. So, the women and children all got out, including my grandmother, her mother, and her grandmother.

When all this commotion started the soldiers came running to the scene and demanded to know what was wrong. But most of them [the Dakota] couldn't speak English and so couldn't talk. This irritated them and right away they wanted to get rough and tried to push my grandmother's mother and her grandmother off the bridge, but they only succeeded in pushing the older one off and she fell in the water. Her daughter ran down and got her out and she was all wet, so she took her shawl off and put it around her. After this they both got back up on the bridge with the help of the others who were waiting there, including the small daughter, Maza Okiye Win.

She was going to put her mother in the wagon, but it was gone. They stood there not knowing what to do. She wanted to put her mother someplace where she could be warm, but before they could get away, the soldier came again and stabbed her mother with a saber. She screamed and hollered in pain, so she [her daughter] stooped down to help her. But, her mother said, "Please daughter, go. Don't mind me. Take your daughter and go before they do the same thing to you. I'm done for anyway. If they kill you the children will have no one." Though she was in pain and dying she was still concerned about her daughter and little granddaughter who was standing there and witnessed all this. The daughter left her mother there at the mercy of the soldiers, as she knew she had a responsibility as a mother to take care of her small daughter.

"Up to today we don't even know where my grandmother's body is. If only they had given the body back to us we could have given her a decent funeral," Grandma said. They didn't though. So, at night, Grandma's mother had gone back to the bridge where her mother had fallen. She went there but there was no body. There was blood all over the bridge but the body was gone. She went down to the bank. She walked up and down the bank. She even waded across to see if she could see anything on the other side, but no body, nothing. So she came back up. She went on from there not knowing what happened to her or what they did with the body. So she really felt bad about it. When we were small Grandma used to talk about it. She used to cry. We used to cry with her.

Things happened like this but they always say the Indians are ruthless killers and that they massacred white people. The white people are just as bad, even worse. You never hear about the things that happened to our people because it was never written in the history books. They say it is always the Indians who are at fault.

An excerpt such as this challenges the emphasis of the *status quo*. This account does not contradict the many written texts on the subject, but contributes details not seen elsewhere, details that shift the focus from the "Indian atrocities," which are provided in rich detail in histories written by non-Indians, to "white atrocities" and Indian courage. It exemplifies the nature of the oral tradition in Dakota culture, as it is the story of one family, one lineage, reflecting the ancient village structure and the community that united those with a collective identity and memory. This account by itself will not change the course of American history, or create a theory for or framework from which the rest of the Plains wars may be interpreted. It is not even representative of the "Dakota perspective." Instead, it is one family's perspective that in combination with other families' stories might help to create an understanding of Dakota views on this event and time period. Certainly these stories shed light on the behavior and actions of members of my family that have led up to the present moment.

As I listened to my grandmother telling the last words spoken by her great-great-great-grandmother, and my grandmother's interpretation, "Though she was in pain and dying, she was still concerned about her daughter and little granddaughter who was standing there and witnessed all this," I understood that our most important role as women is making sure our young ones are taken care of so that our future as Dakota people is assured. I learned that sometimes that means self-sacrifice and putting the interests of others above your own. It also was clear through this story and others that although these were and continue to be hard memories to deal with, always there is pride and dignity in the actions of our women.

In addition, my connection to land and place is solidified with each telling of the story. As a Dakota I understand that not only is Mni-sota a homeland worth defending, but through the stories I learn where the blood of my ancestors was spilt for the sake of the future generations, for me, my children, and grandchildren.

Because these stories are typically not told in the history texts, we also must recognize we are responsible for their repetition. The written archival records will not produce this information. These stories are not told by people who have been "conquered," but by people who have a great desire to survive as a nation, as Dakota people. Consequently, these are not merely interesting stories or even the simple dissemination of historical facts. They are, more important, transmissions of culture upon which our survival as a people depends. When our stories die, so will we.

In my last real visit with my grandmother, several months before she was hospitalized in her final days, she recited this story again. I was moving to New York to begin my graduate education, and it was as if she were reminding me where I come from. In the same way, these stories served to validate my identity in a positive way when, as a girl, I was confronted with contrasting negative images of the "Sioux" in school texts. These stories have stabilized me through graduate school and reminded me why I am involved in this sometimes painful process. One of the last video clips we have of my grandmother is of her telling one of our Unktomi stories to my daughter in Dakota. When I watch that scene it becomes apparent to me that the learning of these stories is a lifelong process and, likewise, the rewards of that process last a lifetime.

The contributions of stories such as this should be recognized as celebrations of culture, as declarations of the amazing resiliency and tenacity of a people who have survived horrible circumstances and destructive forces. Some of the greatest stories are those told by Native people and serve as challenges to the rest of the world to be so strong. Native people have an unbreakable belief in the beauty and the significance of our cultures, and this is reflected in our stories. They are testimony to the richness, variety, detail, and complexity of the interpretations of history. Our role as historians should be to examine as many perspectives of the past as possible—not to become the validators or verifiers of stories, but instead to put forth as many perspectives as possible. But, the greatest lessons of these stories are to the young people, the children, and grandchildren of the elders and storytellers, who will gain an understanding of where they came from, who they are, and what is expected of them as a Diné, as an Apache, as a Laguna, as a Choctaw, and as a Dakota.

Indigenous Families in the Borderlands: Concows and Native Hawaiians in Gold Rush California

BY DAVID A. CHANG

The 1860s, 1870s, and 1880s were marked by two movements that were causally related yet contradictory: huge waves of global migration in tension with nation-states' increased efforts to consolidate authority over their borders. Three villages and hamlets—one at Irish Creek in El Dorado County, California; one at Waiākea in Hilo, Hawai'i; and one at Wushi in Xiangshan, China—exemplify this tension and illustrate its meanings. Tracing the connections that linked these three places demonstrates the utility of using borderlands to understand the complex relationship between global migration and restrictive border making in the nineteenth century. Each of these places might be considered a borderland, and examining them as such can demonstrate how borderlands scholarship turns our attention to important yet easily neglected meeting places in history and opens our eyes to the complexities and ambiguities of social relations in those places....

[B]orderlands history risks obscuring the histories of indigenous peoples whose lands had been colonized or were at risk of colonization, such as nineteenth-century American Indians and Kānaka Maoli (one of the principal

David Chang, "Borderlands in a World at Sea: Conkow Indians, Native Hawaiians, and South Chinese in Indigenous, Global, and National Spaces," *Journal of American History* (September 2011): 384–403. By permission of Oxford University Press on behalf of the *Journal of American History*.

Hawaiian-language terms for indigenous Hawaiian people). Such people lived within or at the margins of nation-states but often not at places that Americans recognize as borders. Recognizing people as indigenous in a borderlands context becomes more complex and more urgent given the fact that they often moved beyond the borders of their original homelands under compulsion (as in the case of the Concow) or were citizens of nations that, while struggling against colonialism, were still recognized as territorial sovereigns (as in the case of Hawai'i).

Reconceptualizing borderlands research to center American Indians and Kānaka Maoli points to the need to look at the process by which today's borders were imposed over indigenous people by settler-colony nation-states—nations such as the United States where settlers claimed colonized lands, not as outposts of a distant empire but rather as their homeland and that of their descendants....

[I]f we aim to understand fully the historical processes of creating settler colonial nations and making boundaries around them, we must extend the process of tracing connections to look not only at migrants but also at indigenous people. They, too, must be understood in the context of the networks that border making severed, the intimacies that colonialism engendered, and in the context of the homelands that settler colonial border making appropriated.

... [S]tart in what many might call a borderland space and ... follow the paths out of town to see where they lead. This essay works toward that end, beginning in a place that some historians might not accept as part of the borderlands: El Dorado County, California, just west of Lake Tahoe. El Dorado County is five hundred miles from the Mexican border, but in 1860 the connection was closer, as it had only been twelve years since Mexico had ceded Alta California to the United States. Yet, ... this was hardly a place where only white Americans, American Indians, and Mexicans competed for space.... [T]he gold rush was "among the most multiracial, multiethnic, multinational events that had yet occurred within the boundaries of the United States." News of the discovery of gold brought many men and a few women from the eastern United States, Mexico, Chile, Argentina, China, Australia, the German states, Britain, Hawai'i, and a dozen other places around the globe. These gold-seekers and other newcomers entered an already nationally and racially diverse space occupied by American Indian people, Mexicans of various racial backgrounds, and white settlers.

The 1860 manuscript census ... reveal that clustered near Irish Creek in El Dorado County was a settlement of some of the poorest and least powerful residents in the region: a group of twenty-three men and one woman born in the Sandwich Islands—as the Hawaiian archipelago was known in the United States at the time. The census reveals nothing about these Kānaka Maoli—other than their birthplace, ages, and occupation (as miners). It provides not even a means to trace their identities because they are listed under such Anglo-American names as Charles and Mary Aaron, Frank Harrison, and Thomas Boyd, at a time when few Kānaka Maoli had such names. Only by searching the Hawaiian-language newspapers published in Honolulu can we discover their names and begin to understand their situation. The *Nupepa Kuokoa* of 1862 reported that these Kānaka Maoli (and one man, H. J. Ua, from Mangaia in the Cook Islands) had, just a few miles from Coloma, California, built very humble homes and planted vegetable gardens in which they cultivated Western crops. In the U.S. Census, this settlement appears to be an isolated enclave, populated mostly by bachelors. Hawaiian-language newspapers, however, suggest that the Kanaka Maoli of El Dorado County were tied to a network of Kānaka Maoli settlements in California and to local American Indian people.

These connections can best be illustrated with the story of a young woman whose names were transcribed in the Hawaiian-language newspapers as Lakaakaa and as Hitokane. She was a Concow ... born around 1844; her homeland, the Concow Valley, was in Butte County, California, one hundred miles north of El Dorado and twenty-five miles north of a place that white Americans called Oroville ("gold city"). To Concow people such as Lakaakaa, the area was not gold country; it was home. They had not come from afar to seek fortune, but instead had found themselves inundated by foreigners in search of a precious metal. Some native people joined the search for gold, but in the 1860s many Concow still followed a seasonal round of activities—fishing, hunting, foraging for plant foods, and especially gathering and processing acorns—or they did so to the extent possible. The gold seekers' digging and settlement disrupted the fish, plants, oaks, and game on which native Californians depended, and whites' violence threatened Indian people directly. It was dangerous for native people to move about their homelands. It is no wonder that the white American trader Alonzo Delano reported that in the early 1850s, whenever groups of women and girls left a Concow village to gather food, they brought "one or two men, to act as a kind of body-guard." Whites killed, raped, and enslaved California Indians with impunity, causing California's native population to fall by about 80 percent between 1848 and 1860. In 1854 the federal government forced many of the Concow to relocate to Nome Cult Farm, which eventually became the Round Valley Reservation, where many Concow still live. In 1862 Concow people fled the reservation for their homeland near the town of Chico. The next year, the Civil War veteran Capt. Augustus Starr was ordered to bring them back to Round Valley. He left Chico with 461, but he arrived with only 277. The brutality of that forced march is still commemorated today.

By 1854, Lakaakaa's family was so impoverished that she began to frequent the settlement of some Kanaka Maoli gold miners to obtain food. The site of the camp is probably near Oroville, at a place remembered today as Kanaka Bar, near the mouth of Kanaka Creek, in the shadow of Kanaka Peak—place names attesting to the important presence of Kanaka Maoli miners in the region. She could communicate with the Kānaka Maoli because they spoke the Concow language well, which suggests that relations between the two groups were ongoing. When Lakaakaa was ten, the Kānaka Maoli extended their practice of *hānai* adoption to her, making her kin and giving her a new Hawaiian name, Waiulili. Perhaps they were motivated by sympathy for a starving child, perhaps by a wish for female domestic labor, or perhaps by some mixture of the two.

In any case, by 1857, when she was about thirteen, she was married to a Kanaka Maoli named G. H. Kamakea. Marriages at that age were not unknown in either Concow or Kanaka Maoli practice, and given the impoverishment of the Concow and the scarcity of prospective brides for the Kānaka Maoli, the pairing would have created advantages for both sides. The couple had two sons, Samuela and Kamakea Jr. When her husband died in 1859, Waiulili married again, this time to another Kanaka Maoli named A. E. Mahuka. With Mahuka, Waiulili had a daughter, Rebeka. They left the Concow homeland, moving sixty miles southeast, to another Kanaka Maoli settlement not far from Placerville, on Irish Creek, a stream named for yet another people active in the gold rush.

In their move, the couple and their children crossed an important boundary dividing the Concow territory from that of the Nisenan—although the whites among whom Waiulili moved may not have understood this. Indeed, the refusal of non-Indians to recognize bounded native territories has been a hallmark of American colonialism, one that still runs through many historical accounts of the Indian past. The Concow, like their neighbors the Nisenan, the Maidu, the Yana, and the Nomlacki, occupied recognized homelands that were linked by trade relations. The Concow historically traded with the Maidu and the Wintuan peoples, exchanging arrows, bows, and deer hides for others' pine nuts, salmon, and abalone shell. Yet the Concow and their neighbors were also separated by boundaries that demarcated the territories of societies where authority was widely distributed. We might fail to see those demarcations if we proceed from Western assumptions that boundaries are artifacts of centralized political power. They were, however, real because Indian people recognized them. Like other boundaries, these were subject to transgression or dispute, which only serves to underscore their importance. The Concow homeland was further divided by the boundaries of groups of villages, ... each of which had its own recognized territory over which it had exclusive hunting and fishing rights. Indeed, each week a pair of Concow men were appointed to patrol for poachers on the village-community's land. Neither the boundaries that divided village-communities and peoples nor the networks that linked them appear on the gold rush–era state and county maps. The colonial processes of making state and county jurisdictions, and the incursions of outsiders, depended on ignoring such boundaries and linkages. To counter that obliteration, we can remember that Waiulili moved from the area of the Concow village of čá-mpïli to the vicinity of the Nisenan village of Koloma.

The Kanaka Maoli settlement there is the hamlet that appears indistinctly in the U.S. census of El Dorado County for 1860. By that time, Lakaakaa had entered the Kanaka Maoli community through adoption and marriage and had taken a Hawaiian name. She appears to have followed the Hawaiian practice of hānai adoption when she gave one of her children, a boy named Kamakea after his father, to fellow settlement resident J. D. Kenao. In doing so, Waiulili followed a Kanaka Maoli way of using adoption to extend kinship bonds. (It is also possible that Concow adoption and kinship practices were in action here.) Waiulili was fluent in Hawaiian, and her mixed-ancestry children likely were also, as that was the language of the settlement in which they lived.

Yet Waiulili and her children hardly cut themselves off from other Concow people. In 1862, for example, Waiulili's toddler daughter, Rebeka, spent time with other Concow and traveled with them in their subsistence work of acorn gathering and fishing. Meanwhile, Waiulili's mother had moved to the settlement at Irish Creek to live with Waiulili and her second husband, Mahuka.

These movements repudiated efforts in the 1860s and 1870s to use reservation borders to confine California Indians and affirmed the networks that linked them to other native Californians and the Kanaka Maoli. When Waiulili, her mother, and her children moved about California, one of the things they were doing was choosing *not* to move to the Round Valley Reservation. The agents of the Office of Indian Affairs there tried to make the reservation border a hard-and-fast line separating Indians on the inside from whites and Indians on the outside. It was a line that was distinct from but in important ways anticipated

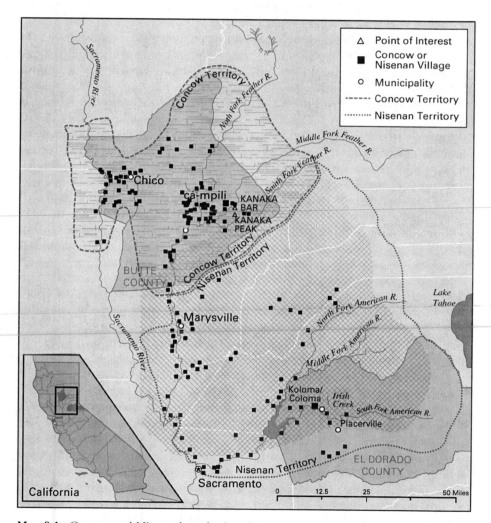

Map 9.1 Concow and Nisenan homelands and Butte and El Dorado Counties, California, ca. 1860. *Map by Matt B. Lindholm, Cartography Laboratory, Department of Geography, University of Minnesota, Minneapolis. Data from Robert F. Heizer, ed.,* Handbook of North American Indians, *vol. VIII: California (Washington, 1978), 371, 388.*

the kind of border control the United States would erect on its external boundaries in the coming decades. The correspondence and reports of the agents reveal that in their minds this internal-external border served multiple purposes, very much in keeping with Philip J. Deloria's characterization of the reservation as simultaneously "a relocation camp," "a concentration camp," and "a reeducation camp." It would ideally appease white settlers who wanted off-reservation Indians such as Waiulili confined to reservations, but it also protected Indians from what agents considered to be the destructive actions and influences of whites—most prominently alcohol, prostitution, and abduction. In accordance with the policy of the Commissioner of Indian Affairs, the Round Valley Reservation agent and Methodist minister J. L. Burchard tried to enforce a strict border control policy: whites could enter the reservation only with his permission and Indians could leave only with a pass. He deemed Indians who left by other means to be "escaping," and he had them pursued. To Burchard, a strong border was a civilizing tool backed by other means of discipline, including the lash. He unapologetically declared in 1875 that he and every previous agent at the reservation whipped Indians because there was no adequate facility in which to jail them. Yet as Burchard's comment reveals, Round Valley Reservation agents were unable to restrict Indians fully, spatially or otherwise.... Round Valley Reservation Indians [as we shall see in the next chapter of this book], regularly moved beyond reservation boundaries for wage or subsistence work and in the process maintained and even expanded spatially widespread social networks of native people from a number of California tribes. Waiulili's story illustrates this network from the perspective of off-reservation Indians. Though sometimes living in predominantly non–Indian communities, they used movement across boundaries to maintain their web of relations with other native people, and they brought new people, such as Kānaka Maoli, into that network by making them kin.

Yet Waiulili was also immersed in her local context in El Dorado County, and in late 1861 she became a dedicated believer during a Christian revival there. The Kanaka Maoli had been exposed to Protestant missionaries from New England as early as 1820, and many had converted to the new faith in varying degrees. Perhaps they encouraged Waiulili in her new faith, or perhaps her conversion spurred their devotion. In either case, we have a Concow woman in Nisenan country brought into the fervor of Christian revival along with a Kanaka Maoli settler community in California that had earlier been converted by New England missionaries in Hawai'i. By any measure, this story exemplifies the kind of complexities and ambiguities that make borderlands such fertile sites of research.

In April and May 1862 a smallpox epidemic devastated the settlement, killing four people [including] Waiulili and her birth child Kamakea. At the time of the epidemic, Theodore Gulick, a white missionary from Hawai'i, was visiting the settlement. He reported in a missionary-sponsored Hawaiian-language newspaper in Honolulu that "we laid the earthly physical home of Waiulili beneath the earth, with worship to the Lord, and hope for her resurrection." Waiulili's mother, Lemaine, wanting a more visible and palpable source of comfort, declared: "If Rebeka is not brought so that I might see her,

her grandmother will die." In that time of crisis, the Concow grandmother summoned her Concow granddaughter, a half—Kanaka Maoli girl with a name that marked her as the child of Christians. Yet Rebeka was one hundred miles to the north, in the Concow homeland, staying with other Indian people who were engaged in the summer salmon harvest. So Mahuka led Lemaine, a party of other Hawaiians, and the missionary to Butte County to fetch his daughter.

The tragedy was not over for Lemaine, however. A struggle over the custody of the now-motherless Rebeka ensued, revealing how American colonial and gender power hierarchies infused the marriages and other linkages that the Kanaka Maoli settlers and the Concow had established among themselves. In most California native societies, and thus probably among the Concow, when the mother of a young child died, the maternal grandmother raised the child. In this case, however, Mahuka wanted Rebeka. Lemaine objected "with the very strong demand that Rebeka be left with her." Rebuffed, "Lemaine took Rebeka, with the plan of going far and maybe hiding her in the brush." The missionary reporter interpreted this as an attempted abduction, chased down Lemaine, and turned Rebeka over to her father. The contest over Rebeka was surely deeply personal. Just as certainly, the struggle for a child, which pitted the Concow against the Kānaka Maoli—two peoples beset by the demographic collapses that followed contact with Western powers and settlers—was also a struggle for a future. Here, the intervention of a white American missionary favored Western patrilineal patterns and the Kānaka Maoli, with whom he had long-term ties.

In some ways, the life and death of Waiulili seems like a classic borderlands story, one in which people and histories converge and make new realities. Yet in this story two important liabilities of the term "borderland" emerge, apparent in the two elements that make up the compound word. The first is border. The United States—Mexico border was not the defining reality in the region: the Kānaka Maoli were far from the watery borders of their homeland, and this story begins with Waiulili at Kanaka Bar, well within the Concow homeland. The term "borderland" focuses attention on two nation-states, even when many other nations are involved. Moreover, only some of these nations could boast their own state apparatus of border control; nations such as the Concow could not. Thus the word "border" privileges two state actors that are admittedly important but hardly the most crucial reference points, while it obscures the fact that border regions are also frequently the homeland of an indigenous people and the place of settlement of many other peoples, including indigenous people from elsewhere.

This brings us to the second element of the term "borderland": land. It was not the land that carried the Kānaka Maoli, the French, the Germans, the Chileans, the Chinese, or even many of the Americans and Mexicans most of the way to their place of encounter with the Concow. It was water. Ships brought them across the ocean, riverboats carried them up the Sacramento and Feather Rivers, and streams led them to the shallows where they panned for gold. This long, watery pathway to the Sierra Nevada Mountains alerts us to the need to think on a broader spatial scale. Indeed, we must think on as broad a scale as the migrants did before they boarded ships to go to California. Granted, this was still the western edge of the United States, and in the 1860s white

Americans were arriving in significant numbers via land, but to emphasize that fact is to naturalize the presence of people of European descent in eastern North America. To understand the nineteenth-century United States for what it was—a settler colony nation-state—it is essential to place the land in the context of the oceans and to place the white Americans in El Dorado County in the context of European maritime and trade expansion worldwide during the previous three centuries. Rather than emphasizing the presence of the two bordering nations, the term "borderland" should ideally lead to an effort to place them in a broader perspective that demonstrates how nations and their territorial claims are themselves historical creations.

We must remember that the story we have traced thus far took place on American Indian land—the Concow territory where Waiulili was born, and the Nisenan territory where she later moved with Mahuka—but we must also follow the paths that led outsiders to that area and see where they lead us. Choosing the example of Waiulili's first husband, Kamakea, the path will lead us out of the gold-country hills to the Sacramento River southwestward along the river to San Francisco and then across the Pacific Ocean via steamship to Honolulu on the island of Oʻahu. Tracing Kamakea back home requires another short ocean trip, this time to the harbor of Hilo, on the island of Hawaiʻi, and then on a short walk to Waiākea. This is the place Kamakea would have called his "one hanau," the sands of his birth.

Waiākea was an ancient ahapuaʻa (an administrative and economic division under the Hawaiian political system) that neighbored Hilo. By 1872, Hilo had become the leading town on the island, boasting 4,400 inhabitants. In 1848 the privatization of land, a process known as the Mahele, displaced most Kānaka Maoli from their homes, and many moved to towns such as Hilo for employment. Some towns were also the centers of missionary activity. In 1824 the American missionaries Joseph Goodrich (from Wethersford, Connecticut) and Samuel Ruggles (from Brookfield, Connecticut) established the Waiākea Mission Station. This was the base from which missionaries converted Kānaka Maoli, probably including Kamakea.

The population of Hilo was predominantly Kanaka Maoli: an 1872 census report lists about 4,000 of the approximately 4,400 inhabitants as "Hawaiian" or "part Hawaiian." This included landless commoners and also the families of landed aliʻi (chiefs) who had moved to town. Two small but prominent foreign elements lived in the town: about eighty white missionaries and merchants (mostly Americans, but some Europeans), and a larger group of about 300 Chinese. Chinese settlers first began coming to the archipelago in very small numbers in the 1780s, but the first Chinese that left any lasting mark in Hilo arrived in the 1830s. By 1840 two or three Chinese settlers were running a sugar-growing and processing operation just outside of Hilo. The owner of the operation was Kuakini, an aliʻi nui (high chief) and the royal governor of Hawaiʻi. In 1845 another sugar plantation was begun by Lau Fai, more generally known as Hapai—a Hawaiianized version of his Cantonese given name. He also operated a store in Hilo. A native of Guangdong Province and a Christian convert, Hapai was married to an aliʻi named Iehu.

She was a granddaughter of Kamanawa, one of the highest-ranking chiefs of the early nineteenth century and a man who had assisted Kamehameha I in his rise to kingship over all of the Hawaiian islands in 1810. As such, historians have emphasized that Iehu gave Hapai the access he needed to land and influential people in the islands.

This fits a pattern of marriage between foreign traders and native women repeated not only by Chinese on the fringes of the Chinese empire, in Hawai'i, and elsewhere in the Pacific, but also by European and white American traders among Native Americans in North America. Historians have noted that in such marriages, foreign traders gained access to native people's resources and social networks. Hapai obtained these advantages, and he was able to marry a woman far younger than he, which may have functioned as a measure of his wealth. Yet Iehu also gained advantages by marrying Hapai, including entrée into the growing commericial economy and the ability to raise children who could participate in Chinese commercial networks yet remain part of the native Hawaiian community. Intermarried nineteenth-century Chinese merchants such as Hapai—and there were many—occupy a complex position historically. They came primarily as sojourners, but many stayed on to prosper as settlers, becoming both the leading edge of Asian settler colonialism in Hawai'i and (through their marriages to Hawaiian women) ancestors of generations of Kānaka Maoli. In 1840 Hapai and Iehu named their first son George Washington Akau Hapai, a name

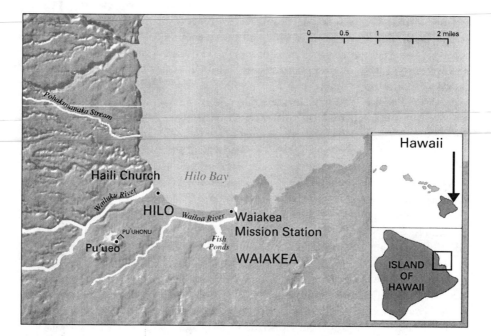

Map 9.2 Hilo, Hawai'i, and surrounding areas in the nineteenth century. *Map by Matt B. Lindholm, Cartography Laboratory, Department of Geography, University of Minnesota, Minneapolis.*

that speaks of his multiethnic background, the international orientation of his parents, and the influence of Anglo-Americans on them.

That influence included Protestant Christianity. In 1859 the elder Hapai was the largest contributor to the reconstruction that transformed the Waiākea Mission Station into what is now Haili Church. The couple almost certainly knew another family born of a marriage between a Kanaka Maoli woman and a Chinese man, Kahaulelio and C. Y. Aiona. C. Y. Aiona was a native of Xishan in Xiangshan County in the Pearl River delta. Like Iehu and Hapai, Kahaulelio and C. Y. Aiona were a locally important family. C. Y. Aiona was one of the wealthiest men in the Hilo area, having prospered as a merchant and sugar planter who built up a store on the Hilo waterfront, ten stores in nearby villages, and a plantation. Local community members called on these wealthy families in time of need. Just as they had asked Hapai to help with the building of a church, they called on Kahaulelio and C. Y. Aiona to take on the task of raising a boy named Awana in 1880.

Here, I can draw on my own genealogy to trace the story farther. Awana was my greatgrandfather, the child of yet another union of a Xiangshan man and a Kanaka Maoli woman, Chang Hu and Ellen Ahu. In 1880, after Chang Hu died of smallpox, Kahaulelio and C. Y. Aiona adopted Awana, who was about four years old. He was not the first child they had taken in; they were already the hānai parents of Chang Apana, who grew to become the Honolulu detective who inspired the fictional character Charlie Chan. Much is unclear about all of these relationships. C. Y. Aiona was somehow related to Chang Apana and may also have been related to Awana's father. They all had the same ancestral village. Seen in this light, the transfer of custody may be one example of the efforts of many Chinese Hawaiian families to keep their children—especially their firstborn sons—embedded in Chinese life and networks. On the other hand, it is also possible that the connection between the families was through Kahaulelio and Ellen Ahu, Awana's birth mother. Indeed, hānai adoption often entailed one woman transferring a child to the family of another woman to whom she was already connected. Furthermore, testimony on Awana's hānai brother Chang Apana consistently centers Kahaulelio and Hawaiian relationships: Chang Apana "grew up in the family of Kahaulelio," was "cared for and mothered by Kahaulelio, the wife of Aiona," and Kahaulelio, with no surviving children, was eager to care for Chang Apana "according to the Hawaiian custom." All of this reinforces the notion that the transfer of Awana may have expressed Hawaiian practices and purposes instead of, or perhaps in addition to, Chinese ones. In any case Awana was likely raised speaking the Hawaiian language, first by his birth mother, Ellen Ahu, and then by his hānai mother, Kahaulelio Aiona.

Waiākea, Hilo, and Hawai'i during the 1860s, 1870s, and 1880s can demonstrate how useful it is to examine borderlands as part of the history of migration, border making, and global networks.... Clearly Hawai'i was a meeting place of empires and peoples, and their coming together created hybrid new realities ranging from intermarried Chinese and Kanaka Maoli families to the creolized language that is commonly known as pidgin.

Even so, as was the case for the California gold country in this era, the idea of a borderland seems to neglect the indigenous history and the multiethnic complexity born of extensive maritime linkages that characterized Hilo in this period. Most fundamentally, Hawai'i was a sovereign nation with a population that ... vigorously asserted and defended its independence throughout the nineteenth century. Neither sovereignty nor physical distance from other land masses meant isolation, however. Linkages of political alliance, class (merchant to merchant), language, religion, and kinship reached out in every direction—toward Native America, white American Protestant churches, and China. These connections were superimposed over the deep ties that Hawai'i shared with the rest of Oceania, a region Epeli Hau'ofa describes as a "sea of islands" bound together by a unifying Pacific. These oceanic ties even endured migration to the Sierra Nevada Mountains, where H. J. Ua—whose homeland was almost three thousand miles south of Hawai'i —lived and labored among the Hawaiians of El Dorado County. Thus Hawai'i was deeply immersed in regional and global networks and faced the constant danger of colonization. It would be ludicrous to call Hawai'i a borderland, but it can reveal much about how to think about the places that are labeled borderlands and their connections to the outside world....

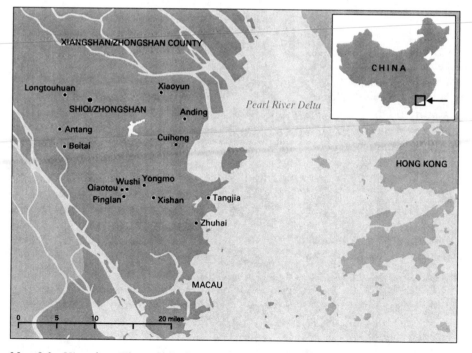

Map 9.3 Xiangshan (Zhongshan) County, Guangdong, China, in the nineteenth century. *Map by Matt B. Lindholm, Cartography Laboratory, Department of Geography, University of Minnesota, Minneapolis.*

As the examples here demonstrate, nodes in global networks sometimes come most clearly into view when we consider sources generated far from the place under consideration: Hawaiian-language newspapers reveal much about El Dorado County that English-language sources do not … family histories are a powerful tool for studying the interaction of these spaces organically.

Family history also points to the interplay of gender, race, and nation in this story. Marriages and adoptions across groups of different origins were crucial to these sites and to the networks between them. Men travelled more than women, but it was the marriages of Lakaakaa/Waiulili (a Concow woman), of Ellen Ahu (a Kanaka Maoli woman), and of Awana's wife, Chang Lum See that built the networks that spanned El Dorado, Hilo, and Xiangshan. Marriages such as these would be labeled "interracial" or as "miscegenation" today, but we must be careful to see that those labels—and the racial and national borders that those labels enforce—were not yet fully effective for the kinds of people I consider here. They certainly were not barriers to them marrying in the way they did.

The long-term meaning of such marriages and the families they created is also instructive. In California, the power of American racial categorization meant that people who traced their ancestry to both Kānaka Maoli and American Indians disappeared from the public record until indigenous activists reinserted them during the late twentieth century. In 1850, almost immediately after becoming a state, California adopted an antimiscegenation law forbidding marriage between whites and blacks. In the 1850 and 1860 federal censuses, some Kānaka Maoli escaped these categorizations; enumerators simply did not enter a race for most of them on the forms. Soon, however, American racial categories were imposed on them. During the 1852 state census, enumerators labeled as "black" almost all California residents born in Hawai'i . The same race label was placed on Kānaka Maoli in the 1880 federal census—including Edward or Eduin Mahuka, most likely Waiulili's widower. Racial categorization was part of the same consolidation of borders that led to the passage of the Chinese Exclusion Act in 1882. Up to the present day, some California Native American communities sustain memories of the families that were created by the blending of Kānaka Maoli and Indians. At least one Kānaka Maoli seems to have joined the Concow community during the early twentieth century, making a family with a woman from Round Valley Reservation. Other California Indians did not remember the connection to Kānaka Maoli; according to one man who was active in the effort to secure state and federal recognition for "the Konkow Valley Band of Maidu," that past was unknown to Concow in the early twenty-first century. While the outcome for native communities was ambiguous, for the American state it was not. It sorted individuals into discrete racial categories, making the way people crossed or disrupted those categories politically invisible.

In Hawai'i , families of mixed Chinese and Kanaka Maoli descent remain visible and known, but the racial categories imposed by American colonialism and American immigration law powerfully shaped their history. In the 1870s, 1880s, and 1890s an anti-Chinese movement gained steam in Hawai'i , fueled by West Coast American racism and whites in the Hawaiian government. Though the movement succeeded in placing limits on numbers of immigrants, it failed in its efforts to halt marriages between Chinese and Kānaka Maoli. Some Kānaka Maoli supported the anti-Chinese movement, but the demands of white planters for Chinese laborers, combined with the close links between the Chinese and the people and leadership of the independent Hawaiian kingdom, placed restraints on its legislative success. After American annexation of Hawai'i in 1898, however, American laws barring new Chinese immigrants were vigorously enforced....

Near the end of *Borderlands/La Frontera,* Anzaldúa writes:

> To live in the Borderlands means you
> are neither *hispana, india, negra, española*
> *ni gabacha....*

Instead, she writes, living in the borderlands means one is mixed: *"mestiza, mulata,* half-breed." Of course, this is not true. Some people in the U.S.-Mexican borderlands do not occupy mestizo/a racial positions. Some (both mixed-ancestry and not) are *indio/a* (Indian) On the next page, Anzaldúa strikes a truer note: "To survive the Borderlands, you must live *sin fronteras,* be a crossroads."

Historians would do well to heed her exhortation. Borderlands history, by simultaneously refusing to be limited by borders and refusing to ignore their power, offers a unique opportunity. Tracing the making and unmaking of the kinds of networks that linked global nodes in such places as Irish Creek, Waiākea, and Xiangshan lays bare the forces—as global as the trade in gold, sugar, and labor and as intimate as marriages and adoptions— that shaped these spaces into nodes in a globalizing world that was segmented by border lines. We might not see the interplay of these global and intimate forces if we look at these places as the separate borderlands of just the United States and Mexico (El Dorado County) or the United States and Oceania (Hilo), or as merely a place that people left behind to make their living elsewhere (Xiangshan). All of this demonstrates the power of making global history local and making local history global, of placing indigenous people at the center of our study of the modern world, and of remaining attentive to the interplay of global networks and national boundaries. As we do these things, borderlands seem ever more expansive, the paths between them come more sharply into focus, and the need for us to follow those paths becomes clearer.

◈ FURTHER READING

Anderson, Gary Clayton. *The Conquest of Texas: Ethnic Cleansing in the Promised Land, 1820–1875* (2005).

Begait, Robert, and Clarence Woodcock, eds. *In the Name of the Salish and Kootenai Nation: The 1855 Hell Gate Treaty and the Origin of the Flathead Indian Reservation* (1996).

Blackhawk, Ned. *Violence Over the Land: Indians and Empires in the Early American West* (2006).

DeLay, Brian. *War of a Thousand Deserts: Indian Raids and the U.S.-Mexican War* (2008).

Hauptman, Laurence M. *Between Two Fires: American Indians in the Civil War* (1995).

———. *The Iroquois in the Civil War: From Battlefield to Reservation* (1993).

Hurtado, Albert. *Indian Survival on the California Frontier* (1988).

Knack, Martha. *Boundaries Between: The Southern Paiutes, 1775–1995* (2001).

LaVere, David. *Contrary Neighbors: Southern Plains and Removed Indians in Indian Territory* (2000).

Lindsay, Brendan C. *Murder State: California's Native American Genocide, 1846–1873* (2012).

Madley, Benjamin. "California's Yuki Indians: Defining Genocide in Native American History." *Western Historical Quarterly* 39 (2008): 303–32.

Magliari, Michael. "Free Soil, Unfree Labor: Cave Johnson Couts and the Binding of Indian Workers in California, 1850–1867," *Pacific Historical Review* 73 (August 2004): 349–89.

———. "Free State Slavery: Bound Indian Labor and Slave Trafficking in California's Sacramento Valley, 1850–1864," *Pacific Historical Review* 81 (May 2012): 155–192.

Miles, Tiya. *Ties That Bind: The Story of an Afro-Cherokee Family in Slavery and Freedom* (2006).

Miller, Susan. *Coacoochee's Bones: A Seminole Saga* (2003).

Phillips, George Harwood. *"Bringing Them Under Subjection": California's Tejón Indian Reservation and Beyond, 1852–1864* (2004).

Rensink, Brenden. "The Sand Creek Phenomenon: The Complexity and Difficulty of Undertaking a Comparative Study of Genocide *vis-à-vis* the Northern American West," *Genocide Studies and Prevention: an International Journal* 4:1 (Spring 2009): 9–27.

Saunt, Claudio. *Black, White, and Indian: Race and the Unmaking of an American Family* (2006).

Silva, Noenoe. *Aloha Betrayed: Native Hawaiian Resistance to American Colonialism* (2004).

Trennert, Robert. *Alternative to Extinction: The Federal Indian Policy and the Beginnings of the Reservation System, 1846–1851* (1975).

West, Elliott. *The Contested Plains: Indians, Goldseekers and the Rush to Colorado* (1998).

Whaley, Gray. *Oregon and the Collapse of Illahee: U.S. Empire and the Transformation of an Indigenous World, 1792–1859* (2010).

Wilkinson, Charles. *The People Are Dancing Again: The History of the Siltez Tribe of Western Oregon* (2010).

Yarbrough, Fay *Race and the Cherokee Nation: Sovereignty in the Nineteenth Century* (2007).

CHAPTER 10

Resistance, Restrictions, and Renewals On and Off Reservations, 1865–1890

In the 1850s, American Indians encountered pressure from the United States to move to reservations. The United States conceived of reservations as concentrated parcels of land isolated from American settlement and migration. After the Civil War's conclusion, an influx of people into the American West and economic changes attending industrialization accelerated the effort to separate Native peoples from American settlers. The Homestead Act of 1862 beckoned thousands of Americans to the Great Plains and attracted immigrants to the United States. The completion of the first transcontinental railroad in 1868 placed even more pressure on Native lands. Many American Indian nations, such as the Lakota and Chiricahua Apache, used co-ordinated military strikes to resist American expansion and confinement to reservations. However, not all Indians responded militarily. Some Native leaders, such as Barboncito (Diné), opted to move to reservations and effectively negotiated for a reservation in a location of their choice. Native peoples in California, Nevada, and Oregon adjusted to the economic, social, and political changes that attended reservation life by turning to wage work and farming. Other Native peoples revital-ized religious beliefs in an attempt to blunt the effects of American expansion. If the United States envisioned reservations as places to isolate American Indians, American Indians con-ceived of reservations as spaces in which to assert sovereignty.

Whether they chose military resistance or accommodation, Native peoples certainly faced constraints on their way of life in the late nineteenth century. As early as 1871, Congress declared that the United States would not sign more treaties with Native peoples; it would still negotiate agreements, but the change in nomenclature—from treaties to agreements—signified that times had changed. With Geronimo's final surrender in 1886 at Skeleton Canyon, Arizona, just north of the boundary between Arizona and the state of Sonora in Mexico, and the Wounded Knee Massacre on the Pine Ridge Reservation in 1890, an era truly had come to an end. Could the federal government have made other choices or achieved other results? Why might some Native communities have fought while others chose different tactics?

◈ DOCUMENTS

These documents present Native perspectives on the reservation era. Document 1 shows how the Diné (also Navajo) leader Barboncito successfully negotiated with United States officials for the Diné to leave the prison camp at Bosque Redondo, New Mexico, and return to their homeland in northeastern Arizona. According to Barboncito, what were the consequences for the Diné and the land if they returned to their homeland? Document 2 reveals how American settlers in Nevada violated the Pyramid Lake Reservation's boundaries and attempted to convince Paiutes to leave. How did Native leaders attempt to prevent outsiders from illegally using their land, and how successful were their efforts? While Barboncito and the Paiute leaders negotiated with federal officials, Lakota leaders on the Great Plains chose to militarily resist American expansion. Document 3 explores how government officials understood the conflict with the Lakota. What were the sources of discord between the Lakota nation and the United States? In Document 4, Mountain Wolf Woman (Ho-Chunk) describes the work and labor strategies her family used in the late nineteenth century. How did Ho-Chunk (also Winnebago) women organize their labor? Did these strategies differ from those employed by Round Valley Indians (see Bauer essay below)? In Document 5, three Apaches— Ace Daklugie, Charlie Smith, and Jasper Kanseah—present oral historical testimony about their remarkable counterpart, Geronimo. Why did Geronimo avoid living on a reservation? What did other Apaches think about Geronimo and his choices? Finally, in Document 6, Lakotas describe the 1890 Wounded Knee massacre. How did Lakotas respond to late nineteenth-century reservation conditions? How did the United States military conduct itself at Wounded Knee?

1. Barboncito (Diné) Demands that the Diné Leave Bosque Redondo, 1868

Barboncito said: Our grandfathers had no idea of living in any other country except our own, and I do not think it right for us to do so, as we were never taught to. When the Navajoes were first created, four mountains and four rivers were pointed out to us, inside of which we should live; that was to be our country, and was given to us by the first woman of the Navajo tribe. It was told to us by our forefathers that we were never to move east of the Rio Grande, or west of the San Juan rivers, and I think that our coming here has been the cause of so much death among us and our animals; that our god, when he was created, (the woman I spoke of,) gave us this piece of land, and created it especially for us, and gave us the whitest of corn and the best of horses and sheep. You can see them (pointing to the other chiefs;) ordinarily looking as they are. I think that when the last of them is gone the world will come to an end.... I thought at one time the whole world was the same as my own country, but I got fooled in it; outside

---

Message from the President of the United States Transmitting A Treaty Between the United States and Chiefs and Headmen of the Navajo Indians, concluded June 1, 1868, Executive Documents, 40th Congress, 2nd Session.

my own country we cannot raise a crop, but in it we can raise a crop almost anywhere; our families and stock there increase, here they decrease. We know this land does not like us, neither does the water. They have all said this ground was not intended for us; for that reason none of us have attempted to put in seed this year. I think now it is true what my forefathers told me about crossing the line of my own country. It seems that whatever we do here causes death ... A rattlesnake bite here kills us; in our own country a rattlesnake, before he bites, gives warning, which enables us to keep out of its way, and if bitten, we readily find a cure; here we can find no cure. When one of our big men die, the cries of the women cause the tears to roll down on to my moustache. I then think of my own country.... We have all declared that we do not want to remain here any longer. If I can complete my thoughts to–day, I will give ... [General William T. Sherman] my best thanks and think of him as my father and mother. As soon as I heard of your coming, I made three pair of moccasins and have worn out two pair of them since. As you see yourselves I am strong and hearty, and before I am sick or older I want to go and see the place where I was born. Now I am just like a woman, sorry like a woman in trouble; I want to go and see my own country. If we are taken back to our own country, we will call you our father and mother; if you should only tie a goat there, we would all live off it, all of the same opinion. I am speaking for the whole tribe, for their animals from the horse to the dog, also the unborn; all that you have heard now is the truth and is the opinion of the whole tribe. It appears to me that the General commands the whole thing as a god; I hope therefore he will do all he can for the Indian; this hope goes in at my feet and out at my mouth; I am speaking to you (General Sherman) now as if I was speaking to a spirit, and I wish you to tell me when you are going to take us to our own country....

That is the way I like to be, and return the commissioners my best thanks. After we get back to our country it will brighten up again, and the Navajoes will be as happy as the land, black clouds will rise and there will be plenty of rain. Corn will grow in abundance and everything look happy. To-day is a day that anything black or red does not look right, everything should be white or yellow, representing, the flour and corn.

2. Paiutes Explain How Settlers Threaten to Usurp Land on Pyramid Lake Reservation, 1875

Sir: I [Indian Agent C.A. Bateman] have the honor to report that on yesterday a large number of the Indians of [the Pyramid Lake Reservation] gathered at the agency to receive instructions relative to their duties and have a talk about the security of this reservation to them.

C.B. Bateman to Commissioner of Indian Affairs, March 8, 1875, Letters Received by the Office of Indian Affairs, 1871–1907, National Archives and Records Adminsitration, Washington, D.C.

During the conference many things were brought out by the Indians which may be well for the Department to know; the following questions and answers explain themselves:

Agent question to Indian Tom—Did you have a letter written to me from Winnemucca?

Ans.—Yes!

Ques.—What did you say in that letter?

Ans.—The Indians have been told by Capt. Bill that all the Indians were to be driven away from the Truckee reservation, and the Indians believe the story, and I wanted you to write and tell me.

Agent ques. to Capt. Bill—Who told you that the reservation was to be broken up?

Ans.—... [Bowers] said that the reserve was broken up—sure—and he was glad of it as he would get his old ranch and fishing ground.

Ques.—How did Bowers know the reservation was broken up?

Ans.—He said he saw paper talk—that the Commissioner—heap talk in a book.

Ques.—Did he show you the book with the talk?

Ans.—No, he said he saw it in town and that Col. Cary had told him so also.

Ques.—Did this Col. Cary ever talk with you?

Ans.—Yes, he said the reservation was broken up and was glad of it—and that he had come to jump my ranch and hold it this time—he said—he would claim it, but I might stay and work it. He didn't care what became of the other Indians as they would all be driven off from their land, and we would go too if he hadn't "jumped it" as other white men wanted it and he "jumped" to keep them off.

Ques.—Did any one else ever talk to you?

Ans.—Yes! Nugent talked to me at Bowers' house—I asked him if the reservation line run below his house—Bateman tells us that it does by the map. Nugent says, Bateman lies—the line goes above the bridge on the slough—Bowers says the same, that the line only runs to the bridge—Nugents bridge. Bowers says the reservation line does not take in the lake.

Ques. to Capt. Joe—Who built that house at your place?

Ans.—Jim Lewis.

Ques.—What did Jim Lewis say when he built the house.

Ans.—He said he was going to build a house on my claim and was going to buy fish. I told him Indians did not want to sell him fish—and for him to take his lumber away—that one store was enough. Jim Gregory (trader) pretty good. Government say only one store and that he (Government) told Gregory to run that.

Ques.—Did you ever talk to any one else?

Ans.—Yes. I talked with Bevier—he told me not to have anything say to the men that were putting up the store and to tell the Indians (in council that day) to remain quiet and wait and hear what Mr. Bateman said when he came from Wadsworth where he was awaiting telegrams which would tell us all.

Question to Capt. Jim (virtually Chief)—What do you say about this matter?

Ans.—I want this reservation to stay. I want to live here and do what the Government tells me. Don't want any white men on the reserve. I like white man that Government says to stay here. No more—all Indians want that store to go—go quick. Jim Gregory pretty good—his store pretty good—no want any more.

Question to all the Indians—Has the Government been your friend?
Ans.—Yes.

Question—Did any one ever give you plows, teams, flour, beans, coffee, sugar, bacon, &c., &c., beside the Government?

Ans.—No—that is the reason we don't want Bowers or Nugent and such men come on here—they used to be here for the Government. We didn't get anything then, nothing not fish even. We all want our homes forever. We want to die here. We will do just what the Govt. tells us if they will let us keep our farms and catch fish.

Ques.—Will you all now go to work the same as if nothing had happened?

Ans.—Yes—but we want all of those white men put off and not have them come on this place any more.

Ques.—Will you, when you wish to leave the reservation, come to me and get a pass? The Government says the Indians must do so.

Ans.—Yes, anything the Government says, we will do—if we can keep our homes.

3. George Manypenny, Commissioner of Indian Affairs, Discusses United States Conflict with the Lakota, 1876

In the early part of the winter of 1875–76, many Indians from the different agencies went out with the consent of their agents to hunt buffalo in this unceded territory. They had the right to do this under the treaty. There was more reason for them to go at this time, because there was an insufficient supply of provisions at the agencies. December 6, 1875, the late Commissioner of Indian Affairs sent instructions to the several agents to notify the Indians in the unceded territory to come to the agencies before the 31st of January, 1876, or that they would be regarded as hostile. This letter reached the Cheyenne River agency on the 20th and Standing Rock on the 22d. Agent [Henry W.] Bingham says, under date January 26, 1876, that "the Indians have never been so quiet or friendly-disposed as they are now, and the intimation of a renewal of hostilities was a surprise not only to me but to all of the Indians under my charge." The runner who was sent by Agent Bingham to notify the Indians to return to the agency was not able to return himself until February 11, 1876. He brought back word that "the Indians received the invitation and warning in good spirit and without any exhibition of ill feeling. They answered that they were then engaged in hunting buffalo and could not accept the invitation at present, but would return to the agency early in the spring."

It does not appear that any one of the messengers sent out by the agents was able to return to his agency by the time which had been fixed for the return of the Indians. It is very easy to understand why the most friendly Indians should hesitate to traverse a pathless country without fuel or shelter, at a time of year

"Message from the President of the United States Communicating the Report and Journal of Proceedings of the Commission appointed to obtain certain concessions from the Sioux Indians," Senate Executive Document, No. 9, 44th Congress, 2nd Session, December 26, 1876.

when fearful storms endanger human life, and with the knowledge that they would find a limited supply of provisions at the agency. In General [Philip] Sheridan's report of November 25, 1876, we find that he states that on acccount of the terrible severity of a Dakota winter the Army were compelled to suspend operations. If our soldiers were frost-bitten and unable to remain in the field even with their comfortable clothing and supply-train, we can judge whether it was practicable for women and children to cross this inhospitable wilderness in the dead of winter.

It is an undoubted truth that there are large numbers of Indians who are now absent from the agencies. They are of three classes:

1st. The larger part made up of those who go every year to hunt the buffalo in the country along the tributaries of the Yellowstone, as provided in the treaty;

2d. Those who became alarmed and left the agencies when they saw large bodies of troops camped among them; and

3d. Those who voluntarily left the friendly Indians and joined the fortunes of Sitting Bull. The absence of these Indians from the agencies when the recent census was taken is liable to mislead Congress in making their estimates for the future support of the Sioux Indians.

The charge is made that the agency Indians are hostile, and that they have furnished ammunition and supplies to the Indians with Sitting Bull. When we remember that during a very considerable portion of this year there was a deficiency of provisions at all the agencies, and that Indians left with the knowl-edge and consent of the agents to procure food, we cannot believe that the hostiles received their supplies from agency Indians, nor do we believe that the Indians have procured their improved arms and ammunition at the agencies. There is water-navigation for 3,000 miles through this territory, and an unguarded border of several hundred miles along the Canadian frontier. So long as the Indians will sell buffalo-robes at a low price and pay two prices for guns, the greed of white men will furnish them. It is gross injustice to the agents and the Interior Department to accuse them of furnishing arms and ammunition for Indians to fight our Army and murder our citizens.

4. Mountain Wolf Woman (Ho-Chunk) Describes Women's Work and Labor in Wisconsin, c. 1890

In March we usually travelled to the Mississippi River close to La Crosse, sometimes even across the river, and then we returned again in the last part of May. We used to live at a place on the edge of the Mississippi called Caved In Breast's Grave. My father, brother-in-law and brothers used to trap there for muskrats. When they killed the muskrats my mother used to save the bodies and hang them up there in great numbers. When there were a lot of muskrats then they used to roast them on a rack. They prepared a lot of wood and built a big fire. They stuck four crotched posts into the ground

Mountain Wolf Woman, Sister of Crashing Thunder: The Autobiography of a Winnebago Indian (University of Michigan Press, 2001, 1961).

around the fire and placed poles across the crotches. Then they removed the burning wood and left the embers. They put a lot of fine wood crisscross and very dense on the frame. On this the muskrats were roasted, placed all above the fireplace. As the muskrats began roasting, the grease dripped off nice and brown and then the women used long pointed sticks to turn them over and over. The muskrat meat made a lot of noise as it cooked. When these were cooked, the women put them aside and placed some more on the rack. They cooked a great amount of muskrats. When they were cooled, the women packed them together and stored them for summer use.

In the spring when my father went trapping on the Mississippi and the weather became very pleasant my sister once said, "It is here that they dig yellow water lily roots." So, we all went out, my mother and sisters and everybody. When we got to a slough where the water lilies were very dense, they took off their shoes, put on old dresses and went wading into the water. They used their feet to hunt for the roots. They dug them out with their feet and then the roots floated up to the surface. Eventually, my second oldest sister happened upon one. My sister took one of the floating roots, wrapped it about with the edge of her blouse and tucked it into her belt. I thought she did this because it was the usual thing to do. I saw her doing this and when I happened upon a root I took it and did the same thing. I put it in my belt too. And then everybody laughed at me! "Oh, Little Siga is doing something! She has a water lily root in her belt!" Everybody laughed at me and yelled at me. My sister had done that because she was pregnant. I suppose she did that to ward off something because she was pregnant. Thus she would not affect the baby and would have good luck finding the roots. Because I saw her do that, I did the same thing, and so they teased me.

When they dug up a lot of roots in this fashion they put them in a gunny sack, filling it half full and even more. Then we carried them back to camp and my mother and all my sisters scraped them. The roots have an outside covering and they scraped that off and sliced them. They look something like a banana. The women then strung the slices and hung them up to dry in order to store them. They dried a great amount, flour sacks full. During the summer they sometimes cooked them with meat and they were really delicious....

At the time we were there when mother and father planted a garden, the blueberries ripened and we picked blueberries. There were pine trees all around where we lived, the kind of pine trees that are very tall and look as if they had been trimmed all up the trunk almost to the top. That is the way it used to be around our home. The pine trees were very dense and there was no underbrush. Under the trees the blueberries grew in profusion. All the Indians picked blueberries. They came carrying boxes on their backs and when they filled the boxes they left. At that time they used to come to our house for water, and when they brought the water up, the turning wheel would say, "gink, gink, gink, gink."

All the berry pickers carried boxes on their backs. The boxes were square and were divided into four square compartments. There were two holes on opposite sides of the box and cords were strung across these holes. They called these boxes waŋkšíkwak 'ʔín, that is, carry on a person's back. They used to carry them by horseback too, a pair slung in front and in back of the person riding the horse. This is the way they went to town to sell the berries. There they bought food for themselves, bringing the berry boxes back full of groceries. This is the way that they earned money.

They were paid a good price; fifty cents a quart is the price they used to get toward the beginning of the season, and as the season wore on, toward the end, they got a quarter. They saved their money and they even bought horses. Some of the Indians had no wagons and that is why they let the horses carry the berries, but some of them had wagons. Thus the Indians came through history. That is the way they procured food for themselves. They saved food and they saved money.

When various foods were ripe the people dried them. They also steamed things underground. They harvested a lot of corn and carried it home on their backs. When I was a little girl our family was large. I was the youngest and I had three older brothers and two older sisters. Another older sister and I were the younger ones. When they harvested the gardens, they harvested a great amount. They steamed the corn. In the evening they dug a pit and heated stones there in a big fire. They put the stones in the pit and when the stones became red hot they took out all the wood and embers and put in the corn husks. Then they put in the fully ripe corn and covered it with more husks. Finally they covered it with the earth that had been dug out. They covered the pit but they left four holes in which they poured water. We used to hear the red hot stones make a rumbling sound.

Then, very early in the morning they opened the pit with great care. They removed the earth very carefully and finally when they reached the husks they took them out. Eventually they reached the corn and it was thoroughly cooked. It was really hot! They took the corn out and put it on the husks. Sometimes other people heard about it and worked with my family. The helpers came and spread out a big piece of canvas on which they put the corn. Then they used metal teaspoons or clam shells to scrape the corn off the cobs. They used to dry it and after it was dried you could see sackfuls of corn standing here and there. They dried the corn in the sun and put it in white flour sacks. Some corn was allowed to remain on the stalks after it was ripe. This they saved for seed. In addition to saving seed they made hominy of this dried corn. They mixed it with ashes and popped it to make hominy....

They used to dry blueberries ... they did not sell. They dried the blueberries and cooked them in the winter time. The blueberries were boiled with dried corn and I used to think this was delicious. That is what we used to eat.

They used to dig a hole to save whatever they were not going to use during the winter. They kept out whatever they thought they would need for that winter and they saved in the hole what they would eat in the spring. Seed was also buried in the ground. They made a hole and buried things in it and took them out as they were required. "Dig up that which is buried," they used to say.

They also dried Indian potatoes. My grandmother and my mother's younger sister and I used to gather them. Indian potatoes grow wild, where it is wooded with dense hazel bushes, near creeks. The vines of the Indian potatoes are like strings stretched out, a lot of strings extending in all directions. That is the way the vines grow, tangled up around the bushes. The women would try poking here and there with a hoe and then they would hit upon them. The potatoes would be linked to each other as if they were strung together. Then they would dig a lot of them. After they dug them up, they cut up the links and dried them. When they cooked these things they added sugar and boiled them until the water was gone, and then we peeled off the skins. Oh, they were really delicious things!...

When I was small the Winnebago generally went to pick cranberries after they were through taking care of their gardens. We used to do that too. When we arrived at the marsh there were many Indians who camped together there and picked cranberries. The men used rakes and the women picked by hand. As the women were picking and they reached the edge of the ditch, they all sat on the edge of the ditch in a long row, side by side. They picked ahead of themselves in a straight line, a bushel-sized box at each woman's side. They would put aside as many boxes as they thought they would fill so they would not run out of boxes. They left their boxes as they filled them, and if you looked down a line you could see the row of filled boxes. As they filled each box they took along another empty box. At noon they went back to the camp to eat. Some people even brought their lunches along and ate there at the marsh. I used to think it was great fun when we took food and ate outside.

That is what people did in the fall. They were making money to save. When they finished there they went deer hunting. They were trying to earn money for themselves and they probably earned quite a bit but I did not know what they were earning. The women used to pick into a big dishpan and when it was full it was emptied into the box. We children used to pick too. We used small pails. Wherever mother sat, I used to sit next to her and I would pick cranberries. When I filled the pail I emptied it into mother's bushel box. My sister did the same thing on the other side of mother. That is what I used to do.

When we were there a peddler of general merchandise often came around. When he said the word for a white man's shirt, he would say, "šorot." He was a white man with black hair and black mustache and he did not know how to speak English. When this peddler came they would all call out, "Oh, šorot is here!"

The Indians were making money and that is why they used to come around and sell things. Somebody came around selling pies. I used to think that was very nice. Mother often bought things from these peddlers and then we used to eat pie. After all, the Indians were using campfires outside and could not bake pies and cakes, and so they had a bakery shop there at the marsh....

After cranberry time they went on the fall migration to hunt deer. That is what we always did, we went travelling to hunt deer. At that time my father did not have to buy any deer license. They never used to pay for such things. When they went deer hunting the white people did not spy on them. That is how it used to be at that time. They killed as many deer as they deemed necessary. We used to travel a certain distance east of Neillsville where there used to be a woods. There were not many white people around at that time. That is where we used to go in the fall. That is where we used to live and almost immediately the hunters used to bring in deer. They wrapped the deer in autumn leaves and carried the deer on their backs. As they were approaching you could see the red leaves moving along here and there, as they came home with the freshly killed deer. Just as soon as we arrived, the first day, they always brought home game. It was always this way. Sometimes they even used to bring in a bear.

5. Ace Daklugie, Charlie Smith, and Jasper Kanseah (Chiricahua Apaches) Remember Geronimo, n.d.

[Ace] Daklugie

Not until after the death of my father, Juh, did Geronimo become very prominent. After that he just took over. He was a Bedonkohe and never was elected to the chieftainship. Naiche was chief, but he was very young—too young for the leadership. It took a man to lead the Chiricahua. Geronimo was of middle age, a well-known fighter and superb leader, and he was also a Medicine Man. No White Eyes seem to understand the importance of that in controlling Apaches. Naiche was not a Medicine Man; so he needed Geronimo as Geronimo needed *him*. It was a good combination. Geronimo saw that Naiche was accorded the respect and recognition due a chief and that he always occupied the seat of honor; but Geronimo planned the strategy, with Naiche's help, and made the decisions. Of course, had Juh or Geronimo been chief, nobody could have usurped their prerogatives. But don't forget that not being a Medicine Man was a great handicap to Naiche.

Several years after our capture, and after I returned from school, I lived in Geronimo's village and was his confidant and interpreter. I accompanied him everywhere he went. When he took pneumonia at Fort Sill and was sent to the hospital, Eugene Chihuahua sat beside him during the day and I at night. And he died with his hand in mine. Even in his delirium, he talked of those seventeen men who had eluded five thousand men of the army of the United States for many years; and eluded not only them, but also twenty-five hundred Mexican soldiers—seventy-five hundred men, well armed, well trained, and well equipped against seventeen whom they regarded as naked savages. The odds were only five hundred to one against Geronimo, but still they could not whip him nor could they capture him.

But I am Geronimo's nephew and there are people who might think that I am biased. Go see Charlie Smith. As a child he and his mother were captured by Geronimo's band. Charlie was with Geronimo and Naiche about a year, I think, before going to Florida.

Charlie Smith

... I'll never forget that winter. Geronimo would line the boys up on the bank, have us build a fire and undress by it, and then make us plunge into the stream, breaking the ice as we went. The first time he did this, I thought that the ordeal

From *Indeh: An Apache Odyssey* by *Eve Ball*. New edition copyright © 1988 by the University of Oklahoma Press, Norman.

would be over when he let us get out of the water. But no—time after time we warmed ourselves by the fire and returned to the icy water. There were times when I just hated him. Geronimo would stand there on the bank, with a stick in his hand. What for, I don't know; I never saw him strike anybody. But we knew he might and that was enough. Nobody defied Geronimo.

Was I present during the fighting? Geronimo had the women and children along, and of course they saw what happened. If pursued, he, as did all Apaches, tried to protect them by sending them ahead; but ordinarily, when fighting occurred, it was because he laid an ambush, and every one of the band was there. Some of the women were very good shots—good fighters, too. Lozen, sister of Victorio, was called The Woman Warrior; and though she may not have had as much strength as one of the men she was as good a shot as any of them.

When actually on the warpath the Apaches were under very strict rules. Even words for common things were different. Women would go with their husbands, but they could not live together. No unmarried woman was permitted to go with them. Lozen? No, she was not married; she never married. But to us she was as a Holy Woman and she was regarded and treated as one. White Painted Woman herself was not more respected. And she was brave! Geronimo sent her on missions to the military officers to arrange for meetings with him, or to carry messages.

When Geronimo crossed the border into New Mexico or Arizona, it was usually to get ammunition. I do not think that he wanted to kill, but there were cases when he had no choice. If he were seen by a civilian, it meant that he would be reported to the military and they'd be after us. So there was nothing to do but kill the civilian and his entire family. It was terrible to see little children killed. I do not like to talk of it. I do not like to think of it. But the soldiers killed our women and children, too. Don't forget that. There were times that I hated Geronimo for that, too; but when I got older, I knew that he had no choice.

Stealing horses was fun. I was not quite old enough to get in on that, and how I envied those who were! It was usually the boys, too, who shot the fire-arrows to set houses ablaze. I never saw that done but twice, though. I did see many, many people killed. I wish I could forget it. Even babies were killed; and I love babies.

But Geronimo was fighting not only to avenge his murdered mother, wife, and children, but for his people and his tribe. Later there were Apaches who were bitter against Geronimo, saying that it was his fault that they were sent to Florida and were prisoners of war for twenty-seven years. Well, if they'd had the fighting spirit of Geronimo, they need not have been sent. The big difference was that he had the courage to keep on and they were quitters. Some of them have "gone white" and blame Geronimo for everything. I don't respect them. They were cowards. I won't name them. I am ashamed that they are Apaches.

And don't forget that Geronimo knew that it was hopeless. But that did not stop him. I admire him for that. He was a great leader of men, and it ill becomes the cowardly to find fault with a man who was trying to keep them free. And don't forget that he was fighting against enormous odds, or that nobody ever captured him.

Jasper Kanseah (nephew of Geronimo)

My father died before I was born, and my mother died when they drove us like cattle from Cochise's reservation to San Carlos. I had nobody but my grandmother and she had to walk. I was little, and when I couldn't keep up she carried me. She told me that Geronimo was my uncle, but I didn't remember him till he came to San Carlos. When he came my grandmother had already gone to the Happy Place, and I had nobody. But Indian women were good to me, and even when they were hungry they gave me some of the food their own children needed. We never went hungry till we got to San Carlos; and there we almost died because there was no food.

I think that I was eleven when my uncle, Geronimo, came and took me with him. And he gave me to Yahnosha to be his orderly and learn to be a warrior. I stayed with Yahnosha and cooked his food, and got his horse and fed and watered it; and I never spoke unless somebody asked me a question. And I ate what was left. No matter what happened, I didn't complain. And even when I talked I had to say it differently. (On the warpath we don't talk as we do most of the time, but differently.) I had to think what Yahnosha wanted next and then get it for him before he told me. But I was proud to be taught by a great warrior and I tried to do everything right.

I knew Geronimo and I knew that he was the victim of liars. He was lied about by many of his own people for whom he was fighting. He was betrayed by them. He was betrayed by [General Nelson] Miles. I am not sure but that he was betrayed by [General George] Crook, though some think not. But I know that he was lied to by Miles. That man did not do what he promised. Geronimo was a really great fighting man, and Miles was a coward. Everything he needed for his troops was provided for him and them, but Geronimo had to obtain food for his men, and for their women and children. When they were hungry, Geronimo got food. When they were cold he provided blankets and clothing. When they were afoot, he stole horses. When they had no bullets, he got ammunition. He was a good man. I think that you have desperados among you White Eyes today that are much worse men and are more cruel than Geronimo.

6. Lakotas Describe the Wounded Knee Massacre, 1891

TURNING HAWK, PINE RIDGE (MR. COOK, INTERPRETER).   [Big Foot's] people were coming towards Pine Ridge Agency, and when they were almost on the agency they were met by the soldiers and surrounded and finally taken to the Wounded Knee Creek, and there at a given time their guns were demanded. When they had delivered them up the men were separated from their families, from their tepees, and taken to a certain spot. When the guns were thus taken and the men thus separated there was a crazy man, a young man of very bad influence and in fact a nobody, among that bunch of Indians fired his gun, and

---

"Report of the Commissioner of Indian Affairs," House of Representatives, Executive Document 1, Part 5, 52nd Congress, 1st Session.

of course the firing of a gun must have been the breaking of a military rule of some sort, because immediately the soldiers returned fire and indiscriminate killing followed....

All the men who were in a bunch were killed right there, and those who escaped that first fire got into the ravine and as they went along up the ravine for a long distance they were pursued on both sides by the soldiers and shot down, as the dead bodies showed afterwards. The women were standing off at a different place from where the men were stationed, and when the firing began those of the men who escaped the first onslaught went in one direction up the ravine, and then the women who were bunched together at another place went entirely in a different direction through an open field, and the women fared the same fate as the men who went up the deep ravine.

AMERICAN HORSE.   The men were separated as has already been said from the women, and they were surrounded by the soldiers. Then came next the village of the Indians and that was entirely surrounded by the soldiers also. When the firing began, of course the people who were standing immediately around the young man who fired the first shot were killed right together, and then they turned their guns, Hotchkiss guns, etc., upon the women who were in the lodges standing there under a flag of truce, and of course as soon as they were fired upon they fled, the men fleeing in one direction and the women running in two different directions. So that there were three general directions in which they took flight.

There was a woman with an infant in her arms who was killed as she almost touched the flag of truce, and the women and children of course were strewn all along the circular village until they were dispatched. Right near the flag of truce a mother was shot down with her infant; the child not knowing that its mother was dead was still nursing, and that was especially a very sad sight. The women as they were fleeing with their babes on their backs were killed together, shot right through, and the women who were very heavy with child were also killed. All the Indians fled in these three directions, and after most all of them had been killed a cry was made that all those who were not killed or wounded should come forth and they would be safe. Little boys who were not wounded came out of their places of refuge, and as soon as they came in sight a number of soldiers surrounded them and butchered them there.

Of course we all feel very sad about this affair. I stood very loyal to the Government all through those troublesome days, and believing so much in the Government and being so loyal to it, my disappointment was very strong, and I have come to Washington with a very great blame on my heart. Of course it would have been all right if only the men were killed; we would feel almost grateful for it. But the fact of the killing of the women, and more especially the killing of the young boys and girls who are to go to make up the future strength of the Indian people, is the saddest part of the whole affair and we feel it very sorely.

I was not there at the time before the burial of the bodies, but I did go there with some of the police and the Indian doctor and a great many of the people, men from the agency, and we went through the battle field and saw where the bodies were from the track of the blood.

◈ ESSAYS

Beginning as early as 1850, many American Indians moved to reservations—either voluntarily or involuntarily—rather than offer a military resistance to the United States. Reservations required Native peoples to adjust their social, political, economic, and cultural lifeways to new circumstances. In particular, they faced pressures from the federal government to conform to an assimilation policy that insisted that Native peoples transform themselves into Christians and farmers. Native peoples adjusted to these changes in many ways. In the first essay, William Bauer (Wailacki and Concow of the Round Valley Indian Tribes), professor of history at the University of Nevada, Las Vegas, explores how northern California's Round Valley Indians temporarily left the reservation to work in nearby hop fields. How did federal officials respond to Round Valley migrant labor? What meanings did Round Valley Indians invest in migrant labor? In the second essay, Tracy Neal Leavelle, professor of history at Creighton University, demonstrates that other Indians modified their economies and social practices on reservations. The residents of Oregon's Grande Ronde reservation showed their commitment to make necessary changes and adaptations in order to make the reservation their own. How and why did Round Valley and Grande Ronde strategies differ? Was one more successful than the other in charting a path of self-determination?

Off the Reservation: Migrant Labor and Native Communities in California, 1865–1887

BY WILLIAM J. BAUER, JR. (WAILACKI AND CONCOW)

In 1877, Round Valley agent John Burchard reported: "A gentleman came here from a distance of 50 miles to get Indians to pick hops; he said he had some Indians that did not belong to this reservation engaged in picking his hops, but they received a stick with notches on it, and a feather tied to it, inviting them to a dance, to hop fields, and all engagements were abandoned, and this gentleman had to look to reservation Indians to help him in his work." In some ways, such a letter might not be surprising. Throughout North America, farm owners and agricultural employers constantly worried about the labor supply and sought out viable sources of temporary workers. However, Burchard's missive fails to explain why hop growers considered Round Valley Indians a potential migrant workforce or indeed why Round Valley Indians worked in the hop fields for the next sixty years. Round Valley oral histories hold some clues.

It was cool and rainy in March 2002, a day that was nearly the opposite of typical for working in the hop fields, as Concow Francis Crabtree described his

William Bauer, *We Were All Like Migrant Workers Here: Labor, Community and Memory on California's Round Valley Reservation, 1850–1941* (Chapel Hill: University of North Carolina Press, 2009), 80–105.

youth spent picking hops. Francis, who wore a classic western-style button-up shirt on the day of our interview, is a rather tall, thin man, with flecks of black in his grey hair, precisely cut in military fashion, betraying his World War II service, of which both he and his wife Jean are immensely proud. As we sat in his kitchen in Redwood Valley, less than twenty miles from the hop fields, with coffee warming our conversation, Francis's mischievous grin led us back to the hop fields. "Oh yeah, that is what I did in the summer when I quit the railroad," he said. "Come down and run around in the hop fields." Although hop picking was a seasonal occupation fraught with hot and irritating working conditions and exploitative relationships, it meant something more to Round Valley Indians, as Francis's roguish smile implied. Round Valley Indians used hop picking to earn cash wages, maintain kinship ties, and create a sense of community in northern California.

Round Valley Indian participation in the hop industry affords one of the best ways to examine the intersection of wage work and community in the nineteenth and twentieth centuries. The history of hop production in California and the distinctive "hop culture" enabled Round Valley Indians to forge the bonds essential to the maintenance of their communities. From tilling the soil to training the vines to picking the crop, Round Valley Indians worked in all facets of hop production. While operating under the particular demands of the crop, Round Valley Indians integrated wage labor into their seasonal household economies and divided their work among family members. Once the daily task of picking hops concluded, Round Valley Indians engaged in big times that connected Round Valley Indians to one another and to other northern California Indians. Thus, hop picking offered Round Valley Indians the opportunity to earn a living and maintain community connections.

... Round Valley oral histories revealed their own hop-picking culture. Picking hops, more than other occupations in Round Valley, dominated labor discussions in Indian oral history and tradition. Working in the hop fields was a generational experience, akin to attending off-reservation boarding schools, which united Round Valley oral histories. Round Valley Indians shared these memories and stories with California Indians from Manchester, Hopland, Ukiah, and Fort Bragg. Round Valley and Mendocino County Indian picking culture emphasized family and kinship, depicted hop picking as a traveler's narrative, critiqued the uneven economic relations in Mendocino County, and demonstrated their industriousness. If anything, Indian workers insisted that they, and not white workers, were the permanent fixtures of the hop fields.

California's hop industry began in the aftermath of the gold rush. In the early nineteenth century, hop cultivation was located primarily in the eastern and midwestern United States, in places such as New York and Wisconsin. In 1855, Wilson G. Flint, a transplant from New York, planted hops along the Sacramento River. For the next fifteen years, hop production expanded in northern California and was considered a windfall for the towns of Ukiah and Hop City.... Although the passage of Prohibition curtailed hop production, a strong European market buoyed the industry until President Franklin D. Roosevelt repealed the Eighteenth Amendment and the Volstead Act in 1933. In 1940, Mendocino

County produced 1.6 million pounds of hops.... Thereafter, hop production declined because of changing tastes for beer, international competition, and the opportunity to plant more profitable crops, such as wine grapes. By 1965, no farmer in Mendocino County planted hops.

The nature of the hop plant meant that growers had to adhere to a particular system of organizing crop production. Hops are a perennial climbing plant. New plants sprout in spring, require harvest in late summer, and die in fall. Used primarily to flavor beer, hops adapted well to the mild California climate....

Considering the geographic location of hop cultivation in California, it is unsurprising that hop growers turned to Round Valley Indians to provide work on their farms....

In 1892, the *Ukiah Press* recognized the role of Mendocino County Indians in the hop industry: "The [hop] picking is being done by whites, Indians and Chinese, in the ratio of about *five, two, and one.*" ... [P]erhaps one-quarter of Mendocino County's workforce was Indian.... Indians may have disappeared from the agricultural workforce in other parts of California, but they remained vital in Mendocino County.

In fact, Mendocino County hop growers preferred to hire Indians, as the letter to Burchard suggested in 1875. There were several reasons for the privileged hiring of Indians. For one, Mendocino County Indians were not Chinese, the pariah of California's agricultural workforce in the late nineteenth century. In 1882, the same year as the Chinese Exclusion Act, Ukiah newspapers praised Mendocino County hop growers: "Our hop men are entitled to credit for the stand they have taken on the Chinese question.... They sat themselves resolutely against employing Chinese, and at infinite trouble have secured Indian and other help." Anti-Chinese sentiment persisted in Mendocino County for more than a decade after the United States restricted immigration. In 1893, an anti-Chinese riot in Ukiah attempted to drive the Chinese population from the region. With one cheap workforce disappearing from the region, hop growers logically turned to Indians to supply labor to their industry. Indeed, Mendocino County Indians appeared to be an ideal hop-picking workforce. Although Indians did not work with particular alacrity, hop expert Daniel Flint argued, they minimized waste and saved growers money. Additionally, Indian workers appeared to be docile. Mendocino County hop advocate Ninetta Eames noted: "The general verdict among the hop growers is, that an Indian is as 'straight as a string'—no sticks or leaves in their sacks, and no likelihood of finding a stray match carelessly or intentionally mixed with the fragrant contents." White employers believed that Indians, unlike other agricultural workers, were not predisposed to lash out against their employers, manipulate their earnings, or foment dangerous forms of resistance. Finally, hop growers did not worry about Indian laborers staying around once the season finished. When Indians picked the last hop of the season, they returned to the Round Valley Reservation or other rancheria communities.

Hop growers' explanations about Indian behavior fail to fully explain why Round Valley Indians worked in the hop industry. For, from beginning to end, Round Valley Indians participated in the hop culture. In January or February, plowmen broke the ground and planted the seeds in rows seven to eight feet apart, Pomo Al Want remembered: "I was thirteen years old, plowing hops with a walking plow and two horses. That's hard work for a kid. I worked from sunup till sundown." Once the crop sprouted, workers "trained" the hop vines. At first, hops "grew up" individual wood poles, a process called "poling." However, this was costly and labor-intensive, as farmers needed to make new poles each year. Hop growers looked about for cheaper and more efficient ways to grow the crop and decided on a trellis system. Farmers planted posts at intervals and workers connected the posts by stringing wires along the base and top of the posts. Another series of strings linked the two wires that were parallel to the ground. Rather than constantly replacing costly wood posts, farmers only had to replace the strings.

After building the trellises, workers "trained" the hop vines to climb the strings. Pomo Al Want remembered that Indians divided their labor by gender and age: "[Ranchers] hired women and children to come and train the hops, work the hops, hoe around the hops.... They pruned 'em, then they'd tie strings on the wires and they'd tie down three strings onto this vine and all the way through and they'd train these onto each string." As Want explained, the first stages of hop culture adhered to Round Valley Indian household economies. Plowing the fields and training the vines provided job opportunities to all members of an Indian household. Men typically plowed the fields, while Indian women and children had the annual springtime job of training hop vines. Such work injected cash into Indian households and enabled families to work together.

After training, there was a respite until the picking season began in late August. Once the hops ripened, Indians left Round Valley and traveled south to Hopland and Ukiah and then worked their way back to the reservation. One of the first such occurrences was in August 1875, when agent J. L. Burchard reported that 120 Indians had left the reservation to pick hops. It is probable that Round Valley Indians learned about the job from ... Pomos, who, after moving to the reservation, migrated to and from the reservation to find work and interact with family members. The seasonal nature of hop picking created rhythms of activity for the community. In late August, everyone in Mendocino County—Indian and non-Indian, government agent, hop grower, and hop picker—knew that Round Valley Indians were leaving the reservation for Ukiah's hop fields.

Hop picking provided a way for some Indian men to embellish customary leadership practices. Initially, captains led migrant Indians to the hop fields, functioning much as padrones. In 1878, agent Henry Sheldon held a meeting on the Round Valley Reservation to ascertain the Indians' opinion about transferring the Office of Indian Affairs (OIA) to the War Department. Sheldon reported that all the captains or chiefs were present except for John Brown, the Yuki and Wailacki captain, who, along with sixty other Yukis and Wailackis, was picking hops in Ukiah....

In 1893, Brown contracted with L. F. Long to pick hops for the Liverpool, London, and Globe Insurance Company in Ukiah. Long pledged to provide flour and beef for Indian workers on the trip to and from Ukiah, pay Yuki workers one dollar per hundredweight, and pay Brown an extra one dollar per day for bringing fifty workers. That same year, Jim, a Wailacki captain, made similar arrangements with Frank Youree, a saloon owner in Covelo, and Concow Dan Wright contracted to work on Patrick Cunningham's hop ranch. In their capacity as padrones, captains functioned as intermediaries between their tribes and hop growers, thus building the social ties necessary for the creation of community.

In the late nineteenth and early twentieth centuries, Round Valley Indian migration strategies changed. Rather than relying on captains to make arrangements with growers, workers found their own ways to the fields. The development of new transportation methods aided in this process. Concow-Pomo Kathy Cook recalled that her family took advantage of the transportation ranchers provided: "They would have a truck go around and pick all the people up at their homes early in the morning.... He would haul them down there like migrant workers or something." The advent of the automobile enabled hop growers to circumvent the Indian captain. Relying on hop ranchers and their automobiles to get to work, however, was a costly proposition since ranchers sought to recoup their transportation costs. In 1893, workers whom ranchers picked up earned one dollar per hundredweight, whereas workers who came to the camps on their own made $1.10 per hundredweight. The cost of relying on ranchers for transportation became more problematic when hop wages declined in the late nineteenth century. In 1899, those people whom the hop growers picked up earned eighty cents per hundredweight, while those who arrived at the fields on their own accord earned ninety cents.

Work began early in the morning. Hop growers had a very short window in which to harvest their crop, usually about three to four weeks. If hops dried on the vine and turned red, a process called "rusting," they became virtually worthless on the open market. Growers equipped pickers with a knife, a sack, and a cloth. The "knife man" cut the trellis strings and jerked the hop vines off the wires or strings. Pickers placed the hops in baskets, sacks, blankets, or boxes and, when full, took the hops to the foreman for weighing. Dexterous workers could snatch four or five hop buds off the vines at a time. The owner gave the picker a number and the weight of each sack of hops they picked. Hop growers used this opportunity to inspect the hops to make sure they were clean (without leaves, dirt clods, or sticks), and docked the wages of "unclean pickers." Sometimes, through the day, picking halted because the hop kilns were full—the hops rotted quickly in the sacks. After drying, hops were immediately baled for market. When the workday concluded, Indians retired to their camps.

At first, compensation was actually quite good. Farmers made concessions to Indian workers, such as offering relatively good wages, food, and acceptable camps, in order to attract them to their farms. In the early 1870s, Indians working on Carl Purdy's ranch in Ukiah received fifty cents per day and flour and meat rations. However, the depression of the mid-1870s forced hop ranchers to cut costs, and they looked for ways to reduce their labor costs. Some hop growers experimented with standardized boxes, which could (allegedly) hold a specific amount of hops. By the 1880s, ranchers began paying workers by the hundredweight, rather than the day or box ... Purdy remembered that piece-work was more efficient and economical for ranchers, because they hired 40 workers to do the same amount of work as 120, and they did not have to feed them. Other ranchers argued that Indians reaped the benefits of piecework because those who worked the hardest profited from the new wage scale. Mendocino County rancher and California state representative Barclay Henley.... estimated that Indians earned anywhere from two to four dollars per day under the new wage system....

But, in fact, the new wage system discriminated against Indian workers. For one, piecework required Indians to pick between 200 and 400 pounds of hops a day, whereas previously they had earned a fixed daily wage. Furthermore, Mendocino County Indians reported that they earned considerably less under the piece rate. In 1879, Pomo Charlie Brown stated that he and seventy-two workers earned $600 in thirty-six days picking hops in Ukiah and Hopland. This equaled a little more than eight dollars per person or twenty-two cents per day. If the day wage had still been in effect, Pomos would have collectively earned more than $1,300, or eighteen dollars per person. Pomo Charlie Bourne provided similar statistics, informing government officials that his party of one hundred Pomos made $800 (again eight dollars per person), but he neglected to mention how long his party worked in the fields. Clearly the shift in pay rates undermined Indian earning power. Pomo hop pickers earned less than one-half of what they had previously made, and ranchers no longer provided food and other supplies.

The effect of the change from the day rate to the piece rate worsened over time as hop wages stagnated in the late nineteenth century. In 1882, the *Ukiah City Press* reported that Indians earned $1.25 per hundredweight. Twenty years later, as the hop industry went into a depression, pickers earned only one dollar per hundredweight. Wages hovered at the same rate in the twentieth century. By 1926, the wages returned to $1.25 per hundredweight, but only for those workers who stayed the entire season. If they left before the entire crop was picked, Indians earned only one dollar. It could hardly be said that hop wages kept up with late nineteenth- and early twentieth-century inflation. Depending on the index, Round Valley Indian hop pickers saw their earning power decline by between 50 and 70 percent between 1882 and 1926.

As with any job, hop picking produced some critical remarks from Round Valley Indians. Wailacki-Pomo Arvella Freeman was unequivocal on the subject of picking hops: "Oh yeah. I hate hops. I found some down here, down here [by] the rodeo grounds [in Round Valley], there are hops down back in the brush. I got some and put them out there [in my garden], and I said, 'oh I don't know why I did this.' I hated hops, so I tore them down. I hated hops." Other Indians did not go to this extreme, but many remembered disliking aspects of the job. Round Valley Indians recalled that hop-picking wages were extremely meager. Cahto–Little Lake–Nomlacki Aloya Frazier remembered: "Pick hops all day and go down and buy an ice cream, and that was our profit." Aside from low wages, working conditions were uncomfortable. Concow-Nomlacki–Little Lake–Tolowa Robert Anderson recalled: "It was hot work, especially in the hops…. [There was] no shade." Summertime temperatures in Mendocino County can top one hundred degrees, making for an extremely uncomfortable experience. In addition to the summer heat, the early morning truck rides were hard on young and old. Wailacki Norman Whipple remembered that the truck picked him up at 4:30 in the morning. For those who did not camp at the fields, the transportation made for extremely long days. Indian workers frequently left for work before the sun rose and came home long after the sun set.

But some Indians fondly remembered hop picking. Concow Acie Hoaglen recalled: "I didn't like that prune business too much. Too much work. I didn't mind the hops." The positive memories of hop picking stemmed, in part, from the economic importance of the job. Pomo Myrtle Shively noted: "It was great fun for children. You got to keep your own money." Intermixed with this seasonal agricultural labor, Indians worked on sheep and cattle ranches and supplemented these jobs with a diverse household economy. Indian families hunted deer, rabbits, and hogs; fished in the Eel River for salmon and steelhead; traveled to the coast to harvest food; produced household and craft items; and raised gardens. Although these myriad activities permitted Round Valley Indians to hold the capitalist economy at arm's length, they always left the reservation in late summer, heading to the hop fields to earn cash. Families used the wages from hops to buy important household staples and, in the twentieth century, purchase school clothes for children. Hops provided a stable and seasonal job opportunity, remaining an important economic strategy for more than sixty years.

Hop picking forged social ties essential to the creation of community. Spouses sometimes met in the hop fields. Concow–Little Lake Wayne Cox remembered: "My father was Irish and he lived in Ukiah, and he ran a pear ranch, hops and pears. That's how he met my mother, because my mother came from a migrant worker family. They would haul the Indians out in the trucks to the Ukiah area, where they could harvest the crops." Picking hops provided opportunities for members of the opposite sex to meet, court, and eventually form their own families. Some children were even born in hop fields. Pomo Annie Ramon gave birth to the famous basket weaver Elise Allen in the hop fields outside of Santa Rosa. These new families continued to travel to these work sites as a family unit. Pomo Al Want recalled: "We used to pick hops in Covelo and then we picked in Ukiah. That's when we had a pretty good sized family then, my wife and I. We had six children." Families also used kinship networks to find work in Mendocino County. Nomlacki–Little Lake Bobbi Anderson said: "After the hops were done [in Round Valley], we moved on to Ukiah…. My uncle George Want was a foreman there. And he'd come and pack us all in a big truck, we'd all go there, and he'd have a house for us to stay in. We stayed down there and my dad was kind of like a foreman, until the prune crop was done and then we come home." Hop picking produced a cycle of family formation. Spouses met in the fields, children were born there, and the children then accompanied their parents to the fields.

Once in the fields, families pooled their labor power. All family members, regardless of age or gender, worked. Pomo Lorraine Lockhart, for instance, recalled that four of her six children accompanied her to the Ukiah hop fields. She considered her twelve-year-old daughter, Gloria, her best work hand. Pomo Mabel Ball also remembered the family organization of labor: "My mother went to take hops in this hot weather. She don't want to leave us down there [in Manchester] because we're under age and by ourselves. So we went there to pick hops." Mendocino County Indian hop pickers also made concessions for the elderly. Older Indians had a chair on which to sit and a three-foot-tall canvas basket for their hops. The knife man cut down several strings of hops around the elderly person, who sat in the chair and picked the surrounding vines clean. No one else touched the vines reserved for the elderly. Round Valley Indians ensured that all family members, young and old, earned money during the hop season.

After combining their labor, most Indian families pooled their wages. Wailacki Norman Whipple said that wages went into the "family pot," with which they purchased school clothes. Pomo Lawrence McCoy recalled that families who worked together stood to make much more than the lone migrant worker: "A family didn't make more than a hundred, hundred thirty dollars in about ten days picking. A single person, he wouldn't make much more than thirty or forty dollars."

Others used family labor to diversify their economic pursuits. Wailacki June Britton recalled: "The family [picked hops], but [my dad Gus Russ] didn't. He stayed here [on the family ranch]. There were four of us, I guess, [my brother] Leroy didn't get in the hops. He had work at home to do." Similarly, Little Lake–Cahto–Nomlacki Barbara Pina's family did not camp out at the Hop Ranch: "We had the farm to take care of. That was a morning, noon, and night project." Often, farm work had to be completed before hop picking began: "We were milking ten to twelve cows at that time. Mom and Dad and [my brother] Pie were over in the Sacramento Valley ... working in the rice. Then we went and picked hops for our [school] clothes. It only lasted about two weeks but we still had those cows to milk." Hop picking was vitally important to Round Valley Indian families but not their only source of income....

If hop picking united families, it also brought interaction between Round Valley Indians and other Native peoples in Mendocino County. "I enjoyed the company of being out amongst people [picking hops] and I enjoyed the money," Wailacki June Britton stated. "We didn't associate with many people, we were raised up on [the north] end of [Round Valley].... [Our parents] never took us no place. We stayed home. If I could get out and pick hops I could see different people." Indeed, Round Valley Indians returned to certain job sites in order to socialize with family members and friends. Seasonal wage labor allowed Pomos to maintain ties with their homelands and kin who had not removed to or had left the reservation. Pomo Myrtle Shively remembered: "There we met all the other friends, our Indian friends and relatives." Yet it was not only Pomos picking hops. Yukis, Wailackis, and Concows also traveled to Ukiah to meet family and friends, creating pan–Indian connections in Mendocino County.

Hop-picking season permitted Round Valley and Mendocino County Indians to participate in big time events. Concow Francis Crabtree recalled: "I don't know if I made a dollar a day [picking hops]. That was all fun work, just something to get by in, in the summer, just to run around." Pomo Lawrence McCoy agreed: "The good old hop picking days. You know, we liked that. These kids get out of school, get a vacation. We had that river down there. That's what we liked. Run down there and swim." Grass game was one of the most popular events during these big times. Pomo Robert Renick said: "They had the [grass game] gatherings in the old days wherever they camped. Different hop fields. Saturday night and Sunday. Get paid Saturday anyway." Yuki–Little Lake–Pomo Leland Fulwider also remembered the close connection between grass game and hop picking: "The grass game players, everybody wanted them and then they would, like, hop season time come up in and bring a big old truck, hard wheel trucks. They would take them to Ukiah, Lake County and all around there, end up gambling, after they finish work, they'd play grass game."

... Round Valley Indians celebrated the conclusion of hop picking by consuming alcohol. In 1883, agent Henry Sheldon complained: "General good order prevailed except some excesses in drinking during hop-picking." Although highly critical of Round Valley Indian drinking patterns, Sheldon pointed out that Round Valley Indians drank alcohol at predetermined and specific moments of the year. Round Valley Indians also imbibed alcoholic beverages when participating in nonwork activities. Concow Claude Hoaglen chuckled: "I played [grass game] when I got older and after I got to drinking wine." Wailacki-Concow Doran Lincoln recalled that when he worked at the Hop Ranch in Round Valley people stayed up late into the night playing grass game and drinking whiskey.

Hop picking also sustained important religious and cultural practices. Doctors, for instance, worked clandestinely off the reservation. Some Indians accused Yuki Ralph Moore of leading a secret "Devil Society" on the Hop Ranch and teaching people how to concoct poisons. If Moore was indeed a poison doctor, he used the workplace to pass on cultural knowledge. Other poison and sucking doctors worked more openly during hop-picking time. Wailacki-Pomo Arvella Freeman witnessed a doctor in action at the hop fields. Pomo Lulu Johnson was sick with pneumonia, so the family called for a female doctor from north of Round Valley. Arvella remembered:

> [The doctor] told [Lulu], cause [Lulu] wore a rag around her head all the time, and she told [Lulu], she said, "What time does your head hurt? You remember the time where you camped one time when you folks went to Ukiah to pick hops." [Lulu] said, "yeah." She said, "Well, do you remember the people that lived next to you, that camped next to you?" [Lulu] said, "Well, yeah, kinda." She said, "Well, they sent a curse on you. They poisoned with a rattlesnake." And she said, "I'm going to take that away from you." And she did. And after that, no scars or nothing left. And Lulu said that every certain time that would

squeeze, that was that snake, squeezing her head. [Lulu] said she, that woman didn't ask for no money or nothing. She said, "Well, whatever you can give me or whatever, you can't pay it's all right." They had some pretty little Indian baskets, so they gave her a basket. I seen that with my own eyes.

As Arvella's story illustrates, hop picking offered opportunities for Indians to settle old grudges and "poison" their co-workers. But it also permitted sucking doctors to combat the poison and restore balance to their world. Such options did not always exist on the reservation, where religiously minded agents attempted to stamp out American Indian religious practices....

Oral histories recorded ways in which Indians deflected some of its worst manifestations and articulated a distinctive "picking culture." Hop picking was a universal experience—an occupation in which all Round Valley Indians of a certain age participated. "Everybody used to go down there and work," Concow-Pomo Kathy Cook stated. "It gave everybody a job. They were like migrant workers. Like they do now with Mexican people, that was how the Indians used to work." Kathy conveyed that hop picking produced a sense of belonging to Round Valley Indians. She described her work experience in a plural sense and noted that all community members worked in the fields. Other Mendocino County Indians made similar observations. Pomo Harriet Stanley remembered: "There were a lot of other Indian people camping. They'd come from all over, because they picked the seasonal crops, like the hops. That's how you got to know people from different areas." Hop picking also attracted northern California Indians from rancherias and communities in Mendocino County. The central place of hop picking in many oral histories illustrates that Round Valley Indians shared their picking culture with other reservation residents and with Indians from other parts of the state.

For Round Valley and Mendocino County Indians, migrating to the hop fields forged crucial connections to place. Pomo Robert Rennick described migrant labor as a traveler's story: "My grandparents would go [pick hops], three of us; we would have to walk because the horse couldn't pull a wagon load up the hill. Then you got to wait, stop the cars—very few cars them days. We'd go Willits Road, or Comptche-Mendocino Road down to Comptche then straight across to Fort Bragg." Traveling to the hop fields required Indians like Rennick and his family to travel across the landscape, which he invested with new meanings. When in the fields, Round Valley Indians incorporated hop ranches into their conception of place and geography. Concow-Nomlacki–Little Lake–Tolowa Robert Anderson remembered: "A lot of the families, I can remember yet, we'd be picking hops down there at the old Johnny Johnson ranch, and a lot of the Indian people would be camped down by the river and they would stay all summer.... And the Indians, I can remember them, a lot of the families from here, just like a little community down along the river, everybody camped out, you know." As Anderson suggests, a new place— the hop-picking camps along the Russian River—offered new opportunities for Round Valley Indians to maintain community in Mendocino County.

The experience of migrant labor forged ties within the family. Wailacki June Britton explained: "I went [to pick hops with my mother]. We went as a family.... We didn't pick hops until we got older. She didn't go until we got older and then we would all go and pick." Nomlacki–Little Lake Bobbi Anderson agreed: "I was living with my mother at the time, it was my mother and I, and we would go down there with some of her friends and we would work in the fields down there and pick hops." For both Anderson and Britton, hop picking united family members, who migrated together to the fields. Additionally, hop picking enabled Round Valley Indian women to contribute to the household's coffers.

The emphasis on family enabled Round Valley Indians to blunt aspects of unfree labor. Little Lake–Cahto–Nomlacki Aloya Frazier recalled: "But you know, a lot of people don't know this either, that is why George Ells, [George] Bauers, and old Ed Gravier, a lot of these old Indians that was their bankers, they'd loan you fifteen cents. That is why these old Indians went to the old ranchers, they were their bankers. They'd handle their money and their business." His sister, Barbara Pina, added: "They were good people." Certainly, the system of debt imperiled Indian workers, who found themselves beholden to white ranchers in Round Valley and Mendocino County. However, by insisting that "they were good people," Aloya and Barbara asserted that the social networks that connected Indians to their employers, rather than the exploitation that resulted from such relationships, was the most significant aspect of this relationship. Employers became part of the Indian community. Indians expected and demanded these gifts and loans because they helped families get through the winter.

But kinship ties only went so far in protecting Round Valley Indians from economic exploitation, and sometimes other, subtler, forms of resistance were necessary. Pomo Elizabeth Willits remembered that every evening during the hop-picking season storeowner Edward Gravier drove his wagon to Round Valley's Hop Ranch and sold meat, vegetables, and watermelons to Indian workers when the day's work concluded. On one occasion, Dixie Duncan told Gravier that in order to boost sales he should yell out in the Yuki language, "I'm bringing good meat. Come and get it." However, Duncan actually taught Gravier to say, "I'm bringing rotten meat. Come and get it." Gravier, of course, did not understand the Yuki language or, perhaps, the chuckles and declining sales he encountered thereafter. For Duncan, though, this was a safe way to make Gravier look like a heel and to resist economic domination. Duncan obviously felt comfortable enough to use the Yuki language to poke fun at someone who could charge usurious rates for meat and other groceries by entering the Yuki language into what scholar James Scott calls the "public transcript." Duncan attempted to cause people to not buy groceries from Gravier but did so in a way that meant everyone—perhaps even Gravier when he discovered the ruse—could have a good laugh, at Gravier's expense.

In some ways, the Round Valley and Mendocino County Indian hop-picking culture resembled that of non-Indian hop pickers. Ethel Docker, a non-Indian woman who grew up in Ukiah, remembered that hop picking was a terribly uncomfortable job: "[Hops and vines did not] care where they stick.

Your neck is just as good a place as any and with the sack tugging at your waist line and the temperature well toward 100° this may give you some idea of the pleasures of picking hops." Although she never claimed to tear down hop vines like Arvella Freeman, Docker agreed with Indian workers that working in the hops field made for a difficult workday. Whites also recalled the conviviality and camaraderie of picking hops, as did June Britton and others. Frank Holland stated: "Much of the pleasure of picking hops came from the association with your fellow workers, many of whom chose to camp in tents stretched under trees along the river[;] cooking over an open campfire made picking season seem almost like a specialized vacation with pay." Docker had a similar memory: "Anyone wanting to go hop picking could go by signing up with the bosses. The hop owners would move their camping things out to the field where they would pick a camp spot not too far from the river, near a good swimming hole. There were many peddlers and delivery trucks that came to the field from town, so the campers didn't have to go to town for supplies. Many people never left the field from the time they went out till the time they came home." Like Round Valley Indians, Holland and Docker remembered hop picking as both an opportunity for recreation and an uncomfortable work situation.

But Round Valley and Mendocino County Indian oral histories reveal a different picking culture from that of the white pickers. Take, for example, one particularly irritating aspect of the job: what it did to the worker's skin. John E. Keller, a non-Indian, recalled: "Several of the Keller sisters went [to the Russian River] to pick hops as a family project to earn extra spending money. I went and worked with them one day, but that was it for me. That night, I broke out with hop rash—my skin was sensitive to the rough hop vines." Indian memories of the rash, however, differed. Concow Francis Crabtree recalled: "I didn't like picking hops, no I didn't care about that. But I just did it, anyway. You get hop poison on your hands, you know little scratches, and they'd swell up and itch. All we did it just to make a little money." Pomo Mabel Bell from Manchester similarly recalled: "Picking hops, though, it was so warm. Those things are sharp. If you don't wear no long sleeved shirt or gloves, they scratch you. Some people get poison with that. My uncle, it's poison for him to pick hops. He can't work." Hop irritations did not discriminate between Indian and white skins, but Indians imbued hop picking with a specific cultural meaning by calling the irritation "poison" rather than a "rash." In northern California Indian communities, touch transmitted illnesses and explained medical maladies. The rash was not a physical ailment; it was a supernatural one. In the case of picking hops, the forces of nature—plants and the land—poisoned people, causing the skin to swell and itch. It is unsurprising that hops might poison Indian workers. After all, horticulture erased traditional harvesting areas from Mendocino County's landscape and forced Native peoples to look for other economic outlets.

In other areas, too, Indian and non-Indian memories of hop picking diverged. Non-Indians remembered hop picking as a temporary job, something to which they did not necessarily return on an annual basis. After suffering the rash, Keller never returned to the fields. Recall the description of hop wages as "pin money," which further contributed to the idea that, for white workers, hop picking was a temporary affair. Additionally, non-Indian workers saw themselves on equal footing with their employers. H. E. Holland remembered: "There was a sense of freedom, you met your employer twice daily, you were not a slave working for someone, you were a helper working with a farmer to harvest his crop." Holland saw himself as a free white worker. He compared his place in the labor market with that of a slave, indicating that he was above servile status. Holland also noted that agricultural labor was a more democratic job than factory work. Rather than laboring under the anonymous gaze of the factory foreman, white agricultural workers like Holland interacted with their employers.

For Round Valley Indians, hop picking possessed other meanings. Picking hops contradicted the stereotype of the "lazy Indian." Pomo Elizabeth Willits noted: "Had to pay the grocery bills so we had to work or you don't eat. You had to work for your living. Didn't lay around the house, do nothing. You had to get out and do something. So from that day on I worked until the end of the training of the hop fields. That's all I worked in, the hops here." Similarly, Pomo Lawrence McCoy noted that parents did not always condone recreation in the hop fields: "Mother, lot of times, she come down the river with a big loop hop vine, run us all out of the river up in the hop fields. Work! That was just in our blood, that's all!" By refuting the "lazy Indian" stereotype, Willits and McCoy insisted that industriousness provided for Mendocino County Indian survival.

Round Valley and Mendocino County Indians also refuted the attempts of the growers' associations to "whiten" the workforce. Pomo Al Want described the workers who trained and hoed the hop fields: "They were practically all Indians. A few whites, not too many." Pomo Robert Renick agreed with this description of the hop-picking workforce: "People come from Covelo, Lake County, Santa Rosa; some come from clear down Hoopa, some come up from Fresno. Traveling through or something, I don't know. All of them were Indians. There was no whites." But, of course, non-Indians did pick hops, something that other Indians remembered. Concow-Pomo Kathy Cook noted: "A few non-Indians worked in there that was poor and that wanted to work." For Round Valley and Mendocino County Indians, though, hop picking was not the egalitarian experience that Holland described above. Instead, hop picking created a racialized landscape. Pomo Edna Guerrero recalled: "The Indians would start on one side of the fields and the white people on the opposite side, and they would all work toward each other." Whites and Indians worked on opposite sides of the hop fields, in Guerrero's memory, in an almost antagonistic manner. Furthermore, Indian workers commiserated not with the growers, but with poor whites and contemporary Mexican migrant workers. Here, Round Valley and Mendocino oral histories and traditions directly challenged the historiography of California agricultural labor. Rather then rendering Indians invisible in the narrative, Indian oral stories washed white workers out of the history. Indians argued that they, not white workers, were the permanent features of the hop-picking workforce.

For nearly seventy-five years, Round Valley Indians made annual peregrinations to the hop fields of the Ukiah Valley. Earning a penny per pound, Indian families worked long hours at the scratchy work to provide food and clothes.

Once the workday concluded, Indians socialized, consumed alcohol, and played grass game. But they lacked control of their lives. Agents tried to keep Indians on the reservation, while hop growers used debt and fixed wages to control Indian workers. It was quite apparent to most observers that Round Valley Indians constituted a class of California farmworkers. Indeed, hop picking was an integral part of Round Valley's, and Mendocino County's, oral tradition and collective memory. Myrtle McCoy, a Pomo woman from Ukiah, stated, "You know, nowadays, these kids that grow up don't know hop fields and all," reminding future generations of Mendocino County Indians of the work and sacrifices that their parents, grandparents, and great-grandparents made to survive in a changing world.

On the Reservation: Agriculture and Adaptation in Oregon, 1856–1887

BY TRACY NEAL LEAVELLE

"The Americans will never leave us alone. Let us not concern our hearts.... We will take [Grand Ronde].... [W]e will make it our own place." These words represent a dramatic decision and transformative vision that emerged in the Native communities of western Oregon in the 1850s. A member of the Tualatin band of Kalapuyans, perhaps Peter Kinai, recalled them for linguist Albert S. Gatschet in 1877. Gatschet's informant related an episode in which the respected Tualatin elder Ki-a-kuts consulted the Tualatins during their treaty negotiations with Joel Palmer in 1855. Ki-a-kuts asked the other members of the band if they wanted to trade their land around Wappato Lake for a portion of the Grand Ronde Valley. Despite reluctance to abandon their native lands, they resolved to accept the new, hopefully more secure home and transform their lives. The year following the treaty council, the Tualatins and other Indians from throughout western Oregon commenced the long project to make Grand Ronde their own.

Between 1856, when the first Indians settled at the Grand Ronde Reservation, and 1887, when the Dawes Act initiated a comprehensive program of allotment, Grand Ronde residents formed a new cultural homeland. They created a reservation culture that looked ahead to a modern Indian future while also relying on the strength of past traditions. In the 1850s the Native peoples of western Oregon's interior valleys recognized that they lived in an age that would not allow them to follow easily in the paths of their ancestors. They traded their vast lands and a life of gathering and hunting for a valley haven and the opportunity to make new lives. In facing the chaos of beginning this endeavor and making the transition to reservation life, the Indians of Grand Ronde demonstrated creativity, flexibility, and initiative. They selectively

"'We Will Make It Our Own Place': Agriculture and Adaptation at the Grand Ronde Reservation, 1856–1887," by Tracy Neal Leavelle, is reproduced from *American Indian Quarterly* with permission from the University of Nebraska Press. Copyright 1999 by the University of Nebraska Press.

adapted their culture to meet the physical, social, political, and emotional demands of their situation. They actively pursued an agricultural life and accepted Christianity, yet they also hesitated to send their children to agency schools and continued to seek the advice and the healing powers of Indian doctors. Contrary to the commonly held view that hunter-gatherers resisted incorporation of agriculture into their lives, the Indians at Grand Ronde made agriculture the foundation for an independence that allowed them to mold a new Indian culture and identity that gave meaning to the reservation experience.

Reservations have often been perceived as places of decline and dependence, as sites where Indian peoples confronted an incomplete assimilation within a larger society that abused or ignored them. Critics observe that economic development and Indian agriculture on most reservations have never been adequate. They note that residents often have been dependent on an inconsistent and unfeeling government for support. In the late nineteenth and early twentieth centuries, reservation agents and Indian Office inspectors blamed persistent traditional cultural attitudes among their Indian wards for these failures. Furthermore, historians of the early reservation period have frequently portrayed the reservation experience as destructive, lamenting the loss of Native cultural traditions and the dearth of appropriate and meaningful replacements. The Navajos of the late nineteenth century, who maintained a relative independence through the expansion of stockraising, are a prominent exception to this pattern. Generally, however, it is easier to recall the dramatic decimation of California's Indian communities, Big Foot lying dead in the snow at Wounded Knee, the racist assumptions of assimilationist government programs, and the tragic loss of Native lands throughout the country. Although bleak images have a foundation in the difficult and challenging realities of reservation life during the last century and a half, Indians turned these prisons into homelands, important "places where a native identity could be maintained and passed on to new generations."

In recent years, historians of the reservation era increasingly have tried to counter the simplistic image of defeated and despondent Indians by emphasizing the adaptability of Indian communities. These scholars reject crude acculturation and persistence models as unrealistically static interpretive frameworks that reduce Native peoples to passive objects of government policies and victims of changing social and economic conditions. Highlighting the new strategies, symbols, and identities created and employed in making the transition to reservation life paints a more subtle, three-dimensional portrait that restores agency to Indian individuals and communities. The story of Grand Ronde offers a particularly vivid example of people drawing from a deep well of cultural creativity to assert some control over their destinies in a time of limited options and difficult choices.

On 19 January 1856, twenty Luckiamute Indians arrived in the Grand Ronde Valley, at the headwaters of the South Yamhill River, to settle on just over 60,000 acres of land reserved for the exclusive use of the Indians of western Oregon. Coming in a difficult winter season of dampness and cold, they found only unprepared and overwhelmed government agents to greet them and canvas tents for shelter. Two weeks later some three hundred Upper Umpquas and

Yoncalla Kalapuyans ended their long trek to Grand Ronde from the river valleys of southern Oregon. At the end of March, 395 Rogue River Indians from numerous bands stumbled into the reservation after a month-long journey of over 250 miles. During the next several months, armed escorts drove hundreds more Indians to the reservation. The violence of the Rogue River Wars that flared in the interior and coastal valleys of southwestern Oregon between 1853 and 1856 had defeated many Indians. Others, like the Kalapuyan bands that held on to scattered plots of land in their native Willamette Valley, had to make way for the thousands of incoming immigrants who coveted their rich lands. In June 1857, after many of the coastal Indians and most of the Rogue River Indians moved west to the recently formed Coast Reservation, a census listed the Indian population of Grand Ronde as close to twelve hundred.

The people who settled the reserve shared many cultural traits and traditions. The Indians of western Oregon were gathering and hunting peoples who relied on a variety of food resources to meet subsistence needs. From the spring through the fall, families and bands lived in transitory camps. Women, children, and probably older men harvested food staples such as camas and wappato roots, acorns and berries, while men fished and hunted. In the winter months, bands settled in villages for annual ceremonies and a period of social visiting. The villages, consisting primarily of patrilocal extended families, formed the basic unit of political organization. Gradations in wealth and prestige between chiefs, commoners, and slaves marked social distinctions within the societies. Wealthy men and village leaders owned slaves and could have more than one wife. The Indians of western Oregon also shared similar beliefs in the guardian-spirit powers available to shamans and, sometimes, to other individuals. Exchange, intermarriage, and intermittent cooperation fostered connections between the many Indian groups of western Oregon.

The bands that arrived at Grand Ronde were culturally and socially familiar to each other, but variations in these broad cultural patterns and in historical experience gave each band a unique heritage. The mix of subsistence items, the content and form of religious beliefs and winter ceremonies, and the emphasis on wealth gradations varied from band to band. The many languages spoken by the Grand Ronde bands represented the most dramatic element of cultural diversity on the reservation. The settlers of Grand Ronde spoke many mutually unintelligible languages. The Kalapuyan bands alone spoke three different Kalapuyan languages. As for other bands, the Clackamas of the lower Willamette Valley spoke Upper Chinookan, the Upper Umpquas were Athapaskan, and the Cow Creeks and Rogue Rivers of southern Oregon utilized Takelman dialects. The Molalas of the western Cascades spoke yet another tongue, and people of mixed French and Indian ancestry often used Canadian French. In western Oregon and at Grand Ronde people relied on Chinook jargon, the lingua franca of the region, to cope with this linguistic diversity. Consequently, shared cultural practices and attitudes and the common reservation experience helped the Indians of Grand Ronde overcome the challenges of this diversity to forge an Indian identity rooted in the place and the history of their valley home.

Joel Palmer, who in 1853 became Superintendent of Indian Affairs for the Territory of Oregon, directed the removal of Indians to the Grand Ronde

Reservation. Palmer faced the difficult task of halting the conflicts between Indians and White settlers in the territory. He concluded that separating the antagonists represented the only hope for peace in the fertile valleys and resource-rich mountains of western Oregon. Moreover, he believed that separation and confinement on reservations offered Indians their only chance for survival as well as the opportunity to ascend to a better, more "civilized" life. Between 1853 and 1855, Palmer worked incessantly to negotiate treaties with the Indians of western Oregon that extinguished their title to the land and opened it for continued American settlement. He signed treaties with the Rogue River Indians, the Cow Creek band of Umpquas, the Umpquas and Yoncalla Kalapuyans, the many Kalapuyan bands of the Willamette Valley, and the Southern Molalas. The territory the Indians ceded included virtually all of Oregon between the main ridges of the Cascades and the Coast Range. On 30 June 1857, President James Buchanan signed an executive order making Grand Ronde the permanent home for these bands.

Reservation policy was well developed in the United States when the Grand Ronde agency opened. Policy makers believed reservations offered a reasonable solution to the problems then plaguing relations between Indians and Whites in the West. Confinement of the Indians reduced and regulated their contact with Whites. Reservation advocates thought a strict separation would reduce tensions and end deadly confrontations. Reservations, it seemed, were the only alternative to the otherwise inevitable extinction of the Indian race. Close containment and control of Indians had the additional benefit of making them available for programs of civilization designed to produce sedentary Christian agriculturalists on the pattern of the idealized yeoman farmer. In this view, reservations were the crucibles of "civilization" out of which new Indian communities and societies would emerge to become part of the expanding Republic.

Agriculture was at the very heart of this government policy of directed culture change well into the twentieth century. The government wanted hunting and gathering peoples like the Indians of western Oregon to give up their seasonal migrations and settle permanently to farm and raise stock on individual plots of land scattered across the reservations. The government expected men to conduct the agricultural labor while women managed the family's domestic economy. Reservation agents intended that Indians learn the value of private property and disciplined labor and hoped that communal ties to clan, band, and tribe would give way to a more individualistic ethos of personal improvement and economic advancement. While their parents worked in field and home, many children attended schools ostensibly designed to reinforce these lessons of modernity. They learned English, other academic basics, and sometimes the skills needed to run an agricultural operation. Teachers worked to suppress Indian languages and other expressions of Native culture and tried to instill in their students the accepted habits of White Christian America.

In the late nineteenth century, with the expansion of the allotment program and the growth of the boarding school movement, these efforts to transform Indians intensified. The ultimate goal was to assimilate them into American society as agricultural producers and citizens and bring about the final breakup of the reservations themselves. The Indian Office followed closely these various comprehensive and complementary policies at Grand Ronde.

In their first years on the reservation, the diverse bands that settled at Grand Ronde faced the numerous challenges of beginning and sustaining agricultural operations. Although preparations for opening the reservation in 1856 were simply inadequate for the large number of Indians who settled there, a much more serious issue for the long term turned out to be the land itself. When Superintendent James W. Nesmith made his 1858 annual report to the Commissioner of Indian Affairs, he complained that "the soil [at Grand Ronde] is a cold, heavy clay, and unproductive. The position is elevated and exposed to violent sea breezes which, at certain seasons, have a deleterious effect upon the growing crops." Unpredictable weather and difficult soil conditions often conspired to reduce yields on Indian farms.

Although some individuals and bands had experimented with stock raising and perhaps with farming before going to Grand Ronde, most, if not all, needed instruction in agricultural techniques. The guidance they received, however, was inconsistent at best. Farmers hired to teach the Indians and to run the agency farm came and went with alarming frequency. The salary was low, the work was difficult, and alternative opportunities were abundant in Oregon. Treaty stipulations that required the agent to employ farmers for the Indians ran out after five years for all bands except the Upper Umpquas, Yoncallas, and Southern Molalas. For these bands the provision for keeping a farmer ended after only ten years.

The lack of proper equipment and sufficient working stock also presented enormous obstacles to efficient subsistence production. In a deposition taken in an 1862 investigation into allegations of incompetence against the reservation agent, several band leaders expressed disappointment at not being supplied with the means to work their land satisfactorily. The grain the Indians managed to raise under these trying conditions often could not even be milled on the reservation. Despite the promises of reservation agents and the expectations of the superintendent, the grist mill was not completed until 1858, and for years thereafter it was constantly in disrepair.

By the late 1860s and early 1870s, however, many people began to enjoy some success in their agricultural endeavors. In September 1869, in response to rumors that they would be removed to make way for Whites, representatives of thirteen bands had a letter written to President Ulysses S. Grant to make "known some of [their] desires, hopes, and fears." In the missive, they told Grant, "We now know how to farm, how to build our houses and barns, how to cook and sew…. The land produces well…. We have built houses and barns and many of us have made rails and fenced our lands, believing that this was to be our home." Grand Ronde Agent Charles Lafollett predicted that the year's harvest, despite some problems with the weather, would support all but the elderly and the orphaned, who would need government support. He estimated that the Indians had at least eight hundred acres of wheat, five hundred acres of oats, and fifty acres of potatoes and other root vegetables under cultivation.

To supplement the products of farming, the Indians continued many of their traditional subsistence practices. Women and children gathered berries, dug camas and wappato roots, and collected edible seeds and plants, all important items in the pre-reservation diet. The men hunted and fished in the area, taking deer, elk, and small game from the forests and trout and salmon from the mountain streams. In 1862 an agent had allowed the Indians to begin making seasonal fishing excursions to the Salmon River near the coast, and in 1865 they constructed a road to the fishery and made further improvements at the site.

Indians at Grand Ronde complemented such subsistence activities with wage labor in a new seasonal cycle. During the summer months, after the crops were in the ground, hundreds of people obtained passes from the agent and left Grand Ronde for the Willamette Valley to work for White farmers. Men chopped wood and worked in the fields as laborers, an important opportunity to learn and polish agricultural skills while earning cash. Labor was in such short supply in Oregon that they reportedly received fair wages for their work. For their part, women cooked, did laundry and housework, and gathered Native food items. Women also sold handwoven baskets to Whites, made with traditional materials in the patterns and forms their White customers desired.

The money the men and women earned was crucial not only in the short term to help make ends meet from year to year, but also in reaching the long-term goal of establishing successful agricultural operations and nourishing and maintaining a fragile independence. Their harvests did not yet produce the surpluses necessary to generate an income from participation in the market, and the government did not supply many of their basic needs, such as clothes. In a council held in 1871 with Felix R. Brunot, a member of the Board of Indian Commissioners, Joe Hutchings complained that the agents had not done anything for them. He reportedly said, "You see our houses; we worked outside and made money and bought them.... Our people go outside and get horses, and they get harness [sic], and plow with them." Henry Kilke remarked, "I have a wagon; I bought it. My house I got the same way. My clothes I bought; the Government never gave me any of them.... Now we want to know what we will get for our lands [given up in treaties]. We need a gristmill, harness and horses, and plows and wagons, and that is all we want."

Many of the Indians at the agency also wanted individual allotments. The focus on the disaster that occurred with implementation of the General Allotment or Dawes Act—the widespread alienation of Indian lands and a decline in Indian farming—has obscured the history of allotment prior to 1887. Concentration on the generally poor outcome of the Dawes Act itself has resulted in neglect of Indian perspectives on allotment before and after the destructive act. The loss of Indian land in the twentieth century was as dramatic at Grand Ronde as elsewhere, but these terrible consequences lay beyond the horizon during the reservation's first three decades. For many people at Grand Ronde, allotment appeared to offer stability and some guarantees for their future in a reservation agricultural community. Allotment also seemed to promise eventual acceptance as full citizens of the state and nation.

The treaties with the Kalapuyans and the Umpquas provided for the survey and allotment of reservation land, to be done at the discretion of the U.S. president, in plots from 20 to 120 acres in size. As early in 1860, Agent John F. Miller had assigned small portions of land to individuals in an effort to encourage farming, but the allotment of the reservation as called for in the treaties had yet to begin. In response to the delays, people on the reservation consistently agitated for the full procedure to be carried out. In 1862, in the deposition given in the investigation of the Grand Ronde agent, Tom and John Chamberlin of the Rogue Rivers, Quakata of the Molalas, Peter of the Yamhills, and Ki-a-kuts of the Tualatin band expressed a desire among their people for creating individual allotments. Yet, in 1869, the agent noted that several bands still farmed communally fenced lands. In their letter of the same year to President Grant, Grand Ronde leaders complained, "We have been here a long time and do not know where our lands are, therefore we can not improve them. If our lands had been surveyed ... we would have known that they were ... our own land and that we could not be ordered by our Agent to leave them and plow and sow at his pleasure, we would by this time been able to support ourselves."

Government officials, also anxious to implement an allotment program at Grand Ronde, believed it would encourage improvement of lands, further the agricultural program, and move the Indians ever closer to American citizenship. By September 1871, the surveys had finally been completed and only awaited the proper approvals from Washington. A year later, the allotting of lands to individuals commenced under the direction of Agent Peter B. Sinnott. The superintendent of Indian Affairs for Oregon, T. B. Odeneal, was present, and he observed that the Indians were pleased with the program. He further noted that many people would have to build new houses and that most would need to fence their lots. While up to that time their houses had generally been built in clusters according to band, they would in the future be more widely scattered across the valley.

The following year, in 1873, Sinnott reported that the Indians had been so busy constructing houses and barns, putting up fences, and making other improvements that fewer people than usual left the reservation for the now traditional summer work. He gushed, "It is conceded by all who are conversant with Indian affairs who have visited this agency, that the Indians are far in advance of any other tribes of the Pacific coast." Other observers made similar assertions. Perhaps Sinnott was trying to boost his reputation with such a statement, but he had only been on the job for a year and a half and so could not take much of the credit. In any case, the Indians at Grand Ronde had received their allotments and were building what was for them a new kind of community based on the family farm.

Residents also formed other institutions to guide reservation society and to support the transition to a new way of life. In 1869 the leaders who sent the letter to President Grant wrote that the people at Grand Ronde "respect the laws of the whites, as well as our own." In the early 1870s, with the support of the reservation agent, elected leaders of the bands began meeting annually in a legislature, where they gradually put these laws into writing. The preamble to the 1873 legislative record stated that "the laws ... were enacted for the Government of the Indians, to preserve order, to maintain the laws, and to qualify them for the position which they will have to fill as Citizens of the State of Oregon before many years."

Once they were functioning as a legislative body, the representatives indeed began to make laws that met the needs of their community and that respected their own traditions and standards as well as those of the surrounding White society. They passed laws regulating estate issues and divorce, setting the fines for property crimes, assault, rape, and adultery, and banning the possession of liquor on the reservation. They also instituted an Indian court to hear complaints and to punish those who violated reservation law. The court met the first Monday of every month and on each Saturday for cases demanding immediate action. The court directed jury trials that included prosecuting attorneys, witnesses, a sheriff, and a clerk, and a presiding justice. Justices also made administrative rulings and approved contracts between reservation residents.

The legislature tried as well to promote agriculture on the reservation. In 1873 it voted to hold an annual reservation fair each September "for the encouragement of the people of Grand Ronde Indian Reservation in farming, stock raising and general improvement." Four years later, the legislature set up a fund in the treasury to make short term loans to reservation residents. Some of the fund was held in wheat and oats, ten bushels of which could be borrowed on the promise of returning twelve bushels to the treasury after harvest. Another law passed in the same session set the rules for use of a threshing machine, which anyone could utilize for a percentage of the crop. The machine increased the community's independence by reducing the need to hire the equipment and time of outsiders to process the harvest. Grand Ronde Indians also operated four reapers of their own.

By the late 1870s and early 1880s, the agricultural community at Grand Ronde was maturing. The development of a largely self-sustaining community was necessary because treaty support ended for the Rogue River bands after sixteen years and for the other bands after twenty. Future appropriations would come only at the discretion of a budget-conscious Congress. In 1877 Agent Sinnott reported that the Indians met 90 percent of their subsistence needs through agricultural pursuits, with the remaining 10 percent coming from fishing, hunting, and gathering. According to Sinnott, the government issued no rations. The following year he estimated that the Indians obtained 95 percent of their provisions through farming and again he issued no rations. He reported that farmers had 3,000 acres under cultivation on the reservation and that they owned over 600 horses, 28 mules, 339 head of cattle, and over 400 sheep.

Reservation residents enjoyed displaying this wealth. The Reverend R. W. Summers, who visited the agency on the Fourth of July, 1877, described a bounteous feast and celebration the Indians held. Groups of people entered the festival grounds in processions, wearing "their most gorgeous garments." They invited Summers "to view the tables neatly spread with spotless linen and a lavish display of china & dainties." They informed him that the tables would look even better once the cakes and pies were laid out. A boy of fourteen mounted a wagon and recited the Declaration of Independence before the crowd. Someone then gave a speech that was in some ways an Indian declaration of independence. The orator pointed to the orderly community they had built at Grand Ronde and said they loved their homes and wished to live and die there. They had given up their former possessions for this place and would not, he said, be taken from their homes and moved to some other location to make way for greedy Whites. Like other Indian communities in the United States, the people of Grand Ronde employed the Fourth of July holiday and festivities for their own purposes. In the context of the great American festival, Grand Ronde residents celebrated connections to their new homeland, recognized progress, and looked ahead to the future.

Inspectors from the Indian Office in Washington, on their tours of Western reserves in the early 1880s, noted the transformation of the previous twenty-five years. One commented in 1880 that Grand Ronde was "the first Indian agency yet visited by [him] where *all of the Indians* live in houses, understand the English language and engage with reasonable diligence in civilized pursuits. The first one where all are able to support themselves and want to become citizens." An inspector reported in 1882 that Indians marketed a grain surplus in the nearby towns of Sheridan and Dallas.

Many reservation residents believed, however, that they could still improve their situation considerably. Some were anxious to obtain larger allotments so they could expand their operations, and concern over the permanency of the allotments that they already held continued to irritate them. Agent Sinnott admitted in 1879 that the allotments in severalty were not legally binding on the government. Although he argued that the government had a moral obligation to protect the possessions of the Indians, he concluded that, "if their removal becomes absolutely necessary," they should be compensated for their improvements. Regardless of any promises of compensation, the idea that they could be moved from their new homes without their consent disturbed the Grand Ronde Indians. In 1877 the orator at the Fourth of July festival called on the government to honor its commitment. Ten years later the Indians met with an inspector from the Indian Office and expressed their continuing fears that they would lose their farms.

Agriculture and the possession of land formed the foundation for building a viable and sustainable community at Grand Ronde, but the Indians asserted themselves in other areas as well. While schools were central to the civilizing mission the Office of Indian Affairs promoted, the Indians at Grand Ronde were skeptical consumers of the educational opportunities offered on the reservation. Government officials viewed schools as the most valuable tool for effecting the long-term transformation of Indian cultures that was the ultimate goal of reservation policy. Officials considered adults difficult to change because they often continued to manifest an interest in familiar Native traditions. Children became the focus of the educational project. Agents and teachers especially favored boarding schools in which children would be delivered from the "pernicious" influences of home and family. At boarding schools Indian students could receive a total education that included, in addition to the basics of reading, writing, and arithmetic, intensive practice in the agricultural and domestic arts, as well as the moral instruction deemed so important by those who perceived little of value in Native cultures.

Authorities opened a school within a year of beginning operations at the agency, but the teachers experienced continual frustration. John Ostrander reported that when he took charge of the school in August 1856, there were eighty students who attended irregularly. He complained that "they seemed to think it our sole business to minister to their wants, and that they were doing us a favor by attending school." Further problems erupted in 1857. According to Ostrander, an Indian medicine woman blamed him for a disease infecting the Indians. "The doctress," he explained, "said she distinctly saw the sickness that afflicted the tribes issue from the trumpet which I sounded to announce the hour of school, and settle like a mist upon the camp; and should I continue to sound it, in a few days all the Indians would be in their graves—the camp desolate." He quickly stopped using the trumpet, but over the years, as instructors came and went and schools opened and closed, agency teachers continued to complain about the mixed reception they and their institutions received on the reservation. The Indians of the Grand Ronde community shared with other Indians throughout the United States an ambivalent attitude toward the government's educational project.

In 1874, with religious denominations ascendant in the implementation of Indian policy in the United States, Catholic nuns from a succession of orders took charge of the reservation boarding school, also known as the manual labor school. The Sisters of the Holy Names of Jesus and Mary arrived in 1874 and worked until 1880, when their order recalled them. Sisters from St. Benedict's convent in Minnesota followed with less than a year of service. In 1882 the boarding school came under the direction of the Mount Angel Benedictine Sisters of Oregon.

Agent Sinnott, a Catholic himself, claimed the sisters soon had the school in a prosperous condition. Yet, according to his own statistics, the school was never even close to capacity. In 1879, for example, he recorded a school-age population at Grand Ronde of 180. The boarding school could accommodate fifty students and the day school thirty-five, but only thirty students attended school one month or more during the year, and average attendance was limited to twenty-five. The day school was not even open.

Agents and educators could only convince the Indians at Grand Ronde to send their children to agency schools when it served personal, family, or community interests. Statements at a council held in 1860 to determine whether the Indians preferred the current teacher or wished to bring a Catholic priest to the reservation revealed some of the things they considered important. Of the fourteen Indian leaders present for the conference, six stated they preferred a priest, but five men wanted neither the teacher nor a priest. Louis Nipissing, an Umpqua leader, refused to send his children to school because the Indians had not first been consulted on their needs and desires, but he was interested in securing the services of a priest. Joseph Sanagratti, a leader of a Kalapuyan band and one of the five opposed to maintaining a teacher, suggested, "In place of throwing away our money for schools as we have had, I would rather have the money used for the completion of the Grist Mill." Subsistence concerns and autonomy were simply higher priorities than having their children educated and indoctrinated in government schools.

However, some parents did send their children to school, indicating that they perceived benefits in doing so. Building the reservation community made certain skills quite valuable. Learning to speak, read, and write English and mastering basic math would have been important for the negotiation of the practical matters and bureaucratic challenges of running a farm and living on a reservation. The people who obtained these skills could then act as cultural brokers, as mediators between Indian and White worlds. In the manual labor school boys had the additional opportunity to learn agricultural skills in the school garden. Female students concentrated on the domestic arts. Parents probably sent their children to the schools long enough to learn these valuable skills, but otherwise expected them to contribute to the maintenance of the household. Some parents may also have used the boarding school, where children at least received some clothing and regular meals, as a survival strategy during lean months and years.

In their encounters with Christianity, the Indians at Grand Ronde also displayed skepticism. While many people eventually embraced it to one degree or another, Native traditions continued to hold an important place in reservation lives, and new indigenous religious movements offered further alternatives for spiritual renewal and community life. In 1860 Catholic priest Adrian J. Croquet arrived from Belgium to open a mission at Grand Ronde and stayed for the next thirty-eight years, working tirelessly to build and sustain a Christian Indian community. While itinerant Catholic and Protestant missionaries and interactions with settlers and Indian agents of various denominations exposed the Indians to Christianity, Croquet's arrival marked the beginning of a more intensive encounter with the Christian faith. Croquet, for his part, believed he was engaging in a struggle with two dangerous spiritual foes, the Protestants on the one hand and unbelief and spiritual delusion on the other, with the very souls of Grand Ronde's Indians hanging in the balance. Writing to a friend he said, "Now is the time to take possession of the missions, as the Protestants are on the alert and they may get a foothold before we do.... May the Black Robes come, therefore, to preserve the tawny children of the forest from the poison of error that is sure to be spread among them."

Croquet's modest mission station at Grand Ronde clearly attracted many people, but the initial burst of enthusiasm seemed to fade over the next few years. An analysis of Croquet's sacramental register, in which he listed each baptism, marriage, confirmation, and burial, shows that he baptized ninety people at Grand Ronde in his first year and ninety-four in his second. Most were children under the age of sixteen. However, at least twenty-three in the first year and another twenty-three in the second year were people who were near death and received virtually no religious instruction prior to the rite. In the third, fourth, and fifth years, the majority of baptisms were of this type, and the total number of baptisms fell dramatically. Croquet baptized only about 20–25 percent of reservation residents in the first five years of the mission.

In October 1862, Croquet dedicated the first church at Grand Ronde, St. Michael the Archangel. A year later he reported that fifty to sixty people attended Sunday services each week, but he deplored the apparent lack of enthusiasm for his project. By 1866, when he still was not making the progress he hoped for, Croquet complained that a "Catholic missionary has no longer the influence with these Indians that he would have upon still savage tribes; they have come and yet come too much in contact with men who, if not hostile, are at least indifferent to the Catholic religion; and they seem to have contracted a fair dose of these men's religious indifference."

Eventually, however, Croquet's presence and considerable patience seemed to have a major impact. A report for the Board of Indian Commissioners from 1873 indicated that a substantial majority of Indians had become members of the Catholic Church, and attendance at Sunday services had jumped to an average of 250. The arrival of Catholic nuns in 1874 to manage the manual labor school provided another intimate point of contact between the Indians and the Catholic religion. In 1883 the Indians, with assistance from the Catholic Church, constructed a new house of worship for the community. Agent Sinnott felt confident that the church, after over twenty years of labor, was flourishing and that Catholicism had largely supplanted Native beliefs and practices in daily life at Grand Ronde.

Yet Sinnott's successor, J. B. McClane, complained that two large dance houses were hidden in the hills above the valley. Indians from Grand Ronde and from other reservations held ceremonies in them lasting several days. McClane said they had even constructed a boarding house to shelter the participants. These ceremonies may have been related to the revitalization movements that attracted followers at Grand Ronde and at the adjacent Siletz reservation beginning in the 1870s. People from Grand Ronde learned the Ghost Dance in northern California in 1871. This prophetic movement probably influenced the Earth Lodge cult, which first came to the reservation in 1873 and was known locally as the Warm House Dance. Agent McClane, like others before him, tried to prohibit the Indians from participating in these rites and confronted the Indian doctors in an attempt to discredit them. McClane recognized what some people had known for a long time: There was a mix of belief and practice among the Indians, many of whom found meaning and value in traditions both new and old.

In the mid-1870s Reverend Summers conversed with Father Croquet on this subject and recorded that most of the Indians had finally accepted baptism, but that many, especially the older men and women, "mingled with the old religion the comforting assurances of [Catholicism]." Summers also spoke to an Indian man who described the dances and ceremonies held every autumn by men on the reservation at a lodge secluded in the forest. Another resident named two Indian doctors who continued to practice on the reservation. Agency physicians had no trouble drawing patients to Western healing traditions, but Native doctors and traditional healing practices offered an alternative and a supplement that many people found appropriate and useful. Traditional healing arts and Native ceremonialism persisted at least through the first decade of the twentieth century at Grand Ronde.

Living in a reservation community that was both Indian and "modern," the Indians of Grand Ronde carefully evaluated their choices in a search for utility and meaning. Summers visited a house of mourning in the mid-1870s where "a little girl, great grandchild of an ancient patriarch named To-ót-ly, lay on her little white bier, with candles at the head and foot, but dressed in a full suit of native garments[,] not an atom of civilization ... about her." He asked the mother why the child was dressed in Native clothing, when all the Indians now wore American attire. She reportedly replied, "while they lived on earth it did not matter. They no longer followed their own customs, therefore why cling to their own dress?" She explained that "after death it was different. If her child went to the other world in white people's clothing, they would think she was white, and put her in the pale faces' heaven, and she did not want her little child there. She wanted her to go to the Indian's heaven where she would be with her own people and be happy." This woman could live outwardly as her White neighbors in the Willamette Valley, but, within her, she still nurtured a distinctly Indian self-identity that explained her place in the world, infused her experiences with meaning, and guided her on a path into the future, even beyond death.

By 1887, on the eve of the new government allotment program outlined in the Dawes Act, the people of Grand Ronde had constructed a prosperous community based on an agricultural life. They received very little direct government support and, therefore, had to be largely self-reliant. The lack of government assistance was not the only incentive to develop this quality. The Indians of Grand Ronde, by working within the limitations of the reservation environment to create a sustainable community, cultivated the ability to make institutions work for their interests. They thus achieved a measure of independence.

The process of building such a community encouraged the emergence of a common identity grounded in reservation experiences. Allotment scattered families across the valley on independent homesteads and stretched traditional band affiliations. In 1878, the Indian legislature switched from representation by band to a system based on the division of the valley into three legislative precincts with three representatives each. Intermarriage between bands fostered bonds of kinship, as they had prior to the reservation period, and community celebrations promoted social exchange. Declining use of tribal languages and the general adoption of Chinook jargon as the community's symbolic Indian language further supported a new identity. Moreover, an increasing proportion of residents had been born and raised on the reservation and knew no other way of life. Band affiliation may still have retained importance for some people, but there was a growing sense that they were *from* this place, that it was part of them. The reservation experience transformed the people of many bands into Grand Ronde Indians.

Not everyone responded with the same enthusiasm to the challenges of erecting an agricultural community at Grand Ronde, nor did they achieve the same results. Some people aspired to wealth and prestige and reached for positions of leadership within the community. Social distinctions, important in the pre-reservation period, were significant at Grand Ronde as well. A wealthy and respected man, for instance, could no longer take several wives nor purchase slaves at Grand Ronde, but he could be elected to the legislature or preside over the court. Replacing the slaves at the bottom of the economic ladder were a number of people, primarily the aged and the orphaned, who depended on the government or the charity of neighbors to survive. For these impoverished people, the weakening of traditional band ties and an increase in individualism would not have been welcome developments. A few people, like a small band of Rogue River Indians led by John Chamberlin in 1862, became dissatisfied with reservation life and so missed their native lands that they sought, unsuccessfully, to resettle them. Not even memories of the violence and blood-shed of the 1850s or the presence of numerous White homesteaders kept them from trying to return to their homeland. Some people left the reservation for years to live and work in the farms, villages, and towns of western Oregon.

The people who stayed created a viable community for a new and different world. In the mid-1850s the Native peoples of western Oregon's interior valleys, pressured by American settlers and government agents, faced a chaotic and restrictive situation, but they still had choices. They decided to exchange the troubles of their homelands for the challenges of a long experiment in personal transformation and cultural adaptation. Once settled at the agency, individuals and groups made choices that tended to enhance self-determination and increase independence.

As the Grand Ronde case illustrates, culture can be both conservative and elastic when people confront disorder and the unknown. While culture structures experience and provides the means to interpret it, it also serves as a rich resource for adapting to changing circumstances and unfamiliar environments. The process of selective adaptation at Grand Ronde included both innovation and cultural continuity. On the surface, the Grand Ronde Indians gave up their traditional system of gathering and hunting for the cultivation of wheat, oats, and potatoes. Yet they developed a new yearly cycle that included Native foods as well as an annual migration to the Willamette Valley. They molded institutions, even those that government agents imposed on them, to serve their needs. In many cases, the reservation program of directed culture change only reinforced decisions the Indians had already made themselves. The government and its agents often lagged behind the Indians in response, timing, and vision, actually limiting the ability of the Indians to make desired adjustments to reservation life. In any case, by 1887, the Indians of Grand Ronde had developed a way of life animated and defined as much by their own standards and goals as by the policies and decisions of government agents. Although experiences at Grand Ronde forever altered the Indian societies of western Oregon, Indians also shaped the nature of those changes and maintained a Native identity.

While the Grand Ronde Indians fashioned an agricultural community that generally impressed observers, Indians at other agencies in Oregon and throughout the West frequently struggled without the same success to adapt to reservation life and to meet their needs through agricultural development. A combination of factors, many of which were absent at other Indian reservations, created the conditions that allowed the Grand Ronde Indians to achieve many of their goals. Most importantly, they had arable land. The soil at the agency, while not ideal, could be productive when cultivated with patience and skill. Abundant rainfall in most years made large irrigation works unnecessary. The valley floor contained enough land to support the community during good years. The Grand Ronde Indians managed to retain the land on which they built their dreams until the twentieth century, when they finally faced the loss of land that savaged so many other Indian communities as well. The Indians at Grand Ronde also took advantage of the opportunity to learn agricultural skills alongside White farmers in the Willamette Valley. The cash they earned for their labor purchased needed supplies and implements that the government failed to provide....

... Federal allotment policy and pressures from Whites who desired access to rich Grand Ronde land produced severe difficulties in the twentieth century. The loss of land eventually eroded the foundation for independence the people had forged, requiring further adaptations. The Grand Ronde community endures to this day, however, having survived the loss of land and even termination. The story of this reservation community should not be examined as if everything were leading inevitably to these future troubles. In making the transition to reservation life, the people of Grand Ronde created a community strong enough to weather the coming challenges.

When the Grand Ronde resident shared his memories of the 1855 treaty council with the visiting linguist, he explained that his people, the Tualatins, had determined to accept the Grand Ronde Valley in exchange for their native lands. He recalled that the people decided, "[W]e will make it our own place." After thirty years in their reservation home, the inevitable delays and setbacks balanced by numerous accomplishments, the Indians of Grand Ronde had, indeed, made it their own place.

◈ FURTHER READING

Bauer, William. *"We Were All Like Migrant Workers Here": Work, Community and Memory on California's Round Valley Reservation, 1850–1941* (2009).

Bighorse, Tiana. *Bighorse the Warrior* (1990).

Bray, Kingsley. *Crazy Horse: A Lakota Life* (2006).

Colwell-Chanthaphonh, Chip. *Massacre at Camp Grant: Forgetting and Remembering Apache History* (2007).

Denetdale, Jennifer Nez. *Reclaiming Diné History: The Legacies of Navajo Chief Manuelito and Juanita* (2007).

Fisher, Andrew. *Shadow Tribe: The Making of Columbia River Indian Identity* (2010).

Gentin-Pilawa, C. Joseph. *Crooked Path to Allotment: The Fight Over Federal Indian Policy After the Civil War* (2012).

Greene, Jerome A., ed. *Lakota and Cheyenne: Indian Views of the Great Sioux War, 1876–1877* (1994).

———. *Washita: The U.S. Army and the Southern Cheyennes, 1867–1869* (2004).

Hämäläinen, Pekka. *The Comanche Empire* (2008).

Hardorff, Richard G., ed. *Lakota Recollections of the Custer Fight: New Sources of Indian-Military History* (1997).

Jacoby, Karl. *Shadows at Dawn: An Apache Massacre and the Violence of History* (2008).

Kavanagh, Thomas W. *Comanche Political History: An Ethnohistorical Perspective, 1706–1875* (1996).

Knack, Martha. *Boundaries Between: The Southern Paiutes, 1775–1995* (2001).

Larson, Robert W. *Red Cloud: Warrior-Statesman of the Lakota Sioux* (1997).

McCrady, David. *Living with Strangers: The Nineteenth-Century Sioux and the Canadian-American Borderlands* (2006).

Moore, William Haas. *Chiefs, Agents, and Soldiers: Conflict on the Navajo Frontier, 1868–1882* (1994).

Ostler, Jeffrey. *The Plains Sioux and U.S. Colonialism from Lewis and Clark to Wounded Knee* (2004).

Paul, Eli R., ed. *Autobiography of Red Cloud: War Leader of the Oglalas* (1997).

———, ed. *The Nebraska Indian Wars Reader, 1865–1877* (1998).

Pearson, J. Diane. *The Nez Perces in the Indian Territory* (2008).

Rand, Jacki. *Kiowa Humanity and the Invasion of the State* (2008).

Rankin, Charles E., ed. *Legacy: New Perspectives on the Battle of the Little Bighorn* (1996).

Roberts, David. *Once They Moved Like the Wind: Cochise, Geronimo, and the Apache Wars* (1993).

Robinson III, Charles M. *A Good Year To Die: The Story of the Great Sioux War* (1995).

Shepherd, Jeffrey P. *We Are an Indian Nation: A History of the Hualapai People* (2010).

Smoak, Gregory. *Ghost Dances and Identity: Prophetic Religion and American Indian Ethnogenesis in the Nineteenth Century* (2006).

Stamm, IV, Henry E. *People of the Wind River: The Eastern Shoshones, 1825–1900* (1999).

Utley, Robert W. *Geronimo* (2012).

———. *The Indian Frontier of the American West, 1846–1890* (1984).

———. *The Lance and the Shield: The Life and Times of Sitting Bull* (1993).

Welch, James, and Paul Stekler. *Killing Custer: The Battle of the Little Bighorn and the Fate of the Plains Indians* (1994).

West, Elliott. *The Last Indian War: The Nez Perce Story* (2009).

Wishart, David J. *An Unspeakable Sadness: The Dispossession of the Nebraska Indians* (1994).

CHAPTER 11

Education, Land, and Sovereignty in the Assimilation Era, 1890–1920

As the federal government and U.S. military confined American Indians to reservations, federal officials and reformers who saw themselves as "friends of the Indian" attempted to assimilate Native peoples into the larger American society. These reformers considered private property, Christianity, the English language, and the opportunity to farm or learn a useful trade to be central to American values and success. The effort to assimilate American Indians took place on three fronts. First, the General Allotment Act of 1887, popularly called the Dawes Act, followed the model of the Homestead Act of 1862. The Dawes Act broke up communally held reservation lands and allotted parcels of land to individual families. The government could sell any unallotted land to non-Indian farmers. Second, on- and-off reservation boarding schools instructed Native students in English and attempted to inculcate Anglo-American values. Finally, the U.S. Congress and Supreme Court limited Native peoples' ability to exercise tribal sovereignty. Perhaps nowhere can we see these assaults more clearly than in Indian Territory. Initially, the Dawes Act exempted the Five Tribes (Cherokee, Chickasaw, Choctaw, Creek, and Seminole) in Indian Territory, but in the 1890s a commission headed by Henry Dawes called for the allotment of their lands and the end of tribal sovereignty. Cherokees, led by Principal Chief S. H. Mayes, protested against the division of lands and the United States' attempt to usurp Native authority. They called attention to the impressive institutions the Cherokees had established following their removal to Indian Territory. Even given these and other achievements, the United States forced the Five Tribes to submit to allotment; by 1907, the dream of separate statehood had vanished when the new state of Oklahoma swallowed Indian Territory. Under the rapidly changing circumstances of the period, did federal policymakers have other choices? Was the course they chose the only pragmatic one?

Even with all the difficulties that attended this period, it is important not to portray the assimilation era solely in bleak terms. On the national level, Indians created new organizations, including the Native American Church and the Society of American Indians, that offered creative religious and political responses to this new age. Within different Indian communities, people faced compelling questions. They made far-reaching decisions about the *nature of leadership, the kind of economy they could develop, and how they would educate their children. Largely unnoticed, individuals and families weathered the trying period and in many instances built foundations for further revitalization in the years to come.*

◈ DOCUMENTS

Although the majority of non–Indians of the nineteenth century supported the General Allotment Act of 1887 (the Dawes Act), many Native people and scholars today agree that it was ill advised. For those reservations that came under its provisions and the subsequent policies designed to further reduce Native landholdings, the results usually were disastrous. Indians in the area that later comprised the lower 48 states lost two of every three acres that they held before 1887. Document 1 provides Dawes' rationale for pursuing allotment. A reading of the Act, which is excerpted in Document 2, gives a firsthand sense of the era's federal objectives. Although the U.S. Congress initially exempted Cherokees and the other Five Tribes from the provisions of the General Allotment Act, Native people in Indian Territory had only a temporary respite. Non-Indian intruders in Indian Territory continued to demand the division of the tribal estate. In 1893 Congress created a commission, chaired by Dawes, to negotiate with these Indian nations. The Cherokees knew this commission imperiled their lands and institutions. As Document 3 reveals, they defended themselves with great eloquence, but it would be to no avail. The Dawes Commission soon began to allot Cherokee land.

In the late nineteenth and early twentieth centuries, Indigenous people in the United States faced pressures on their land and sovereignty not only in places like Oklahoma, but also in areas that were further west still—even out across the Pacific. The history of Native Hawaiians provides an excellent way to understand the varied experiences of Indigenous people. In Document 4, the deposed Queen Lili'uokalani (Kanaka Maoli) describes the United States' coup against her government and seeks compensation for this injustice. Why did the United States overthrow Lili'uokalani? Did Lili'uokalani's strategies differ from those of the Cherokee leaders?

In addition to U.S. claims on their land and sovereignty, American Indians encountered the United States' efforts to reeducate their children. Government officials forced Indian children to attend federal and mission schools. Students and families responded in a variety of ways to these schools. Some of these schools were located near their homes, but others were hundreds or even thousands of miles away. Until the early twentieth century, Richard Henry Pratt's Carlisle Indian Industrial School in Pennsylvania furnished a model for many of these institutions. In Document 5, Shoshone Dorothy Peche describes her time at a boarding school on Wyoming's Wind River Reservation. How did school officials attempt to assimilate Native students into United States society? How did the students interact with one another at the school? Boarding schools were a family experience, as Document 6 demonstrates. Nomlacki Minnie Wilburn of the Round Valley Reservation pleaded with her son Clarence to leave the Sherman Indian Institute in Riverside, California, and return home for the summer. How did boarding schools affect students' families back on the reservation?

1. Henry Dawes Supports the Allotment of the Cherokee Nation, 1885

Now, that the Indian can be made something of, I want to tell you what I have seen during the last summer. I spent my vacation among the five civilized tribes, as they are called.... [After Indian Removal,] the United States gave them a patent to that land [in Indian Territory]—an absolute deed. I have seen the original of it; it is just as perfect as any deed you ever held. They were, from that time, absolutely and permanently fixed there ... they have wrought out a government on their own soil without our help. The fundamental idea was that they stood upon their own land, and knew it could not be taken away from them. They have a principal chief and a written constitution, and a legislature elected once in four years; it is composed of a Senate and House. They have a Supreme Court, a County Court, and a school system of which compulsory education is a feature. It compels every child within school age to attend school, which is taught in the English language. They have a high school for girls and one for boys, in buildings that would be respectable in Massachusetts. In one of these buildings, ... I saw one hundred girls taught by Indian teachers, superintended by a white woman. I heard Indian girls recite to an Indian teacher in Moral Philosophy. I went a few miles away to a high school for boys, one class of which were laying out surveys, and it was beyond my comprehension whether they were good or bad; another class was reciting Latin; some of them are sent, at the expense of the Government, into the States for education. I once heard a Senator of the United States,—and not a great while ago, and he was born in Massachusetts and educated there—I heard him in the Senate of the United States denounce this appropriation for Indian schools, declaring that there was not an instance of an Indian who had been educated and made to take care of himself. I heard Mr. Garrett, of Princeton, introduce that Senator to this High School and tell them that he was the silver-tongued orator of the United States. He told them of their possibilities and capacities, and how to work out their problem. I had a further satisfaction when we called a pure-blooded Indian before us, and he discoursed upon what had been done by their people. The same Senator asked him: "Where did you get your education ?" "At Dartmouth College, Sir." The head chief told us that there was not a family in that whole Nation that had not a home of its own. There was not a pauper in that Nation, and the Nation did not owe a dollar. It built its own capitol, in which we had this examination, and it built its schools and its hospitals. Yet the defect of the system was apparent. They have got as far as they can go because they own their land in common ... under that there is no enterprise to make your home any

Proceedings of the *Third Annual Meeting of the Lake Mohonk Conference of the Friends of the Indian, Held October 7 to 9, 1885* (Philadelphia: Sherman & Co., Printers, 1886), 42–43.

better than that of your neighbors. There is no selfishness, which is at the bottom of civilization. Till this people will consent to give up their lands, and divide them among their citizens so that each can own the land he cultivates, they will not make much more progress.

2. Cherokee Delegates Defend Their Land and Institutions, 1895

To the Senate
And House of Representatives
of the United States Congress:

... These are times of imminent danger to those institutions of government and tenure of property that the Cherokees have brought with them from the darkness of time immemorial, modified somewhat by the enlightened influences of your great constitution but distinctive still as Cherokee institutions. The Cherokees are fully alive to the situation, and they know that unless in some way congress shall become acquainted rapidly with their true condition, all that they hold dear of country and people will be swept away by the hands that they have heretofore confidently looked to for protection, and which have in gentleness and friendship been so often extended to them. For some reasons that we cannot explain, the Cherokees have been traduced and grievously misrepresented by persons high in authority, from whom we have had every reason to expect fair statement. It is natural to love the country one lives in, if that country protects life, promotes happiness, and insures equality. When a people are found who are intensely patriotic, it can be taken for granted that their government gives them such assurances. The Cherokees are such a people; there is not upon the face of the earth today a people more thoroughly contented with their condition than the Cherokees. In his humble western home, sequestered from the mad rush one sees in the east, you will find the Cherokee a sober, industrious, religious gentleman, earning his daily bread by honest labor upon the soil, of which he is equal owner with every one else in the nation, irrespective of superior advantage such as wealth, opportunity, or education gives.

He believes in common education; such as is natural with his ideas of common property. Therefore, under the constitution adopted in 1839, we find this provision: "Religion, morality, and knowledge being necessary for good government, the preservation of liberty, and the happiness of mankind, schools, and the means of education, shall forever be encouraged in this nation." Faithful to the idea here expressed, the history of the advancement of the educational interests of the Cherokees for the last fifty years cannot but please the mind and heart of him who loves his fellow-man for the good that he promises. Now, notwithstanding the pall that the civil war threw over the land, the progress of the Cherokee schools and facilities for common education has been marked and rapid. Now, with a population of 40,000 Cherokees, we have over one hundred common schools, running nine months a year, with capable,

---

This document can be found in the Cherokee Papers, Oklahoma Historical Society, Oklahoma City, Oklahoma.

competent teachers, generally comfortable school houses, where all of necessary appliances, books, etc., are supplied by the Cherokee nation; a male and female college, of brick and stone, at a cost not exceeding each year over $150,000, afford to the youth of both sexes an opportunity of higher education; an orphan asylum of sufficient size to accommodate every orphan of school age in the nation, which has cost over $100,000, have now an attendance of over 2,000 orphans. We have also an asylum for the infirm and unfortunate (a home for these poor stricken people). At the male seminary this year there [are] over one hundred and eighty young men, at the female seminary over two hundred of our girls. The several missionary societies have not less than fifteen or twenty schools in the various parts of our country, encouraged by generous gifts of land upon the part of the Cherokees. To these earnest Christian workers in our midst we also appeal, in our time of extremity for national existence, to assist us in refuting the false charges made with no other motive, we believe, than to induce congress to withdraw its powerful protection from us, that we might become easy prey of unscrupulous avarice and greed, as the hungry beast devoured his milder companion of the forest. These religious denominations among us, who brought to us the beautiful Christian religion, who witnessed the sowing of its seeds and now behold its plant of vigorous growth in the full bearing of its fruits, can bear us witness of the many false charges of retrogression, immorality, lawlessness, and crime among the Cherokees. We ask, when our enemies traduce us and when grave charges of malfeasance in public offices and trust are hurled at us, that you will require specific proof to accompany the accusation.

Churches are everywhere, organized throughout our land, and their efficient and powerful auxiliaries, the Sabbath schools, are conducted every Sunday in our various churches and school-houses, where the same lesson papers are used that your children study throughout this land and elsewhere. All of this, with the exception of the missionary efforts among us, to which we largely contribute, is done at no expense whatever to the United States, but entirely at the expense of the Cherokees. Is it to be doubted that a people fostering and encouraging such institutions have all the finer sensibilities of education and Christian manhood that will be found among similar communities in the States? Could a nation of irresponsible, corrupt, criminal people produce such conditions? Are these the results of the evil and corruption that the Dawes Commission assert pervade the very atmosphere down there? We earnestly ask that before laying the axe to the root of the tree you yourselves have planted and carefully attended, that you examine the fruits thereof and take not the word of some persons controlled by envy, and in a moment of irritability against us for not blindly following their suggestion, consent to and advise our destruction. We submit that in the nature of things, it would have been impossible for the Dawes commission to have found no good existing in our country, yet not one redeeming word do we find in their report, if there is any. Did they not see us in the worship of the same God they worship? Did they not hear us while with bowed heads we implored the intercession of the Son of God? Then why have they with the black veil of corrupt charges obscured the good that honor would have compelled them to acknowledge if they found it?

In our governmental affairs we have followed in the footsteps of your people; our form of government is as yours, with its three departments, executive, legislative and judicial, where the same authorities govern and the same methods and rules obtain, perhaps somewhat modified, as among you. It may be that at our legislature some of your practices have been adopted, and it may be that some of our methods in the struggle for office may partake of the taint we sometimes hear charged against your legislatures. Walking in your footsteps, it could hardly be expected that, in following the good you practice, some of your evils may not have also left their mark. We pursue some short cuts in office down there sometimes that would hardly receive the approbation of a legislative reformer; but that we are one half as corrupt as the Dawes commission represent us we emphatically deny, neither can we admit that we are to any degree as corrupt as the newspapers assert of your average legislatures....

The Cherokees wish to call your attention to the size of their present country. Within our country as at present bounded there are less than five million acres of land; our population is thirty thousand; the estimate of the number of acres includes river beds, and portions, and all that would be necessary for public travel and commerce. At a glance it will be seen that we have now less than one hundred and sixty acres to the head. The proportion of the arable land to that unfit for cultivation is, by the most liberal estimate, not exceeding one to four, so it will be seen that today the Cherokees have less than forty acres of tillable land to the individual. We invite your close attention to this fact, for not the least among the influences seeking the destruction of our government and the opening of the country is the hope that homes may thereby be obtained for the white people who would come in. It could not be so in the Cherokee nation; we have not now more than will suffice the immediate necessities of our people; nor could we consent to part with any more land whatever without gross injustice to our poor, who depend upon agriculture and stock-raising for subsistence. There is no necessity for a town-site law in the Cherokee nation. The statement by the Dawes commission that towns had been erected, costly business houses and residences built in the Cherokee nation by non citizens is absolutely false with not a single exception. We have half a score or more of beautiful towns in the Cherokee nation, beautifully and symmetrically surveyed, containing many substantial and even fine structures; but all has been done by citizens of the nation, and such buildings are not occupied or owned in any manner by aliens, nor have they any money in them. Our towns have good systems of municipal government, the result of liberal legislation on the part of the national council. A municipal government is run by a mayor and a board of aldermen, and called a town council. The quiet and neatness of our towns commend us to all our visitors. There are no white aliens doing business among us, other than those engaged in farming; we do not, as alleged, invite them into our country; we do not invite or use their money in building our towns; we put every impediment we can in the way of their coming among us; we do not need them in our midst, but we are a hospitable people, our friendship extends beyond the lines of our country, and in our acts of hospitality we sometimes harbor in our midst coming in the guise of friends, who, through motives of envy and covetousness, subsequently advise our undoing. Our country is indeed fair to look upon; to us its lovely valleys, limpid streams, flowing prairies, waving forests, and grand hills are an Eden. There, over fifty years ago, with specious promises of everlasting protection, you planted us, literally driving us from our homes in the mountains of Georgia, Tennessee, and North Carolina. "As long as the grass grows and water runs," wrote General Jackson, "shall the country remain yours." "No state or territorial line shall ever surround you," were the words [of] your minister who induced us to go to that country, and his words are engrafted into the treaty. Now, after the lapse of fifty years, when the bodies of those who made these promises to us have been consigned to the tomb, and their names have taken their places in history, many of them for all time, you, their children, tell us, the children of those with whom they treated, that your parents did not mean all they said, and were only preparing a temporary solution of the questions they were pretending to settle....

S. H. Mayes,
Principal Chief,
and other delegates

3. The General Allotment Act (Dawes Act), 1887

An act to provide for the allotment of lands in severalty to Indians on the various reservations, and to extend the protection of the laws of the United States and the Territories over the Indians, and for other purposes.

Be it enacted by the Senate and House of Representatives of the United States of America in Congress assembled, That in all cases where any tribe or band of Indians has been, or shall hereafter be, located upon any reservation created for their use, either by treaty stipulation or by virtue of an act of Congress or executive order setting apart the same for their use, the President of the United States be, and he hereby is, authorized, whenever in his opinion any reservation or any part thereof of such Indians is advantageous for agricultural and grazing purposes, to cause said reservation, or any part thereof, to be surveyed, or resurveyed if necessary, and to allot the lands in said reservation in severalty to any Indian located thereon in quantities as follows:

To each head of a family, one-quarter of a section;

To each single person over eighteen years of age, one-eighth of a section;

To each orphan child under eighteen years of age, one-eighth of a section; and

To each other single person under eighteen years now living, or who may be born prior to the date of the order of the President directing an allotment of the lands embraced in any reservation, one-sixteenth of a section: *Provided,* That in case there is not sufficient land in any of said reservations to allot lands to each individual of the classes above named in quantities as above provided, the lands

---

This document can be found as the General Allotment Act, February 8, 1887, *U.S. Statutes at Large* 24: 366–391.

embraced in such reservation or reservations shall be allotted to each individual of each of said classes pro rata in accordance with the provisions of this act: *And provided further,* That where the treaty or act of Congress setting apart such reservation, provides for the allotment of lands in severalty in quantities in excess of those herein provided, the President, in making allotments upon such reservation shall allot the lands to each individual Indian belonging thereon in quantity as specified in such treaty or act: *And provided further,* That when the lands allotted are only valuable for grazing purposes, an additional allotment of such grazing lands, in quantities as above provided, shall be made to each individual.

Sec. 2. That all allotments set apart under the provisions of this act shall be selected by the Indians, heads of families selecting for their minor children, and the agents shall select for each orphan child, and in such manner as to embrace the improvements of the Indians making the selection. Where the improvements of two or more Indians have been made on the same legal subdivision of land, unless they shall otherwise agree, a provisional line may be run dividing said lands between them, and the amount to which each is entitled shall be equalized in the assignment of the remainder of the land to which they are entitled under this act: *Provided,* That if any one entitled to an allotment shall fail to make a selection within four years after the President shall direct that allotments may be made on a particular reservation, the Secretary of the Interior may direct the agent of such tribe or band, if such there be, and if there be no agent, then a special agent appointed for that purpose, to make a selection for such Indian, which election shall be allotted as in cases where selections are made by the Indians, and patents shall issue in like manner.

Sec. 3. That the allotments provided for in this act shall be made by special agents appointed by the President for such purpose, and the agents in charge of the respective reservations on which the allotments are directed to be made, under such rules and regulations as the Secretary of the Interior may from time to time prescribe, and shall be certified by such agents to the Commissioner of Indian Affairs, in duplicate, one copy to be retained in the Indian Office and the other to be transmitted to the Secretary of the Interior for his action, and to be deposited in the General Land Office....

Sec. 5. That upon the approval of the allotments provided for in this act by the Secretary of the Interior, he shall cause patents to issue therefor in the name of the allottees, which patents shall be of the legal effect, and declare that the United States does and will hold the land thus allotted, for the period of twenty-five years, in trust for the sole use and benefit of the Indian to whom such allotment shall have been made, or, in case of his decease, of his heirs according to the laws of the State or Territory where such land is located, and that at the expiration of said period the United States will convey the same by patent to said Indian, of his heirs as aforesaid, in fee, discharged of said trust and free of all charge or incumbrance whatsoever....

Sec. 6. That upon the completion of said allotments and the patenting of the lands to said allottees, each and every member of the respective bands or tribes of Indians to whom allotments have been made shall have the benefit of and be subject to the laws, both civil and criminal, of the State or Territory in which they may reside; and no Territory shall pass or enforce any law denying any such Indian within its jurisdiction the equal protection of the law. And every Indian both within the territorial limits of the United States to whom allotments shall have been made under the provisions of this act, or under any law or treaty, and every Indian born within the territorial limits of the United States who has voluntarily taken up, within said limits, his residence separate and apart from any tribe of Indians therein, and has adopted the habits of civilized life, is hereby declared to be a citizen of the United States, and is entitled to all the rights, privileges, and immunities of such citizens, whether said Indian has been or not, by birth or otherwise, a member of any tribe of Indians within the territorial limits of the United States without in any manner, impairing or otherwise affecting the right of any such Indian to tribal or other property....

Sec. 8. That the provision of this act shall not extend to the territory occupied by the Cherokees, Creeks, Choctaws, Chickasaws, Seminoles, and Osage, Miamies and Peorias, and Sacs and Foxes, in the Indian Territory, nor to any of the reservations of the Seneca Nation of New York Indians in the State of New York, nor to that strip of territory in the State of Nebraska adjoining the Sioux Nation on the south added by executive order....

4. Queen Lili'uokalani (Hawaiian) Protests the United States' Annexation of Hawai'i, 1905

The undersigned, a Hawaiian by birth, and by virtue thereof a legalized subject of the United States of America, enjoying life under the protection of its flag and the Constitution and laws thereof, hereby respectfully petitions the honorable Congress of the United States of America, and prays that this petition and claim relative to her official and personal status and legal rights whatsover in the premises under the Constitution and laws may be examined and inquired into, scrutinized, adjusted, and finally settled according to the principles of common justice and equity, and by what ex parte means those rights became involved.

That prior to January 17, 1893, a constitutional monarchy existed in the Hawaiian Islands; that Hawaii was a free and independent sovereign State, recognized as such by all the enlightened powers of the world, especially so by the Government of the United States of America, for upwards of nearly three-quarters of a century, and that Hawaii ever enjoyed the most cordial and friendly relations with those powers.

That upon said January 17, 1893, a few of the foreign influential citizens of Honolulu secretly got together and led others in a conspiracy to overthrow the constitutional government of Hawaii, thereby committing acts of treason.

That they knew full well such overt acts were unconstitutional and contrary to the authority of the monarchical government of Hawaii; but they had sought the aid of the American minister resident, John L. Stevens, to support them, who

---

"Claim of Liliuokalani," *Senate Documents*, Document No. 66, 59th Congress, 1st Session (1905).

in turn made known the wishes of the conspirators to Capt. G. C. Wiltse, of the cruiser *Boston*, then stationed in the harbor of Honolulu, and ordered him to land her forces, which was obeyed....

Once on shore the forces of the United States of America were marched to and immediately in front of the royal palace, where petitioner then resided, being opposite to the government building. At or a little prior to this time the government building was taken possession of by the conspirators, from whence a proclamation was read purporting to declare the establishment of a provisional government, whose vice-president made a demand upon petitioner's marshal and the members of her cabinet to deliver up the arms and ammunitions of war of the monarchical government, at the same time informing them that the provisional government had been recognized by the American minister resident of the United of America, John L. Stevens. The petitioner was also called upon by the same person to surrender the reins of her government and to follow the orders of the provisional government.

Being in much fear and within sight of the American forces that were halted in front of the royal palace, it was made evident to petitioner and every one else that if a negative answer had been made at the time to his demand there would have been a bloody riot; and whereas the said American minister resident, John L. Stevens, had previously recognized, supported, and provided the provisional government with the forces and arms of the United States of America; therefore, in order to avoid spilling the blood of her loyal subjects, and owing to such aid being given the conspirators by said minister resident, petitioner acquiesced to his demands and gave up the reins of government, but only on condition then reserved that a protest be filed, and was filed, with the United States Government against the acts of its minister resident, John L. Stevens; and that accordingly such protest was approved by petitioner's cabinet on said January 17, 1893, and duly submitted to the administration in Washington, praying it to inquire by what authority petitioner was divested of her rights, and by what authority the aid of the American minister resident in Hawaii was extended to the conspirators....

That from the time of the filing of petitioners protest against the overthrow of the monarchical government on January 17, 1893, up to the filing of this petition, now nearly thirteen years, no adjustment of the rights herein mentioned has been made by the Government of the United States of America.

That petitioner being rightfully the reigning sovereign under the constitution and laws of the Hawaiian Islands, then an independent sovereignty, was in receipt of a large and lucrative annuity, besides which she was in receipt for her exclusive use of all and singular the rents accruing from the Crown lands by virtue of law and they formed no part of the Hawaiian Government revenues prior to said overthrow.

That from the time of said overthrow and up to the present time petitioner has been wholly deprived of the aforesaid income revenues; that she has suffered greatly in mind, body, and health, and in addition thereto her private estate has been and is reduced to poverty and want; that petitioner asks compensation for all the wrongs done and for damages sustained.

That petitioner is advised, and therefore respectfully suggests the sum of $10,000,000 as a proper and reasonable amount in settlement for all the damages and losses sustained by her, and in consideration therefor she hereby solemnly agrees to and with the United States of America to relinquish all her claims of whatsoever kind or nature.

That in consideration of the premises and in common with all other subjects of the Territory of Hawaii the petitioner submits to the present form of government erected since the annexation of Hawaii to the United States of America, and that petitioner has ever since been a loyal and obedient subject under the Constitution and laws of the same and under the constitution and laws of the Territory of Hawaii.

Finally, relying upon such settlement as ought to be based upon the principles of right and justice she now submits her case to the Congress of the United States of America, trusting that it shall render equity, justice, and right in the premises with reasonable dispatch.

Petitioner comes now before your honorable body without the aid of an attorney at law for the reason that she is without means to pay for further legal advice or services, having already paid out large sums of money in that respect. (But it ought not to take a legal talent or mind to gain the attention of Your Excellency the President of the United States or of the Congress of the United States of America.) Petitioner prays that it may please Your Excellency the President and the Congress of the United States of America to look favorably on this petition.

5. Dorothy Peche (Shoshone) Recalls Attending a Government Boarding School, c. 1917

... [The government school] wasn't a very nice place at all. It was unsanitary and then they bathed as many kids as they could get into one tub ... 'Cause that was all there was, one bath tub, at that time. And then there was an older girl over seven or eight kids and all in the same water. Oh, there's a lot of things like that....

And you dasn't say anything because you'd get punished every time that you turned around....

For speaking your own native language for one thing and you were severely punished for that....

They would put you in the ... "jail." It was a room down in the basement with no windows or anything and they'd give us bread and water for.... 'till they said it wasn't so or something. They kept you there until you said that you didn't mean what you said or was supposed to have said that.... Then they would caution you not to say it again and then there was a lot of Indian girls, like us, we totally forgot that we was Indians, you know, our language....

I had a sister that was everlastingly down there, because she was one of these feisty ones. She would fight back, you know, and call them names and all that....

And she was down there and she was everlastingly fighting somebody or somebody was fighting with her.... [Another girl] was just the meanest human on earth when she was going to school there. She was one of the older girls that

Warm Valley Historical Project, American Heritage Center, University of Wyoming.

was over a number of small ones, you know. When we were just treated like slaves at times, and then at other times we were treated like we were in the army, you know, we marched and we were in uniforms, I guess from over here ... this is ... on ... this was an army post somewhere.

... And then the girls were in the hickory ... the everyday dress was ... you only had two dresses, that was the hickory, like this old ticking, you know that they put on pillows....

And those were our everyday clothes and then we had our uniforms that we wore to church on Sunday or on parade and we was everlastingly parading, you know. Marching ... and we did that all the time, several times a day, you know. Marched here and marched there. We got to be real marchers ... I'll tell you! ....

And some of those little ones, you know, it was really hard on them. 'Cause the big ones ... was just as mean as she could be. If they stepped out of line or fell down, she would raise the devil with them. And then the matron just stood up for [the older girls], that's what she was supposed to be doing, just like an officer or something in the army. [She] would yell at you, just like you was in the army.

... And in those days, they'd round the kids up, the Indian kids up, and made them go to school, you know, whether they wanted to go or not, or their parents. They just took you and put you down there. That's the reason there was a lot of them there. And I know, my sister, she ran away a couple of times but they got her and brought her back. [Another girl] ran away every time she turned around. And they were so mean to her. That's why she ran away. And then she always had poor eyes, you know, she couldn't see good in the first place and they didn't care whether you could see good or not. She couldn't do anything in school. She couldn't keep up with her grades or anything. She couldn't see! She always had bad eyes....

She wore ... a fence post, for a long time. It was about that big around and about as long as a fence post and she wore that for a long time and she kept running away anyway. She just got to where she could just handle that post like nothing. And she ran away anyway and then they put two of them on her. One on each ... until Rev. [John] Roberts came down there one Sunday for Sunday school, for church on Sunday, you know. And boy! He raised the devil out there! But they still kept her and her posts....

One on each leg. And she used to jump out of the window with those two posts. Occasionally, she got to where she didn't care, you know. And she had a boyfriend.... He was in the background somewhere. I don't know where, out in the haystack or somewhere, I don't know exactly. They used to kid him about being in the haystack all the time. I don't know.... And then he helped her from the outside because a lot of them girls that run away did. They'd tie their sheets together and there'd be boys waiting outside to pick them up. And then the boys would get into... That's how they got into dormitories too, those boys. Some of the boys down there. Some of the bigger boys. They would get into the dormitories, crawled up the sheets, the girls ... some of those girls would tie all their sheets together and bring them up to the dormitories. It would scare the rest of us half to death. Afraid of them, because ... I must have been about ten or twelve years old, I think that I was in fourth grade. Somewhere along in there. And they had the meanest teacher down there that ever lived.... She looked just like a witch. Skinny and ... well, just like a witch. She was mean. She was everlastingly popping the kids on the hand with a ruler, you know. I know [some boys] used to get into a fistfight with her ... and then they would get punished too ... I suppose. That was going on all the time, at the school. You couldn't learn anything because there was so much fighting and ... and there was certain kids that they just picked on all the time. The teachers, you know, and never gave them a chance to learn anything. I don't think I learned a thing down there but mopping floors and washing dishes and that sort of thing. It wasn't very pleasant at all....

They had some boys in jail there, just like they had the girls, ... on bread and water because they had done something and quite a few of them boys was from the Cheyenne Reservation.... And he was always in jail and they was basketball players and football players and they were everlastingly being punished. They couldn't go to games or anything. That's the way they got even with them....

We had an Arapaho girl that come to school ... she was one of the older girls and she sneaked food out of the kitchen and put it in her bloomer legs around here [laughs] and then, down to the basement and poke it through, you know, where the pipes come through the wall in the basement. She'd push the food in through there for a lot of those kids in jail, boys and all....

Me and my sister, we would have been awfully hungry if it wasn't for Marie. She'd sneak food out for us once in a while, whenever she could. Like a sandwich or something....

Oh, everything was boiled. Gravy ... meat boiled in ... and then gravy, meat in the broth, most of the time, that's all. And then oatmeal. They never had any sugar down there. They had syrup down there and they would pour syrup on everything. It was like feeding a bunch of pigs, if you ask me, lots of times. But it was, World War I was on that he time and everybody was having a hard time. But that was a self-supporting school down there. They raised everything down at that school. There was no excuse for it ... That's just the way they treated us Indians. That's the way ... the whole thing of it....

World War I, was going on and my dad volunteered to go to the war and mom had two kids, two small kids, besides Alice and I and they put us there. He brought us down on horseback. And then ... he came once during all the school season to see us. And we never saw mom. And we had long hair, Alice and I had hair.... Our hair was dragging on the floor, just like my mother, she had long hair too. And we got lousy down there. Oh! And they just grabbed our braids and cut them off, the matrons down there. Talk about mad! Mom was ready to fight when she seen us when we got home. She never seen us until school was out and then they wanted to keep me there the following summer on a detail. They kept several kids there, you know, during the summer time. But mom wouldn't let them. They said ... she said no, they'll come home....

She explained it to them that dad was supposed to be going to war and she had to have some kids. I was the oldest one and they had to have me to help and we lived up there at Crow Heart, just under the hill.... We had a house there,

... That was supposed to be my allotment, but, they never allotted it to me. I don't have any allotment. A lot of us don't....

You weren't supposed to speak [your language]. They were trying to make white people out of us! ... They were trying to change us.... There was a lot of them was ... forgot about their language. My husband was a Flathead Indian ... They put him in ... His mother and father separated and he was abused something terrible because he couldn't talk English. He talked French all the time and he completely forgot his language because he said they beat him and made him kneel in a broomstick handle, hours at a time and he got whipped several times, he said with a wet towel....

When you can't speak it ... And then being small, like I was, I suppose it had something to do with it, because you just ... You just forget.... Block it out of your mind and do as they do. As you were supposed to do down there. That's the way it was....

My mother was a Bannock and she spoke ... I never did hear her speak her language at all. Of course, she went away to school, too. She went to Carlisle, too....

Well, for one thing, Oh, there's a lot of things, like food. We used to, I used to go with my grandma and we'd dig ... we'd go every ... spring, I think it was spring, we went and we'd gather roots like the sago bulbs and bitter roots and all those kinds of things for our food, you know. And you just lost track of all that and you even forgot what the thing was, what you were looking for, like. You have to know what you were doing, and you'd forget. Oh, there's just a lot of things ... And the way you dressed ... and the way you acted lots of times.

... Alice and I had these two great big braids that hung down our backs, plum to the floor and they cut it off and that just ... Oh, that was something awful to us! It was just like cutting our throats [laughs], because we didn't believe in wearing ... and we weren't brought up to have short hair ... and there was just a lot of things.... It was Depression time, ... my dad made us kids' shoes so that we could go to school. We had a terrible time. He made his shoes for us, Alice and I, so that we could go to school. And we made our own clothes. And I think that we had one outfit that we wore to school and as soon as we got from school, we took it off and our middies were washed and done up for the next day and our skirts were all cleaned so that we'd have it for the next day of school. That's after we left the school down there.

6. Minnie Wilburn (Nomlacki) Wants Her Son, Clarence, to Come Home from the Sherman Indian Institute, 1918

My Dear Son,
Will write you a letter to let you know that we are sending the money to [Round Valley Reservation school superintendent Walter] McConihe for your return transportation. You say you want to work down there [in southern California]. There is lots of work up here. Ben wanted you to work with him,

---

Minnie Wilburn to Clarence Wilburn, 1918, Student Case Files, National Archives and Records Administration, Laguna Niguel, CA.

said that you both could make a hundred dollars a piece a month. And we want you to come. Besides Tina is coming the middle of June and we will all be together once again. There is a lady and her little boy coming with Tina. We've been very busy putting in garden, planted lots of beans, corn, potatoes and everything. There hasn't been but one little rain this spring. We are praying for a rain so everything will come up. One patch of potatoes is up, have radishes to use. Papa and John [went] after the horses today. Papa is going to ride Nig to Traver's. He is fat now. Buck is fat. I expect he will throw you off now. Queen has a colt. We sent John after your dog Buck the other day and Tom wouldn't give him up. He said you owed him $6.00 and that if we payed him the $6.00 we could have him. Looks like when you pruned the orchard that would pay for that. He promised you half of the fruit and you didn't get any. I know all the time that he wouldn't want to give him up. We wanted him to catch coyotes with.

He said you tryed to sell him to Ned for $5.00. You get him Clarence when you come. I'll bet he's the best dog of the three. The reason Tom wants him, the coyotes are getting thick here.

[Your siblings] Tommie & Ruby are playing with some little chickens. They just got back from school. Emma has a cold. Papa complains all the time with his breast. He wants you to come and take up a homestead. The land here will be throwed open to settlement the 20 of June. You know we haven't but little range to run our stock on. Be sure and let us know when you will arrive at Dos Rios so some of them can meet you at Covelo.

Well Dear I hope this letter will find you well as it leaves me. Love & kisses from all as ever, your loving Mama.

Write soon now.

xxx R.W. xxx T.W.

P.S. we send the money to McConihe, $25.00. [Sherman Institute Superintendent Frank] Conser wrote that it would be necessary for us to send it before you came.

◈ ESSAYS

The essays that follow emphasize important aspects of late-nineteenth- and early-twentieth-century assimilationist policies and Indian responses to the demands of this transitional period. The first essay comes from Brenda Child (Red Lake Ojibwe), a professor of American Indian Studies at the University of Minnesota, whose widely acclaimed account, *Boarding School Seasons: American Indian Families, 1900–1940*, underlines both the enormous problems boarding schools posed for Indian pupils and their families as well as the strength of those families. Child presents damning details of life in these early institutions, drawing from the wealth of correspondence between students and their families.

Malinda Maynor Lowery (Lumbee), a professor of history at the University of North Carolina, explores the ways in which migrant Indian workers from North Carolina's Robeson County maintained their "Indian" identity in the face of assimilationist pressures and Jim Crow segregation. Lowery reminds us that some American Indians still lived east of the Mississippi and that they, like their western counterparts, encountered racism and economic marginalization. How did Robeson County Indians create community in the Jim Crow South? How did they use the South's racial hierarchies to establish their "Indian" identity?

Ojibwe Children and Boarding Schools

BY BRENDA CHILD (OJIBWE)

Boarding school education came to the Ojibwe people, the Anishinaabe, during a turbulent period in their history. The General Allotment Act, passed in 1887, and subsequent legislation had worked to erode the traditional, communal method of tribal landholding in favor of individual ownership on reservations. Few reservations escaped allotment. One notable exception was that of the Red Lake band in Minnesota. As historian William Watts Folwell commented about Red Lake in 1930, "It is still Indian country." For tribes across the United States, as well for many Ojibwes, the results of allotment policies and withdrawal of the protective trust relationship were an often devastating loss of country. Ojibwes in the Upper Midwest, whose seasonal economies were already challenged after being removed to new territories or having their reservation holdings reduced, could ill afford the environmental destruction and dispossession that unfolded in northern Minnesota, Wisconsin, and Michigan after the turn of the century. Land fraud was rampant, and the interests of ecocidal timber companies dominated the political landscape of the woodlands.

By 1920, the once-luxuriant pine trees in the north had been cleared from many reservations. The land base of Ojibwes had declined precipitously, and new Euro–American landowners, beneficiaries of tribal losses, populated the region. Ojibwes were expected to settle down to work as small farmers. This was not a real possibility for many Indians. Lands were so diminished in size that nothing more than a small garden was feasible for most families. Tribes complained that the allotment process itself had been unfair, that high-quality and valuable land had been lost to Indians. Undeniably, remaining reservation lands were frequently far too poor to farm. For example, in Wisconsin during the 1920s, the Lac du Flambeau Reservation was so covered by stumps and brush that the cost per acre of removing the old growth and timber company debris would have exceeded the value of the land. Lac Court Oreilles Ojibwes, who were also left with meager farming land, and the Lac du Flambeau band mostly relied on the traditional economy, tourist work, or off-reservation jobs for support. Red Cliff residents had such poor agricultural lands that most Ojibwes there were forced to labor off the reservation in the fishing and lumber industries.

The story was similar for many Ojibwes in Minnesota. After the devastation of their vast timber lands and the extensive land fraud perpetrated upon the bands congregated at the White Earth Reservation, most residents depended on wage labor or were forced to abandon the reservation entirely due to lack of opportunity. At Leech Lake, 437 allotments had been abruptly transferred from individual trust "for the benefit of the people" of the state when the Minnesota National Forest was created by an act of Congress in 1908. Twenty years later, without intended irony the park was redesigned the Chippewa National Forest.

The increased poverty and landlessness of many Ojibwes both threatened and confirmed the strength of the traditional economy. The seasonal rounds of hunting, fishing, making maple sugar, harvesting fruits and wild rice, this familiar and revered work, remained central to reservation life and Ojibwe identity in the twentieth century. Nett Lake Ojibwes, who were left with a fair amount of swampland after their allotments had been made, still retained ownership of some of the finest wild rice stands in the Great Lakes. Few Nett Lakers were able to maintain adequate gardens, but traditional subsistence activities, tourism, and off-reservation labor maintained the band. Nett Lake also increased its land base slightly in the postallotment period. The people living on the rocky Superior coast at Grand Portage fared somewhat worse. Their reduced reservation was diminished to the extent that by the 1930s, the several hundred band members there owned little more than three acres per person of the original tract that had been reserved for them by treaty in 1854.

As historian Melissa Meyer has argued, if the "government's programs of assimilation had a chance to succeed anywhere, White Earth should have become an experimental showcase" because of its incredibly rich and diverse environment of fishing lakes, rice stands, forests, and fertile farmlands. Historians have documented the corrupt history of the postallotment era at White Earth, a time when the regional pine cartel, Minnesota politicians, the federal government, local banks, and residents mingled interests to defraud conservative Ojibwes of their land and timber. Unfortunately, the corruption and fraud at White Earth was not exclusive to the reservation or even to Minnesota, but instead became part of a larger pattern of tribal dispossession in the nation.

The effects of this immense exploitation of people, land, and resources reverberated in Ojibwe country for many years. Out-migrations from reservation communities, increased participation in wage labor, and a continued degradation of wild-rice stands and other environments contributed to a deterioration of the seasonal economy. As deforestation progressed in the rustic timber and lake country, tourism contributed to tribal incomes in northern Minnesota, Wisconsin, and Michigan. Ojibwes worked at a number of off-reservation odd jobs and many found new sources of income as loggers, millers, and farm workers. Even so, seasonal changes still inspired many Ojibwes to harvest wild rice and blueberries, turn sap into maple syrup, and track deer in fresh snow.

The lives of Ojibwe people in the Upper Midwest were transformed as a result of new land tenure policies and the educational programs designed by the federal government to assure the success of allotment. Ironically, policies and practices of the assimilation years dismantled the economies of self-sufficient people who had for generations successfully educated their children in the cultural knowledge, values, and economic tradition best suited to the integrity of the woodland environment. A new educational agenda from Washington, which mandated forced acculturation away from that source of learning, would create unprecedented sources of stress for Ojibwe families and jar their distinctive cultural foundation.

Throughout most of the boarding school era, Ojibwe families encountered new economic conditions while some migrated to different homes. White Earth, the home of Mississippi, Gull Lake, Pembina, and Otter Tail Pillager bands, never fully realized the plans of Minnesota politicians who hoped to merge all Minnesota Ojibwes, except for those at Red Lake, on a single reservation. Still, migrations to the reservations "peaked in 1891 and again in 1893–1894," causing the population to double "between 1890 and 1920." The reservation was also characterized by ethnic diversity, as Metís families formed a significant community at White Earth. This community, considered among the many people who profited from the exploitation of the reservation, maintained large households with more children than their conservative Ojibwe "cousins."

Conservative families tended to be patrilineal, nuclear, with fewer children, but they identified a greater number of "dependents" in the census of 1910. The census indicated "a rise in the number of extended households" at White Earth after the economic descent precipitated by the land fraud. Widening poverty and landlessness within the community motivated conservatives to incorporate extended family and other tribal members into their households. Reckoning kin in the "Indian way" was often an informal process in a culture that respected cousins as brothers and sisters. The virtues of generosity and flexibility had always served the Ojibwes well.

Poverty, diaspora, and disease were the combined legacies of dispossession at White Earth and other reservations in the United States. In the boarding school era, tuberculosis replaced smallpox as the largest health threat to Indians. It has been estimated that one in every twenty Ojibwes was infected with the deadly disease shortly after the turn of the century. Deaths from pulmonary disease multiplied at White Earth between 1910 and 1920. In 1915, a doctor found 130 cases of it among the 898 Ojibwes he examined on the Bad River Reservation in Wisconsin. Studies conducted during the 1930s still revealed alarmingly high rates of tuberculosis among Indians in Minnesota. The suffering was widespread among Ojibwe communities, as evidenced by the high rates of the disease found at Fond du Lac and Grand Portage. At Nett Lake, an estimated 30 percent of the population was afflicted with tuberculosis. Approximately 15 percent of Minnesota Indians contracted tuberculosis at some point during their lives.

Tuberculosis statistics for Ojibwes were grim, but other communicable diseases also ravaged Ojibwe communities in the early twentieth century, including syphilis, gonorrhea, and trachoma. The Bureau of Indian Affairs, charged with providing medical care for Indians, often placed the blame on American Indians themselves for their poor state of health. The bureau attributed high rates of disease, child morality, and early death to the ignorance of an "immoral," superstitious people who preferred medicine men to government physicians and rejected vaccinations and the concept of cleanliness. The few poorly paid physicians and other health care personnel who served Indians could little alter the crisis in health care that existed on many Ojibwe reservations. Indian people were continually afflicted by diseases, such as trachoma, that were not problems for the majority population in the United States. Communities were particularly vulnerable to epidemic disease, as evidenced by the high death rates during the influenza pandemic of 1918.

During times of crisis, Ojibwe families had historically relied on the generosity of family members and the community at large. When new patterns of homelessness emerged at White Earth and other reservations after the turn of the century, time-honored methods of caring for the needy and adopting parentless children proved inadequate. Disease disrupted family life and other long-standing Native institutions. The ranks of the poor, sick, widowed, and orphaned grew. All too often, husbands, wives, and even older siblings were left with large families to maintain after the death of a spouse or parent. Overcrowding became a common feature of Ojibwe households, and many remaining allotments, some of them held by minor children or vulnerable to tax forfeiture, were secure only temporarily.

During these trying years for American Indians, some promoters of assimilation still looked to boarding school education as a panacea for many social problems, if they lacked the reformist zeal of the previous generation. The idea was conceived decades before that boarding school education, which removed young children from the tribal environment, would "civilize" and prepare Indians for citizenship while providing them with a practical, vocational education. It was widely assumed that vocational education not only suited the "native mentality" but would also help to solve the nation's so-called "Indian problem" by training the growing number of impoverished and landless Indians for wage labor.

Early in the era of forced assimilation, coercion was often used to gather Indian children to the far-away schools. Rations, annuities, and other goods were withheld from parents and guardians who refused to send children to school after a compulsory attendance law for American Indians was passed by Congress in 1891. Boarding schools in the Midwest were seldom located in areas close to Indian communities, making the transition traumatic for children. Visits from parents were rare events in the lives of boarding school students, especially those from very poor families. Assimilationists argued that the task of "civilizing" Indian children would be easier and lapses into tribal ways less likely if students stayed away from their homes and relatives until their education was complete.

Indian parents across the country responded in strikingly similar ways to the residential school concept. For the most part, they proved to be tenacious. They often refused to surrender their children to government authorities, especially the very young, and resisted boarding school education. Stories have filtered out of the Southwest that describe how rural tribal children had to be virtually kidnapped from their parents in order to be taken to the alien schools. In her autobiography, Helen Sekaquaptewa recalled that Hopi children were taught by their parents to play a game similar to "hide and seek" to avoid the police. The most painful story of resistance to assimilation programs and compulsory school attendance laws involved the Hopis in Arizona, who surrendered a group of men to the military rather than voluntarily relinquish their children. The Hopi men served time in federal prison at Alcatraz.

Ojibwe students were often rounded up by the reservation police before being sent to boarding school. Nina King of Red Lake recalled being removed after police came to her home. Certainly coercion was a popular method used to recruit early boarding school pupils, and in 1907 Commissioner of Indian Affairs Francis Leupp still endorsed the use of force in bringing children to school when families would not cooperate with voluntary measures.

Historian Frederick Hoxie has shown that the enthusiasm of reformers for boarding school education waned considerably after the turn of the century in favor of reservation day schools. Reformers and policy-makers began to doubt that full assimilation for Indians was possible. Boarding schools of this era imparted low expectations, and the goal of Indian education became to provide students with primary skills or channel them into a limited number of vocational trades. As expectations diminished, boarding school attendance remained a common experience for American Indians through the 1930s. More children attended day schools, but unfortunately, the bureaucracy was slow to respond to the new trend of reservation-based education. Euro-American reformers lost their initial enthusiasm for the transforming power of Indian education, and budget cuts undermined plans for vocational training. Non-Indian officials and teachers maintained a consistent level of disdain for tribal institutions and languages until a new wave of reformers led by John Collier infiltrated Indian education. Hoxie has suggested twentieth-century boarding schools became "an empty remnant of the reformers' original design." For most Indian students, government boarding schools provided them with a minimal education and a minimum of care.

Like other tribal people in the United States, Ojibwes were primarily educated in off-reservation schools in the late nineteenth and early twentieth centuries, and a still-significant number of children were in residential schools in 1940. A survey conducted at Red Lake in the late 1920s indicated that over 40 percent of the adult residents who had received formal education had been to one of the off-reservation government schools. By 1930, attending Flandreau, Wahpeton, or another school had become an arrangement common for people in the Red Lake community....

Ojibwe families, known for strong kinship ties, only reluctantly sent their children to distant boarding schools even when persuaded it was for their best interest. Although most parents preferred to have their children remain at home or be educated on the reservation when that was an option, it is also evident that a great many Ojibwe families decided based on sheer hardship to send their children away to boarding school. The presence of so much disease on reservations widowed women and men before their time, and, ironically, many Indians began to use the boarding school as a refuge for their children during a family crisis.

There are many examples in the government archives of letters from families in distress who sought help from boarding school officials. When a Wisconsin Ojibwe father who had been recently widowed wrote to the superintendent of Flandreau in South Dakota, he described an unfortunate but all-too-common situation for American Indians living on early-twentieth-century reservations.

> I have lost my wife and left me with six children.... I would like to ask
> you to send these little folks over to you two or three years so I can get
> along. It is hard for me [to] stay here alone home because children not

used home alone when mother gone. When I am going working out it hard for them ... and this all I ask you if you have a place for them.

Under these sad circumstances, it is not difficult to imagine why a father would ask to place his six children in a residential school, even though it may have meant a separation of several years.

While facing a similar crisis, another father turned to Flandreau's superintendent for help in February 1924, just a week after the death of his wife.

I am writing you to see if you can do me a favor by taking my daughter in your school it would be a big favor to me as my wife died Feb. 4th and have no way of taking care of the girl we cant stay at home as it is very lonesome for her.... Therefore I am asking you this favor, to turn my daughter over in your care.

Indian women were sometimes faced with the predicament of having to relinquish custody of their children to government boarding schools. Again, the death of a spouse was often the compelling factor. When a woman found it impossible to support a large family after the death of a husband, she could be reassured by the idea that clothing, a regular diet, and a stable place to live would be provided for her children. As one woman confided to her granddaughter at Flandreau, she thought the girl would have "better eats" at school than if she were to live at home.

Writing from a reservation in South Dakota, a Lakota woman described the many hardships she suffered after the death of her husband, who left her as the sole caretaker of seven children. The mother, Mrs. Bad Moccasin, wrote the superintendent of the school at Flandreau, where her son and daughter were students:

I am always glad to hear from my children saying they are improving in their studies and that they sure are taking interest in it. That's what I want them to do is to take interest in their studies so they can learn and try to make man and woman out of themselves as those children have lost their father when they were little, and I have brought them up the best I can.

Due to her own illness, Mrs. Bad Moccasin was no longer able to earn a living for her large family but hoped her children would be someday able to support themselves as well as their younger siblings. She wanted her children to be educated and learn a trade at school. Indian families viewed government boarding schools as the only alternative for their children, one of the few opportunities for young people from rural areas to be educated and develop skills for future employment.

A six-year-old White Earth Ojibwe boy, Wallace, was first sent away to boarding school when his widowed mother was not able to care for him or his five siblings, aged three to seventeen. At the time Wallace entered Flandreau as a teenager, his application form said he had "no fixed home other than [the] Wahpeton Indian School" in North Dakota. Wallace did not return to White Earth; instead he lived his entire childhood and adolescence in government boarding schools.

When Wallace turned nineteen, he entered the army and was sent to Fort Snelling in Saint Paul, Minnesota. In a postcard to the Flandreau school from its longtime student, Wallace, a veteran of government institutions cheerily wrote, "I'll be in uniform by the time you receive this card. Ft. Snelling is a nice place. Lots of freedom, good food (best in U.S.) and two cities to visit." In his message, Wallace fondly referred to his alma mater as "My Shangri-la." That boarding schools proved to be a haven for some children, like Wallace, stands as a somber testimony to the poor quality of reservation life for Ojibwe families in the early twentieth century.

There are many signs that the fabric of Ojibwe community life persisted only under great stress during the boarding school era. For generations, Ojibwe families and other tribal people had traditionally made room for parentless children in their households. Orphans were treated with kindness, and little distinction was made between "natural" children and those adopted. Often, adoptees were blood relatives who simply went to live with a grandparent or aunt and uncle after a parent died. But as family life suffered during the early reservation, postallotment, and Great Depression years, traditional methods of absorbing orphaned children into the extended kinship group were not always possible. For a society that regarded caring for relatives as a virtue, with tender devotion to both the young and the elderly, this was a troubling sign.

When Ojibwe families could no longer maintain traditional methods of adopting orphans, more children were sent away from Indian communities to live and be reared in government boarding schools. Reservations like White Earth in northern Minnesota, devastated by allotment and plundering timber companies greedy to gain title to Indian lands, were unable to provide homes for all their deserving children. When a little White Earth boy, Clifford, described by a social worker as a "half starved undernourished child" was sent to the Pipestone boarding school in Minnesota after the death of his father, a note on his application read, "The boy is absolutely homeless with no relatives to care for him."

Orphaned children often applied to government boarding schools as family networks failed. A young Lac du Flambeau Ojibwe boy, Woodrow, went to Flandreau after numerous family members died, leaving him and a sister orphaned. Because his natural mother died when the boy was small, he already resided with foster parents on the reservation. After the death of his foster father, Woodrow explained that his mother "can't afford to pay board tuition or transportation to and from Ashland the nearest school."

Ojibwe family life was complex and blighted with instability on early-twentieth-century reservations. Children, left alone after the death of parents, were frequently shuttled from one home to another on the reservation as those families met with death or hardship, too. When Bernice, a young Ojibwe girl from Reserve, Wisconsin, applied to boarding school at Flandreau, it was because her shattered family could find no alternative.

Bernice's mother had died in 1924 of tuberculosis. Her father had remarried, giving Bernice a stepmother and eventually two younger siblings. When her stepmother died in 1929 of pneumonia, Bernice and two half-brothers went to live with their maternal grandmother, since their father was unemployed. The grandmother had also taken in the children of two of her recently widowed sons. At the time of Bernice's application to Flandreau, her younger brother,

Antoine, a second-grader, was found to have an active case of pulmonary tuber-culosis. Though Bernice had been a good student at the local school in Hayward, Wisconsin, achieving above average scores in science, history, arith-metic, English, and music, she stopped attending classes during the winter months because she lacked proper cold-weather clothing. By the time she entered Flandreau as a ninth-grader, Bernice reportedly did not "have a place that she [could] actually call her home nor [had] her living conditions been satisfactory." By going to school in South Dakota, Bernice hoped to attend clas-ses regularly and to study home economics.

Mrs. Mary Twobirds, a Bad River Ojibwe woman from the community at Odanah, Wisconsin, sent several of her grandchildren to Flandreau beginning in the 1920s. Described as a "very intelligent old lady" by the local agent on the reservation, Mrs. Twobirds had raised six of her grandchildren after the death of her daughter, the children's mother. She frequently counseled her grandchildren about the importance of an education and reminded them that she would not always be able to provide for them. Mrs. Twobirds explained: "I am the guard-ian of these poor children since [their] mother died. I took care of them. I'm [their] grandmother and I've worked hard to raise these children on my own. Sent them to school here, our school here only goes as far as 8th grade."

A determined woman, Mrs. Twobirds bought a second-hand car to retrieve her grandchildren during the summer vacation. While driving from northern Wisconsin to South Dakota, they even "tipped over once, on a certain curve." Mrs. Twobirds lived twelve miles from the nearest high school in Ashland, Wisconsin, and daily transportation back and forth from school was problematic for the family, particu-larly during the northern Wisconsin winters. For the Twobirds grandchildren, Flandreau represented an opportunity for them to complete their schooling....

A surprising number of students, older and orphaned, were not being cared for by adults at all when they enrolled in boarding school. In 1913, Joseph High Elk of Eagle Butte, South Dakota, asked to enter Flandreau after having taken "care of myself since I was old enough to work." Years later, when a teenage Menominee, David, enrolled at Flandreau in 1936, the agent at Keshena, Wisconsin, reported that he was "without parents [and] has no home." The hard-working Menominee boy had been trying to support himself while he attended a local high school. The agent wrote that David had "used practically all of his money paying for board and lodging while attending a nearby high school, and we have decided that he can no longer afford to pay such expenses."

Alphonse Caswell, one of many former Flandreau students from Red Lake, decided to go away to school after his parents died. Alphonse planned to learn a trade and then return home to Red Lake to care for his younger brother and sister, Louis and Priscilla, who resided with relatives. As a young man, Alphonse strongly felt responsible for his younger siblings and assumed the roles of his late parents. By the time of his graduation, Alphonse was described as "an exacting workman, capable of thinking for himself," and with "a pleasing personality." As it turned out, Alphonse's time at Flandreau greatly influenced his later life. After graduation he married a young woman from White Earth, Ethelbert Branchaud, whom he had met while she attended the Pipestone boarding school, just a few miles away from Flandreau. Later, Alphonse's younger sister Priscilla went to Flandreau. Flandreau was undergoing change in the 1930s, developing into a more sympathetic institution, and Alphonse successfully kept his family together with some help from the school. The Caswells remained a close and loving family....

Some Ojibwes tried to make a living on the reservations, whereas others decided to make their way in the cities. In the 1920s, it was not unusual for the growing number of urban Ojibwe parents, especially women, to enroll their children in boarding schools. These women, often single mothers, had left reservations like White Earth, and migrated to urban centers in order to find work to support their families. Once in the city, women generally could find work only at low-paying, menial jobs. In cities like Minneapolis, Milwaukee, and Chicago, Indian women usually lacked the family networks of the reservation, which made finding care for their children and supporting a family an increased burden.

When women did not receive support, financial or otherwise, from the father of their children, they had few alternatives other than to send them home to live with relatives or to enroll them at Indian boarding schools. This was the case for one Ojibwe mother living in Saint Paul, Minnesota, who left an abusive husband after he tried to assault their twelve-year-old daughter. In the aftermath of this crisis, the woman asked to send her daughter and another child to Flandreau while she looked for work.

In 1924, a single mother of several children labored in the linen room of the Ryan Hotel in Saint Paul while two of her sons attended school at Flandreau. As she explained,

> I have had the sole support of my three boys for the last six years.... I never had no help from their father ... with the exception of the little he has sent for them this spring. I have had to care and work for them while they were small ... but I am just like an old mother bear and will fight for my children.

Given her precarious economic situation, this parent felt boarding school was best for her boys and she was "real proud of the good work they have been doing this year."

Boarding school became a solution for many urban Indian women when they were not able to support a family. In 1925, a woman with two daughters, aged fourteen and eleven, living in Milwaukee asked to enroll her children at Flandreau. As she said, "I am living in the city, trying to keep my two little girls and sending them to school, but with what little funds I have I can not do justice to them or myself so I have been thinking of your school."

The following letter, written in 1925 by an Ojibwe woman who had relocated to Minneapolis, illustrates some of the problems Indians encountered as they moved to new, urban areas. The mother, originally from White Earth, felt that the urban environment was a bad influence on her child. As she explained to the administrator at Flandreau:

> I have my boy Herbert ... from White Earth, with me and I have come to the conclusion that this city life is not conducive to his moral welfare.

His grandmother ... is not able to give him the proper care on account of [forgetfulness] or else I would send him back to the reservation. My sincere wish is that he enter your institution so that he may obtain the proper training to success....

For a variety of sound reasons, students ... often chose to attend off-reservation Indian schools. The small towns of northern Wisconsin and Minnesota have an unfortunate history of discrimination against Indians. When students felt unwelcome in nearby public institutions due to racism against Indians, government boarding schools offered a less threatening environment. Rural students had many serious issues to consider when deciding on a school, including their own proximity to public school facilities or the inability of some local schools to offer the upper grades.

Sometimes children were attracted to boarding schools when siblings or cousins were already students. At times boarding school students actively recruited new pupils when they came home for summer vacation. In August 1921, before the start of a new term, a young Lakota boy from Greenwood, South Dakota, wrote to his superintendent wondering if "you want a boy to go to school that is in third grade and another boy in second grade. If so let me know before Sept ... both of these boys are 8 ... years of age."

A few students, such as George White Bull, carefully considered their educational options before deciding on a particular school. In 1913, the young boy from Porcupine, South Dakota, wrote to ask to be enrolled at Flandreau, after attending Ogalalla boarding school for four years but saying he no longer got "much out of it."

I am going to write to you and asked you how I can come to school and so wish you would give me the proportion to come I play in band for two or three years and I'm just in fifth grade and I am very glad to learned little more if I can I have looked over all the non-reservation schools but I dont think I can go any wheres but to come over to your Flandreau Indian School as I thought this School will give me a little more education so that I can make an honest living when I get out. I know several Indian boys from here that had been there before and as they tell me about how the School is over there and so I thought I will get my learning from you Well Sir I wish you would kindly send me some blanks so that I can fill them up The very first thing I want to do when I get over there is to join the band.

It was very common for siblings, cousins, or friends to attend the same boarding school, which alleviated some of the isolation most students encountered at off-reservation schools. In 1913, Simon Antelope of Greenwood, South Dakota, enrolled his fourteen-year-old son at Flandreau as well as a neighbor's son who "talks English and reads it." Mr. Antelope commented that the boys were "both full Indian but are used to work on farm." In a similar request made in June 1914, a North Dakota father sent the ten-dollar fare for the summer return of his son Waldo and asked to send another boy back with him in the fall who was "a little younger than him but smart and talk good English."

Some children, especially those with a poor family life, grew tired of their situation on the reservation and asked to be sent away to school. Josephine, a teenager from Wisconsin, was reportedly "anxious to go to school away from the reservation" and felt that the "classical courses offered at the local parochial school" did not "benefit" her, and "wanted to begin high school work with a vocation in mind." Josephine's family was poor and received support from their agency.

The complexity of Native American life and the multitude of problems Indians encountered throughout the boarding school era are all too obvious from the letters received at Flandreau and Haskell. In many cases, it is apparent that boarding schools created problems for Indians, but clearly in other instances the institutions provided a solution, however temporary, to some of their most crucial dilemmas. American Indians at times resented boarding schools, and rightly so, but they also found them useful. In times of family crisis or economic hardship, Indians could turn to boarding schools for help. Ojibwes and members of other tribes found a place for these institutions after the era of forced assimilation had passed.

Throughout the boarding school era, Indian parents and students hoped education would provide them with the skills to earn a living in order to cope with reservation conditions. After reservations were reduced in size or allotted, the most frequent result was poverty for Indians. When families could not earn an adequate living on the reservation or in the city, they often enrolled children in boarding schools as a temporary or long-term solution to some of their most pressing problems. Parents expected that in boarding school basic needs would be met in the form of food, clothing, a rudimentary education, and the opportunity to learn a trade. Even modest expectations on the part of parents were sometimes disappointed.

Reservation life proved to be a constant struggle for American Indians in the early twentieth century. Disease and poor health care combined to take the lives of many Indians at a young age. The high death rates reached a crisis point in many Indian communities. Traditional methods of absorbing needy individuals into the larger kinship network were not always possible as early death and increased poverty overwhelmed Ojibwe family life. In many instances Indian parents died young, and children were left without caretakers. Boarding schools often took in needy and orphaned children.

Ojibwe communities were situated in remote regions of the northern states. School facilities, especially high schools that were designed to serve the non-Indian community, were seldom conveniently located for Ojibwe students. During the notoriously harsh winters in these regions, it was nearly impossible to expect children to attend schools miles from home on a regular basis. Again, Indian students and their families had few alternatives other than education in a residential school.

Ojibwe students sometimes chose education in a government boarding school because of the familiarity and security of an all-Indian environment. Ojibwes from northern Wisconsin and Minnesota often complained of the discrimination they experienced in local white communities. There is little doubt that government boarding schools, although often antagonistic toward tribal cultures in many ways, also provided a friendly environment because of the intertribal composition of the student body. The decision to enter a government boarding school could be made by a reservation official, a struggling parent or guardian, or a personally motivated student. But, once reached, the boarding school path was frequently rocky, and there were few signs of an easy passage for beginners.

Creating Community and a Native Identity in Jim Crow Georgia, 1890–1920

BY MALINDA MAYNOR LOWERY (LUMBEE)

In 1890 a group of Croatan Indians, now called Lumbees, migrated from their home in Robeson County, North Carolina, to Bulloch County, Georgia. These families left voluntarily, walking the railroad lines, following the turpentine industry from North Carolina to southeast Georgia, where this community of approximately one hundred established a new home and built a school and church to solidify their place. In this period Georgia, and the South as a whole, legally encoded racial segregation and threatened to force Bulloch County Croatans into a black or white identity. But rather than assimilate into the larger black or white communities of Bulloch County, Croatans maintained an identity as Indians and eventually returned home to Robeson County in 1920. The story of their sojourn in Georgia raises questions about how Croatans perpetuated a sense of themselves as a distinct "Indian" people. That distinctiveness depended on markers we ordinarily do not associate with Indian communities. How did they maintain a distinctive identity, away from their homeland, in a region that countenanced only two racial categories, "white" and "colored"? Rather than claiming that an unbroken connection to a place sustained their Indian identity, Croatans used the segregation of the Jim Crow South to build social institutions—a school and a church—to distinguish themselves from non-Indians and reinforce their community ties....

Croatans followed non-Indian North Carolinians to southeastern Georgia to work in the naval stores industry. Indian men and women had learned turpentine skills in Robeson County, and they held nearly every occupation in Bulloch County's naval stores industry. Prior to the Civil War North Carolina produced the highest quality and quantity of naval stores, but in the 1880s manufacturers began leaving the state to search for virgin pine and higher profits. In 1880–81 North Carolina produced 62 percent of the United States' gum naval stores, and Georgia produced 24 percent. Within ten years, however, output reversed: North Carolina produced 40 percent, and Georgia became the leading producer in the South, with 52 percent. Bulloch County's newspapers reported the leading turpentine manufacturers' connections to North Carolina—the society pages detailed when these elite men and their wives returned to North Carolina for family reunions and when North Carolina relatives visited them. Georgia naval stores manufacturers were particularly well connected to southeastern North Carolina, the home of the Croatans; many hailed from Cumberland, New Hanover, Bladen, and Robeson counties.

Malinda Maynor Lowery (Lumbee) "People and Place: Croatan Indians in Jim Crow Georgia, 1890–1920." *American Indian Culture and Research Journal*, 21 (Spring 2005): 37–64.

Bulloch County's earliest reference to its new Indian immigrants described Croatan families. In 1890 the local paper identified a group of Croatans working for Graham McKinnon and Sion A. Alford. McKinnon and Alford may have been from Robeson County and brought Croatan laborers with them to Bulloch County. The article described the Croatans as "about the color of Indians, and the women and children who are not exposed much to the sun are real bright in color. The men and women have straight hair, and are intelligent people." Croatans, the author wrote, "are said to be honest and industrious. They stick to each other, and don't mix much with the negros.... They are a distinct race in North Carolina, where their homes are, and are supposed to be a mixture of Indian and Portuguese."

Whereas whites distinguished Indians from blacks according to skin color and ethnic lineage, Croatans separated themselves from both whites and blacks based on kinship. Since apparently Croatans did not appear black, whites had little reason to label them as black and thus force them into the racial hierarchy. This left room for Indians to claim their Indian identity voluntarily by perpetuating their kinship networks rather than relying on demonstrating their "Indianness" by avoiding association with blacks. The presence of families at McKinnon and Alford's operation was not a common characteristic of turpentine camps as historians have described them or as the 1900 census data demonstrate. In 1900 children made up 33 percent of the Indian population, compared to 26 percent for both the white and black populations. In 1900 a higher proportion of Indian than black turpentine workers were married, and, in fact, most Indians had at least three children.

Croatan families in turpentine camps contrasted sharply with the experience of black turpentiners. Previous scholarship has described turpentine laborers as primarily single black men who migrated with the industry. While some black families resided in the turpentine camps, the overwhelming majority of Bulloch County's black turpentine laborers were single and lived in independent households or households headed by one male and three or four male boarders. Black turpentiners who chose to settle in southeast Georgia often married local Georgians, but both spouses in Indian households were typically from North Carolina: 64 percent of Indian females and males with no occupation were born in North Carolina. Indians married other Indians, suggesting that they wanted to stay connected to North Carolina and to their Indian identity.

Marriage to other Indians was important in the Croatan community because of what it signified for kinship relations and the maintenance of community. Each Croatan spouse was obligated to a host of Robeson County kin. Croatan marriage represented an alliance of families that ensured the continuance of inherited first and last names, an important marker of Indian identity to outsiders, as well as occupations, talents, and community roles. Croatans' large, fluid families with strong bonds between grandparents and grandchildren offered social stability and economic flexibility. Migrating families refused to relinquish their attachments to extended family in Robeson County because such a loss threatened a family facing an uncertain economic future in a new place. By contrast, young single men dominated the black turpentine labor force. Croatans moved in families in order to better maintain Indian identity in the new place; staying connected to home through family was a way to replicate the social landscape they had known in Robeson County.

Some Indians brought their spouses and families with them to Georgia, but others maintained connections by moving back and forth seasonally. They used turpentine labor as temporary employment to improve their economic situation at home. Steve Maynor, an Indian from Robeson County, is one example. He married Magnolia Bullard in Bulloch County in 1893. In 1894 Steve owned no property and paid one dollar in poll tax in the Sinkhole District in Bulloch County, where several other Indians lived. After 1894 Steve disappeared from the documentary record, suggesting that Steve and Magnolia met in Bulloch County and left after 1894. In fact, Steve and Magnolia were both Indians and met in Robeson County, where Steve worked for Magnolia's father as a plowboy. Steve left Robeson County about 1892, hoping to escape a threat from Magnolia's father. Magnolia loved Steve and followed him to Georgia, where they married. She then returned home and set up house in Robeson County, a newly married and pregnant woman. Steve, meanwhile, worked in Georgia another year and then returned to North Carolina with money to support his family.

This story illustrates the significance of Croatans' connection to their Robeson County home for their identity, and it adds a dimension to Croatan migration— not only did Steve's connection to home preserve his Indian identity in the new place, but it also strengthened identity in the old place. For Steve and Magnolia, Bulloch County was a refuge from trouble, where they salvaged their relationship and amassed a nest egg with which to build a home in North Carolina. Other Indians already residing in the Sinkhole District probably recruited Steve. This social network made Sinkhole a comfortable place for Magnolia to come to beyond the reach of her father, where she and Steve could marry among friends. Money that Steve made in Bulloch County ensured a more comfortable life in Robeson County. Robeson County was the couple's constant reference point, and their social network allowed them to perpetuate their Indian identity in Georgia.

In 1897 Sarah Oxendine wrote her brother, Daniel Webster Oxendine, a plaintive letter. He was in Bulloch County working in turpentine. She told him that the whole family was sick and that some of their Robeson County neighbors had died. "[Y]ou cum home," she wrote. "You can get work to do here and we will be together in our trubels and that will be a cumfret to us." She asked him, as well as "Edy" and "Exey Ann," perhaps other relatives, to send money and to do it "rite at once." If he did not return, "som of us you will never see in this world and I am sorry you went to GA." Sarah sounded desperate. Her detailed report of the family's sickness, the news of the neighbors' deaths, her repeated appeals to her brother to return home, and her requests for money, not only from him but from others, indicated her fear that her own life and that of her whole community were falling apart. Her survival depended on her brother's connection to his home.

Polie Lowery wrote a spirited letter to her father in Robeson County that offered a wholly different view but reinforced Croatans' reliance on their Robeson County connections. Whereas Sarah Oxendine suggested that the home place was falling apart, Polie Lowery regarded her new home—Powell Turpentine camp—as full of possibilities. After she arrived in Georgia in 1900, she wrote cheerfully, "I got hear Safe.... Send Me word if mamma is got Satis-fide yet[.] Send me word How all of the folks is[.]" She continued, "Eliz[abeth?]

Sayed To tell Fletcher that He can Git a plenty of Boxes Puling or chiping.... Theair is Plenty of Hausen [housing]." Her strong connection to her family led her to recruit another neighbor or relation—Fletcher—to join her and Elizabeth in Georgia. There were plenty of turpentine "boxes," she wrote, referring to the receptacles that collected the pine tree gum that they distilled into turpentine. Fletcher could "pull" or "chip," two low-skill occupations on turpentine farms, and the plentiful camp housing made Georgia's longleaf pine forests a potentially attractive escape from a household where "Mamma" was never "Satisfide." Polie ended by asking her father to "write soon and fail not to." Polie's survival perhaps depended on her ability to leave home, but it also rested on her connections to home. Both letters reveal reasons that people from Robeson County migrated to Georgia—hard economic times, a difficult relationship—but both writers wanted to keep the bonds with family and home strong.

The families of Steve Maynor, Daniel Webster Oxendine, and Polie Lowery found various ways to keep their connections to Robeson County, whether through sending money home that they earned, recruiting family and friends to join them, or physically moving with spouses and children to their new place. Kinship bound these individuals to a larger community that they desired to recreate in their new place.

At first, many Indians did not move to Bulloch County and settle together in one place because lumber camps were dispersed and Indians could not always choose where to live. Within the county, mobility appeared quite high in the early years of migration. During the 1890s a few Indians paid taxes year after year in the same district, but the vast majority moved from district to district, or their names only appeared once and not again for several years. Moreover, few blacks and no identifiable Indians owned more than five or ten dollars' worth of household furniture during the 1890s. Low property ownership tended to characterize both Indians and blacks, whereas only a relatively small proportion of whites owned no property in this period. Turpentine laborers moved so frequently, and most of them were paid so little, that acquiring property must have been virtually impossible. Between 1900 and 1910, however, the critical years of economic change in Bulloch County, Indians seemed to have a choice about where to settle, and they began to coalesce in one area, the Sinkhole. There they formed a community expressed in their occupations and social institutions.

Bulloch County's economic climate shifted about this time. Georgia's naval stores production peaked in the 1890s, and manufacturers began to search for virgin pine elsewhere in the Southeast. In 1899 manufacturers were elated by "what they saw in the way of turpentine and timber prospects" in Florida and reported that they "may invest some money down that way." One company moved to Alabama, taking with it black laborers who were in debt to their employer "in various amounts aggregating about $200, and attachments were taken out on the negroes' furniture to collect these amounts." For black turpentiners, unlike many of their Indian counterparts, their status and their futures were defined by the fortunes of the turpentine industry.

Economic activities contributed to racial designations in the minds of non-Indians, and the disassociation of Croatans from the turpentine industry made race appear a less-rigid category and more fluid. For example, E. J. Emanuel, a Croatan, worked as a woods rider, a skilled and high-status occupation usually reserved for whites. Between 1898 and 1905 the tax returns listed this Croatan man as "Colored." From 1898 to 1900 he owned no property. The 1900 census listed him as white. In 1901 he acquired $7 worth of furniture and $8 worth of livestock. In 1904 he moved to the Sinkhole District and bought more property: $15 in furniture, $3 in livestock, $10 in tools, and $4 in other property. In 1905 he apparently sold everything except his furniture, which had increased to $50 in value. In 1909 Emanuel, listed as a white taxpayer, owned $45 worth of furniture and $150 in livestock. In 1910 the census listed him as a mulatto farmer. On tax records Emanuel was "Colored" when he worked in turpentine and owned little or no property; in the census his occupation may have encouraged the enumerator to list him as white. But by 1910 a "mulatto" racial category had emerged for Croatans, and the enumerator described him as a mulatto as he moved up the economic ladder to farming.

Emanuel's various designations reveal that the relationship of the Croatans to other races in the county was an important element in their community development and that racial identity fluctuated according to economic and social status. Like other Croatans, E. J. Emanuel, a skilled turpentine worker, did not use his potential ability to "pass" as white to migrate with the industry when it left Bulloch County. He likely believed that Bulloch County promised other economic opportunities and that the racial climate did not present impediments to his continued identity as an Indian. If the economic climate provided him with an opportunity to live in an Indian community as an Indian, Emanuel chose that life rather than life as a white man apart from his community. Croatans sustained identity by exploiting more than their racial ambiguity—the county's transition from turpentine to cotton gave them an opportunity to control their own economic resources and build their community.

Between 1898 and 1905 agriculture began to shape the county's social, economic, and political life. The transition from naval stores to agriculture was slow and uneven. Both turpentine and cotton flourished in the first years of the twentieth century, but by 1905 cotton had absorbed the attention of most Bulloch County residents. Croatans resisted migrating with the turpentine industry and stayed to become tenant farmers with the Adabelle Trading Company, a prominent merchandising, cotton, and naval stores operation. Tenancy with this company gave Croatans an opportunity to maintain their internal social networks and control their own labor, their main economic resource.

The Adabelle Trading Company began as the Foy & Williams Company. Foy & Williams exemplified Bulloch County's economic transition and provided Croatans with a place to take advantage of economic change and racial ambiguity to assert a community identity. McKinnon and Alford's 1890 Croatan laborers perhaps joined Foy & Williams's workforce as early as 1895, when Graham McKinnon apparently sold his turpentine still and livestock and returned to Robeson County. Croatans found relatively stable employment with Foy & Williams. Between 1900 and 1910 large numbers of Indians settled in the Sinkhole District near Foy & Williams's property; in fact, whereas only 22 percent of the Indian population lived in Sinkhole in 1900, 80 percent lived there in 1910. The high number of Indians in these districts contrasts with the pattern in the 1890s, when Indians who were engaged in turpentine production lived in various parts of the county. Croatans used Foy & Williams's prosperity to begin developing a separate community.

Foy & Williams represented the kind of "New South" enterprise that fostered an economy in which both whites and nonwhites could participate. As outsiders to Bulloch County's black and white world, Croatans found a stable existence possible in this racially mixed social and economic place. Foy & Williams not only produced naval stores from the remaining pine forest, but they also rented land to tenants and operated a general store, post office, cotton gin, sawmill, grist mill, and livestock business. A 1901 advertisement read as follows:

> Right Goods, At Right Prices, is what everybody wants.
> We Have Them.
>
> On account of running a mercantile business in connection with our naval stores firm, we are enabled to buy goods in large quantities, thereby securing better prices. A large force in the way of teams, salesmen, etc., is necessary in the carrying on of the turpentine business. Therefore we are enabled to handle the stock of merchandise at little or no additional expense, and we have decided to give our customers the benefit of this saving. We now have an experienced business man in charge of our store who is in a position to handle your business in a manner which we will assure you to be satisfactory.
>
> Call on us and be convinced that we can save you money on any goods usually kept in a general store.
>
> Foy & Williams,
> Adabelle, GA.

Foy & Williams employed a simple strategy to draw customers—the "right goods" available to "everybody," with a progressive, commonsense explanation of company business practices. Throughout the South general stores depended on white and nonwhite customers; although whites excluded them from politics, nonwhites could participate in the economy by taking advantage of the conveniences that the general store offered. Croatans, misfits in Bulloch County in so many ways, found a relatively comfortable place in an economy driven by large companies like Foy & Williams. As the county's dominant industry changed from turpentine to cotton and merchandising, Croatans used the racially mixed marketplace to begin developing their own community. Rather than move with the turpentine industry, they stayed to develop a "people" in a new place and to create social institutions that marked a distinctive Indian community. Sometime between 1900 and 1909 Croatans literally planted their community by establishing a cemetery on Foy & Williams's property.

Male and female occupational roles mirrored the changes in Bulloch County's economic life. Whereas black and white women increasingly went to work after 1900, the percentage of Croatan women who worked remained stable. Further,

Croatans had the lowest percentage of female workers of any race in the county in both years. Indian women chose to fulfill more domestic, community-building roles after turpentine left the county in contrast to their black and white neighbors, who used cotton's prosperity as an opportunity to gain more income for their families by working outside the home as farm laborers or semiskilled domestic help. Correspondingly, the numbers of Croatan children born in Georgia increased dramatically after 1900, whereas the white and black native-born population stayed roughly the same. Croatan women had more children and increased the number of kin perhaps because of their desire to construct a community based on the county's new economy, which made a settled existence possible. In any event Croatan women made a distinctly different choice from white and black women.

Croatan men also changed occupations according to the county's economic transition. In 1900, just prior to the departure of turpentine from the county, turpentine labor occupied the vast majority of both Croatan and black men. By 1910, however, most Croatan and black men worked in farming, either as tenant farmers or sharecroppers; only a few remained in the county's small turpentine industry, probably working for the Adabelle Trading Company. The growth of Croatan farmers compared to black farmers does not appear significant on the surface, but tax data show an important difference. After turpentine left, much of the county's black male population left with it. Bulloch County's nonwhite adult male population dropped 35 percent between 1902 and 1903 because of the exodus of turpentine laborers. These data suggest that by 1910 comparatively more blacks than Indians worked in turpentine; perhaps Indian men chose to switch to farming because of their wives' desire to develop a settled community. Indian women understood the cotton boom's potential prosperity and may have encouraged their Indian husbands and brothers to get out of turpentine.

Men and women of all races found alternative means of subsistence after turpentine's departure, but the Croatans' transition to farming did not translate into an increase in land purchases as it did with whites and blacks. Tax data show "Colored" landownership to be on the rise throughout the first decade of the 1900s. Between 1895 and 1905, however, only a few Indians acquired furniture and livestock, the vast majority owning no property at all. Although there were one or two Indian landowners in the region, Indians by 1910 farmed rented land or worked as farm laborers, possibly for the Adabelle Trading Company. Renting, rather than owning, indicates that the Bulloch County Croatans were not intent on establishing firm roots in the county, but neither did they want to move on with the turpentine industry, as many blacks did. Instead, they saw renting land and farming cotton as a way to provide their increasing numbers of children with a kin-based, agricultural community similar to what they had known in Robeson County.

Blacks did not always simply "choose" to move on with turpentine or stay to farm cotton; wider social forces had an important impact on their economic choices, just as they impacted Croatan choices. In parts of southern Georgia, local white racial attitudes "could limit or enhance blacks' opportunity to buy property,"... The intervention of the local white community in the form of anti-black violence, debt peonage, disfranchisement, and competition affected black landownership. Southeast Georgia residents excluded blacks from economic opportunity, hoping to open the cotton economy to white yeoman farmers. In 1899 the *Bulloch Herald* reported an unwelcome presence of black laborers in Statesboro: "There are too many negro quarters in this town," one reporter wrote, "and they continue to spring up. There are now not less than ten, and there is talk of establishing others right in among the white residents of the town."

While white hostility did not apparently limit Indians' opportunity, Indians did not choose to invest their earnings in Bulloch County soil. Rather, they invested in their connections to Robeson County and in the growing Indian community around the Adabelle Trading Company. Renting prevented them from planting roots in Bulloch County and kept their connection to Robeson County possible. Landownership was not necessary for community, as it had been in Robeson County. Furthermore, if identity rested in part in a Robeson County connection, as it had in the 1890s, landownership implied severance with that community and jeopardized their identity as Indians in their new place.

Croatans could perpetuate a group identity in Bulloch County because their white neighbors were ambivalent about them and demonstrated little interest in them. Racial status and racism emerged as an important factor in Croatans' ability to negotiate their identity. The prosperity of cotton agriculture and companies like Foy & Williams also opened up an economic space within which Croatans could find a sense of community. Gradually, Indian strategies to enhance and protect their community identity began to center on social institutions that the cotton economy and their employment at the Adabelle Trading Company made possible. Croatans did not express their relationship to place through landownership but rather through the construction of educational and religious institutions that facilitated the social inclusion and exclusion necessary to create a distinctly Indian community. Under Jim Crow, Croatans embraced race and racial categories to include and exclude community members. Croatans' use of these institutions helped mediate social change when their economic livelihood changed from longleaf pine forests to cotton fields.

Building religious and educational institutions led Croatans into an engagement with the racism that began to dominate Bulloch County in the early twentieth century. During these early years of legal segregation, whites were not the only group assigning racial and social status—Croatans' own process of racial categorization produced a separate school and church in Adabelle and led them to embrace racism as a part of their cultural identity. Croatans adopted segregationist ideology to protect their ethnic community identity. While a Croatan-only church and school looked like a black or white institution from the outside, from the perspective of those who constructed them, these institutions marked their section of Bulloch County as a distinctively Indian area and served to perpetuate a sense of Indian community. The church and school also helped maintain ties to Robeson County—preachers and teachers visited back and forth, and they established a regular correspondence to keep Robeson Croatans informed. As social institutions independent of place, the Indian school and church linked Croatans' old and new homes and made it possible for them to maintain an Indian identity.

In 1909 an Indian preacher from Robeson County visited the Adabelle community. "The pine forests of Georgia," he reminded his readers, "induced many citizens to leave Robeson County several years ago, [and] among these were many of the Indian race. While some have returned to their native country, large numbers remain abroad in various states. An occasional homecomer brings glorious reports of the absent ones." The preacher articulated the sense of place and attachment to community that Indians in Robeson felt—Indian people traveled from "their native country ... abroad," beyond the community's borders and into foreign territory. He observed that the Bulloch County Croatans perpetuated this group cohesion. They had a small Indian church with eighteen members when he had held an eight-day revival and baptized fourteen new people. The preacher's visit brought the total number of church "members"—that is, baptized Christians—up to thirty-two. In addition to these thirty-two baptized church members, the congregation included family members that had not been baptized. Actual church attendance and participation was between fifty and seventy people, a healthy number for an unaffiliated church. Religious activities were similar to those in Robeson County and Protestant churches throughout the South. Croatan ministers preached every other week, baptized congregational members, organized a Sunday school, and held revivals. The strength of this Indian institution reflected the community's cohesion.

By 1910 Croatans had opened a school on Adabelle Trading Company property. One Indian resident of Bulloch County wrote to the *Robesonian*, Robeson County's newspaper, that the school and church were fully segregated and that "they have from 6 to 7 months ... of school during the year and I find the children seem to take a great interest in their school work." The school offered a classical education, with debating societies, patriotic music, dialogues, and recitations, all supervised by Indian teachers from Robeson County. The school's principal, C. L. Oxendine, was also an Indian, and closing ceremonies regularly featured Indian speakers, perhaps from North Carolina. Other letters commented on the excellent attendance at the school and anticipated an increase in population, "which will afford more and better schools." Letters to the *Robesonian* interspersed news of school and church events with obituaries and reports of relatives visiting from Robeson County. They announced Sunday fish fries and celebrations at the end of the school year. Indian social life revolved around the school and the church in Adabelle.

The social ramifications of Indian-only education, however, went much deeper than get-togethers among Indian people. Indian-only education marked the community's social boundary. Bulloch County appropriated no financial support for the school in its early years; Indians had to provide their own teacher salaries, materials, and building facilities. In Robeson County Indian schools, which received minimal state funding, the need to raise funds brought the community together and instituted local control. Croatans' active construction of their own schools in Robeson County suggests that Bulloch County Croatans employed a similar approach to education and social cohesion, but they relied more on local whites to facilitate their community.

Whites were not a daily presence, but they had an impact on the school. The Adabelle school occasionally welcomed non-Indians to attend its activities, and the white county school superintendent spoke at closing exercises on at least two occasions. Another letter writer reported "white people present" at closing exercises, where the featured speaker was S. A. Hammonds, a Croatan. On the whole, whites seemed uninvolved in the school's operations and were present only on public occasions, but they eventually made the school viable financially. The county appropriated funds for a separate Indian school in 1914, and W. M. Foy's heirs apparently donated the land to the Adabelle Indian community for their church/school and cemetery. Influential whites clearly saw the value and purpose of an Indian-only school and allowed it rather than forcing Indian children to attend black schools, as local whites attempted to do in Robeson County until the mid-1880s.

Croatans did not just want education; they wanted Indian-*only* education. Indians' sense of themselves as a people made their own school a necessity, in both Bulloch and Robeson counties. Indian-only education served the same purposes in both places—it allowed Indians to maintain control over their children's education and over those accepted as Indian. One Bulloch correspondent wrote: "While days of sunshine seem to flow we Indian people of Bulloch County, Ga., are trying to do a better work and a greater work, especially for the education of our children and bringing them up to a higher standard of life." By invoking "we Indian people," the writer articulated the group's conscious community identification and intense focus on transmitting that identity to Indian children who, if they were born in Georgia (as many increasingly were), knew nothing about the home place of Robeson County. In the absence of their children's knowledge of the home place and in a county where their racial identity was ambiguous, Bulloch County Croatans found another way to make sure that children understood who they were. They created institutions that reinforced Indian social networks. Furthermore, maintaining an Indian-only school required the community to decide who was Indian and who was not; these decisions differentiated Indians from non-Indians in a shared geographical space. Segregationist ideology assisted them in this effort.

Croatans sustained their own school by recognizing the racial hierarchy and assuring whites of their perceived superiority. They employed a time-tested social strategy [of] "making white friends." By gaining white friends, such as the school superintendent or local white ministers who occasionally addressed students, Croatans established an identity as "not black" in the minds of local whites and secured their school's continued existence. A publicly printed letter from C. L. Oxendine, the Adabelle Indian school's principal, to the county school board revealed this strategy. He "highly appreciate[ed]" the county's "kindness" in appropriating $25 per month and complimented the school board as a "most kindly set of gentlemen" who gave the Croatans "every consideration." He described his people as believing in "agriculture, education, and all enterprises that tend to lift a people to a higher standard of progressiveness, intelligence and Christian character." Oxendine appears to be an assimilationist, not an uncommon strategy for any American minority group in this period. He appealed to the qualities espoused by the mainstream at this time—"progressiveness, intelligence and Christian character"—reassuring readers that Croatans aspired to the same things that whites had already achieved, and by virtue of their slowness in achieving them, they were still inferior to whites. At the same time, Oxendine demonstrated that Croatans were superior to blacks, as Bulloch County whites debated the benefit of educating blacks at all. His compliments to the school board affirmed whites' perception of their superiority. Oxendine's assimilationist veil, however, served a larger purpose by ensuring that Indians had a separate school and a sense of themselves as a people. Racism did not force Croatans to abandon their cultural identity. Instead, they manipulated racism to serve their own community agenda.

Croatans found their own social place in a new geographic area by taking advantage of Bulloch County's economic transition and its racial dynamics. Rather than simply being victimized by these ideologies, Croatans took an active role in establishing their place in the racial hierarchy. Given the economic and political circumstances of the time, that hierarchy must have seemed like a social fact, in spite of its dissimilarity from their own approach to identity. In order to preserve that approach in a shared environment, where they could not physically isolate themselves from foreign cultural influences, they embraced hierarchy and manipulated race to their own ends.

As World War I came to a close, Croatans' "in-between" status in Bulloch County changed. C. L. Oxendine's strategy of accepting the racial hierarchy worked to sustain an Indian-only place, but an Indian named Warren Dial challenged that hierarchy and consequently affected the entire community. Sometime between 1917 and 1920, Warren Dial went into the town of Statesboro to get a haircut. He walked into a white barbershop around 1:00 p.m. "He was sort of dark skinned," recalled James C. Dial, a Lumbee and distant relative of Warren Dial. When the barbershop closed around 6:00 and Warren Dial still had not had a haircut, "he just tore the place up." James Dial continued, "Back then the whites they had something like the Ku Klux Klan and … they came out to [Adabelle] trying to find him. And that generated some hard feelings between the races, then, and it sort of put the Indians at some disadvantage." James Dial remembered other stories about visits the Klan made to Adabelle: "Some of the white Ku Klux Klan … would come out at night … and search the place. And some of the Indians fought back, you know, with the guns."

Dial's violent challenge to segregation and the Klan's vigilante response demonstrated that Croatans' negotiated identity was about to come to an end. Before his outburst the county's white power structure had acquiesced to the Croatans' insistence that they were "not black," but afterward, the Klan attempted to send Warren Dial—and the whole Croatan community of Adabelle—the message that they would be treated like blacks if they challenged the racial hierarchy. If whites could so easily redefine an anomalous group as black—especially one that, according to the 1890 newspaper reporter, did not even "look" black—the biracial dichotomy seemed hardly authentic or "natural." Warren Dial not only threatened segregation, but he also endangered the fiction of the immutable biological characteristics that made racial segregation necessary. Rather than accommodate segregationist attitudes further, the Croatan community implemented another strategy to maintain their sense of distinctiveness.

That strategy was to move home to Robeson County. The comfortable racial ambiguity that Croatans had found in Bulloch County was over. Whereas the racial hierarchy had assisted Indians in maintaining their distinct community, without having to claim racial purity or aboriginal connection to the land, the racial hierarchy actively began to threaten their community's survival. Rather than accept a racial category that did not acknowledge their identity, Croatans abandoned their economic prosperity and returned to Robeson County.

Warren Dial's explosion, however, may have been simply coincidental with other social developments. Even as early as 1911 the community was looking toward home: "They have not forgotten their old home," one correspondent wrote of the Croatan community; "they are preparing themselves to move back." The Adabelle Trading Company closed its doors in 1917. Perhaps their assurance of stable work had disappeared; perhaps the rumors of the boll weevil, which finally hit Bulloch County in 1919, drove them north, back to Carolina. Perhaps the population growth that had supported the school began to decline. Regardless of the motivation, Indians such as E. J. Emanuel, Christianne Oxendine, Ashley Jacobs, and his brother Will, all of whom had arrived in Bulloch County twenty years earlier as Indians, returned to Robeson County, where their descendants live today as Indians. The sojourn in Bulloch County had not destroyed their community identification. Indians' connections to home, their ability to make economic choices that secured those connections, and their creation of social institutions that reinforced ethnicity enabled them to preserve a community identity that led them back to Robeson County by 1920.

In a landscape that they shared with non-Indians, Croatans did not take their community's identity for granted, nor did they blend in with one or another dominant ethnic identity. They continually reinforced their distinctiveness as a community by employing strategies as diverse as maintaining long-distance kin ties and accommodating racial segregation. Even as place seemed unimportant to these migrants, their focus on maintaining a relationship between the old place and the new place and their ultimate return home testifies to the centrality of place in their sense of distinctiveness.

Almost seventy years after the last Croatan families left Bulloch County, Georgia, Lumbee descendants of this community demonstrated their connection to this distant place by visiting the cemetery that their ancestors established on Adabelle Trading Company property prior to 1910. They cleaned the graves and offered prayers to honor their dead kin. This pilgrimage encapsulates one of the Bulloch County Croatans' strategies for maintaining identity—reinforcing and strengthening kinship connections—but it also reflects the role of place in Croatan identity. To maintain the kinship connections, Lumbee descendents believed that it was critical to reconnect to the place where their ancestors rested. The cemetery's founders used the place to mark their community's separateness in foreign territory and to reinforce their kinship ties; they then used the economic and social changes brought by cotton agriculture and Jim Crow to preserve those connections. By resisting turpentine migration and simultaneously refusing to buy land, Croatans asserted their control over their economic resources and demonstrated a willingness to adjust to available opportunities rather than allow their community to dissolve. The Adabelle Indian school and church further fostered Indian identity by marking community in a physical way so that community members could recognize where they belonged, as well as to whom they belonged. Croatans' response to economic and social circumstances reveals that their ability to perpetuate their distinct community had as much to do with their status relative to other races as it did with internal cultural values. While their Robeson County homeland was constantly present in their lives, Croatans in Bulloch County used the homeland's social networks to perpetuate and strengthen a group identity in a new place.

◈ FURTHER READING

Adams, David Wallace. *Education for Extinction: American Indians and the Boarding School Experience, 1875–1928* (1995).

Bloom, John. *To Show What an Indian Can Do: Sports at Native American Boarding Schools* (2000).

Britten, Thomas A. *American Indians in World War I: At Home and at War* (1997).

Bsumek, Erika. *Indian-Made: Navajo Culture in the Marketplace, 1868–1940* (2008).

Burnham, Philip. *Indian Country, God's Country: Native Americans and the National Parks* (2000).

Cahill, Cathleen. *Federal Fathers and Mothers: A Social History of the United States Indian Service, 1869–1933* (2011).

Chang, David. *The Color of the Land: Race, Nation, and the Politics of Land Ownership in Oklahoma, 1832–1929* (2010).

Child, Brenda. *Boarding School Seasons: American Indian Families, 1900–1940* (1998).

Churchill, Ward. "Genocide by Any Other Name: North American Indian Residential Schools in Context," In *Genocide, War Crimes, and the West: History and Complicity*, Adam Jones, ed., 78–115 (2004).

Clark, Blue. *Lone Wolf v. Hitchcock: Treaty Rights and Indian Law at the End of the Nineteenth Century* (1994).

Deloria, Philip. *Indians in Unexpected Places* (2004).

Eastman, Charles. *From the Deep Woods to Civilization: Chapters in the Autobiography of an Indian* (1916).

Ellis, Clyde. *A Dancing People: Powwow Culture on the Southern Plains* (2003).

————. *To Change Them Forever: Indian Education at the Rainy Mountain Boarding School, 1893–1920* (1996).

Gilbert, Matthew Sakiestewa. *Education Beyond the Mesas: Hopis at the Sherman Institute, 1902–1929* (2010).

Greenwald, Emily. *Reconfiguring the Reservation: The Nez Perces, Jicarilla Apaches, and the Dawes Act* (2002). .

Hagan, William T. *The Indian Rights Association: The Herbert Welsh Years, 1882–1904* (1988).

————. *Quanah Parker, Comanche Chief* (1993).

Harmon, Alexandra. *Rich Indians: Native People and the Problem of Wealth in American History* (2013).

Harring, Sidney. *Crow Dog's Case: American Indian Sovereignty, Tribal Law, and United States Law in the Nineteenth Century* (1994).

Heaton, John. *The Shoshone-Bannocks: Culture and Commerce at Fort Hall, 1870–1940* (2005).

Hosmer, Brian C. *American Indians in the Marketplace: Persistence and Innovation Among the Menominees and Metlakatans, 1870–1920* (1999).

Hosmer, Brian C. and Colleen O'Neill, eds. *Native Pathways: American Indian Culture and Economic Development in the Twentieth Century* (2004).

Hoxie, Frederick E. *A Final Promise: The Campaign to Assimilate the Indians, 1880–1920* (1988).

————. *Parading Through History: The Making of the Crow Nation in America, 1805–1935* (1995).

Iverson, Peter. *When Indians Became Cowboys: Native Peoples and Cattle Ranching in the American West* (1994).

Jacobs, Margaret. *Dark Mother to a White Race: Settler Colonialism, Maternalism and the Removal of Indigenous Children in the American West and Australia, 1880–1940* (2011).

———. *Engendered Encounters: Feminism and Pueblo Cultures, 1879–1934* (1999).

Keller, Robert. *American Protestantism and United States Indian Policy, 1869–82* (1983).

King, C. Richard, ed. *Native Athletes in Sport and Society* (2005).

Lewis, David Rich. *Neither Wolf Nor Dog: American Indians, Environment and Agrarian Change* (1994).

Littlefield, Jr., Daniel F. and James W. Parins. *Native American Writing in the Southeast: An Anthology, 1875–1925* (1995).

Lomawaima, K. Tsianina. *They Called It Prairie Light: The Story of Chilocco Indian School* (1994).

Lowery, Malinda. *Lumbee Indians in the Jim Crow South: Race, Identity and the Making of a Nation* (2010).

Mann, Henrietta. *Cheyenne-Arapaho Education, 1871–1982* (1997).

Mathes, Valerie Sherer. *Helen Hunt Jackson and Her Indian Reform Legacy* (1990).

Mathews, John J. *Sundown* (1934).

McDonnell, Janet A. *Dispossession of the Indian Estate, 1887–1934* (1991).

Meyer, Melissa L. *The White Earth Tragedy: Ethnicity and Dispossession at a Minnesota Anishinaabe Reservation, 1889–1920* (1994).

Mihesuah, Devon A. *Cultivating the Rosebuds: The Education of Women at the Cherokee Female Seminary, 1851–1909* (1993).

Mitchell, Pablo. *Coyote Nation: Sexuality, Race, and Conquest in Modernizing New Mexico, 1880–1920* (2004).

Moses, L. G. *Wild West Shows and the Images of American Indians, 1883–1933* (1996).

Oakley, Christopher Arris. *Keeping the Circle: American Indian Identity in Eastern North Carolina, 1885–2004* (2005).

Porter, Joy. *To Be Indian: The Life of Iroquois-Seneca Arthur Caswell Parker* (2001).

Raibmon, Paige. *Authentic Indians: Episodes of Encounter from the Late-Nineteenth-Century Northwest Coast* (2005).

Riney, Scott D. *The Rapid City Indian School, 1898–1933* (1999).

Sackman, Douglas. *Wild Men: Ishi and Kroeber in the Wilderness of Modern America* (2010).

Schneider, Khal. "Making Indian Land in the Allotment Era: Northern California's Indian Rancherias," *Western Historical Quarterly* 51 (Winter 2010): 429–50.

Shurts, John. *Indian Reserved Water Rights: The Winters Doctrine in Its Social and Legal Context, 1880–1930* (2000).

Silva, Noenoe. *Aloha Betrayed: Native Hawaiian Resistance to American Colonialism* (2004).

Standing Bear, Luther. *My People, the Sioux* (1928).

Stremlau, Rose. *Sustaining the Cherokee Family: Kinship and the Allotment of an Indigenous Nation* (2011).

Trachtenberg, Alan. *Shades of Hiawatha: Staging Indians, Making Americans, 1880–1930* (2004).

Trennert, Robert A., Jr. *The Phoenix Indian School: Forced Assimilation in Arizona, 1891–1935* (1988).

Zitkala-Sa. *American Indian Stories* (1921).

CHAPTER 12

New Deals and Old Deals,

1920–1940

The 1920s saw the emergence of a new kind of reformer, one who began to understand what Indians across the country had known for decades: that federal policy had failed, and failed badly. Native communities had lost most of their land. Trachoma, tuberculosis, and other diseases plagued reservations. Boarding schools separated children from their families. Tribal governments, where they even existed, had remarkably limited powers. The Bureau of Indian Affairs continued to discourage tribal religions, languages, arts, and crafts. In the face of these failures, a reform movement originating in Pueblo country at the beginning of the 1920s led to a full-scale investigation of Indian affairs.

In 1933, the leader of this new reform movement, John Collier, a newcomer to Indian country, was named Commissioner of Indian Affairs. Although Congress and conservative forces in the West blocked some of his initiatives and he received mixed reviews from Indian communities, Collier held this position longer than any other person ever would. Collier's so-called Indian New Deal rejected the assimilationist period's ideals. It mirrored the New Deal itself in emphasizing community, the arts, and more careful use of the land. In addition, Collier called for Indian religious freedom, advocated bilingual and bicultural education, and supported the right of Native communities to retain separate land bases. Indeed, Collier tried to add to and consolidate Indian reservation land holdings. He also embraced cultural pluralism more fully than his predecessors. Like many reformers, though, Collier thought he knew best. He often imposed his own ideas, ignoring or failing to solicit the advice of Native people. More than half a century after he resigned his position as Commissioner, Collier remains a controversial figure in Indian country. Why did some Indians and many non-Indians resist Collier's reforms?

◈ DOCUMENTS

In the 1920s, the federal government, stung by widespread criticism of its Indian policy, asked Lewis Meriam, Henry Roe Cloud (Ho–Chunk), and his associates to investigate conditions in Indian country. Meriam's survey, published in 1928, became known informally as the Meriam Report. Its criticisms helped to spur reforms during Herbert Hoover's administration and more extensive reforms during Franklin Delano Roosevelt's presidency. Document 1 is reprinted from the introduction to that report. In 1929, the U.S. Senate responded to the Meriam Report with a nationwide investigation of Indian affairs. A committee of senators arrived in Wisconsin and interviewed doctors regarding the health conditions of Native people in that state. Some of their findings appear in Document 2. Who bears responsibility for reservation health conditions?

The primary piece of legislation passed during the Indian New Deal represented a compromise between Collier's aims and a cautious Congress. Document 3 is taken from that law, known as the Indian Reorganization Act (or the Wheeler–Howard Act, after its congressional sponsors). The remaining two selections speak to some of Collier's initiatives and philosophies. In Documents 4 and 5, Rupert Costo (Cahuilla) and Ben Reifel (Brule Lakota) offer contrasting judgments of Collier and the Indian New Deal. Costo and Reifel exchanged their views at a conference held in 1983 to mark the 50th anniversary of the Indian New Deal. Costo was an activist and publisher, while Reifel served as a congressman from South Dakota and as Commissioner of Indian Affairs.

1. Lewis Meriam Summarizes the Problems Facing American Indians, 1928

An overwhelming majority of the Indians are poor, even extremely poor, and they are not adjusted to the economic and social system of the dominant white civilization.

The poverty of the Indians and their lack of adjustment to the dominant economic and social systems produce the vicious circle ordinarily found among any people under such circumstances. Because of interrelationships, causes cannot be differentiated from effects. The only course is to state briefly the conditions found that are part of this vicious circle of poverty and maladjustment.

Health.   The health of the Indians as compared with that of the general population is bad. Although accurate mortality and morbidity statistics are commonly lacking, the existing evidence warrants the statement that both the general death rate and the infant mortality rate are high. Tuberculosis is extremely prevalent. Trachoma, a communicable disease which produces blindness, is a major problem because of its great prevalence and the danger of its spreading among both the Indians and the whites.

Living Conditions.   The prevailing living conditions among the great majority of the Indians are conducive to the development and spread of disease. With

Lewis Meriam, "General Summary of Findings and Recommendations," from *The Problem in Indian Administration,* Johns Hopkins 1928, pp. 3–8.

comparatively few exceptions the diet of the Indians is bad. It is generally insufficient in quantity, lacking in variety, and poorly prepared. The two great preventive elements in diet, milk, and fruits and green vegetables, are notably absent. Most tribes use fruits and vegetables in season, but even then the supply is ordinarily insufficient. The use of milk is rare, and it is generally not available even for infants. Babies, when weaned, are ordinarily put on substantially the same diet as older children and adults, a diet consisting mainly of meats and starches.

The housing conditions are likewise conducive to bad health. Both in the primitive dwellings and in the majority of more or less permanent homes which in some cases have replaced them, there is great overcrowding, so that all members of the family are exposed to any disease that develops, and it is virtually impossible in any way even partially to isolate a person suffering from a communicable disease....

Sanitary facilities are generally lacking. Except among the relatively few well-to-do Indians the houses seldom have a private water supply or any toilet facilities whatever. Even privies are exceptional. Water is ordinarily carried considerable distances from natural springs or streams, or occasionally from wells. In many sections the supply is inadequate, although in some jurisdictions, notably in the desert country of the Southwest, the government has materially improved the situation, an activity that is appreciated by the Indians.

Economic Conditions.   The income of the typical Indian family is low and the earned income extremely low. From the standpoint of the white man the typical Indian is not industrious, nor is he an effective worker when he does work. Much of his activity is expended in lines which produce a relatively small return either in goods or money. He generally ekes out an existence through unearned income from leases of his land, the sale of land, per capital payments from tribal funds, or in exceptional cases through rations given him by the government. The number of Indians who are supporting themselves through their own efforts, according to what a white man would regard as the minimum standard of health and decency, is extremely small. What little they secure from their own efforts or from other sources is rarely effectively used.

The main occupations of the men are some outdoor work, mostly of an agricultural nature, but the number of real farmers is comparatively small. A considerable proportion engage more or less casually in unskilled labor. By many Indians several different kinds of activity are followed spasmodically, a little agriculture, a little fishing, hunting, trapping, wood cutting, or gathering of native products, occasional labor and hauling, and a great deal of just idling. Very seldom do the Indians work about their homes as the typical white man does. Although the permanent structures in which they live after giving up primitive dwellings are simple and such as they might easily build and develop for themselves, little evidence of such activity was seen. Even where more advanced Indians occupied structures similar to those occupied by neighboring whites it was almost always possible to tell the Indian homes from the white by the fact that the white man did much more than the Indian in keeping his house in condition.

In justice to the Indians it should be said that many of them are living on lands from which a trained and experienced white man could scarcely wrest a reasonable living. In some instances the land originally set apart for the Indians was of little value for agricultural operations other than grazing. In other instances part of the land was excellent but the Indians did not appreciate its value. Often when individual allotments were made, they chose for themselves the poorer parts, because those parts were near a domestic water supply or a source of firewood, or because they furnished some native product important to the Indians in their primitive life. Frequently the better sections of the land originally set apart for the Indians have fallen into the hands of the whites, and the Indians have retreated to the poorer lands remote from markets.

In many places crops can be raised only by the practice of irrigation. Many Indians in the Southwest are successful in a small way with their own primitive systems of irrigation. When modern highly developed irrigation systems have been supplied by governmental activities, the Indians have rarely been ready to make effective use of the land and water. If the modern irrigation enterprise has been successful from an economic standpoint, the tendency has been for whites to gain possession of the land either by purchase or by leases. If the enterprise has not been economically a success, the Indians generally retain possession of the land, but they do not know how to use it effectively, and get much less out of it than a white man would.

The remoteness of their homes often prevents them from easily securing opportunities for wage earning, nor do they have many contacts with persons dwelling in urban communities where they might find employment. Even the boys and girls graduating from government schools have comparatively little vocational guidance or aid in finding profitable employment.

When all these factors are taken into consideration it is not surprising to find low incomes, low standards of living and poor health.

Suffering and Discontent.   Some people assert that the Indians prefer to live as they do; that they are happier in their idleness and irresponsibility. The question may be raised whether these persons do not mistake for happiness and content an almost oriental fatalism and resignation. The survey staff found altogether too much evidence of real suffering and discontent to subscribe to the belief that the Indians are [reasonably] satisfied with their condition. The amount of serious illness and poverty is too great to permit of real contentment. The Indian is like the white man in his affection for his children and he feels keenly the sickness and the loss of his offspring.

The Causes of Poverty.   The economic basis of the primitive culture of the Indians has been largely destroyed by the encroachment of white civilization. The Indians can no longer make a living as they did in the past by hunting, fishing, gathering wild products, and the extremely limited practice of primitive agriculture. The social system that evolved from their past economic life is ill suited to the conditions that now confront them, notably in the matter of the division of labor between the men and the women. They are by no means yet adjusted to the new economic and social conditions that confront them.

Several past policies adopted by the government in dealing with the Indians have been of a type which, if long continued, would tend to pauperize any race. Most notable was the practice of issuing rations to able-bodied Indians. Having moved the Indians from their ancestral lands to restricted reservations as a war measure, the government undertook to feed them and to perform certain services for them which a normal people do for themselves. The Indians at the outset had to accept this aid as a matter of necessity, but promptly they came to regard it as a matter of right, as indeed it was at the time and under the conditions of the inauguration of the ration system. They felt, and many of them still feel, that the government owes them a living, having taken their lands from them, and that they are under no obligation to support themselves. They have thus inevitably developed a pauper point of view.

When the government adopted the policy of individual ownership of the land on the reservations, the expectation was that the Indians would become farmers. Part of the plan was to instruct and aid them in agriculture, but this vital part was not pressed with vigor and intelligence. It almost seems as if the government assumed that some magic in individual ownership of property would in itself prove an educational civilizing factor, but unfortunately this policy has for the most part operated in the opposite direction. Individual ownership has in many instances permitted Indians to sell their allotments and to live for a time on the unearned income resulting from the sale. Individual ownership brought promptly all the details of inheritance, and frequently the sale of the property of the deceased Indians to whites so that the estate could be divided among the heirs. To the heirs the sale brought further unearned income, thereby lessening the necessity for self support. Many Indians were not ready to make effective use of their individual allotments. Some of the allotments were of such a character that they could not be effectively used by anyone in small units. The solution was to permit the Indians through the government to lease their lands to the whites. In some instances government officers encouraged leasing, as the whites were anxious for the use of the land and it was far easier to administer property leased to whites than to educate and stimulate Indians to use their own property. The lease money, though generally small in amount, gave the Indians further unearned income to permit the continuance of a life of idleness.

Surplus land remaining after allotments were made was often sold and the proceeds placed in a tribal fund. Natural resources, such as timber and oil, were sold and the money paid either into tribal funds or to individual Indians if the land had been allotted. From time to time per capita payments were made to the individual Indians from tribal funds. These policies all added to the unearned income of the Indian and postponed the day when it would be necessary for him to go to work to support himself.

Since the Indians were ignorant of money and its use, had little or no sense of values, and fell an easy victim to any white man who wanted to take away their property, the government, through its Indian Service employees, often took the easiest course of managing all the Indians' property for them. The government kept the Indians' money for them at the agency. When the Indians wanted something they would go to the government agent, as a child would go to his parents, and ask for it. The government agent would make all the decisions, and in many instances would either buy the thing requested or give the Indians a store order for it. Although money was sometimes given the Indians, the general belief was that the Indians could not be trusted to spend the money for the purpose agreed upon with the agent, and therefore they must not be given opportunity to misapply it. At some agencies this practice still exists, although it gives the Indians no education in the use of money, is irritating to them, and tends to decrease responsibility and increase the pauper attitude.

The typical Indian, however, has not yet advanced to the point where he has the knowledge of money and values, and of business methods that will permit him to control his own property without aid, advise, and some restrictions; nor is he ready to work consistently and regularly at more or less routine labor....

2. Wisconsin Residents Detail the Poor Health Conditions of Native People, 1929

Dr. H. G. Mertens [of Bayfield, Wisconsin testifies]:

[The Red Cliff Reservation] is only a small one and is now a part of the township of Russell, Bayfield County. A few years ago the reservation was thrown open and is now within the incorporated township of Russell. There are about 35 or 40 farmers there, white farmers I mean, and the balance are Indians. The Indians of course do not pay taxes; the Indians living within Red Cliffe village don't pay taxes. Every tax certificate is turned delinquent to the county, nobody will buy these certificates, and consequently the white farmers have to bear the tax burden. Taxes are so high that they are now confronted with the proposition of closing one of the schools....

These Indians here are in a bad condition physically due to disease because of the fact that they have had no medical supervision for years. The last 10 years they were on the reservation the Government had a [contract] physician to whom they paid $600 a year to go on the reservation one day a week. The Indians of course did not come in on the day set aside for them and did not propose to pay for treatment at other times and as a result [the physician] was doing all their work and dishing out his medicine all year for the small salary he was allowed. The Government, however, had a stock of medicines which they could have furnished if they wished to do so. Before that time the physician from the La Pointe Agency would come down to Bayfield by train and take a rig from there and drive out to the reservation, necessarily he would cut his visits as short as possible in order to catch the train back. These Indians here now have no Government physician of any kind, they are getting old and destitute and many of them are afflicted with different diseases and naturally these diseases are spread among the white people of the community.

... At the present time I am in charge of the Tri-County Tubercular Sanitarium maintained by Bayfield, Iron, and Ashland Counties. The Indian population of those three counties will not average 1½ to 2 per cent of the total population in the three counties, ... however, 12 per cent of the patients in this sanitarium are Indians afflicted with T. B. We have about 250 to 300 Indians at Red Cliffe and Bayfield, and I believe there are fewer physicians in Ashland

Survey of Conditions of the Indians in the United States, Part 5, July, 1929.

County or on the old Odanah Reservation than we have up here. Most of the Indians we get in the sanitarium are discovered real sick and are a menace to their neighbors, the most of whom are white people. Nowadays, of course, there is more effort made to get them to a sanitarium, not only for the purpose of a cure, but for the safety of their family.

... Many of the white people when taken to the sanitarium pay their own way. If they can not afford to pay $15 a week they pay a third, but [the] Indian pays nothing. They are all county charges.

... Two years ago last winter a meningitis epidemic broke out; the weather was cold, and we had a lot of snow. I was called to a place 3 or 4 miles from town and the roads were so bad that I almost had to hire a team to get there.... I had six, seven, or eight families in which there was meningitis. That, as you know, is a very dangerous disease. I had to get out there and these cases had to be isolated.

Now, these people were in very destitute circumstances and in two instances I recall I had to dig down in my pocket and supply oranges for the children to keep them from getting scurvey. The town officers had made no provisions for these people and I had to take care of them for about four months. I made numerous trips out there in all kinds of weather and my bill considering the time I spent, changing my clothes each time before going and coming back, the bad roads and hard times I had getting out there to them, and so forth, would have amounted to at least $1,200, basing it on a reasonable charge of $5 a visit. I sent a bill to Mr. Everest with the request that he send it to the Commissioner of Indian Affairs. I think my bill was around $300, and the commissioner advised me that after a thorough investigation it was found that these people were not wards of the Government and that I would have to look to local authorities for compensation. This is just one illustration of the generosity of the Federal Government. Now, I submit to you gentlemen, that the poor white farmers living in this locality are in no sense to blame for the poverty and destitution among these poor Indians. If the Indians had any money they did not spend it with us and we should not be asked to take care of their old, indigent, and sick. We have about all we can do without taking care of the Indians, but unfortunately we are located in an old Indian reservation and for the sake of humanity we are obliged to saddle a burden which rightfully belongs to the Government. It is certainly most unfair to ask [us] to do so, and it seems to me that the least they could do would be to establish a hospital in this territory, for taking care of tubercular Indians and some established hospital to take care of these Indians charging them only the actual cost of their care. I am sure if they would do that that everyone in this community would feel very grateful. I had one boy in the hospital for four months, every time he tried to work he was sent home and he was found to be in an advanced stage of T. B., they of course could not take care of him at home neither could they afford to send him away and I finally induced the county to send him as a county charge to a sanitarium, which cost about $60 a month or $14–18 a week; that boy was the only support of his parents and when he left they had nothing to eat, and I finally prevailed upon the county to pay them $20 a month.

So far as getting any of that money back is concerned, that is out of the question. It is just such cases as this that we have to deal with continually, and it is certainly a most unfair and unreasonable proposition to expect any local community to bear the brunt of the destitute Indian problem. We feel, without question, that they should be taken care of by the Government and that they are responsible for their welfare. We are always confronted by the Government with the plea "lack of funds," which we consider is just an excuse to saddle the tax burden and care of these Indians on the white people of the various communities unfortunate enough to be located on or adjacent to an Indian reservation....

There is just one more thing I might mention in connection with the health problem; there are a great many Indian children attending our public schools, and they are our chief problem in health work; not only that but the burden of expense in educating these children is borne by the whites. These Indians live in town; their children have the same advantages as the whites, yet they pay no taxes. I am sure that not over 2 per cent of the Indians pay taxes. We feel that the Federal Government should assume the burden of taking care of these Indians whether they are wards of the Government or not. I have been dealing with the Indians for 22 years up here, and I believe that the Government has gone about the Indian problem in the wrong manner. Up until a few years ago we had seven Government employees in the town where I live and it seemed to me that they were spending a lot of money for everything except what it should have been spent for, and no good came of it.

3. The Indian Reorganization Act (Wheeler–Howard Act), 1934

To conserve and develop Indian lands and resources; to extend to Indians the right to form business and other organizations; to establish a credit system for Indians; to grant certain rights of home rule to Indians; to provide for vocational education for Indians; and for other purposes.

Be it enacted by the Senate and House of Representatives of the United States of America in Congress assembled, That hereafter no land of any Indian reservation, created or set apart by treaty or agreement with the Indians, Act of Congress, Executive order, purchase, or otherwise, shall be allotted in severalty to any Indian.

Sec. 2. The existing periods of trust placed upon any Indian lands and any restriction on alienation thereof are hereby extended and continued until otherwise directed by Congress.

Sec. 3. The Secretary of the Interior, if he shall find it to be in the public interest, is hereby authorized to restore to tribal ownership the remaining surplus lands of any Indian reservation heretofore opened, or authorized to be opened, to sale, or any other form of disposal by Presidential proclamation, or by any of the public-land laws of the United States: *Provided, however,* That valid rights or claims of any persons to any lands so withdrawn existing on the date of the withdrawal shall not be affected by this Act: *Provided further,* That this section shall not apply to lands within any reclamation project heretofore authorized in any Indian reservation....

"Wheeler-Howard Act," July 18, 1934, U.S. Statutes at Large, 48: 984.

Sec. 4. Except as herein provided, no sale, devise, gift, exchange or other transfer of restricted Indian lands or of shares in the assets of any Indian tribe or corporation organized hereunder, shall be made or approved: *Provided, however,* That such lands or interests may, with the approval of the Secretary of the Interior, be sold, devised, or otherwise transferred to the Indian tribe in which the lands or shares are located or from which the shares were derived or to a successor corporation; and in all instances such lands or interests shall descend or be devised, in accordance with the then existing laws of the State, or Federal laws where applicable, in which said lands are located or in which the subject matter of the corporation is located, to any member of such tribe or of such corporation or any heirs of such member: *Provided further,* That the Secretary of the Interior may authorize voluntary exchanges of lands of equal value and the voluntary exchange of shares of equal value whenever such exchange, in his judgment, is expedient and beneficial for or compatible with the proper consolidation of Indian lands and for the benefit of cooperative organizations.

Sec. 5. The Secretary of the Interior is hereby authorized, in his discretion, to acquire through purchase, relinquishment, gift, exchange, or assignment, any interest in lands, water rights or surface rights to lands, within or without existing reservations, including trust or otherwise restricted allotments whether the allottee be living or deceased, for the purpose of providing land for Indians.

For the acquisition of such lands, interests in lands, water rights, and surface rights, and for expenses incident to such acquisition, there is hereby authorized to be appropriated, out of any funds in the Treasury not otherwise appropriated, a sum not to exceed $2,000,000 in any one fiscal year....

Title to any lands or rights acquired pursuant to this Act shall be taken in the name of the United States in trust for the Indian tribe or the individual Indian for which the land is acquired, and such lands or rights shall be exempt from State and local taxation.

Sec. 6. The Secretary of the Interior is directed to make rules and regulations for the operation and management of Indian forestry units on the principle of sustained-yield management, to restrict the number of livestock grazed on Indian range units to the estimated carrying capacity of such ranges, and to promulgate such other rules and regulations as may be necessary to protect the range from deterioration, to prevent soil erosion, to assure full utilization of the range, and like purposes.

Sec. 7. The Secretary of the Interior is hereby authorized to proclaim new Indian reservations on lands acquired pursuant to any authority conferred by this Act, or to add such lands to existing reservations: *Provided,* That lands added to existing reservations shall be designated for the exclusive use of Indians entitled by enrollment or by tribal membership to residence at such reservations....

Sec. 9. There is hereby authorized to be appropriated, out of any funds in the Treasury not otherwise appropriated, such sums as may be necessary, but not to exceed $250,000 in any fiscal year, to be expended at the order of the Secretary of the Interior, in defraying the expenses of organizing Indian chartered corporations or other organizations created under this Act.

Sec. 10. There is hereby authorized to be appropriated, out of any funds in the Treasury not otherwise appropriated, the sum of $10,000,000 to be established as a revolving fund from which the Secretary of the Interior, under such rules and regulations as he may prescribe, may make loans to Indian chartered corporations for the purpose of promoting the economic development of such tribes and of their members, and may defray the expenses of administering such loans. Repayment of amounts loaned under this authorization shall be credited to the revolving fund and shall be available for the purposes for which the fund is established. A report shall be made annually to Congress of transactions under this authorization.

Sec. 11. There is hereby authorized to be appropriated, out of any funds in the United States Treasury not otherwise appropriated, a sum not to exceed $250,000 annually, together with any unexpended balances of previous appropriations made pursuant to this section, for loans to Indians for the payment of tuition and other expenses in recognized vocational and trade schools: *Provided*, That not more than $50,000 of such sum shall be available for loans to Indian students in high schools and colleges. Such loans shall be reimbursable under rules established by the Commissioner of Indian Affairs....

Sec. 16. Any Indian tribe, or tribes, residing on the same reservation, shall have the right to organize for its common welfare, and may adopt an appropriate constitution and bylaws, which shall become effective when ratified by a majority vote of the adult members of the tribe, or of the adult Indians residing on such reservation, as the case may be, at a special election authorized and called by the Secretary of the Interior under such rules and regulations as he may prescribe. Such constitution and bylaws when ratified as aforesaid and approved by the Secretary of the Interior shall be revocable by an election open to the same voters and conducted in the same manner as hereinabove provided. Amendments to the constitution and by-laws may be ratified and approved by the Secretary in the same manner as the original constitution and bylaws.

In addition to all powers vested in any Indian tribe or tribal council by existing law, the constitution adopted by said tribe shall also vest in such tribe or its tribal council the following rights and powers: To employ legal counsel, the choice of counsel and fixing of fees to be subject to the approval of the Secretary of the Interior; to prevent the sale, disposition, lease, or encumbrance of tribal lands, interests in lands, or other tribal assets without the consent of the tribe; and to negotiate with the Federal, State, and local Governments. The Secretary of the Interior shall advise such tribe or its tribal council of all appropriation estimates or Federal projects for the benefit of the tribe prior to the submission of such estimates to the Bureau of the Budget and the Congress.

Sec. 17. The Secretary of the Interior may, upon petition by at least one-third of the adult Indians, issue a charter of incorporation to such tribe: *Provided*, That such charter shall not become operative until ratified at a special election by a majority vote of the adult Indians living on the reservation. Such charter may convey to the incorporated tribe the power to purchase, take by gift, or bequest, or otherwise, own, hold, manage, operate, and dispose of property of every description, real and personal, including the power to purchase restricted Indian lands and to issue in exchange therefor interests in corporate property, and such further powers as may be incidental to the conduct of corporate business, not inconsistent with law, but no authority shall be granted to sell, mortgage, or lease for a period exceeding ten years any of the land included in the limits of the reservation. Any charter so issued shall not be revoked or surrended except by Act of Congress.

Sec. 18. This Act shall not apply to any reservation wherein a majority of the adult Indians, voting at a special election duly called by the Secretary of the Interior, shall vote against its application. It shall be the duty of the Secretary of the Interior, within one year after the passage and approval of this Act, to call such an election, which election shall be held by secret ballot upon thirty days' notice.

Sec. 19. The term "Indian" as used in this Act shall include all persons of Indian descent who are members of any recognized Indian tribe now under Federal jurisdiction, and all persons who are descendants of such members who were, on June 1, 1934, residing within the present boundaries of any Indian reservation, and shall further include all other persons of one-half or more Indian blood. For the purposes of this Act, Eskimos and other aboriginal peoples of Alaska shall be considered Indians. The term "tribe" wherever used in this Act shall be construed to refer to any Indian tribe, organized band, pueblo, or the Indians residing on one reservation. The words "adult Indians" wherever used in this Act shall be construed to refer to Indians who have attained the age of twenty-one years.

Approved, June 18, 1934.

4. Rupert Costo (Cahuilla) Condemns the Indian New Deal, 1986

… The IRA [Indian Reorganization Act of 1934] was the last great drive to assimilate the American Indian. It was also a program to colonialize the Indian tribes. All else had failed to liberate the Indians from their land: genocide, treaty-making and treaty-breaking, substandard education, disruption of Indian religion and culture, and the last and most oppressive of such measures, the Dawes Allotment Act. Assimilation into the dominant society, if by assimilation we mean the adoption of certain technologies and techniques, had already been underway for some hundred years. After all, the Indians were not and are not fools; we are always ready to improve our condition. But assimilation, meaning fading into the general society with a complete loss of our identity and our culture, was another thing entirely, and we had fought against this from the first coming of the white man.

This type of assimilation would be the foregone conclusion of the Indian Reorganization Act. Colonialization of the tribes was to be accomplished through communal enclaves subject to federal domination through the power

Rupert Costo remarks in Kenneth Philp, editor, *Indian Self Rule: First Hand Accounts of Indian-White Relations from Roosevelt to Reagan*, 1986, pp. 48–52.

of the secretary of the interior. Now this view of the IRA is now held by practically all of the historians who write the history of the IRA era.

The record shows otherwise. All one must do is to read and study the hearings held in the Congress, the testimony of Indian witnesses, the evidence of life itself, the statements of the Indian commissioner, and the practically identical tribal constitutions adopted by, or forced upon, the Indians under the IRA. In these constitutions the authority of the secretary of the interior is more powerful than it was before the so-called New Deal. No wonder the Indians called it the Indian Raw Deal.

The IRA did not allow the Indians their independence, which was guaranteed in treaties and agreements and confirmed in court decisions. It did not protect their sovereignty. Collier did not invent self-government: the right of Indians to make their own decisions, to make their own mistakes, to control their own destiny. The IRA had within it, in its wording and in its instruments, such as the tribal constitutions, the destruction of the treaties and of Indian self-government.

There are those who believe that most of the Indians who opposed the IRA were members of allotted tribes who had been economically successful with their allotments. This is a simplistic response, and one that displays a serious lack of understanding of Indian affairs and history. Allotments certainly did not originate with the Dawes Act. They also were established in treaties. The Dawes Act did, however, force Indians into the allotment system, with a guarantee that they would have to sell their land, either through taxation or by sheer physical force. Those who survived created what they had always wanted, an estate for themselves and their children, a type of insurance against being moved again like cattle to other lands and the chance to make a decent living on their own land....

On May 17, 1934, in hearings before the Senate, the great Yakima nation, in a statement signed by their chiefs and councilmen, said, "We feel that the best interests of the Indians can be preserved by the continuance of treaty laws and carried out in conformity with the treaty of 1855 entered into by the fathers of some of the undersigned chiefs and Governor Stevens of the territory of Washington." Now these are only a few examples of some of the testimony given by Indian witnesses and by most of the tribes. Many refused to even consider the IRA and rejected it outright.

But the commissioner of Indian affairs reported to the House of Representatives on May 7, 1934, that, "I do not think that any study of the subject with all of the supporting petitions, reports, and referendums could leave any doubt that the Indian opinion is strongly for the bill." He then proceeded with this outright falsification of the facts, saying, "In Oklahoma I would say quite overwhelmingly they favor the bill." Both Congressmen Roy Ayres of Montana and Theodore Werner of South Dakota disputed those statements. They showed that Collier was falsifying the facts.

During April 1934, the tribes that had bitterly opposed the IRA attended some of the ten meetings held by the commissioner of Indian affairs throughout the country. Here, as evidence shows, they were subjected to Collier's manipulations. In May, they came before the House of Representatives and completely reversed themselves. In fact, they gave a blanket endorsement to the Indian Reorganization Act. The congressmen, in shocked disbelief, prodded them again and again. Finally they asked, "If the proposed legislation is completely changed into an entirely different act would you then also endorse it?" The Indian delegates, according to many of their tribesmen and tribeswomen said, without any authority of their people, "Yes. Even then we would endorse it." In short, at least two of the tribal delegates gave a blanket endorsement of the IRA in advance of the final legislation. How did this happen? I can tell you how it happened. They received promises that were never kept. They received some special considerations and they felt the arm of the enforcer ordering them to accept or be destroyed. That was Collier's way, as I very well know.

In California, at Riverside, forty tribes were assembled. All but three voted against the proposed bill. Collier then reported that most of the California tribes were for the proposed bill. The historical record was falsified, and his falsification was swallowed whole by Kenneth Philp who also stated in his book that "several mission Indians, led by Rupert Costo, agreed with an unsigned three-page circular sent around the reservation which claimed Collier's ideas were 'communistic and socialistic.'" The implication is that this was a sneaky, underhanded job. The truth is that there was a complete cover letter with that circular, signed by me and my tribe. We were outraged at the provisions of the proposed bill.

It is a curious fact that, in all the ten meetings held with Indians over the country, in not one meeting was there a copy of the proposed legislation put before the people. We were asked to vote on so-called explanations. The bill itself was withheld. We were told we need not vote but the meetings were only to discuss the Collier explanations. In the end, however, we were required to vote. And I suppose you would call this maneuvering self-rule. I call it fraud. The Hupa Indians of northern California had two petitions on this proposed bill. One was to be signed by those supporting it; the other, by those who opposed it. In neither case had anyone seen the actual bill, but they rejected it on a massive scale on the basis of explanations alone.

The Crow rejected the IRA and stated for the record in a letter to Senator Burton K. Wheeler, one of the sponsors of the bill, "That under the Collier-chartered community plan, which has been compared to a fifth-rate *poor farm* by newspapers in Indian country, the Indian is being led to believe that they, for the first time in history, would have self-government." But according to the bill, any plans the Indians might have for such self-government would have to be first submitted to the interior secretary or commissioner of Indian affairs for supervision and approval. Self-government to this extent was already accomplished through the tribal councils and tribal business committees, which, by the way, were organized and functioning long before Collier manifested his great interest in the Indians in general.

Now at these councils, Indians discuss matters they consider of vital interest and initiate measures for better management of their affairs, but no action may become effective without the approval of the commissioner of Indian affairs, or the secretary of the interior. Where is the advantage of an almost similar system bearing John Collier's name? Can we say that this power of the interior was forced upon the commissioner in the final proposed bill? No, not at all. His original bill contained not less than thirty-three references making it obligatory for the interior secretary to approve vital decisions of the tribes.

It is a matter of record that in California Indians were afraid to come to meetings for fear of losing their jobs if they showed disapproval of the Collier proposed bill. On the second day of the Riverside meeting, the Collier enforcers would not allow us to speak, and according to one report of an Indian organization, "they almost threw Rupert Costo out." Another element of the Collier enforcer policy is found in the warning to civil service employees in the BIA by Interior Secretary Ickes that they would be dismissed if they spoke out against Bureau policies on the proposed bill....

5. Ben Reifel (Brulé Lakota) Praises the Legacy of John Collier, 1986

While I was a boy growing up on the Rosebud Indian Reservation, we had the most sickening poverty that one could imagine. Tuberculosis was a killer of Indians. The people on the Pine Ridge Reservation and at Oglala were eating their horses to survive. Impoverishment was everywhere.

I remember going to Oglala in 1933 as a farm agent. The superintendent of the reservation, a gentleman by the name of James H. McGregor, looked to me almost as a son. After I graduated from college with a degree in agriculture, he recommended that the commissioner appoint me to be a farm agent. The reason he wanted me to be a farm agent was because, in this particular district on the Pine Ridge Reservation, all of the 1,300 people, except two or three mixed-blood families, had conducted their business with a farm agent who was a graduate of Carlisle by the name of Jake White Cow Killer. He talked Sioux and Lakota in all of his communications with these people. He was a member of the village in that area. McGregor wanted someone who could speak the language.

I was only twenty-five years of age, and the old timers would come in to have their dances. They could have dances only on Saturday night. Bert Hills Close to Lodge came in and said, "I want to get permission to have a dance tonight for our group in the village." I had just received a copy of a telegram signed by John Collier, Commissioner of Indian Affairs. It said, "If the Indian people want to have dances, dances all night, all week, that is their business." So I read it to him. Bert sat there, stroked his braids, looked off in the distance, and he said in Lakota, "Well, I'll be damned." The interesting part of it was, if they did not have the dance Saturday night, they would have a dance a month later, because they felt they were on their own. The Indian policemen were not going to police anybody, and it was just too much for them to have self-determination about their own dances.

Speaking of the benefits of the Indian Reorganization Act, we now have more young men and women in universities and colleges. Some of them are represented here. When I was in college in 1928, I could count the number of Indian students, at least from our reservation, on the fingers of your hand. Now they are in the hundreds and up to the thousands at universities and colleges around the country. We also have community colleges on five or six of our reservations.

The Flandreaux Santee Sioux Indian Tribe is made up of a group of about a hundred families that came into the Dakotas during the massacre in Minnesota [in 1862]. They homesteaded along with the whites around the Flandreaux

Ben Reifel remarks in Kenneth Philp, editor, *Indian Self Rule: First Hand Accounts of Indian-White Relations from Roosevelt to Reagan,* 1986, pp. 54–58.

Indian School. When the Indian Reorganization Act was finally passed, they got a leader and they went to us for assistance. They accepted the act and drafted a constitution, by-laws, and a charter. They also took advantage of the Indian land purchase provisions, and they bought farms around there. And then housing was made available under a rehabilitation program for the people who were needy. They got houses on their forty-acre tracts. Last month, under the Supreme Court decision for the Seminoles, they could have bingo. So they are now making good money playing bingo, and the state cannot touch them. This is because the Indian people have rights under the trust responsibility.

But getting back to the Indian Reorganization Act, there was in 1934 an Indian congress at Rapid City to discuss the Wheeler-Howard bill. Walter V. Woehlke, John Collier, and Henry Roe Cloud, a Winnebago Indian, were there. Henry Roe Cloud was probably one of the few Indians at the time that had a doctor's degree. I was quite impressed with him. Henry Roe Cloud had recently been appointed the first Indian to be the superintendent of the Haskell Institute.

And I remember Rev. Joseph Eagle Hawk, one of the dear friends of mine in the community. He was a fine gentleman and a Presbyterian minister. Speaking of Indians not having a right to express themselves, we held this meeting at Rapid City for three or four days. I took leave to go up there because I wanted to see what it was all about. When Roe Cloud finished explaining part of the bill, Rev. Joe Eagle Hawk got up and said to Roe Cloud:

> You know, when we used to ship cattle to Omaha, Nebraska, they
> would go down to the slaughter house and they had a goat and they
> would lead a goat through the slaughter. The cattle would follow the
> goat in, the goat's life would be saved, and all the cattle would be killed.
> I think that is what you are, this Judas goat.

And he said that before the commissioner. I was impressed.

One of the things discussed at Rapid City was establishing some kind of official constitutional tribal government. When I grew up as a kid on the reservation, we had general tribal councils. What did they talk about when they came together? They passed a resolution asking the secretary of the interior, or the federal government, to allow them to have an attorney to represent them in their claims. When they had any tribal monies in place, the congressmen, about election time, would come around and say we will get you a per capita payment. They would then get a per capita payment, because at that time our Indian people, since 1921, even before that in South Dakota, were entitled to vote in the general election. If there was some of the tribal land to be leased, the general tribal council would come together and pass a resolution.

When I was a kid, there was also an old fellow called Chief High Bald Eagle. In those days we had an Indian trader store and a post office with counters and cages. Old High Bald Eagle was sitting up there with his legs crossed. He must have been about eighty or ninety years old; he looked like two hundred to me. We were having what we called a Scattergood dam constructed not too far away from our home. They were having a big tribal council meeting, and someone said to High Eagle in our language, "Why are you not up there at that big meeting?" He said, "When I was a young man years ago, when things were really important, then our leaders got together. But now, when a child gets constipated just about August eating chokecherries and it gets so his bowels are all stuck up, they have to have a council meeting on it." That is about as important as I thought the council meetings were on the Rosebud Reservation. That was also true at Pine Ridge. So I was impressed with Collier's idea that Indians would get together and form some kind of governmental operation where they would democratically elect their own people and select their own leaders.

I was also concerned over the years about the tribal courts. Tribal court judges were appointed by the superintendent or the Indian agent. There was no appeal from them. Before the Indian Reorganization Act came along, I remember my brother was thrown in jail because he lived close to where there was a big fight going on and they thought he was a part of it. My younger brother came in where I was working in a store, and he said, "Hey, our brother George is in jail." So what did I do? I knew the superintendent lived near by because I was a close friend of his son. I went over there, and he said, "What happened, Ben?" Well, I told him what happened, and he wrote out a little note which I gave to Andrew Night Pipe, who was the chief of police. Andrew Night Pipe unlocked the door and let my brother go home. That was the sort of thing that was going on, and I felt we needed a better judicial system.

I was really impressed with the original draft of the so-called Wheeler-Howard bill. In it was a section where there would be a circuit court that would move from one reservation to another. Funds would be provided for this court to operate. Under the federal system, there would be the right of appeal from the local court just like any other court. There would be none of this business that goes on where the judges are appointed by the superintendent or the tribal council. The revised bill was cut from forty or fifty pages to just about eleven pages. The court system and several other things were taken out.

After the Rapid City meeting, I asked the superintendent for permission to talk about the bill with the people; he agreed. But he felt that there was a little red tinge to all of this, because one of the remarks he made to me was "I do not mind the little red schoolhouses as long as they are not red on the inside." Nevertheless, he was very supportive of my going out and explaining this bill. Of course, there were those on the reservation who were very opposed to it. And there were those who were for it. Think of me, only twenty-five years old, getting up there arguing with the old timers such as American Horse. I do not know who all the rest of them were. I felt that this was something we could support.

Conditions have improved. Tribal councils have been organized. They are fighting among themselves, but as Floyd O'Neil said, this is no different than Congress. In South Dakota, some tribal councils cannot even write checks, because they are tied up in fussing over who is going to be in control. That is no different than in California where the governor was not going to make payments to employees. The legislative body would not go along. It took the Supreme Court of the United States or the federal court to order them to make payments to the employees....

◈ ESSAYS

Perhaps one of the Indian New Deal's most controversial aspects was Collier's support of livestock reduction on the Navajo Reservation. In the first essay, Marsha Weisiger, the Julie and Rocky Dixon Chair of U.S. Western History at the University of Oregon, explores the gendered nuances of livestock reduction. How did livestock reduction affect Diné women? How did Diné women resist livestock reduction? In the second essay, John R. Finger, a professor emeritus of history at the University of Tennessee, highlights some of the dilemmas the Indian New Deal posed for Native communities where the gospel of individualism had won many adherents. By the 1930s, Indian lands were much less isolated, and communities such as the Eastern Cherokee also had to confront the mixed blessings brought by an influx of tourists. Collier's emphasis on tribalism earned praise from some members of the tribe, while others, such as Fred Blythe Bauer, bitterly opposed the commissioner's initiatives.

Diné Women and Livestock Reduction in the New Deal Era

BY MARSHA WEISIGER

IN 1936, LOCAL NEWSPAPERS in Winslow, Arizona, and Gallup, New Mexico, reported that the women were inciting a revolt on the Navajo Reservation. For three years, John Collier, the commissioner of Indian Affairs, had pressured Navajos to slash herds in an effort to conserve severely overgrazed rangelands. Now trouble was brewing, the *Gallup Independent* claimed, in the language of yellow journalism, "due to the dissatisfaction of the squaws over Collier's policies." Evidence of this simmering rebellion is admittedly meager. Very few Navajo women spoke English, and the government officials who created much of the historical record tended to ignore them. But the few clues that do surface here and there are suggestive. Consider the account of a community meeting near Kayenta, where perhaps 250 Diné (as they call themselves), nearly all of them men, had gathered. Before them stood Denehotso Hattie. Although almost blind from trachoma, she was the meeting's "unquestioned, dominating leader," and an "aggressive and vigorous speaker." Pointing her finger at E. R. Fryer, the newly appointed superintendent of the Navajo Service, Hattie denounced the government's plan for range management. She spoke so heatedly and rapidly that Fryer's interpreter, Howard Gorman, could not keep up, or perhaps Gorman was reluctant to translate her invective. Nonetheless, it was clear that the woman did not blame government officials alone. She scolded Diné men, too, pointing at them as they hung their heads. Diné councilmen and community leaders had acquiesced to the wholesale slaughter of stock and the confinement of flocks into grazing districts, bringing poverty and despair to their people. Hattie held them all accountable.

Marsha Weisiger, "Gendered Injustice: Navajo Livestock Reduction in the New Deal Era." *Western Historical Quarterly* 38 (Winter 2007): 437–55.

This story illustrates the significant, but often overlooked, part that Diné women played in resisting and remembering the environmental injustice known as Navajo livestock reduction. The term "environmental justice" is usually reserved for the recent political movement to fight for poor and marginalized racial and ethnic communities that bear the burden of our society's toxic wastes and other environmental hazards. But noxious neighborhoods are not the only sites of environmental injustice.... Today, the indigenous peoples of the American West and *Nuevo Mexicanos* define their ongoing struggles against the federal agencies that dispossessed them from their lands and livelihoods as battles for "environmental justice," a useful, if sometimes unsettling, way of viewing conservation conflicts. Significantly, women have been on the vanguard of the environmental justice movement in the American West and throughout the nation, as they were on the Navajo Reservation. The story of Navajo livestock reduction illuminates the gendered politics of conservation and the crucial contribution of women's resistance to the failure of the New Deal program to save the soil.

John Collier's conservation program, to be sure, sought to address an environmental and impending human calamity. He and his men felt compelled to decrease herds drastically because Diné had allowed their animals to overgraze the land, which, especially when coupled with climate change beginning in the late-nineteenth century, acutely accelerated erosion. Climate change—a long period of intense drought followed by a new pattern of high-energy, convective summer storms—likely initiated the network of arroyos that even now scar the land. According to tree-ring data, the 1870s and 1880s had been extremely dry, although punctuated by years of considerable rain. Then came the severe drought of 1899–1904, with scant snow and rainfall. Some years saw almost none. Not since the 1660s—and before then, the 1250s—had the region suffered such painful drought. With so little moisture, plants weakened, setting the stage for rapid erosion when intense summer downpours brought flash flooding. Such storms came regularly during the prolonged wet period of 1905–1920—the likes of which had been unseen for nearly a century. Compounding the damage, some of the highly erodible sandstones in the area proved particularly sensitive to these climatic shifts.

The effect of livestock on this brittle environment was cumulative and dynamic. When livestock continuously defoliate favored forbs, grasses, and shrubs, they eventually kill the native vegetation they prefer and encourage the invasion and spread of less palatable plants, both native and exotic. As vegetation density decreases, larger areas of soil become exposed to the baking sun, making them more arid. And as the patches of bare ground become wider, the wind begins to carry away the topsoil. As early as the first decades of the 1900s, increasingly crowded flocks on the reservation—amplified by a handful of wealthy stockowners—and competition from Anglo-American and Hispanic ranchers on the reservation's fringes had depleted forage, restructured plant communities, and allowed greasewood, snakeweed, and other unpalatable and sometimes toxic weeds to flourish.

Many Diné had discerned this degradation. Some called for the exclusion of competitors from the "Checkerboard" on the reservation's periphery, a patchwork of Navajo, federal, state, and privately-owned lands, and for expansion into new areas, much as ranchers have done throughout the history of the American West. Some called for the development of stock water so that poorly watered areas could be used for grazing. Others placed faith in their belief that the ceremonies that reenacted the creation of the earth could reestablish order in the natural world and restore *hózhó*, or beauty and balance. Still more had remained largely unaware of the altered landscape, in part because ecological change often occurs incrementally, escaping notice. Nonetheless, by the 1930s, nearly one million sheep and goats, or their equivalents in horses and cattle, ranged across the Navajo Reservation, and the damage triggered by overgrazing and climate change could no longer be ignored.

Collier believed that if the range continued to deteriorate, sheep and goats would starve, and ultimately, so would Navajos. As he admonished the Navajo Tribal Council, the grasses and soils were important "because if they go everything else goes—everything, including your own human life." He cared deeply about the fate of the Navajos. An anti-modernist like many social reformers of his generation, he believed that Native communities, particularly Navajos, somehow captured a purer, more authentic way of life. In the 1920s, he had described the Navajos as paragons of self-sufficiency and cultural integrity, a beacon for the larger society to follow. They had "preserved intact their religion, their ancient morality, their social forms and their appreciation of beauty." That way of life, however, depended mightily on the land. He had to act quickly to restore the range, he felt, for the future of an entire people hung in the balance.

Yet in their haste to respond to an environmental crisis, Collier and his conservationists unwittingly made matters worse, ecologically and culturally. Among their many mistakes, they ignored the importance of long-established cultural patterns, disparaged local knowledge and cultural understandings of nature, and refused to listen to Navajos' advice in implementing the livestock reduction program. Significantly, they disregarded women. The fact that women really mattered in Diné society—that they had the power to sway communities—never fully penetrated the consciousness of New Deal policy-makers. True, Collier recognized their central place in Diné social organization and economy. And yet, when he and his staff sought Navajo approval of the conservation program, they excluded women from the decision-making. That was a mistake. Indeed, Howard Gorman, who was an assistant to Superintendent Fryer and later the chairman of the Navajo Tribal Council, observed that the conservation effort "failed largely because women of the tribe were not won over to Commissioner Collier's program."

In ignoring women, Collier and Fryer followed a path laid out by earlier policy-makers. Since the mid-nineteenth century, the Bureau of Indian Affairs had endeavored to transform Native societies by stripping women of their power as agricultural producers and hide processors and transforming them into good housewives. The Dawes Act, for example, sought—with limited success—to create patriarchal families by allotting lands only to male heads of households. And on the Navajo Reservation, the bureau had instituted an all-male tribal council in the 1920s to approve oil leases and decide other important matters.

Collier challenged the principle of cultural assimilation that governed Indian affairs, and yet he never questioned its patriarchal underpinnings....

Indeed, some of the problems historians have attributed to factionalism among powerful men were likely the result of the influence of women. Throughout the New Deal era, frustrated government officials complained that the Navajo Tribal Council vacillated from one meeting to the next, first agreeing to the government's plans, then demurring. That change of heart can be explained by Diné women's outcry against stock reduction. Between 1934, when range riders began seizing Navajo goats, and 1943, when the tribal council voted to suspend stock reduction, women goaded the council to resist the government through their participation in community meetings, petition drives, and acts of disobedience.

Diné lived in a matricentered society.... Women stood at the center of almost all aspects of Diné life and thought: spiritual beliefs, kinship, residence patterns, land-use traditions, and economy. Their most important deity was— and is—Changing Woman, who created the Diné and their livestock and gave them their central ceremony, Blessingway. Diné traced descent exclusively through their mothers, and a newly married couple generally built their hogan near the wife's family, creating closely-knit networks of mothers, daughters, and sisters. But women's power did not rest merely on female solidarity. Women were important to economic production, and significantly they controlled the means of their own production: livestock and land. Diné acquired use-rights to grazing land through matrilineages headed by elderly women. And women typically owned a large share of the sheep and almost all of the goats. These herds sustained lives: they provided food for families and produced the wool that women transformed into blankets, which by the early-twentieth century had become valued trade goods. Living in a society that measured wealth and prestige in livestock, those women who owned especially large flocks thereby amplified their autonomy and authority within their rural communities. They did not take demands to reduce those flocks without a fight.

Rebellion against stock reduction did not arise immediately, and even then, it did not appear everywhere. The program's initial phase in the winter of 1933–34 was largely voluntary. With funds from the Federal Emergency Relief Administration and the Agricultural Adjustment Administration, Collier's agents and local traders purchased more than 86,500 sheep from Navajo stockowners. That was somewhat fewer than the goal of 100,000 head, but for the most part, Diné stockowners willingly sold their unproductive culls to the government, which even purchased old gummers that traders would never buy. In essence, the federal purchases replaced the fall market for lambs, a market that had dwindled to nothing since the beginning of the Great Depression.

Not everyone who gave up their sheep did so all that willingly, however. Frank Lenzie, who supervised reduction, reported that "considerable opposition to the disposition of their stock was voiced by a large number of Indians in all parts of the Navajo country, their feeling being that the delegates did not have the right to obligate them to such a course." One of the bureau's stockmen, Carl Beck, reported that women particularly resented the idea that a handful of men had promised they would sell their sheep. Women owned their own flocks, and no one had the right to tell them what to do with their property. But it was not only women who objected. In some quarters, people complained that they were being reduced to poverty, for tribal council members (many of whom were themselves large stockowners) encouraged everyone to reduce 10 percent of their herds across the board, rather than asking the wealthiest to shoulder the burden.

Still, for the most part, this initial reduction went smoothly, seducing Collier into thinking that Navajos understood the need for the program, or at least readily followed the tribal council's lead. And yet it would have been wise for him to listen more carefully to the Navajo Tribal Council. One delegate after another had tried to advise him that his broader plan to dramatically decrease herds would never find acceptance among the Diné. Henry Taliman, from Oak Springs, put it most emphatically. "Under no consideration," he warned, "will the Navajos favor reducing their livestock." He knew full well that the people back home opposed stock reduction. "They are just so afraid this thing is going to be carried out so they begged me especially not to accept this program." Collier apparently pressured Taliman to change his mind during a closed executive session that evening. No minutes were kept of that discussion, so we have no way of knowing what transpired, but when the council reconvened the next day, Taliman himself presented the resolution calling for cooperation with Collier's program. The commissioner declared victory and went home. Had he instead heeded Taliman's warning, he might have better prepared to avoid all out war.

The turning point in women's rejection of Collier's program came in 1934, when the government issued a mandate to nearly eliminate their goats. The Diné valued goats in ways that Collier and his men never fully grasped. Conservationists targeted these animals because they had little market value and damaged both rangelands and forests. And yet, for many Diné, goats measured the difference between feast and famine. Many subsistence herds consisted largely of goats, because they were hardier and survived winters better than sheep and so were more dependable as a source of food. Families could drink goat's milk and eat goat cheese and meat while reserving their sheep to breed or barter at the local trading post. The loss of those goats would prove devastating.

Only a faint note of protest arose, however, at the March meeting of the Navajo Tribal Council, and even then, Collier seemed to quiet the councilmen's fears. Jacob Morgan—who would soon emerge as the leading voice of the beleaguered smallholder and Collier's nemesis—expressed concern for those with few sheep and many goats. "I have been wondering," he remarked, "if it would not be possible in some way to think of these people." Henry Taliman suggested that they table the issue until they could discuss it with the people back home and then "act upon how the livestock can be reduced to the best satisfaction of the people." Chee Dodge, the wealthiest stockowner among the Diné and widely respected as a leader, thought that the council could resolve the issue now by sparing those with flocks smaller than 100 head. Collier listened thoughtfully to these concerns (it would be one of the last times he would do so) and responded that it might even be possible to help poorer families by replacing goats with sheep acquired from large stockowners. That would eliminate goats and yet give families enough livestock to live on. Collier's assurances laid the council's fears to rest, and the men unanimously resolved to encourage their people to sell half their goats, with the proviso that the delegates would ask the people back home to "consider the matter and devise ways and means" for carrying out the program.

The council's resolve would not last long. Back home, the men quickly discovered that the people who owned goats had no intention of giving them up without a fight. Both Carl Beck, the BIA stockman, and C. N. Millington, national head of the Indian Emergency Conservation Work program, who attended several community meetings, noted that women were especially vocal in their criticism of the council's decision to sacrifice their goats. Women owned the vast majority of these animals, and they felt betrayed by the men who had promised to cut their herds. Some women resolved to reduce their flocks in their own way by eating lots of goat meat, and they set about butchering the animals for home consumption. But all this talk of selling off their goats left them feeling anxious and powerless.

When the council again convened at Crownpoint and later at Keams Canyon, the mood was tense. Throngs of as many as five or six hundred Diné women and men came to observe, their numbers spilling out under the trees. Large crowds often came to these meetings, but now the council members seemed more keenly aware of the people's interest in the proceedings. Indeed, the night before the Keams Canyon meeting, the council met with a gathering of angry people, who apparently accused the men of failing to represent them. Some of the women and the older men had pleaded with the councilmen, demanding to know how they were to support themselves without their goats. So as this series of meetings opened, the councilmen did their best to explain to the bureau that few favored goat reduction, and they struggled with officials to find some kind of middle ground.

Albert Sandoval, a representative from the Southern Navajo jurisdiction, hoped to find another solution. He asked whether it would be possible to reduce the goats by eating them and by selling butchered meat to the reservation schools. He figured that if each family ate six head of goats and sheep per month, over the course of a year the Diné could reduce the entire stock population by almost half, not counting the annual reproduction of lambs and kids. Collier's representative at that meeting, James Stewart, replied that such an approach would take too long, and besides normal consumption had never brought a decrease in annual livestock numbers. But Sandoval stood his ground and requested more time to consider the proper course of action, pointedly calling Stewart's attention to the fact that the council's agreement to reduce goats had specified that the people themselves would devise the method for cutting their herds down. Sandoval challenged Stewart, and the crowd greeted his defiance with laughter and applause.

Goat reduction would come to symbolize stock reduction and would color the image of the entire conservation program. Poor planning of goat reduction hindered Collier's men from the outset. One major problem was the remote locations of many herds, which made it difficult to drive them to railheads. In one notorious incident, BIA stockman Carl Beck purchased 3,500 head of goats and sheep around Navajo Mountain, an utterly remote area on the extreme northwestern edge of the reservation. Before long, Beck realized that the animals would never survive the long trek to the nearest passable road, where they could be picked up by truck. So he herded them into a box canyon, ordered them shot en masse, and left them to the coyotes, buzzards, and crows. Stories like this one— substantiated by piles of bones littering the ground—along with rumors of government agents burning goats alive reverberated across the reservation.

Diné women owned almost all of these flocks of goats, so they experienced particular anguish as their goats were slaughtered. In oral histories, witnesses describe scene after scene of women weeping over their livestock. Howard Gorman later shared his recollection of events at the Hubbell Trading Post near Ganado: "It was a terrible sight where the slaughtering took place," he told a visitor. "Near what is now the Trading Post was a ditch where sheep intestines were dumped, and these were scattered all over. The women folks were crying, mourning over such a tragic scene." These women did not soon forget the powerlessness they felt at the hands of government agents.

Collier first felt their wrath at the ballot box. The cornerstone of his Indian New Deal was the Indian Reorganization Act, a laudable—if sometimes culturally misguided—program to create tribal councils, promote economic development, and foster self-determination. When in 1935 it came time to vote on whether to take part in the IRA, the Navajos narrowly rejected the measure. Many Diné understood the election as a referendum on stock reduction and on Collier himself. Particularly in the eastern and northern jurisdictions of the reservation, where goat reduction had been especially devastating, people registered their anger by voting against the IRA. Upon defeat, Collier himself recognized that women may well have tipped the balance. Many, Collier discovered, had thought that a vote for the act was a vote for continued stock reduction, and he confided that it was this belief that "undoubtedly controlled the votes of a great many of the older Indians, particularly the women."

Women continued to voice their indignation as conservationists imposed maximum limits on the numbers of livestock each family could graze. By 1936, range managers estimated that the reservation could carry roughly 560,000 sheep and goats, or their equivalent in cattle and horses. (Each sheep or goat was one "sheep unit"; since cattle and horses required more forage, each counted as four or five sheep, respectively.) And yet after years of effort to cut the number of stock, more than 918,000 sheep units remained. The Navajos still needed to bring the stocking pressure down by nearly 40 percent. To do so, administrators established the "maximum permit number" for each family, using a calculation that took into account the number of stock a family could possess if the carrying capacity were divided equally, adjusted by the number of animals that those with even smaller flocks actually owned. Those who had fewer animals could keep all of them but acquire no more. Families with more than the maximum had to remove the surplus stock from the reservation either by selling them or (for those few who could afford it, like Chee Dodge) by leasing pastures elsewhere.

Bringing the number of stock down to the land's carrying capacity required an accurate count of the animals, recorded at dipping vats and branding round-ups.

This became the official register for a grazing permit system designed to convey or withhold land-use rights forevermore. Administrators wanted an authoritative register of ownership because they had long been frustrated with what they saw as Indian chicanery. In the late 1920s, the BIA had imposed a grazing fee on especially large flocks to no avail. Many bureau employees believed that Navajos had circumvented those regulations by claiming that large herds were in fact clusters of smaller, individually owned flocks of a few hundred head. Those tactics, officials thought, had stymied efforts to levy grazing fees and thereby discourage enormous herds.

In truth, of course, each family member actually *did* own her or his own flock and pooled their animals to herd them or take them through the dipping vats. One woman, whom the ethnographer Gladys Reichard called "Dezba," tried to explain Diné conceptions of ownership to a government worker. When Dezba and her family took their sheep to the Ganado vat just before the first stock reduction, an agent told her that, by his count, she had 810 sheep and goats. But Dezba begged to differ. She clarified that they were not all hers: some belonged to her husband, others to her brother, and still more to her two daughters and her two sons. She herself owned only 125 head. But nothing she said convinced the man, and he walked off in disgust. Government officials, in fact, seemed almost mulishly unwilling to comprehend the complex fabric of the Navajo economy, which wove together communal conceptions of land use and obligations of reciprocity with highly autonomous notions of livestock ownership. That failure to grasp basic property concepts caused a good deal of animosity that might have been avoided.

Instead of crediting actual owners, federal officials assigned possession of an entire family flock to the federally designated "head of household." Generally, that person was a man. Only widowed, divorced, or unmarried women could be registered stockowners. A few married women made it onto the list by taking their sheep and goats through the dipping vats themselves. But their designation did not last long. Take 'Asdzáá Yazzie, for example. She lost her chance at a permit when her husband amended the record to include his sheep, which had been counted erroneously with someone else's flock. On learning of the error, the district supervisor deleted her from the register and issued a permit in her husband's name. Crediting men with the family flock reflected long-time BIA practices and the patriarchal values of the Mormon superintendent of the Navajo Service, E. R. Fryer, not those of the matricentered Diné. In Fryer's eyes, when a man and a woman ran their flocks together, they became a single economic unit, headed by a man. To his credit, Fryer followed this logic through the twists and turns of Navajo marital relationships. When a couple divorced, the woman reasserted and regained a recognized autonomy. Even polygamous women who lived apart from their husbands in independent households could gain permits for their flocks. And yet, when a woman shared her hearth with a man, or even with her natal family, she lost an important measure of her autonomy: her independent grazing rights.

As word spread that the registration of sheep heralded a new and dramatic program for reducing livestock, many Diné became defiant. Resistance flared especially in those districts where large numbers of herds exceeded stingy stock limits, some as low as 61 to 83 sheep units. In the northern districts, the BIA arrested a handful of stockowners and sentenced them to six months in jail for interfering with the round-up of horses and cattle. The most infamous case involved Hastiin Tso, Mister Big Man, the vice president of the Twin Lakes chapter (a local political and community center), who refused to take his sheep to the dipping vat for the official count. To make an example of Big Man, Fryer asked the tribal court to issue a warrant for his arrest. As Big Man stopped in Gallup on his way home from a protest meeting, three Navajo policemen attempted to take him into custody. When he resisted arrest, the officers beat him with blackjacks and a pistol. The tribal court dismissed the case, in part because the police had been outside their jurisdiction. The story of the attack, nonetheless, lingered in the minds of Diné as a vivid reminder of the power of the state.

Diné also blamed their leaders for failing them. Tall Woman remembered this era with reluctance and regret. Her husband, Frank Mitchell, a renowned healer, or hataałii, and a tribal councilman, had been one of the leaders, and "he and the other leaders really took the brunt of it," she recalled. "People were very, very angry[,] and they started saying nasty words to all the leaders, blaming them. Even though Frank explained the order came from Washington, for some reason people blamed him. They even threatened to harm him and his children because of it. Those things worried me greatly." Yet Mitchell himself agreed with the conservationists that overgrazing had nearly denuded much of the land. So "he kept telling us he had to do his job; the People were going to have to listen and obey those instructions. He said if they didn't, the reservation would have no future; the land would never recover and everything would come to an end." Even in decades later, she added, "People still talk about the stock reduction and the suffering it caused. In our family, we don't talk about it very much because it brings back the hardships it caused for Frank … and others who had to enforce those orders. It wasn't right that people blamed them for causing it; the overgrazing did it. But some of the People couldn't understand that, so they blamed all the leaders, from Washington right on down … to the headmen in the local areas." Mitchell ruefully remembered those times, too. He, himself, had received a permit for only ten sheep and two horses, and yet his neighbors accused him and the rest of the council of urging the government to reduce *their* livestock and not their own. Only a few strong Diné men could weather the impending storm.

Resistance grew as officials implemented the new grazing program. In early 1938, supervisors of the various grazing districts began issuing official certificates granting grazing rights, printed on special "safety paper" in government green and stamped with a red seal. Many Diné rejected these outright. Some refused to accept their permits; others burned them in campfires. At Sheep Springs, Diné men allegedly threatened the range riders who distributed them, and in the northern area around Aneth, men assaulted a range rider while on his route and destroyed the detested documents. Much later, in 1945, violence flared again around Teec Nos Pos, where angry stockowners, including at least one woman, bound and beat government officials. Range riders and the Navajo police were part of the problem. Often their unnecessarily rough treatment of stockowners sparked violence, and Fryer did little to restrain them.

But surprisingly few sparks flared, considering how high emotions ran in these years. Indeed, the most common form of protest was the all-American petition drive. At trading posts, chapter houses, day schools, and ceremonial dances, Diné signed petitions denouncing stock reduction, John Collier, and the entire New Deal. As early as 1937, when the official livestock counts began, men and women—thousands of people altogether—gathered at chapter houses to register their dissent. Most could not write, so they marked these petitions with their thumbprints, which since the early 1900s had replaced the traditional "X" for signing important documents. We have little to tell us about these protest meetings, but the thumbprints themselves are suggestive. At each chapter house or trading post, more than 40 percent of those who came to convey their displeasure were women. We can imagine these women in their colorful Pendleton blankets as they waited patiently to make their mark. They likely gossiped with one another and discussed the troubles they had feeding themselves and their children ever since John Collier demanded that they give up their goats. At one chapter house, Bah stood with twelve other women, among them Rachel Tsosie, ´Asdzáá Łtsoii, and Yił Deezbaa´. John W. Goat was next, but then came five more women eager to make their feelings known. This scenario repeated itself again and again as women and men waited their turn to stick their thumbs onto the black pad of ink and express their anger.

Jacob Morgan helped organize at least some of these campaigns, apparently in concert with New Mexico Senator Dennis Chavez. Both men harbored a deep antipathy toward Collier. Educated at Hampton Institute, Morgan resented Collier's tilt toward the leadership of traditional headmen, instead of the products of boarding schools, like himself, and he believed that the move away from assimilation would handicap the Diné in the modern world. Chavez, for his part, viewed Collier's efforts to expand the reservation eastward into the Checkerboard as a threat to his constituency, Hispanic and Anglo-American ranchers. Because Chavez and Morgan supported the protests, Fryer and others with the Navajo Service dismissed the petition drive out of hand as a political vendetta and no more. Fryer believed that the Navajos had no idea of what they were signing and that the petitions represented the sentiments of "not more than twenty-four people." It is true that Morgan clearly influenced and perhaps orchestrated these meetings. And yet, it was a mistake to disregard the Diné as merely dupes in a political struggle. Several of the preambles to these petitions specified that the people gathered specifically to voice their objections to stock reduction. And in a few locations, women and men offered personal notes attesting to their heartfelt refusal to allow the government to "execute" their horses or take more of their stock. Even though people may have signed after listening to a rousing diatribe against Collier and his New Deal program, their sentiments were no less sincere.

As range riders began to distribute permits, Diné were stunned at the extremely low numbers of livestock that the government allowed. In one heavily overgrazed district near the eastern Checkerboard, a family could own no more than 61 sheep units including their horses, each of which counted as five units. About one-third of the population, some with as few as 38 sheep and goats, would have to reduce their flocks if they kept 1 horse for each family member. Three other districts allowed fewer than 90 sheep units; even the most generous permits authorized only 280.

These limits, of course, reflected the amount of available forage and the population of stock-owning families. They were low largely because overgrazing had severely damaged easily erodible land or because the soils made grasses lean already. But the small permits came as a staggering shock, nonetheless.

Diné did not take this drastic reduction of their sheep quietly. A delegation from Oljato, Navajo Mountain, and Kayenta raised money to go to Washington, D. C., where they arranged an audience with Eleanor Roosevelt, whom they begged to intervene. One of the delegates, a woman named 'Asdzáá Nez, explained to Roosevelt through an interpreter: "Our sheep are our children, our life, and our food." This theme of providing for families echoed in the words of women across the reservation. One woman wept as she vented her anger in 1940. Ever since Collier came to the reservation, she told sociologist Floyd Pollock, "we have seen nothing but trouble." The loss of her sheep meant that she could barely feed her family of six children. "This may sound awful for me to say," she added, "but I really hate John Collier.... When I think of what he has done to us, I realize that I could even kill him myself just like I could kill a mad dog. I don't like to feel about anyone the way I feel toward John Collier, but he has ruined our home, our lives, and our children, and I will hate him until the day I die."

The summer of 1943 opened a new chapter in range management on the Navajo Reservation. The Tribal Council, chaired by Chee Dodge, passed a series of resolutions that repudiated stock reduction and much of the conservation program. One Diné woman was so moved by the council's courage that she asked to speak before the council. Congratulating the delegates, she exulted, "I have always wanted our Navajo people to come together and unite[,] and today I believe they have done so." When Collier took office, the Diné had lacked a strong political organization. Now they proved united against New Deal conservation.

Diné defiance brought an end to stock reduction and the enforcement of grazing restrictions. The resistance included not only famous leaders like Jacob Morgan, but also the countless women and men who stood in line to express their thoughts with their thumbs. This rebellion against the conservation program would live on in collective memory. As grandmothers and grandfathers passed down stories to their grandchildren, few would recall Collier's effort to lay the groundwork for Native nationalism, preserve religious freedom, protect Navajo landowners on the Checkerboard, or even open up wells. Instead, they would reflect on the days when they had lots of sheep and curse Collier for destroying their pastoral way of life.

Ruth Roessel, a Diné educator and political leader, has done as much as anyone to keep those memories of environmental injustice alive. In 1974, she published a collection of oral histories with the provocative title, *Navajo Livestock Reduction: A National Disgrace*. In that book, she argued that the cruelty and callousness of stock reduction was an injustice that Americans had yet to acknowledge. "Americans deplore injustice and gross violations of human rights," she observed in her foreword. "We wring our hands and demand congressional action" for the protection, she went on, of those rights in foreign lands. "Yet, within the past 30 to 40 years, one of the most devastating attacks on individual and group rights took place on the Navajo Indian Reservation with hardly a murmur of protest. In this instance, as in most cases of the type, Americans' defense was, 'We didn't know what happened.' " Her pointed subtitle—*A National Disgrace*—and Broderick Johnson's illustrations depicting violence, powerlessness, and grim scenes of animals burned alive made a strong political statement. As their recollections make clear, the Diné experienced stock reduction in different ways, depending on where they lived, their degree of geographical isolation, their social position, their wealth, their gender, their education, and so forth, and their *personal* memories of that era reflect those differences. But the heavy-handedness with which the federal government carried out this program helped produce an overpowering *collective* memory of terror, betrayal, loss, and grief. That collective memory continues to complicate efforts to conserve Navajo rangelands.

Of course, Collier had the best of intentions when he launched his most ambitious New Deal program on the Navajo Reservation. Livestock, drought, and arroyo-cutting rains had gnawed the land, and as he grasped this serious threat, he felt an almost messianic impulse to act quickly before the area became another Dust Bowl. Adding to his sense of urgency had been the sudden availability of federal conservation funds, which he rightly feared might soon evaporate. Collier intended to save Navajo life, both literally and culturally, by saving Navajo land. And yet, as the old adage goes, the road to hell is paved with good intentions.

Collier only belatedly, and imperfectly, comprehended the meanings livestock held for Diné, and he never fully fathomed long-established patterns of stock ownership. It is not trivial that he and the conservationists always spoke of the Navajo pastoralist using the male pronoun; stockowners were sheep *men*, even though the commissioner was well aware that Navajo women owned their own sizeable herds. By controlling their own means of production and unmediated access to matrilineal grazing areas, women enjoyed economic autonomy and a good measure of power within their families and communities. Women, moreover, stood at the center of a distinctive social landscape in which their opinions actually mattered. When conservationists imposed measures to reduce stock without even consulting these women, they provoked a resistance that would, in the long run, foster chronic erosion. In the 1990s, a Diné man with the Navajo Department of Forestry told the ethno-geographer Patrick Pynes that most people now will not "touch grazing issues on the reservation with a ten foot pole."

The New Deal conservation program could not possibly have worked as long as policymakers ignored the values and ideas of the Navajo people. When conservationists high-handedly imposed measures that were profoundly antithetical to Diné culture, they helped begin the process of their program's unraveling. That is perhaps the central lesson of this episode in the environmental history of the American West. In our quest to restore ecological diversity and conserve land, we cannot ignore the people who make their living from it. That constitutes environmental injustice, which—as this story suggests—also has ecological consequences.

In their crusade to save the land, federal agencies rendered the Navajos nearly powerless over their lives. And that is an essential characteristic of environmental injustice. As with the struggle of the Western Shoshones against nuclear testing on their reservation or the efforts of the Hualapai to retain rights to the Colorado River, the underlying issues are power and control. Notice how the Navajo story differs from that of Anglo ranchers, who reluctantly came under the Taylor Grazing Act during the same period. Those ranchers gained a powerful voice in the administration of public lands, which they themselves managed, and thus controlled, through local committees. By contrast, federal conservationists managed every aspect of the Navajo range program. The resulting economic and cultural impacts of stock reduction and grazing management proved reprehensible, a shock from which the Diné are only now beginning to recover. In their myopic focus on restoring the land, New Deal conservationists lost sight of the fact that a truly sustainable relationship with the natural world requires an ethical relationship with the land, with those who people it, and with the cultures that give it meaning.

The Eastern Cherokees and the New Deal

BY JOHN R. FINGER

Franklin D. Roosevelt brought a jaunty optimism to the presidency and a bold New Deal featuring myriad agencies for coping with the depression. Amid these sweeping changes was an "Indian New Deal" designed by John Collier, Roosevelt's commissioner of Indian affairs. A native southerner and former New York City social worker, Collier had been impressed by the richness and variety of the immigrants' cultural heritage and had become a proponent of cultural pluralism. No longer should our nation strive for a homogenized, uniform citizen emerging from the melting pot of America. Instead, national culture should be a blend, reflecting certain common values—respect for equality under the law, for example—and varied ethnic attributes. By the 1920s Collier had developed a fascination with the Puebloan tribes of the Southwest and emerged as an impassioned spokesman for Indian rights. Extrapolating from his earlier experiences with immigrants, he believed Indians could be a vital part of American culture while retaining much of their tribal identity. His familiarity with Puebloan folkways had also given him respect for communalism as an agent of cultural bonding and cooperative change. Communalism or tribalism, he thought, might operate as an effective restraint on rampant American individualism.

Good progressive that he was, Collier also wished to address the Indians' many social, economic, and educational problems. A persistent critic of the Indian Office, he had supported the systematic analysis of reservation problems conducted by Lewis Meriam and applauded many of the conclusions in Meriam's published 1928 report. Thus Collier's background suggested that his approach as Indian commissioner would reflect both the fervor of progressivism and an appreciation of ethnic and cultural diversity.

The cornerstone of the Indian New Deal was the Wheeler-Howard Act of June 18, 1934, often called the Indian Reorganization Act (IRA). A decisive about-face from previous policy, it affirmed the validity of Indian cultures, formally abandoned the already discredited allotment policy, and promoted Indian progress within a modern tribal context. With the end of allotment the reservations would become sacrosanct communal societies. In some cases they would even be enlarged. Tribes were encouraged to write their own constitutions, organize as corporations, and apply for federal loans for economic development. Meanwhile the new administration would deemphasize off-reservation boarding schools and promote practical, socially responsible education among the Indians themselves. This included encouraging traditional crafts and skills as a means of preserving tribal culture and also earning money. Like many New Deal programs, then, the IRA combined old and new ideas with a bold willingness to experiment.

One of the most remarkable features of the IRA was a provision allowing tribes to vote on whether they would accept the new law and thus be eligible for its benefits. Never before had Indians been encouraged to exercise their own judgment in policy matters relating to themselves, and a number of tribes disappointed Collier by voting against the IRA—in part for the novelty of saying no to the federal government and partly because of questions about how the new policy would actually be implemented. Initially, however, the Eastern Band had only mild objections. It was willing to incorporate under federal law, despite satisfaction with its state charter, but wanted certain practices to continue: state law enforcement on the reservation, tribal operation of a new handicraft guild, and heirship rights to possessory claims. Otherwise, agent Spalsbury noted, the concept of corporate self-government struck a responsive chord: "These Indians have been operating under a similar organization for many years and believe in it." In May 1934 the tribal council approved the pending Wheeler-Howard bill, and on December 20 the entire tribe likewise endorsed the recently passed act by a vote of 705 to 101. Counting absentee ballots, 806 out of an estimated 1,114 eligible voters went to the polls, better than 72 percent. Support was lopsided in all six communities as well as among the 60 absentee voters. Harold E. Foght, the current Cherokee agent, reported satisfaction "with the way the Indians turned out and voted, particularly as the mountain roads were in bad condition after several days of rain and snow." He anticipated quick adoption of a new tribal constitution and charter of incorporation to replace the existing 1889 state charter.

To many Eastern Cherokees, the most important facet of the Indian New Deal was the creation of new jobs on the reservation. Tribal unemployment had become particularly acute in the last months of Hoover's administration, and about the only income came from the agency's own limited road building. Fortunately, many of Roosevelt's famous "alphabet agencies" provided employment and relief to Indians as well as other Americans. One of John Collier's first steps as Indian commissioner was to establish the Indian Emergency Conservation Work Program (IECW), an adjunct of the Civilian Conservation Corps (CCC). Often called the Indian CCC, the IECW was, at Collier's insistence, "Indian-built, Indian-maintained, and Indian-used" and devoted exclusively to relief measures on reservations. It was quite prominent on Qualla Boundary and provided employment in reforestation, fire and erosion control, road building, and similar programs. More than 500 Eastern Cherokees applied for the 100 full-time positions, and to benefit the maximum number of Indians Harold Foght set up two shifts, each working two weeks a month. Later it became necessary to limit even further the hours any one individual could work.

Other New Deal agencies like the Works Progress Administration (WPA) and the Public Works Administration (PWA) also allocated funds to the Department of the Interior for similar job programs on reservations. Even with all this, employment lagged badly. Late in 1936 only 135 out of about 650 eligible Eastern Cherokees had jobs—mostly on roads, the IECW, and a new hospital project. Yet the efforts at relief continued, and between 1933 and 1941 various New Deal agencies pumped a total of about $595,000 into the North Carolina reservation. Nationwide, the Indian CCC alone spent some $72 million among American Indians.

With passage of the Johnson-O'Malley Act in 1934, Collier's Indian Bureau encouraged state and local agencies to share in providing many Indian services. The state of North Carolina, for example, contracted with the United States Public Health Service and the Department of the Interior to furnish additional medical care for the Eastern Band. By 1938 the state had a district health unit operating out of Waynesville and a resident field nurse on the reservation who visited even the most remote Cherokee homes. For the first time almost every Cherokee child received a medical examination and necessary immunizations, while prenatal care and treatment for venereal disease became readily available for adults. As in the past, state and county officials also continued to provide most tribal law enforcement, though sheriffs were sensitive to the fact that Indians paid no taxes. Less successful were federal efforts to interest white public school systems in admitting Cherokee pupils under the Johnson-O'Malley Act. As agents often pointed out, prejudice against Indians was simply too strong in Bryson City and Sylva.

Taking advantage of the IRA's desire to maintain and even enlarge reservations, the Eastern Band made an effort during the 1930s to acquire more tillable land to accommodate its inflated membership rolls. Some Indians talked about selling the more remote tracts in Graham and Cherokee counties and using the proceeds to buy better—and more defensible—property closer to Qualla Boundary. And on several occasions the tribe offered marginal though scenic property to the Great Smokey Mountains National Park in exchange for farmland, especially around Ravensford. The tribe was never able to make the exchanges it wanted, but it did eventually pay $25,000 for the 884-acre Boundary Tree Tract as a site for tribal tourist industries. While bargaining with the park service, the Cherokees also attempted to use New Deal agencies to acquire some 23,000 acres south of Qualla Boundary and in Graham County. Arrangements were nearly complete when, according to Harold Foght, the government dealt "a great blow" to Cherokee aspirations by deciding against it.

One revolutionary phase of the Indian New Deal of particular importance to the Eastern Band was its encouragement of Native American traditions, crafts, religion, and self-identity. In contrast to the early 1920s, when the Indian Office warned Indians to cease their "useless and harmful" dances and ceremonies, Collier explicitly encouraged Indian religious freedoms and preservation of tribal cultures. To the disgust of many missionaries and longtime reformers, he issued a circular in January 1934 directing the Indian Service to show an "affirmative, appreciative attitude toward Indian cultural values." Furthermore, "No interference with Indian religious life or ceremonial expression will hereafter be tolerated. The cultural liberty of Indians is in all respects to be considered equal to that of any non-Indian group." Tribal arts and crafts should be "prized, nourished, and honored."

Responding to this new directive, Harold Foght advocated teaching Indian history in Cherokee schools and creating a museum to exhibit craft work from other Indian schools in the United States. This "would lend an understanding and inspiration to the children that would be difficult to get in any other way." As for Cherokee religion and traditions, he later explained, "We are thus going out of our way to have meetings with the older Indians who are rapidly dying off to have them transmit in permanent form what they still retain from the ancient national epic of creation, their guiding supernatural spirit and the world hereafter as reward for noble deed and worthy living." Then, in a comment accurately reflecting the new ideology, he added, "Unfortunately, the Cherokees have not been a conservative religious group holding onto their ancient religion."

Cherokee crafts had been a matter of keen interest to Indian agents, tourists, and others well before the depression. Across the mountains in Gatlinburg, Tennessee, the predecessor of the Arrowmont School fostered traditional mountain crafts, an emphasis blending nicely with the new awareness of Indian culture. By spring 1932 R. L. Spalsbury was trying to organize a crafts guild among the Eastern Cherokees so they could become an auxiliary of the Southern Mountain Hand Craft Guild in Gatlinburg. Spalsbury confidently predicted that the new transmountain road from Knoxville and Gatlinburg would bring more tourists to Qualla Boundary and create greater demand for Cherokee crafts; the new Indian guild and its affiliation with the larger organization would help meet these demands. Unlike before, when Indians often bartered crafts for supplies at local stores, the new arrangement would allow them to bring their wares to the guild storehouse, where they would receive cash. The guild would then sell the crafts at enough of a markup to pay expenses and allow for future expansion. Using funds borrowed from the tribe, the guild was finally organized in the summer of 1933 and operated out of a storeroom in the new council house then nearing completion. It was the predecessor of the crafts guild that today handles much of the Cherokee artistic output.

Spalsbury and Harold Foght followed up these early efforts to promote Cherokee handicrafts. There were crafts classes in the tribal schools, an attempt to anticipate tourist demands, and frequent inquiries from the Indian Office regarding the state of Cherokee artistic creativity. Goingback Chiltoskey, a woodcarver and one of the most famous artists of the Eastern Band, received much of his instruction and encouragement during this period. Likewise, Roosevelt's New Deal gave a moral and financial boost to artists throughout America. On the other hand, the employment programs of the Indian New Deal sometimes detracted from Cherokee crafts. The government employed instructors in basketry and pottery part time at the boarding school but then lured them away with higher-paying opportunities elsewhere. Spalsbury advocated raising the instructors' salaries from twenty-five to fifty cents an hour, with at least fifteen hours of work a week. Yet New Deal programs continued to work at cross purposes. As Harold Foght noted in summer 1934, "I find that only a limited number of the reservation Indians are engaged in basketry and weaving, and very few in pottery making. This is probably due in part to the fact that the men have had remunerative work on Government projects in recent years."

Nourishing Indian handicrafts was simply one part of a larger program to transform Cherokee into a tourist center. As early as 1932 R. L. Spalsbury was anticipating future needs by advocating development of a plan for leasing attractive business sites in town and at Soco Gap. One problem was the number of whites already operating businesses under arrangements made with individual Indians before the government assumed trusteeship over the reservation. By spring 1933 the tribal council had decided that 10 percent of the consideration for all business leases would go into the tribal treasury to help with relief, and Spalsbury was requiring white businessmen to obtain traders' licenses from his office.

Completion of a modern highway system into Cherokee was of course critical and by late 1935 the Appalachian Railroad had finally liquidated its holdings and surrendered its right-of-way for the new and more direct highway linking Bryson City and Cherokee. Whenever the long-discussed highway from Soco Gap was completed, Cherokee would also be a convenient gateway for motorists approaching from the east. In anticipation of these developments, the council voted to appropriate $50,000 of tribal funds to undertake an "industrial development" program in Cherokee. Basically it entailed tearing down some of the old shacks and constructing new tourist-related facilities, including a hotel, trading post, craft shop, and service station. The council intended to oversee all phases of construction, the leasing of concessions, and landscaping. One objective was to drive out of business R. I. McLean, a white trader who operated a large general store and trading post on a small parcel of land in the heart of the business district; this had never been part of the reservation. Harold Foght said that McLean had long been "a thorn in the flesh" of other traders, whom he regularly outsmarted. The Indians at first were willing to start legal proceedings to force McLean to sell out, but Principal Chief Jarrett Blythe soon decided that if the tribe could open a new cooperative store as part of its industrial program, McLean would sell of his own volition. Little did Blythe realize that his program would soon come under attack by some fellow Cherokees as undemocratic and even subversive.

Whatever the accomplishments of the Indian New Deal, some Eastern Cherokees became disenchanted because it fostered tribalism at the expense of individualism, decisively eliminated the prospect of allotment, and appeared to be a "return to the blanket." They found themselves joining a rising chorus of opposition to Collier's programs among many acculturated Indians throughout the United States. Ironically, these dissenters found support among some poorly educated or conservative Indians who saw the Indian Reorganization Act not as an affirmation of tribal ways but as a suspicious new tactic adopted by an always devious federal government. What emerged on many reservations, then, was an alliance of convenience between certain acculturated and traditionalist Indians to resist the IRA. On the Eastern Band's reservation all that was required was an individual to crystallize such latent fears and resentment. Fred Blythe Bauer was the individual.

Bauer was born in December 1896, the son of Rachel Blythe Bauer, a Cherokee mixed-blood, and Adolphus Gustavus Bauer, a northern-born white architect who designed a number of important state buildings after moving to Raleigh. When his mother died just two weeks after his birth, Bauer was sent by his distraught father to Qualla Boundary to live with James and Josephine Blythe, who adopted him. Blythe was Rachel Bauer's brother, and his wife was the daughter of former principal chief Nimrod Jarrett Smith. Fred Bauer grew up with his cousin Jarrett Blythe (who was ten years older), attended Carlisle, and during World War I served with the army air corps in France. Afterward he taught and coached at various Indian institutions around the country.

By the early 1930s Bauer and his wife Catherine were employed at the school in Mount Pleasant, Michigan, and when it closed they returned to Qualla Boundary, where their intelligence and forceful personalities quickly ensured their prominence. R. L. Spalsbury was delighted to provide a teaching position on the reservation for Catherine, and her husband worked on a variety of relief projects, including construction of reservation highways. Before long, however, the couple became open and persistent critics of the Indian New Deal. Fred Bauer had always been a progressive who, culturally at least, was a "white Indian." To him full and unconditional Indian citizenship meant a good education, allotment of reservation lands, distribution of tribal assets, private initiative in business and government, and an end to Indian Office bureaucracy and paternalism. Anything less was un-American and unacceptable. In his eyes Collier's romantic notions of tribalism were not only un-American but communistic. Not surprisingly, Bauer quickly enlisted allies among other white Indians and suspicious conservatives willing to believe the worst about federal Indian policies. Of necessity they found themselves frequently at odds with the principal chief, who steadfastly backed most New Deal programs. That man was none other than Bauer's cousin and adoptive brother, Jarrett Blythe. It was a scenario befitting a Greek tragedy.

The catalyst for Bauer's campaign against Collier and the Indian New Deal was the new educational program on the Cherokee reservation. In September 1932, before Roosevelt's election, agent R. L. Spalsbury had posed a basic question: "What is the proper educational program for this reservation?" He had an answer. In line with the Meriam report and other critiques of Indian education, he called for "a complete reorganization" that would reduce the role of the boarding school at Cherokee and emphasize "close contacts between the school and the home" by means of day schools. Somewhat paradoxically, he finally concluded this could best be accomplished by improving the local road systems, closing the two existing day schools, converting the boarding school into a consolidated day facility, and busing in students who lived in Bird Town, Big Cove, and the Jackson County communities along Soco Creek. "This has all the merits of a consolidated school in any community," Spalsbury said. "It provides close daily contacts between the school and the home. It permits the children to maintain their home contacts while getting their education and suggests that the school might extend its influence easily by reason of these contacts to the improvement of the home life of the adults." It would also be cheaper than the current boarding system and would free several dormitories for other uses. For an indefinite period, however, Spalsbury admitted it would be necessary to retain boarding facilities for a few orphans, refugees from broken homes, and pupils from remote tracts in Graham and Cherokee counties. Whatever the merits of his proposals, the lame-duck Hoover administration had no intention of undertaking such costly changes on the Cherokee reservation. Instead, it authorized construction of a new day school in Soco Valley.

John Collier's regime likewise rejected the notion of a large consolidated Cherokee school and opted for expanding and improving existing day schools and making them more responsive to community needs. Spalsbury quickly proved himself a disciple of the new administration by defining tribal education in the broadest possible terms. Sketching the preliminary outlines of an idealized program for the Eastern Band, he said, "Our program of education will be wider than the classroom. It will take in the home, the fields, the forest, the churches, the tribal organization, and every individual entitled to participate in the tribe. Community wide in its ramifications, it will aim to better and improve the economic, social, sanitary and spiritual condition of these people." As he admitted, "This is a large order." Schoolwork would reflect the Cherokees' own environment and would not require such things as foreign languages or "higher mathematics." Spalsbury hoped to add grades eleven and twelve to the boarding-school curriculum during the next two years and, assuming the school could hire the necessary instructors, to teach both written and spoken Cherokee at those levels. As the agent put it, "On the background of [Cherokee] racial inheritance we should build a structure of knowledge, skill and attitudes dovetailing into their environment so that they will be able to make the best use of it without waste."

Spalsbury saw the "adult phase" of the new program "centering around the home and the family. These are the two primary social units that must be strengthened and developed." But the agent had only a vague idea of how this might be accomplished, and he acknowledged that everyone connected with the Indian New Deal would "have to attack and develop" the problem. One thing he knew for certain:

> Rugged individualism must give way to social cooperation. The social element is dominant. An individual can only develop in organized society. If this means anything, it means that the social organization of the community must receive major attention. The Cherokees have some most commendable features in their social life which should be preserved and extended. Their community club organizations for mutual help in times of trouble or need are examples of this. As their social stability rests on the strength of the home and family, every effort should be made to improve their economic and moral condition. Health and sanitation are important elements to be stressed throughout.

Spalsbury's successor, Harold Foght, was equally diligent but more practical in attempting to set up an educational system that conformed to the broad-gauged objectives of the Indian New Deal. He emphasized prevocational and vocational instruction in agriculture, forestry, and the mechanical arts. Basically he ignored curriculum formats and requirements in other North Carolina schools, thinking it "wasteful and positively foolish … to ape" them. An

ominous foreshadowing of future events occurred when students at the boarding school and some Cherokee parents protested, to which Foght replied that
they simply did not understand "the real situation." He was preparing Cherokee children for the realities of reservation life, but if there should be "a young
Indian boy or girl who shows outstanding gift in certain cultural or professional
fields, we would recommend such students for transfer from Cherokee to
white high schools willing to accept Indian students."

Foght quickly found himself bewildered and beleaguered by a rising tide of
opposition to the new school programs. In part it was a matter of his own
"stern" personality, in part a reaction to the aggressive, radical nature of Collier's entire administration. The welter of anxieties and uncertainties relating to
the Indian New Deal had suddenly coalesced and focused on the issue of education. And it was on this issue that Foght first directly confronted Fred and
Catherine Bauer. Catherine had proved a very good substitute teacher in the
spring of 1934, and Foght had had no qualms about recommending her for a
full-time position at the new Soco Day School. By spring 1935, however, she
and one or two other reservation teachers openly opposed the educational program. Her husband and a number of white Indians were meanwhile holding
meetings and, according to Foght, making "insidious insinuations and false
statements" and inducing many parents to sign a petition against the new programs. The exasperated agent dealt with his most immediate problem by firing
Catherine Bauer, claiming she had been insubordinate and had "joined in the
movement to discredit the new system of education." He asked the acting
director of education within the Indian Office to investigate the matter himself,
adding that "the Tribal Council, from the Chief down, is standing by us and
look upon the whole matter as impertinent interference on the part of a few
discontents."

Bauer meanwhile had gone at his own expense to Washington, conferred
with Collier, and received no satisfaction. Back in Cherokee, he and others organized a "Cherokee Indian Rights Association," which held a strike against tribal
schools; some parents were persuaded to protest the IRA educational program by
withdrawing their children from classes. Amid the furor, the tribal council
appointed a committee to look into the situation, and it prepared a report generally supporting Foght's educational program. For those favoring an education
emphasizing assimilation rather than tribalism, Bauer made the case most
cogently in a congressional hearing a few years later: "Suppose you, a white,
born in a white community, see only white people, attend white schools, have
only white associates. After you attain manhood you are suddenly dropped down
in China, India, or Africa, with people of a different race, language, and social
customs. Do you think you would be accepted without question into the social,
economic, and political life of that community? And be happy there?" Cherokee
children, Bauer argued, should attend public schools with white children to be
better prepared for the "real world." The problem, as Bauer no doubt realized,
was that schools in Swain and Jackson counties did not admit students who were
phenotypically Indian. Withdrawal of the Cherokee reservation and the new
national park from Swain County tax rolls had drastically reduced the local tax

base, and quite apart from any racial animosity, county officials were not inclined to provide public services for the Cherokees.

A prominent ally of the Bauers was William Pearson McCoy, a white Indian from Bird Town who operated a small restaurant in Cherokee, where authorities seized two slot machines in summer 1934. Foght labeled him and Fred Bauer "the chronic trouble maker[s] of this reservation" and indeed they were to be persistent enemies of the Indian Office for years to come. But the list of Foght's critics went considerably beyond those two and included certain discontented parents and even a few teachers. Outsiders also had unkind things to say. A Tulsa woman, Mrs. R. M. Hill, appeared on the reservation during Foght's initial troubles with the Bauers and, according to the agent, seemed to be a religious crank who wanted the school day to begin and end with prayer. She also "launched upon a tirade against the teaching of Bolshevism and certain communistic practices in our schools, all of which was so preposterous that it was difficult for me to refrain from taking the whole matter in a jocular vein." Mrs. Hill's chief target was a teacher of industrial geography who had discussed the Soviet Union and had a pupil prepare a report on its economic system based on a book from the teacher's own library. A bit defensively, Foght acknowledged that "Communism and Bolshevism have no place in the report or in the book, but the word 'Russia' was evidently sufficient to set our objectors on edge. Anyhow, they had filled this woman with a lot of nonsense."

Charges that the IRA was promoting communism were reiterated by Fred Bauer and the American Indian Federation (AIF), an organization he had joined and whose assistance he solicited in the spring of 1935. The AIF was a national association of Indians of diverse backgrounds and viewpoints who happened to agree on three basic objectives: removal of John Collier from office; repeal of the IRA; and most important, abolition of the Office of Indian Affairs. Founded in Oklahoma in 1934 in response to the IRA, it was headed by Joseph Bruner, a wealthy, acculturated Creek who came from a traditionalist background. The "brains" of the AIF was its energetic publicist and Washington lobbyist Alice Lee Jemison, a Seneca who was also part Cherokee. Like Bauer, many AIF members perceived Collier and the Indian bureau as obstacles to Indian individualism and modernity. The IRA, they believed, fostered a bureaucracy and paternalism that stifled initiative and self-reliance. They argued forcefully for the Indian's "emancipation" and complete integration into white society. Others opposed the Indian New Deal because it seemed to violate treaty rights that guaranteed preservation of their identity as tribal Indians. A favorite attention-getting ploy of the AIF was a right-wing rhetoric that accused Collier and his program of being atheistic, communist inspired, and pawns of the American Civil Liberties Union.

In June 1935 the AIF asked the Senate Committee on Indian Affairs to investigate the situation in Cherokee and distributed a circular titled "Collierism and Communism in North Carolina" to every member of Congress. Eventually, at hearings before the committee in April 1936, the AIF charged that the "present Indian Bureau program involves 'atheism, communism and un-Americanism in the administration of Indian Affairs both at Cherokee and in general.'" Harold Foght and others at Cherokee were supposedly trying to destroy private ownership of property, promote collectivism, deny free speech, substitute social science for Christianity in the schools, and "subversively" teach sex.

Though the Senate committee proved unresponsive, the AIF continued its efforts to uproot the IRA on the Cherokee reservation. In January 1937 Alice Lee Jemison wrote North Carolina's Senator Josiah Bailey that "the regime at Cherokee" had become "autocratic and tyranical" as well as vindictive: "Those who have opposed their program at Cherokee have been denied work of any kind and every possible barrier has been thrown in their [way] to prevent them from earning a livelihood through individual enterprise." When Bailey asked Collier to respond, the Indian commissioner said Jemison's allegations were "arbitrary fictions in most cases. They are so wild and bizarre that an answer to them carries one into the realm of detective stories." On February 15 and 17 the Senate committee held additional hearings on the Cherokee case and focused on allegations about communist teachings in Cherokee schools, the IRA's support of native conjurers at the expense of modern medicine, and agency assaults on Christian belief. Similar accusations were made at hearings in 1938, 1939, and 1940, and Jemison claimed she spoke for about three hundred disgruntled Cherokees.

Amid these charges and countercharges, Fred Bauer was daily becoming more influential. Nowhere was this more apparent than in a tribal election of August 1935 on a proposed new constitution under the Indian Reorganization Act. Bauer and his allies waged what Foght characterized as "a campaign of falsehood and misrepresentation" that resulted in a decisive defeat of the constitution, 484 to 382. In Cherokee there were 74 votes for the constitution and 79 against; in Bird Town 54 for and 121 against; Paint Town 22 for and 92 opposed; Wolf Town 54 pro constitution and 129 con; Big Cove 97 for and 32 against; Graham County (Snowbird) 78 for and 2 against; and 2 absentee ballots in favor and 29 in opposition. Foght thought it significant that Graham County and Big Cove, "the two precincts inhabited by the full-blood Indians were the only two to vote right.... They seem still able to think for themselves. Birdtown, which is the stronghold of the white Indians gave a better vote for the Constitution than did either Painttown or Wolfetown, which ordinarily line up right on a proposition."

Foght had no trouble explaining why there had been such a remarkable turnabout after the overwhelming tribal support shown for the IRA less than a year before. In an obvious reference to the Bauer-Pearson McCoy group, he said "the real cause was after all a campaign of falsehood and misrepresentation that has been carried on by a certain faction well known to you for a long time. The only astonishing thing to me is that the propaganda used could so utterly mislead people who ordinarily do their own thinking." Despite his embarrassment, Foght said many Cherokees hoped for another election, "as it will not be long before these people will see the mistake they have made." But he was wrong. The Eastern Cherokees never adopted a new constitution and instead continued to operate under their amended 1889 state charter.

Just a few days after rejection of the constitution, Foght and the Collier program received another blow when Fred Bauer was elected vice chief of the Eastern Band. As an added insult, Pearson McCoy became a new councilman. The only real consolation to Foght was the reelection of Principal Chief Jarrett Blythe, a staunch IRA supporter. (Like many other Americans, the Eastern Cherokees have never shown much consistency in voting for their leaders.) Bauer's enemies attempted to block his swearing in because tribal law required the vice chief to have at least one-half Cherokee blood, and the Baker Roll listed him as three-eighths. The most persuasive evidence, however, suggests that Bauer was only one-quarter Cherokee. Part of the confusion over his ancestry resulted from the romantic tales surrounding his mother's marriage to Augustus Bauer, their supposed ostracism by Raleigh society, and Rachel's untimely death. According to stories circulating in the 1930s, she had been a full-blood Indian "princess." Perhaps these tales explain why several witnesses assured the tribal council that Rachel Bauer's son was a half-blood and therefore legally qualified for office. The council acquiesced, and the candidate quickly assumed his position as vice chief.

Bauer immediately made his presence felt by convincing the council to rescind the resolution of the preceding year appropriating $50,000 for construction of new tourist facilities. Foght almost sputtered with rage, but he was helpless to prevent reduction of the construction program to a face-saving standby basis. Bauer's obstructionism then took a different turn as he launched a campaign to halt plans for a new "park-to-park" highway across the reservation. This scenic mountain route, the Blue Ridge Parkway, would eventually stretch 469 miles from the Shenandoah National Park southwest of Washington, D.C., to the Great Smoky Mountains National Park. Late in 1934, after considerable controversy and lobbying, secretary of the interior Harold L. Ickes selected Cherokee as the terminus for the Smokies.

Originally the reservation section of the parkway was to be the long-needed state highway from Soco Gap to Cherokee, for which North Carolina had obtained a right-of-way sixty feet wide. The state then planned to reconvey the property to the United States. To the Cherokees' amazement, however, the National Park Service insisted on a much wider route along Soco Creek that would gobble up valuable farmland and potential business sites. It would also virtually wipe out the main street of Cherokee and necessitate moving back existing commercial buildings to the Oconaluftee's floodplain. Tribal access to the parkway, moreover, would be limited. Amid such revelations the Cherokees decided against the park demands, which Foght called "little less than confiscatory." Secretary Ickes pointed out the obvious benefits of such a road but said he would not force it on the Indians, who continued to hope the state would undertake construction of its own highway along the original right-of way. To this extent, at least, Foght and Blythe found themselves in rare agreement with Bauer. For a while it seemed the parkway would not cross the reservation at all.

By early 1937, however, negotiators had worked out a compromise proposal involving a land exchange between the tribe and the national park. The Cherokees would give the park some marginal acreage in return for long-coveted parkland near Ravensford. Then, in exchange for their properties along the necessary right-of-way, as well as North Carolina's promise of just compensation for damages, the affected Cherokees would receive part of the Ravensford lands. A bill allowing such an exchange was duly introduced in Congress, while Foght lined up a majority of councilmen to approve the plan. Then, to his shock and indignation, three of his staunchest supporters changed their minds during a Sunday adjournment and helped defeat the measure, six to five. Foght believed they had been threatened by the Bauer faction. Furious, he alluded to Bauer's lack of sufficient Cherokee blood to hold office, then asked, "Now would the Office of Indian Affairs sanction an attempt to displace him at this time, or shall the majority continue to suffer these unwarranted proceedings directed by him and two others[?]"

In an apparent effort to overcome Bauer's opposition, the House amended the pending bill to authorize the land exchanges if approved by secret ballot in a tribal election within sixty days of the bill's enactment. It was passed in August 1937, much to Chief Blythe's chagrin. He gave three reasons for opposing it. First, the Indians did not understand the act "and have been misinformed in regard to same"; second, because of past injustices the Cherokees were suspicious "of any proposition put to them by the Indian Office"; and third, section 2 of the bill stipulated that the results of the election would be final, "and since it is my belief that it will surely lose at this time, I do not think it wise to hold the election." The election never took place, probably saving the parkway from outright rejection by the Cherokees. Obviously Blythe recognized the potency of Bauer's opposition.

Finally, a new compromise emerged in 1938. Under this plan North Carolina would build a highway through Soco Valley, while the parkway would follow the mountain ridges surrounding Qualla Boundary and then descend to Ravensford, where it would connect with the road through the national park. This would give the Eastern Cherokees virtually everything they wanted: a new highway through Soco providing direct access to the park and leaving Indian tourist businesses intact, and a new parkway offering unobstructed views of mountain grandeur as well as alternative access to the park and reservation. Clyde M. Blair, Foght's successor as agent, canvassed all council members, including Fred Bauer, and expected unanimous approval. But much to his surprise, the council rejected the proposal nine to two. The only explanation given Blair was that some Cherokees feared the state would later turn control of the Soco highway over to the park service. In all likelihood Bauer was responsible for this misimpression. Both Blair and Chief Blythe were frustrated and disappointed.

George Stephens, publisher of the *Asheville Citizen*, was even more distressed, fearing Cherokee intransigence might mean loss of a parkway that promised millions of dollars for the regional economy. He believed that both Fred and Catherine Bauer had "inherited the ancient grudge of the Indians against the white man" and that their arguments had befuddled the average Cherokee. Furthermore, it was his understanding that the Bauers intended to ask North Carolina newspapers to publish articles they had written attacking the Indian Office. Stephens thought such diatribes would "so stir up the Cherokees that it will be impossible to ever get any cooperative action from the Indians on the Blue Ridge Parkway." He asked Curtis B. Johnson of the *Charlotte Observer* to delay publication of any such articles "until present negotiations are definitely settled." Johnson agreed to cooperate.

Congressman Zebulon Weaver was even more determined to have the parkway. He introduced a bill that would, if necessary, appropriate tribal lands for the project. The secretary of the interior would select lands for the parkway right-of-way in consultation with the tribal council but was not bound by its wishes. He would then convey those lands to North Carolina. In congressional hearings in July 1939, Weaver insisted he had no intention of harming the Eastern Band. "All I desire is to bring this road down there to them where more than a million people will pass over and through there during the year. Except for this roadway, they are isolated." Spokesmen for North Carolina said they were willing to pay the Band a total of $40,000 or $30 an acre, whichever was greater, for the compromise right-of-way; testimony demonstrated that this was much more than the land was worth. Under Weaver's bill, the Cherokees were allowed to use part of this money to buy more productive lands from the national park.

True to their sometimes exasperating tradition of playing both sides of an issue, the Band had delegated both Chief Blythe and Vice Chief Bauer to represent them. The former, predictably, favored the proposed compromise as "a very generous offer." Bauer, now a candidate for chief in the upcoming tribal elections, had a platform of not alienating any tribal lands and proposed a parkway route that would be entirely outside the reservation. When asked why two Cherokee representatives should have such different views, Bauer said Chief Blythe was a central figure in the tribe's "relief setup" whose "bread and butter comes from the Government pay check." But neither the testimony of Bauer nor that of Alice Lee Jemison could stop the parkway. The bill finally passed the House in early August without specifying a route. Then it awaited Senate action, leaving the Band a choice of taking immediate steps toward approving the compromise offer or running the risk that the secretary of the interior would select a route less attractive to the tribe.

This situation played into the hands of Jarrett Blythe, who was running against Bauer for reelection as principal chief. Blythe was probably the most popular political figure ever to hold office on the Cherokee reservation, a man Clyde Blair characterized as "very level-headed" and intelligent, "who has the best interest of the Indians as heart and who thoroughly understands the relationship between the Federal Government and the tribe." Against another opponent and in other circumstances, Fred Bauer might have been a more viable candidate. As Blair had conceded in 1938, Bauer exercised "a strong influence with the Council due largely to the fact that he is emotional, dramatic, clever and capable of very persuasive speech." But that had been a year earlier, when things were going Bauer's way. Now it was clear the parkway would be built on reservation land, with or without Cherokee approval—and possibly on terms far less generous than the compromise proposal. Blythe clearly favored the compromise, and the prospect of receiving a large sum of money for largely uninhabited, unproductive lands along that route must have swayed many Cherokees. Nor did it make matters easier for Bauer that he had recently coauthored a booklet published by William Dudley Pelly, head of the Silver Shirts of America, a pro-Nazi and virulently anti-communist and anti-Semitic organization. The booklet's title revealed its thesis: *Indians Aren't Red: The Inside Story of Administrative Attempts to Make Communists of the North Carolina Cherokees.* Although Clyde Blair doubted it would have much impact on the Indians, he reported that Congressman Weaver was asking for an investigation of Pelly's publishing company.

Whatever Bauer's problems, in all likelihood Jarrett Blythe would have beaten him—and anyone else—easily. One astute observer believed Bauer could have run against Blythe 150 times without winning. It was no contest. Not counting the Graham County returns, Blythe polled 707 votes in the September 1939 elections to 161 for his adoptive brother. Equally important, almost all of the new council members supported Blythe and the compromise right-of-way. Bauer's days of significant tribal authority were over, though his machinations and vocal opposition to the Indian Office would continue for another thirty years.

Besides losing the election, Bauer and his followers also failed in their efforts to promote a Cherokee education reflecting mainstream American culture. By 1939 the school system, although modernized in terms of its facilities and certain administrative procedures, unabashedly geared its education to reservation life rather than outside opportunities. The boarding school now had grades eleven and twelve but emphasized vocational education and Cherokee arts and crafts. More than previous administrations, the Collier regime had also attempted to provide elementary education for all reservation children without disrupting family ties. Access to expanded and modernized day schools at Big Cove, Bird Town, Soco, and Snowbird was much easier than in earlier days, and many children now attended classes who otherwise would have been overlooked. This in turn helped reduce the number of boarders at the central school to 140, while another 260 students—mostly older children—were bused in each day. For the present, at least, the Indian Office realized that few Cherokees would be allowed to attend public schools with whites. During the preceding decade, out of $2,351,000 of nonrelief federal money spent on the Band through the Bureau of Indian Affairs, more than $1,255,000 had been for education.

To Clyde Blair and other Indian Office employees, Bauer's eclipse and the unquestioned leadership of Jarrett Blythe must have brought enormous relief. Blair found the new tribal council to be diligent, cooperative, and willing to follow the advice of the chief. At the first meeting Blythe made it clear that he saw resolution of the right-of-way issue as a priority, and the council proved agreeable. In February 1940 it unanimously ratified what was essentially the compromise plan and, as a bonus to the Indian Office, denied that Alice Lee Jemison or any other outsider represented the Band. Congress promptly approved the new parkway route, and the Cherokees eventually had their Soco Valley highway as well.

Whatever one thinks of Bauer, his opposition to the initial parkway plans clearly had the support of a tribal majority, as well as Chief Blythe and agents Foght and Blair. Such a proposal would have strangled tribal business enterprise in both the Soco Valley and the town of Cherokee. For better or worse, the compromise allowed the present strip development of commercial enterprise along reservation highways. When the real tourist boom began after World War II, the Cherokees would be prepared. The most enduring legacy of the New Deal among the Eastern Cherokees was the groundwork it laid for that boom.

◈ FURTHER READING

Biolsi, Thomas. *Organizing the Lakota: The Political Economy of the New Deal on the Pine Ridge and Rosebud Reservations* (1992).

Blaine, Peter, Sr., with Michael S. Adams. *Papagos and Politics* (1981).

Bsumek, Erika. *Indian-Made: Navajo Culture in the Marketplace, 1868–1940* (2008).

Burnham, Philip. *Indian Country, God's Country: Native Americans and the National Parks* (2000).

Collier, John. *From Every Zenith: A Memoir and Some Essays on Life and Thought* (1963).

Deloria, Vine, Jr. *The Indian Reorganization Act: Congresses and Bills* (2002).

———— and Clifford Lytle. *The Nations Within: The Past and Future of American Indian Sovereignty* (1984).

Farr, William E. *The Reservation Blackfeet, 1882–1945: A Photographic History of Cultural Survival* (1984).

Fisher, Andrew. *Shadow Tribe: The Making of Columbia River Indian Identity* (2010).

Hall, Edward T. *West of the Thirties: Discoveries Among the Navajo and Hopi* (1994).

Hauptman, Laurence M. *The Iroquois and the New Deal* (1981).

Horne, Esther Burnett and Sally McBeth. *Essie's Story: The Life and Legacy of a Shoshone Teacher* (1998).

Hosmer, Brian C., and Colleen O'Neill, eds. *Native Pathways: American Indian Culture and Economic Development in the Twentieth Century* (2004).

Iverson, Peter. *Diné: A History of the Navajos* (2002).

———— and Monty Roessel. *"For Our Navajo People": Diné Letters, Speeches & Petitions 1900–1960* (2002).

Kelly, Lawrence C. *The Assault on Assimilation: John Collier and the Origins of Indian Policy Reform* (1983).

Knack, Martha. *Boundaries Between: The Southern Paiutes, 1775–1995* (2001).

La Farge, Oliver, ed. *The Changing Indian* (1942).

McNickle, D'Arcy. *The Surrounded* (1935).

Meeks, Eric. *Border Citizens: The Making of Indians, Mexicans, and Anglos in Arizona* (2007).

Oakley, Christopher Arris. *Keeping the Circle: American Indian Identity in Eastern North Carolina, 1885–2004* (2005).

O'Neill, Colleen. *Working the Navajo Way: Labor and Culture in the Twentieth Century* (2005).

Osburn, Katherine M. B. *Southern Ute Women: Autonomy and Assimilation on the Reservation, 1887–1934* (1998).

Ostler, Jeffrey. *The Lakotas and the Black Hills: The Struggle for Sacred Ground* (2010).

Parker, Dorothy R. *Singing an Indian Song: A Biography of D'Arcy McNickle* (1992).

Parman, Donald L. *The Navajos and the New Deal* (1976).

Philp, Kenneth R., ed. *Indian Self-Rule: First-Hand Accounts from Roosevelt to Reagan* (1986).

————. *John Collier's Crusade for Indian Reform, 1920–1954* (1977).

Purdy, John Lloyd. *The Legacy of D'Arcy McNickle: Writer, Historian, Activist* (1996).

Roessel, Ruth, ed. *Navajo Livestock Reduction: A National Disgrace* (1974).

Rosier, Paul. *Rebirth of the Blackfeet Nation, 1912–1954* (2001).

Schrader, Robert F. *The Indian Arts and Crafts Board: An Aspect of Indian New Deal Policy* (1983).

Shepherd, Jeffrey P. *We Are an Indian Nation: A History of the Hualapai People* (2010).

Talayesva, Don C., with Leo Simmons, ed., and Robert V. Hine and Matthew Sakiestewa Gilbert. *Sun Chief: The Autobiography of a Hopi Indian* (2013).

Taylor, Graham D. *The New Deal and American Indian Tribalism: The Administration of the Indian Reorganization Act, 1934–1945* (1980).

Underhill, Ruth Murray. *Singing for Power: The Song Magic of the Papago Indians* (1938).

Weisiger, Marsha. *Dreaming of Sheep in Navajo Country* (2009).

CHAPTER 13

Wars Abroad and at Home,
1941–1960

When World War II began, the Indian New Deal already had lost its impetus, as had the New Deal itself. The nation's attention turned to the international conflict. Indians responded to the war, with thousands of Native men and women serving in the armed forces and thousands more working in war-related industries. Wartime experiences deeply affected many people, altering how Native people saw their communities and themselves. Indians took collective pride in the achievements of soldiers such as Clarence Tinker (Osage) and Ira Hayes (Akimel O'odham), as well as the accomplishments of the Navajo codetalkers during the Pacific campaign. The Codetalkers based their code on the Navajo language and relayed messages with speed and accuracy. The Japanese never broke the code. Indian success in adapting to the exigencies of wartime encouraged others to see them as just like everyone else.

This perception proved to be a double-edged sword, for if it encouraged greater respect it also promoted a renewed push for assimilation. In 1946, the Indian Claims Commission (ICC) Act seemed to promise a redress of past injustices. However, the federal claims court denied many suits or provided Native nations with very limited compensation. Most Indian communities were disappointed with the results. The ICC was part of the process by which the federal government attempted to end its involvement with Indian communities. The effort to end federal trust responsibilities for Indian reservations—a policy generally labeled termination—initially gained some support from Native people who were tired of Bureau mismanagement and constraints. Unfortunately, the form that termination took differed drastically from what most Indians had in mind. At the same time, some Indians moved from rural areas or reservations into urban centers. This movement was sometimes voluntary and sometimes pushed by Bureau officials who saw reservations as economic dead ends, and who also saw urbanization as a means of expediting assimilation. The shock waves of this period also had the ironic consequence of catalyzing Indians' political activism and their development of their own economies on their own terms. As with the earlier assimilationist period of the late nineteenth and early twentieth centuries, this era proved to be a complex time, one that historians are only now beginning to comprehend more fully. What is this time period's legacy?

◈ DOCUMENTS

World War II promoted significant changes in Indian country. In Document 1, Diné Keith Little describes his experiences as a Codetalker in World War II. What did Little have to accomplish in order to become a Codetalker? How did Little reconcile his experience as a Codetalker with the history of assimilation policies? Yankton Dakota anthropologist and linguist Ella Deloria recognized the significance of the war years. Document 2 is an excerpt from her book *Speaking of Indians*, published in 1944, in which she perceptively addresses the impact of the war. Document 3 is the most significant piece of legislation for Native peoples of the 1950s: the so-called Indian Freedom Act or Termination. Ruth Muskrat Bronson, a western Cherokee who played a vital role in the newly established National Congress of American Indians, spoke out strongly against termination. Her protest against the end of federal trusteeship comprises Document 4. In Document 5, Northern Cheyenne leader John Wooden Legs emphasizes the importance of the tribal land base. In Document 6, Mary Jacobs (Lumbee), continues the story of the Lumbee, the people discussed in a Chapter 11 essay. Here, Jacobs explains how the city of Chicago could become a home for her family.

1. Codetalker Keith Little (Diné) Emphasizes the Importance of the Navajo Language in World War II, 2004

I was raised in Tonalea area. That's on the western part of the Navajo reservation and north of Tuba City, Arizona. I was raised by my sister; my mom and dad had died before I got to know them. I have three sisters and one brother—two of them passed away.... I was raised, ... herding sheep, livestock, do a lot of chores and things like that.

... one day I ran away and went to—caught a ride to Tuba City and went to the boarding school and tell them I wanted to go to school.

... they were very strict about talking in your own language, Navajo, and I could not talk Navajo at school. So that kind of makes you—forces you to learn English, you know, at whatever levels you can, the fastest way you can; and I did that. I learned a few words like, "going to the wash room," "washing up," saving "hello" and saying "good morning" and things like that ... the school is what I wanted, and I think the reason is that he said, "Go to school, learn to be like a white man, do things like the white man." And I see white people wearing clean clothes, have a nice haircut and they always wear a white shirt or something like that and they were always in authority too. So I figured well, the essence of the thing was that the older peoples say that when you learn to talk and listen, work like a bilagaana [white people], someday you going to be like that. So that's the way I wanted to be....

Keith Little Collection (AFC/2001/001/28922), Veteran's History Project, American Folklife Center, Library of Congress, Washington, D.C.

... a couple of days after my 18th birthday I left school and enlisted into the Marine Corps in Gallup, [New Mexico]....

Just about the time I was finishing my boot camp, the drill instructor was kind of nice that day and he asked me, "Are you American Indian?" I told him, "Yes sir." "Are you a Navajo by any chance?" "Yes sir." "Well," he says, "the United States Marine Corps wants Navajos real badly." He says, "I understand they make good scouts." So all the guys—all my platoon mates, they heard what the man said. So when we got dismissed I really got a ribbing for asking to be—have my rear end shot out some day behind enemy lines or something like that....

I was told to go to a circle number so-and-so on the parade ground in San Diego Marine Corps Recruit Depot. So I took my stuff over there and found it and there was a bunch of Navajos standing there waiting. A couple of them I had been to school with in Tuba City. So it was a good time to see them, make [me] kind of happy. We got on a truck and they hauled us up to Camp Pendleton. They put us in a—they dropped us off at a barrack, told us to report to somebody in there. There was nobody there during the day, in the afternoon—late in the afternoon. And whoever that was keeping the house there told us to wait, just wait. Put your sea pack right there and wait until the company comes back. And about 4–5 o'clock, somewhere in there, we heard some marching coming and we stood out there and looked at the men. And they were [all] Navajos. And we of course, we wondered about, are all these people going to be scouts?

... the Navajo company was there in the signal school and they all did the same thing. And a lot of times we went out at night carrying radios and we would practice our message sending, things like that. Sometimes somebody else would come around, a non-Indian would come around, and try to train us in radio maintenance, things like that....

One of the things that they tell you is kept ... don't say anything about what we're doing, not to anybody, not even to your girlfriend. Don't speak what we are doing into her ear.

... all the military units were clans. The Navajo clans were used for military units and one of them was [debeh lizini]—I think it was a squad.... And then there was one edge water, [tabaha], for regiment I think it was. I'm not too fluent on that anymore, but these were—this is only an example. Then they had military weapons. Say Navy; a Navy serviceman was called white cap—[cha le gai]. And then the ships—you got battleships—a big fish [lo tso], a submarine as iron fish [besh lo], then they have names for Destroyers, mosquito boats, cruisers—everything that pertained to sea life. So I guess they were all kinds of fish....

It is a whole lot faster. The ordinary, the conventional military code in comparison, the Navajo code always beats them, and you know if you match the two together, for the simple reason that conventional code has to be changed, updated, maybe a day, two days, maybe a week, scramble words and numbers....

... my first duty was being assigned to battalion commander. A guy—an old man from Texas, I was his personal radio man. And in other words, wherever he is I have to follow him around....

I was always afraid, but the thing about it is that a radioman is always a marked person by the enemy. So if they see a radioman they want to shoot him.

So you're going and somebody tells you that there's a safe place there so you run in there. And when you're ready to go again somebody beats you on the shoulder or something and you take off again. So in a way you get seasoned up to where is a safe place, but when you first get into the battle you kind of—there's that bewilderedness, you know. "What is the safe thing to do?" or "Will I get shot doing something"—something may come from the air and shoot you to pieces. These are constant reminders, but you lose that kind of—you lose that attitude simply because you're trying to save yourself. You know, you're always kind of looking out for the next spot to go....

None of us—none of the Navajos have ever been recognized for their efforts for their contributions, no matter how hard—how faithful you are in the unit, nobody recognizes in you in rank, promotion, or recognition of any kind. I think the reason is that ... nobody is supposed to know about the Navajo code at all....

However, we got into the communication school with the rank that we got, most all of us stayed with it all the way....

Private first class or private. Hardly anybody got beyond that....

I think it was 1969 or 1968, ... The 4th Marine Division decided to honor their Navajo code talkers. So they asked all the Navajo Code Talkers, as many as possible, to come to a 4th Marine Division reunion in Chicago. And—not enough of us got together so all Navajo code talkers at the Marine Corps were asked to attend, and they provided a plane I heard. About that time I got sent out of the country so I did not attend, but the guys came back with a great big medallion, a gold medallion or a copper medallion that had 4th Marine Division and Ira Hayes riding a horse on the back. And later on, all the Navajo code talkers as possible got together in Window Rock and we got our medallion there. So we treasure those medallions to this day....

[After the war], I wandered around for a while, did odd jobs, then I went back to school and graduated from high school in Chilocco, Oklahoma, in 1947....

After I graduated from high school, then went to work at different kind of jobs, employment, searching around for something better to do. And I finally went back to school, got a job ... as a teacher at the Inter-Mountain Indian School in Utah. The Navajo nation, at the time, they were having a crafts program of educating all their young kids, from 6 all the way through to 21 I think it was. And many of them were teenagers, young adults. And I had a class of the young adults in Brigham City, Utah at the Inter-Mountain Indian School, teaching them to talk English and write English, teaching them words and things like that....

... [W]hen the program was phasing out I just didn't want to be in the classrooms so I got out of there and became a logger for the Navajo Nation....

I was what you call a CEO. I got a position as a logging manager and also did a lot of work for Indian timbers, Indian tribes that have timber, and I became the president of the organization. They call it National Indian Timber Council. And became a member of the board of directors. At one time I was there four years as the president, and I served on the board 16 years. That's why I was in Washington, DC a lot....

I think it was July the 27th, 2001. These people, the surviving members of the original 29 that were recruited for the pilot project of the Navajo code, were recognized by the President in Washington, DC. And the President made a remark that they—in the gratitude of doing very, very, very difficult work for developing the code they were being recognized, and that they will be remembered for a long time....

I think we are making the effort that the young people don't really know about their heritage, and that's what we're working on. We are the people that use the Navajo language to make contribution to the war efforts for the freedom of our nation. And many people take it for -what we have, you know, the freedom, many people take it for granted. It's there, but what it takes is sacrifice of somebody in order to make it—to enjoy the things that we have....

I have a real feeling that I was able to be a marine, and not knowing what I was going to do. All I was going to do was maybe carry a rifle or a machine gun and shoot, but I ended up not using my weapon. But my weapon was my language, and that language probably saved countless lives.

2. Ella Deloria (Yankton Dakota) on Indian Experiences During World War II, 1944

All the Indians today may be thought of as divided into the same three groupings found among any other class of citizens—those who are left at home, the men and women in the services, and the workers in war industries. Let me tell you about them.

First, some glimpses of the people at home, who carry on there, praying, working, and comforting one another as they meet the inevitable hardships and sorrows that come to all in war. I receive many letters from my Dakota kith and kin telling me what goes on among that particular tribe. One says quite naturally, in speaking of a recent drive from Rosebud to Rapid City, "Of course it was a long slow ride in the cold, at thirty-five miles an hour, but we made it all right." I know that road. It is long, monotonous, and deserted. Nobody on earth would ever know if they speeded along, as usual, at fifty miles an hour. But they had been asked not to do so in order to conserve gas and tires for the sake of the boys; so they obeyed. It was not smart to cheat.

Then I have the story of a woman whose only son was the first from that reservation to be killed in action. In her intense grief, she reverted to ancient customs, so long given up, and demeaned herself by cutting off her hair, wearing her oldest clothes, and wandering over the hills, wailing incessantly. Nor would she be comforted. Did the people do anything? Certainly. In the old-time manner, which they now carry over into their church, they made a feast and invited the bereaved mother. After a memorial service in the church they went down to the guild hall. There the elder men and women, strong in their faith and given to such exhortation, made speeches addressed to her, as is the traditional manner of condoling with those who mourn. "I do not presume to make light of your great sorrow, my relative," said one earnest Christian woman, "but to remind you of God's love." And so the woman's silent weeping subsided. They washed her tear-stained face and partook of food with her, all in decent quiet, for this was a ceremony. "Then

Ella Deloria, *Speaking of Indians*. Copyright © 1944. Published by The University of Nebraska Press.

they all collected gifts for her, mostly food," the letter ends, "and she told them she felt lots stronger now because they had talked to her and comforted her."

Another letter tells what happened after a four-engine bomber burst into flames high over a little Dakota chapel and fell blazing and crashing to the ground not far off. Everyone in it was lost. The Dakota catechist immediately rang the bell and the people came running. When he saw that all hope of rescue was gone he said to them, "My relatives, let us go into the church." They took their places, some weeping softly for the nameless victims. Then he read prayers from the burial office in the native tongue amid a stillness that was absolute but for the fire still crackling outside. The families of the boys in that plane might like to know that prayers were offered for them first by Christian Dakotas.

In no line of any letter is there the least sign of discouragement or despondency over their hardships. The people see singly: "There's a job to be done. So let's get at it. Never mind about *us* now."

Next, the second group: the young men and women in the services. The reports come thick and fast about them and their record shows that they are more than doing their best. They are constantly being cited for heroism and given the various army and navy decorations. The Secretary of the Interior, Harold L. Ickes, writes of them:

> The inherited talents of the Indian make him uniquely valuable. He has
> endurance, rhythm, a feeling for timing, coordination, sense perception,
> an uncanny ability for getting over any kind of terrain at night, and,
> better than all else, an enthusiasm for fighting. He takes a rough job and
> makes a game of it. Rigors of combat hold no terrors for him; severe
> discipline and hard duties do not deter him.

That is a generous and, I believe, fair appraisal, but for one word that may strike a false note, "an enthusiasm for fighting." For me that flavors too much of the old notion of savage bloodthirstiness, consciously or unconsciously imputed indiscriminately to all Indians. It does not seem a fair way to represent modern Indian boys who had known only peace. "An enthusiasm for action when the aim is plain" would be truer.

I see a little paper each month, *Victory News*, edited by a talented Dakota girl, an A.B. from Carleton College. Her staff are all Dakotas. It is mimeographed by them on the reservation and is the organ of the Victory Club of Rosebud, through which the people work together to send cheer and home news to the boys all over the world. Think of it, a little Indian paper with a mailing list that covers the globe! There are similar papers at other places. These clubs prepare army kits and write personal letters to the boys without parents and to those whose parents cannot write.

Here are a few random excerpts from service men's letters, which *Victory News* quotes monthly:

Pfc. Anthony Omaha-Boy is "glad for God's protection." Pfc. Laverne Iron Wing is studying French and Italian between times! Robert Schmidt is a gunner on one of Uncle Sam's flying forts. Sgt. Gilbert Feather asks "that we all pray God to bring us safely back to the good old U.S.A." Pvt. Albert Bad Hand ends, "I haven't seen my Indian pals since I came over. I am aching to see one so that I can chat with him in Dakota."

The *Martin Messenger Weekly*, of Martin, South Dakota, carried this letter from Paddy Starr, in Hawaii, addressed to his catechist. It shows that the boys feel responsible for their home church: "You may think I have forgotten everything back home. No. I bear every one of you in my heart. I'm enclosing a money order for $15.00, of which $5.00 is for the Men's Society, $5.00 for the Women's Auxiliary, and $5.00 for the Young People's Fellowship. I'm doing my part over here. In prayers I want every one of you to do your part."

Indian boys are in every branch of service. From General Tinker, who lost his life at the very start of the war, down to the last private, they qualify for any post and are serving everywhere, courageously.

Indian girls are Red Cross nurses, WACS, and WAVES. They, too, are everywhere. When a missionary's wife asked where his sister was now, a little full-blood boy answered quite casually, "In Iceland." Iceland was now part of his world.

These new experiences of Indian youth raise some vital questions about their training, and this may be a good place to stop and consider them.

Before the war some of the educational planning was directed to a very special kind of life. It was predicated on the common statement, "Ninety per cent of the Indians return to the reservation anyway," the assumption always being that there is little need of training them for the outside world since they will not be in it. The course of study and training was thus devised for the limited, expectable needs of reservation life. And now, see where the young people are! How well prepared were they for the world at large? It seemed a good idea at the time, no doubt. But in future a course of study that corresponds in all essentials to the requirements of the various state boards of education might be safer—and fairer to the Indians in the long run.

We might well ask ourselves, "Why do they return to the reservation, anyway?" Well, partly it is that pull toward home and family, a universal human need but peculiarly accentuated in the Indian nature from centuries of close family and clan and *tiyošpaye* life. But that is not all. It is also because Indian young people had not been prepared to get into American general society and feel at home in it. If they had known the ordinary, commonplace things that other American youth take for granted, they would not have felt ill at ease and lonely there. If one is not familiar with the allusions and casual references that pepper the conversation of a particular group, one is bound to feel left out. Indian people are by nature reticent and retiring; when they feel a lack of social ease and self-confidence, they want to run away from the crowd, knowing they are ill-prepared to hold their own. It is not enough to be a good mechanic or a well trained stenographer at such times.

I sometimes listen to quiz programs on the radio to see if I can answer the questions. It challenges me to find out the things I miss. I don't like *not* to know the answers. Some Americans know them; why not I? That is the way I think other Indians feel. That is how some parents have been feeling of late. They have been saying they want their children to learn what the other children in their state are required to learn. They can teach them all the Indian lore and language they themselves choose, they say, and do a better job of it. They want the schools to concentrate on things the children cannot learn at home. I think they have something there.

The war has indeed wrought an overnight change in the outlook, horizon, and even habits of the Indian people—a change that might not have come about for many years yet. For weal or woe, the former reservation life has been altered radically. As it looks now, that idea of a special course of study set up for Indians alone shows up a bit negatively as a kind of race discrimination. What is right and necessary for the majority of American school children and is made available to them ought not to be denied to other American children. It is a challenge, moreover, to be expected to measure up, the same as anyone else, rather than to have allowances continually made on the basis of race.

The third group we are considering here, the workers in industry, are numerous and important. Whole families have moved into the cities and are meeting problems they have never faced before. As workers they are valuable. Skillful with their hands at tasks requiring meticulous care, they are extremely accurate, patient, dependable. If they are a split second more deliberate than some others, they make correspondingly fewer mistakes that might prove fatal. They will not stop to bargain for themselves; it is not in their tradition to think of self first; and they will not grumble. They will never do anything to hinder the war effort. They are too peculiarly American for that.

One of their problems is that of paying rent. They find it an irksome concomitant to living away from their own homes. They have never paid rent before. Naturally they try to find the least expensive places—with the result that they sometimes find themselves among undesirable neighbors. And of course there are numerous other problems. What to do with their children and adolescent girls in these surroundings is one of the hardest problems. How to get wholesome entertainment is another, and where to go to church, a third.

These Indians are earning "big money" now, and for many of them it is their first experience. They like it and will want to keep on earning and being able to buy, out of their own efforts entirely, what they desire, instead of waiting endlessly for their money from leases handled by the agency.

But do they all know how to take care of their money? What knowledge have they of practical business? Can they budget wisely? Many of them have till now had little chance to handle money, since the agency office has always managed even personal accounts for the majority of them.

And then what of the great problem they share with people on every continent—the new ordering of their life when their sons and daughters return from the armed services and the war industries are closed?

What will the workers in war plants do then? Many will doubtless want to stay in the cities, having become urbanized and liking it. Some will doubtless get on there; but others may quite possibly force out of work. Reticent and uncompetitive, as some of their tribal societies have made their people, perhaps they will have their jobs snatched by the aggressive and blatant type of workers who are used to competition.

The vast majority will probably want to go home. It is natural to want to be near one's own people. Many Indians cannot yet feel complete with just their little family, their spouse and children. They have been used to thinking in terms of the larger family groups for many generations. Even while they work their hearts turn homeward. "This is transitory," they think. "We will soon be home again." For many, that means the reservation, and it seems very good to them, however drab and bare it may look to outsiders. It will be good it get into their own homes, be they ever so humble. At least they won't have to feel beholden to landlords and will be able once again to reckon without rent. Owning one's own home will take on a new meaning.

The boys and girls in distant lands must be thinking of home, too. Perhaps for the first time they really appreciate having lands and houses. Their own sojourn in areas of great destruction where they see throngs of pitiful refugees will make them extra thankful for America and for their reservation homes.

Numbers of these young people will want to get back and do something about the life in their old communities. For now they have seen things, not only pitiful but also thought-provoking things: how people get along; how they work without letup to improve their places; how they manage to own some livestock and take good care of it; and how they grow things on every spare inch of ground and garner every berry and grain, loath to lose even one. Wonderful object lessons! Those who have been away will want to copy them when they come home.

Being with other people is indeed an eye opener to many things. The boys and girls have had a chance to see how they measure up in the life of average American communities, and they have begun to realize what their churches and schools have done for them. They went to school in the past because it seemed they must, and they occupied themselves with whatever was taught them. They had no choice about it; but then they had no basis for making a choice anyway. Some of it has certainly stood them in good stead, but other parts of it looks now like so much waste. They might have learned certain other things, instead, for which they now feel a definite lack. They know now, too, that they never went far enough in any one thing, nor deep enough into fundamentals. That was why they disqualified for this or that type of specialized training, even though they knew they could do it because they had a natural feel for it.

They will come back with perspective. They will see their churches and schools in a new light. They will appreciate what those agencies have tried to do for them. Now they will be able to say just what they require of them. There will be a new call to government to help them with their land and economic problems, since they will be ready and eager for help. There will be a new call for schools, for now they know what they need, what they missed in the past, and what their children must not miss in the future. They have fought and suffered for their country. They are Americans, and they will want to be treated as such....

3. House Concurrent Resolution 108 Terminates the Trust Relationship, 1953

Whereas it is the policy of Congress, as rapidly as possible, to make the Indians within the territorial limits of the United States subject to the same laws and entitled to the same privileges and responsibilities as are applicable to other citizens of the United States, to end their status as wards of the United States, and to grant

---

Indian Affairs: Laws and Treaties, Vol. VI. Laws (Washington, D.C.: Government Printing Office), 614–15.

them all of the rights and prerogatives pertaining to American citizenship; and Whereas the Indians within the territorial limits of the United States should assume their full responsibilities as American citizens: Now, therefore, be it

Resolved by the House of Representatives (the Senate concurring), That it is declared to be the sense of Congress that, at the earliest possible time, all of the Indian tribes and the individual members thereof located within the States of California, Florida, New York, and Texas, and all of the following named Indian tribes and individual members thereof, should be freed from Federal supervision and control and from all disabilities and limitations specially applicable to Indians: The Flathead Tribe of Montana, the Klamath Tribe of Oregon, the Menominee Tribe of Wisconsin, the Potowatamie Tribe of Kansas and Nebraska, and those members of the Chippewa Tribe who are on the Turtle Mountain Reservation, North Dakota. It is further declared to be the sense of Congress that, upon the release of such tribes and individual members thereof from such disabilities and limitations, all offices of the Bureau of Indian Affairs in the States of California, Florida, New York, and Texas and all other offices of the Bureau of Indian Affairs whose primary purpose was to serve any Indian tribe or individual Indian freed from Federal supervision should be abolished. It is further declared to be the sense of Congress that the Secretary of the Interior should examine all existing legislation dealing with such Indians, and treaties between the Government of the United States and each such tribe, and report to Congress at the earliest practicable date, but not later than January 1, 1954, his recommendations for such legislation as, in his judgment, may be necessary to accomplish the purposes of this resolution.

Passed August 1, 1953.

4. Ruth Muskrat Bronson (Cherokee) Criticizes the Proposed Termination of Federal Trusteeship, 1955

If the official policies of the Federal Government, as reflected by the current policies of the Bureau of Indian Affairs and the actions of the 83rd Congress, continue to be pursued the American Indian (like that other living creature associated with him in history, the buffalo) is likely, similarly, to continue to exist only on the American nickel.

The tragedy is that this may come about through misunderstanding of the issues involved in the proposed termination of Federal trusteeship over the Indian. These issues have been almost completely obscured in a miasma of confusion caused by conflicting financial interests, conflicting opinions on proper psychological solutions, and of justice itself. And, most important of all, caused by uninformed sentiment.

The average American is noted for his sympathy with the underdog. He is also apt to have romantic sentiment for the American Indian. Add to these two admirable qualities a vague sense of guilt for the actions of his forebears in ousting the original inhabitants of the rich land they adopted and for the long and

This document can be found in Ruth M. Bronson (Cherokee) on Termination, National Congress of American Indians Papers.

shameful history of broken treaties with these dispossessed, and you have a tendency toward impulsive action based on a desire to make amends. If this action is founded on superficial or inaccurate knowledge rather than on thoughtful study or familiarity with fact and reality the result can be exceedingly serious, even disastrous, for the Indian. This is true in the case of the termination bills since these jeopardize the Indian's very existence and unquestionably would lead to his eventual—literal—extinction.

There is even widespread misconception as to what is involved in the Federal trusteeship. The casually informed citizen, dedicated to fair play, feels there is something definitely insulting in labeling an adult a ward of the government, as though he were being branded as too incompetent to function without a guardian. Actually, today's Indian enjoys all the major rights and obligations of every American citizen: the right to vote, for instance; to move freely about the country (that is, to live on a reservation or not, as he chooses); the right to sue in court and to make contracts, to hold office; the obligation to pay taxes, and to fight and die for his country in the armed forces.

In addition, he has special privileges, which is what trusteeship boils down to, which he gained by bargaining with his conquerors. In the not so distant past the Indians agreed to end their fighting and cede land to white settlers in exchange for certain defined, inalienable lands and specified services which the Indians could not provide for themselves and which are provided by the States and local communities for non-Indian citizens. It is hard to see how benefits make a "second class" citizen out of an Indian, especially when preferential treatment seems not to jeopardize the status of veterans, farmers, subsidized airlines and steamship companies, manufacturers protected by tariffs, or the businessmen with rapid tax write-offs.

On the contrary, it would seem to be our established political philosophy that the economic well-being of particular groups is a legitimate concern of the Federal government—all this aside from the fact that, in the case of the Indians, it is a matter of solemn treaty.

In addition to the treaties which established reservations as the property and home of the Indian people, the Reorganization Act of 1934 affirmed the partnership of Indian tribes and the Federal Government. Consolidating numerous individual treaties that had been effected with Indian tribes over the years, the Indians were granted by this Act the right to exist as distinct communities, with their own properties, culture, and religion, and the promise of certain services to be furnished by the Federal Government normally furnished [to] other citizens by the states was reaffirmed and enlarged upon.

In the 83rd Congress there was a concerted effort to abrogate this Act, by means of over 100 bills claiming to "free" Indians. Tens of those bills proposed termination of trusteeship over specific tribes. Five of them were passed and signed by the President. All of the bills follow the same pattern. They were introduced by less than a handful of men, but were designed to cut down the Indian on many fronts: the family, the band, the tribe and at State level. They would destroy the tribal organizations, abolish tribal constitutions and corporations formed under the Act of 1934 and void Federal-Indian treaties. Government supervision of the sale of Indian property and expert guidance on the development of natural resources which has been provided up to now would also be cut off, thus exposing the individual Indian, the weak as well as the strong, to exploitation by the unscrupulous and those more knowledgeable in the commercial ways of a highly complex and competitive society. This would take away from him the protection that was preventing further depletion of his last remaining resources. Such a loss would be the country's as well as the Indian's, since conservation along with guided expert development would cease.

In addition, there would be a cessation of education, health and welfare services now supplied by the Federal Government, guaranteed by treaty and sorely needed, without assurance that these would be provided by the States or local communities....

Actually very few voices are raised against eventual termination of trusteeship over the Indians. The Indian people themselves, the friends of the Indians, and the authorities on Indian affairs who are deeply concerned about the trend toward termination are frightened and deeply disturbed, not only because of the inequities contained in the legislation proposed in the 83rd Congress, but at the haste, without proper safeguards or study in relation to the conditions of individual tribes.

And most of all, we are deeply concerned that termination is being decided upon *without the consent,* nay, over the protests, of the Indians concerned. Too often when Indian consent is given it has been obtained by unfair pressures amounting to nothing less than administrative blackmail, as in the case of two tribes which accepted termination bills because they were denied their own funds until they consented. This seems to them a shocking violation of faith.

The informed feel that there should be an attack on the major forces that are keeping the Indian from realizing his potentialities: ill health, lack of educational opportunities, widespread poverty. By attacking these problems at the root, they feel the day will be hastened when the Indian people will no longer need the protection of a special relationship with the Federal Government.

Termination of trusteeship, they believe (if it should be undertaken at all), should be carefully planned-for well ahead of the event, after thorough study, with the agreement of the Indians, the Federal agencies involved, the States and local government units, and the other organizations who would assume responsibility for providing the services now given by the Federal Government. Maintenance of the tribal integrity, if this is what the Indians want, must be assured in any program looking toward their future healthy integration into the American way of life. The consent of the Indians, moreover, should not be obtained by pressure amounting to duress such as was used last year in the cases of Menominee and Klamath when it was made clear to these two tribes that they would be permitted to withdraw their own money in the United States Treasury only if that withdrawal was coupled with "termination."

More than one theorist has stated that "the solution to the Indian problem" is the absorption of the Indian into the culture, race and society of the European-oriented American way. Shouldn't the Indian have something to say about this? Should the Indian be forced to give up his beliefs, his way of conducting his affairs, his method of organized living, his kind of life on the land he is a part of, if he chooses not to? Shouldn't the Indians have the same right to self-determination that our government has stated, often and officially, is the inalienable right of peoples in far parts of the world? Do we apply a different set of principles, of ethics, to the people within our own borders? ...

5. John Wooden Legs (Northern Cheyenne) Outlines the Fight to Save the Land, 1960

I am not proud of myself for anything. I am a humble man. But I am proud to be a Cheyenne.

In the old days my people fought hard to defend their homeland. The Cheyennes were a small tribe—but fast on horseback. They came and went like a tornado. That is why the soldiers shot down old people and children when defeat came. The soldiers did not stop until my people were helpless.

Sixty years my people stood looking down at the ground. Hope was running out of them the way blood runs. I heard an Indian Bureau employee say, "The Northern Cheyenne Tribe is in the process of dissolution." He said that in front of me. He thought I did not know what he meant....

I will tell you what it means to be a Cheyenne. Then you will understand what it means to my people to be back on the war ponies—going somewhere.

The white people living near us call the Cheyennes "those poor devils over on the reservation." Sometimes they call us "no-good Indians" and say we do not know how to use our land and the sooner we sell it to white men the better. Even our Bureau Area Director thinks that about us. He wrote me a letter that said my people should not try to keep their land. He said we should let white men buy all over our reservation, so that the Cheyennes could live next door to these white men and learn to be just like them.

To us, to be Cheyenne means being one tribe—living on our own land—in America, where we are citizens.

Our land is everything to us. It is the only place in the world where Cheyennes talk the Cheyenne language to each other. It is the only place where Cheyennes remember same things together.

I will tell you one of the things we remember on our land.

We remember our grandfathers paid for it—with their life. My people and the Sioux defeated General Custer at the Little Big Horn. There never was an Indian victory after that. But the Army hated us. I think they were a little afraid of us too. They took my people away from Montana. They took them to Oklahoma Indian Territory. The people were sick there in all that heat and dust. They asked to go home again, but they were locked up in a military prison instead. Then Little Wolf and Dull Knife broke out of the prison, and they led the people on the long walk home. Montana is far away from Oklahoma, and they had no horses. They had no warm clothes, and many froze to death in the snow. They had nothing to fight with, and most of them were shot by the soldiers. A whole Army hunted them all the way. My grandmother told me she walked holding a little girl by the hand on each side. She had to keep pulling them out of the line

Reprinted by permission of the Association on American Indian Affairs.

of the soldiers' bullets. 300 of my people left Oklahoma. 100 came home. After that the Government gave us the reservation we live on now.

Now you can understand why we are fighting to save our land today. This fight is not against soldiers. It is a fight to stop land sales.

The General Allotment Act was passed in 1887. It is said that the Government could take away any reservation, and give every member of the tribe a piece of it, with the right to sell it to white men in twenty five years. In the southwest the Apache and other tribes never had their land allotted. These tribes have good economic development programs today. Their people are not turning into landless gypsies....

Our Cheyenne land is cattle country. Sensible people knew it would be wrong to take cattle land like ours and divide it up into little pieces—big enough for grazing rabbits, but not cattle. Allotment was held off for the Cheyennes until 1926. My people did not know what allotment was. 25 years had to go by before individual Cheyennes could sell their pieces of our homeland out of Cheyenne ownership. Nobody worried until 1955—except white ranchers and speculators. They were waiting to defeat my hungry people with dollars the way soldiers defeated them with bullets. Then in 1955 the life and death fight of our Northern Cheyenne Tribe started.

When I tell you about the fight remember this. Cheyennes don't sell pieces of our homeland because they want to take their land sale money and go away from the people to life. They spend their land sale money on food—clothes—old cars to get around in....

In 1955 the first tracts of Northern Cheyenne land were put up for sale by the Indian Bureau. Our people told us, the tribal council, to save the reservation any way we could—by asking the Bureau to stop Cheyenne land sales, by having the tribe buy up any land that was going to be sold. The tribal council liquidated our tribal steer enterprise, and we wanted to use $40,000 from this to keep the first Cheyenne land from being sold. The Bureau would not release our money to us in time for us to bid on the land. And they refused to hold up the land sale until our money was released. The Bixby Tracts were 1,340 acres of our best grazing and with water, and they were sold to a Mr. Norris for $22,458. A year later Mr. Norris offered to sell the land back to us again—for $47,736, a $25,278 profit. By then the tribe couldn't afford to buy back the Bixby Tracts, because the Billings Area Office of the Bureau was putting other tracts of our land up for sale as fast as they could. We had to bid on those tracts with the money we had. So far—from 1958 to 1959—the tribal council managed to hold our reservation together by bidding on every piece of land that went up for sale. In 1959 we borrowed $50,000 from the Indian Revolving Loan Fund at 4% interest. We knew this money will not be enough to buy all the land that ever comes up for sale. We thought we could save our homeland for a little while longer—and then the end would come.

The tribal council remembered the people told us to save the reservation. We prayed and thought. Then we wrote a plan to save the land the Cheyennes came home to from the Oklahoma. The people approved the plan. The Keeper of the Sacred Hat blessed it, and he is our holiest man.

Our plan is the Northern Cheyenne 50-Year Unallotment Program. It is a plan to make our reservation unallotted again in 50 years. The plan asks the

Bureau to make us a 50-year loan of $500,000 at 2½% interest for land purchase. We have proved that we can repay this loan in 50 years or less out of income from the land the tribe will be buying. In the 50 years that the plan will be going on, we asked the Bureau to stop all Cheyenne land sales except to the tribe, and the tribe obligates itself to buy all land that individual Cheyennes want to sell. We also asked the Bureau to stop the approval of all fee patents during the period of the plan—and we asked them to allow members of the tribe to buy, sell and trade land among themselves without being forced to take it out of trust.

That plan could save our land. It will not cost the Government anything. The Government divided up our land so that it could be sold to white men in pieces. Now we are willing to buy every piece back again out of our own money.

We took our plan to the Interior Department—to Assistant Secretary Roger Ernst. He congratulated us for planning for ourselves. He said the plan would be approved if we could show that we could repay the loan we asked for.

We asked the Indian Bureau to stop all land sales on our reservation immediately, so that our lands would not be slipping away while we waited to get our loan. The Interior Department said the Bureau would do that. Right after we heard this good news, the Billings Area Office of the Bureau advertised 13 tracts of land for sale. The Association on American Indian Affairs told us to trust the Interior Department because Secretary Seaton and Secretary Ernst were men of their word. The Association was right. My people will tell the story of a thing that happened for a long time.

The land sale was advertised. Certain white men were wheeling around like buzzards waiting for the bidding to start. The Cheyennes could not talk—they were so angry and sad. Then all at once the land sale was called off—by a telephone call from Washington. You would have to be a Cheyenne to know what it meant when the Government in Washington kept its word—helped us against the Bureau in Montana. At first the people whispered the news to each other. Then they said it out loud. I never saw the Cheyennes as happy as that. I was never as happy myself in my whole life. I think all of us had a picture of the Government helping us save our land, then helping us with a plan to make our Cheyenne community a good part of America.

It is good for us to have that picture of how life can be for us. It will keep us strong in the fight ahead....

My people are fighting to save their land. They are not fighting Congress or the Interior Department....

6. Mary Jacobs (Lumbee) Relates How Her Family Made a Home in Chicago, n.d.

On Christmas day in 1952 my parents, Willard Cummings and Lora Neil Brooks, were married in Dillon, South Carolina. On the next day, my parents left Robeson County to make Chicago their new home. As a child I never thought about the courage or sense of self that my parents must have had to

Reprinted with permission from the author.

complete that seemingly simple act of moving away from home for the first time. They had come from very simple beginnings. My dad was 22 when he married my mom. He was the third child of Newton Cummings and Flora Ann Lowry. My father's parents were sharecroppers moving up from a one-mule farm to a two-mule farm. Finally my grandparents were able to realize a dream and bought their own 100-acre farm in the Prospect community. They had fourteen children; seven girls and seven boys. All but one of my father's siblings (a brother) would live to adulthood.

My mother was 18 when she married my father. She was the second-youngest child of Andrew Worth Brooks and Mary Jane Locklear. My mother's father operated a crane, and he helped build highways across several states, including Oklahoma and Virginia. My grandmother, my mom's mother, stayed in Pembroke raising their twelve children; only nine would survive to adulthood.

My parents were born during the Depression and their schooling took place in segregated schools. Everyone was poor and few people had the opportunity to better themselves through higher education. During my parents' school years there were the three school buses that rode through Pembroke: one for whites, one for blacks, and one for Indians. My father had attended both of the local high schools for Indians in Robeson County, Pembroke and Prospect High School, but never completed the degree. My mother did graduate from Pembroke High School and even attended a semester of college at Pembroke State University.

Now re-named the University of North Carolina at Pembroke (UNCP), UNCP has the distinction of being the only state-supported college created for the education of Indians. UNCP was established in 1887. It was called the Croatan Normal School. Croatan was one of many names by which the state recognized Robeson County Indians. The legislation that created the Normal school stated that Lumbee people had to purchase the land and erect a building for their school; both of which were completed within the legislative two-year deadline.

While my parents were growing up, Pembroke State represented the only chance for higher education in Lumbees in North Carolina. The college was a school for teachers and teaching represented one of the few career paths open to Lumbees at that time; the career options were preaching and farming. For those Lumbee men without the required education, the military offered a good alternative.

My father went into the army during the Korean War. He served one term (three and half years), during which he wrote to my mother. He had had dreams of being a veterinarian and during the war he served as a medic. Going to medical school was not in his future since no school in North Carolina would accept him and he did not have the money to go out of state. After the war he returned to Robeson County and began working doing carpentry work. Today carpentry work (hanging sheet rock and finishing work) is still a popular area for young men with little education in Robeson County. The work was and is seasonal and sporadic at best.

While working, my father heard about a school in Chicago from Peter Dial, a young Indian man from the Prospect area who had attended there. The school was the Allied Institute of Technology, a trade school, on Michigan Avenue. Peter also gave my father the address of a boarding house where he had lived while he had attended the school. So my parents left Robeson County with the address of the school and the name and address for a place to live.

My mother said that she recalled feeling very apprehensive about moving to Chicago. She had never lived outside Robeson County and wondered if she and my father would be accepted by their neighbors, because Indians were not accepted by whites in and around Robeson County at that time.

They spent New Year's weekend with my great uncle Coolidge Mack Cummings (my father's paternal uncle), his wife Van, and their children in Louisville, Kentucky. Coolidge was a pastor in a "white" church there. It would be several years before he would return to Robeson County to pastor an Indian church. Over the years in Chicago, my parents would visit Uncle Coolidge in Kentucky often.

On the last day of 1952 my parents drove into Chicago. They had an address for an apartment house that Peter Dial had given them; it was 1418 West Jackson. My father said that the woman who ran the apartment house just happened to have an available apartment. They signed the lease. That same week my father went to Allied Institute to sign up for classes. Since he had not contacted the school earlier, he did not know that the school term had already started and he would have to wait one term before he could enroll. Meanwhile, both he and my mother looked for work.

First Jobs

My father's first job in Chicago was at a plant that made coils for bedsprings. The plant was on Pulaski, but since my parents had a car he was able to get from their apartment to work until he was in an accident. My father recalled that a "drunk" ran into him and the car was totaled. After that he found a job closer to their apartment. That job was in a tool and die shop on Madison, at about the 1200 block west.

My mother worked for a catalog company, the Alden catalog, across the street from the apartment. She was able to do the work, but felt that the management was too overbearing. None of the workers in the shop were allowed to speak to each other and all of their breaks were timed. She felt as though every minute was regulated. She left the first job and then went to a small company that printed bank certificates and hunting licenses. She proofread the materials after they were printed. But after getting pregnant, she stopped working because the fumes from the ink made her ill. She would not work again until all of her children were in school.

About a month after moving to the city, my father began attending school at the Allied Institute. He was able to use his GI benefits to pay for school and completed his A.A. degree in Industrial Engineering. Immediately after completing the degree, he got a job with Scully-Jones, a family owned company that designed and made tools for other industries. Later Scully-Jones became a part of Bendix Corporation. My father would stay with the company for twenty-four years before leaving that job to move back to Robeson County.

Keeping in Touch with Home

Mom said that most of their neighbors in Chicago were poor whites from the south: Kentucky, Tennessee, and Mississippi. She recalled that poor southern whites were most of the people that they met, but whenever they heard about another Lumbee person in the city they would make an effort to meet them and visit with them. My mother said that both her parents and my dad's parents would write them and let them know about other Indians (Lumbees) from home living in or traveling through Chicago.

My mother recalled visiting H. B. Jacobs (she could not remember his full name), a Lumbee man who had served in World War II and married a woman he met in Germany. The Jacobs lived on Adams, near my parents' apartment. There was also Morrison and Odessa Maynor, who lived just north of Kimball Avenue. Then in 1958, my mother's nephew Samuel Brooks came to Oak Park to attend college at Emais Bible College, a brethren college located in that suburb (my mother's family attended the brethren church in Pembroke). My mother's elder brother, Venus Brooks, was pastor of the brethren church in Pembroke and he wanted his son, Sam, to attend a brethren school. Samuel would marry a white woman from Oak Park and live in that suburb for most of his life.

My parents were able to meet a lot of Lumbee people moving to Detroit or living in Chicago for brief periods who were there for work. While my parents knew of Indians from other tribes living in the city, they did not make much effort to seek them out. My parents grew up in a generation of Lumbee that did not consider themselves "real Indians" because "real Indians like the ones in the movies wore feathers and lived on reservations in the west."

Before there was a real movement among the Lumbee to recover lost traditions and consider themselves a tribe, the people relied on familial ties for identity. That is, your family group (large groupings of families descended from some major figure) determined your identity as an Indian.

My father recalled that few people asked him about his race, but when they did he said he was a Cherokee Indian from Robeson County. He recalled "that's what they told us we were." Cherokee Indians from Robeson County was one of the many names that the Lumbees had to use until the state and federal government would allow the Lumbees to name themselves in 1956.

But my parents did not rely on a tribal identity to know who was Lumbee; rather people were known only by "who their people were." At that time (and to an extent this is still true), when Lumbee people first met they introduce themselves by telling who their parents and grandparents (and sometimes other relatives who might have been well known in the community) were. Knowing who another Indian's "people" were placed that person in their proper context. With that information you knew where they probably lived in the county, went to school, and which familial church they attended. It also gave information about what kind of work they probably did and, to an extent, the familial reputation (being smart or other personal characteristics) that might extend to that individual as well. That is why my parents were able to keep in touch with events and people from "home" that they might not have known otherwise.

But my parents did return to Robeson County after moving to Chicago. For all of the twenty-five years that they lived in Chicago and later Maywood, they returned "home" almost every summer. I remember well leaving home at 2 or 3 A.M. to begin the trip to Pembroke. It would usually take us 18 or more hours of driving and we would not stop until we reached "home." To all Lumbees of my parents' generation and to most today, Robeson County is always called "home." When I returned there people usually ask "How long will you be home this time?" And my parents and in-laws usually want to know "when are you coming home?" They are referring to our family home in Pembroke, but they are also referring to Robeson County as a larger home for Indian (Lumbee) people.

My Return to Chicago

My parents had eight children. I was their last child; the youngest or "baby" of the family. I was born in Chicago, like all my brothers and sisters, but considered Pembroke my home. My parents moved back to Robeson County when I was thirteen years old and I attended junior high, high school, and college in North Carolina. I met my husband (another Lumbee person) there and we were married in my mother-in-law's living room.

I decided to move to Chicago after being accepted into the doctoral program in Social Work at the University of Chicago. I really had mixed feelings about moving here. After my husband and I were married we moved to Southern California and had been living there for six years. I did not know a lot about the U. of Chicago before moving there and I was not sure that I would like it. I did know that Chicago had an Indian community, but I did not know any Lumbee people here except my sister.

My sister, Stephana, was the third eldest child in our family and she never moved to Robeson County with the family. She was already married to a white man she has met at church, and they stayed in Illinois after we moved. All of my other siblings and family were living in Robeson County (and still are).

However, after moving here, I did meet other Indian people, but my sister and I are the only Lumbee people here that we know. My first cousin Samuel Brooks passed away in the mid-1980s and his widow and children still live near Oak Park. My sister and I do visit with them. In addition to school, I work with a group in the Indian community in Chicago who are trying to create more Indian foster parent homes for Indian children, the Native American Foster Parent Association (NAFPA).

I, unlike my parents, grew up during a period of great traditional recovery in Robeson County. Lumbees were more in touch and aware of themselves as a tribal group and were a growing political force in national tribal politics as well. Although Lumbees are still not federally recognized, we do have a national reputation because of all the work that individual Lumbee people do at a national level with various Indian communities and in Washington, D. C. Upon moving to Chicago, I told people here in the Indian community I was Lumbee; they recognized my tribe and I felt very welcomed by the Indian community here.

Today, my parents do not come to Chicago often, but do visit here with my sister and me and our families on occasion. I think their hope is that we will finally return to Robeson County to live permanently, but they understand that returning is not always possible. There are still rather limited employment opportunities in Robeson and the surrounding counties. In addition, the jobs there do not pay well and there are still a lot of racial tensions in the community, especially between whites and Indians.

I hope that I will return to Robeson County or at least the state of North Carolina someday, but for now I am happy to be living and attending school in Chicago. I, like my parents, consider Chicago a temporary stop on the way back home.

◈ ESSAYS

The first of these two essays, "Building Toward Self-Determination: Plains and Southwestern Indians in the Mid-Twentieth Century" by Peter Iverson, represents an early revisionist view of the termination period. A professor emeritus of history at Arizona State University, Iverson argues here that despite the many problems the era posed, and sometimes because of those very dilemmas, the mid-twentieth century was a time when Indian individuals and communities established the foundation for self-determination. This essay is one of the first reinterpretations of the era. It moves away from a total emphasis on victimization toward paying greater attention to Indians' ability to respond creatively and productively to the demands of the time. In addition to termination, Native peoples encountered federal policies that intended to relocate them from reservations and into cities. In the second essay, Myla Vicenti Carpio (Jicarilla Apache and Laguna Pueblo), a professor of American Indian Studies at Arizona State University, examines how Laguna Pueblos maintained ties to their reservation and resisted colonization in Albuquerque, New Mexico. Vicenti Carpio points out that, though Laguna Pueblos had been urbanized early in the twentieth century, they refused to surrender their identity or connections to Laguna. Why did Laguna Pueblos move to cities, in particular to Albuquerque? How did urban Pueblos create social, political, economic, and cultural ties to their rural homeland?

Building Toward Self-Determination: Plains and Southwestern Indians in the Mid-Twentieth Century

BY PETER IVERSON

[The mid-twentieth century] is often referred to in the literature as the era of termination. During this time, many members of Congress and the Truman and Eisenhower administrations made sporadic but persistent efforts to reduce or eliminate federal services and protection for American Indians. The public rhetoric spoke of liberating the Indians by reducing governmental interference. Termination sought to immerse Indians in the mainstreams of their counties and

Peter Iverson, "Building Toward Self-Determination: Plains and Southwestern Indians in the 1940s and 1950s," *Western Historical Quarterly*, vol. 16, April 1985, pp. 163–73. Reprinted with permission.

states. This crusade resulted in significant hardships for many Indians. Tribes such as Menominees in Wisconsin or the Klamaths in Oregon saw their reservation status ended. Indians who relocated to cities, with or without federal sponsorship, confronted many dilemmas. State and local agencies proved unwilling or unable to shoulder responsibilities previously bestowed upon the federal government. Economic development programs on reservations usually did not markedly improve unemployment, housing, and other critical problems.

Yet to label these years as the termination era and to emphasize so exclusively the negative aspects of this generation is to present an incomplete picture. We cannot ignore federal policy in our consideration of any period, for it always has an important effect. But the 1940s and 1950s are more than a time of troubles. Just as new research is starting to reveal the late nineteenth and early twentieth centuries as a time when Indians in many areas made important and necessary adjustments to continue their lives as Indians, so too a closer examination of this more recent era shows it to be a period in which tribalism and Indian nationalism were reinforced. Indeed, to a significant degree, the threat and the enactment of terminationist policy often strengthened rather than weakened Indian institutions and associations. In addition, the attitudes of state and local officials, as well as the perspectives of urban residents, encouraged Indians throughout the nation to recognize increasingly their common bonds and needs.

During the 1940s and 1950s, then, Indians in growing numbers tried to identify and take advantage of their own economic resources and tried to affirm their identities as members of tribes and as Indians. They rejected the conventional wisdom that they would be "less Indian" if they gained more education, acquired new jobs, or moved to a new residence. Actually, greater contact with the larger American society promoted greater awareness that the English language, new technological skills, and other elements of the American culture could be used to promote a continuing, if changing, Indian America.

A review of Indian actions in two important regions—the Plains and the Southwest—reveals a vital maturation in Indian leadership and a reaffirmation of Indian identity in the 1940s and 1950s. Far from vanishing, Indians emerged from this generation more determined than ever to be recognized on their own terms. The more publicized activism of the late 1960s and 1970s thus may trace its origins to these ostensibly more quiet years.

World War II marks a critical turning point in modern American Indian history. Indians took great pride in their involvement in the war effort. For example, Cecil Horse, a Kiowa, remembered his son John winning a bronze star and a purple heart and in turn receiving from his people a war bonnet and a give away ceremony in his honor. Navajos celebrated their Codetalkers' role in the Pacific. In a publication of November 1945, the Office of Indian Affairs recorded the military honors earned by Indians and the investment by Indians in more than $17 million of restricted funds in war bonds. It quoted the instructions of Private Clarence Spotted Wolf, a Gros Ventre killed on December 21, 1944, in Luxembourg:

> If I should be killed, I want you to bury me on one of the hills east of
> the place where my grandparents and brothers and sisters and other

relatives are buried. If you have a memorial service, I want the soldiers to go ahead with the American flag. I want cowboys to follow, all on horseback. I want one of the cowboys to lead one of the wildest of the T over X horses with saddle and bridle on. I will be riding that horse.

The war generated more than memories and emotions. It meant that Indians had become more a part of the larger world in which they lived. As Ella Deloria, the Dakota linguist, wrote in 1944: "The war has indeed wrought an overnight change in the outlook, horizon, and even the habits of the Indian people—a change that might not have come for many years yet." Through the service, through off-reservation experiences, and through wage work, Indian perspectives and Indian economies began to change. Returning veterans and other participants in the war effort recognized the significance of better educational opportunities. Navajo Scott Preston put it simply: "We have to change and we have to be educated."

Change also demanded organization. Indian delegates from fifty tribes, hailing from twenty-seven states, met November 15–18, 1944, in Denver to organize the National Congress of American Indians. In the words of one of the congress's first presidents, N. B. Johnson, the delegates set "an example for speed, diplomacy and harmony." Within four days, they "adopted a constitution and formally launched the organization in an effort to bring all Indians together for the purpose of enlightening the public, preserving Indian cultural values, seeking an equitable adjustment of tribal affairs, securing and preserving their rights under treaties with the United States, and streamlining the administration of Indian affairs." In subsequent meetings in Browning, Montana, in 1945 and Oklahoma City in 1946, those in attendance proved to be, according to Johnson, "a cross-section of Indian population: old and young, full-bloods, mixed-bloods, educated and uneducated Indians from allotted areas and others from reservations," all of whom "were dissatisfied with many phases of the government's administration of Indian affairs." Improved health care and educational opportunities, protection of Indian land rights, and increased Indian veterans' benefits were advocated. The National Congress of American Indians urged the U.S. Congress and the current administration "not to enact legislation or promulgate rules and regulations thereunder affecting the Indians without first consulting the Tribes affected."

Such, of course, would not be the case. In both the Truman and Eisenhower administrations, the federal government proceeded to pass legislation and carry out policies contrary to the will of the vast majority of American Indians. For many Americans, the Indian war record had prompted concern that Indians be treated fairly. O. K. Armstrong's influential article in the August 1945 *Reader's Digest* urged America to "Set the American Indians Free!" House of Representatives Majority Leader John W. McCormack read Armstrong's piece advocating the removal of "restrictions" from Indians and wrote to his colleague, W. G. Stigler, that he was "interested in seeing justice done for all—and this applies with great force to our fine American Indians." Cherokee/Creek historian Tom Holm has properly summarized what happened: "In the end, fighting the White man's war gained sympathy for American Indians but it also fueled a fire that they did not want and eventually found difficult to extinguish."

While they were not without effective allies, Indians had to lead the fight against Public Law 280, House Concurrent Resolution 108, and other features of termination. Protests against such measures soon resounded throughout the West. Through a variety of means, Indians attempted to ward off the implementation of a policy they realized could bring them great harm. In the early years, voices from tribal councils and business committees rang out against a specific action in a particular locale. For example, Richard Boynton, Sr., and George Levi of the Cheyenne-Arapaho business committee telegrammed Oklahoma congressman Toby Morris to protest against the impending closing of the Cheyenne-Arapaho school in El Reno. Kiowa leader Robert Goombi argued that abolishing the Concho Indian School would be counterproductive. Yet, as the wider pattern of the era emerged, multitribal associations were strengthened as a more effective means of presenting a more powerful Indian voice.

The National Congress of American Indians (NCAI) therefore continued to expand in its influence in the years that followed its establishment in 1944. Plains and Southwestern Indian peoples remained active in the executive ranks of the organization throughout the 1940s and 1950s. In the mid-1950s over half the elected members of the executive council would come from regional tribes, including the Osages, Gros Ventres, Gila River Pimas, Taos Pueblos, Blackfeet, Oglala Sioux, and Cheyenne-Arapahoes. Colorado River tribes, Hualapais, Omahas, and the San Carlos Apaches appointed additional representatives. Oglala Sioux Helen Peterson served as executive director; Papago Thomas Segundo was regional representative.

The NCAI filled two critical functions. It helped Indians speak out against termination, but it also advocated programs that would contribute to Indian social, political, and economic revitalization. Through publicity releases from its Washington office, specially called tribal forums, and other means, the congress directly confronted the forces favoring termination. John Rainer from Taos Pueblo thus in 1950 attacked Commissioner of Indian Affairs Dillon Myer for imposing "drum head justice" upon Indians by denying tribes the power to choose their own attorneys.

The organization did more than criticize. It manifested a maturing capacity to articulate counterproposals when it offered suggestions to reduce Indian poverty, improvements for health care and educational facilities, and provisions to use reservation resources more effectively. A specific example—the Point Nine Program—was formulated and adopted by the congress in November 1954. It addressed critical questions relating to such matters as land and water resources, planning, credit, land purchase, and job training. Pointing to the assistance provided by the United States to underdeveloped countries around the world, Helen Peterson and other leaders demanded that this country apply the same principles within its borders.

Indians addressed the issues of the day through other forums as well. The Association on American Indian Affairs, under the direction of Oliver La Farge, helped publicize both the dangers of federal policy and Indian moves to oppose it. Thus when the NCAI mobilized Indian representatives from twenty-one states and Alaska to come to Washington, D.C., on February 25–28, 1954, to protest impending legislation, *Indian Affairs*, the newsletter of AAIA, not only gave extensive coverage but also proper credit to NCAI for its actions. Other institutions and organizations put together symposia for the examination of contemporary Indian well-being. Tribal spokesmen from the Plains and the Southwest participated vigorously in such gatherings, be it the annual meeting of the American Anthropological Association in Tucson in 1954 or the annual conference on Indian affairs at the University of South Dakota's Institute of Indian Studies.

By the end of the era, new forums had been sought for the expression of Indian views. In 1961 representatives from sixty-four tribes, totaling approximately seven hundred delegates, met in Chicago to create the Declaration of Indian Purpose. They did not all agree with one another, but the so-called Chicago Conference was an important landmark in modern Indian affairs because of its size and its impact upon many of the participants.

Another example is the National Indian Youth Council (NIYC), which came into being soon thereafter. The NIYC had its roots in the annual conferences of the Southwest Association on Indian Affairs, beginning in 1956. This one-day session at the St. Francis Auditorium in Santa Fe brought Indian community people together with high school and college students, with the latter speaking to the former about their studies and the applicability of these studies to the communities. From this local beginning, the conference became regional in its focus in 1957 and was called the Southwest Regional Indian Youth Council. The council held annual conferences in the spring until April 1961 when the last meeting was held in Norman, Oklahoma. According to the Tewa anthropologist Alfonso Ortiz, "It was a core group from these youth councils, augmented later by alumni of D'Arcy McNickle's Indian Leadership Training Programs, who founded the NIYC in Gallup after the American Indian Chicago Conference was held in June."

Other experiences and associations prompted heightened pan-Indian feelings. Relocation programs to American cities brought Indians into contact with non-Indians indifferent to tribal distinctions. Prejudice sometimes spurred pan-Indian identification. The formation of Indian communities and intertribal marriages in the cities also could foster such sentiments.

The Cherokee anthropologist Robert K. Thomas and other observers have noted that this movement frequently had a "pan-Plains" quality to it. Thomas also suggested that within the Southwest something of a "pan-Puebloism" could be perceived. Pan-Indianism, as it continued to evolve during this time, could be "very productive, as nationalist movements often are, in literature and the arts," but it also developed institutions dealing with non-Indians. One such development was the growth of powwows—a source of pleasure and pride for participants and enjoyment and education for spectators.

A final example of the pan-Indian movements in the 1940s and 1950s that should be cited is the Native American Church. It found significant support within the Plains and the Southwest, and leaders for the organization frequently hailed from these regions. At the tribal level, the Native American Church increased its membership during this period. Many Indians looked to participation within the peyote religion as a way of accommodating the various demands of modern life and reaffirming their identities as Indians. In Montana perhaps half the Crows and many Cheyennes embraced the church. Adherents included prominent tribal leaders such as Robert Yellowtail, Crow, and Johnnie Woodenlegs,

Northern Cheyenne. Frank Takes Gun also emerged as an important, if controversial, church leader.

Attitudes toward the practice of the faith varied considerably, to be sure, from one Indian community to another and within communities. In the Navajo nation, the peyote religion grew considerably in its membership during the 1950s, despite an antagonistic stance taken against it by the tribal chairperson, Paul Jones. Raymond Nakai gained the chairmanship in 1963 in part because he pledged to stop harassing the Native American Church. On the Wind River reservation in Wyoming, Northern Arapahoe political and traditional leaders became more conciliatory toward the well-established practice. As was true in many tribes, the Arapahoes often added the Native American Church to prior participation in other religious ceremonies, be they Christian or traditional.

The reservation continued in the 1940s and 1950s as a centrally important place for religious observances, but for other reasons as well. The guiding philosophy of federal policy dictated that reservations were economic dead ends. After all, people were supposed to relocate because there were not enough jobs being generated at home. Since the land, families, familiarity, and, indeed, everything that went into the definition of home continued to be valued so deeply, Indian communities within the Plains and the Southwest endeavored to keep more of their citizens at home. While organizations such as the NCAI could advocate local development of resources, such development had to be prompted and managed.

Navajo economic and political development has been described elsewhere in some detail. In the face of termination, Navajos who distrusted state governments and desired to maintain a working ethnic boundary between themselves and whites had little choice during the era but to pursue a more nationalistic approach. With large sums newly available to the tribal treasury from mineral revenues, the Navajo tribal government became far more ambitious. Federal assistance through the long-range rehabilitation program also assisted internal Navajo development. While the 1960s and 1970s would bring more fully to fruition some of these plans and programs, the 1940s and 1950s were crucial in the reinforcement of a working tribal identity and a commitment to a revitalized tribal economy.

Arts and crafts came to command a more important place in many tribal economies in the Southwest. For the Navajos, silversmithing and weaving continued to be vital sources of income. Pottery also gained widening acclaim, particularly at San Ildefonso, but also in other Pueblo communities along the Rio Grande and at some of the Hopi villages. Silverwork at the Hopi and Zuni pueblos, basket weaving especially among the Papagos and Walapais, the paintings of such artists as Fred Kabotie, Hopi, and Harrison Begay, Navajo, and the sculpture of Alan Hauser, Apache, also found appreciative audiences. Though the boom in Indian art had yet to arrive, a kind of foundation had been established.

Cattle ranching represented another important element in economic development. On the San Carlos Apache reservation, the cattle industry underwent significant alteration. The tribal council in October 1956 approved Ordinance No. 5-56 to reorganize and consolidate existing associations and implement various reforms in grazing regulations and practices. Improved range management could be combined with maintenance of cooperative efforts among the people of San Carlos. Cattle sales created some income for most families in the tribe. The quality of the Apaches' Herefords consistently attracted cattle buyers from throughout the West and generated a positive image of the Apaches to the non-Indian residents of Arizona.

Similarly, the Northern Arapahoes gained greater control over their tribal ranch established during the Indian New Deal. With the assistance of an attorney, the tribe eventually was able to hire a ranch manager and to have the ranch trustees be Arapahoes appointed by the Arapahoe business council. This sizable operation returned a consistent profit to each Arapahoe. As with the San Carlos Apaches, the ranching enterprise contributed to tribal self-esteem, the status of the tribal government, and an enhanced view of the Arapahoes among outsiders, including the Shoshones who shared the Wind River reservation.

In 1950 the tribal council of the Pine Ridge reservation in South Dakota passed a tax of three cents per acre for grazing privileges on tribal lands. The tax met with strenuous objections by white cattle ranchers. In the face of such opposition, the Department of the Interior quickly assigned responsibility of collecting the tax to the Sioux. By 1956 white ranchers had challenged the tax in court, but in the following year the U.S. District Court judge ruled against them, contending that Indian tribes were "sovereign powers and as sovereign powers can levy taxes."

Greater assertion of Sioux power was not limited to Pine Ridge. Under the leadership of Chairman Frank Ducheneaux, the Cheyenne River tribal council approved a firm resolution against Public Law 280. Both on Rosebud and on Pine Ridge, tribal voters in 1957 overwhelmingly defeated the assumption of state jurisdiction in South Dakota on Indian reservations. Opposition to repeated efforts to institute state jurisdiction led in 1963 to the formal organization of the United Sioux Tribes.

By 1959 the Rosebud Sioux tribal chairman, Robert Burnette, had filed complaints of discrimination under the Civil Rights Act of 1957 before the Civil Rights Commission. Burnette contended that Indians in South Dakota had been excluded from juries, had been beaten and chained in prisons, and generally had been greeted as people without equal rights in the state. While the commission was not very responsive to Burnette's allegations, the very act of publicly challenging local conditions indicated that a more activist stance would be assumed in the 1960s.

In the Dakotas, Wyoming, Arizona, and elsewhere, then, the growing importance of attorneys could be observed. For many tribes the establishment of the Indian Claims Commission in 1945 had prompted their first acquisition of some form of legal counsel. While the Bureau of Indian Affairs in the 1950s had often discouraged tribal use of attorneys or tried to dictate the choice of a specific firm, by decade's end it was clear that legal assistance would play a vital role in many realms of tribal life.

Williams v. *Lee* is a useful example of this evolution. Called by Chemehuevi attorney Fred Ragsdale "the first modern Indian law case," *Williams* v. *Lee* involved a non-Indian trader on the Navajo reservation who sued a Navajo in the state court to collect for goods sold on credit. While the Arizona Supreme Court ruled in favor of the trader, the U.S. Supreme Court reversed this decision. Justice Hugo Black, on behalf of the Court, stated: "There can be no doubt that to allow the exercise of state jurisdiction here would undermine the authority of the tribal courts over Reservation affairs and hence would infringe on the right of the Indians to govern themselves." This landmark decision served as a crucial statement in support of tribal sovereignty, presaging additional legal battles to be waged in the years to come.

In any reappraisal of the 1940s and 1950s, it is important to not overstate the case. The negative aspects of the period remain, even with the vital developments outlined above. And in a treatment of this length, some events of magnitude must be slighted. For example, the damming of the Missouri River created great hardship for the Indian peoples of that area. Scholars have correctly underlined the problems that seemed to exist everywhere, from the most isolated reservations to the largest city.

Nonetheless, a more careful examination yields a more balanced picture. In overdramatizing the difficulties of the time, we may not give sufficient credit to the enduring nature of Indians in this country. By the end of the 1950s, tribal resources were more studied and better understood; tribal council leadership was often more effective. The Salish scholar and writer D'Arcy McNickle appreciated the transition that had taken place. He spoke in 1960 of the growing Indian movement toward self-determination. Indians in the future, he suggested, would "probably use the white man's technical skills for Indian purposes." McNickle affirmed that "Indians are going to remain Indian ... a way of looking at things and a way of acting which will be original, which will be a compound of these different influences."

The 1940s and 1950s witnessed not only change in Indian policy and a resurgence of pressures to assimilate Indians into the larger society, but they also saw maturation and growth of Indian leadership at the local and national levels and efforts to develop tribal institutions as well as a reaffirmation of identity, and a willingness to adapt and change in the face of new conditions. In the immediate future, seemingly new demands would resound for self-determination. Yet these demands were firmly based upon a foundation gradually constructed in the previous generation.

Fighting Colonization in the Urban Southwest: Laguna Pueblos in Albuquerque

BY MYLA VICENTI CARPIO (JICARILLA APACHE)

The federal government's relocation program, coupled with its termination policy, attempted to usurp indigenous lands and indigenous cultures. Beginning in the 1950s, relocation and termination provided a way for the government to withdraw "legally" from its federal trust responsibility and impose a policy of assimilation on indigenous peoples. Terminating trust responsibilities, borders, and "Indianness" sent a clear message that the federal government intended for American Indians to cease to exist as cultural and self-determined peoples. The federal government's formula was to get Indians off the reservations and the federal dole—if no one lived on the reservations then there would not be a need for

Myla Vicenti Carpio, "Countering Colonization: Albuquerque's Laguna Colony," *Wicazo Sa Review* 19 (Fall 2004): 61–78. Reprinted with permission of the author and the University of Minnesota Press.

public funds to support social, educational, and land management expenditures on those lands. Seeking to absorb indigenous peoples into mainstream society, the relocation program aimed to send them from reservations to urban areas where they would provide vocational training, a place to live, and a job. As with other policy eras, indigenous people and the federal government had very different ideas on the meaning of relocation.

No matter the reasons for moving, relocation, with or without the federal relocation program assistance, failed to completely assimilate indigenous people into American society. The myriad experiences of those who migrated to the cities and those who stayed on reservations created dynamic relationships between urban life, indigenous identities, and reservation life. Unfortunately, early studies of relocated Indians simplistically characterized assimilation in terms of success (staying) or failure (returning).... The notion of the reservation Indian versus the urban Indian utilizes colonialistic labels of progress that posit the "good" Indian against the "bad" Indian. Those who stayed in the city were "successful" despite unmeasured living conditions and situations; the only important criterion by federal standards was that they stayed. Failure meant leaving the city and returning to the reservation. Consequently, the urban Indian was seen as the assimilated Indian no matter what his or her socioeconomic and cultural status.

As a result, the reservation/urban dichotomy denotes an urban Indian experience as being completely distinct from, and less authentic than, reservation life. The reservation is believed to generate "authentic Indians," ones who know their culture, practice their religion, and speak their language while always challenging the colonial policies of the federal government. Conversely, the dichotomy posits urban identity as being separate from the reservation; creating a home in the city represents a changed identity, removed from the reservation, giving rise to either the assimilated or the generic pan-Indian. As these polar identities become internalized, the process of American colonization further obscures, divides, and devalues indigenous peoples' lived realities.... In this case, the internalization of the reservation and urban dichotomy further divides and devalues indigenous people living in urban centers....

[The] concept of pan-Indian identity limits our understanding of the lived reality of urban indigenousness.... I will focus on the intersection where urban Indian organizations develop community while maintaining and nurturing connections with reservation life and culture. Although relocation was responsible for urbanization among Indians, primarily in the 1950s, the Lagunas began to live away from their reservation in the late 1800s. However, those who left found means to maintain social, economic, and political bonds with their people back home.... Instead of assimilating the dichotomy of reservation and urban Indians, members of the Laguna Colonies live outside their reservation home while maintaining cultural connections through the colony.

Moving to the city does not necessarily end a personal or spiritual connection to the reservation, although living even a short distance from one's home community does pose significant obstacles for maintaining religious, cultural, and language ties. Indigenous urban people have formed different associations and relationships in order to build bridges to home, to a specific culture or a specific people. For some, connections with others are made informally at powwows, church, Indian centers, and bars where diverse indigenous peoples gather.... Others gravitate toward individuals of their own nation or cultural background....

The Laguna Colony furnishes a social support system while offering a way for its members to maintain cultural obligations, language, and some gender roles in a process that bridges Laguna Pueblo with Laguna tribal members living in Albuquerque. The Pueblo of Laguna, consisting of six villages, has a unique history of formally recognizing tribal members, through colony status, who live away from the reservation. This process began when Manifest Destiny reached the Pueblo of Laguna in the form of the 1880 railroad. The rail permanently changed the lives of the Laguna people, though the Pueblo of Laguna saw this contact as a unique opportunity to involve Laguna people within this railroad system construction and operation. In the 1880s, the Atlantic and Pacific railroads began laying track south of Albuquerque. In time, they reached the Laguna Pueblo reservation lands. The Lagunas stopped the construction in order to negotiate a precedent-setting "Gentlemen's Agreement of Friendship" between Laguna officials and the railroad company.

As part of this agreement, railroad officials offered the Lagunas a lump-sum payment as compensation for right-of-way passage through the reservation. In place of this payment, the Atlantic & Pacific Railroad, later named the Atchison, Topeka, and Santa Fe (AT&SF) Railway, and the Laguna leadership fashioned a renewable annual verbal agreement to allow passage through the Laguna reservation. In exchange for right-of-way, the railroad company employed any Laguna who wanted to work at building and maintaining the railroad system. Workers had jobs "so long as the governor of their pueblo granted the workers his approval."

The agreement introduced Lagunas into the wage-earning economy, but it also took them off the reservation. While many Lagunas laid track and then returned home, others worked in several areas of the railroad operation: in construction and as mechanics, clerks, and conductors. They moved from New Mexico through Arizona and into California, to cities along the route, including Gallup, Winslow, Holbrook, Barstow, Richmond, and Los Angeles. The Atlantic & Pacific Railroad Company employed many Laguna men and women while continuing to renew their handshake agreement, or "watering the flower" as the Lagunas called it. Once a year, Lagunas and representatives for the AT&SF did actually meet face-to-face, usually at the railroad corporate office, to shake hands and reaffirm their contractual agreement.

Laguna leaders anticipated the emigrants' needs for a home away from home, so they included a provision in the agreement to include housing off the reservation. In this way, the pueblo maintained a formal connection with the workers. Like the later federal relocation program, the railroad company's idea of adequate housing did not consist of houses; the railroad put aside boxcars on railroad property, which became homes for many Laguna and Acoma railroad workers and their families. The Acomas, whose reservation stood just west of the Laguna lands, and the Lagunas stayed near one another, partly to recreate their proximity at home, but also out of a linguistic kinship—both speak dialects of the Keresan language. In order to create a home away from home, the Lagunas decorated and fashioned the boxcars into residences for their families. Their homes represented life away from the pueblo with no forgetting of their origins. The railroad communities consequently became cultural communities that sustained Laguna language, culture, and ceremonies.

In the early 1900s, the communities of Laguna railroad workers asked that the Pueblo of Laguna formally recognize them as colonies of the pueblo. Laguna formally recognized the colonies in Gallup, New Mexico; Winslow, Arizona; Barstow, California; and Richmond, California. Pueblo approval of the Laguna railroad workers' communities served as the basis for a more structured community. Formal recognition allowed for both an actual and a psychological connection to home. They continued some social dances in the meeting hall that was, of course, a converted boxcar. Colony members used this same meeting hall to host deer dinners, meetings, and feasts. The hall must have echoed from the drumbeats of the deer and corn dance songs; beats that bounced off the floors and ceilings to be absorbed by those in attendance. Residents even built Indian ovens to make Pueblo oven bread, supplying the smells and foods of home. In fact, many members of these original colonies eventually become Albuquerque colony members.

Katherine Augustine, who later became a member of the Laguna Colony of Albuquerque, spent her summer vacations from the Albuquerque Indian School as a youth in the Laguna Colony of Gallup where her parents worked during the 1940s. A small front deck led to the entrances of each family's two-room boxcar. Inside, homes had wood stoves for cooking and heat. Outside, wood piles supplied the necessary wood, clotheslines stretched from the boxcars to barbed wire fences, and the occasional horno, or beehive oven, sat ready to bake bread. Families shared men's and women's community bathrooms equipped with bathtubs, showers, and toilets. The boxcar homes had electricity, but people carried water from a spigot next to the bathhouse.

Fathers worked at the railroad and most women took care of the homes, children, and occasionally others. Katherine Augustine remembered, "Sometimes they made sandwiches for the Hobos who got off the freight trains." While some of the children went to the boarding schools in Albuquerque or Santa Fe, other students went to Gallup public or Catholic schools. The children in Gallup sought entertainment at Catholic Indian Center dances or the Sunday afternoon movies at the Chief or the El Morro theaters with a cherry Coke before going home....

The roots of the Laguna Colony of Albuquerque are similar to those of the Laguna railroad colonies. Both types of colony represent the reciprocal relationship between members off and on the pueblo and their connection to pueblo community and culture. For many, economic circumstances on the reservation were such that many of them decided to leave the reservation in search of employment. A larger number of Lagunas lived in Albuquerque than in the other colonies because of the availability of railroad jobs. In addition, students from Albuquerque Indian School, a boarding school where many Laguna youth were sent, often stayed in the city after graduation. For example, female students who remained became nurses, teachers, or worked in wealthy families' homes. Males often found employment in railroad, mechanical, retail, or agricultural occupations. Many of those who returned to the reservation worked for the Bureau of Indian Affairs or the Indian Health Service on the reservation and elsewhere.

As the number of Lagunas living in Albuquerque increased as the 1900s progressed, many of them felt a need for unity and interconnectedness. Laguna Pueblo is only forty miles west of Albuquerque; however, that distance is immense in terms of being away from one's culture, language, and relations. Many Laguna urbanites viewed the distance from their pueblo as an undesirable aspect of city living that could promote a sense of cultural disassociation, and they exercised their right to seek recognition as stated in the Laguna Constitution in Article III, section 5, which discerned "populations" of adult pueblo members located outside the boundaries of Laguna Pueblo. To mitigate the distance, Lagunas in Albuquerque sought colony recognition from the Pueblo of Laguna in the 1940s. The pueblo saw no purpose in recognizing a colony so "close" to home, but as a result of uranium deposits on Laguna land and the eventual royalties from that uranium, the Laguna Colony of Albuquerque was created and recognized in 1955.

In the late 1940s and early 1950s, the Cold War spurred the federal government's search for domestic uranium deposits. In New Mexico, uranium was located near Grants, then eventually on the Laguna reservation near the village of Paguate. The discovery of uranium brought much-needed economic opportunities to the pueblo, and in the early 1950s, the Anaconda Mining Company contracted with the Pueblo of Laguna to extract the uranium. This agreement provided royalties to Laguna Pueblo, and soon after the Laguna people wanted the royalties distributed. Before uranium, however, the tribe had experienced little economic development or garnered surplus funds. As a consequence, the Laguna Pueblo constitution stated that the tribe would never distribute tribal funds. In order to change the tribal funds restriction, the Pueblo needed to revise their constitution.

Elders on the council called in a number of Laguna individuals living outside the Laguna reservation to help the tribal council revise the constitution. Ulysses Paisano was one of those members. He recalls:

> There were two guys from Winslow, Arizona, one from Santa Fe, and the main thing was to try to help the council. How to get the job done, to distribute the money. So we had to hire a lawyer, and the government lawyer also helped us a lot. The first thing we [had] to do was to revise the old constitution, it was outdated.... Of course, up to that time the tribe had little money. So revising the constitution, of course, took a lot of work [and] it took many years. In fact ... it took about five years. Finally, we [had] to set up a tribal roll in addition to the constitution revision.

The old constitution had specified several colonies: Gallup, New Mexico; Winslow, Arizona; Barstow, California; and Richmond, California; but they did not include Albuquerque. Ulysses Paisano asked the council and then Laguna governor, Tom Daily, about the possibility of setting up a colony in Albuquerque. At first, the tribe did not see the feasibility of such a request. They felt Albuquerque was close enough for pueblo members to drive home for community obligations. With some persuasion, pueblo officials approved the colony on December 31, 1955.

> We weren't organized at all. And so the councilmen kind of objected because they [thought] we were too close [to Laguna Pueblo]. [They] said, "you can come to meetings, village meetings." But we argued with them that it was too costly to run out there. So they finally agreed to let us set up a new colony in Albuquerque.

Authorized to set up a Laguna Colony in Albuquerque, pueblo officials notified everyone in Albuquerque about the matter. Ulysses worked at the Albuquerque Indian School, and the superintendent let them hold their first meeting on February 15, 1956, in the Albuquerque Indian School gymnasium. John Paisano Sr., the governor of the Pueblo of Laguna, also attended. Ulysses stated:

> And if I remember right there were about eighty-five people who showed up. That's how many Lagunas were here then. And we established the colony right then and there and elected the officers. They elected me as chairman and so I served as chairman after that, I guess about four times. So that's how we got started.

According to the Laguna Colony of Albuquerque bylaws, the purpose of the organization "is to establish the principal line of communication between the Pueblo government and the Colony members." In order to keep up that communication, the tribal council and village officials regularly send copies of the meeting minutes to the colonies. Moreover, colony bylaws stipulate that members must adhere to the Laguna Pueblo constitution, ordinances, customs, traditions, and other applicable regulations, meaning they are still responsible for fulfilling tribal obligations. More important, the colony served to promote and provide educational, cultural, and charitable services to its members while "preserving the culture of the Pueblo in an urban setting."

The colony takes seriously its mission to maintain Pueblo customs and beliefs away from the reservation. The committees and activities within the colony illustrate one venue through which nonreservation Lagunas maintain cultural continuity. The colony relates and adheres to the Pueblo of Laguna through community or communal customs of shared responsibilities. In the pueblo, community work was and continues to be valued as important. For instance, during early spring before planting crops and gardens, on one mutually chosen day, all the men in each village come together to clean the irrigation ditches. As with all desert areas, water is a treasure. Since agriculture was the main form of subsistence for the Pueblos, along with hunting, the uninhibited flow of irrigation water to crops was the lifeline of the people. Cleaning the irrigation ditches not only brought the community together, but was basic to physical survival. The Lagunas of Albuquerque had a duty to return to their reservation and participate in the communal ditch work.

Despite the bylaw makers' intent, wage work has an effect on community obligations, especially since both men and women live or work away from the pueblo. This condition has an impact on some of the responsibilities, particularly those of men, in the pueblo or villages: these include cleaning the plaza where many ceremonies take place, digging graves for funerals, and attending village meetings. The men digging the graves receive recognition for their labor through gifts of food, drink, and cigarettes while they work. Each man in the village assumes these responsibilities, though some exceptions exist with age and handicap. To encourage participation, pueblo officials post signs along the road to inform everyone of the time of the next village meeting and impose a fifteen-dollar fine for those who fail to participate. Tribal officials collect these dues at the time of per capita distribution.

One intersection of the Laguna Colony's dual cultural landscapes can be seen in the interactions between the colony and pueblo officials. Recently, the mayordomo at the village of Paguate asked the past chairman, David Melton, to send him the attendance records of the Albuquerque Laguna Colony meetings. The mayordomo assured the chairman that attendance at colony meetings would count toward the attendance of the Paguate Village meeting. Perhaps the other villages will eventually follow this kind of recognition of the validity of the Albuquerque Laguna Colony meetings. Melton, the current chairman, hopes that pueblo officials will recognize the political potential of Laguna Colony members in the form of voters and other educational and political assets. This communication and recognition strengthens, nurtures, and maintains connections between Lagunas living on and off the pueblo.

Laguna Colony strives to maintain connections and communications with the pueblo through many avenues. Colony leadership works at the political level through increased communication and shared spaces. David Melton envisions the colony and the pueblo having more communication, a two-way conversation, with the pueblo recognizing more and more the needs and aspirations of the colony. He wants office space, preferably at the Indian Pueblo Cultural Center, to permanently house the colony's governmental and policy documents. Currently, a file cabinet with past minutes and documents is simply passed around as the vice president's term ends and begins because there is no central location to store it. Melton believes that office space can benefit the tribal officials who come to Albuquerque on business. Instead of renting expensive office spaces in town, they could use Laguna Colony space. This, in turn, would create a closer, more personal relationship between on- and off-reservation officials.

Colony membership incorporates and appreciates all inhabitants of the Albuquerque Laguna community. It includes enrolled members of the Pueblo of Laguna residing in Albuquerque, other members of Laguna Pueblo, associate members, and those on the board of directors. The colony acknowledges non-Laguna spouses and children of members with associate memberships. The associates play an invaluable role in the colony, especially with the cultural and state fair committees. Both colony and associate members have voting privileges.

The board of directors, consisting of a chairman, vice chairman, secretary, treasurer, and a member elected at large by the membership, governs the Laguna Colony. The officers conduct meetings, appoint committees, develop and present for approval the annual budget for colony funds, and create financial management plans for investments and disbursement. Most of these actions need approval by colony membership. As a governing body, the board of directors consists of colony members, and so also includes members of the Pueblo of Laguna.

In December of each year, all colony members, including associate members, elect the board of directors for a one-year term. The colony chairperson is the principal contact between the colony and Laguna governor and the tribal council. The chairperson fulfills this duty by meeting at the pueblo with the governor and council. Also, the chairperson manages affairs for the colony from matters as small as state fair products to communications with the pueblo. The vice chairperson fulfills the duties directed by the chairman and keeps an inventory of colony equipment, such as a PA system, file cabinet, and other acquired items. The chairperson and vice chairperson arrange meeting agendas, decide who will receive and read the council and village minutes at the meetings, and deal with the projects and decisions that arise. The secretary, of course, takes the minutes of the meetings, maintains a permanent file of minutes and colony membership information, and keeps the pueblo officers informed of colony administrative changes and events. The treasurer handles money matters, such as deposits, record keeping, disbursements, and reports. The board of directors appoints two sergeants-at-arms to prepare and clean up the meeting area while maintaining peace and order at the meetings. Last, the board member-at-large serves as liaison between colony members and the board of directors.

Within the past twenty years, an important change involving the role of women in political office has taken place within the colony, one that has significantly influenced tribal politics at Laguna Pueblo. Up to the early 1990s, men held the positions of chairman and vice chairman. Then in 1992, the Albuquerque Laguna Colony elected its first woman chair. Interestingly, Ulysses Paisano held the first chairmanship, and his daughter, Cheryl Paisano, became the first woman chairperson. Lagunas still regard this recognition of women leadership as a major feat. Traditionally, the responsibility of Laguna leadership falls on the men. Reflecting on the significance of election to that office, Cheryl commented:

> Daddy and I were just talking, saying how he was the first chairman and years later I was the first woman chairman. Because up until then the colony didn't have [a woman chair]. We had women officers, but we didn't have a woman chairman, and I've been secretary and I've been vice chairman for several years. And so I was selected, and it was really interesting because back then when the news got out at the pueblo that the colony had a woman chairman they said, "How come we don't have women officers?" And so a lot of things have evolved since then. And so eventually they did allow women to run for a secretary and the other officers, but not governor or anything like that.

Laguna voters eventually approved women's eligibility to run for tribal secretary, treasurer, interpreter, and tribal council representatives. Women within the pueblo still do not hold governing positions as they do within the Laguna Colony, but such differing standards of governance between the pueblo and colony illustrate their ongoing mutual relationship as one characterized not just by agreement but also by discussion and debate.

The structure of the Laguna Colony of Albuquerque tries to emphasize Laguna cultural and social cohesiveness within the colony and its connectedness with the pueblo. Colony committees—Sunshine, Social, Arts and Crafts, Recreation, Education, Cultural, and State Fair—provide a space where members maintain the communal custom of shared responsibilities to each other and to Laguna culture. Each committee, in its own way, plays an important role in building a cohesive community to accomplish these aims. For example, the Sunshine committee, consisting of only one person, keeps track of colony members who may be sick or in the hospital and of deaths within the colony or the pueblo. That person sends flowers to those colony members and provides a small amount of money to the family at the time of death. Because many Lagunas in Albuquerque who die are buried at the pueblo, that money is important to cover funeral costs. The Sunshine committee also provides familial support in time of economic need.

The Social committee, with help from the State Fair committee, puts together the governor's dinner and the Christmas dinner. Every year, the colony pays its respect to elected tribal officials by hosting the governor's dinner. The colony leaders invite Laguna Pueblo officials, council members, and their families. This function allows Laguna Colony members and tribal officials and relatives to meet and eat good food. At the dinner, the governor gives a brief update on tribal business and concerns and colony members can ask questions. When the governor cannot attend, he sends another official, such as the lieutenant governor or a council member on his behalf. He usually gives words of encouragement and reminders of the colony's political power. As with other social functions, the governor's dinner reinforces the bonds between the colony and pueblo leadership.

The Christmas dinner affords another opportunity for the colony members and friends to maintain relations with one another. Colony members contribute door prizes like Pauline Acoya's tasty, favorite cookies and Marie Aragon's beadwork. Dan Atsye leads Christmas carols and plays Santa for the kids. These dinners provide important opportunities for family and friends of all generations to come together, even giving young people a place to meet and fall in love. Cheryl Paisano remembers that "Roland Johnson's son and Dan Atsye's son were best friends ...; a family that lived at Isleta but were part Laguna came to the functions and stuff. So the guys met the sisters at one of the Christmas parties. And they ended up dating." Eventually, the young men married these two sisters.

The Cultural committee organizes a program to teach the Laguna language and culture. Many of the Laguna Colony members grew up in Albuquerque outside the reservation and either never learned the Keresan language or only know "bits and pieces." Even if Laguna was their first language, it is difficult to hold on to it when you do not speak it every day. Thus, the language classes provide an opportunity to use the language or a place to learn or improve their skills. Before Roland Johnson returned to Laguna to serve as the governor of Laguna, he taught the language and culture class. Recently, Dan Atsye has supplemented the language class by emphasizing Laguna origin stories, clans, and family structures. The committee, using a grant from the University of New Mexico, has created a curriculum for the language, placing fluent speakers with nonfluent speakers for weekly classes to teach the language and culture. Dan Atsye has also made audiotapes designed to teach colony members and others the basics of the Laguna language.

Another committee handles education, contributing to colony members' postsecondary education through a small scholarship fund. Committee members review scholarship applications, which require the applicant to be in attendance at six meetings and be a Laguna Colony member. The colony also helps its members with scholarships for work-related meetings and courses, especially education that encourages the use and persistence of Laguna language and culture. Student scholarships, funded through the money made at the state fair concession booth, total $550 each semester for college students.

The Arts and Crafts committee maintains a program that gives colony members an opportunity to either learn or teach crafts. In order to offer specific classes, the committee considered paying class fees for members who can then return to teach the class at the colony. The classes provide a social environment for participants to learn different types of artwork including quilting, weaving, beading, and moccasin making. Other classes teach members how to prepare different foods, such as tamales and Easter pudding. Recalling her experiences, Cheryl Paisano stated:

> I taught beadwork. And then Grace Andrews let us meet at her house and we had an embroidery class … and cross-stitch. Bruce Paisano … taught us how to do weaving, and Grace's husband made the looms for us. I think they really need to get the people more involved, like we did with the cross-stitch. Initially it was a learning experience, and after that it got to be a social thing like a quilting bee or something. People would just look forward to [meeting], the women especially, getting out at night. And, too, they would tell stories, they would tell of things that happened before. A lot of it was cultural[ly] related and those kinds of things are really neat. We grew a lot. I miss some of those ladies; they aren't with us anymore.

The colony provides an atmosphere, events, and programs that enable family and friends to come together in an urban setting. These gatherings also helped its membership to maintain gender boundaries. While the Laguna Colony committees and groups contribute to social and cultural camaraderie, no other project unites or embodies the Laguna Colony of Albuquerque as much as the state fair Laguna Colony concession stand. At the beginning of its history, the colony had little money to manage its affairs. In the colony's first mass mailing, leadership had "to ask everyone to chip in for postage and stationary." To raise needed funds, the

Laguna Colony leadership looked toward the New Mexico State Fair, held annually in Albuquerque, as a possible economic avenue. With Ruth Paisano's hard work, the colony set up a concession booth and sold food to fairgoers.

The New Mexico State Fair has become increasingly and legitimately multicultural. Recently, the fair's cultural umbrella has expanded to include the African-American pavilion, which displays the history and contributions of African-Americans to New Mexico history. The state fair also houses the Spanish and Indian villages, with both areas offering ethnic foods, music, and dances. Walking into the Spanish Village, fairgoers are immediately met with a large selection of New Mexican and Mexican food booths that offer enchiladas, tacos, rice, burritos and much more. Vendors also surround the square to sell items from Mexico and northern New Mexico. Throughout the day and evening, dance and music programs illustrate the colorful Hispanic culture. Similarly, the Indian Village has numerous food booths ranging from Laguna, Jemez, and Navajo foods as well as arts vendors from different Indian nations and Peru. It is also a popular attraction with its fry bread, music, and dances. Daily, different dance groups from Laguna, Mescalero Apache, Zuni, and Hopi perform, as well as various contemporary bands. During the weekend, a small powwow takes place in the recently renovated performance and audience areas.

With such a large venue, it is no wonder that the Laguna Colony saw the money-raising potential. Profits provided operating costs to send out meeting announcements and a newsletter, as well as funding educational scholarships to encourage and support colony members at postsecondary institutions. For the colony, the fair promoted community cohesion, cultural expression through food and arts, and funds for continuation. Most important, perhaps, the Laguna Colony members had to draw on one another, working together as Laguna people to run a busy seventeen-day business.

The Indian Village in the late 1950s consisted only of square footage of prime New Mexico dirt and dust. The Indian Village had few or no buildings in which to sell foods or crafts; food booths constituted whatever one constructed. The first booths in the Indian Village were run by the Council of American Indians, the Navajo Club, and the Laguna Colony. The men would go out and build ramadas from which the colony would sell food. Remembering those early days, Cheryl Paisano commented:

> The men would do a ramada-type of thing where they cut the poles and the booth was covered with branches and the side is where they fried the bread.... They had a tarp out there, and they had gas stoves.... I was in high school then, and I remember going out there to help. Sometimes it would be raining and that rain would hit the pots and hot oil would just splatter and stuff. Eventually, [it was] enclosed and then the fairgrounds helped a little more and they included electricity.

From those early days of the Laguna Colony fair booth, the group worked together with cooperation across ages and genders.

Running the concession booth took work. It meant constructing the booth, preparing the food, and vending. Talking with colony members about the booth, all comment about the amount of work, but more important, they speak of the fun and cohesion it produced within the colony. Most of the work was done by hand, men and women working together. Making the chile stew for thousands of orders meant bushels of green chile had to be prepared. The men roasted the Hatch green chile, and the women peeled and bagged them. Cheryl Paisano noted:

> There were times that's what we did [worked] all day. The men would roast all the chile, and the women would peel it, cut [it] up and bag it. People would take x amount home and put it in their freezers, and as they needed that they would bring it in. And I remember one night, I swear we did twenty bags, sacks of chile. We didn't have a whole lot of help. We started out about eight in the morning, and we were usually done by maybe four or five, and then they would have a steak fry. But that time we were there until ten o'clock at night, and there was chile everywhere. So people ended up taking sacks home to peel at home, then we had to try to round it all back up. But I remember people turned their car headlights into the booth so that we had some light so we could see what we were doing.

In this process, even children helped by placing a spoon and fork in a napkin that was passed out with purchased stews and Indian tacos.

The next largest endeavor is the fry bread. Making fry bread is a relatively simple process: just mix flour, salt, and baking powder with milk or water, flatten and fry. That is, until you need enough dough to yield three hundred or more servings. That yield takes twenty-five pounds of flour, handfuls of baking powder and salt, and lots of water. The ingredients must be mixed thoroughly, rolled out, then placed in the hot oil. Grace Andrews remembers:

> We used to have these big tubs where people would mix this big dough for the fry bread. There would be ten to twelve people all lined [up] rolling out the dough because sometimes people would order five or six fry bread at one time. That's our biggest seller actually, is the fry bread. And of course now Laguna tacos is another big one.

Rolling the dough is hard work, and everyone must work together. Even with such a large volume of dough to work, colony members and friends maintained support and camaraderie. Cheryl Paisano remembers:

> We would have to roll those things out by hand, and they would mix by hand. It was a lot of work. I mean, everybody pulled together and we would be laughing. In fact, I had a friend of mine volunteer, and she came and helped. She was rolling her bread, and you know you have to flip it and do all these other things to roll it. And her [dough] kept shrinking, and so she worked on hers for about five minutes, so finally one of the ladies said, "Wouldn't you rather serve the drinks?"

Eventually, the colony invested in an industrial-sized mixer and two rollers. The mixer took the place of the big tubs and a few people struggling to combine the ingredients. People still need to roll out and flap the dough, but the rollers took out an initial step, making it easier for the rolling people.

Two shifts work the state fair. The day shift works from eight to four and the night shift works four to nine on weekdays, four to ten on weekends. In the past, workers were colony members volunteering their time to the concession stand. Many took their vacations during the state fair time so they could work at the colony booth. It is mostly retired people who work, but scholarship recipients and the executive board would also come in and volunteer. However, in recent years, volunteerism has given way to paid participation. Many work or go to school and cannot take time off to work the concession stand.

While the colony constantly adjusts to the many forces that bring change, they have remained cohesive and ardent in maintaining their ties to Laguna Pueblo and in flourishing as a community. The Laguna railroad colonies were created as a way for off-reservation community members to maintain cultural and political connections while away from the pueblo. These Lagunas remained bound to the pueblo, thereby perpetuating Laguna culture, history, and language. The Laguna Colony of Albuquerque likewise has kept its cultural and political connections to the Laguna Pueblo. These ties can especially be seen at the meetings, at which a range of generations participates, from elders to grandchildren. You see relatives sitting together, sisters, mothers, daughters, sons, cousins, husbands, and wives. The colony leadership makes a serious attempt to keep the group together and to hear all different voices. In lively discussions, respect is always given to those who speak up.

The colony encourages ties to the pueblo through communication, activities, or participation in feast day dances. It seeks to "make a good showing for the Colony to demonstrate the importance of the Pueblo world in our daily lives." Tribal village meeting minutes inform Albuquerque Lagunas of the events at the pueblo. Furthermore, chairman David Melton has pushed for a two-way communication between the Pueblo and the colony, in addition to the usual one-way communication in which minutes are read at the Laguna Colony meeting. The Albuquerque Laguna Colony is now trying to send its minutes to village leaders in order to express their opinions on pueblo business. "Let them know we still exist" is the idea behind creating such two-way communication.

The relationship between Laguna Colony and the pueblo has demonstrated a strikingly different use of the colony as a means of cultural preservation. Imperial colonies facilitated political and economic expansion as a "new political organization created by invasion," exploiting and subjugating indigenous peoples. Colonies, as hegemonic structures, "became imperialism's outpost, the fort and the port of imperial outreach." In America, European powers used settlement colonies toward the economic exploitation of indigenous resources and the utilization of cheap land and labor. Spanish, Mexican, and American colonization arrived through European colony structures invading indigenous lands. In the Southwest, the numerous indigenous nations understood the destructive capacity of colonial settlement. The Pueblo of Laguna utilized this concept not for hegemonic expansion, but rather to counter white America's continuing colonial pressures on their land and culture.

The history and lived experiences of the members of Laguna Colony of Albuquerque illustrate the dynamic intersections of reservation and urban life. Within these intersections colony members maintain and nurture cultural connections from Albuquerque and oppose destructive dichotomous identities that divide and isolate many indigenous peoples. Many still return home to Laguna to participate in the ceremonies, remaining connected to the pueblo along with the colony. The Laguna Colony of Albuquerque has experienced many changes in its brief history but has creatively adapted to those changes with the ongoing support of the pueblo.

◈ FURTHER READING

Arnold, Laurie. *Bartering with the Bones of Their Dead: The Colville Confederated Tribes and Termination* (2012).

Beck, David. *Seeking Recognition: The Termination and Restoration of the Coos, Lower Umpqua, and Siuslaw Indians, 1855–1984* (2009).

Bernstein, Alison R. *American Indians and World War II: Toward a New Era in Indian Affairs* (1991).

Blackman, Margaret B. *Sadie Brower Neakok: An Inupiaq Woman* (1989).

Blu, Karen. *The Lumbee Problem: The Making of an American Indian People* (1980).

Brophy, William, and Sophie Aberle, eds. *The Indian: America's Unfinished Business* (1966).

Burnham, Philip. *Indian Country, God's Country: Native Americans and the National Parks* (2000).

Cowger, Thomas W. *The National Congress of American Indians: The Founding Years* (1999).

Deloria, Ella. *Speaking of Indians* (1944).

Fixico, Donald L. *Termination and Relocation: Federal Indian Policy, 1945–1960* (1986).

———. *The Urban Indian Experience in America* (2000).

Hauptman, Laurence M. *The Iroquois Struggle for Survival: World War II to Red Power* (1986).

Knack, Martha. *Boundaries Between: The Southern Paiutes, 1775–1995* (2001).

Kohlhoff, Dean. *When the Wind Was a River: Aleut Evacuation in World War II* (1995).

LaGrand, James. *Indian Metropolis: Native Americans in Chicago, 1945–75* (2005).

Lawson, Michael L. *Dammed Indians: The Pick-Sloan and the Missouri River Sioux, 1944–1980* (1982).

McMillen, Christian. *Making Indian Law: The Hualapai Land Case and the Birth of Ethnohistory* (2007).

Meeks, Eric. *Border Citizens: The Making of Indians, Mexicans, and Anglos in Arizona* (2007).

Metcalf, R. Warren. *Termination's Legacy: The Discarded Indians of Utah* (2002).

Mitchell, Donald Craig. *Sold American: The Story of Alaska's Natives and Their Land 1867–1959: The Army to Statehood* (1997).

Oakley, Christopher Arris. *Keeping the Circle: American Indian Identity in Eastern North Carolina, 1885–2004* (2005).

Peroff, Nicholas C. *Menominee Drums: Tribal Termination and Restoration, 1954–1974* (1982).

Philp, Kenneth R. *Termination Revisited: American Indians on the Trail to Self-Determination, 1933–1953* (1999).

Rosenthal, Nicolas. *Reimagining Indian Country: Native American Migration and Identity in Twentieth Century Los Angeles* (2012).

Shepherd, Jeffrey. *We Are an Indian Nation: A History of the Hualapai People* (2010).

St. Pierre, Mark. *Madonna Swan: A Lakota Woman's Story* (1991).

Thursh, Coll. *Native Seattle: Histories from the Crossing-Over Place* (2008).

Trennert, Robert A. *White Men's Medicine: Government Doctors and the Navajo, 1863–1955* (1998).

Ulrich, Roberta. *American Indian Nations from Termination to Restoration, 1952–2006* (2010).

Valandra, Edward. *Not Without Our Consent: Lakota Resistance to Termination, 1950–59* (2006).

Vicenti Carpio, Myla. *Indigenous Albuquerque* (2011).

Wilkinson, Charles. *Blood Struggle: The Rise of Modern Indian Nations* (2005).

———. *The People Are Dancing Again: The History of the Siltez Tribe of Western Oregon* (2010).

CHAPTER 14

Taking Control of Education, Land, and Lives, 1960–1981

During the 1960s and the 1970s, American Indians became more visible to the larger American society. Protest movements, including the occupation of Alcatraz Island in 1969 and of the village of Wounded Knee in 1973, gave prominence to younger Native activists. At the same time, reservation communities sought new ways to revitalize their economies and safeguard their rights. The growing awareness of Native people during this period occurred on a national scale, and it affected not only large federally recognized entities but also smaller communities through-out the United States, many of them in the East and the South, who sought full recognition from the federal government. Indian groups attempted to regain control over sacred sites, such as Blue Lake for Taos Pueblo, and they pushed for the realization of traditional hunting and fishing rights, especially in the Pacific Northwest and the Upper Midwest. Why did Indian individuals and communities feel so strongly about these matters?

The prominence of television and the creation of Indian newspapers, which quickly gained national readerships, facilitated a new degree of publicity for what had once been local-ized struggles for change. Indians adeptly fostered and utilized media attention. At the same time, tribal newspapers offered a forum for the discussion of vital issues. Indian writers, artists, and musicians gained unprecedented audiences for their work. As more and more Indian students attended colleges and universities, they gained new training that better equipped them, and often their home communities, to face the future. Beginning with the establishment of Navajo Community College (now Diné College) in 1968, tribal colleges emerged on many reservations. New legal service programs, Head Start, and other initiatives yielded other possibilities for meaningful, lasting change. Why were these new programs important?

◈ DOCUMENTS

Clyde Warrior (Ponca) was a fiery young Indian leader of the 1960s who had little patience with those who equivocated in the face of the challenges facing Native peoples. In Document 1, Warrior, the president of the National Indian

Youth Council, presents a critique and a call to arms. By the decade's end, Indian activism had entered a new phase. The "Proclamation of All Tribes" on Alcatraz Island in 1969, presented in Document 2, underscored Native dissatisfaction with federal trusteeship. Occupation of the famous island brought international attention to the Indians' grievances, even if Native people could not hold the island in the long run. Alaska constituted another contested area. Oil discoveries and a rapidly increasing non–Native presence put unprecedented demands and pressures upon traditional Native subsistence economies. In Document 3, Emil Notti (Athabaskan), future president of the Alaska Federation of Natives, describes how non–Natives hindered Alaska Natives' subsistence economies. He concludes with a demand for Alaska Native self-determination. Ultimately, Native activism, as evidenced by Warrior, Alcatraz, and Notti, initiated a shift in federal policy. Document 4, President Richard Nixon's statement in support of self-determination without termination, has been the executive branch's stance on Indian policy since the 1970s. In 1961, the Menominees of Wisconsin launched a drive to restore their lands to reservation status. After a 12-year battle, their success in 1973 in overturning the termination of their reservation marked an important victory for American Indians everywhere. Ada Deer, who later headed the Bureau of Indian Affairs, led the fight for restoration. In Document 5 she explains how the Menominees achieved this triumph. In Phoenix, Arizona, meanwhile, Native students and their parents attempted to gain control over their education. In Document 6, Michael Hughes (O'odham and Hopi) remembers his experiences in the off-reservation and urban schools in Phoenix. How do his experiences compare with those of students in the early twentieth century? How did the urban environment alter the education of Native students?

1. Clyde Warrior (Ponca) Delineates Five Types of Indians, 1965

Among American Indian youth today there exists a rather pathetic scene, in fact, a very sick, sad, sorry scene. This scene consists of the various types of Indian students found in various institutions of learning throughout American society. It is vary sad that these institutions, and whatever conditioning takes place, creates these types. For these types are just what they are, types, and not full, real human beings, or people.

Many of you probably already know these types. Many of you probably know the reasons why these types exist. This writer does not pretend to know why. This writer can only offer an opinion as to names and types, define their characteristics, and offer a possible alternative; notice alternative—not a definite solution. All this writer is merely saying is he does not like Indian youth being turned into something that is not real, and that somebody needs to offer a better alternative:

Type A—SLOB or HOOD. This is the individual who receives his definition of self from the dominant society, and unfortunately, sees this kind in his daily

From "Which One Are You? Five Types of Young Indians," by Clyde Warrior, from *ABC: Americans Before Columbus*, II, No. 4, December, 1964. Reprinted with permission.

relationships and associations with his own kind. Thus, he becomes this type by dropping out of school, becomes a wino, steals, eventually becomes a court case, and is usually sent off. If lucky, he marries, mistreats his family, and becomes a real pain to his tribal community as he attempts to cram that definition [of himself] down the society's throat. In doing this, he becomes a Super-Slob. Another Indian hits the dust through no fault of his own.

Type B—JOKER. This type has defined himself that to be an Indian is a joke. An Indian does stupid, funny things. After defining himself, from cues society gave him, he proceeds to act as such. Sometimes he accidentally goofs-up, sometimes unconsciously on purpose, after which he laughs, and usually says, "Well, that's Indian." And he goes through life a bungling clown.

Type C—REDSKIN "WHITE-NOSER" or THE SELL-OUT. This type has accepted and sold out to the dominant society. He has accepted that definition that anything Indian is dumb, usually filthy, and immoral, and to avoid this is to become a "LITTLE BROWN AMERICAN" by associating with everything that is white. He may mingle with Indians, but only when it is to his advantage, and not a second longer than is necessary. Thus, society has created the fink of finks.

Type D—ULTRA-PSEUDO-INDIAN. This type is proud that he is Indian, but for some reason does not know how one acts. Therefore he takes his cues from non-Indian sources, books, shows, etc., and proceeds to act "Indian." With each action, which is phony, we have a person becoming unconsciously phonier and phonier. Hence, we have a proud, phony Indian.

Type E—ANGRY NATIONALIST. Although abstract and ideological, this type is generally closer to true Indianness than the other types, and he resents the others for being ashamed of their own kind. Also, this type tends to dislike the older generation for being "Uncle Tomahawks" and "yes men" to the Bureau of Indian Affairs and whites in general. The "Angry Nationalist" wants to stop the current trend toward personality disappearance, and institute changes that will bring Indians into contemporary society as real human beings; but he views this, and other problems, with bitter abstract and ideological thinking. For thinking this [he] is termed radical, and [he] tends to alienate himself from the general masses of Indians, for speaking what appears, to him, to be truths.

None of these types is the ideal Indian....

It appears that what is needed is genuine contemporary creative thinking, democratic leadership to set guidelines, cues and goals for the average Indian. The guidelines and cues have to be *based on true Indian philosophy geared to modern times*. This will not come about without nationalistic pride in one's self and one's own kind.

This group can evolve only from today's college youth. Not from those who are ashamed, or those who have sold out, or those who do not understand true Indianism. Only from those with pride and love and understanding of the People and the People's ways from which they come can this evolve. And this appears to be the major task of the National Indian Youth Council—for without a people, how can one have a cause?

This writer says this because he is fed up with religious workers and educationalists incapable of understanding, and pseudo-social scientists who are consciously creating social and cultural genocide among American Indian youth.

I am fed up with bureaucrats who try to pass off "rules and regulations" for organizational programs that will bring progress.

I am sick and tired of seeing my elders stripped of dignity and low-rated in the eyes of their young.

I am disturbed to the point of screaming when I see American Indian youth accepting the horror of "American conformity," as being the only way for Indian progress. While those who do not join the great American mainstream of personalityless neurotics are regarded as "incompetents and problems."

The National Indian Youth Council must introduce to this sick room of stench and anonymity some fresh air of new Indianness. A fresh air of new honesty, and integrity, a fresh air of new Indian idealism, a fresh air of a new Greater Indian America.

How about it? Let's raise some hell!

2. A Proclamation from the Indians of All Tribes, Alcatraz Island, 1969

To the Great White Father and All His People—

We, the native Americans, re-claim the land known as Alcatraz Island in the name of all American Indians by right of discovery.

We wish to be fair and honorable in our dealings with the Caucasian inhabitants of this land, and hereby offer the following treaty:

We will purchase said Alcatraz Island for twenty-four dollars (24) in glass beads and red cloth, a precedent set by the white man's purchase of a similar island about 300 years ago. We know that $24 in trade goods for these 16 acres is more than was paid when Manhattan Island was sold, but we know that land values have risen over the years. Our offer of $1.24 per acre is greater than the 47 cents per acre the white men are now paying the California Indians for their land.

We will give to the inhabitants of this island a portion of the land for their own to be held in trust by the American Indian Affairs and by the bureau of Caucasian Affairs to hold in perpetuity—for as long as the sun shall rise and the rivers go down to the sea. We will further guide the inhabitants in the proper way of living. We will offer them our religion, our education, our life-ways, in order to help them achieve our level of civilization and thus raise them and all their white brothers up from their savage and unhappy state. We offer this treaty in good faith and wish to be fair and honorable in our dealings with all white men.

We feel that this so-called Alcatraz Island is more than suitable for an Indian reservation, as determined by the white man's own standards. By this we mean that this place resembles most Indian reservations in that:

1. It is isolated from modern facilities, and without adequate means of transportation.

This document can be found in Peter Blue Cloud, ed., *Alcatraz is Not an Island*, (Berkeley, CA: Wingbow Press, 1972).

2. It has no fresh running water.

3. It has inadequate sanitation facilities.

4. There are no oil or mineral rights.

5. There is no industry and so unemployment is very great.

6. There are no health care facilities.

7. The soil is rocky and non-productive, and the land does not support game.

8. There are no educational facilities.

9. The population has always exceeded the land base.

10. The population has always been held as prisoners and kept dependent upon others.

Further, it would be fitting and symbolic that ships from all over the world, entering the Golden Gate, would first see Indian land, and thus be reminded of the true history of this nation. This tiny island would be a symbol of the great lands once ruled by free and noble Indians.

What use will we make of this land?

Since the San Francisco Indian Center burned down, there is no place for Indians to assemble and carry on tribal life here in the white man's city. Therefore, we plan to develop on this island several Indian institutions:

1. A Center for Native American Studies which will educate them to the skills and knowledge relevant to improve the lives and spirits of all Indian peoples.

2. An American Indian Spiritual Center which will practice our ancient tribal religious and sacred healing ceremonies....

3. An Indian Center of Ecology which will train and support our young people in scientific research and practice to restore our lands and waters to their pure and natural state....

4. A Great Indian Training School will be developed to teach our people how to make a living in the world, improve our standard of living, and to end hunger and unemployment among all our people....

Some of the present buildings will be taken over to develop an American Indian Museum which will depict our native food & other cultural contributions we have given to the world. Another part of the museum will present some of the things the white man has given to the Indians in return for the land and life he took: disease, alcohol, poverty and cultural decimation (As symbolized by old tin cans, barbed wire, rubber tires, plastic containers, etc.)....

In the name of all Indians, therefore, we re-claim this island for our Indian nations....

Signed,
Indians of All Tribes
November 1969
San Francisco, California

3. Emil Notti (Athabaskan) Describes Economic Changes in Alaska and Calls for Self Determination, 1968

The native people [of Alaska] who for centuries have made their living off the land can no longer do so. The decline of game animals due to increased pressures of hunting from the urban areas and by trophy hunters has made it difficult for natives to make a living by subsistence hunting. The native people who for 10,000 years made a living off of the land by subsistence hunting are now prevented from doing so because of artificial game regulations that are foreign to the native people and the penalties for breaking these regulations are severe in terms of money fines.

The native people along the Yukon who hunt moose by boat and outboard motors find that the game is being hunted out and being driven into remote and inaccessible areas by the press of hunters equipped with float planes and tracked vehicles. When a family does not get a moose in the fall it is like the city supermarket without meat on the shelves for a period of 6 months because the moose is a main staple for many months of the year. This is only one example of the encroachment of modern civilization on the old way of life. And just as the territory needed land to make the transition from the statehood, the natives need land to make the transition from a subsistence economy to a wage economy.

The decline of hunting and the encroaching civilization would not be so bad if it brought with it a means to offset the loss of the subsistence way of life, but unfortunately this is not the case. The Federal Field Committee for Development Planning in Alaska found in a study published in 1967 that there was 60 percent unemployment among the native people in Alaska. This unemployment is a crisis of major proportions to us and should prompt immediate action to correct the situation.

But, unfortunately, it has not. Another facet of the native method for subsistence living has hit an alltime low. That is the salmon fishing industry. The responsibility for the ruin of the fishing industry lies with the Federal Government. It took place under the control of the Bureau of Commercial Fisheries. Furthermore, the ruin of the industry was done against the will of the people of Alaska. Who by referendum, voted to abolish the cause of the ruin, the fishtrap. The Alaska salmon industry was the world's greatest salmon industry, but it was ruined under Federal control and the industry that was a major employer of the Alaska native has been ruined to the point that the State is seriously considering closing the salmon season to commercial fishing. Salmon industries and fishing boats employed many hundreds of native Alaskans. Canneries that ran to capacities are now running with skeleton crews and many have closed their doors. Fishtraps were allowed to operate 24 hours a day, 7 days a week. The ruining of the industry has put many natives out of work and has not been replaced by other means of making a living.

The decline in a subsistence way of life for the native people and the ruining of a basic industry that supported the natives leaves many people without means of making a living. In many areas of Alaska it costs $1 a gallon for fuel. It also costs $15 a case for milk. Without a means for making money and without a way of making a subsistence living. The native people are facing a daily crisis just to

"Alaska Native Land Claims," Senate Hearing, February 8–10, 1968, 90th Congress, 2nd Session.

survive and the situation is getting worse as Alaska develops and grows in population. Unless relief is forthcoming it is not inconceivable that we may have starvation in the most affluent country in the history of the world....

Settlement of the land problem is the remedy for solving the problems. I visualize sawmills coming into being to start a housing program. I visualize native businesses beginning to alleviate unemployment. There is a whole economy to be developed in rural Alaska and outside capital is reluctant to take the risk.

It is going to take the capital of the people who live in those areas to develop the economy. I can think of no better way to put revenues from the Continental Shelf to work than to bring relief to those areas that need it so desperately.

Controls by Federal agencies over the resources and lives of native people in Alaska has not met with any success though the reasons can always be rationalized away by those responsible for the failures. But the fact remains that they have failed in every instance. Two notable specifics are the canneries in southeastern Alaska where all canneries under BIA guidance have not made any money and do not hope to make any money. The BIA insisted on selecting the managers for these canneries. They do the buying and marketing and they do these in a manner different than private industry does and they never have made any money.

The BIA also is reluctant to approve attorney contracts for those places that have tried to hire attorneys.

Another example of a Government run program is ANICA, Alaska Native Industries Cooperative Association. After 20 years of existence it still can barely show a profit and those businessmen who have looked at the operation believe that it is hampered by administrative rules and regulations of questionable value.

I point these things out because there is a strong feeling among the native people in Alaska, that they want to have control of their own destiny. And if there are going to be mistakes made, we want to make them, not let the bad decisions be made in Juneau, or even farther away, in Washington. D.C. I stand here before you to state in the strongest terms possible that the representatives here today, of 50,000 native people in Alaska do not want paternal guidance from Washington, D.C. We feel we have the ability to make our own way and once we get a fair settlement for our lands, it will enable us to operate our businesses. At first, no doubt, with the aid of competent advice, until our own men learn business management....

There is no question in my mind that we need the Bureau of Indian Affairs in many instances in Alaska and at this point we cannot get along without them. But I feel if a settlement comes that we do not need a veto by them on business decisions.

4. President Richard Nixon Advocates Self-Determination for Native Nations, 1970

To the Congress of the United States:

The first Americans—the Indians—are the most deprived and most isolated minority group in our nation. On virtually every scale of measurement—

http://www.presidency.ucsb.edu/ws/print.php?pid=2573. Accessed April 24, 2012.

employment, income, education, health—the condition of the Indian people ranks at the bottom.

This condition is the heritage of centuries of injustice. From the time of their first contact with European settlers, the American Indians have been oppressed and brutalized, deprived of their ancestral lands and denied the opportunity to control their own destiny. Even the Federal programs which are intended to meet their needs have frequently proven to be ineffective and demeaning.

But the story of the Indian in America is something more than the record of the white man's frequent aggression, broken agreements, intermittent remorse and prolonged failure. It is a record also of endurance, of survival, of adaptation and creativity in the face of overwhelming obstacles. It is a record of enormous contributions to this country—to its art and culture, to its strength and spirit, to its sense of history and its sense of purpose.

It is long past time that the Indian policies of the Federal government began to recognize and build upon the capacities and insights of the Indian people. Both as a matter of justice and as a matter of enlightened social policy, we must begin to act on the basis of what the Indians themselves have long been telling us. The time has come to break decisively with the past and to create the conditions for a new era in which the Indian future is determined by Indian acts and Indian decisions.

Self-Determination without Termination

The first and most basic question that must be answered with respect to Indian policy concerns the historic and legal relationship between the Federal government and Indian communities. In the past, this relationship has oscillated between two equally harsh and unacceptable extremes.

On the one hand, it has—at various times during previous Administrations-been the stated policy objective of both the Executive and Legislative branches of the Federal government eventually to terminate the trusteeship relationship between the Federal government and the Indian people. As recently as August of 1953, in House Concurrent Resolution 108, the Congress declared that termination was the long-range goal of its Indian policies. This would mean that Indian tribes would eventually lose any special standing they had under Federal law: the tax exempt status of their lands would be discontinued; Federal responsibility for their economic and social well-being would be repudiated; and the tribes themselves would be effectively dismantled. Tribal property would be divided among individual members who would then be assimilated into the society at large.

This policy of forced termination is wrong, in my judgment, for a number of reasons. First, the premises on which it rests are wrong. Termination implies that the Federal government has taken on a trusteeship responsibility for Indian communities as an act of generosity toward a disadvantaged people and that it can therefore discontinue this responsibility on a unilateral basis whenever it sees fit. But the unique status of Indian tribes does not rest on any premise such as this. The special relationship between Indians and the Federal government is the result instead of solemn obligations which have been entered into by the United States Government. Down through the years, through written treaties and through formal and informal agreements, our government has made specific commitments to the Indian people. For their part, the Indians have often surrendered claims to vast tracts of land and have accepted life on government reservations. In exchange, the government has agreed to provide community services such as health, education and public safety, services which would presumably allow Indian communities to enjoy a standard of living comparable to that of other Americans.

This goal, of course, has never been achieved. But the special relationship between the Indian tribes and the Federal government which arises from these agreements continues to carry immense moral and legal force. To terminate this relationship would be no more appropriate than to terminate the citizenship rights of any other American.

The second reason for rejecting forced termination is that the practical results have been clearly harmful in the few instances in which termination actually has been tried. The removal of Federal trusteeship responsibility has produced considerable disorientation among the affected Indians and has left them unable to relate to a myriad of Federal, State and local assistance efforts. Their economic and social condition has often been worse after termination than it was before.

The third argument I would make against forced termination concerns the effect it has had upon the overwhelming majority of tribes which still enjoy a special relationship with the Federal government. The very threat that this relationship may someday be ended has created a great deal of apprehension among Indian groups and this apprehension, in turn, has had a blighting effect on tribal progress. Any step that might result in greater social, economic or political autonomy is regarded with suspicion by many Indians who fear that it will only bring them closer to the day when the Federal government will disavow its responsibility and cut them adrift.

In short, the fear of one extreme policy, forced termination, has often worked to produce the opposite extreme: excessive dependence on the Federal government. In many cases this dependence is so great that the Indian community is almost entirely run by outsiders who are responsible and responsive to Federal officials in Washington, D.C., rather than to the communities they are supposed to be serving. This is the second of the two harsh approaches which have long plagued our Indian policies. Of the Department of the Interior's programs directly serving Indians, for example, only 1.5 percent are presently under Indian control.... The result is a burgeoning Federal bureaucracy, programs which are far less effective than they ought to be, and an erosion of Indian initiative and morale.

I believe that both of these policy extremes are wrong. Federal termination errs in one direction, Federal paternalism errs in the other. Only by clearly rejecting both of these extremes can we achieve a policy which truly serves the best interests of the Indian people. Self-determination among the Indian people can and must be encouraged without the threat of eventual termination. In my view, in fact, that is the only way that self-determination can effectively be fostered.

This, then, must be the goal of any new national policy toward the Indian people: to strengthen the Indian's sense of autonomy without threatening his sense of community. We must assure the Indian that he can assume control of his own life without being separated involuntarily from the tribal group. And we must make it clear that Indians can become independent of Federal control without being cut off from Federal concern and Federal support. My specific recommendations to the Congress are designed to carry out this policy.

5. Ada Deer (Menominee) Explains How Her People Overturned Termination, 1974

... Termination occurred in 1954, it became finalized in 1961. Our people have had a strong sense of identity as a group, also a strong adherence to the land. We live in one of the most beautiful areas in this entire country, even if I have to admit it myself. But, we have beautiful lakes, streams and forests. Senator Nelson, who is a great environmentalist, became so concerned about the development [building and selling cabins and land to outsiders] that was starting to take place that he introduced and pushed through Congress the Wild Rivers Act, and made the Wolfe River which runs through our area part of this, so the development would stop. In 1961, our tribe, which at that time was composed of 3,270 members, had 10 million dollars in the treasury. We were one of the wealthiest tribes in the country and paid for almost all of our services that were provided by the Bureau of Indian Affairs. We had a lumber mill and our land was intact. This changed. First of all, our land and assets were taken out of trust. Our areas are approximately 234,000 acres. This became a separate county in the state of Wisconsin. We are now the poorest county in the state and the poorest in the nation. Again, to make the story short, it's been an economic, political, a cultural disaster, and instead of taking away federal supervision and giving tribal supervision, as you would think by looking at the resolution, and at the termination law, this did not occur. The trust was taken away; all the protection and services of the Bureau of Indian Affairs were taken away, and a very oppressive and private trust was thrust upon us. First of all, we became a county. Our people had no experience in county government, did not understand how a county functioned, what the responsibilities, the obligations of county government were. Many people had no experience in business enterprise. A separate tribal corporation called MEI, Menominee Enterprises Incorporated, was established. However, this was not controlled by the Menominees because we had another group called the Menominee Common Stock and Voting Trust which was established. This consisted of seven members, four white and three Indians. Now, in most corporations, the individual owners elect the board of directors but this did not occur here. The board of directors was elected by the Menominee Common Stock and Voting Trust. Now, to add insult to injury, there were many people declared incompetent. For example, we had a man who was blind who was declared incompetent without due process of law. Some people ran around and made a big list, shipped it to the Bureau of Indian Affairs and it was authorized, so we have many people who are incompetent, we also have the minors, the children under 18. These votes were controlled by the First Wisconsin Trust Company of

This document can be found in Ada Deer (Menominee), "How the Good Guys Won," *Journal of Intergroup Relations* 3 (1974), pp. 41–50.

Milwaukee. So from 1961 to 1970, we were controlled by white banking and financial institutions. The only participation that the Menominees were able to have in the tribal affairs was to elect one trustee per year at the annual meeting. It was very frustrating. The hospital was closed, many of the youngsters were consolidated into attending one school, the dropout rate has been phenomenal, we've had many serious problems as a result of termination. It has accentuated the values of competitiveness, selfishness, greed, and it's had a disastrous effect not only on our people as a group, but on many individuals. Many people have gone off to Milwaukee, Chicago and other areas across the country.

However, that thing that galvanized us into action was the fact that our board of directors got into a partnership with land developers. Land developers are not only a problem to the Indians but to every single person in this country, because we don't have enough land that's beautiful that we can preserve for everyone. I think that every one of us ought to be concerned about this…. To increase the tax base, we had some fast-talking developers coming up there. We have an area of over 80 natural lakes; they created an artificial lake. They channeled some of these; it's an ecological disaster. The lakes are continually changing. They're pumping water from one to another. The shoreline trees have been destroyed in many areas. We've got motor boats, snowmobiles, pollution, terrible situations. Two thousand lots were slotted for sale and we started demonstrating. We demonstrated, we marched, we started to use the press, we formed a grass roots group called DRUMS, "Determination of Rights and Unity for Menominee Shareholders." This is a real grass roots group, because there were several of us that got together in 1970 and decided that no matter what we felt, it was important to fight for our land and people….

Restoration has three points: (1) putting our land assets into trust, (2) making us eligible for federal services, such as education and health services, and (3) giving us federal recognition as a tribe. Our bill was introduced last year, but we didn't get through the entire legislative process because of the presidential campaign. It was re-introduced again this year in May….

I especially tell this to Indian people because it's a typical response of bureaucrats and other people that work with you. They say, "You can't do it, it's going to take a lot of work and there's no way you can change the system." This is not really true. We have chosen another path and this is to beat the system. Now it's taken four years, and in a way, I feel like I've been preparing for this all my life, because my background is a social worker, community action person, and in social action every now and then you have to put your money where your mouth is, and I feel that we as Indians have to practice our Indian values, which is concern for your tribe, and be involved when it's of vital importance. Now, this has meant that several of us have had to change our lives around. I was in law school; the people that I was starting with are going to be graduating this year and will be joining the legal profession. My car is falling apart, some of the others' cars are falling apart, but along with this we are about to achieve the most significant victory in all of American Indian history. On Tuesday of this week, the House passed our act, the Menominee Restoration Act, with a vote of 404 to 3; everybody wants to know who the three that voted against it and how did I let them get away….

We started, first of all, tracking every single Menominee that we could. We called people, we made home visits. First we got two people elected into the Voting Trust. The second year we got four people. Even with four of eleven, they elected me the chairperson of the group. They decided then to proceed with this lobbying effort. Now, the platform we ran on was the stopping of land sales, restoration and Menominee Restoration. Last year, we took over and have been working very hard since that time. We have gone around to all Indian groups, major Indian groups in the country, conducted extensive speaking campaigns—we're learning how to use the media too—and it's been very exciting to be a part of this. It's also very exhausting, but on the other hand, it's worth fighting for. It was such a great pleasure to meet and sit in the House gallery last Tuesday to see the whole United States Congress voting on something that one small Indian tribe brought to their attention. I think it's very significant not only for the Menominee tribe, for all Indian tribes, but for American people as a whole, because I was mentioning to Senator Mondale last evening, we were talking about our legislation that we were about to win, and he said, "Yes, it looks like the good guys are going to win," and we are. Now we've done this in a very interesting way and approach. We decided to approach this on a bi-partisan basis, because we feel that everyone's to blame for Indian problems. We went to the Republican Party platform hearing last year in Miami and we got a statement from the Republican platform stating their recognition of Menominee problems and promising a complete and sympathetic hearing of our plea. We received a good reception at the Democratic Party convention, and in the Democratic platform there was a statement opposing the policy of termination. Then we conducted a drive to get as many people of both parties as we could on our legislation, and it was very interesting to see. We've got about 50 people as sponsors from the House and we have everyone from Bella Abzug to Collins, from Illinois. We did the same thing in the Senate, we have people like Senator Goldwater and Senator Kennedy, and all the Republican members of the Senate Interior and Insular Affairs Committee as sponsors of our legislation. Again, this is an incredible accomplishment which can only be attributed to making the system work, I assume that people are on our side until they prove themselves. I think it's very important to understand that people will take different positions depending on the issue and then of course, you kind of blitz them and you use a little humor in your lobby. I learned a lot. I didn't start out being a lobbyist, but if you care enough—I've told everybody that I would do anything to promote the legislation. So one day it was, I decided, be-kind-to-BIA day. I went out and bought two pounds of candy and started out with the headquarters—this was before it was taken over—I said to the guard, "I'm starting out with headquarters here and I'm going to sweeten you up a little," and I gave him some candy. Of course, he'd been letting me park there in the BIA parking lot, and usually you have to get all kinds of permits and permissions, etc. I smiled at him and he smiles at me, and every now and then it does, even though we live in a chauvinist society which we're changing, every now and then it does help to use some of your feminine wiles. Anyway, he was very nice and he allowed me to park there, so then I went to see all the secretaries.

By the time I got to the top floor, I only had two or three pieces of candy left. So you have to use kind of a light touch in all of this lobbying, and we do have some bumper stickers which we have been selling and distributing around the country. We have to have visibility, and I feel that there is not enough of us Indians, so we have to make our presence count. We feel that it is important to keep our issue before the public, and I've met many interesting people on airplanes and in airports as a result of this. Now, I've given you kind of the high-lights, the problems that has engendered this, what we've done about it and in essence, I would say that any citizen in this country can take action on an issue if you're ready to get involved and ready to move on it....

6. Michael Hughes (O'odham/Hopi) Describes Schools in Phoenix, 2001

[O]ne time, when I was about 14, I think, this doctor [laughed] from the Indian Hospital who I was friends with came by my house at Christmas time and he said "I'm going to San Francisco, you want to come with me?" And I said "Yeah, okay." So I said to my mom, "I'm going to San Francisco with this doctor." She said "Well. Okay. Just be careful." ...

So we got in his jeep and drove across the desert to San Francisco and stayed with some of his friends in San Francisco—he had gone to medical school over there. And we stayed with them for, I don't know, 3 or 4 days. And during that time, that was when ... [Indians were] occupying Alcatraz. And so we went down and took the boat over there and got over there and checked it out, walked around at Alcatraz....

I specifically remember our high school textbook. I think there was—it was a pretty big textbook on American history. I think there were two sentences on Indians in the whole book. And one was at the very beginning, when the Pil-grims came over and they met the Indians, and then another one was in the 1800s when the settlers were trying to settle and the Indians were being hostile to them, always fighting with the settlers, and I remember writing in my book [Bullsh**]. [Laughed.]....

[My mother] grew up in Flagstaff [a town in northern Arizona]....

She moved with us down here to Phoenix and raised us down here....

[S]he just felt that if she stayed on the Hopi reservation with us kids that she would be on welfare. And she didn't want to do that. And my dad had run off, so, she just decided to move with us kids down to Phoenix. And so she brought us down here, and I was about 5 years old then. We slept in our car for a couple of nights and finally found a real inexpensive place to live and stayed there....

[S]he started going back to school, learning different things. First she got into medical records and so she worked in hospitals for a long time, and then she went back to school and she got a bachelor's degree in social work and

Michael Hughes (O'odham/Hopi), interview by Steve Amerman, 8 June 2001 and 26 June 2001, tapes and transcripts in Labirola National American Indian Data Center, Hayden Library, Arizona State University, Tempe, AZ. Reprinted with permission.

then she went out and got her master's degree. In fact, she got her MSW [Master's in Social Work] in '73 which is the same year that I graduated from high school. So, during that time I was going to high school, she was going to college at A.S.U. [Arizona State University] and so I would have a lot of contact with A.S.U. and her fellow students, people like that....

[My mother] didn't go to boarding schools, but my grandparents did. My grandmother left the Hopi reservation when she was 6 and didn't return at all even for visits until she was 16.....

I really liked going to school [in Phoenix] when I was a little kid. 1st, 2nd, and 3rd grades were just a lot of fun to me. And then, 4th grade, I started out in 4th grade and I'll never forget this teacher I had named [Ms. V.] She was just like this angel woman, a wonderful, nice teacher. And every year, they would have you take these tests, you know, see where you were at, what kind of work you could do. And after we took the tests in the fall, um, well, the way my mother says it, and I don't remember this part, but she thought the school thought I had cheated on my test so they made me take it again and I hadn't cheated but I scored really high, so they called in a psychologist and I remember him giving me this intelligence test, I don't know, a Stanford IQ test or something like that. So I scored really high. And so they asked me if I would be interested in just moving on to the 5th grade, in that same year, when I was 9 years old. And I said "Yeah, okay." So, I did that, and what happened was, while the other kids were going to recess I was going over to the 5th grade class and they asked me "What do you like?" and I think I said "math and science and reading" so they would have me go to those classes as sort of a transition and then, finally about halfway through the school year they said "Well, let's just put you in the 5th grade." And that was a real turning point for me because that was just a bad experience, a very bad experience. And then, what happened was, up until then, I was just sort of this happy-go-lucky, well-adjusted kid, but then I moved into this class [where] #1, I was the smallest guy in the class, because I was a year younger than everybody; #2 I didn't fit in anywhere because, you know, by that time, all your groups are settled, you know, who's into what kind of stuff; and #3 I was this egg-head, who was real different, this strange guy who's supposed to be super smart, and people didn't know how to approach me; and #4 my skin was brown, and everybody else's skin was white except for just, I remember, just maybe two other Indian kids and a couple Mexican kids, so I just didn't fit in and some of the older boys would pick on me and I started having fights with them and that went on into the 6th, 7th, and 8th grades. And what I remember about 6th, 7th, and 8th grades was a combination of enjoying science and math, and then fighting....

I don't know if there's any typical experience of going into the schools. I don't know how typical mine was. It was kind of strange in some ways. [Laughed.]

◈ ESSAYS

Throughout the twentieth century, American Indians struggled and, in many ways, successfully controlled their educational experiences. In the late-twentieth century, these conflicts moved from reservations and off-reservation boarding schools to urban schools. In the first essay, Steve Amerman, professor of history at Southern Connecticut State University, reveals the myriad and complex ways in which Native peoples carved out an Indigenous space in Phoenix, Arizona, schools. How did Indian educational experiences in the late-twentieth century differ from those earlier in the century (see Chapter 10)? If anything, the effort to control education in Phoenix was emblematic of the larger struggle for sovereignty in the United States. In the second essay, Daniel Cobb, professor of American Studies at the University of North Carolina, documents the efforts of a diverse group of Native peoples to demand sovereignty. Looking at often-ignored spaces and people, Cobb traces the discourse of sovereignty from the American Indian Chicago Conference to the politics of Standing Rock Sioux Vine Deloria, Jr. How did the Native struggle for sovereignty reflect the Cold War politics of the 1960s? How did Native peoples achieve sovereignty in the 1960s?

Making an Indian Place in Urban Schools

BY STEPHEN KENT AMERMAN

"I can still remember walking with my mom to Longview Elementary School for the first day of school," said Martha Sadongei, thinking back to her childhood in the 1960s. "I remember seeing all these kids, all these parents," she recalled. "It was crowded, and it was noisy, with the echoing little hallways—they were short hallways but there was still a lot of noise. And I remember my mom taking me to the classroom. I don't remember being scared. I just remember her taking me and finding the room, and that was it. She just said, 'This is where you're going to start school, so just listen to what they say, and I'll be back. I'm not leaving you. I'll be back, but you need to go to school.'" Reassured by her mother's words, Martha Sadongei took her seat in her new classroom and prepared to listen to what her teacher had to tell her.

In one sense, Martha Sadongei's story is like the story of almost every American child in the twentieth century. In other ways, however, it is different. Martha Sadongei is an American Indian, the child of a Kiowa father and a Tohono O'odham mother. Yet her story is not only different from that of non-Indian children but also from that of many Indian children. Instead of attending a federal boarding school or a reservation school, as did many Native youths in the twentieth century, Sadongei attended a school in the heart of a large city: Phoenix, Arizona. Even though there were tens of thousands of Native Americans like her who attended urban public schools between 1945 and 1975, historians have been rather slow to learn their stories.... This is no small oversight, for by 1970 the number of urban Indians in the United States was nearly the same as the number of reservation Indians. Phoenix, is an especially good place to start listening to urban Indian schooling stories, for it emerged in the post–World War II years as a city with one of the largest urban Indian populations in the nation....

Although Phoenix's Native American community grew steadily after World War II, rising from 808 in 1950 to nearly 8,000 in 1970, educators seem to have been generally unaware that there were significant numbers of Indian students in their schools. A survey of the minutes of the meetings of the Phoenix Union High School System (PUHSS) board of education for the years 1953 to 1973, for example, reveals only a handful of very cursory mentions of Native American students. The tendency of Indians in Phoenix schools to be "invisible" to non-Indians reflected the tendency of urban Indians to be "invisible" to Phoenicians in general. After meeting with leaders of the Native American community in 1968, for instance, the city mayor remarked that he was "surprised to learn that there [were] between 8,000 and 10,000 Indians living in the Phoenix metropolitan area."

This ignorance of urban Indians, when coupled with the American public's lack of accurate knowledge of American Indians in general in the 1950s and 1960s, sometimes manifested itself in troubling ways in Phoenix's schools. Some Indians, for instance, actually reported being commonly mistaken as Mexican American.... Lola Allison, a Blackfoot ... who attended Phoenix schools in the 1960s and early 1970s, attested to the tendency of some Anglos to confuse Indians with Mexicans. "Since I was from Montana and not from here, I didn't look like Indians here," she said. "And so people would think I was Mexican until I would tell them. We were kind of mixed in with the Mexicans. They kind of swallowed us up in those days."

Another possible consequence of urban Indian "invisibility" was that educators, perhaps because they assumed there were no Indians in their classrooms, seemed prone to engaging in insensitive portrayals of Indian history and culture. For Martha Sadongei, this happened one particular November. In a grade school ritual that is still practiced today, Sadongei's teacher had her students dress up as Pilgrims and Indians to honor the Thanksgiving holiday. She divided up the class and placed Sadongei with the Pilgrims.

Other Phoenix schools showed their insensitivity to Indian cultures in other ways. At Central High School, just a few blocks away from Longview Elementary, students engaged in a yearly celebration known as Maverick Day. Maverick Day, which existed at least into the 1970s, attempted to honor popular, and largely mythical, Anglo-American versions of the history of the "Wild West." It involved beard-growing contests for young men, a "Sagebrush Swing" dance, skits, mock gunfights, the selection of a Rodeo Queen, a pie-eating contest (the connection to the "Old West" is more difficult to see in this case), and dressing in "cowboy" garb. Indian stereotypes, and donning Indian "costumes," were also a part of the festivities. The 1961 yearbook caption reads, for example, "It's Maverick Day, and all you dudes in Eastern clothes are gonna' be thrown into the Corral," preceded by the dictum, "Go west, young man, go west, but watch out for hostile Indians!" Such attitudes were echoed in the 1970 yearbook as well, which reported that, "Sheriff Jim Christenson and his posse went after the paleface Indians that happened to be visiting our campus. And it came to pass that these officers of the law killed the Indians and placed those without proper dress in jail." One wonders how such portrayals affected the forty-five Native American students who attended Central High School that year.

We do not have to wonder how some Phoenix Indian students viewed the way in which their teachers and textbooks presented Indians.... Michael Hughes, of O'odham and Hopi ancestry, offered a particularly direct assessment. "I hated history in high school," he said, remembering his student days from the late 1960s and early 1970s. "I just considered it to be white supremacist indoctrination. I didn't consider it to be history at all." Hughes recalled one of his textbooks in particular:

> It was a pretty big textbook on American history, but I think there were only about two sentences on Indians in the whole book. And one was at the very beginning, when the Pilgrims came over and they met the Indians, and then the other one was in the 1800s when the settlers were trying to settle and the Indians were being hostile to them, always fighting with the settlers.

When one examines some of the textbooks that the Phoenix schools used, one begins to get a sense for Daychild's and Hughes's frustrations. In 1965, the PUHSS school board approved the adoption of a text entitled *The Growth of America*, a 1959 Prentice Hall publication. *The Growth of America* was one of many books that were scrutinized by Jeannette Henry in her 1970 publication, *Textbooks and the American Indian*. Henry, an Eastern Cherokee, published the book through the Indian Historian Press, a press established by her and her husband, Rupert Costo (Cahuilla) in the early 1960s.... Henry was relatively mild in her evaluation of the PUHSS's chosen text, compared to her often-scathing critiques of many other textbooks. *The Growth of America*, she wrote, did provide a "fair treatment ... concerning Tecumseh and the Indian war." Still, it fell short of her desired standards. "The approach is European. Contributions of Indians to American life and to the world [are] generally not treated, except the admission that the Iroquois contributed to the founding of the nation through the philosophy of their confederacy," her analysis reads. "No treatment of the Indian today."

Students in the PUHSS took courses in American history and Arizona history. One text that was used in these courses was *Arizona Pageant: A Short History of the 48th State*, written by Madeline Paré and Bert Fireman.... Paré and Fireman published *Arizona Pageant* in 1965, still a time when few Euro-American historians were stopping to think about how American Indians might view their histories. Their book, not surprisingly, reflects that fundamental deficiency. The authors, for example, frequently referred to southwestern Indians as violent "savages." They described Geronimo's actions as a "rampage" of "savagery," and wrote that the famous Apache leader "could be trusted no more than a fierce animal." They also adopted a long-standing Euro-American attitude toward Native cultural traditions, which held that, although Indian cultures could be intriguing, they were still inherently inferior to Euro-American cultures. They called the Hopi Snake Dance, for instance, a "weird ritual" that was "steeped in magic," and referred to Pueblo spiritual views as "superstitions." As for attention to twentieth-century Arizona Indian history, let alone the migrations of Indians to Arizona cities such as Phoenix, there was none.

When non-Indian Phoenicians did notice Indians in their classrooms, they often viewed them merely as stereotypes, a tendency that textbooks similar to the ones previously mentioned must have helped foster. Tricia Palmer ..., Omaha ..., attended Longview Elementary.... Although the marital friction and alcohol problems of her parents made Palmer's childhood household an often-unsettled place, Palmer's grandmother helped make it sufficiently stable and affirming. "I was raised in a warm home, with nice things around—not expensive things, but Indian things," she said. "Then, I'd go to school, and it was like entering a whole other world." She recalls being fascinated with the relative affluence of most of her Anglo classmates. "A lot of the people that went to Longview in those days went to the Phoenix Country Club," she noted, then added:

> I adored them. I wanted their clothes. They had matching everything. I wished my mom would come pick me up from school in tennis clothes, because that's what their mothers would do. They would come to school in their tennis clothes and take their kids to dental appointments. I never got to go to dentist appointments!

But Palmer also remembers that while the lifestyles of her classmates attracted her, she repelled the classmates. "If I sneezed accidentally on one of them," she said, "they'd go 'eww!' and they'd make a big thing about it, saying, 'You're Indian! Yuck! You're making me sick!'" She summed up her feelings on her elementary schooling experience with the following statement: "At home, Indian families treat their children very well, with a whole lot of love and warmth, and a lot of encouragement. You're always feeling reinforced and praised. So, when you walk out the door, it's like someone throwing a glass full of water at you. You hit the white world, and it's not a very nice world." For Palmer, the unpleasant memories continued to affect her into her adult life. "Even today," she said, speaking in 2000, "if I walk into a room of white people, at meetings or a conference or something, and I'm the only minority there, that insecurity that developed at Longview School starts bubbling up, like I'm still not good enough to be around white people. It bubbles up at me, and I stand at the door, and I have to work to push it back down. It's like a demon that always pops up."

Being visible to educators as an Indian also could mean being automatically labeled as academically deficient. Upon beginning first grade, for example, Martha Sadongei was immediately placed into a lower track. After one month of witnessing Sadongei easily and quickly accomplish the teacher's assignments, the school finally put her into the high-track classroom. Although this was the right move for her academically, the change made the young Sadongei somewhat apprehensive. She explained:

> It was so interesting because I do remember, in the low group, there were—there were never that many Indians at Longview when I was going through there—but at least in that low group, there were Hispanic kids, so I saw more brown kids in that low group. But then when I went to [the high-track] group, it was just almost all white in there. And that's when I kind of got nervous.... I was more nervous going into that new classroom than [I was on] the first day of school.

Other Phoenix Indians corroborated Sadongei's general experiences. Michael Hughes told of how, as a fourth grader, he sat down with his classmates at Washington Elementary with a number 2 pencil in hand and proceeded to take the required standardized test. He earned a high score, and recalled, "The way my mother says it—and I don't remember this part—she thought that the school believed I had cheated on my test." The school made Hughes re-take the exam. "So, they made me take it again…," he said. "They called in a psychologist, and I remember him giving me this intelligence test—I don't know, a Stanford IQ test or something like that." Hughes again did exceptionally well, prompting the school to ask him if he would not mind joining the fifth graders, skipping the rest of the fourth grade.…

Diane Daychild did not tell of her testing results being questioned, but she believed that she had encountered a more subtle kind of stereotyping in the Phoenix schools. Her experience is an example of how even a seemingly positive stereotype is still, nevertheless, a stereotype. In high school, she enjoyed art classes and developed a good relationship with her art instructor. The teacher even tried to assist her in gaining entrance to the prestigious Institute of American Indian Arts in Santa Fe, a school that has been associated with famous artists such as Allan Houser and Fritz Scholder. Daychild, however, was not convinced that she belonged in the company of Houser and Scholder. She felt that, although she was competent as an artist, she did not possess the talent to make a career out of it. When she acted on this assessment and decided to drop art class in order to pursue a college preparatory track, her teacher seemed to take it personally. "She really was pretty pissed off at me," Daychild said, laughing a bit. "She said, 'I suppose you want to be a nurse and change bedpans for the rest of your life.'" Daychild still enjoys art and sometimes wonders if she should have continued developing her abilities. But she also wondered if popular notions of Native Americans as people who are somehow genetically programmed to become artists might have clouded her art teacher's well-meaning goals for her. "It's just something that's sort of interesting to think back on," she said. "You know, I think that, with that field, there's sort of a stereotype that Indians are artistic, that it's just natural for them, and that's what she might have been thinking."

In addition to the challenges that the Anglo-dominated urban world posed to Native Americans, some challenges also arose from within the Native community. For many Indian children, one of the greatest struggles was to understand and learn about their distinctive ethnic identity. In several cases, there was a link between this and another aspect of the history of Indian education: the boarding schools. After all, many of the Indians who moved to Phoenix had attended federal boarding schools, and some of them carried those particular educational lessons with them. They then imparted these lessons to the children they were raising in the city.

Michael Hughes's mother, Aleene, who was raised in the city of Flagstaff before moving to Phoenix as an adult, was someone who experienced boarding school legacies through her parents. In the early decades of the twentieth century, her mother, a Hopi, attended Sherman Indian School and her father, who was Tohono O'odham, attended Carlisle Indian School. Their experiences at those schools seemed to affect their attitudes toward Aleene's education in powerful ways. They were, for instance, strict—even severe—disciplinarians. Speaking of his grandparents, Michael Hughes explained that "both of them had been raised by disciplinarians in the boarding schools, and basically, you were just punished for everything and marched around and stuff like that. And then they raised my mother the same way. You know, you hit first and ask questions later. So she was raised pretty rough." The boarding schools also made them value vocational education over a more academic one. "Most of their education was an industrial type education," Hughes said, and added:

> My grandfather was trained to be a worker in a factory, and my grandmother was trained primarily to be a domestic.... So they didn't really value higher education that much.... And I remember my mother telling me that she would try to read books at home and my grandfather would tell her it was a big waste of time. She needed to get out in the yard to pull weeds and stuff like that. When she was going to school, they had real ... ambivalent feelings about it. They never really understood what she was doing and didn't know whether to support her or not.

In addition to learning to disdain book reading and to "hit first and ask questions later," Michael Hughes's grandparents also learned to denigrate parts of their Indian identities. Michael's grandmother in particular actively tried to distance herself and her family from Native culture. "My grandmother and ... one of my aunts ... were both real fundamentalist Christians," Michael noted, "and so they really discouraged us from having a lot to do with other Hopi people, especially if they were non-Christian."

... Diane Daychild was also brought up with a boarding school influence. Her aunt and uncle, who were responsible for most of her upbringing, had attended such schools, and one of the legacies they passed on concerned language. "As far as teaching me my language," Daychild said, "their thoughts were that they both had to go through so much for speaking their language—corporal punishment and other kinds of verbal abuse from the teachers and the missionaries—that they felt that it would be better if I did not learn our language, because it would be better for my transition to the larger community. So they didn't speak it with me, or they would only speak it when they didn't want me to know what they were talking about." In terms of her O'odham culture in general, Daychild reported that her aunt and uncle did take her on monthly trips to the reservation, which helped her learn at least something about her heritage. Overall, however, she believed that her understanding of her Native identity was minimal by the time she graduated from a Phoenix high school in 1965.

As it happens with many people, it perhaps took leaving "home" for Daychild to realize just how much she did not really know about that "home" and its heritage. After graduating from high school, Daychild in 1967 accepted a position as a counselor at an upstate New York summer camp for African American children from the Bronx. "They were just regular kids," she said. "But they were special in that they had always lived in the city. Most of them—maybe they went down South to see their grandparents occasionally—but most of them had just been raised in that urban environment." In that respect, their experiences had not been too dissimilar from hers. In that extended stay away from central Arizona, Daychild not only taught the summer campers but also was taught by them. She believed, for example, that she was successfully concealing her discomfort about being so far away from the place she knew, until one day in art class a young camper told her, "I know you're homesick." Daychild was impressed. "I said, 'Really? How can you tell?' And she said, 'Because you keep drawing mountains and cactus.'" Daychild laughed at the memory. "And I said, 'Oh, yeah. I guess so!'" Similar to most children, the Bronx youths were not shy about asking questions of Daychild and her fellow Indian counselor, especially when they found out that they were both American Indians. "They were real curious. They asked about the way we lived, and why my hair didn't frizz up when I washed it, they wanted to hear us 'talk Indian,' and stuff like that. I knew a few words, but then I thought, gosh, maybe I should know more about myself." She added, "It was real interesting, because, actually, when I think about it, that's sort of when I started thinking about 'Well, who in the heck am I?'"

Delores Johnson, a Hopi, also wrestled with issues of identity, not so much for herself as for her children. Similar to Aleene Hughes, Johnson was an urban Indian who grew up in Flagstaff whose parents were products of boarding schools. As with Daychild, language issues were a notable boarding school outcome. Johnson recalled that, as a child in Flagstaff in the 1940s and 1950s, she and her siblings spoke Hopi with their grandparents, but their parents mainly used English. This partly helps explain why, when Johnson moved to Phoenix and began raising her own children in the 1960s and 1970s, she let English be the main language in her home. A second factor, though, was that she married a Maricopa man, so English was their common language.

Raising children in the city without making a concerted effort to teach them their parents' languages or cultures could have interesting and unsettling consequences. Johnson was made acutely aware of this one day when her eldest child returned from elementary school with an intriguing question. She recalled:

> He came home from school one day—I think he was in the first or
> second grade—and said, "My best friend, he's a Mexican. And this other
> guy at my school is a colored boy. And this other guy is a white boy."
> And then he said, "What am I? I'm brown, but what am I? I know I'm
> not white." And my husband and I said, "What? You're Indian. You're
> half Maricopa and half Hopi. You're American Indian." And he said,
> "Well, where are my feathers then?"

Delores Johnson and her husband were understandably taken aback. "It dawned on us that we had never talked about who we were, that we had never talked about who they were," she said....

At the opposite end of the spectrum, ... some urban Indian children had their "Indianness" challenged not by Mexican Americans or by Anglos but by other urban Indian children. Martha Sadongei was one such child. In 1972, she graduated from the Osborn Elementary District and began her high school studies at North High School. The move to North, which had rapidly changed from being a virtually all-Anglo school in the late 1960s to being a school with large non-Anglo populations by the early 1970s, was a rather "shocking experience," Sadongei said. "I had been so used to being one of few Indians, and one of few minorities even, at Longview.... And, so then I went to North High, and I had never seen so many blacks in my life, so many Mexicans, or even so many other Indians." She was also struck by what she calls the "ruggedness" of the North students. "You know, they were streetwise," she said. "And they knew about 'inner city school survival.' ... And here I was: I came from this very soft white side to get thrown in with these 'rugged' groups."

Though she had grown up around some other Indian families in her part of the city, she found it difficult at first to relate to many of the Indians at North High. Some of them, she felt, were swept up in the "militant" attitudes of 1970s Indian activism. Sadongei and her younger sister suddenly had their identities challenged in a different way than they had been at Longview Elementary. "Because, one, we didn't speak our Native language, and, two, we didn't come from a reservation, and didn't have a lot of ties to those two things, they would tell us, 'Oh, you're just a little white girl,'" she recalls. Sadongei maintains that, for the main Native group at North High in these years, being a "real Indian" also meant rejecting the teachings offered at a Euro-American educational institution such as North High. "That was really my first experience of being torn down by my own," she said, "of getting that sense that, 'Who do you think you are because you want to go to class? Don't you know that you should be cutting? Education is not worth it.'" Sadongei and her sister began to abandon the more proper clothing that they had usually worn at Longview and began dressing in the jeans and sneaker attire that most of their Native peers at North High preferred. Martha Sadongei also started skipping class on a regular basis. Though her mother had passed on to her an intense love for reading as a young child, she cut so many reading classes that she failed the course and was placed in a remedial reading program for her sophomore year.

Sadongei's pastor, however, must have believed in Sadongei even in that troubled part of her childhood. Joedd Miller, an Anglo who ministered at a Phoenix church that the Sadongei family and other Indian families attended, knew Margaret and the rest of the Sadongeis well and was convinced of their determination. The Sadongeis, he said in a 2001 interview, "would have made it in life if they had a row of tanks in front of them." Miller's words could have actually spoken for many of the Indian children in the city. They all saw their paths blocked by "tanks" of various sorts, but they found productive ways of moving past them, whether by adjusting to the reality of the city, resisting the city's pressures outright, or doing a bit of both.

One manner of adjusting to the reality of being an Indian in an urban school was to develop social networks within those schools, even if demographics dictated that those social networks might be partly or largely non-Indian. Sadongei and her sister certainly made friends with non-Indians, perhaps out of necessity as much as by design, because she believed her elementary school only had one other Native American student at the time. "We mingled with everybody," she said. Mary Astor, of Laguna and O'odham ethnicity, also made connections with her elementary school classmates in the late 1940s. Even some fifty years later, in 2001, she retained warm memories of them. Looking at an old photo of her almost entirely Anglo class, she simply said, "We all went to school together. These are all my friends." She has kept in touch with at least one of those friends throughout the years.

Michael Hughes had significant interactions with his non-Indian peers. He described the high school he attended in the early 1970s, East High School, as being similar in terms of ethnic composition and economic status to the schools that Astor and Sadongei attended. "It was mainly Anglo, and pretty solidly middle class," he said. It was also a school with the sort of cliques that one now associates with most American high schools. "The jocks were a real big group in school," he recalled, "and then there was sort of this fringe group of students who were interested in intellectual kinds of stuff, and so I hung out with some of those people." As with adolescent American peer groups throughout the twentieth century, music was a common interest for Hughes and his friends. In terms of popular music, however, Hughes's group found the early seventies to be somewhat troubling times. "I remember that, to me, that was the tail end of what I considered to be the rock [music] that I had really liked," he said. "Jimi Hendrix, Cream, Jefferson Airplane, that was sort of dying out. People were getting more into Rod Stewart, Cat Stevens, and Elton John. And I just couldn't get into those guys." He recalled a day when, out of boredom, he decided to listen to some of the records that one of his mother's boyfriends had left behind at their house. Included in the collection were jazz and blues LPs by people such as Miles Davis, John Coltrane, and Howlin' Wolf. "I said, 'Wait a minute, I remember this stuff!'" The records rekindled his appreciation for such music, an appreciation that his friends at East High shared. Some even attempted to play the tunes themselves. "One guy played sax and one guy played trombone, and so we would just hang out and listen to them and to the records," Hughes remembers.

Although Hughes and many other Indian students socialized extensively with Anglos, many also said that they felt a certain solidarity with other non-Anglo students. Lola Allison attended Emerson Elementary that counted few African Americans and Mexican Americans—and even fewer American Indians—in its enrollment. Allison made friends with one of the few African American boys among her classmates because, she felt, they could relate to each other's common experiences of prejudice. Still, she maintains that she had friends from various ethnic groups.

Other students had more interactions with other nonwhite students simply because they attended schools that were more ethnically diverse than the school that Allison, for instance, attended. In the two neighborhoods that Diane Daychild's aunt and uncle raised her in, one east of downtown and one west of it, Mexican Americans formed the majority of residents. Daychild developed social ties accordingly. "My friends were pretty much Mexican people, because that's where I lived," she noted. "I know a little more Spanish than I do Pima."

Where the ethnic composition of Lola Allison's elementary school was considerably less diverse than Diane Daychild's schools, however, the ethnic composition of Allison's high school—Phoenix Union—was actually considerably more diverse than Carl Hayden High School, Daychild's alma mater. Allison's mother had purposefully chosen her grade school *because* it tended to cater to middle-class—and even upper-middle-class—Anglos. Confronted with a choice between Emerson, a school that had been home to such prominent Arizona families as the Udalls, and a mainly "minority" public school near their neighborhood, Allison's mother selected the institution that she believed could offer her daughter a superior education. For her choice of high school, however, Lola departed from her mother's philosophy. After completing eighth grade, most of Allison's classmates from Emerson would attend North High, which in 1967 (several years before Martha Sadongei would go there) was still a mainly Anglo and middle-class school. But Allison passed on North and opted instead to attend Phoenix Union, where Anglos were a minority. "White people were the minority at Phoenix Union because nobody wanted to send their kids there," she said. "It was predominantly Mexican and black with a few Asians and a few Indians." Allison welcomed the new demographic environment. "My freshman year I was finally around brown people," she noted, "and it was so wonderful. It was totally different from my elementary school. I felt valued and I felt empowered."

Although forging friendships and associations with non-Indian students—white and nonwhite—must have helped Indian children adapt themselves to the urban school environment, it did not necessarily preclude them from acknowledging their identity as Indians. Allison, for instance, greatly appreciated the multiethnic nature of her city high school. Yet this appreciation did not come at the expense of her sense of ethnicity. Allison was disturbed when some of her Indian classmates chose to identify themselves as Mexican American rather than Indian. "It still angers me that you would want to hide something that I find to be an asset," she explained. "I like being an Indian. But a lot of people don't, I guess."

Allison's mother helped her feel better about being Indian, demonstrating that not all urban Indian parents had been swayed, or at least completely swayed, by the assimilationist boarding-school legacies. On one hand, Allison felt that her mother was able to provide her with only a limited education on Indianness. "She liked it here in Phoenix," she said. "She liked it a lot." Allison's mother embraced many of the ways of her new Euro-American urban home and evidently did not feel a great concern to teach Lola and her siblings how to make traditional Blackfeet beadwork, clothing, or food, for instance. "No, she was happy with frozen foods," Allison asserted, chuckling. On the other hand, Allison says that, although her mother may not have sat her down to listen to traditional Blackfeet stories, she did teach her about some of the recent history of the tribe: about, for example, the massacres and diseases that the Blackfeet suffered at the hands of US soldiers at the close of the nineteenth century. Allison learned enough from such stories to know that she was not getting the complete versions of Indian-Euro-American interactions in her Phoenix public-school textbooks and classrooms.

Allison's mother was certainly not alone among Phoenix Indian parents. Many others, whether they had experienced boarding schools firsthand or not, similarly tried to pass on a sense of Indian identity to their city children. Native Americans moved to Phoenix and other cities primarily for economic reasons, after all. They came for jobs because jobs were scarce on their reservations. Most did not come to lose their culture or to make their children lose their culture. Even if assimilationist attitudes had seized hold of some, as earlier examples in this article attest to, they may not have wanted a total cultural loss. In any case, Delores Johnson and her husband were among those who, similar to Allison's mother, felt that Indian culture was something worth passing on to their children. When their son came home from school asking, "What am I?" and "Where are my feathers then?" they did not simply shrug their shoulders and give up on teaching him about their cultures. On the contrary, the moment galvanized them into action, for that child and for the eight who would follow. "After that," Johnson said, "we would talk more about who we were with the rest of the kids.... That was kind of like an eye opener for us."

In Tricia Palmer's case, it was her grandmother who played an especially large role in her cultural education. This grounding must have helped sustain her when she was told by her white elementary-school classmates that she "was making them sick" because she was an Indian. Palmer's grandmother lived with her and her mother. "She spoke her language," she noted. "She taught me Omaha values, though I didn't know it at the time. She taught me how Omaha women should be." Palmer's grandmother passed away when Tricia was ten years old, and her mother dealt with her death in the traditional Omaha way. She took Tricia with her back to the Omaha Reservation in northeast Nebraska for a four-day, four-night funeral, which included a peyote ceremony. The ceremonies left a deep impact on Palmer but at the same time marked the passing of one of her most important cultural teachers.

Martha Sadongei received cultural teachings from her family as well. "Mom was always teaching us our culture and telling us there was nothing shameful about it," she noted. Especially in their preschool years, Martha said that she and her siblings would listen to their parents tell stories from both the Tohono O'odham and Kiowa traditions. "She read to us every night," Sadongei said. "We just loved to listen to her read to us. And so every night was a big treat, whether she was going to read us a story or tell us a story. Every night, it was that way." Non-Indian traditions were also part of the teachings, for some of the stories Martha's parents told were from the Bible. At any rate, even by the first grade, Sadongei's education about her Indian identity was enough to prompt her to react when her teacher made her wear a Pilgrim's hat for Thanksgiving. "I remember distinctly ... being disgusted because I had to wear a Pilgrim woman's hat," Sadongei said. "There was just something maybe innate in me that said, you know, 'This just is not right. I should not be wearing a Pilgrim woman's hat.'" She continued:

> My sister and I had that same memory of having to do those Pilgrim hats....
> In our own 6-year-old thinking, we knew that this was just not right. It
> made us uncomfortable. But we did it. We hated it.... And as soon as we
> could, we took off those stupid little white construction paper hats.

Michael Hughes's mother helped give him a foundation for fending off challenges to his sense of identity. Aleene Hughes seemed to form her interest in her Indian culture in spite of her parents' efforts to deemphasize it. It is even possible that it was, to some extent, her way of rebelling against them. She raised Michael to be a bit of a rebel as well, and he smiled to think of her parenting. "She gave me a lot of very mixed messages," he said, grinning. "One of the mixed messages was: she wanted me to be part of society, to be successful, and go to school, and do all of that stuff; and then the other part was, she wanted me to fight against society. And there was never really any clear connection of how those two things lined up."

Aleene Hughes found various ways to teach Michael and his sister about their Native heritage. Michael remembered her talking to him often about Indian history. She would, for instance, show him the books—he specifically remembers the book *Our Brother's Keeper*, edited by Edgar Cahn—being published in the late 1960s that were seeking to revise the traditional Euro-American interpretation of Indian-white relations. Aleene also took her son to hear some of the Indian activists who came to town to deliver guest lectures. He recalled in particular attending a speech delivered by Lehman Brightman, a Lakota who was the head of the American Indian Studies Department at the University of California, Berkeley. Brightman acknowledged that there were many Anglo employees and teachers who were "good" and "sincere" but passionately called attention to general mistreatments of American Indians by Anglo bureaucrats and educators. "What they teach in this country is European history disguised as American history," he said. "You don't read anything in the history books about the Indians. You don't read anything about the blacks." Foreshadowing goals that Michael Hughes would later vigorously pursue himself, Brightman urged non-Indian educators to hire more Indian teachers and to work more diligently to incorporate Native American culture into their curriculums. Echoing words that more and more American Indian leaders were saying louder and louder in the 1960s and 1970s, he told the crowd, "You've got a damn proud heritage and you ought to be damned proud of it."

Hughes's mother, through her own example and by letting Michael listen to people like Brightman, also seems to have taught him that it was all right to speak out if you disagreed with someone or something, for example, a teacher or a textbook. Duly inspired, Hughes wrote a pointed comment in the pages of his high school history book, the one that relegated Indians to two measly sentences. The comment, he reported, was simply the word "Bullsh[**]." As for his high school history teacher, Hughes described him as a "nice person," but a person who did not hesitate to bring his socially conservative views into the classroom. "He would talk about how people who were on welfare were lazy, and I would always raise my hand and I'd say 'Well, when I was a kid my dad left and we were on welfare, but now my mother is a social worker. So, I don't think that that applies in all cases.'" On another occasion, the teacher allowed Hughes to take part in a one-on-one classroom debate. His debate opponent was a classmate who Hughes described as a "real straight-arrow kind of guy," a person who "wore a little cross on a necklace" and drove a Rambler. "And we had this debate," he said.

> I don't even remember what the topic was, but I let him lead off and he
> started talking about all the atrocities in history that had been committed by

Hitler against the Jews and by Stalin against the people in Russia and all these really terrible things. And so I sat there listening to him, and then I said, "Yeah, I agree with you. That's a lot like what the United States Army did to the Indians in the 1800s. And so you're right, all these governments have just been horrible." It was just this crazy debate we had.

As the debate continued, and as Hughes continued to criticize the US government for its past and present actions, the teacher finally interjected. "He was just supposed to be listening, but he said, 'Well, wait a minute. If you don't like government, what do you propose?' And I said, 'Well, I think we ought to replace the government with scientists.' I was just saying these outrageous things."

Hughes's somewhat militant posture may have been influenced by his trip, as a teenager, to the 1969–71 Native American protest at Alcatraz Island. At least one of the other people interviewed for this project, Lola Allison, also visited Alcatraz while she was a high school student. The experiences of Hughes and Allison at Alcatraz demonstrate that, as powerful as schools and parents are, not everything a child learns comes from them....

Though they did not know each other at that point, Lola Allison and Michael Hughes may have been on Alcatraz at the same time. Allison had dropped out of her junior year at Phoenix Union High School to take part in the occupation, and she stayed there much longer than Hughes. "That was an education on another level," she said.

I was there for thirteen months.... I was taught all this stuff, all this beautiful stuff about being an Indian that I had always felt, but that nobody had ever sat down and taught me: religion, artwork, mythology.... I learned Indian stories, and to me that was the most important part of being educated as an Indian kid. But I didn't get that until I was sixteen, and I had to go search for it.

Allison did complete high school at Phoenix Union, something she attributed to her mother's firm insistence on obtaining a solid education in the Euro-American system. "In our family, no one dropped out," Allison asserted. "My mom called me and she said, 'Lola, we don't drop out in this family. You have to come back and graduate.' And I just couldn't let my mom down so I came back and graduated." After graduating high school, Allison resumed her activist involvement, visiting places like Washington State to take part in "fish-ins" in the Pacific Northwest. "I went back on the road and went all over the country, east coast to west coast," she said. "It was wonderful."

Martha Sadongei did not go to Alcatraz Island. When she entered North High School in 1972, Indian peers who seemed to be influenced by Alcatraz, Wounded Knee, and the other events of those years had called her a "little white girl." For a while, she and her sister tried to conform to their peers' standards of Indianness, or at least to what they perceived their peers' standards to be. The Sadongei sisters dressed "down" in jeans and sneakers, skipped classes, and received failing grades. Finally, though, at some point in that sophomore year, Martha Sadongei managed to assess her situation, and she remembered her mother's goal—and her own childhood goal—of attending college. "I made the conscious decision to just stop that behavior, and accept that the rest are just going to have to deal with it," she said. "You're going to hear it," she remembers thinking to herself, "but you're going to be better off in the long run. It's not that big a deal what they say anyway."

Yet her Indian peers' views were still a big enough deal that Sadongei did try to find some way of reconciling her interest in succeeding academically with her concern for acceptance by those peers. As she reflected on it, she remarked, "I guess what helped though was that I was somehow able to balance out ... my going to class [with] still being with them." By getting involved in North High's newly formed "Indian Club" and by simply gathering with other Indians at lunchtime, Sadongei felt she was able to strike this balance. In terms of lunch, Sadongei and the other students carved out a Native place in their urban school quite literally. She explained,

> We would get together at lunch time. We would try to work schedules out so that we'd all either take the first or second lunch period, and have our designated picnic tables there, and that would be the meeting point. And we'd get there, and we'd have our markers, and things, and etch things into the table and write all over it and it got to a point where everybody just knew that this was the Indian table, and we all just gathered there mid-day, so to speak.

At lunch and in the Indian Club, Sadongei learned to "[joke] around with them and [tease] them and all that other stuff that Indian youth do when they get together." Gradually, she said, she gained their approval. "But it was almost like it took a couple of years for them to accept me as being Indian. And after that I could go back to being the student and studying and even being the president of the Indian Club and all this sort of stuff and they sort of cut back on some of the slack. And so the last two years weren't as hard as the first two.... But it was not easy making that first two years. [They] were really tough." ...

Making an Indian place in urban schools was not easy, yet not impossible. Their educational experiences correlated in many ways with the more familiar histories of Indian education that have so far been produced: the studies centering on the boarding schools. Similar to the boarding schools of the early twentieth century, urban public schools of the late twentieth century exerted pressure on Indian students to assimilate. And, like many Indian students in boarding schools, many Indian students in city schools found ways of resisting assimilation and maintaining their identities. In other respects, though, the experiences differed. If boarding schools sought to assimilate Indian children in very direct ways, urban schools were somewhat less direct. If "Kill the Indian to save the man" was the notorious mantra of the boarding schools, "Indians? What Indians?" may have been the mantra for city classrooms. Just the simple fact that they were a tiny minority, in other words, provided its own sort of inherent assimilationist pressure. In boarding schools, or in on-reservation schools for that matter, this was not a factor. There, Indians did not have to be concerned, for example, with being "swallowed up by the Mexicans" to paraphrase Lola Allison.

Being a tiny minority presented opportunities as well as challenges. The accelerating increase in Indian contacts with non-Indian cultures is one of the big stories of Indian history in the twentieth century. This increase happened for reservation Indians, certainly, but one could say that it happened even more quickly and extensively for urban Indians and, especially, for their children. They likely had more African American, Mexican American, and Anglo friends than their reservation counterparts, for example. They may have been exposed to Jimi Hendrix, Jefferson Airplane, and Cream a bit earlier than them, too. And, they had a front-row seat to watch and to learn from the 1960s political movements of urban African Americans and urban Mexican Americans.

With tens of thousands of Indian children attending urban schools rather than boarding schools in the twentieth century, these sorts of differences are worthy of our notice. And yet, the two schooling experiences were also linked, as the interviewees in this essay indicated. Some boarding school graduates were among those who moved to cities, and it affected how many of them approached their children's education, sometimes in profound ways.

Through it all, most urban Indian children managed to stay Indian, something that Martha Sadongei's particular journey helps illustrate. Her mother and father had prepared her well for her first day in the "crowded," "noisy," urban classroom, with its "echoing little hallways." She had survived the Pilgrim hat episode to the point that, as an adult, she and her sister were able to look back at it and chuckle. Joedd Miller had been right about her. She "made it in life" even when metaphorical "tanks," be they teachers or other Indian students, did make the path difficult. Martha Sadongei ultimately brought her urban Indian educational experiences full circle. In 1980, fresh from her graduation from college, she returned to the echoing little hallways of Longview. This time, she was the teacher. When November arrived, her students were ready to learn about the story of Thanksgiving. But Sadongei did not have the children don Pilgrim and Indian costumes. Instead, she taught them in detail about the histories and cultures of the indigenous peoples of New England. And the students and their parents loved it.

Perhaps the city schools had made Sadongei different in some ways from Indian children who had attended boarding schools or reservation schools, just as the city schools made all children different. But, Sadongei had also turned around and made the city a little different herself; again, just as all children did. Her story, then, is not just an urban American Indian story. It is also an American story.

Talking the Language of the Larger World: Politics in Cold War America

BY DANIEL COBB

Imagine Standing Rock Sioux activist and intellectual Vine Deloria Jr. sitting on a sofa in his den. A cup of coffee and a row of carefully aligned Pall Mall cigarettes rest on a nearby end table. A box of donuts lies open on a coffee table in front of him. On this brisk fall morning, he is bedecked in a white sweatshirt and matching pair of white sweatpants. Over several hours, he methodically works his way through one smoke after another while telling stories about his tenure as executive director of the National Congress of American Indians during the mid-1960s. This is how I remember my first encounter with one of the towering figures of the twentieth century, a man who shaped not only the course of American Indian history but also the way we think about it. It was October 2001, a little more than four years before his passing.... the two days I spent interviewing him at his home in Golden, Colorado, fundamentally altered the way I conceptualize my work.

This chapter explores four important aspects of the politics of tribal self-determination during the 1960s—the Workshop on American Indian Affairs, the American Indian Chicago Conference, the War on Poverty, and the Poor People's Campaign. The analytical thread holding each of them together derives from one of the many poignant observations Vine Deloria made during our conversations. "At NCAI," he [said], "I was looking for some kind of intellectual format of how you would justify overturning termination and at the same time escape this big push for integration that civil rights was doing." To make this distinction, he situated tribal issues in the context of what he called "an era of resurgent nationalism among dark-skinned people the world over." He remembered telling tribal leaders, "If we're gonna say we're nations and we got sovereignty and our treaties are as valid as other treaties, then we gotta talk the language of the larger world."

In arguing this point, Vine Deloria added his voice to a conversation that had been under way for more than a generation. Indian activists began drawing parallels between themselves and nations emerging from colonialism after World War I, but the advent of the Cold War following the Second World War added a new sense of urgency. In 1954 and again in 1957, Native and non-Native advocacy organizations launched aggressive campaigns for what they called an American Indian Point IV Program, a strategy that invoked President Harry S. Truman's plan to provide technical assistance and scientific training purportedly needed by developing nations to "modernize" their cultures, political systems, and economies. These reformers presented their appeal as more than just an alternative to termination.... They argued that it represented a Cold War imperative: if the United States expected to prevail in its ideological contest with the Soviet Union in Latin America, Asia, Africa, and the Middle East, they argued, it would have to demonstrate to the rest of the world that it treated the indigenous peoples within its own borders with justice and honor.

Among the earliest and most eloquent advocates of this position was D'Arcy McNickle. Born on the Flathead Reservation to a Cree mother and Scots-Irish father in 1904, McNickle entered the Indian Service during the 1930s, just as Commissioner of Indian Affairs John Collier initiated the Indian New Deal, a wide-ranging reform agenda that intended to bolster tribal self-government. McNickle helped to found the National Congress of American Indians in 1944, before resigning from the Bureau of Indian Affairs (BIA) ten years later, disgusted by the advent of termination.... Like Deloria, McNickle believed that Indians shared "the world experience of other native peoples subjected to colonial domination." In the 1950s he set about extending "the process of decolonization to the United States" through an organization called American Indian Development (AID).

In 1960 McNickle committed AID to sponsoring the Workshop on American Indian Affairs, a six-week program for Indian college students, initiated by University of Chicago anthropologist Sol Tax in the summer of 1956. At the outset, the workshops endeavored to offer course credit through the University of Colorado, provide an incentive for Indian youths to complete their degrees, and cultivate a new generation of leaders—a particularly important goal, given the threat that termination posed to many Native communities. The workshops metamorphosed into something greater still after Robert K. Thomas, a Cherokee doctoral candidate at the University of Chicago, placed his mark on the curriculum.... Through a combination of reading about Robert Redfield's anthropological work in Latin America, studying under Edward Spicer and Sol Tax, and reflecting on his own personal experiences, Bob Thomas began thinking about American Indians as a folk people adjusting to contact with and colonization by an urban industrial society.

Thomas contended that Indian students, like their peers in so-called underdeveloped countries, traditionally received vocational training to learn specific skills. When they did go to college, they dropped out in inordinately high numbers because they felt marginal, and they felt marginal because of the messages they received about who they were and where they did or did not fit in. Under his direction, workshop students learned that they were not forsaking their relatives or somehow abandoning Indian culture by going to and succeeding in college. "These kind[s] of bullshit dilemmas are false and come from high school teachers," he seethed. When students recognized that the problems they confronted personally, within their families, and in their communities were not their fault and that they were not alone, they could see these problems for what they were, objectify them, and deal with them "intellectually instead of in a personal, secret, unformalized way." Social science would make this possible by serving as a vehicle for the liberation of their minds and, with it, the redemption of their communities.

The curriculum Bob Thomas constructed compelled students to confront the idea of internal colonialism and to apply it to analyses of federal policies, their own communities, and even themselves. In 1962 Thomas asked workshop students to "[d]escribe the consequences for the world and social relations of a folk people under a colonial administration" and, even more pointedly, asked, "Is it possible for a government, given a colonial situation, to determine the destiny of the governed people and also to terminate their colonial status with success?" The final exam in 1963 read: "Compare the structure and consequences of colonialism or minority group status in one of the following: India, Kenya, Ghana, Maori in New Zealand, aboriginal people in the Philippines, with the structure and consequences of the relationship between either American Indians or a specific group and the wider American society."

D'Arcy McNickle later remarked that the workshop experience served as "an awakening" for many of the students who attended. The essays they wrote during their summers in Boulder lend credence to his assessment. "I had never before thought of the Indians as compared to colonialism," Frank Dukepoo (Hopi) reflected. "I thought colonialism existed only in the older countries like southern Europe or in places such as Africa." Clyde Warrior (Ponca) detected similar resonances. "Another thing I learned is that all over the world tribal peoples are coming in contact with the outside world," he noted, "and basically they all have the same reactions." What this young person—who was instrumental to the formation of the National Indian Youth Council in August 1961—meant by "same reactions" was, of course, rebellion. Makah tribal member and NIYC member Bruce Wilkie explained why: "[A]s long as there is a colonial agency set up to administer to Indian affairs," one of his papers read, "there will always be an Indian social problem."

In a perceptive essay written in 1962, Sandra Johnson, another Makah from the Neah Bay area, extended a Cold War analogy to this discourse on colonialism and wove it into issues of identity. "It is not that Indians reject white culture, per se. It is that they reject white culture when they are forced to adapt to it by losing what they are and [what] they value. One does not painlessly reject oneself," she asserted. Searching for an appropriate metaphor, she asked how non-Indians might respond to the prospect of being forced to live under Soviet domination: "Many would cry, 'Better dead than Red.' And yet, another battle between the Reds and the Whites is being fought within our own borders. Given this different context it may be easier for white citizens to understand our cry which would sound more like, 'Better Red than dead.'"

The workshop's emphasis on decolonization and ethnic pride clearly informed students' rejection of termination and assimilation. Moreover, many of the "Workshoppers," as they called themselves, carried these ideas with them as they went on to become elected tribal leaders, educators, doctors, lawyers, documentary filmmakers, artists, writers, and founders of activist organizations such as the National Indian Youth Council. From this generation arose persons who, over the course of the succeeding fifty years, would become influential promoters of change in Native America—youth activist Clyde Warrior, tribal leaders Mel Thom and Bruce Wilkie, filmmaker Sandy (Johnson) Osawa, former Institute of American Indian Arts president Della (Hopper) Warrior (Otoe-Missouria), lawyer Browning Pipestem (Otoe), tribal college administrator Phyllis Howard (Mandan), Stockbridge-Munsee community leader Dorothy Davids, Mary Hillaire (Lummi), Evergreen State College's first Native staff member, and many, many others.... All of them have been active in decolonizing a wide range of spheres, from art and education to mass media and federal–Indian relations.

A second example of how international affairs shaped Indian politics during the 1960s can be found in the American Indian Chicago Conference. Seizing upon a United Nations proclamation that the 1960s would be the "Decade of Development," Sol Tax proposed a meeting that would bring delegates from across Indian Country to Chicago in order to finalize a comprehensive

"Declaration of Indian Purpose." This statement would, in turn, be presented in person to John F. Kennedy, the newly elected president of the United States. The National Congress of American Indians endorsed the idea in December 1960, and D'Arcy McNickle quickly took the lead in authoring a draft document. Then, during the spring, Sol Tax coordinated a series of regional meetings in which Indian and non-Indian people discussed and critiqued it. Long an advocate of the Point IV philosophy, McNickle infused the initial statement with the spirit of international development. The final declaration even resurrected the Cold War imperative by intoning, "[T]he problem we raise affects the standing which our nation sustains before world opinion."

Looked at from a different perspective, the Chicago conference reveals still another dimension to politics in Cold War Native America. Indeed, one of the untold stories of the event is the extent to which it was plagued by the politics of anticommunism. If the Chicago conference's proponents sought to harness the Cold War as a means of advancing a progressive agenda, its detractors used the fear of communist subversion as a bulwark against change. Earl Boyd Pierce, general counsel of the Cherokee Nation of Oklahoma, proved instrumental in this regard. Born and raised in Ft. Gibson, a small town in Muskogee County, Oklahoma, he saw himself as a champion of the American way of life, venerated Federal Bureau of Investigation director J. Edgar Hoover, and kept an autographed copy of the zealous anticommunist's book, *Masters of Deceit*, in his personal library. Although he actively pursued Cherokee legal claims against the federal government, he was suspicious of strident acts of protest, such as civil rights demonstrations and antiwar rallies.

The Chicago conference came under close scrutiny in January 1961 when the Inter-Tribal Council of the Five Civilized Tribes convened in Muskogee, Oklahoma. Detecting a nefarious scheme, Cherokee principal chief W. W. Keeler, an executive for Phillips Petroleum, recalled a trip to the Soviet Union he had taken in August 1960: Some Russians "took me aside and explained to me how they would like to work with me in working out plans to set up some *Indian Republics* here in the United States. [T]hey talked about *freeing the Indians* ... they had the idea Indians are held as prisoners ... they spoke of the Indians in leg-irons...." But that was not all. "They said it came from the reports of the *University of Chicago*." Earl Boyd Pierce added his own premonition that Sol Tax, D'Arcy McNickle, and others intended to lay a "booby trap" in Chicago that would culminate in nothing less than "an overall Governmental State."

With deep suspicions in tow, Pierce traveled to Chicago in February to attend a meeting of Indian leaders who had been chosen to serve as the steering committee for the conference. He proceeded to bait the participants and to underscore that Indians were no longer sovereign nations—that they must remain loyal to the United States government. Repeatedly, the Cherokee general counsel argued that the Interior Department and the Bureau of Indian Affairs should be consulted before Indians took any definite actions. By being too forceful, he feared, they would come off as "an unhappy minority." Pierce had to leave before the steering committee disbanded, and he suspected rightly that he had earned their derision. He also knew that a tape recorder had been running throughout all but the first session. Upon his return to Oklahoma, he requested copies. An incredible game of cat and mouse followed, with Pierce pursuing what had become, in his mind, a "black plot against him" and assistant coordinator Nancy Lurie, an anthropologist and a former student of Sol Tax, doing all in her power to forestall the inevitable surrender.

In the months that followed, opponents of the Chicago conference spread rumors that Tax, a Jew whose socialist parents emigrated from Germany, was a communist in disguise. If Pierce could not destroy the conference by whispering such intimations, he resolved personally to see that no one advanced a radical agenda. When the hundreds of tribal delegates finally descended on Chicago in June 1961, he and his allies worked diligently to secure passage of a stridently anticommunist "American Indian Pledge" that ultimately prefaced the "Declaration of Indian Purpose." In ultrapatriotic prose targeting Tax and his allies, it denounced "the efforts of the promoters of any alien form of government." When representatives from the Chicago conference finally had their personal meeting with John F. Kennedy, it appears that the "American Indian Pledge" was the only part of the declaration the president actually read.

This aspect of the Chicago conference suggests that the intersection between domestic and international politics did not occur merely in the realm of ideas. Rather, it literally shaped behavior and, with it, the course of events. In this instance, the Cold War served as a powerful backdrop. Just as decolonization informed the organizers' embrace of development through democratic self-determination, fear of communist subversion inspired its opponents.

Another unanticipated manifestation of these ideational border crossings—one that extended into the realm of action—can be found in the strategy Vine Deloria carved out for the National Congress of American Indians. Upon assuming the executive directorship in 1964, not only did he adopt rhetoric reminiscent of that found in anticolonial movements across the globe, but he also used similar approaches for affecting change. In a study of Cold War foreign policy, historian John Lewis Gaddis observed that although "Third World" countries could not challenge the Soviet Union or the United States militarily, they could manipulate these world powers "by laying on flattery, pledging solidarity, feigning indifference, threatening defection, or even raising the specter of their own collapse and the disastrous results that might flow from it." Under Deloria's direction, the NCAI engaged in precisely this kind of veiled resistance by adopting a carefully orchestrated play-off system involving several government agencies.

President Lyndon Baines Johnson unwittingly handed him the primary vehicle he would use to push for reform, when Johnson launched and then proceeded to escalate the War on Poverty.... Deloria immediately formed a significant relationship with James J. Wilson, an Oglala Lakota brought in to oversee all the War on Poverty's Indian programs in the spring of 1965. Channeled through what Deloria called "inside-outside politics," they seem to have agreed to use each other in order to manipulate the federal bureaucracy from within rather than confront it from without. Both of them well knew that the War on Poverty—and particularly the Community Action Program, given its direct funding of tribes and emphasis on local initiative—offered a potent critique of wardship and paternalism. Having the dubious distinction of being the quintessential symbol of these unsavory concepts, the Bureau of Indian Affairs became the central focus of their attacks.

The political strategy Wilson and Deloria devised evidenced itself during the National Congress of American Indians' annual convention in Scottsdale, Arizona, in November 1965. Through the spring, summer, and fall of that year, the Office of Economic Opportunity, which served as the administrative headquarters to the War on Poverty, was embroiled in tremendous controversy, in large part because of the explosion of the Watts riot in Los Angeles. Members of Congress and city mayors intimated that federal money was being used to incite racial and class conflict. At the same time, the rising cost of the war in Vietnam meant potential budget cuts for the War on Poverty. R. Sargent Shriver, the director of the Office of Economic Opportunity, found himself fighting two battles. First, he argued with President Lyndon Johnson over how much money it would take to win the antipoverty campaign. Second, he had to struggle with city mayors and congressmen to save the grassroots-centered approach of Community Action.

Vine Deloria and Jim Wilson understood that they could leverage these struggles to advance tribal interests. Networking with other Washington insiders, they suggested to R. Sargent Shriver that he attend the NCAI convention and use it as an opportunity to fight back. Given the depth of bitterness directed toward BIA paternalism and the popularity of Community Action in Indian Country, there could be few better places for Sargent Shriver to reaffirm his commitment to the idea of maximum feasible participation of the poor. This calculated maneuver paid off. "He was almost like a conquering hero returning," one observer remembered of Shriver's arrival at the convention. Deloria had a similar recollection of the event. "I can remember him coming into the hotel, and, by God, it took him ten minutes to get up on the podium.... All these people wanted to show him pictures of their projects or talk to him. Everybody was just shaking hands with him. I hardly had a chance to say two words to him, and I was running the whole thing...."

Shriver used his address to proclaim the Office of Economic Opportunity's commitment to tribal self-determination. Reservation communities, he argued, could be likened to underdeveloped nations, and, therefore, the same kinds of prescriptions for change applied to them. "[W]hite imperialism, white paternalism," he argued in a thinly veiled reference to the BIA, "cannot be replaced by the paternalism of experts, the imperialism of professionals." He also said, "The money is yours—because the whole basis of the poverty program is self-determination—the right of the people—individually and collectively—to decide their own course and to find their own way." Deloria considered Shriver's performance a tremendous success. The War on Poverty received the positive media coverage it needed, while he gained additional leverage to use against the established bureaucracy. With OEO on his side, Deloria recalled, he could go to the BIA and say, "Okay, we'll listen to the commissioner, but this better be good."

Vine Deloria allowed the Office of Economic Opportunity to cultivate a romantic image of Community Action. But did that mean he really believed in it? Consider this remembrance.... "I never liked most of the OEO people cause they were so ... snobby, and they were all Ivy League people, you know?" They might talk a good game about empowerment and representation, he remembered, but they had no idea what it was like to live in poverty. "[If] you took one of these OEO guys and put him in the towns we grew up in, they'd make a total ass of themselves," he stated flatly. "They'd be run out of town in a half hour."

This observation needs to be balanced with the following exchange Deloria had with a non-Indian social scientist named Murray Wax. Wax took particular umbrage at the War on Poverty's Head Start preschool program, basing his assessment on extended on-site evaluations in centers across Indian Country. "I have looked closely at poverty programs on Indian reservations and I assure you they violate the fundamental principle of Indian self-determination," he wrote to Deloria. "Do Indian parents really need Head Start programs so as to transform their children into Whites?!?" Deloria offered a response rich with irony. "I don't believe you are understanding what is taking place in regard to poverty programs and Indianism—the more educated they get, the more nationalistic they get also," he wrote. "Head Start just provides us with a chance to get them a solid basis for becoming nationalists 2 years sooner."

Vine Deloria not only talked the language of the larger world but also walked the walk. "In any fight with an institution, the institution will always win because it's going to be there longer than you," he later explained.... "So you gotta screw up the way it operates itself, turn it in on itself, create a crisis for it. And then, they'll give you what you want and alter things." In public addresses, congressional testimony, formal resolutions, and the pages of the NCAI's publications, Deloria proceeded to use innuendo, warnings of impending crises, fulsome praise, and caustic ridicule to play Congress, the Interior Department, the Bureau of Indian Affairs, the Office of Economic Opportunity, and even tribal leaders against one another. "The only way we're going to get anywhere," he later said in justification of this approach, "is to praise one agency while kicking the ass of another and get those two competing with each other."

This logic was certainly operative in Scottsdale in 1965, but another event in April of the following year may provide the single best example. By the spring of 1966, heightened anxieties over the resignation of one Indian Affairs commissioner and the appointment of another, rumblings of support for termination in the Senate, and rumors of the BIA's designs to take over the Office of Economic Opportunity's Indian programs permeated Indian Country. Amidst this tumult, Interior secretary Stewart Udall organized a policy meeting for federal employees and interested congresspersons in Santa Fe, New Mexico. Arguing that Indian people deserved the right to have a voice in making decisions that affect their lives, Deloria requested permission to send NCAI observers to the four-day conference. To his exasperation, Udall declined.

Deloria had had enough. Likening the Interior Department to a giant piñata, he remembered thinking, "Let's take the closest thing we have and hit that thing as hard as we can and see what's going on." To do so, he called an emergency meeting. In short order, two hundred representatives from sixty-two tribes descended on Santa Fe to hold countermeetings a mere three blocks away from Udall's closed session. Taking the civil rights movement as his model, Deloria sought to create a "media phenomenon" that would dramatize the BIA's complete disregard for basic democratic principles. For three days, the NCAI railed against the Indian bureau as a reporter from the *New York Times* recorded every detail.

Throughout the confrontation, members of the NCAI juxtaposed the "spectacular success" of local initiative via Community Action with the BIA's penchant for paternalism. The *New York Times* articles, according to Deloria, delivered the following message: "Here are the Indians who are managing their own affairs, and they've got poverty programs and everything. Here's the Bureau trying to put them back in the nineteenth century." Praising the War on Poverty while criticizing the Indian bureau fostered the kind of competition that Deloria hoped would prove advantageous to tribes. To be sure, the Office of Economic Opportunity could ill afford to lose one of the few friends it had left, and the last thing the much maligned BIA needed was to appear to be perpetuating dependency.

In the wake of Santa Fe, Deloria continued the strategy. "Certainly there has been no single program or theory of government that has caused such excitement on Indian reservations in 100 years as the Poverty Program," he expounded in the pages of the *NCAI Sentinel*. But in keeping with the strategy employed by other developing nations during the Cold War, he added a dire warning: "There is now a good chance for wholesale collapse of enthusiasm on reservations if the basic philosophy of the OEO is changed to conform to what is happening in the large cities." Through the spring and summer of 1966, black–white coalitions fragmented, calls for Black Power and welfare rights peaked, and the inner cities exploded. Through it all, the National Congress of American Indians continued to cultivate an image of Indians as the one minority group that Lyndon Johnson's administration could safely champion without fear of white reprisal. Why? To advance a nationalist agenda to promote tribal sovereignty.

After Vine Deloria resigned from the NCAI in 1967 to pursue a law degree at the University of Colorado, John Belindo (Kiowa/Navajo) carried his efforts forward. In March 1968 the organization scored a victory when President Johnson issued "The Forgotten American," the twentieth century's first presidential statement devoted exclusively to Indian affairs. The address did not renounce termination outright, but it did indicate that the Johnson administration wanted to end the debate by committing the federal government to a policy of "self-help and self-determination." Showing himself to be equally adept at leverage seeking, Belindo assured Johnson's advisers that if the NCAI were given an audience with the president, then it would "include quotes like 'The Johnson Administration has done more for Indians than any other president'" and would also "support the President's Viet Nam stand." Following closely on the heels of the disastrous Tet Offensive in Vietnam, this must have been inviting, indeed.

The Poor People's Campaign, a massive six-week protest in the heart of Washington DC, revealed that even as the NCAI's patient incrementalism seemed to be producing results, the political climate was becoming increasingly radicalized. Less than two months after Johnson issued "The Forgotten American," thousands of poor whites, blacks, Chicanos, and American Indians converged on the capitol, taking up residence in Resurrection City, a makeshift community located just off the National Mall, and in churches and schools throughout the city. Together, they marched, picketed, testified before Congress, conducted sit-ins, and allowed themselves to be arrested—all in an effort to expose what they considered to be the grave injustices visited upon those who lived in America's shadows. Over the course of the Poor People's Campaign, a demonstration was staged outside the Supreme Court to protest the anti-treaty fishing rights *Puyallup* decision, and a spontaneous sit-in occurred at the Bureau of Indian Affairs headquarters.

Indian involvement in what many perceived to be a primarily African American demonstration created deep divisions within tribal communities. The National Congress of American Indians, as well as a number of tribal governments, refused to endorse the Poor People's Campaign. Although Vine Deloria understood the Indian participants' anger and reasons for being there, he questioned their tactics. "The temptation to be militant overcomes the necessity to be nationalistic," he later wrote in *Custer Died for Your Sins*. "Anyone can get into the headlines by making wild threats and militant statements. It takes a lot of hard work to raise an entire group to a new conception of themselves. And that is the difference between the nationalists and the militants."

Mel Thom did not see it this way. On May 1, 1968, Thom—a participant in the American Indian Chicago Conference, a student in the Workshop on American Indian Affairs, a founding member of the National Indian Youth Council, and director of the Walker River Paiute Community Action Program—stood as one with a multiracial delegation of the poor called the Committee of One Hundred as it met face-to-face with members from President Lyndon Johnson's cabinet. In an impassioned speech delivered before representatives from the Bureau of Indian Affairs, Thom spoke of poverty as a product of internal colonialism. "There is no way to improve upon racism, immorality and colonialism; it can only be done away with," he railed. "The system and power structure serving Indian peoples is a sickness which has grown to epidemic proportions. The Indian system is sick. Paternalism is the virus, and the Secretary of the Interior is the carrier...."

By drawing analogies between Indians and others, and particularly by locating the struggle of Native people squarely in the context of decolonization, Mel Thom followed in the tradition of D'Arcy McNickle, Sol Tax, Robert K. Thomas, and even Vine Deloria Jr., though he came to a different conclusion. As he wove together issues regarding race, poverty, identity, and power, he made a demand not only for self-determination but also for national liberation. The time for talking was over. "The day is coming when we're gonna move," he warned during a second encounter with government officials, this time representatives from the Office of Economic Opportunity. "And when we move, like I said, watch out!" As Mel Thom hammered his fist against a table, he offered an accurate premonition of things to come. Later that summer, in Minneapolis, Minnesota, members of an embattled urban community formed an organization they eventually called the American Indian Movement, and in California a small contingent of college students launched an abortive attempt to occupy and lay claim to Alcatraz Island as Indian land.... The rest, as they say, is history.

This analysis of the Workshop on American Indian Affairs, American Indian Chicago Conference, War on Poverty, and Poor People's Campaign illuminates several new dimensions of American Indian politics and activism during the 1960s. It shows how a generation of Indians and non-Indians situated themselves and the struggle for tribal self-determination in the context of domestic controversies involving race, class, and war, as well as global concerns over the rights of indigenous peoples and the Cold War. But talking the language of the larger world, no matter how conceptually powerful it proved to be, did not necessarily produce results—for it was one thing to speak, another to be heard, and still something different to be understood. Indeed, as Mel Thom stood in solidarity with the Committee of One Hundred, he had reached the point of exasperation for the very reason that Indian people had been listened to but not understood. Despite drawing analogies and assiduously pointing out parallels, the dominant society simply could not or would not make the translation. It is a problem that continues to this day.

◈ FURTHER READING

Akwesasne Notes. *Trail of Broken Treaties: BIA, I'm Not Your Indian Any More* (1974).

————. *Voices from Wounded Knee, 1973, in the Words of the Participants* (1974).

Amerman, Stephen Kent. *Urban Indians in Phoenix Schools, 1940–2000* (2010).

Bilharz, Joy A. *The Allegany Senecas and Kinzua Dam: Forced Relocation Through Two Generations* (1998).

Brugge, David M. *The Navajo–Hopi Land Dispute: An American Tragedy* (1994).

Campisi, Jack. *The Mashpee Indians: Tribe on Trial* (1991).

Castile, George P. *To Show Heart: Native American Self-Determination and Federal Indian Policy, 1960–1975* (1998).

Cobb, Daniel M. *Native Activism in Cold War America: The Struggle for Sovereignty* (2008).

Cobb, Daniel M., and Loretta Fowler, eds. *Beyond Red Power: American Indian Politics and Activism Since 1900* (2007).

Davis, Julie L. *Survival Schools: The American Indian Movement and Community Education in the Twin Cities* (2013).

Deloria, Philip J. *Playing Indian* (1998).

Deloria, Vine, Jr. *Behind the Trail of Broken Treaties: An Indian Declaration of Independence* (1974).

————. *Custer Died for Your Sins: An Indian Manifesto* (1969).

————. *We Talk, You Listen: New Tribes, New Turf* (1970).

Gonzalez, Mario, and Elizabeth Cook-Lynn. *The Politics of Hallowed Ground: Wounded Knee and the Struggle for Indian Sovereignty* (1998).

Gordon-McCutchan, R. C. *The Taos Indians and the Battle for Blue Lake* (1991).

Harmon, Alexandra. *Indians in the Making: Ethnic Relations and Indian Identities Around Puget Sound* (1998).

Janda, Sarah Eppler. *Beloved Women: The Political Lives of LaDonna Harris and Wilma Mankiller* (2007).

Johnson, Troy R. *The Occupation of Alcatraz Island: Indian Self-Determination and the Rise of Indian Activism* (1996).

Johnson, Troy R., Joane Nagel, and Duane Champagne, eds. *American Indian Activism: Alcatraz to the Longest Walk* (1997).

McNickle, D'Arcy. *Wind from an Enemy Sky* (1978).

Momaday, N. Scott. *House Made of Dawn* (1968).

Nagel, Joane. *American Indian Ethnic Renewal: Red Power and the Resurgence of Identity and Culture* (1996).

Ramirez, Renya. *Native Hubs: Culture, Community and Belonging in Silicon Valley and Beyond* (2007).

Rosier, Paul. *Serving Their Country: American Indian Politics and Patriotism in the Twentieth Century* (2009).

Sayer, John William. *Ghost Dancing the Law: The Wounded Knee Trials* (1997).

Shreve, Bradley G. *Red Power Rising: The National Indian Youth Council and the Origins of Native Activism* (2011).

Silko, Leslie Marmon. *Ceremony* (1977).

Smith, Paul Chaat, and Robert Allen Warrior. *Like a Hurricane: The Indian Movement from Alcatraz to Wounded Knee* (1996).

Smith, Sherry. *Hippies, Indians, and the Fight for Red Power* (2012).

Steiner, Stan. *The New Indians* (1968).

Stern, Kenneth S. *Loud Hawk: The United States Versus the American Indian Movement* (1994).

Welch, James. *The Death of Jim Loney* (1979).

———. *Winter in the Blood* (1974).

Wilkinson, Charles. *Blood Struggle: The Rise of Modern Indian Nations* (2005).

CHAPTER 15

Identity, History, and Economic Development in the Twenty-First Century

If the final two decades of the twentieth century reflected challenges for American Indians, they also demonstrated conclusively that in many ways American Indians could face a new century with optimism. In 1980, Native peoples confronted complex and essential questions about education, health care, employment, housing, and their relationship to other Americans. By 2010, many Native nations used revenues from enormous gambling facilities to assume more control over social services, economic development, and cultural renewal. In 1980, the United States census counted approximately 1.3 million American Indians in the United States. By 2010, that number had increased to more than 5 million. This marked not only an enormous population growth in three decades but also the moment when North America's Indigenous population had rebounded to their pre-1492, precontact numbers. Indeed, then-Democratic presidential candidate Barack Obama's campaign stop on Montana's Crow Reservation in 2008 demonstrated conclusively that American Indian nations possessed demographic, political, and economic clout in the twenty-first-century United States.

Although debate continues about Indians' place and status in America, there is no doubt, early in the twenty-first century, that the image of the vanishing Indian has proved a myth. In 2004, the National Museum of the American Indian opened on the mall in Washington, D.C. Native art, music, and literature have flourished. An unprecedented number of contemporary Indians have entered medicine, law, engineering, and other professions. Powwows, rodeos, and other forums have evolved to permit people from different tribes the chance to interact, compete with, and learn from one another. More than 500 years after Columbus, American Indians remain as distinct entities in North American life.

◈ DOCUMENTS

In the late-twentieth century, economic development was a pressing concern within Indian communities. The first two documents in this chapter address the debate about on-reservation gaming. In Document 1, Eddie Tullis of the Poarch Creek Band of Creek Indians details the important benefits that Creeks derived from their bingo hall in Alabama. How did gaming help Creeks? How did gaming support non-Creeks? Not everyone supported the expansion of Indian gaming in the twentieth century, no matter how much it helped Native and non-Native communities. In Document 2, Senator Harry Reid of Nevada (a state that relies heavily on gaming for state revenue) argues for greater state, rather than federal, control of reservation gaming. Many of Reid's arguments influenced the passage of the 1988 Indian Gaming Regulatory Act, which required Native nations that wanted to establish a Class III, Las Vegas–style gaming establishment to enter into a compact with the state.

In addition to economic development, other issues came to the forefront of American Indian communities in the twenty-first century. James Riding In (Pawnee), a professor of American Indian Studies at Arizona State University, has gained national prominence for his role in pushing for the repatriation of sacred and secular objects to their proper place within Indian communities. In Document 3, Riding In offers his perspective on this vital concern. The question of identity—who is and is not an Indian—also generated considerable debate. In Document 4, Kanaka Maoli Kai'opua Fyfe testifies in front of the United States Senate in opposition to the federal government recognizing Native Hawaiians as American Indians. Why does he resist federal recognition? Land issues also remained significant in the twenty-first century. The late Elouise Cobell (Blackfeet) outlines the history of land litigation, beginning with the Dawes Act and culminating with a suit against the federal government for the misappropriation of American Indian monies in Document 5. In Document 6, Steve Russell (Cherokee) sparks a heated discussion with a seemingly offhand remark about Mexicans and Indians. How does the United States–Mexico border complicate issues of Indigenous identity in North America? Charlene Teters (Spokane) has been outspoken in her concern about the use of Native symbols and images of Native people. She has campaigned tirelessly in an effort to educate non-Indian individuals about the offensiveness of employing Indians as mascots for athletic teams. In Document 7, she raises a question about what kind of history we should (and should not) celebrate.

1. Eddie Tullis (Poarch Band of Creek Indians) Outlines the Benefits of Bingo and Gaming, 1985

I would encourage this committee and Senator [Dennis] DeConcini's staff to proceed with all deliberate speed and effort on this bill [to establish federal standards and regulations for the conduct of gaming activities within Indian Country] for two reasons. One is for this Congress to reassert the fact that it is this

"Gambling on Indian Reservations and Lands," Committee on Indian Affairs, 99th Congress, 1st Session (1985).

Congress that should deal with Indian tribes throughout the country and not renege that responsibility to some of the States where we see a lot of the mechanisms of that State controlled by overzealous, misdirected public officials who do not even have the respect for the courts that they are charged to uphold. So I think it is very critical that we have legislation passed through this Congress in the very near future.

On a personal note, I would like to tell you that the Poarch Band of Creek Indians began operation of a high stakes bingo operation on our reservation on April 13 of this past year. I can truly say that there has been a remarkable change in the status of the Poarch Band of Creek Indians. For the first time in the history of the tribe, we now have unobligated funds that the tribal council can use to do those things that are really a priority in our community, and we have already begun to see a significant change in not only the attitude but in the ability of our people to address some of their needs.

Since the fourth day of December last year, we have put into the local economy in excess of $2.4 million. This is money that has been brought into the economy of a very economically depressed county. Due to the fact of that economic input the tribal community as well as the county commissioners or the board of county commissioners of our local county, the mayor and the city council of the local community in the nearest town to us, the local district attorney, the county judge, have all been supportive of the establishment of high stakes bingo on the Poarch Creek Reservation.

I also want to say that high stakes bingo has had a significant impact on the unemployment in my tribe and the local community. We now have 129 people employed. Forty-one of those are tribal members, 88 of them are nontribal members. Tribal members are employed in all levels of the management. The top manager of our bingo operation is a nontribal member, but that was a necessity due to the fact that we did not have a tribal member that had any single experience operating a bingo operation.

We do have a management company that has a 5-year contract. We feel very comfortable now after only 2 months of operation, that when that 5 years is up, the Poarch Band of Creeks will be a totally tribally operated and owned operation.

2. Senator Harry Reid Requests State Control of Indian Gaming, 1987

I consider [Indian Gaming] to be of the utmost importance, both to the future of my State, the State of Nevada, and our very important industry, and also the integrity of the United States and to the well being, honor and safety of those who occupy Indian lands.

I am here to state a position that States regulate gaming on all lands within a State, and against any exception to that rule. I approach the question with a somewhat unique perspective, since I served as chairman of the Nevada Gaming Commission for 4 years.

"Indian Gaming Regulatory Act," Committee on Interior and Insular Affairs, 100th Congress, 1st Session (1987).

The Nevada Gaming Commission is the ultimate policy maker for Nevada gaming. Based on that personal experience, I am convinced that regulation of gaming operations is at best an extremely complex, expensive and arduous task.

Even in a small State like Nevada, it requires commitments of literally millions of dollars and many hundreds and hundreds of employees, including investigators, surveillance personnel, accountants and attorneys, as well as a large and well trained clerical staff.

Between ... Nevada and New Jersey, there will be in excess of $100 million spent this year to regulate gaming operations....

This is in contrast to the bill that is before us, that calls for $2 million, and so I would suggest, Mr. Chairman, that the presentation of legislation requesting $2 million to control this is nowhere near the mark, especially when you have the gaming in Nevada and in New Jersey in a geographical setting that makes control somewhat easier. The Indian reservations, of course, are spread all over this country.

Without ... millions and millions and millions of dollars, effective regulation is not only difficult, it is impossible. Lack of that effective regulation is an open invitation to organized crime to move into lucrative areas where the commodity is cash, and corruption reaps tremendous profits....

In Nevada, for over 50 years, we have repeatedly experienced the heavy baggage borne by those who assumed the duty of regulating gaming. We have seen mobsters move in and skim cash from casino accounting rooms, an operation which allows them to launder money and reap illicit profits at the same time.

We have seen attempts by organized crime to dominate gaming related unions and to obtain illegal control of casinos through improper loans, as well as threats and intimidation. We have seen onetime honest businessmen overwhelmed and corrupted by the ever probing tentacles of organized crime.

The battle has been continuous and all consuming. It is never won and completely over.

As chairman of the Nevada Gaming Commission, my commission took action on what we believed were casinos controlled by organized crime. We imposed what were at the time the largest administrative fines in the history of the United States. We fought with legions of attorneys to shut down subvertive casinos and to clean up their operations.

I experienced some personal discomfort ... as a result of those battles. My life was repeatedly threatened, and I was forced to obtain FBI and police protection on a continuing basis.

What really bothered me, however, were the threats and attempts against my family. My wife, as an example, discovered at one time a bomb attached to our car. My children constantly walked in fear to school many, many times under police protection.

And it hasn't been only me alone that has had these experiences.... Bob Broadbent, who used to be Under Secretary of the Interior, when he was county commissioner in Clark County, Nevada, was a repeated target of threats, and as did I, he carried a gun for protection.

Commissioner George Schwartz, who served with me on the commission, also had a bomb placed on his car. Those are a few of the incidents during my short tenure.

As recently as last year, Ned Day, a Las Vegas columnist, who repeatedly challenged and exposed the mob, awoke one morning to discover his car had been torched. That, of course, was the bad news, Mr. Chairman. The good news is that he was not in the car when it was torched.

The mob, you see, well, they may appreciate constitutional protection when we catch them, but doesn't believe in freedom of the press. My job, and the job of the regulators in Nevada, was to protect the people of Nevada from the thugs and hoodlums who tried to muscle their way into Nevada gaming.

Today, our job before this committee is to protect the public and potential owners of gaming establishments on Indian lands from these same, what I believe to be dark forces. I cannot and do not believe that small tribal groups of 20, 50 or even a few hundred individuals, often living in isolated communities, will be able to withstand the physical and financial onslaught of the sophisticated organized crime syndicates and operatives, who are a constant threat against the integrity of Nevada gaming.

I want to urge this committee to leave the power of regulation of gaming where it should be, in the hands of the States, which have the resources of money and personnel to adequately and effectively control any gambling they care to make legal.

If States have not legalized some form of gaming, then the chances are they do not believe it should be permitted within their borders. The various legislatures are certainly most well fit to analyze their resources and reaction of their populace on a statewide basis. No small group, of whatever origin, should be permitted to undercut that fundamental legislative decision.

Some will tell you that this a question of Indian sovereignty, and that the Federal Government should do nothing which might imply a role for other governmental entities. That argument is at best disingenuous ... the Federal Government has the legal authority and moral obligation to ensure that tribal enclaves do not become sanctuaries for organized crime. It is our duty to prevent a situation where State authorities stand by impotently while their citizens are victimized, and that the mob flaunts its operations before their helpless gaze.

... I am not engaging in exaggeration or in hyperbole. Unless control of gaming remains with the States, the hope for controlling organized crime in this country will be lost forever.

3. James Riding In Presents a Pawnee Perspective on Repatriation, 1996

The acts committed against deceased Indians have had profound, even harmful, effects on the living. Therefore, as an activist and historian, I have had to develop a conceptual framework for giving meaning and order to the conflict. The foundation of my perspective concerning repatriation is derived from a combination of cultural, personal, and academic experiences. An understanding of Pawnee religious and philosophical beliefs about death, gained through oral tradition, dreams, and research, informs my view that repatriation is a social justice movement, supported by native spirituality and sovereignty, committed to the amelioration of the twin evils of oppression and scientific racism. Yet, I am neither a religious fundamentalist nor a left- or right-wing reactionary. Concerning repatriation, I simply advocate that American Indians receive what virtually every other group of American enjoys; that is, the right to religious freedom and a lasting burial.

My training as critical scholar provides another cornerstone of my beliefs about the nature of "imperial archaeology." My writings cast the legacy of scientific body snatching within the realm of oppression. Oppression occurs when a set or sets of individuals within the dominant population behave in ways that infringe on the beliefs, cultures, and political structures of other groups of people. Acts of stealing bodies, infringing on spirituality, and resisting repatriation efforts represent classic examples of oppression.

Although exposed to years of secular interpretations about the nature of the world and the significance of archaeology for understanding the past through formal Euroamerican education, I have continued to accept Pawnee beliefs about the afterlife. To adopt any other perspective regarding this matter would deny my cultural heritage. I cannot reconcile archaeology with tradition because of the secular orientation of the former as well as its intrusive practices. Unlike archaeologists who see Native remains as specimens for study, my people view the bodies of deceased loved ones as representing human life with sacred qualities. Death merely marks the passage of the human spirit to another state of being. In a 1988 statement, then Pawnee President Lawrence Goodfox Jr. expressed a common perspective stressing the negative consequences of grave desecration on our dead: "When our people die and go on to the spirit world, sacred rituals and ceremonies are performed. We believe that if the body is disturbed, the spirit becomes restless and cannot be at peace."

Wandering spirits often beset the living with psychological and health problems. Since time immemorial, Pawnees have ceremoniously buried our dead within Mother Earth. Disinterment can occur only for a compelling religious reason. Equally critical to our perspective are cultural norms that stressed that those who tampered with the dead did so with profane, evil, or demented intentions. From this vantage point, the study of stolen remains constitutes abominable acts of sacrilege, desecration, and depravity. But racist attitudes, complete with such axioms as "The only good Indian is a dead Indian," have long conditioned white society to view Indians (as other non-whites) as intellectually inferior subhumans who lacked a right to equal treatment under legal and moral codes. Complicating matters, value judgments about the alleged superiority of the white race became interlocked with scientific thought, leading to the development of oppressive practices and policies.

Consequently, orgies of grave looting occurred without remorse. After the Pawnees removed from Nebraska to Oklahoma during the 1870s, local settlers, followed by amateur and professional archaeologists, looted virtually every

Pawnee cemetery they could find, taking remains and burial offerings. Much of the "booty" was placed in an array of institutions including the Nebraska State Historical Society (NSHS) and the Smithsonian Institution.

We have a right to be angry at those who dug our dead from the ground, those who established and maintained curatorial policies, and those who denied our repatriation requests. Last year, my elderly grandmother chastised white society in her typically reserved, but direct fashion for its treatment of our dead. After pointing to an Oklahoma bluff where many Pawnee relatives are buried, she declared, "It is not right, that they dug up all of those bodies in Nebraska." What she referred to can be labeled a spiritual holocaust. When anyone denies us our fundamental human rights, we cannot sit idly by and wait for America to reform itself. It will never happen. We have a duty not only to ourselves, but also to our relatives, our unborn generations, and our ancestors to act. Concerning repatriation, we had no choice but to work for retrieval of our ancestral remains for proper reburial and for legislation that provided penalties for those who disrupted the graves of our relatives.

Yet our initiatives sought redress in a peaceful manner. In 1988, Lawrence Goodfox expressed our goals, declaring "All we want is [the] reburial of the remains of our ancestors and to let them finally rest in peace and for all people in Nebraska to refrain from, forever, any excavation of any Native American graves or burial sites." In our view, reburying the disturbed spirits within Mother Earth equalizes the imbalance between the spiritual and physical worlds caused by the desecration.

4. Kai'opua Fyfe Opposes Federal Recognition of Kanaka Maoli (Native Hawaiians), 2000

Aloha, greetings to the Hawaii Congressional Delegation and members and staff of the Senate Committee on Indian Affairs and the House Resource Commitee....

To preface my remarks [concerning Native Hawaiian federal recognition], I cite what has become my personal self-determination mantra,

First thing, Na kanaka Hawai'i maoli must achieve unity of purpose; from there the sky is the limit.

That being said, I must inform you that I cannot support [federal recognition.]

These measures were drafted and submitted to Congress without incorporation of the manao of Kanaka Maoli. These measures were drafted and submitted to Congress prior to the achievement of that absolutely mandatory "unity of purpose."

Basically, [federal recognition] is not pono, [it is] not appropriate, and ... not grounded in any way in the manao of the Na kanaka Hawaii maoli. Instead, [it is] grounded in the environment of fear and greed that runs rampant today. Fear of the loss of Federal funding for native Hawaiian programs. Greed for the

---

"Native Hawaiian Federal Recognition," Senate Hearing 106–753, Part 1 (August 28, 2000).

anticipated riches to be gained as a result of Federal recognition as indigenous native Americans.

If we only like money, short-term, these measures are the way. If we like long-term open options for self-determination based on that pono "unity of purpose," we must oppose them.

I cannot support [federal recognition].

On July 30, I participated in the development and adoption of a position statement by the executive council of the 'Aha Hawai'i 'Oiwi. It has been officially distributed by mail to all of you. No doubt you will hear numerous references to it throughout the balance of this week's hearings. The following are excerpts from that statement:

The 'Aha Hawai'i 'Oiwi shares the common concern for the protection of the benefits of the native Hawaiian people, but not at the expense of the loss of self-determination as defined under international norms.

With due respect for your efforts, and those of Senator Daniel K. Inouye, and Representative Neil Abercrombie, the 'Aha Hawai'i 'Oiwi cannot support [Senator Daniel Akaka's] recognition bill, ... or the companion measure ... as introduced on July 20, 2000, which measures define the rights of native Hawaiians as synonymous with those of native Americans.

And,

Further, this bill attempts to duplicate and replace the actions of the 'Aha Hawai'i 'Oiwi, an entity duly empowered by twenty two thousand two hundred and ninety four registered Hawaiian voters; thus this bill usurps these taro roots efforts, this native initiative.

Further, I fully support the following manao as expressed by Reidar H.K. Smith, an active delegate to the 'Aha Hawai'i 'Oiwi. He is one of the several delegates who represent the kanaka Hawai'i maoli who reside outside of Hawai'i ka Pae 'Aina.

Reidar says:

One hundred and two years ago the U.S. Congress passed a joint resolution annexing Hawaii as a Territory. Nobody ever bothered to ask the Hawaiian people what they wanted. Some of the leaders of Hawaii at that time thought that being a U.S. Territory would be best for the Hawaiian people. These leaders thought that, like children, Hawaiians weren't ready to decide for themselves or make such an important decision. Our kupuna were never offered the vote to accept or reject that congressional resolution. Yet, their petitions against annexation (still on record) show they would surely have rejected it.

Today the U.S. Congress and some of our leaders in Hawaii are trying to do it again. They propose to recognize us as native Americans to give us indigenous rights and save some entitlements already approved by Congress. What they don't tell us is this may also take away our rights to the ceded lands, shorelines, ocean economic zone, and gathering rights. This bill also diminishes the greatest right of the Hawaiian people, the right of self-determination. Hawaiians have the right to choose between indigenous rights or the right to reestablish our sovereign nation and then choose the type of government for our nation. We even have the right to choose to remain with the status quo.

I oppose this bill as presently written, says Reidar, because it puts the cart ahead of the horse. It determines what rights Hawaiians will receive and then calls for a roll of all Hawaiians who will choose which form of government we want on our reservation. Why not get that roll first so that Hawaiians can make both decisions? This time let the Hawaiian people decide. The 1993 U.S. apology bill asked for reconciliation and offered the next move to the Hawaiian people, not to this Congress. "This bill is deja vu 1898 all over again."

Mahalo a nui loa for your time and consideration.

5. Elouise Cobell (Blackfeet) Describes the History of Land Litigation, 2008

In 1887, the Congress passed what was called the Dawes Act, or the Allotment Act, in which parcels of land that was already owned by Indian tribes were divided up and redistributed to individual Indians, and at that particular point in time, basically, the government, the Secretary of Interior said, "You Indians are all stupid, and you're not able to manage your own funds, so we will manage these funds to the best fiduciary duties." Well, as time went by, of course, that's not what happened. And many individual Indians, for number of years, have continued to ask the questions: Why can we get an accounting of our money? I know we have land, I know we have resources on our land, but what's happening to our money? And there was never any answers.

... I was the treasurer of the Blackfeet Indian tribe for a number of years, and so I saw many of the elderly people coming to me, asking, "Can you help us? Can you help us? Can you write letters for us? We're not getting our money. We need food for our families. We need medical attention for our families, but we can't get our money from the government, from the Indian agent." And I continued to write letters for individual Indian people, because I felt that they were totally underrepresented. They didn't have the education and the know-how to get any answers.

... I began this entire campaign of trying to get answers for individual Indians on what happened to their money and why weren't they getting it. I visited with the administrations, many administrations. I talked to Congress.... I did everything possible. And finally, the only alternative that I could ever — the last alternative, because I've never sued anybody in my entire life, is that I determined the only way that we were going to get justice is to file this class-action lawsuit, and that's what I did in 1996 on behalf of over 500,000 individual Indians.

So, basically this lawsuit is for three simple things — is, one, to give individual Indians — to compel the United States government to fix the accounting systems that are broken, that are broken and are not capable of managing our money for us. The second part of the lawsuit was to give individual Indians an accounting for their money. And the third part of the case was, if there is

---

"Federal Judge Rules US Government Owes Group of Native Americans $455 Million for Unpaid Royalties on Drilling for Oil and Gas," August 12, 2008, Democracy Now! democracynow.org.

restitution due as a result of this accounting, then restitution has to be paid to individual Indian people.

In 1999, we won the first part of the case, which is compelling the United States government to fix the accounting systems, although they have not done that yet, but we won that.

The second part of our case was determined on January the 30th [2008]. Can the government actually do an accounting? And the judge ruled ... that it's impossible for the government to give us an accounting. There's so many things wrong with the systems. And as you mentioned earlier, you know, there are zillions of reports from inspector generals, from the Government Accounting Office, from independent accounting firms, that this is a mess. This is the worst accounting nightmare that anybody had ever seen. And they continue to report all kinds of conditions: fraud — you know, who knows where the money went? ... the money goes into Treasury. The Treasury was using our money for other purposes, such as reducing the national debt. They were absolutely not getting any information from the Department of Interior of where this money—or who owns this money and where this money should be paid to.

In the meantime, ... in our Indian communities, people are living in dire poverty. People that have oil wells pumping in their backyards are not receiving their money. And they don't have homes. They can't send their children to school. And it's a very sad condition. It doesn't take you very long to drive through an Indian community and see all these wonderful resources, but seeing our communities living in dire poverty. And then, after you find out — and what we found out through this lawsuit is the fact that, well, the government was just using our money to reduce the national debt, because the inept Department of Interior was not sending information to the Treasury so that they could draw the checks to the right people.

So, the third part of the case is what we just finished up in June, the trial that we just finished up, which is basically the monetary recovery. OK, as a result of — since the accounting is impossible, what is owed individual Indians?

6. Steve Russell (Cherokee) Argues for a Hemispheric Indigenous Identity, 2010

Republican Gov. Jan Brewer has just signed a law that empowers, or, I should say, requires Arizona police officers to stop anybody they suspect may be an undocumented person and demand papers. For people insufficiently light complexioned, it will be like the old Soviet Union, where internal passports were required for travel. In my formative years, during the Cold War, I thought the freedom to travel from one end of the continent to the other without having some bureaucrat demanding "papers" distinguished the Free World.

Then I learned about the Indian nations whose homelands cross the United States and Canada border, who retain the right to cross under the Jay Treaty.

Steve Russell, "Don't Visit Arizona Without Your Papers," *Indian Country Today*, April 2010; Steve Russell, "Raising Arizona for Brown People," *Indian Country Today*, May 2010. Reprinted with permission from the author.

The Indian nations whose homelands cross the U.S. and Mexico border are not as well-fixed. The best legal argument they have is by implication in the Treaty of Guadalupe-Hidalgo, but they have historically managed to live in peace because deserts and sparse population made the border fairly insignificant in the days before drug smugglers and terrorists.....

If I am forced to visit Arizona while this license to harass brown people is in effect, I shall have to as a matter of principle speak only Spanish to police officers. Having spent the last 10 years in the Midwest, my Spanish needs a lot of brushing up. I presume that if I get arrested they will find my white card [Certificate of Degree of Indian Blood] and my blue card [Cherokee National Registry] at the booking desk and decide that I'm a U.S. citizen.

However, that presumes they know the geographical location of the Cherokee Nation and they know that Indians were declared to be U.S. citizens by Congress in 1924. While I've heard some Indians complain about that declaration, my understanding of the context is that Indians were drafted to serve in the U.S. military in World War I but were not allowed to vote. The Indian Citizenship Act, of course, did not resolve the voting rights of Indians because the states still resisted.

This digression about citizenship and the right to vote circles back to Arizona. It's commonly known that Indians in Arizona finally got the right to vote in an Arizona Supreme Court decision in 1948, the lawsuit having been brought by Frank Harrison, Yavapai. It's less commonly known that Harrison had attempted to register before serving in World War II and was denied.

The privileges of citizenship were slow to come for Indians while the responsibilities came right away. It's hard not to think of the island-hopping campaign in the Pacific, some of the toughest combat of WWII. The Navajo code talkers served through that campaign at a time when Arizona was still denying them the vote. Now, it appears that Arizona Indians who visit the cities will have to be careful about being brown in a no-brown zone, whether or not they are veterans.

It would be hilarious watching Gov. Brewer claim that this law can be enforced without racial profiling if I had fewer relatives who could get profiled. Make no mistake: This law is not aimed at Europeans without papers, even though by its plain words a German tourist could be locked up for leaving her Phoenix hotel without her passport. This law is aimed at Mexicans and the blood of Mexicans is primarily American Indian....

... [A] Tohono O'odham person in Sacaton or a Navajo person in Chinle will have little to fear. In a small town, you are known to be who you are. However, you take your chances in Phoenix or Tucson. I wonder how the enforcement will go around the spectacular national parks in Arizona that drew visitors from all over the world? ...

Several people took umbrage at my passing statement that the blood of Mexicans is primarily "American Indian." [They were] right in that this detracted from my main point.

I must first observe that Mexico is in America.

Then the question becomes the ratio of *Indio* to *Hispano*. Did you think the conquistadores brought their wives? Most of the literature puts the ratio at

80/20, and you have to realize this is in the context of pervasive color prejudice, giving persons of *Indio* blood strong reasons to deny it as soon as it became deniable by a combination of distance and color. So the records would tend to understate mixed blood Indians trying to avoid discrimination and full blood Indians avoiding being counted entirely. We can say a lot of bad things about the Spanish, but they kept excellent records compared to the U.S.

The marriage records I've seen from Spanish colonial times list Indians not by "race" but by tribe.

Leaving aside written evidence, my time working with the United Farm Workers tells me that many agricultural workers (those workers of lowest status) who come from Mexico do not speak Spanish but rather their native languages. My work with the Kickapoo Traditional Tribe of Texas brought me into contact with individuals for whom English was their third language, after *Kikapú* and Spanish.

Most Mexicans are Indians, folks. They may deny it and we may deny it but that's the fact. They are the offspring of the Natives and the colonists and, unlike in the U.S., the colonists were a tiny minority in the gene pool.

7. Charlene Teters (Spokane) Asks "Whose History Do We Celebrate?" 1998

"We took the liberty of removing Don Juan de Oñate's right foot on behalf of our brothers and sisters at Acoma Pueblo."

—*Anonymous letter to the* Albuquerque Journal, *Jan. 8, 1998*

This year marks the Cuartocentenario, the 400th anniversary of the incursion of the Spanish conquistador Don Juan de Oñate from Mexico into what is now Texas, Arizona, and New Mexico. Recently, however, New Mexicans on the verge of a year-long series of celebrations were shocked by the action of an unidentified group whose members sawed off the right foot of a bronze statue of Oñate in the Española Valley north of Santa Fe.

New Mexico, home to one of the largest contemporary American Indian populations, was quickly reminded that Indian people are still here—and that we are not always docile. The disfiguring of the statue also resulted in a quick and powerful history lesson for mainstream America. One of many brutal truths selectively omitted from most history books is this: in 1599, Oñate attacked Acoma Pueblo in retaliation for the death of his nephew, ordering that the right feet of all men in the pueblo above the age of 25 be chopped off.

History is very powerful. The manner in which it is presented has the ability to inspire or deflate, to move nations to love, joy, anger, or hatred. The vast majority of Americans know very little about how this continent—originally peopled by thousands of diverse Indian nations—came to be what is now the United States. This ignorance serves to perpetuate the doctrine of Manifest

Reprinted with permission from *Indian Artist*, Summer 1998, Vol. IV, No. 3, pp. 14–15. Copyright © 1998 Indian Artist, Inc.

Destiny, the supposedly inevitable conquest of North America and the islands of the Pacific and the Caribbean. Twenty-five years ago, from Wounded Knee, South Dakota, the American Indian Movement decried the absence of American Indian history in the nation's classrooms. Even today, many remain willfully ignorant of it.

I embrace the concept of personal destiny. I am a survivor, not a victim. And yet during my public school experience, the presentation of American history deeply influenced my self-esteem, as it did for many Native children. I remember trying to become invisible as teachers told stories of brave settlers, untamed lands, and savage, uncivilized Indians. Washington State history simply did not include American Indian history. To this day, it remains largely ignored or distorted in most American schools.

While growing up in Washington State, I also felt the impact of a powerful mural portraying the explorers Lewis and Clark pointing to the western horizon in the direction of my homeland in Washington State. That same mural depicts Indians and other people of color bowed in an all-too-typical posture of servitude before the two glorified travelers. The caption beneath it reads, "The first civilized men to look upon the Inland Empire."

Now, many year later, I still feel the sting of ethnocentric propaganda in public art. As an artist, I know the power of art used to reinforce heroes, icons, and political ideology. All across the United States, bronze statues, monuments, and murals celebrate conquests and commemorate the fulfillment of Manifest Destiny.

Art also has a history of effective use in social activism. As the nation celebrates numerous anniversaries—the Quincentennial of Columbus's landing in America, the Oklahoma Land Rush, the California Gold Rush, and the Cuartocentenario—the question is: how do we Indians find appropriate ways to mark these events in our collective history? How do we reconcile that some of America's heroes are not *our* heroes? Glorifying Indian killers feels to us like glorifying Hitler.

Cutting the foot off the Oñate statue in the face of public celebrations forces the issue that there is another side to the notion of conquest. Native artists have often used art to express their own reactions to historical events. But such expression often appears in subversive forms, as our dissenting voices are still largely unwelcome in such national festivities.

Another dissenting voice is Edgar Heap of Birds, a Cheyenne-Arapaho conceptual artist, who responded to Oklahoma's 1989 Land Rush celebrations with a series of five billboards that spelled out the words, "RUN OVER INDIAN NATIONS, APARTHEID OKLAHOMA." Like the sawing off of Oñate's foot, Heap of Birds's caustic message didn't stand in the way of reenactments, parades, and speeches, but it gave voice to a strong and widespread sentiment that was missing in the state-sanctioned celebrations.

Art also provides more mainstream ways of expressing dissent. In a break from tradition this year, the Oakland Museum in California is presenting a series of programs giving expression to California's untold stories. With the museum's blessing, Maidu artist Harry Fonseca has created a body of work entitled *The Discovery of Gold in California*, which explores the impact of the Gold rush on

California's Indian population. Similarly, the American Indian House Gallery in New York City is planning a summer exhibition that will express two histories simultaneously: that of the Indians and that of the colonizers.

These two exhibitions are steps in the right direction, because our history is very different from that of the colonizers. For Indians to celebrate many events in American history requires either that we have historical amnesia or that we grant amnesty for the atrocities committed on our populations. The cost of either of these alternatives is too great to pay. It is time we all began acknowledging a more balanced history than that provided by schoolbooks and supermarket tabloids. Together, let us find more ways to honor the victims and survivors of the legacy of conquest, who are also American citizens.

◈ ESSAYS

Two issues have been of particular concern to Native nations at the start of the twenty-first century. First, Native nations have faced continued efforts to limit their sovereignty. In the first essay, Eileen Luna-Firebaugh (Cherokee and Choctaw), a professor of American Indian Studies at the University of Arizona, explores the many ways in which Native nations have asserted their sovereignty across the international borders of Canada and Mexico. How have Native nations pushed for sovereign rights over international borders? How successful have these efforts been? A second issue for Native nations in the twenty-first century has been economic development. In the second essay, Nicolas Rosenthal, a professor of history at Loyola Marymount University, describes how gaming has empowered and enriched Native nations of southern California and identifies some of gaming's potential pitfalls. How does gaming in southern California compare with that in Alabama (Document 1)?

The Border Crossed Us: Identity and
Sovereignty on the Borders of Indian Country

BY EILEEN LUNA-FIREBAUGH (CHEROKEE AND CHOCTAW)

For many years, the Tohono O'odham Nation in Arizona has transported tribal members from Mexico to the United States through traditional border crossings for medical treatment. The nation is the only one in the United States that grants full enrollment to its people who are citizens of Mexico. Thus, Mexican citizens who are enrolled members are legally entitled to access health and other services provided by the tribe to all its members.

Since the recent militarization of the U.S.–Mexico border, these routine visits have become more rare and more dangerous. Frequently now, the tribal

Eileen Luna-Firebaugh (Choctaw-Cherokee), "The Border Crossed Us: Border Crossing Issues of the Indigenous Peoples of North America," *Wicazo Sa Review* 17:1 (2002): 159–81. Reprinted with permission of the author and the University of Minnesota Press.

employees who provide the transportation for Mexican O'odham Nation members have been stopped and harassed by U.S. Border Patrol agents. These agents, operating on the lands of the O'odham Nation, have made the nation's elders and others who suffer from tuberculosis, diabetes, and other life-threatening diseases return to Mexico if they lack U.S. documents. This insistence on official U.S. documentation, rather than recognizing Tohono O'odham Nation membership identification, strikes at the heart of Indian sovereignty....

While traditionally it is common for nation-states such as Canada, the United States, and Mexico to protect their borders, the requirement that official documentation be proffered for simple, short-term visits has not been required for most citizens of the North American continent.... However, with the hysteria that has resulted from the "Drug War" and the widespread fear of "illegal immigrants," the United States has militarized its northern and southern borders. This militarization has resulted in inconvenience for all border crossers, but has made border crossing by the continent's indigenous extremely problematic.

Enhanced and restrictive border crossing procedures are an assault on indigenous sovereignty as well as an assault on the cultural integrity of native societies. The laws of Canada, the United States, and Mexico restrict contacts between the indigenous as citizens of their nations, and as members of families, clans, and religious groups that predate the colonization of the North American continent. The new laws (and regulations) also increase the level of danger for the indigenous. Those who continue to use traditional border crossing areas are in danger of being shot by U.S. Border Patrol personnel, U.S. military, or vigilante citizen groups. For a young Texas shepherd named Ezequiel, U.S. military personnel who opened fire while he tended his goatherd along the Texas-Mexico border cut life short. His death, and the deaths of others, is a result of the increased militarization of the U.S.-Mexico border.

The treaties and agreements that set the international boundaries between the nation-states of the North American continent were negotiated and signed *only* by the colonizers. The indigenous of these border regions, whose lands these borders transect, were not consulted, nor were they signatories to any treaty or agreement. This stands in clear opposition to their rights as nations who were, at that time, fully sovereign, and whose status as sovereign was recognized in later treaties between them and the colonizers. In addition, the fact that some indigenous nations are mentioned in the colonizers' treaties and some are not, or that some indigenous nations later negotiated separate treaties or agreements to protect their right to access their traditional lands on either side of the borders, has contributed to a patchwork approach to border crossing rights. While in some cases treaties or agreements have largely resolved the problem for some indigenous groups, the general failure of the colonizing governments to allow indigenous input into the resolution of border issues has furthered the assault on the sovereignty of indigenous nations of the North American continent.

The laws that require declaration of citizenship or official documents issued by the colonizing powers are a denigration of the nationhood of indigenous peoples. A declaration of citizenship in the Tohono O'odham, Mohawk, Blackfeet, Yaqui, Kickapoo, Cocopah, Kumeyaay, or other indigenous nations, in response

to a question asked by border officials, often results in extended delay and intensive interrogation. Thus all but the most committed indigenous activist is forced
to simply respond "U.S.," "Mexico," or "Canada" to a request for identifying
citizenship.

The assertion of the right to cross the international border without undue
delay is a long-standing problem. The indigenous nations of the Americas have
attempted to resolve this problem through treaties, legislation, negotiations, and/
or direct action. The problem has different parameters on the northern and
southern borders of the United States, largely due to historical legacies. The legislative approach has had varying levels of success, with failure often a result of
federal action or lack thereof, and sometimes attributable to tribal inaction or
disagreement. Negotiation and direct action have been effective in some ways,
particularly in focusing attention on legal, cultural, and historical inequities,
although they result in limited agreements affecting indigenous nations on a
piecemeal basis. These approaches have focused attention on the inequities.
The development of a concerted approach by indigenous nations and peoples is
necessary if the problem is to be finally resolved.

The indigenous nations of the North American continent have been pursuing different avenues. For some, enhanced activism is reaching a boiling point.
Other indigenous peoples are asserting the rights of their citizens and of their
nations in a formalized, legalistic manner. The manner in which these assertions
of rights may best proceed needs to be considered. The critical question is
whether it is proper for nation-states to deny indigenous peoples access to their
traditional sites, regardless of which side of an international border they are on,
or to restrict their family contacts or the continuance of their religions and cultures. These issues for the indigenous of the North American continent must be
addressed if indigenous cultures and traditions are to survive....

Prior to the setting of the U.S. borders with Canada and Mexico, indigenous peoples had traditional territories with boundaries that were recognized
and honored by their neighbors. Villages and other types of settlements existed
where water, agricultural possibilities, and trade made the location reasonable.
When, however, the international borders were drawn up, little if any regard
was given to the separation of native villages, and native nations were not consulted. The lines imposed by the colonizers ignored traditional hunting lands,
areas of resource procurement, and religious sites....

The fiction of new boundary lines extended even to the renaming of the
indigenous peoples; for example, the Blackfeet in the United States were
named the Blood in Canada. The lines also created division and divisiveness.
While the Blackfeet were originally one people, this artificial division began to
erode their self-identity, and they have come to see themselves as separate peoples. The colonizing nations afforded their indigenous groups different rights,
which caused further erosion in the continuity of tradition and peoplehood,
and also led to factionalism. Indigenous groups have resisted this separation of
peoples and have continued their struggle to remain cohesive.

The experiences of some indigenous peoples split by the borders were very
different from the Blackfeet. For some the cultural ties of the people were

maintained. For others the ties were severed, the impacts on the culture and traditions were horrific, and there were economic consequences. We will examine these experiences and the ways in which some of these nations have tried to resist the assertions of authority by colonizing powers.

The United States and England signed over twenty treaties to delineate the northern border. Rights of the indigenous are mentioned in two, the Treaty of Amity, Commerce, and Navigation of 1794 (otherwise known as the Jay Treaty) and the 1814 Treaty of Peace and Amity (also known as the Treaty of Ghent). The Jay Treaty establishes the right of free passage across the border to Indians dwelling on either side of the border, by either land or inland navigation, into the territories of either Canada or the United States, to navigate all the lakes, rivers, and waters of each country, and to freely engage in trade or commerce with other indigenous nations. No custom duties are to be assessed against the personal property of any Indian exercising their right to cross. The Treaty of Ghent restored the rights set forth in the Jay Treaty, which had eroded due to the War of 1812.

The United States and Canada treat the Jay Treaty differently, the Canadian government recognizes the rights for Indians per se, and the United States interprets the rights within a political context. The rights and the specific meaning and application of the provisions of the treaty have been addressed and readdressed in the courts of these two nations in a number of legal cases. There has also been legislation that has established restrictions of the rights set forth in the treaty.

Subsequent to the Treaty of Ghent, and prior to 1924, Canadian Indians were allowed free passage into the United States without the production of immigrant visas. However, political winds shifted in the United States during the 1920s, and with the passage of the 1924 Immigration and Naturalization Act, aliens (including Canadian Indians) who were ineligible for citizenship were not permitted as immigrants. This legislation, coupled with the Citizenship Act of 1924, which awarded U.S. citizenship to all Indians born within the boundaries of the United States, was interpreted to mean that Canadian Indians could no longer cross the U.S. border freely, despite the rights guaranteed in the Jay Treaty and the Treaty of Ghent.

The reaffirmation of Jay Treaty rights began again with the U.S. Supreme Court ruling in *U.S. ex rel. Diabo v. McCandless*. In *Diabo,* the plaintiff, a Canadian Mohawk, challenged his deportation under the 1924 Immigration Act, citing the Jay Treaty's guarantees. The court held that the right of free passage in traditional indigenous homelands is an inherent aboriginal right, even where an international border has been created subsequently. In language that emphasized the Court's holding, the Court stated:

> [T]he rights of Indians [are not] in any way affected by the treaty,
> whether now existent or not. The reference to them was merely the
> *recognition* of their right, which was wholly unaffected by the treaty,
> except that the contracting parties agreed with each other that each
> would recognize it.... From the Indian['s] viewpoint, he crosses no
> boundary line. For him, this [boundary line] does not exist.

This right of free passage for indigenous peoples on the northern border was then codified in changes to the Immigration and Nationality Act. However, later amendments to this act further restricted free passage rights. The 1952 act, perhaps reflecting the assimilation and termination era of the time, restricted free passage to those Indians who met a 50 percent blood quantum requirement. This has gradually been changed, perhaps as a result of the era of self-governance, to now allow free passage to any Indian who possesses a tribal membership identification card.

The treaties that exist between Canada and the United States, with regard to the border crossing rights of affected indigenous, have been tested far more often than those treaties that exist between the governments of Mexico and the United States. While the issues for the U.S.-Mexico border may appear to be less complex, that is an illusion. There is only one treaty, with the Kickapoo Tribe of Texas, that deals with the right of passage for the U.S.-Mexico border. The rest of the border area and the indigenous nations of this region are without any guidelines set forth in treaties or legislation. The result is chaos, a patchwork of executive and administrative agreements, and failed legislation that is difficult to understand or resolve.

In the southern border area, traditional indigenous homelands became subject to Spanish colonialism, then in 1821, as a result of Mexico's independence, they came under the authority of the Mexican government. Although the traditional homelands were recognized, the indigenous peoples were considered citizens of Mexico. No tribal sovereignty was considered or honored. Most of the homelands in Sonora and Chihuahua were then lost, largely through the policy that Mexican citizens were required to apply for land grants. The indigenous, probably due to their geographic remoteness, inability to speak Spanish, and migratory nature, either failed to receive notice of the land grant process or had no knowledge of it.

The Treaty of Guadalupe-Hidalgo in 1848 split part of the lands off from Mexico. It required that the United States honor the land grants extended by the Mexican government and covered the lands of the Rio Grande, from the Gulf of Mexico to the Pacific. The long-settled Pueblos of New Mexico had received land grant homelands. However, no land grants were created for the Yuman, Apache, O'odham, Kumeyaay, or other indigenous peoples of the region who did not live in villages. The new border split the traditional homelands of these indigenous peoples, and they were left without any right of free passage.

While the histories of the northern and southern borders are distinct, indigenous peoples experienced problems in common: economic, cultural, and demographic. These problems are the result of the impact of colonialism/imperialism on peoples and culture, their historic resettlement patterns, migration patterns, individual lives, and on the individual and cultural responses to colonialism. The indigenous communities were seriously affected by the creation of international borders. Dislocation, encroachment on the land, loss of traditional homesteads, inability to control and traverse over traditional lands, colonization, loss of mobility and traditional contacts became the norm. Conflict between indigenous and colonial governments became entrenched. Over time, as many Indian peoples began to think of themselves as Canadian, Mexican, or American first and indigenous second, the traditional relationships among relatives eroded, and distinctions were perceived.

The individual experiences that some groups of indigenous peoples faced illuminate the situation for most, if not all, of the peoples of the border regions.

The nations chosen for this article are ones that have been politically or legally involved in this issue and have undertaken direct action and/or legal and legislative attempts at resolution.

Members of the Blackfeet Confederacy were split by the creation of the U.S.-Canada border. Six bands were on the Canadian side and only one within the boundaries of the United States. While there were few problems with regard to retaining the right to cross the border at will, most obstacles relate to the import and export of certain tariff-free goods, native traditions, and religious ceremonies. Blackfeet ceremonies are commonly conducted with participants from all bands from both sides of the border and require the use of special ritual paraphernalia. According to their tradition, only men are allowed to touch the sacred bundles used in the ceremonies. When ceremonial bundles are carried across the border, this tradition has sometimes been violated by female customs officers.

In order to resolve the problem of import-export regulations and inspection, in the 1980s the Blood Tribe established a border committee, composed of band members, to negotiate for the passage of legislation in Canada. To date, this effort has been unsuccessful. The efforts have also included a call by confederacy leaders from both sides of the border for an Indian-only border crossing between Alberta and Montana. These initiatives are ongoing at this time.

The land of the Mohawk of the Saint Regis Indian Nation is split between New York State and Quebec. Even though the Mohawk utilized these lands traditionally, the Canadian government has taken the position in court cases that they moved into Canada subsequent to the Jay Treaty. The Canadian government has thus contended that the Mohawk may not avail themselves of the protections granted by the treaty.

The Mohawk Indian Nation has no official U.S. customs crossing. Mohawks have generally taken direct action by crossing their traditional lands at will and disregarding the imposed borderline. They have taken the position that the Mohawk Nation is sovereign and undivided. Since 1815, they have asserted that the border is largely irrelevant, a notion that was not functionally opposed nor directly challenged by the nation-states.

Prior to the militarization of the U.S. border in the 1990s, citizens of the Mohawk Nation had full access to all Mohawk land whether those lands were within the territories of Canada or the United States. The Oka crisis in March 1990 inflamed a situation that was already intense. The U.S. Immigration and Naturalization Service (INS) has repeatedly entered Mohawk lands in pursuit of undocumented aliens and those who smuggle them across the U.S.-Canada border. This intrusion into Mohawk lands continues to date and is as yet unresolved.

The Mohawks have also asserted their rights under the Jay Treaty to take personal goods across the border without payment of customs duties. They have engaged in the transportation of cigarettes for sale, without payment of tax, and in the transportation of immigrants in noncompliance with the immigration laws of the United States. This upping of the economic ante by the Mohawk resulted in the heightened enforcement and legal response by the nation-states in the 1990s. From this case, it appears that the nation-states are unconcerned about indigenous peoples until economic interests are at stake.

In 1848, subsequent to the U.S. war with Mexico, the Treaty of Guadalupe-Hidalgo was signed. This treaty ceded the land south of the Gila River to Mexico, thus locating all O'odham land in Mexico. This became a problem for the United States when it decided that a southern rail route to California was needed. As a result, in 1853 the United States purchased almost 30,000 acres in Mexico. The Gadsden Purchase included approximately half of the Tohono O'odham traditional home-lands. The rest remained in Sonora, Mexico. This division of the O'odham lands resulted in a border area that is longer than that of the state of New Mexico and Chihuahua.

The effect was devastating for Mexican O'odham people and their culture. Contacts between families were severed and the political history and government structure diverged sharply. The land base of the Mexican O'odham was eroded, and religious and cultural connections to land on both sides of the border were lost to those on the other side.

In order to rectify this situation, the Tohono O'odham adopted and enrolled the Mexican members in the tribe. The Mexican O'odham vote in tribal elections and receive services provided in the U.S. O'odham health clinic. The O'odham maintain an unofficial border crossing on tribal lands that, while known to U.S. Customs, is not regulated by the U.S. government.

The culture, history, and traditions of the Cocopah are inextricably linked to the Colorado River. They were a seminomadic people who farmed in the floodplain of the river, with villages extending into what are now California, Arizona, Sonora, and Baja California. Those Cocopah who found themselves on the northern side of the U.S.-Mexico border were able to retain their lands, while those on the southern side lost control of their lands and were forced to live within the encomienda system.

Cocopah communities and clans were first split by the Gadsden Purchase, with the majority in Mexico and a small group in the United States. The border originally meant little, and the Cocopah moved freely along the river. However, in the late 1930s, the INS cracked down on this free passage and effectively split the people into two nation-alities. After the crackdown, the Cocopah developed an unofficial agreement with the INS that allowed for freedom of passage of Mexican Cocopah into the United States.

The Cocopah were impacted by heightened border crossing controls earlier than other border tribes, possibly because their land is adjacent to a primary river-crossing area. Control of the water of the Colorado was crucial for the United States, particularly during the 1930s when there was rampant agricultural and residential development of Southern California. Thus, due to the accident of geographical location, the Cocopah were seriously affected at a much earlier date than other indigenous nations along the borders.

Due to historic migration patterns, some tribes experience border crossing problems even if the border did not split their traditional lands. The Yaqui, or Yoeme, were one such affected people.

The Yaqui were originally centered in the Yaqui River valley near Guaymas in Sonora with a culture that focused on agriculture. The Yaqui were traders and traveled throughout northern Sonora and southern Arizona. After contact the Yaqui entered into an alliance with the Spanish Jesuits and soldiers against the Apache. This alliance did not ease the relationship between the Yaqui and the new state of Mexico, however. During the late 1800s Mexican expansion forced the relocation of many bands of Yaqui and scattered the people across Mexico and into the United States. Others were pushed into the mountains where they waged a guerrilla war against hacienda families and the Mexican military. Some Yaqui relocated to Arizona, settling in and around Tucson and Phoenix. Cultural and religious ties between the villages and bands on both sides of the border continued, however, even in the face of great difficulty.

The ability to conduct ceremonies is essential for the lands to truly become and remain a homeland. For some ceremonies to be held, it is necessary for participants to travel from one nation-state to the other. The increased militarization of the southern border of the United States has resulted in travel restrictions and cultural and religious disruption.

The Kickapoo originated in the Great Lakes region and moved from place to place as a result of broken land treaties and a desire to resist the forces of colonization. Some Kickapoo were forced to live in Kansas and Oklahoma, while others fled to Mexico in the 1800s.

In 1832 U.S. Army officials granted tribal members in Mexico the "right of safe conduct" to cross the border into the United States. An 1850 land agreement between the Mexican government and the Kickapoo south of the border granted tribal members the same rights as Mexican citizens and a small reservation in Coahuila. This arrangement has continued to this day. Legislation during the 1990s guaranteed rights of passage for Mexican Kickapoo.

During the 1940s the Mexican Kickapoo were forced to relocate again. Due to a protracted drought and rapid industrialization in the area of their reservation, Mexican Kickapoos began to work in the United States as migrant laborers. Their right to cross the border encouraged their hire through the Bracero program. Many worked in the agricultural fields of the United States during the harvest season and returned home to their reservation during the winter.

The Kumeyaay reside in scattered villages in Baja California and in rancherias and reservations in Southern California. The Kumeyaay traditionally were coastal people, living along the Pacific Ocean. They were ultimately forced inland into eastern San Diego County and further into Mexico.

Until 1993 Kumeyaay routinely crossed from their homes in Baja California into San Diego County, using inexpensive border crossing cards that they obtained from the Instituto Nacional Indigenista (INI), the Mexican counterpart of the Bureau of Indian Affairs (BIA). Unfortunately, the U.S. Border Patrol apprehended non-Kumeyaay using these passes and subsequently refused to accept them, forcing Kumeyaay to obtain Mexican passports for border crossing. The cost of the passports, and the inability of many Kumeyaay to provide the necessary documentation to obtain them, has resulted in a severe restriction of the ability of the Kumeyaay to cross the border.

In their attempts to continue or reestablish the traditional religious, cultural, and social connections with their relatives across the borders of the nation-states, indigenous individuals have faced a number of obstacles. In turn, they have established several means to overcome the nation-state-imposed barriers. Over the years, many indigenous peoples have simply ignored the legalisms of border crossing. Informal crossing gates were opened on tribal land and were generally used by indigenous peoples for tribal purposes. However, the recent increased militarization of the border region by the INS, Border Patrol, and U.S. Customs agents cracking down on undocumented aliens and the drug trade has closed many traditional crossing areas. Along the southern border of the United States, many agents are unaware of the inhabitants' ancient migratory ways and customary rights. They have disrupted long-held understandings of the right of mobility throughout traditional indigenous homelands.

Southwest tribal governments have become concerned about the effects related to this increased border militarization, including stopping, searching, and in some cases the forced return to Mexico of tribal members. In San Diego County, for example, U.S. Border Patrol agents have subjected the Kumeyaay to repeated stops and detentions. This is unacceptable and has resulted in discriminatory behavior. As Mike Connolly, Campo Reservation director of environmental programs stated, "This is our land, and we've been here for thousands of years. It's tough when you're being stopped all the time and asked if you really belong there." Tribes have also been concerned about degradation of tribal land by federal officials, cutting of roads into sensitive and/or sacred lands, and high-speed pursuits over tribal roads, some of which are unpaved, activities that endanger tribal members and livestock.

Indigenous organizations, including the Indian Defense League of America, have taken a confrontational approach to border agents' activities. Members of this organization have, for seventy-one years, organized annual protests along the U.S.-Canada border. Tribal members from the Iroquois Confederacy engage in direct action, making commemorative crossings of the international border at various sites.

Tribal governments have attempted to resolve these issues through meetings and conciliations, which to date have not shown much success. Federal officials have not indicated full support of tribal sovereignty, particularly if it would require seriously addressing tribal concerns. Federal officials have generally responded to the concerns as if they were being communicated by a local government rather than by a sovereign nation. This denies each nation their rights to conduct international relations. Meanwhile Indian peoples on both sides of both U.S. borders have had their routine contacts and social interactions restricted, and border crossing for tribal ceremonies, funerals, and other gatherings have been made much more difficult.

Congressional approaches to resolution of the issues facing the tribes on the southwest border have been spotty at best. The success of the legislative approach depends on the willingness of the federal governments to seriously address the problem, the willingness of the individual tribes to pursue a legislative strategy, and the cooperation of governmental agencies to abide by agreements. For some tribes, the legislative approach has worked well. Legal rights have been established and protected. For others, the approach has been problematic. Legislators have been unwilling to support indigenous rights, or the tribes have faltered in their attempts to convince their own people or legislators of the wisdom of such a strategy.

The legislative strategy has served the Kickapoo well. During the 1950s the INS granted parole status to the Kickapoo, pursuant to the Immigration and Nationality Act of 1952. Parole status allowed tribal members to cross the border freely with tribal identification cards, however, the cards had to be renewed every year and did not grant them permanent rights to cross the border.

In 1983, the Texas Band of Kickapoo Act was passed, which mandated that tribal membership cards would be sufficient for border passage. It further included that the tribe would be a party to the decision about identification requirements. A tribal roll was established, and members on the roll had five years to apply for U.S. citizenship. Once citizenship was granted, a permanent border crossing card was issued. The Kickapoo who were not U.S. citizens received all citizenship rights other than the right to vote and to hold public office.

The act clarified citizenship for members of the band. However, it did not alter their land status or other rights in Mexico. The act makes band members eligible for Indian services and programs, and provides for consent and cooperation with Mexican officials to ensure the provision of appropriate services for the band. The Texas Band of Kickapoo and a separate Kickapoo tribe are now seeking to expand the rights provided for in the act to tribal members who live in the United States but travel to Mexico each winter for traditional ceremonies.

The Tohono O'odham Nation has pursued legislation for a number of years. In 1987 a bill was introduced by Morris Udall (D. Arizona) to clarify the right of free passage for members of the Tohono O'odham Nation. The bill provided for the establishment of a tribal roll, and it would have empowered all those on the roll to pass freely across the U.S.-Mexico border and to live and work in the United States. The Reagan administration had serious misgivings about this bill, however. They wanted border crossing privileges extended only to U.S.-residing tribal members and a restriction of the services that would be provided to Mexican O'odham while in the United States. The tribe agreed to compromise on these two clauses. A third clause became the sticking point. The federal government wanted the O'odham to cross only at official border crossings. For the O'odham this was absolutely unacceptable.

While the crossing at official federal crossing points had not been a problem for the Kickapoo, for the O'odham it was an attack on who they were as a people and as a sovereign nation. The Kickapoo had been in the border area for approximately 150 years, a relatively short time for indigenous inhabitants. The requirement that they pass through at an official crossing was not a cultural or traditional assault. On the other hand, the O'odham had been in the area since time immemorial. They had ancient migratory routes and settlement sites that were still important culturally. The tribe was unwilling to give up these traditional crossing places on tribal land. When this could not be resolved, the tribe requested that the sponsor of the bill pull it from consideration. This assertion of tribal sovereignty and commitment to tradition has become a signpost of the struggle for the O'odham.

In 1998, the Tohono O'odham pursued legislative relief for a second time. The bill, sponsored by Ed Pastor, addressed many of the issues left unresolved in the previous legislative attempt. It included the right of passage at any gate on traditional indigenous lands; allowed the tribe to monitor these traditional gates; directed that federal officials ensure that their practices do not conflict with religious rights, customs, or traditions of the O'odham; required that federal officials negotiate with the tribe over policies and procedures to be followed on tribal lands; and held federal officials liable for damages under

42 U.S.C. 1983 and 1988 for violation of the right of free passage for the indigenous. This bill also suggested an amendment to Title 8 U.S.C. Sec. 1359, adding indigenous peoples on the southern border to those on the northern border who have the legal right to free passage subsequent to the Jay Treaty.

This bill did not become law. The Mexican and U.S. governments failed to support it due to concerns regarding the traditional ports of entry. The Tohono O'odham also had misgivings, particularly related to the treatment of nation members as immigrant aliens if their residence was in Mexico. These and other concerns caused interest to lapse, resulting in the decision of Congressman Pastor not to pursue this legislative bill further.

The Tohono O'odham Nation has written and Congress is now considering the proposal of a new piece of legislation that will not raise the same issues of concern as the last. This bill would amend Chapter 2 of Title III of the Immigration and Nationality Act (8 U.S.C. 1421 et seq.) to read:

> To render all enrolled members of the Tohono O'odham Nation
> citizens of the United States as of the date of their enrollment and to
> recognize the valid membership credential of the Tohono O'odham
> Nation as the legal equivalent of a certificate of citizenship or a
> state-issued birth certificate for all federal purposes.
>
> Sec. 2. Naturalization for Tohono O'odham
>
> Sec. 323(a) Granting of Citizenship. A person who is listed on the
> official membership roll of the Tohono O'odham Nation, a federally
> recognized American Indian Nation located in Arizona, is a citizen of
> the United States as of the date on which such listing occurs.
>
> Sec. 3. treatment of Tribal Membership Credentials. Notwithstanding any other provision of law, the valid membership credential
> issued to a person who is listed on the official membership roll of
> the Tohono O'odham Nation pursuant to the laws of the Tohono
> O'odham Nation shall be considered, for all purposes subject to federal
> law, equivalent to
>
> (1) A certificate of citizenship issued under Section 341(a) of the
> Immigration and Nationality Act (8 U.S.C. 1452(a)) to persons who
> satisfy the requirements of such section; and
>
> (2) A state-issued birth certificate.

The language of this proposed bill explicitly recognizes the inherent sovereignty of the Tohono O'odham and the members of the nation as citizens of the nation. It further establishes that the documents of the nation are all that is necessary for recognition. The bill implicitly pushes back against the incursions of state law into Indian Country, as state-issued documents (such as a birth certificate issued by the state of Arizona) would no longer be required. This would greatly alleviate the problem for many Tohono O'odham, who were born at home during the early years of the twentieth century and do not possess Arizona birth certificates.

Efforts have been made by indigenous peoples to resolve border crossing issues through the process of negotiations. Like legislative efforts, these efforts have met with varying levels of success.

In addition to the new legislative proposal, the Tohono O'odham Nation has initiated a different approach, which attempts to avoid the difficulties inherent in the earlier pieces of legislation. The Tohono O'odham is the only Indian nation on the southern border of the United States that has full enrollment for its members in Mexico. Throughout 1999 and 2000, the nation held public meetings and confidential negotiation sessions with the U.S. and Mexican counsels and the U.S. Immigration Service in an attempt to administratively resolve the border crossing issues for its people.

Through negotiations, the U.S. and Mexican government agencies agreed to accept a birth or baptismal certificate or an identification document issued by the Tohono O'odham in lieu of the normally stringent paperwork required to cross the U.S.-Mexico border. Citizens of the nation who should be given priority for border crossing rights due to chronic medical conditions that required them to travel from their homes in Mexico to the nation's health center in the United States were identified, and the necessary paperwork was produced by the nation. Some 104 persons were so identified. By August of 1999, the U.S. Immigration and Naturalization Service had approved 88 of them for American laser visas. The U.S. and Mexican agencies have also agreed to provide visas for the rest of the nation's members residing in Mexico, approximately 1,238 people. One difficulty with this approach is that the nation is forced to shoulder the cost of establishing the identity of these tribal members, projected to be in excess of $100,000.

There is a further issue for many O'odham. Many activists, some of whom are members of the Council of the Nation, reject the idea that citizens of the nation should have to carry tribal identification papers to cross over their own lands. If this should be approved, the O'odham would become the only people in the United States or Mexico who have to do so.

The Yaqui have made efforts to resolve border crossing issues for their people living in Rio Yaqui, in Sonora, Mexico. The pueblos of the Yaqui Nation of the United States routinely hold religious ceremonies to which ceremonial leaders and participants from Mexico are invited. In many instances, these Yaqui are essential to the ceremonies.

While some ceremonial leaders and participants from Mexico occasionally have been allowed to cross, often they have been refused. The right to cross the border and to carry ceremonial objects has sometimes depended on whether the individual INS officer, or the supervisor on duty, was familiar with the Yaqui and the ceremonial occasion. While the cost for Mexican passports and the inability to produce requisite documents to establish residency and employment are impediments to many Mexican indigenous, the Yaqui face an additional stumbling block. Due to their traditions and their religion, the young men of the Yaqui do not register for the Mexican military. Such registration is required for men under the age of 40 in order to obtain a Mexican passport. These men are thus precluded from crossing the border to participate in ceremonies in the United States.

In 1997 the Yaqui negotiated an agreement with the INS Regional Administration in Arizona. This agreement allowed the Yaqui ceremonial leaders in the United States to identify persons who were invited to the ceremonies and to sponsor their admission into the United States. A letter of sponsorship was sent to INS on a yearly basis, and the right to cross the border was approved.

Although this agreement has been in place for four years, it has not been universally successful. The right of Mexican Yaqui to cross the U.S.-Mexico border still depends on individual INS officials at the regional and border gate level and, unfortunately, the mood that they are in on any particular day.

Cases have been brought by indigenous nations and tribal members to seek to enforce the provisions of the Jay Treaty and the Treaty of Ghent, and to extend those rights to all Indian peoples of the Americas. A recent case sought to clarify that the right of free passage for North American indigenous set forth in the Jay Treaty included the right to purchase and transport goods across the border. Under the treaty, such goods were to be exempt from duty or taxes, so long as they were for personal use. This has changed somewhat, and now the right to transport goods duty-free has been restricted by statute and case law.

In a number of Canadian cases, Canadian Indians were required to pay duty on items for personal use being brought into Canada from the United States. The courts upheld the custom duty since the items being transported (a washing machine, a refrigerator, and an oil heater) were not unusual or unique to Indians. The duty was further upheld since there was no local or municipal ordinance that incorporated the provisions of the Jay Treaty.

In a more recent Canadian case, the former grand chief of the Akwesasne Mohawks challenged the Canadian minister of national revenue over the interpretation of treaties. The plaintiff, Mike Mitchell, asserted that the treaties guaranteed Mohawks duty-free access across the Canada-U.S. border. The Canadian government argued that the Mohawks were immigrants to Canada in 1755 and thus could not claim aboriginal rights in Canada pursuant to the Jay Treaty. The Canadian government also asserted that, as the Iroquoian peoples traditionally charged each other duties to cross their lands, this same right could be asserted by Canada.

The courts of the United States have made similar interpretations of the rights contained in the Jay Treaty. Duties have been attached to Indian-made baskets being brought from Canada into the United States, where the court held that the right to import depends on statutory authority, not the Jay Treaty. In 1977, the U.S. Court confirmed in *Akins v. United States* that a duty applied to goods that were brought into the United States for personal use and not for resale. However, this case let stand a previous ruling by the U.S. District Court of Maine that Indians had the right to pass the border without undue restriction or restraint.

Very recently the right of Canadian Indians to work in the United States was supported by the Arizona courts. In this instance, a Canadian Mohawk had been hired by the Tohono O'odham police department as a police officer. The Arizona Peace Officer Standards and Training (POST) board, which certifies officers, declared that he was not eligible to be a state-certified peace officer because he had not been born in the United States.

The tribe challenged this decision pursuant to the Jay Treaty, which allows natives of the Saint Regis Mohawk Nation to travel between Canada and the United States and to live and work where they choose. While the Jay Treaty was referred to as "old" and "obscure," the Arizona POST board decided to honor its provisions and granted state certification to this officer.

Article 27 of the International Covenant on Civil and Political Rights affirms the right of persons belonging to "ethnic, linguistic or religious minorities … to enjoy their own culture, to profess and practice their own religion [and] to use their own language." For the indigenous of the North American continent, the rights guaranteed in this covenant are clearly violated by the restrictions to travel across the U.S.-Mexico and U.S.-Canada borders.

To use the Tohono O'odham as an example, there are religious sites on traditional lands that lie on both sides of the U.S.-Mexico border. On an annual basis, many O'odham make a pilgrimage to Magdalena de Kino, Sonora, Mexico, a tradition of Sonoran Desert Catholicism. At other times, O'odham travel to Boboquivari, a sacred mountain on O'odham lands north of the U.S.-Mexico border. Those O'odham without the legal right to travel into Mexico or into the United States are clearly inhibited in their right to practice their own religion, as established by the International Covenant on Civil and Political Rights.

The UN Human Rights Committee and the Inter-American Commission on Human Rights of the Organization of American States have also recognized the need to protect indigenous rights. These entities have held their "cultural integrity" norm to cover all aspects of an indigenous group's survival as a distinct culture, understanding culture to include land-use patterns as well as religious practices.

The proposed American Declaration on the Rights of Indigenous Peoples, adopted on June 5, 1997, at the seventh plenary session of the Inter-American Commission on Human Rights of the Organization of American States, specifically sets forth the following:

> Article XVIII. Traditional forms of ownership and cultural survival.
> Rights to land, territories and resources …
> 2. Indigenous peoples have the right to the recognition of their property and ownership rights with respect to lands, territories and resources they have historically occupied, as well as to the use of those to which they have historically had access for their traditional activities and livelihood.

The national indigenous organizations of Canada and the United States have recognized the problem of border passage; however, little has been done politically to try to resolve this issue. In 1988, a regional border rights meeting was held in Idaho, attended by a number of U.S. and Canadian tribes. A policy statement was issued that addressed the right of free border passage of the indigenous, based upon traditional rights of mobility and of the rights guaranteed in the Jay Treaty and the Treaty of Ghent. Certain demands were set forth, including:

1. The right of Indian nations to identify their own nationals
2. The right to be in, travel in, work in, reside in, use the territory of their nations
3. The right to transport their possessions with them and to trade freely with other Indian people
4. The right to receive services in each country on the same basis as other people of their nations

The policy statement contained a number of recommendations that revolved around the creation of a U.S.-Canadian international joint commission, composed of an equal number of representatives from each country and including Native American representation. The commission would have jurisdiction to resolve border disputes or problems, would oversee border stations, and would develop a "cohesive and consistent border crossing policy" for Canada and the United States. While this policy statement was far-reaching and visionary, it unfortunately did not include representation of the indigenous along the U.S.-Mexico border.

One Canadian noted for his criticism of Indian Affairs was quoted as saying in regard to the proposed policy, "This is moving in the wrong direction. I can't for the life of me understand why they would need a special border crossing, unless they're beginning to see themselves as people with no border." This is precisely what began to publicly emerge in the resolve of many cross-border native peoples.

While nothing came of this policy statement, the issue did not go away. Border issues for the tribes along the U.S.-Mexico border were a continuous problem that received substantial publicity. There were also continued free mobility issues along the U.S.-Canada border. Culminating this decade of continued problems, a joint meeting between Canada's Assembly of First Nations (AFN) and the U.S. National Congress of American Indians (NCAI) was held in July 1999. Indigenous representatives from Mexico (and indeed, throughout the world) attended the meeting, giving new hope for a concerted effort to resolve the issue of indigenous mobility across the imposed borders of their traditional lands.

The indigenous nations along the U.S.-Mexico border have, since 1997, been active in Alianza Indígina Sin Fronteras (Indigenous Alliance without Borders). This organization, supported by the American Friends Service Committee, includes representatives from the Yaqui, Tohono O'odham, Texas Kickapoo, Kumeyaay, and Gila River Pima/Maricopa peoples from both sides of the border. It emphasizes the development and maintenance of cultural, religious, and personal ties among indigenous peoples, as well as organizing and supporting the approaches to resolution undertaken by their members.

Statements made by indigenous leaders have been striking in their assertion of traditional passage rights. As Tohono O'odham councilman Kenneth Williams stated, "We were here long before other countries were established.... We are not immigrants. It just so happened that they put the line between us." Chief Ernie Campbell, of the Musqueam Nation, stated, "We did not put any line or border anywhere to separate us. There are no borders among our people." This position was supported by the AFN national chief Phil Fontaine when he declared that the delegates to the joint meeting of NCAI and AFN were "divided by locality but united by common origin and destiny," and further by H. Ron Allen, president of NCAI, when he stated, "We are crossing over this international border that we do not know and do not recognize."

The problem of free movement over international borders exists for many of the indigenous nations of North America. Many of these nations have made repeated attempts to resolve the border crossing issues for their people. Unfortunately, few of these attempts at resolution have been wholly successful....

The joint meeting held by the National Congress of American Indians and the Association of First Nations is an initial step toward effective action. The effort made by Alianza Indigena Sin Fronteras to coordinate and support the efforts of U.S.-Mexican indigenous nations is also worthwhile. However, the efforts are, to date, not coordinated.

Given the imbalance of power held by the federal governments of Canada, the United States, and Mexico, it would be wise for the indigenous nations of North America, through their respective organizations, to coordinate their efforts to resolve this issue. A unified approach by the indigenous nations of this continent, through their empowered organizations, could focus the world's attention on the issue of the right to maintain traditional contacts and ceremonies. This approach could force the colonizers to give new consideration to the traditional rights of the indigenous and to the rights guaranteed in laws and treaties. In this way, advancement might be made not only to the resolution of border crossing issues, but also perhaps to the maintenance and protection of other rights long ignored or forgotten.

Dawn of a New Day?: Indian Gaming in Southern California

BY NICOLAS G. ROSENTHAL

On April 19, 2002, the Cabazon Band of Mission Indians, a small tribe with a reservation 130 miles east of Los Angeles, celebrated the grand opening of the Cabazon Cultural Museum, a multimillion-dollar facility featuring ongoing exhibits, public programs, and performances illustrating the tribe's history. About 100 tribal members and friends, from young to old, gathered in the museum's sculpture garden for ceremonial prayers, songs, and speeches. Joining them was a spokesperson for U.S. Representative Mary Bono, who presented the tribe with a congratulatory proclamation. Writing of the event, the director of Cabazon cultural affairs proclaimed, "A new day has dawned. It is a moment of pride for the Cabazon Band of Mission Indians. Come for a visit and bring your children and grandchildren."

Not long before, few could have predicted this day would come. In 1876 the U.S. government designated 2,400 acres of desert land as a reservation for the 600 followers of Chief Cabazon, a nineteenth-century Cahuilla … leader who settled his people near the town of Indio, California, after railroad interests appropriated the band's water rights. A century later the tribe's enrollment had dwindled to 28, and only a handful of families remained on the reservation, living in mobile homes without electricity or running water. Yet encouraged by

Republished with permission of University Press of Colorado, from Nicolas Rosenthal, "Dawn of a New Day?: Indian Gaming in Southern California," in *Native Pathways: American Indian Culture and Economic Development in the Twentieth Century*, eds. Brian Hosmer and Colleen O'Neill (Boulder: University of Colorado Press, 2004), 91–111; permission conveyed through Copyright Clearance Center, Inc.

the efforts of other Indian groups around the country, a small group of Cabazon leaders saw the potential for harnessing state and federal funds to serve the tribe. Working out of a rented office in downtown Indio, they set off on an ambitious program of long-term economic development. Initial ventures such as jojoba production and shrimp agriculture produced only marginal returns, prompting the tribe to consider goods and services in greater demand. Beginning with a tribal smoke shop in 1979, then a card club, bingo palace, casino, and the opening of Fantasy Springs Casino Resort in 2000, the Cabazon advanced far beyond their initial goals. By 2002 all tribal members had guaranteed employment, housing had been built for members returning to the reservation, a wide range of social services was provided by the tribe, and profits from tribal businesses had been invested in projects meant to revitalize Cabazon culture, including the Cabazon Museum. Once ignored or thrust aside by policy makers, the Cabazon began getting visits from members of Congress, senators, and state officials, who came seeking campaign contributions and espousing pro-Indian positions on a variety of issues.

Over the last two decades of the twentieth century, several other Indian tribes throughout southern California that opened casinos and entered the world of high-stakes gaming shared the Cabazon experience. Although economic development among Indian tribes has a long and complex history, few engagements with the American marketplace have produced such rapid and dramatic results for Indian people. Indeed, these changes occurred so quickly and are so recent that it is premature to attempt a full treatment of the relationship between economic development and American Indian cultural identity. Nevertheless, contemporary events do provide the material for some preliminary observations on Indian gaming in southern California. A brief history of Indian economic development in the region shows how tribes went from poverty and relative obscurity to become operators of multimillion-dollar entertainment complexes. The social and economic impact on Indian and non-Indian communities throughout southern California is becoming apparent, as casinos have provided employment and generated revenue for tribal services and economic development, both on and off the reservation. Politically, gaming has not only provided southern California tribes with the means to achieve the long-touted goals of self-determination and tribal sovereignty but has also made them a force in local, state, and national politics. The cultural implications of Indian gaming are the most difficult to discern at this early date, but evidence points to several trends, including cultural revitalization, retribalization, and a rise in Indian people's influence on American popular culture. If these trends continue into subsequent decades, the Cabazon Tribe's notion of a new day dawning seems fitting, not only in terms of tribal culture but also in regard to the social, economic, and political status of Indian people throughout southern California.

The opening of casino resort complexes offering high-stakes gaming and other forms of leisure and entertainment on Indian reservations in southern California should be seen as the most successful of Indians' recent efforts to develop tribal lands and resources to complement the regional economy. During the 1960s and 1970s, Indian people across the country acquired unprecedented funding for economic development through the national Office of Economic Opportunity and other federal and state programs. Much of this funding went to a younger generation of Indians who worked outside the lines of power developed through years of close association between tribal leaders and the Bureau of Indian Affairs (BIA). Educated in urban universities and radicalized by identity politics, this new leadership sought creative solutions to the economic woes of Indian people. Even within the BIA, an agency with a notorious record when it came to acting in the economic interests of Indian people, there was movement toward support for self-determination, or empowering Indian people to take control of their economic destinies.

These developments were not lost on the thirty or so Indian tribes in southern California, which had long suffered from an almost total lack of economic opportunity on the small, isolated lands that made up their reservations. Over the years the allure of work in nearby towns and cities and powerful regional interests had drained the reservations of residents and resources, and those Indians who remained negotiated unemployment, poverty, and a scarcity of basic services. For many southern California Indians, new prospects for economic development fueled by federal funds raised hopes of self-sufficiency and tribal revitalization. In 1970, representatives from twenty-two California reservations formed Indian Campgrounds, Inc., a chain of Indian-owned campgrounds seeking to compete with the region's non-Indian recreational facilities. Over the next few years campgrounds and RV parks complete with tribal stores, electrical hookups, showers, and other amenities opened at reservations throughout southern California.

Meanwhile, the Chemehuevi Tribe and Colorado River Tribes underwent more sustained economic development projects. Situated along the banks of the Colorado River, both groups built marinas, campgrounds, beach recreational areas, restaurants, and motels. Southern California reservations also became sites of production for regional and national markets. In 1970 the La Jolla Band of Luiseño Mission Indians, the Rincon San Luiseño Band of Mission Indians, and the Pauma Band of Mission Indians announced the establishment of Southwest Indian Enterprise, a firm that would construct prefabricated glass-fiber homes on the Rincon Reservation. A few years later the same three tribes undertook a joint project to develop reservation fruit orchards. In the mid-1970s members of the Pala Band of Mission Indians broke from the tradition of electing a tribal elder as chairman by choosing a much younger man, Larry Blacktooth, for the job. Blacktooth, a recent graduate in business administration from the University of Southern California, initiated a number of economic development projects, including planting alfalfa, flowers, avocado, and citrus trees and opening a number of tribal businesses, including a wholesale nursery, a sand-and-gravel plant, a trailer park, a cable television system, and a Spanish roof-tile manufacturing facility. Geographic isolation, problems of political and economic capital, and fluctuating federal supports limited the size and viability of all these operations. Nevertheless, Indian people throughout southern California, like Indian people throughout the country, clearly were working during the 1970s to integrate their lives and lands into larger regional economies.

Beginning in the 1980s and into the 1990s, tribal economic ventures in southern California bore unprecedented fruit as tribes turned to offering various forms of gambling, culminating in the development of high-stakes, Nevada-style gaming. Encouraged by a favorable district court ruling for a Seminole bingo hall in Hollywood, Florida, in 1980, the Cabazon Tribe opened a card club offering draw poker games that same year. Card clubs were legal under state law but were regulated under city and county jurisdiction, prompting police raids and legal challenges by the city of Indio and Riverside County officials. Over the next seven years the case worked its way through the courts until the U.S. Supreme Court handed down a landmark decision in the case of *Cabazon Band of Mission Indians v. County of Riverside* (1987), asserting the right of Indian tribes to operate games of chance already legal under state law, free from local and state regulation. Congress, aware of the potential expansion of Indian gaming into areas beyond card clubs and bingo halls, moved quickly to pass the 1988 Indian Gaming Regulatory Act (IGRA). IGRA stipulated that social games for minimal prize values associated with traditional ceremonies or celebrations (Class I gaming) fell under the exclusive jurisdiction of Indian tribes; card games and bingo (Class II gaming) were subject to oversight by a National Indian Gaming Commission but could be played free of state regulation on Indian reservations in states that already allowed such gambling; and Nevada-style casino gambling, lotteries, and pari-mutuel betting (Class III gaming) would be permitted on Indian reservations only after a tribe passed an ordinance authorizing gambling activities and negotiated a compact with the state that set the terms for gaming operations. Moreover, Class III gaming was restricted to states that already permitted some form of such activities; for example, after a successful court battle by the Mashantucket Pequot Tribe in Connecticut, it was determined that laws permitting high school students to hold Nevada-style "after-prom parties" were sufficient precedent for allowing tribes to operate table games for high stakes under IGRA. Proponents of Indian gaming in California won another victory in 2000 when 65 percent of state voters approved Proposition 1A, clearing the last legal hurdle to tribal operation of video slot machines and Nevada-style card games.

By 2002, eighteen tribes in southern California had opened Class III gaming facilities, most of which evolved into multimillion-dollar entertainment complexes. The Agua Caliente Band of Cahuilla Indians, for example, spent over $230 million to upgrade and expand its Spa Resort Casino, which lies on nine acres in downtown Palm Springs and offers slot machines, card games, luxury hotel accommodations, spa services, fine dining, and golf. In addition to Fantasy Springs Casino, which features bingo (in English and Spanish), blackjack and other card games, off-track betting, and slot machines, the Cabazon Tribe built an outdoor amphitheater to accommodate boxing matches and musical concerts. During the period 2000–2002, performers included the Doobie Brothers, Bill Cosby, Merle Haggard, George Jones, and Isaac Hayes. In June 2002 the Pechanga Band of Luiseño Indians opened Pechanga Resort and Casino, a $262 million gambling and entertainment facility and the largest tribally owned hotel and casino in the western United States. Replacing a smaller casino built in 1995, the Pechanga Resort encompasses a 1-million-square-foot area, including

65,000 square feet of casino space, 522 hotel rooms, six restaurants, a dance lounge, a 1,200-seat theater, and a 40,000-square-foot convention center. For anyone who remembered the reservations just ten years before the casinos, the changes seemed dramatic—these Indian lands, neglected and all but forgotten by most southern California residents, had become major destination centers, drawing millions of people per year from around the world.

Just a decade and a half after the passage of IGRA, a complete assessment of the economic impact brought on by Class III gaming in southern California is difficult to compile. As part of a legislative analysis for an Indian gaming proposition in 1998, California tribes reported $600 million in gambling profits the previous year, but that number is likely to have grown with the expansion of gaming following Proposition 1A in 2000 and the proliferation of gaming resorts. In any case, tribes are under no obligation to enter their earnings into the public record. Nevertheless, some of the economic and related social implications of Indian gaming are becoming apparent; it remains to be seen if these trends continue into subsequent years and decades.

One apparent benefit of Indian gaming often touted by the tribes themselves is the expansion of employment opportunities and other benefits for both Indians and non-Indians in areas that historically have faced economic hardship. Gaming is the most successful venture in the history of Indian interactions with American capitalism in terms of generating jobs and providing the means for individual self-sufficiency. On the Viejas Reservation, for example, the Viejas Casino eliminated unemployment, which before the advent of gaming had reached 80 percent. Yet whereas most casinos have provided employment to any tribal member willing and able to work, the majority of jobs go to non-Indians, thus creating common interests between Indians and their neighbors. In 2002, Barona Casino, owned by the Barona Band of Mission Indians, maintained 1,500 full-time staff, about 97 percent of whom were non-Indians, making it one of the largest employers in San Diego County. Although many of these were service jobs, the casino offered generous benefit packages that included medical and dental insurance, retirement plans, child care, vacation pay, and English as a Second Language classes. The popularity of gambling has also insulated tribal casinos and their employees against slowdowns in the regional and national economy. Despite a spike in the national unemployment rate and a slowdown in the tourism industry during fall 2001, the Twenty-Nine Palms Band of Mission Indians was predicting steady business for its Spotlight 29 Casino and planned to hire 300 additional workers. Furthermore, notwithstanding an exemption from many forms of taxation, the most successful gaming tribes have pumped substantial amounts of money into local, state, and national economies. In 1999 the Barona Casino purchased $53.9 million in goods and services and paid $3.1 million in payroll taxes. Gaming tribes have also made charitable contributions to non-Indian causes. The Cabazon Tribe, for instance, has supported such groups as the local chapter of the American Diabetes Association, the City of Indio Police Department, United Way of the Desert, Toys for Tots, and the Boys and Girls Club of Coachella Valley, in addition to other local, regional, and national organizations.

Beyond employment, casino profits produce other social benefits for Indian people in southern California. After a century and a half of relying on the Bureau of Indian Affairs for services that were both inadequate and destructive, many tribes gained the ability to determine and provide for their own needs. With casino revenues, the Viejas Band of Kumeyaay Indians spent millions to build and renovate tribal housing, expand tribal offices, construct a community park and senior citizens' center, improve emergency services, and restore the reservation land and watershed. By 2002 the Barona Tribe had committed to provide full medical, dental, and health insurance for all tribal members and their nontribal spouses and dependents, spent $2.5 million on road construction throughout the reservation, and expanded the tribal school to offer tutoring, computer access, a library, and Head Start programs. As long as students maintain reasonable grades, the Cabazon Tribe has paid the educational expense for all its members, from day care through graduate school.

Southern California Indian tribes who have not reaped large profits from casinos have also felt the impact of casino revenues. As a provision of the gaming compacts negotiated with the State of California, Class III Indian casinos agreed to give millions of dollars of gaming revenue to California tribes that have no casinos or that run small gambling operations. In 2001, sixty-eight tribes shared $10.1 million under this plan. A year later more than $39 million had been paid out and earmarked for a variety of tribal services. The Los Coyotes Band of Mission Indians, for example, planned to construct a tribal office building with the money it received or to open a store adjacent to its campground, whereas the Torres Martinez Desert Cahuilla Indians hoped to improve water and sewer services and create a tutoring program for their children. Outside the requirements of state compacts, gaming tribes in southern California have contributed to Indian causes on their own volition. In 1998 the Viejas Tribe, the Barona Tribe, and the Sycuan Band of Mission Indians helped sponsor the annual pow-wow of the Southern California Indian Center, Inc. (an organization serving the needs of Indians living in the Los Angeles metropolitan area), and the Barona Tribe began talks to become involved in the Indian Center's social services programs. During the 2001–2002 winter holiday season, the Pechanga Tribe and the Morongo Band of Mission Indians collected about $40,000 in donations for the Santee Sioux of Nebraska, whose assets had been seized by the federal government in a dispute over the tribe's gaming operation.

Although it is easy and perhaps even justified to emphasize the tremendously positive aspects of Indian gaming—for scholars who have spent their careers exploring the ways in which Indian people have struggled against European and American colonialism, this news from Indian country is staggering—it would be shortsighted to leave the economic side of the story a simple narrative of steady progress, uncomplicated by past, present, and future challenges. The ambiguities at the intersection of tribal, state, and federal jurisdiction have produced the legal foundation for Indian gaming while also leaving the entire enterprise open to future court challenges and federal legislation. Some tribes in southern California have realized this and have made efforts to diversify reservation economies and tribal holdings. The San Manuel Band of Mission Indians,

for instance, formed the San Manuel Bottled Water Group in April 2002 to produce Big Bear Mountain Premium Spring Water. Although awash in profits
from the San Manuel Indian Bingo and Casino, San Manuel tribal chairman
Deron Marquez noted that gaming could be "here today and gone tomorrow,"
and the tribe planned to "do everything possible to get money from gaming and
diversify." Additional efforts at economic diversity have included First Nation
Recovery Incorporated, the Cabazon Tribe's tire-recycling facility, and factory
outlet stores on the Viejas Reservation. Other tribes have been more reluctant
to stake their fortunes primarily on gaming. The La Jolla Tribe opened the smallest Indian casino in southern California, with just thirty slot machines located in
a minimarket on its reservation. Rather than compete with several large Indian
casinos in the area, the tribe decided to use the slots to promote its popular outdoor recreational facilities. For the San Pasqual Band of Mission Indians, gaming
did not pan out as the tribe had hoped. Its relatively small Valley View Casino
made modest-profits, but far short of what the tribe had anticipated. The tribe
planned to expand its operations by building a much larger, $230 million facility
resembling a Mediterranean palace, surrounded by horse trails and vineyards, but
trouble with its business partner, First Nation Gaming of Louisiana, put those
plans on hold. Although usually in the minority, there have been dissenting
voices among tribes contemplating gaming ventures. Karen Toggery, a member
of the Jamul Band of Mission Indians, filed a string of lawsuits beginning in the
late 1990s in an effort to block casino plans and prevent development on the
Jamul Reservation. Distressed by the thought of excavating the grounds where
her relatives lived and were commemorated, Toggery stated, "I'm fighting for
traditions. I'm trying to stand up for what's right." This and other dissenting
voices, the legal status of casinos, tribal economic diversification, and competition
among gaming tribes, among other issues, may all prove crucial for native people
and for scholars assessing the economic and cultural impact of Indian gaming.

Closely related to the economic growth and development fueled by Indian
gaming in southern California have been fundamental changes in the tribes'
political fortunes. Beginning in the 1970s, federal policy and the concerns of
Indian people themselves focused on concepts like self-determination and tribal
sovereignty, or empowering Indian communities to address their own needs and
asserting the rights of Indian tribes to act as sovereign nations. With gaming revenues, southern California Indian tribes advanced toward both these goals.
Through the social services, economic development, education, and community
outreach programs..., the tribes gained considerable control over their day-
to-day lives. A concerted effort has also been made to translate economic success
into increased political power. Speaking at the 2002 Western Indian Gaming
Conference in San Diego, Viejas tribal member Anthony Pico issued a call for
Indians nationwide to work through the courts and state and federal legislatures
to protect and restore Indian rights. Pico outlined a special role for California
tribes, believing they possessed the experience and funds to lead the charge.
Jacob Coin, executive director of the California Nations Indian Gaming Association, agreed, arguing that both recent challenges to tribal sovereignty by the
states and the improved position of tribes with gaming ventures made action

imperative. "Up until now," Coin stated, "tribes have never had the economic wherewithal to make a difference. Before the tribes had resources to contribute to political campaigns, no one cared."

Indeed, one of the big stories of Indian gaming in southern California is that a wide range of politicians suddenly began to care greatly about Indian issues as the tribes ascended to prominent roles in local, state, and national politics. This shift in the political landscape is partially attributable to the necessity for Indian tribes and government officials to enter negotiations following the legalization and proliferation of casinos. The terms of the Indian Gaming Regulatory Act, for example, stipulated that tribes and the state work out gaming compacts, with federal oversight to make sure both sides act in good faith. Once a tribe had signed a compact and decided to build a casino, new relationships had to be formed with county and city governments. In past decades local officials often found little reason to take Indian issues seriously. With the rise of Indian gaming, the same officials developed a host of concerns relating to traffic, crime, the environment, and other possible casino impacts yet found they had little or no jurisdiction in regulating Indian actions. In San Diego County, for example, new relationships between gaming tribes and local officials slowly evolved through trial and error. Early on, when the county ran into a problem with the tribes, it appealed to state agencies like the Department of Alcoholic Beverage Control, state officials such as the governor and attorney general, and the federal Bureau of Indian Affairs—often without consulting tribal leaders. When these efforts failed, county administrators were forced to contact the tribes and sit down to negotiate. Following meetings between county supervisors and the Rincon Tribe, for instance, the tribe agreed to pay $7 million for roadwork to offset the increase in traffic caused by the Rincon River Oats Casino. Moreover, in 2001 the county hired a full-time tribal liaison to develop and maintain lines of communication with local tribes on gaming issues.

The reluctance of state and federal officials to get involved in matters between Indian tribes and local officials could be interpreted as a sign of a growing respect for tribal sovereignty. To a great extent, however, that deference only developed as tribes in southern California became able to put substantial amounts of money into the political system, primarily to support pro-gaming politicians. As early as 1994, California gaming tribes became a force in state politics when they gave $700,000 to their preferred candidate for attorney general in an attempt to unseat an incumbent who had frustrated gaming efforts. California assemblyman Tony Cardenas developed into a leading supporter of an Indian legislative agenda, particularly as an advocate for limiting state regulation on Indian casinos and as an author and supporter of bills to expand gaming on tribal lands. This work helped him garner hundreds of thousands of dollars in contributions for an aborted run to become secretary of state for California in 2001 and thousands more for an election bid to the Los Angeles City Council. In the last days of the tightly contested 2001 Los Angeles mayoral campaign, the [Soboba] Band of Mission Indians spent $100,000 on a postcard campaign supporting eventual winner James Hahn, and the Morongo Tribe aired $200,000 in radio spots against Hahn's opponent, Antonio Villaraigosa, who had failed to support Indian gaming while serving in the California State Assembly. California tribes also spent millions of dollars influencing California voters to pass pro-gaming legislation. Collectively, they raised about $21 million for the passage of Proposition 1A, including $7.7 million from the San Manuel Tribe, $3.5 million from the Viejas Tribe, $2 million from the Morongo Tribe, and $1 million from the Pechanga Tribe.

Although impressive, these numbers pale in comparison with the $68.6 million collected by the tribes to support Proposition 5, a similar pro-gaming measure that passed overwhelmingly in 1998 despite substantial opposition by Nevada gaming interests but which the courts later declared unconstitutional. The magnitude of these contributions is an indication both of how profitable gaming has been for the tribes in recent years and of how much is at stake when it comes to gaming legislation. It also suggests that a few hundred thousand dollars given to a mayoral campaign or to support a candidate for secretary of state may be relatively little when compared with the total amount spent by tribes on political contributions. Indeed, if it is believed that substantial monetary support would be a politician's primary motivation to journey to a sparsely populated reservation in the Colorado Desert, then watching the Cabazon Reservation may be a way to gauge tribal spending on state and national politics. Between June 2001 and May 2002, the Cabazon Band hosted U.S. Representatives Bob Filner (California), Brad Sherman (California), and Patrick Kennedy (Rhode Island); California State Senator Jim Brulte; California Lt. Governor Cruz Bustamante; California Governor Gray Davis; and U.S. Senators Tom Harkin (Iowa) and Tim Johnson (South Dakota). Whereas diversifying the economy is good policy for any nation, this participation in the American political system may be the tribes' best insurance against legislative and judicial shifts that threaten the existence and profitability of Indian gaming....

One of the most obvious signs of cultural activity relating to Indian gaming involves efforts at tribal revitalization. In other words, revenue from Indian casinos has allowed many southern California tribes to invest in attempts to rebuild from over two centuries of cultural genocide brought on by European and American colonialism. The Agua Caliente Tribe, for example, began work in 2002 on a 100,000-square-foot, $37 million facility to document and display its history. For the generation of tribal leaders building the museum, the project took on tremendous symbolic value. Believing Indian identity could be a hindrance to survival in a white-dominated world or faced with disinterested children and grandchildren, many past elders were reluctant to hand down tribal culture. In 1951 the ceremonial leader of the tribe burned the tribe's ceremonial house to the ground, ordered the burial of all sacred ceremonial bundles, and declared the customs and traditions of the tribe finished. The tribe's last ceremonial singer died in 1979 after refusing to teach anyone the songs that detailed the tribe's history and beliefs. Only in the late 1980s, as the tribe's fiscal outlook began to improve and its land base was secure, did the Agua Caliente begin to turn its attention toward attempts to rebuild tribal culture. With gaming revenues, the tribe began Cahuilla language classes, employed older tribal members to teach tribal culture, and drew up plans for the new museum. Efforts at revitalizing tribal culture were also undertaken by the Cabazon Tribe. In addition to its museum, described in the introduction to this chapter, the tribe worked to transform "tribal elder" into an elected position. Beginning in 1989, any retired tribal member with ten years of service to the tribe became eligible for election to the office. Benefits include a lifetime annual salary and a new car, with the understanding that the elder is to represent the tribe at functions and share knowledge of tribal culture with Cabazon youth.

Another cultural development relating to Indian gaming in southern California might be called "retribalization," or the reversal of a decades-long pattern of flight from the reservation and disengagement from tribal life. The social, cultural, and economic opportunities made possible by Indian casinos seem to be attracting tribal members to reservations or retaining reservation residents who might otherwise move out of the area. One example is the Pechanga Reservation, where the population increased from under 100 in the 1960s to 346 in 2000. Individual cases of Pechanga tribal members illustrate this trend. Gary DuBois grew up in nearby San Bernardino County during the 1970s and occasionally visited the Pechanga Reservation for tribal meetings. After attending college in the area, DuBois left for graduate school in St. Louis, then worked in Oklahoma and Washington, D.C. DuBois returned to California and moved onto the reservation for the first time in 1999, becoming cultural resources director for the tribe—a position made possible by the growth of the Pechanga's gaming operations. Russell "Butch" Murphy was raised on the Pechanga Reservation, then went to school in nearby Riverside and settled down to teach in San Diego. In the late 1990s Murphy was able to move back to the reservation when he took a job as tribal spokesman. Marc Macarro also grew up on the Pechanga Reservation, then left for college in Santa Barbara. After graduation he returned to serve the tribe and assumed the office of tribal council chairman.

Although the lives of native people are the most strongly affected by Indian gaming, there have been cultural implications for other residents of southern California as well. Millions of non-Indians, many of whom were once oblivious to the survival of California Indians, have journeyed to southern California Indian casinos and resort complexes, where they have experienced a type of Indian culture firsthand. Even those who have never stepped onto an Indian reservation have felt the cultural impact of Indian gaming. With revenue from casinos, tribes have taken an increasingly active role in the cultural life of southern California's cities, towns, and rural areas. In 2000–2001, for example, the Cabazon Tribe served as the primary sponsor of numerous events throughout the region, including annual festivals like the Riverside County Fair, the Southwest Arts Festival, and the National Date Festival; sports tournaments such as the Bob Hope Golf Classic; and black-tie Beverly Hills awards shows like the annual Diversity Awards, the annual First Americans in the Arts Awards, and a fundraiser for the American Indian College Fund.

The Cabazon Tribe also got involved with the University of California, Riverside, by working with the college on its endowed chair in American Indian history and by developing its forthcoming Native American Research Center. In 2001 the Pechanga Tribe took steps to become partners with the Southwest Museum, the largest repository of American Indian artifacts in the western United States and the oldest museum in Los Angeles. The financially struggling Southwest Museum first explored a deal with the Autry Museum of Western Heritage, but the Pechanga stepped in with a counteroffer that included annual operating costs and the construction of a museum branch on land adjacent to the Pechanga Reservation, which the Southwest Museum favored. By late 2002 the Pechanga had second thoughts on the deal and the Southwest Museum forged a new agreement with the Autry. Nevertheless, the prominent role of the Pechanga in the negotiations reveals that Indian people have returned as major players in the cultural life of southern California after generations of European and American cultural impositions....

The latest beneficiary of Indian gaming in southern California appears to be the Torres Martinez Desert Cahuilla Indian Tribe. Historically, the Torres Martinez has been among the poorest Indian tribes in California. The U.S. government created the Torres Martinez Reservation in 1876 on approximately 24,000 acres of land located 150 miles east of Los Angeles. In 1905 the bursting of a dam on the Colorado River flooded 11,000 of those acres, forming the Salton Sea, a large, saline lake that stayed replenished through agricultural runoff. Over the years, efforts at farming dates and wine grapes, two products grown successfully by non-Indians in the region, failed because of the harshness of the environment or for lack of capital to dig the necessary wells. Although work was available 50 miles away in the Palm Springs area, dirt roads made travel across the reservation slow and arduous. Social services for tribal members were so underfunded that health problems stayed far above the national average, and many adolescents emerged from school unprepared to pursue higher education or compete for good jobs. In the 1990s nearby tribes like the Cabazon, Morongo, and Agua Caliente grew wealthy, but prospects for opening a casino on the reservation seemed dim because of its remoteness from major thoroughfares. By 2001 about 250 of 659 tribal members continued to live on the reservation, many in homes without electricity or running water. For young people like eighteen-year-old Jacob Ward, the reservation offered few prospects for the future. "There's really not much to do here," Ward stated after outlining his plans to leave the area and attend vocational school in Wyoming.

In March 2002, following fifteen years of litigation, the Torres Martinez Tribe had what it hoped would prove to be a dramatic change in fortune. Congress approved a $14 million reparation package to compensate for the flooding of the reservation almost a century earlier. Furthermore, the tribe was granted the right to purchase 640 acres of land for a casino north of the reservation, near Interstate 10, which would be the first Indian gaming center in the country built on nontribal land. During a public ceremony, Secretary of the Interior Gale Norton presented a check for the first payment to the tribe, accompanied by U.S. Representative Mary Bono, the sponsor of the legislation. Tribal chairwoman Mary Belgardo graciously accepted, stating that the "fruits of all our suffering [are] about to come to bear." The tribe planned to use the money to build new homes, invest in the school system, and embark on a program of economic development, with a new casino as the cornerstone. "This is the key that will lift us out of poverty," said Ernie Morreo, the sixty-seven-year-old spiritual leader of the tribe. "I never thought the day would actually come."

Indeed, it might seem a foregone conclusion that the Torres Martinez would follow what by now has become a well-worn narrative in southern California—an Indian tribe suffering from generations of poverty embarks on a venture leading to rapid economic prosperity, political power, and cultural capital. Yet for the Torres Martinez and other Indian tribes in the region, the future is far from certain. The prospect of a casino run by the Torres Martinez exacerbated concerns that the market for Indian gaming is reaching a saturation point, raising possibilities that casinos operating in the same area will have to cut back their operations, compete for business, or find new ways to cooperate. Any such shift in economic fortune is sure to have implications for the individual tribes, in addition to rearranging the landscape of intertribal relations. Without any precedent for an off-reservation Indian casino, the Torres Martinez may face legal challenges, and the tribe still has to negotiate a gaming compact with the state, which could be strained because of the off-reservation issue. Although the political clout of Indian tribes has clearly grown tremendously in recent years, this political influence does not go uncontested. Relationships between California Indian tribes and the state took a turn for the worse during the early 2000s following former governor Gray Davis's veto of a bill that would have added protections to sites in California considered sacred to native people, the filing of a lawsuit by the San Manuel Tribe and the Pechanga Tribe against the state over casino revenue-sharing payments to nongaming tribes, and the state's legal efforts to have California tribes disclose political campaign donations. The cultural implications of gaming ... are likely to intersect with shifts in other realms of tribal life. These and many more questions surround the social, economic, political, and cultural issues raised by the Torres Martinez casino venture and the ongoing development of Indian gaming as a whole. Based on the evidence available at this time, it seems fair to say, as some Indian people have, that tribal gaming in southern California has ushered in the dawn of a new day. As the sun now breaks the horizon and ascends into the sky, however, it remains to be seen what the new day will bring.

◈ FURTHER READING

Alexie, Sherman, *The Absolutely True Story of a Part-Time Indian* (2009).

———. *The Lone Ranger and Tonto Fistfight in Heaven* (1993)

Ambler, Marjane. *Breaking the Iron Bonds: Indian Control of Energy Development* (1990).

Barker, James H. *Always Getting Ready: Yup'ik Eskimo Subsistence in Southwest Alaska* (1993).

Berman, Tressa. *Circle of Goods: Women, Work, and Welfare in a Reservation Community* (2003).

Castile, George Pierre. *Taking Charge: Native American Self-Determination and Federal Indian Policy, 1975–1993* (2006).

Cattelino, Jessica. *High Stakes: Florida Seminole Gaming and Sovereignty* (2008).

Cornell, Stephen E., and Joseph P. Kalt, eds. *What Can Tribes Do?: Strategies and Institutions in Indian Economic Development* (1992).

Dudas, Jeffrey. *The Cultivation of Resentment: Treaty Rights and the New Right* (2008).

Eichstaedt, Peter H. *If You Poison Us: Uranium and Native Americans* (1994).

Epps, Garrett. *Peyote vs. the State: Religious Freedom on Trial* (2009).

Erdrich, Louise. *The Plague of Doves* (2010).

———. *The Round House* (2012).

Fixico, Donald L. *The Invasion of Indian Country in the Twentieth Century: American Capitalism and Tribal National Resources* (1998).

Fowler, Loretta. *Tribal Sovereignty and the Historical Imagination: Cheyenne–Arapaho Politics* (2002).

Grobsmith, Elizabeth S. *Indians in Prison: Incarcerated Native Americans in Nebraska* (1994).

Hale, Janet Campbell. *Bloodlines: Odyssey of a Native Daughter* (1993).

Harjo, Joy, and Gloria Bird, eds. *Reinventing the Enemy's Language: Contemporary Native Women's Writings of North America* (1997).

Harris, LaDonna. *A Comanche Life* (2000).

Hart, E. Richard. *Zuni and the Courts: A Struggle for Sovereign Land Rights* (1995).

Holm, Tom. *Strong Hearts, Wounded Souls: Native American Veterans of the Vietnam War* (1996).

Iverson, Peter. *Riders of the West: Portraits from Indian Rodeo* (1999).

King, Thomas. *Green Grass, Running Water* (1993).

———. *Medicine River* (1990).

Klopotek, Brian. *Recognition Odysseys: Indigeneity, Race, and Federal Tribal Recognition Policy in Three Louisiana Indian Communities* (2011).

Makley, Michael, and Matthew Makley. *Cave Rock: Climbers, Courts, and a Washoe Indian Sacred Place* (2010).

Mankiller, Wilma, with Michael Wallis. *Mankiller: A Chief and Her People* (1993).

Mason, W. Dale. *Indian Gaming: Tribal Sovereignty and American Politics* (2000).

Middleton, Beth Rose. *Trust in the Land: New Directions in Tribal Conservation* (2011).

Mihesuah, Devon, ed. *Repatriation Reader: Who Owns American Indian Remains?* (2000).

Nesper, Larry. *The Walleye War: The Struggle for Ojibwe Spearfishing and Treaty Rights* (2002).

Pickering, Kathleen. *Lakota Culture, World Economy* (2000).

Pommersheim, Frank. *Braid of Feathers: American Indian Law and Contemporary Tribal Life* (1995).

Power, Susan. *Grass Dancer* (1994).

Ross, Luana. *Inventing the Savage: The Social Construction of Native American Criminality* (1998).

Ruppel, Kristin. *Unearthing Indian Land: Living with the Legacies of Allotment* (2008).

Sarris, Greg. *Grand Avenue* (1994).

Smith, Andrea. *Conquest: Sexual Violence and American Indian Genocide* (2005).

Smith, Sherry, and Brian Frehner, eds. *Indians and Energy: Exploitation and Opportunity in the American Southwest* (2010).

Snipp, C. Matthew. *American Indians: The First of This Land* (1989).

Tapahonso, Luci. *Saanii Dahataal: The Women Are Singing: Poems and Stories* (1993).

Tolley, Sara-Larus. *Quest for Tribal Acknowledgment: California's Honey Lake Maidus* (2006).

Wagoner, Paula. *"They Treated Us Just Like Indians": The Worlds of Bennett County, South Dakota* (2002).

Welch, James. *The Indian Lawyer* (1990).

Whaley, Rick, with Walter Bresette. *Walleye Warriors: An Effective Alliance Against Racism and for the Earth* (1994).

Wilson, Waziyatawin Angela. *Remember This!: Dakota Decolonization and the Eli Taylor Narratives* (2005).

Zah, Peterson, and Peter Iverson. *We Will Secure Our Future: Empowering the Navajo Nation* (2012).

MAJOR PROBLEMS IN AMERICAN HISTORY SERIES
TITLES CURRENTLY AVAILABLE

Allitt, *Major Problems in American Religious History*, 2nd ed., 2013
(ISBN 978-0-495-91243-9)

Blaszczyk/Scranton, *Major Problems in American Business History*, 2006
(ISBN 978-0-618-04426-9)

Block/Alexander/Norton, *Major Problems in American Women's History*, 5th ed.,
2014 (ISBN 978-1-133-95599-3)

Boris/Lichtenstein, *Major Problems in the History of American Workers*, 2nd ed.,
2003 (ISBN 978-0-618-04254-8)

Brown/Carp, *Major Problems in the Era of the American Revolution, 1760–1791*,
3rd ed., 2014 (ISBN 978-0-495-91332-0)

Chambers/Piehler, *Major Problems in American Military History*, 1999
(ISBN 978-0-669-33538-5)

Chan/Olin, *Major Problems in California History*, 1997 (ISBN 978-0-669-27588-9)

Chudacoff/Baldwin, *Major Problems in American Urban and Suburban History*,
2nd ed., 2005 (ISBN 978-0-618-43276-9)

Cobbs Hoffman/Blum/Gjerde, *Major Problems in American History*,
3rd ed., 2012
   Volume I: *To 1877* (ISBN 978-0-495-91513-3)
   Volume II: *Since 1865* (ISBN 978-1-111-34316-3)

Fink, *Major Problems in the Gilded Age and the Progressive Era*, 3rd ed., 2015
(ISBN 978-1-285-43342-4)

Franz/Smulyan, *Major Problems in American Popular Culture*, 2012
(ISBN 978-0-618-47481-3)

Games/Rothman, *Major Problems in Atlantic History*, 2008
(ISBN 978-0-618-61114-0)

Gordon, *Major Problems in American History, 1920–1945*, 2nd ed., 2011
(ISBN 978-0-547-14905-9)

Hall/Huebner, *Major Problems in American Constitutional History*, 2nd ed., 2010
(ISBN 978-0-618-54333-5)

Hämäläinen/Johnson, *Major Problems in the History of North American Borderlands*,
2012 (ISBN 978-0-495-91692-5)

Haynes/Wintz, *Major Problems in Texas History*, 2nd ed., 2015
(ISBN 978-1-133-31008-2)

Holt/Barkley Brown, *Major Problems in African American History*, 2000
   Volume I: *From Slavery to Freedom, 1619–1877* (ISBN 978-0-669-24991-0)
   Volume II: *From Freedom to "Freedom Now," 1865–1990s*
   (ISBN 978-0-669-46293-7)

Hurtado/Iverson/Bauer/Amerman, *Major Problems in American Indian History*,
3rd ed., 2015 (ISBN 978-1-133-94419-5)

Jabour, *Major Problems in the History of American Families and Children,* 2005 (ISBN 978-0-618-21475-4)

Kupperman, *Major Problems in American Colonial History,* 3rd ed., 2013 (ISBN 978-0-495-91299-6)

Kurashige/Yang Murray, *Major Problems in Asian American History,* 2003 (ISBN 978-0-618-07734-2)

McMahon, *Major Problems in the History of the Vietnam War,* 4th ed., 2008 (ISBN 978-0-618-74937-9)

McMillen/Turner/Escott/Goldfield, *Major Problems in the History of the American South,* 3rd ed., 2012
   Volume I: *The Old South* (ISBN 978-0-547-22831-0)
   Volume II: *The New South* (ISBN 978-0-547-22833-4)

Merchant, *Major Problems in American Environmental History,* 3rd ed., 2012 (ISBN 978-0-495-91242-2)

Merrill/Paterson, *Major Problems in American Foreign Relations,* 7th ed., 2010
   Volume I: *To 1920* (ISBN 978-0-547-21824-3)
   Volume II: *Since 1914* (ISBN 978-0-547-21823-6)

Merrill/Paterson, *Major Problems in American Foreign Relations,* Concise Edition, 2006 (ISBN: 978-0-618-37639-1)

Milner/Butler/Lewis, *Major Problems in the History of the American West,* 2nd ed., 1997 (ISBN 978-0-669-41580-3)

Ngai/Gjerde, *Major Problems in American Immigration History,* 2nd ed., 2012 (ISBN 978-0-547-14907-3)

Peiss, *Major Problems in the History of American Sexuality,* 2002 (ISBN 978-0-395-90384-1)

Perman/Taylor, *Major Problems in the Civil War and Reconstruction,* 3rd ed., 2011 (ISBN 978-0-618-87520-7)

Riess, *Major Problems in American Sport History,* 2nd ed., 2015 (ISBN 978-1-133-31108-9)

Smith/Clancey, *Major Problems in the History of American Technology,* 1998 (ISBN 978-0-669-35472-0)

Stoler/Gustafson, *Major Problems in the History of World War II,* 2003 (ISBN 978-0-618-06132-7)

Vargas, *Major Problems in Mexican American History,* 1999 (ISBN 978-0-395-84555-4)

Valerio-Jiménez/Whalen, *Major Problems in Latina/o History,* 2014 (ISBN 978-1-111-35377-3)

Warner/Tighe, *Major Problems in the History of American Medicine and Public Health,* 2001 (ISBN 978-0-395-95435-5)

Wilentz/Earle, *Major Problems in the Early Republic, 1787–1848,* 2nd ed., 2008 (ISBN 978-0-618-52258-3)

Zaretsky/Lawrence/Griffith/Baker, *Major Problems in American History since 1945,* 4th ed., 2014 (ISBN 978-1-133-94414-0)

CPSIA information can be obtained
at www.ICGtesting.com
Printed in the USA
FFOW03n1626110216
21397FF